WITHDRAWN

Padua under the Carrara, 1318–1405

Benjamin G. Kohl

Padua under the Carrara, 1318–1405

The Johns Hopkins University Press
BALTIMORE AND LONDON

This book has been brought to publication with the generous
assistance of the Gladys Krieble Delmas Foundation;
and the Andrew W. Mellon Chair in the Humanities
and the Salmon Fund of Vassar College.

© 1998   The Johns Hopkins University Press
All rights reserved. Published 1998
Printed in the United States of America on acid-free paper
9 8 7 6 5 4 3 2 1

The Johns Hopkins University Press
2715 North Charles Street
Baltimore, Maryland 21218-4363
The Johns Hopkins Press Ltd., London

Library of Congress Cataloging-in-Publication Data
will be found at the end of this book.
A catalog record for this book is available from the British Library.

ISBN 0-8018-5703-1

For Judy—at last

Contents

List of Illustrations ix
List of Tables xi
Acknowledgments xiii
Introduction xvii

I. The Early Carrara, 1318–1355

1. Late Medieval Padua: The Setting 3
2. Under Foreign Domination, 1318–1337 39
3. Venice's *Status Noster*, 1337–1355 68

II. Francesco il Vecchio, 1356–1388

4. Seeking Other Allies, 1356–1376 103
5. Signorial Government and Carrara Wealth 132
6. Creating the Carrara Affinity 167
7. Venice's Mortal Enemy, 1377–1388 205

III. Francesco Novello, 1388–1405

8. Exile and Restoration, 1388–1392 245
9. Reconstituting the Carrara Regime 275
10. Ambition and Destruction, 1392–1405 303

Appendixes

1. Contrade of Padua (1320) and Villages of the Padovano (1281) 339

CONTENTS

2. Podestà and Vicars of Padua, 1318–1405   350
3. Sales and Gifts of Carrara Property,
     June–November 1388   354

Notes   365
Glossary   421
Bibliography   425
Index   447

Illustrations

Figures

1. Tower of Palazzo degli Anziani, Padua 6
2. Ponte Molino, North Gate of Padua 9
3. Church of S. Stefano da Carrara 26
4. Giacomo da Carrara beheaded on orders of Ezzelino da Romano in 1240 36
5. Giacomo il Grande da Carrara receives lordship of Padua in 1318 40
6. Painted *carro* stemma and cross of Paduan commune, walls of Cittadella 69
7. Marsilio da Carrara receives lordship of Padua in 1337 70
8. Tomb of Marsilio da Carrara, S. Stefano da Carrara 73
9. Carrara Castello, Monselice 74
10. Portrait of Ubertino da Carrara 76
11. Tomb of Ubertino da Carrara, Church of the Eremitani, Padua 88
12. Portrait of Francesco il Vecchio da Carrara 105
13. Rocca degli Alberi, with walls of Montagnana 110
14. *Portrait of the Aged Petrarch in His Study* 128
15. Loggia of Carrara Reggia, Padua 134
16. *Angel Blessing Pilgrim and Poor Beggar* 138
17. Castello Carrarese, Valbona 146
18. Tower of Carrara Castle at S. Pelagio 146
19. Carrara stemma representing the four cardinal virtues 153
20. Portraits of Fina da Carrara and her daughters 155
21. *Carrarini* of 2 *soldi* 159
22. Two views of upper die for striking *carrarini* in Francesco il Vecchio's mint 160
23. Walls of Cittadella 165
24. Dotti votive painting with Madonna Enthroned 168
25. *The Council of King Ramiro* 180

ILLUSTRATIONS

26. Soldiers of Lupi Family of Parma   184
27. Tomb of Manno Donati, Basilica of S. Antonio, Padua   188
28. *Soldiers Casting Lots for Garments of Christ*   215
29. Notarial act appointing Carrara envoys   227
30. Rationale for Carrara sales, fall 1388   246
31. Portrait medal of Francesco Novello, 1390   269
32. Tomb effigy of Caterina, widow of Bonifacio Lupi, cloister, Basilica of S. Antonio   286
33. Portrait of Francesco Novello da Carrara   305
34. *Adoration of Magi*   314
35. Defaced *carro* stemma, Gate of Castelfranco   336

Maps

1. Padua in the Fourteenth Century   5
2. The Padovano in the Fourteenth Century   11
3. Northern Italy in the Fourteenth Century   60

Tables

1.1. Quarters and *Centenari* of Padua in the Fourteenth Century   7
1.2. Population of Padua in 1320   8
1.3. Hearths in the Jurisdictions of the Padovano in 1281, and Men-at-Arms in 1397   13
1.4. Geographic Origins of the Podestà of Padua, by Term, 1318–1405   19
1.5. Ordinary Officials of the Communal Government of Padua, 1362   21
1.6. Bishops of Padua in the Carrara Period, 1319–1406   25
1.7. Guilds in Carrara Padua   28
2.1. The Carrara I. Branch of Giacomo il Grande and Marsilio il Grande   50
2.2. The Carrara II. Branch of Niccolò and Ubertino   52
5.1. The Carrara III. Francesco il Vecchio's Legitimate Offspring   135
5.2. Balance Sheet of the Carrara Household, 1357   137
5.3. Assets and Cash on Hand, Carrara Household, 1357   139
5.4. Extraordinary Borrowing and Expenditures of the Carrara Regime in 1373   148
5.5. Organization of the Carrara Household, 1380   158
5.6. Output of the Carrara Mint, 1381–1383   161
6.1. The Dotti   170
6.2. The Papafava dei Carraresi   172
6.3. Members of the War Council of July 1372   173
6.4. The Scrovegni   176
6.5. The Lupi, Bonifacio's Branch   179
6.6. The Lupi, Simone's and Antonio's Branch   183
6.7. The Forzatè   190
6.8. The Negri   197
8.1. Carrara Sales of Summer–Fall 1388   250

Tables

8.2. The Carrara IV. Francesco Novello's Offspring 258

9.1. The Carrara V. Francesco il Vecchio's Illegitimate Offspring 298

Acknowledgments

My study of the history of late medieval Padua stretches back for more than three decades, starting with research in the city's archives and libraries as a Fulbright fellow in 1964–65 for a doctoral dissertation on Francesco il Vecchio da Carrara written under the supervision of Frederic Chapin Lane at the Johns Hopkins University. Since then, thanks to various grants and fellowships, I have been able to return to Italy for nearly three years of additional archival and manuscript research in Padua, Venice, Florence, and Rome. I am indebted to the American Academy in Rome for awarding me its Rome Prize Fellowship in Post-Classical Humanistic Studies in 1970–71 and the Gladys Krieble Delmas Foundation for a fellowship to work in Venice in the autumn of 1978. Generous sabbatical leaves from Vassar College permitted me to complete archival research in 1985–86, begin writing this book in January 1990, and finish a draft of it in the summer of 1995.

In Padua I am deeply indebted to Professor Paolo Sambin, who led me in my first steps in Latin paleography in his course at the university and helped introduce me to the holdings of the Archivio di Stato. There I have been aided by a succession of helpful directors—Letterio Briguglio, Bianca Strina Lanfranchi, and, for the past fifteen years, Rita Baggio Collavo. In the Sala di Studio I have benefited from many kindnesses of the staff, who, from the late Orlando Rampin in the 1960s to Gabriella Tursini in the '90s, have shared with me their unrivaled knowledge of the riches of the *deposito*. At Padua's Biblioteca Civica, Director Mirella Blason Berton has been a longtime friend and supporter, facilitating my use of both manuscripts and printed sources. I wish to acknowledge the typical generosity of the late Count Novello Papafava dei Carraresi, who, in the spring of 1965, permitted me to consult the riches of his family's archive. I am much indebted to my fellow historians of medieval Padua for stimulating discussions and many helpful suggestions over the years. I especially wish to thank Sante Bortolami, who has generously shared with me his knowledge of Paduan

Acknowledgments

history and topography, most recently checking the accuracy of the place-names in Appendix 1.

In Venice my research has been greatly helped by my old friend Reiny Mueller, who has generously placed his unique knowledge of Trecento Venetian sources at my disposal and encouraged my work in many ways, most recently giving Chapter 5 a typically penetrating critique that enabled me to eliminate several errors. I recall gratefully discussions over the years at the Frari and the Marciana with Humfrey Butters, Stanley Chojnacki, Paul Hills, Paul Kaplan, Michael Knapton, Michael Mallett, Edward Muir, and Robin Simon. Tracy Cooper took a number of the photographs used to illustrate this book and has been ever eager to share information from her own archival and manuscript research.

As my work progressed, I have presented papers on Carrara Padua and drafts of portions of this book to a number of scholarly audiences: the Warwick University conferences in Venice in December 1978 and November 1985, the International Congress of Medieval Studies at Kalamazoo, Michigan, in May 1985, the History Department of University College, Swansea, in March 1990, the European History Seminar at Syracuse University in April 1990, the First Draft Club of Vassar's Department of History in November 1990, Nicolai Rubinstein's seminar on Italian history at the University of London in March 1991, the Renaissance Studies Group of Wesleyan University in April 1992, and the Mid-Hudson Medieval Seminar in September 1994. I wish to thank the audiences on each of these occasions for their helpful criticism and comments and my various hosts for their indulgence in letting me speak so much on Padua under the Carrara.

To two men of the previous generation—no longer able to read these words—I owe a great debt. Early in our relationship, my mentor Frederic Chapin Lane convinced me that the sort of history I wanted to write had to be founded on painstaking and thorough archival research, informed by a complete knowledge of the secondary literature, presented with the utmost accuracy. That I have taken seriously his injunction never to publish until satisfied that all the sources were consulted accounts, in part, for the length and complexity of this book. Its many imperfections are as much witness to my own shortcomings as a historian as to the ultimate impossibility of any scholar realizing Lane's noble dream. I owe an even greater and more enduring debt to my father, Victor P. Kohl, who tried, by his example, to teach me to cultivate the field of history with the same patient care with which, for forty years, he tilled our farm in Delaware.

In the final stages of this work I received enormous help from John Easton Law, senior lecturer in history at University College, Swansea, who read an early draft of the entire manuscript, saving me from many errors

Acknowledgments

and encouraging me to think that my story of the Carrara regime was worth telling. Two colleagues, Alison Smith of Wagner College and Ronald Witt of Duke University, have read and criticized Chapter 1, helping me to eliminate errors and confusions. In September 1996, Dr. Dieter Girgensohn of the Max-Planck-Institut für Geschichte in Göttingen read the penultimate draft of Chapter 10 and offered many valuable suggestions for improvements.

Since preliminary discussions in October 1993, the executive editor of the Johns Hopkins University Press, Henry Y. K. Tom, has supported my vision of writing a large book on Carrara Padua. The full bibliography, appendixes, illustrations, maps, and genealogical tables are witnesses to Henry's conviction that the history of Carrara Padua is worth presenting on a grand scale. That this is a much better book than the manuscript I presented in the fall of 1995 is a tribute to both the very helpful and extensive comments of the Press's anonymous reader and Henry Tom's sympathetic guidance in enabling me to discover the book I really needed to write. The superb copyediting by Grace Buonocore has materially improved the accuracy of the book.

My most conspicuous debts are to two institutions located in Poughkeepsie, New York: Vassar College and my nuclear family. Since I arrived as a young instructor in 1966, my colleagues and the administration at Vassar have always supported my scholarly endeavors. Vassar's leave system has given me the free time to carry out work in dozens of libraries and the leisure to conceive and write a book on this scale, and its enlightened policy of library acquisitions has built significant holdings in the history of Venice and northern Italy. The library's Interlibrary Loan Office has been unfailing in filling numerous orders for books and photocopies of rare articles. Among my Vassar colleagues, I am indebted to Robert Norton of German for checking my reading of vernacular letters from Charles IV, Robert Brown of Classics for help with some knotty problems of Latin translation, and Nicholas Adams of Art for advice in obtaining illustrations. My colleagues in the Department of History have supported my research and writing in many ways. I am especially indebted to Tony Wohl for his insistence on the importance of the apt quotation and to the department's administrative assistant, Norma Torney, whose constant support enabled me to serve several terms as chair while I undertook this project.

My greatest debt, however, is to my family. My children, Ben and Laura, have lived with me and my book on Padua their entire lives. As youngsters, they seemed to accept summers in a Venetian *pension,* schooling and day care in an *asilo* in Rome, travels across Europe as the natural consequence of a father who also "did history." At first quizzical and later be-

Acknowledgments

mused at my stacks of note cards, sheaves of papers, archaic filing system that assigned folders to each year of the Trecento and each family of Carrara Padua, they have never questioned the enterprise and always tolerated the sacrifices it demanded. As adults they have retained vestiges of their early involvement in the "Padua" project: Ben and his wife, Kim, have developed a zest for travel, and Laura and her husband, Adrian, a taste for things Italian. Even more supportive has been my wife, Judy, who has borne with me and "Padua" for thirty years—with more good-humored forbearance than I have any right to expect. Over the years she has learned to treat my musings on the people and events of Trecento Padua as normal conversation at dinner or during a trip down the New Jersey Turnpike. On her computer she has carefully transformed my messy genealogical tables into models of clarity and elegance. Most of all, Judy has brought her considerable acumen as a teacher of English composition to every page of several drafts of this book, placing me and my readers greatly in her debt. Dedicating this book to her can only be a token of my incalculable debt.

Introduction

> In the contest for power and in the maintenance of an illegal authority,
> the picked athletes came to the front.
>
> —John Addington Symonds, *The Age of the Despots* (1875)

> The rise of the *signori* in the communes of the Veneto did not bring about an
> absolutist form of government in the proper sense of the word but rather
> a constitutional form to which it would not be inappropriate
> to apply the term: diarchy.
>
> —Francesco Ercole, "Comuni e Signori nel Veneto" (1910)

"Athletes and Diarchs": these two images represent the extremes in the historiographical debate on the personalities and regimes of the so-called despots of the Italian Renaissance. The cunning and ruthless Renaissance despot, avid for power and contemptuous of the usual sanctions of law and morality, has long held sway over the popular image of the Renaissance lord. Developed in the late nineteenth century in the liberal, if sometimes sensationalistic, treatments of Renaissance Italy of Jacob Burckhardt and John Addington Symonds, the image of the brutal and illegitimate "despot" has maintained a strangely tenacious hold on the historical imagination. The term *despot* is clearly an anachronism, a concept borrowed by nineteenth-century historians from Greek antiquity, unknown in late medieval Italy, and applied mistakenly to the lords of the early Renaissance. In the fourteenth century, the term *tyrant* was applied to a ruler who held his office without legal right or who exercised excessive and illegal power. Thus, the lord of an Italian city could be a tyrant because he had not gained office by popular election or sanction by a higher authority, such as pope or emperor (*de defectu tituli*), or because he ruled illegally and against the welfare of his subjects (*ex parte exercitii*). In the propaganda campaigns that accompanied the wars between Florence and the Visconti and Venice and the Carrara, *tyrannus* was used widely and recklessly simply to insult and condemn one's

Introduction

enemies. Some major students of the Italian Renaissance still sometimes use the term *despot*, even though the more accurate term *tyrant* is available to denote "bad rulers" of Italian cities. Most recent studies, however, emphasize the constitutional, legal structure of the signorial (one-man) regimes, which came to govern the cities of northern Italy in the late thirteenth and fourteenth centuries. Indeed, I hope that one result of this book will be to banish the term *despot* from the vocabulary of late medieval Italian politics and encourage the adoption of the less charged and more accurate *signore*, or lord.[1]

Subject

This book is a detailed study of one such signorial regime, the nearly century-long rule of the Carrara dynasty over the north Italian city of Padua from 1318 to 1405. My study aims at demonstrating the complexity of the shared authority of the lord and commune of Padua, while admitting that the old commune government lost much of its power in the course of the Trecento. This book takes seriously the application of "diarchy" (dual rule) to define the relation of the early Carrara lords and the Paduan commune, whose magistracies, judiciary, police, and systems of taxation and public works continued to function. There is little evidence to suggest that the election of the first Carrara lords brought about major immediate changes either in the administration of the city or the structure of society.

The book organizes the role of the Carrara dynasty in shaping Trecento Paduan history under four overlapping historical themes: the uniqueness of Padua, or Patavinitas; the crucial importance of Venice's interests and policies in sometimes supporting, sometimes challenging, but always affecting the Carrara dynasty's rule over Padua; the development of a new ruling elite of Padua, supporters of the Carrara to whom I have applied the term *affinity;* and the growth of the regime's authority as a household government directed by friends and members of the Carrara family.

Patavinitas

The first Carrara lord, Giacomo il Grande, was elected "lord and captain general," to defend his city's status as an independent state that claimed sovereignty over a defined territory in northern Italy. Emblematic of this claim was the communal seal of Padua, which revived, in the late thirteenth century, the notion of the definite natural boundaries of the ancient Roman province. Within these boundaries, Padua served as the capital of a 1,000-square-mile *contado*, or area of countryside around a city, in which an agricultural and artisanal economy flourished. Adopting the formula of "lord

Introduction

and commune of Padua" at each election, the Carrara lord was the principal elected official (similar in theory to Venice's doge) charged with protecting Padua's commune, church, university, guilds, and people. But the ability of the Carrara lords to rule Padua and to succeed in their attempt to create a larger state was constrained by the backwardness of Padua's economy and sometimes the inherited structures they were sworn to protect.

The city's greatest asset was its university, which provided statesmen and jurists for the regime, and its most important industry was textiles, which the lord controlled, nurtured, and protected as a major source of wealth. The richly diverse Paduan contado increasingly became part of a territorial state, while its land came under the ownership of Carrara supporters. The communal government carried on many of the more mundane tasks of government, such as the collection of taxes, the administration of civil justice, and public works. The Paduan church and its secular clergy and major monasteries also increasingly became tools of the Carrara regime—with members of the family serving as abbots, priors, and even bishop. The long-term opposition of the commune to the imperial vicars, the Ghibellines in northern Italy in the thirteenth century, identified Padua with the Guelf cause in Italy. The Carrara lords largely continued to support the papacy and its allies, Florence, Bologna, the Este in Ferrara, and later the Angevin kings of Hungary. Thus, commitment to the Guelf cause became an integral part of "Patavinitas" and a rallying cry for Padua and the Carrara lords.

The Importance of Venice

Much of Padua's history was marked by an unequal struggle between the greatest commercial entrepôt of the later Middle ages, Venice, and its agriculturally rich mainland neighbor. In the early Trecento Venice required a pliant buffer state to protect its investors in the Padovano from expansionist mainland lords. As the Scaliger rule over Padua challenged Venice's control of the contado as a source of food, fiber, and raw materials, Venice backed the restoration of the Carrara lords to power in 1337 and came to look upon Padua as "its own state," installing its own patricians as *podestà,* or chief executive officers, of Padua to oversee changes in government and ensuring, through a series of commercial treaties, the privileged position of its own citizens and monasteries as landowners in the Padovano. But the Carrara lords increasingly challenged Venice's dominance, and in 1357 Francisco il Vecchio entered into an alliance with Venice's rival, King Louis of Hungary. Constructing a system of alliances with Guelf regimes in Florence, Bologna, and Ferrara, the Carrara dynasty became Venice's mortal enemy in the last third of the century, supporting Genoa in the Chioggia war and occupying Treviso and Friuli in the 1380s. Padua's wars of aggression so near to home eventually became unacceptable to Venice, which made an alliance with the lord of Milan, Giangaleazzo Visconti, who occupied Padua briefly from 1388 to 1390. Francesco Novello da Carrara reconquered the city with the active support of Florence and tacit agreement of Venice. The Carrara lord's inept policy of territorial aggrandizement following the death of Giangaleazzo Visconti in the early Quattrocento drove Venice to despair of accommodation. The Venetian government eventually adopted a policy of destruction of the hated Carrara house, which reached its climax with its conquest of Padua in 1405 and subsequent extermination of the family.

Affinity

The rule of the Carrara family gradually transformed the ruling elite of Padua. The civil wars of the early Trecento brought about the exile or extinction of many of the older feudal families, whose lands were confiscated and, in turn, bestowed on the regime's supporters, whom I call the Carrara affinity. The term is borrowed from medieval English history, where it is defined as "the servants, retainers, and other followers of a lord, . . . the most important grouping in medieval society."[2] While the contemporary Este regime in Ferrara and Scaliger rulers in Verona extensively employed the techniques of feudalism to gain supporters, bestowing land to gain vassals, the Carrara lords used more informal means of reward to gain supporters, with pledges of fealty rarely required.[3] In Padua the creation of vassals was restricted to a small number of professional soldiers, men-at-arms, who undertook military service in exchange for fiefs of land. Popular methods of rewarding members of the affinity were the awarding of lay tithes by bishops loyal to the Carrara lord, dispensing of taxes and grants of citizenship, bestowal of urban property near the lord's court, farming of excise taxes (*dazii*) to favorites, and appointment to communal offices, such as podestà. As a result many noble foreign lords and soldiers gravitated to Padua during Francesco il Vecchio's rule. The composition of a war council convened at the beginning of the Border War with Venice in 1372 reveals the distinctly military and noble character of the Carrara affinity. Although the Carrara lords' interests in textiles and banking required continued cultivation of Padua's business community, the leaders of signorial Padua followed (as Angelo Ventura has argued) a distinctly "aristocratic vocation."

Statism and the Tools of Rule

Empowered to regulate local customs and abrogate statutes, the Carrara lords left the mundane tasks of the administration of justice and policing to the commune, while claiming wide powers in war and diplomacy for the lord. The promulgation of new statutes in 1362 demonstrated a profound

Introduction

respect for the forms of communal institutions, though the lord now made explicit his authority to alter any statutes or policies against what he deemed was the general welfare. During the 1370s, Francesco il Vecchio completed formation of a territorial state, with the Padovano divided into nine *podestarie* and vicariates, each governed by a magistrate handpicked by the lord. By the 1380s the Carrara lord had formed a powerful household regime staffed by a cadre of jurists, diplomats, and soldiers. Though Carrara wealth and resources were diminished under Francesco Novello (1390–1405), he used many techniques to bolster the prestige and effectiveness of his regime: medallions to commemorate his reconquest, titles, such as *dux Carrarie,* to enhance his stature, and an advanced chancery and able military and diplomatic staff, including many members of his own family, to pursue his renewed ambition to dominate northeast Italy. By the end of the century, the authority of the Carrara regime had penetrated all aspects of Paduan life.

Sources and Method

This study, perhaps more than any other detailed treatment of a late medieval Italian city, has been shaped by the nature of the surviving sources. Carrara Padua is as rich in narrative sources for the city's wars and diplomacy as it is poor in documentary evidence from the regime's chancery and financial offices. The most authoritative and detailed chronicles of the period are two highly partisan narratives by Guglielmo Cortusi and the Gatari, father Galeazzo assisted by his sons Andrea and Bartolomeo. Each was written by intimates of the Carrara regime, who were often eyewitnesses to the events described. Cortusi's chronicle provides a full narrative of Paduan politics from the beginning of the Carrara rule until midcentury; Galeazzo Gatari, a merchant who served as an envoy for the last two Carrara lords, compiled a detailed diary of war and diplomacy, often enriched by his insertion of texts of treaties and membership lists of embassies and councils into his narrative. Several members of the Carrara household composed accounts of specific wars and campaigns: the head of the Carrara chancery, Niccoletto d'Alessio, wrote a history of the Border War of 1372–73, often documented with Francesco il Vecchio's letters and field orders, and two other Carrara intimates (anonymously) treated the Trevisan War and composed a life of Francesco Novello. At the end of the century, Francesco Novello commissioned a collective biography of his forebears, redacted both in Latin and the vernacular, the *Gesta magnifica domus Carrariensis,* and Pier Paolo Vergerio composed, in the humanist tradition of lives of illustrious men, biographies of the Carrara lords who ruled in the first half of the Trecento.[4] Paduan chronicles, which are as detailed and authoritative as

INTRODUCTION

those of any Italian city in the later Middle Ages, have been supplemented by contemporary histories of the cities of Verona, Venice, Milan, Treviso, Bologna, Ferrara, and Florence.

This book largely attempts to tell a story, to "return to narrative," using as its method the rather old-fashioned technique of describing events from what some may see as "unreliable" partisan chronicles. Of course, the nature and significance of the events described have been checked, whenever possible, against documentary sources and the interpretations of modern historians. But in many cases, the accounts of military campaigns and battles, descriptions of funerals and weddings, and the debates of Carrara councils must rely on contemporary chronicles. When the chronicle account (or archival document) seemed to capture the nature of the event, I have often let the sources "speak for themselves," providing quotations in English translation. In composing a narrative based on a mixture of documentary, narrative, and literary sources, I have employed the same method used by my models in the field of political history, historians of late medieval Italy such as Gene Brucker, Philip Jones, and D. M. Bueno de Mesquito.

This privileging of contemporary chronicles has been necessitated, in part, by the poverty of surviving records from the Carrara regime itself. The wholesale destruction of Carrara chancery records, on the order of the Council of Ten, following Venice's conquest of 1405 has required the inescapable paradox of reconstructing Paduan foreign policy largely from Venetian state documents. Venice's policy toward the Carrara regime can be traced through the major series of Venetian legislative bodies: the deliberations and pardons (*grazie*) of the Maggior Consiglio and the Senate's deliberations, both "mixed" and "secret," with some attention to the records of the Collegio, the Avogadori di Comun, and the Procuratori di San Marco. The narrative has also been enriched by the study of the policies of the Carrara regime's principal ally, Florence, especially as expressed in the letters emanating from the Prima Cancellaria under Coluccio Salutati. Thus, the details of Carrara foreign policy are often known only from treaties, diplomatic correspondence, and debates of the councils of foreign powers.

A few crucial texts from the Carrara regime have, however, survived. Three manuscripts originating from the Carrara chancery are known to me: the Trecento communal statutes, the so-called *Statuti carraresi*, a formulary of letters from the early 1380s in the Archivio Papafava dei Carraresi, and the diplomatic correspondence for 1402, contained in the *copialettere carrarese*. As valuable as these texts are for the structure of the communal government in 1362 and the diplomacy of the Chioggia and Visconti wars, the student of Carrara Padua must rely mainly on the registers of the Archivio Notarile. Some hundreds of these survive from the second half

Introduction

of the Trecento and contain protocols of every sort—appointments of envoys, sales, leases, dowries, testaments, deposits with bankers, and contracts with mintworkers and purveyors—which provide many intimate glimpses of the Carrara family, its regime, and its affinity. The papers and ledgers of certain families, the Grompo and Lion, survive in the Archivi Privati Diversi, and many original parchments, chiefly from monastic sources, are collected in the Archivio Diplomatico and Archivio Corona. Rich ecclesiastical records, especially the bishops' grants of lay tithes, are found in Padua's Archivio della Curia Vescovile.

The uneven quality of the surviving documentary record has long challenged the ingenuity of historians of the Carrara Padua. During the eighteenth century two local antiquarians, Giovanni Brunacci and Giuseppe Gennari, compiled a massive manuscript, *Codice diplomatico padovano,* which comprised transcriptions of thousands of medieval documents, with volume 8 especially useful for the Trecento. At the end of the century, Gian Battista Verci brought out, in twenty volumes, his *Storia della marca trevigiana e veronese,* which published, mainly from private collections in Treviso, numerous documents on the Carrara regime. In the early nineteenth century, the local cleric Pietro Ceoldo compiled histories of the Papafava family and the abbey of San Stefano da Carrara, while the "Jacobin" bishop F. S. Dondi dall'Orologio published a history of the medieval Paduan church.

In 1842 the local liberal noble, Count Giovanni Cittadella, published the first extended history of the Carrara regime, colored by local patriotism, love of his subject, and deep dislike of Venice. During the second half of the century, the great Paduan historian and archivist Andrea Gloria published numerous editions of documents from the Trecento in pamphlets and short notes. In compiling his invaluable two-volume *Monumenti della Università di Padova (1318–1405),* Gloria thoroughly exploited the records of the local archives, especially the registers of the Archivio Notarile and other *fondi* mentioned above. But since Gloria aimed at providing names and dates for professors and students at the university in brief extracts, his volumes are mainly useful for their witness lists or documents directly affecting the *studium.* The two foremost Paduan medievalists of this century, Vittorio Lazzarini and Roberto Cessi, have contributed major studies of Venice's policy toward Carrara Padua and its industry, economy, mint, and foreign relations, often publishing archival sources as well. Perhaps the most significant study of medieval Padua is J. K. Hyde's *Padua in the Age of Dante,* to which my book may, in some respects, be viewed as a sequel. The only recent synthesis on Carrara Padua is Luigi Montobbio's *Splendore e utopia nella Padova dei Carraresi,* which (as the title suggests) celebrates the dynasty's art, culture, and court. Finally, Silvana Collodo's essays on late medieval Padua collected under the title *Una società in trasformazione* are models of careful archival research and contribute greatly to an understanding of Carrara interests in the wool industry and its network of supporters.

Thus, my study of the Carrara regime, its wealth, household, and affinity is much indebted to the labors of my scholarly predecessors. But since very few documents from the Paduan archives are published in full, like Brunacci, Gennari, Gloria, and Collodo, I have had to read through scores of volumes of the Archivio Notarile (AN). At first, I concentrated on the personal cartularies kept by notaries who worked in the Carrara chancery: Sicco Polenton (AN 1–4), Zilio Calvi (AN 5–9), Giovanni da Campolongo (AN 31–32), Bandino Brazzi (AN 33–38), Salimbene Zennari (AN 115–120), Pietro Saraceno (AN 256–258), and Marco Guarnerini (AN 525–525bis). These volumes yield valuable material on chancery practices, foreign relations and diplomacy, and Carrara family wealth. They are augmented by documents on the Carrara clan and its Papafava branch in the Biblioteca Civica of Padua, scores of original parchments in the collection *Documenti carraresi* (MS B.P. 990), and five volumes of transcriptions from original notarial contracts (some now lost) made in the eighteenth century by the local antiquarian Giovanni Battista Papafava, *Documenti per servire la storia dei Carraresi* (MS B.P. 928). The study of contracts and ledgers contained in the Archivi Privati Diversi, Archivio Diplomatico, and many other volumes of the Archivio Notarile illuminates kinship and marriage alliances and the business interests and landed wealth of the Carrara affinity Though perhaps not the "daily newspaper" of late medieval Padua (as Paolo Sambin has called them), Padua's notarial records often provide insights into the aspirations and enmities, goals and fears, as well as the wealth and family ties of the ruling family and its elite. The chapters of this book on the Carrara regime and affinity under the last two lords depend massively on the contracts redacted by Padua's Trecento notaries. Ironically, the criticism I made years ago reviewing Kenneth Hyde's book *Padua in the Age of Dante* came back to haunt me as I realized it could also apply to my book *Padua under the Carrara:* "the notarial documents . . . often intrude in the text as dry abstracts of wills and dowries" (*Speculum* 41 [1966]: 750).

The severe (but, I hope, not completely naive) empiricism of my method has perhaps conferred some benefits. The narrative chapters are intended to provide a detailed account of the politics of Trecento Padua comparable to those that Florence, Milan, and other late medieval Italian cities have long enjoyed. The close reading of thousands of surviving notarial acts should enable a more nuanced understanding of the wealth, power, and limits on authority in a signorial regime. The bibliography of both manuscript and printed sources and secondary works provides a full record of my own re-

Introduction

search and may serve as a guide to others undertaking work in Trecento Paduan history. Finally, my sharp insistence on the importance of context, physical and historical, enhanced by the numerous illustrations, may sometimes allow me to convey the reader across the chasm of the centuries and see the leaders of Carrara Padua, as it were, face to face.

Note on Time, Measures, and Money

The Paduan year began at the Nativity of Christ, that is, at the Christmas preceding 1 January, when the year begins now, whereas the year in Venice began on 1 March, two months after it begins in New Style. All dates in this book are given in New Style, but I often add the notation "*more veneto*" with year in parentheses to indicate the year found in the Venetian document.

The basic measure of land was the Paduan *campo*, which was divided into four quarters and 840 *tavole*.

1 *campo* = 3,862.57 square meters = 0.954 U.S. acre

1 *tavola* = 4.60 square meters

The basic measure of length was the Paduan mile (*miglio*), which was divided into 20 *tornature*, 620 *pertiche*, and 3,720 *piedi*. Hence, 1 *tornatura* equals 31 *pertiche*, and 1 *pertica* equals 6 *piedi*.

1 *piede* = 0.3574 meter = 14.2 inches

1 *miglio* = 1,329.5 meters = 0.82 U.S. mile

Measures of capacity were both dry and liquid. The basic dry measure was the *moggio*, which was divided into 12 *staia*. It took 6 *moggii* to make up 1 cartload (*carro*).

1 *moggio* = 347.8 liters = 9.87 U.S. bushels

1 *staio* = 28.98 liters = 0.823 U.S. bushel

The basic liquid measure for wine and oil was the *mastello*.

1 *mastello* = 71.28 liters = 15.68 U.S. gallons

In general, two coinage systems, one based on billon and silver, the other on the gold ducat and florin, obtained in Padua under the Carrara. The everyday system used the pound of petty deniers (*libra denariorum parvorum*), in which 240 *denarii* (real coins) = 12 *soldi parvorum* (money of account) = 1 *libra parvorum* (money of account). Early in his rule, Francesco il Vecchio da Carrara introduced two fine silver coins, the *carrarino*, which was worth two *soldi*, and the *carrarese*, worth four *soldi*. In addition, in the 1390s Francesco Novello introduced two *quattrini*, one worth two, the other four petty deniers.

The conversion between the gold ducat and the pound of petty deniers varied over the century. For example, on 3 June 1374 one ducat equaled 72 *soldi*, while on 20 November 1388 a ducat was worth 88 *soldi*, and on 1 January 1391 84 *soldi*.

Sources: Gloria, *Territorio padovano,* 1:148–55; A. Martini, *Manuele di Metrologia* (Turin, 1883), 437. On coins, see Rizzoli and Pertini, *Le monete di Padova,* 71–74, 84–86. For the conversions between *soldi* and ducat, see Lane and Mueller, *Money and Banking in Medieval and Renaissance Venice,* 1:583, 591–92.

Part I

THE EARLY CARRARA, 1318–1355

Chapter 1

Late Medieval Padua: The Setting

Muson, Mons, Athes, Mare Certos Dant Michi Fines.
[The Musone River, Monte Grappa, the Adige, the Sea Give
Me Definite Boundaries.]

—Motto on the Thirteenth-Century Seal of the Commune of Padua

Land and People of Late Medieval Padua

In the late Middle Ages the city-state of Padua was defined largely by natural boundaries: the Adige River on the south, the Venetian lagoon to the east, the Musone River on the Trevisan border, the foothills of the Alps on the north, and the more mobile frontiers with Verona and Vicenza to the west. The medieval Padovano was somewhat larger than the modern province of Padua, extending to the lagoon in the east and north, comprising 2,600 square kilometers (about 1,000 square miles). In the early centuries of the Christian era, Padua was the second city of the Roman Empire, growing up on the banks of the Meduacus (now the Brenta) River.[1] In ancient times, this major river divided to the northeast of Padua, forming the island on which the city was founded, and divided again near Strà, where the major channel flowed east to the lagoon; the Meduacus Minor ran southeast into the Adige near the Adriatic. The interior branch of the Meduacus (Livy's *flumen oppidi medium,* the current Riviera di Tito Livio and Ponti Romani) formed a major depot for goods as Padua became a military base under Roman, and later Byzantine, authority. At the end of the sixth century, disastrous flooding caused the Meduacus to form a new channel north of the city, while the Bacchiglione, flowing east from Vicenza, occupied the riverbed south of the city, eventually making early medieval Padua into an island. With the barbarian invasions and widespread destruction of the city, Padua was eclipsed by the Lombard capital in neighboring Verona. The resurgence of the city in the high Middle Ages was signaled by the rebuilding of the cathedral and ancient Benedictine house of S. Giustina, as well as the construction of the first circle of city walls at the end of the twelfth century.

Around these walls flowed the Bacchiglione, which divided at the southwest corner of Padua, at the Torlonga (later Ezzelino's Castello), with one branch running counterclockwise to the east and north, through the Naviglio Canal, north at Torricelle, following the course of the old *flumen oppidi medium,* to rejoin the other branch near Ponte Molino. The main branch flowed north around the western edge of the city to Ponte Molino, where it joined the Noventa Canal, eventually flowing into the Piovego Canal, which joined the Brenta at Strà. As Padua outgrew its island center in the thirteenth century, other canals were built to ring the larger city. The Bovetta dell'Alicorno flowed to the eastern terminus of the city at Ognissanti, where it met the Piovego Canal, which served trade from Venice and the eastern Padovano. Trade on the Bacchiglione from Vicenza and the Battaglia Canal, built in the early thirteenth century to connect Monselice from the south, entered the city at Porta S. Giovanni delle Navi, where the city's custom house was located and a guild of boatmen was formed to transport goods.

Although almost all of the Roman city had been destroyed—indeed, an area in the southeast was called Rudena from its extensive ancient ruins—the quarters of medieval Padua probably followed the axes of the ancient city. The north-south axis (or *cardo*) ran from the gate of Ponte Molino through the center near Palazzo Bo to the southern gate at S. Maria in Vanzo, and the major east-west axis (the *decumanus*) ran from Ponte Tadi on the western walls to Porta S. Lorenzo, forming the street to Ponte Corvo, and thence the road to Piove di Sacco and on to the lagoon. At the city center was built the town hall, or Palazzo della Ragione, whose giant roof, like the inverted hull of a ship, loomed over the entire city.[2] Near the Salone, as the town hall was also known, was located much of Padua's retail trade. Open-air markets were held daily in the flanking squares, the Piazze della Frutta and dell'Erbe, with poultry, fruit, secondhand clothes, and arms sold to the north and wine, tools, and vegetables to the south. To the east of the civic center bordering the Naviglio Canal was situated the haymarket in the Piazza de' Noli and the wood and charcoal market in the Piazza delle Legne. There too was located the fish market (the *pescheria*), the grain warehouse (the Fondaco delle Biave), and, by the end of the Trecento, the wool exchange (the *garzeria*). At the ends of the Salone were located other civic buildings: on the west, the debtors' prison, and on the east, a complex of palaces, housing the *podestà* and the smaller communal councils. Here too trade was mixed with government: salt was sold at the Palazzo degli Anziani and ironware at the Palazzo del Podestà. Thus, the civic cen-

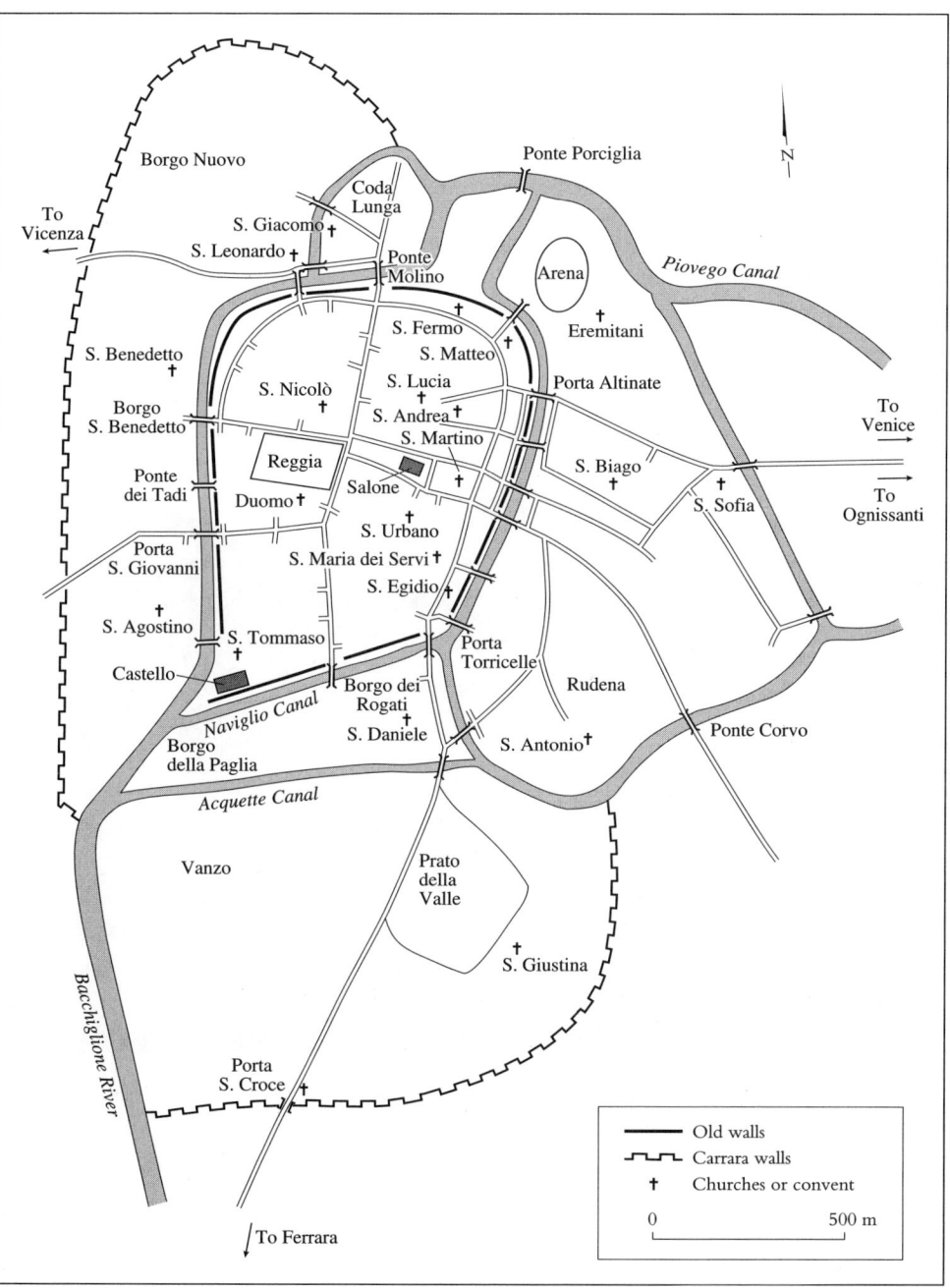

MAP 1. *Padua in the Fourteenth Century*

The Early Carrara

FIG. 1. *Tower of Palazzo degli Anziani, Padua. Photograph courtesy of Judith C. Kohl*

ter combined buildings for policymaking, policing, and the administration of justice with the major retail trades and the provisioning of the city with necessities: food, salt, metals, textiles, grain, hay, wood, and fuel.

To distribute representation on the city council and responsibility for policing the neighborhoods, in the thirteenth century Padua was divided into four quarters, named after three major gates—Ponte Molino, Torricelle, Altinate—and the Duomo. These quarters were further divided into

Late Medieval Padua

TABLE 1.1
Quarters and *Centenari* of Padua in the Fourteenth Century

Duomo	*Ponte Altinate*	*Torricelle*	*Ponte Molino*
Duomo	S. Biagio	S. Martino	Ponte Molino
S. Nicolò	S. Sofia	S. Egidio	S. Fermo
S. Lucia	S. Matteo	S. Daniele	S. Leonardo
S. Tommaso	S. Andrea	S. Croce	S. Giacomo
S. Urbano	Arena	Rudena	Codalunga

Source: Appendix 1, pt. 1.

five wards each (*centenari*), which were obliged to provide volunteer police and firefighters in case of emergency and to raise militia in time of war.[3] The centenari, usually named for the dominant parish church in the area, were further divided into neighborhoods, called *contrade,* the smallest subdivision of the city, often a source of local pride and patriotism. The quarters provided the basis for representation on the communal councils and for jurisdiction over the Padovano, which was likewise divided into four regions, each under the administration of an urban quarter. These administrative units of quarters, centenari and contrade, were adopted by the Carrara regime and remained the basic divisions of Padua into the early modern era.

The most important source for the population of late medieval Padua is a census made in 1320 to assess manpower when the city was under siege by Veronese forces. The census surveyed the city by centenari and contrade to determine the population in each area and the number of men, aged eighteen to sixty, fit for military service. But sometimes only the number of families is given, sometimes the number of "men," occasionally both. Also given are the names of notable citizens and male minors in each neighborhood, providing a list of reliable leaders in the crisis and, incidentally, a valuable source for determining the residence of important families and individuals. The common estimate of at least 35,000 inhabitants has been reached by simply multiplying by three the number of 11,131 "men" stated at the beginning of the survey.[4] But the figure of 11,131 is itself suspect because it does not tally with any possible sum of men or families given in the census. Rather, a close study of the survey (see Appendix 1) shows that the population of Padua was somewhat lower, perhaps no more than 30,000, in 1320. The data given in the survey may be presented in tabular form. The first column lists the number of families in each of the quarters, the second column the number of "men" for those neighborhoods where no families are given, and the third column the number of citizens named with male minors resident in their households.

TABLE 1.2
Population of Padua in 1320

Quarter	Families	"Men"	Citizens (+ Minors)
Duomo	1,580	None	259 (+ 135)
Torricelle	2,014	None	240 (+ 241)
Ponte Altinate	383	1,881	240 (+ 181)
Ponte Molino	28	1,933	194 (+ 152)
Total	4,005	2,714	933 (+ 709)

Source: Appendix 1, pt. 1.

The usual coefficient of 4.5 per household yields a population of 18,023 (4,005 x 4.5) for the households given in the survey. Using a ratio of 3:1 for the "men of arms-bearing age" adds a population of 8,142 (2,714 x 3) for those neighborhoods where figures are given only for men. The total of 26,165 is no doubt too low for the entire city, since in several neighborhoods no figures are given for either families or men. The number of uncounted persons cannot be known, but allowing for 10 percent, the city had a total population of 30,000. At one adult male per household, nearly 7,000 men were resident in Padua in 1320, of whom about 1,000 (or 1 in 7) enjoyed the rights of citizenship. Accepting the calculation of 63,000 persons residing in the countryside at the end of the thirteenth century, the ratio of urban to rural population comes to 1:2.[5]

As the census of 1320 shows, Padua in the age of Dante had greatly outgrown its walled center, creating suburbs on every border. To the north outside Ponte Molino lay the Borgo Nuovo; to the west Borgo S. Benedetto, containing several major religious houses; and to the south the older *borghi* (suburbs) of Paglia and of Rogati. Farther south below the Acquette Canal lay the large area of Vanzo, extending to the city's southernmost gate at S. Croce, containing orchards, vineyards, and fields and the fairgrounds at Prato della Valle, built on the ancient Campus Martius and dominated by the Abbey of S. Giustina. A few hundred meters to the east was erected the great Franciscan house of S. Antonio, between Ponte Corvo and the Rudena. These suburbs were protected by *murus spaldi,* earth and wooden ramparts built at the beginning of the fourteenth century, particularly strong on the west facing Verona. Surrounding the newly walled city was the Paduan *campanea,* a band of suburban rural villages under the direct control of the communal government, farmed by the villagers for urban landlords, who paid the same taxes as the city residents.[6] Thus, the Paduan campanea, also

FIG. 2. *Ponte Molino, North Gate of Padua. Photograph courtesy of Judith C. Kohl*

called the *campione,* developed into an area of intensive cultivation, with vineyards, gardens, and small grain farms providing for the needs of the urban populace. The border of the campanea was defined by stone markers placed 6 kilometers or more from Padua's center at the Duomo. In 1339, at the beginning of the Carrara regime, both the city and campanea of Padua received definition.[7] The city was the area enclosed by walls, of stone or of wood, and its "suburbia." The campanea was the area where the boundary stones were placed or, if these were lacking, where the residents were ac-

The Early Carrara

customed to paying taxes as Paduan citizens. Thus, peasants and landowners of the campanea became a privileged group, exempted from contributing labor for public works as was required of inhabitants of the Padovano.

The Padovano itself was, by geography and administrative custom, divided into several distinct regions. The richest and most spectacular was the Pedevenda, the area of the Euganean Hills, rising to peaks of more than 1,000 meters just to the southwest of the city. In the rich peaty soils of these ancient hills of volcanic origin were cultivated the cash crops of grape and olive, nut and fruit trees. Combining wine making and olive pressing with growing vegetables, legumes, and some grain, the Pedevenda developed into one of those areas of high agricultural productivity located near large cities in the Middle Ages. Here farms were small: the *mansus* (or basic farmstead for one family) was defined as 5 *campi* (or 2 hectares) of vineyard in the hills, but 30 *campi* for arable agriculture. Many influential families from the communal period, the Estensi, Conti, Carrara, Lozzi, and Schinelli, held property here, along with the bishop of Padua, the Abbey of S. Giustina, and other religious houses.[8] Below the hills in the southwest corner of the Padovano was situated the Scodosia, bounded by the Guà River on the north, the Fratta on the west, and the Adige on the south. Of Lombard settlement, characterized by large rural villages, the Scodosia was the most exposed region of the Padovano, protected in the Carrara period by the fortified vicariate of Castelbaldo on the Adige and governed by the podestà of the walled city of Montagnana at its center. Agriculture here mixed sheep and cattle herding with the cultivation of cereals and especially flax for linen and hemp for cordage. Just east of Scodosia lay Este and its villages on the low plain between the Euganean Hills and the Adige, bordered by Monselice, the largest town of the Padovano.

The southeast Padovano was divided between the vicariate of Conselve and the Saccisica, governed by the *podestaria* of Piove di Sacco. The low-lying area around Conselve was filled with woods, streams, and marshes in the Middle Ages, requiring a vigorous campaign of land reclamation and the construction of drainage canals to bring it under cultivation. Its rich loam soil made the area ideal for a mixed agriculture of grain and legumes with grazing of pigs in its woods and cattle and sheep on the large natural pasture called the Patriarcati.[9] Bordering the Venetian lagoon was the region of the Saccisica, governed as an extension of the quarter of Ponte Altinate. Situated on soil of sandy loam, the region was bordered on the south by the Bacchiglione and crossed by a cut of the Brenta, which flowed southeast from Strà into the lagoon at Chioggia. Its many small villages, dominated by the major town of Piove di Sacco, were devoted to cereal and flax cultivation. North of Padua lay the Oltrebrenta, an extension of the

MAP 2. *The Padovano in the Fourteenth Century*

quarter of Ponte Molino, which in the fourteenth century was divided into the vicariate of Camposampiero on the east and the podestaria of Cittadella on the west. The area of rich clay soil bordering the Trevisano was marked by centuriated fields surviving from the age of Roman colonization, each field about 750 meters square. The villages in this area were often no more than large farmsteads, dominated at the beginning of the fourteenth century by the Camposampiero, Dente, and Scrovegni families. The gravelly thin loam of the Brenta Valley made this a region more suitable for grazing and sheepherding than intensive agriculture. The area around Cittadella, which had been founded in 1220 as a frontier bastion opposite Treviso's Castelfranco, was marked by a number of *regole* (common pastures) under the control of the local commune. In all, the medieval Padovano was remarkable for its agricultural diversity, which was reflected in the patterns of settlement and distribution of population.

The principal source for determining the population of Padua's *contado* is the hearth assessment of 1281, made for the purpose of regulating the contributions of individual villages to public works projects such as maintaining roads, bridges, dikes, and, most of all, the drainage canals that crisscrossed the region. This extensive program of public works, later incorporated into the Paduan statutes of 1362, assigned to each village annual corvées on roads and waterways on the basis of the number of hearths (see part 2 of Appendix 1). The total number of hearths from the 396 towns and villages listed was 13,812, which multiplied by the standard coefficient of 4.5 persons per household gives a total population of over 62,000 (13,812 x 4.5 = 62,154).[10] This yields an urban-rural ratio of 1:2. The urban population was even higher if the inhabitants of the larger towns are included: Monselice (1,093 hearths), Piove di Sacco (775), Este (642), Montagnana (410), Pernumia (310), and Conselve (290). With a total area of 2,600 square kilometers (1,000 square miles), the population density of the contado was 24 persons per square kilometer (63 per square mile).

In the course of the late Middle Ages, the city's government developed ever closer administration of the Padovano. In 1276 the Paduan commune had installed its own podestà in the twenty-seven largest villages of the contado, regulating the private jurisdiction that feudal families held. By 1309 the commune required that all criminal court cases had to be tried before the podestà in Padua; civil suits for large amounts also had to be heard in the capital. At the restoration of the Carrara in 1337, there were already podestà installed in Bassano, Monselice, Este, and Montagnana, and probably vicars in other towns of the Padovano.[11] When, about 1370, Francesco il Vecchio da Carrara issued a letter defining the legal competence of local magistrates in civil suits, the entire contado was divided into five

TABLE 1.3
Hearths in the Jurisdictions of the Padovano in 1281, and Men-at-Arms in 1397

Jurisdiction	Hearths (1281)	Men-at-Arms (1397)
Podesteria		
Monselice	1,120	3,600
Piove di Sacco	2,989	6,300
Este	1,078	2,300
Montagnana	935	4,350
Cittadella	1,189	3,150
Vicariates		
Conselve	2,581	5,350
Teolo	1,302	1,400
Arquà	901	1,200
Camposampiero	1,260	5,300

Source: Appendix 1, pt. 2, and Gatari, *Cronaca carrarese*, 456–58.

podestarie and four vicariates.[12] Arranging the hearths and villages of 1281 under these podesterie and vicariates gives the total number of hearths in each jurisdiction, excluding those in the Paduan campanea. At the end of the fourteenth century, a parade muster of all men capable of bearing arms provides another indication of the distribution of population in the Padovano. In both instances, Piove di Sacco emerged as the largest podestaria and Conselve as the largest vicariate (see table 1.3). By the early Quattrocento, vicars were placed in command of the garrison towns of Castelbaldo and Anguillara on the Adige frontier and forts at Mirano and Oriago facing Venice, though these had very small territorial jurisdictions.[13]

Linking the towns of the contado with Padua and the rest of northern Italy was an extensive network of rivers and navigable canals, roads, and bridges. As we have seen, rivers served as boundaries as well as means of communication: the Musone River formed Padua's northeastern frontier with Treviso, and the Adige its southern border with Ferrara. Just west of the Musone flowed the fast-moving Tergola, which turned at Vigonza and became the Serraglio, which in turn flowed into the Brenta Canal near Mira. Originating in the Alps above Trent, the Brenta was the major river of the northern Padovano, linked in the early fourteenth century to the Bacchiglione at Brusegana by the Brentelle Canal, which flowed south from Limena west of Padua. The Bacchiglione flowed around Padua to Codalunga, where the Piovego Canal linked the city to Strà on the Brenta. From Strà, the Brenta flowed in one channel to the lagoon at the ferry station of Fusina opposite Venice, and by another cut southeast to Chioggia. The main course of the Bacchiglione ran south of Padua to Ponte S. Niccolò, on to Bovolenta, whence it flowed into the lagoon at Chioggia.

The major canal south of Padua was the Battaglia, excavated in the late thirteenth century, linking the city's terminus at Porta S. Giovanni delle Navi with Monselice and later extended to Este and Montagnana. From the village of Battaglia was excavated the Vigenzone Canal, which flowed northeast to join the Biancolino Canal at Cagnola, where it ran east to join the Bacchiglione at Bovolenta. All major shipping canals, as well as the canals surrounding Padua, were provided with towpaths to permit haulage of heavy shipborne cargoes. In the course of the fourteenth century, the Bacchiglione became a main route for the transport of persons and goods (and soldiers in time of war), departing from the Venetian lagoon at Chioggia. But maintaining dikes, embankments, and towpaths on the shipping canals paled beside the rural villages' obligation to construct and maintain the numerous drainage canals (*scoli*) that crisscrossed the Padovano. Hundreds of *scoli* were required to drain the low-lying regions of Scodosia, Saccisica, and Conselve. Small canals were also constructed in the Euganean Hills to provide transport and draw off water from marshy areas. Even in the dryer Oltrebrenta a number of short canals and ditches were built to drain water into the Musone, Tergola, and Brenta. In all, about 590 canals measuring more than 1,100 kilometers were built and maintained in the late medieval Padovano, at an enormous cost in time and labor to the peasants of the rural villages.[14]

Supervision of the countryside fell to the city's podestà and his staff, aided by the second half of the Trecento by Paduan citizens, usually Carrara favorites, who served as the podestà and vicars of the major towns of the contado. The podestà of the rural town was its chief judge and magistrate, helped by local officials elected by the adult male villagers for terms of six months or one year.[15] These local officials included the *sindico,* who administered communal property and reported wrongdoers to the podestà, the *massaro* (or treasurer), two consuls, who were in charge of recording all decisions, and two *cataveri,* controllers who checked the commune's accounts and oversaw the regulation of weights and measures. The most numerous local officials were the rural police (*saltuarii*), who numbered ten in Cittadella and twenty-two in Montagnana. This unpopular office, which could be avoided only upon payment of a heavy fine, was charged with arresting those guilty of causing or permitting damages to local property. Especially important was the task of keeping sheep, pigs, and cattle out of vineyards and arable. Most communes appointed salaried herdsmen to tend flocks, which were kept on fallow and waste land or in communal pastures (*regole*) or meadows. This responsibility was defined in great detail in the grazing lands of Cittadella. Conversely, there was much attention to the regulation of growing and processing flax and hemp in Scodosia. The system of mixed agriculture, combining animal husbandry and cereal tillage in most of the Padovano, placed heavy demands on the villagers to protect crops, especially vineyards and orchards, and raise animals at the same time. The generous bounties placed on such predators as wolves and kites underscored the danger of wild beasts in the remaining woods and wastes of the countryside. In general, the statutes of the rural communes provided for the minute regulation of local retailers and professionals: millers, taverners, schoolmasters, and physicians. Each town retained enormous powers of eminent domain, with *ingrossatores* elected annually to regulate common fields and maintain highways, confiscating such land as needed for local improvements. Although the podestà from Padua oversaw policing and higher justice, considerable authority remained vested in the village councils, composed of all taxing-paying males above the age of fourteen, who numbered forty in Cittadella and sixty in Montagnana. There were also meetings of councils in the smaller villages. In 1321 thirty-one men in Camin met to appoint a proctor to represent them in Padua, and in 1330 the council of Polverara elected a representative to treat with the new Scaliger vicar in Padua.[16] Thus, local *vicinancie* (neighborhoods) as well as larger communes enjoyed a measure of self-government in the Trecento.

Despite the measure of self-government accorded the rural communes, most land in the Padovano belonged to owners resident in Padua. In the communal period many areas had been under the de facto influence of local magnate families. As these were reduced in power in the wars of the early Trecento, only a few older families continued to exert major influence: the Carrara south of Padua, the Camposampiero and Da Vigonza in the Oltrebrenta, the Grompo and Este in Scodosia. In the second half of the Trecento, most farmland in the Padovano was acquired by the Carrara affinity, urban professionals, notaries, merchants, judges, and retailers, as well as rentiers and knights, who literally stocked their larders and filled their tables with the products of their rural estates. Although the basic unit of Paduan agriculture remained the *mansus,* the Trecento saw the enclosure of fields and, after the Black Death, the creation of large blocks of tillable land.[17] Much of the countryside was tilled under a three-field system, with winter crops of wheat, barley, and rye followed by spring crops of legumes, millet, and sorghum, while a third field lay fallow. Typically fields of five to fifteen *campi* were enclosed by hedges of vines, fruit trees, poplars, and willows. These enclosed fields at once protected the cereals from grazing animals, provided cash crops of grapes, fruit, and wood, and helped to promote drainage and prevent erosion in the low-lying countryside, often less than 10 meters above sea level.

The relation between the urban landlord and his rural tenant was usually defined by a written contract: a short-term lease of five or ten years (the *locatio*) or a longer lease of twenty-nine years (the *livello*).[18] The long-term lease, which often required a high entry fine, was, in practice, perpetual and often used to rent urban properties and by religious houses to settle distant property on peasants without close supervision. The more common contract was the *locatio,* in which the peasant's obligations were expressed in terms of a portion of the crops delivered to the landowner's home, a cash payment on the feast of St. Justina (7 October, Padua's autumn day of reckoning), and customary gifts in kind (called *onori*), such as capons at Shrovetide, eggs at Easter, or a ham at Christmas. Thus, Paduan agriculture was based on a type of sharecropping, in which the landlord provided land, seed, and sometimes tools to his tenant in return for food, gifts, and cash. Based on a symbiosis between town and country, the rural economy was not extensively monetized, with more than 80 percent of all *mezzadria* (sharecropping) contracts in the fourteenth century providing for payment in kind or in cash and in kind alone.[19] The *soceda* contract also favored the landlord leasing cattle or sheep to his peasants for a term of years (three to five) in return for annual dues in grain and granting half of any offspring of the owner. Landlords' interests sometimes extended to the welfare of their peasants' families, with gifts of dowries to daughters of favorite sharecroppers not uncommon. In the course of the Trecento, as an urban elite linked to the Carrara dynasty largely replaced the older feudal nobility, individual villages came under the rule of a new Paduan *noblesse de robe.*

In addition to native Paduans, Venetian monasteries and lay proprietors developed major interests in the Padovano.[20] Investments in the *terraferma* were especially heavy at the turn of the Trecento, with Venice requiring by treaty that its landowners in the Padovano be permitted to send food and materials duty-free into the *dogado.* For Venetian monasteries, such as S. Zaccaria, payments in rents in kind, especially in wine and olive oil, became the norm, with income earned by sales in the urban market. Throughout the Trecento, extensive holdings of certain Venetian families and religious houses in the Padovano provided Venice with a large incentive to control the affairs of Padua. The Venetian government often viewed the Padovano as its own contado—a toll-free source of food, fiber, and raw materials for its nobles, clergy, and industries.

Late Medieval Padua

The Government of the Paduan Commune

At his election in 1318, the first Carrara lord was explicitly charged with the protection of the Paduan commune, its institutions, and its autonomy. Throughout the Trecento, the commune continued to be the formal instrument of government for Padua and its contado, with its officials undertaking and overseeing the mundane tasks of governing, while the Carrara lord was mainly concerned with war and foreign policy. Thus, the Carrara lords left to the commune a number of areas of responsibility, under the general supervision of the podestà and his staff.[21] The supreme judicial officer and magistrate of the government of Padua was the podestà, a foreign jurist or knight, chosen for a term of six months, originally through a system of nomination and election by the communal councils. The transition from communal to signorial regime was accompanied by placing the election of podestà much more closely under the control of the *signore*. Honesty in overseeing communal property and fairness in the administration of laws and justice remained standard throughout the period, but political allegiance, membership in a Guelf commune, or the nobility of a friendly power became major criteria for appointment during the Trecento. Under Francesco il Vecchio, military ability instead of judicial competence became the prime quality sought in the podestà.

Throughout the fourteenth century, the podestà was expected to oversee the administration of justice and communal property and follow correct judicial procedures. The incorporation of oaths from the communal period in the Carrara code of 1362 underscores that at least lip service was paid to the integrity of the podestà in the day-to-day governance of the city of Padua.[22] The oath to defend the interests of the Paduan commune fell under four general heads: justice, defense, property, and taxes. Under justice, the podestà swore that he and his staff would execute the sentences handed down by the officials of the commune. Under defense, the podestà pledged to keep Padua safe from attack, to keep roads and bridges, ramparts and walls in good repair and, if the need arose, lead the city's army in battle. In overseeing communal property, the podestà swore to permit no theft or embezzlement and to recover any lands or goods that had been illegally alienated. Finally, the podestà agreed to oversee the collection of taxes and customs duties (*vectigalia et dacia*) and prevent the extortion of taxes that were not owed to the Paduan commune. Even more pointed was the inclusion of elaborate procedures for the syndication, or investigation, of the podestà and his staff at the end of their term of office. A citizen board was to investigate and ensure that no favoritism had been shown or that no theft of communal property had occurred. But over the course of the century, the Carrara lord exerted ever greater control over the choice and conduct of the podestà, as an analysis of their geographic origins shows.

The geographic origins of Padua's podestà from 1318 to 1405 reveal major shifts resulting from external political events and changes in regime (see Appendix 2). During the first decades, when the rule of Padua was disputed, the podestà were sometimes chosen from the enemies, sometimes the partisans of the Carraresi. After 1328, under the Scaligers of Verona, podestà were recruited largely from Verona and other cities friendly to the lords of Verona. With the backing of Venice and Florence, the Carrara dynasty retook control of Padua in 1337. For the next two decades, the Venetian government treated Padua as *"status noster,"* with fifteen of its nobles serving a total of thirty-seven terms as podestà. Francesco il Vecchio used the office to install able military commanders who were close friends of the dynasty. For example, Giovanni Manfredi of Reggio served nine terms, Simone Lupi of Parma nine, and Rizzardo Count Sambonifacio of Verona fourteen terms. Since these podestà were more often military captains than judges or legal experts, daily administration often fell to a vice-podestà who held a doctorate in civil law. With the first fall of the Carrara under Visconti conquest in 1388, Milanese soldiers held the office, and with the return of Francesco Novello da Carrara under Venice's auspices in 1390, a succession of Venetian nobles held the office until 1403. Only during his fatal struggle against Venice did the lord of Padua again recruit podestà from Guelf Florence.

Whatever his loyalties and origins, the podestà ruled with a large staff. Each podestà was supported by soldiers, jurists, household servants, and police to bring justice and security to the city and its contado.[23] After 1320 his staff included five judges and five knights, twelve men-at-arms, servants and cooks, and a police force of sixty uniformed officers (*berroderii*). The podestà's salary was £1,000 per month, from which he was also to maintain this retinue, which he housed in a large palace in the center of Padua. In the exercise of their duties, the podestà and his staff touched every facet of Padua's public life. More often than not the podestà's primary responsibility lay not in justice but defense. Military service was compensated according to detailed pay schedules (£8 per diem as a captain in the Paduan army, and £4 per diem as head of a body of horsemen or protecting an embassy), and the commune was to provide restitution if the podestà's horse was killed in battle. In the rules governing official inquiries (*sindicationes*) required at the end of a term of office, the podestà's lay and knightly origins were clearly recognized: "because many podestà of Padua are lay knights and ignorant of law, they are held to make all condemnations and absolutions with the advice of their staff."[24]

The most important judicial officer on the podestà's staff was his vicar,

TABLE 1.4
Geographic Origins of the Podestà of Padua, by Term, 1318–1405

Period	City or Region of Origin						Terms
	Venice	Veneto	Florence & Tuscany	Emilia/ Romagna	Lombardy	Other	
1318–37	3	17	2	5	6	4	37
1337–57	37	0	0	0	0	0	37
1357–88	2	16	10	26	4	2	60
1388–1405	24	8	4	0	3	0	39
Total	66	41	16	31	13	6	173

Source: Appendix 2.
Note: Terms were usually of six months.

who almost always held a doctorate in civil law and served as presiding judge at the highest communal court that met under the communal seal, hence called Sigillo. Here litigation was heard between the commune and its citizens or among citizens on weighty matters, which, in the course of the Trecento, were sometimes appealed to the Carrara lord himself. In the absence of the podestà, the vice-podestà served as judge at Sigillo. The other four judges of the podestà's staff carried out more specialized functions. One judge, who was head of victualing (Vettovaglio), held court at the sign of the unicorn and presided over cases concerning the provisioning of the city, maintenance of roads, bridges, and canals, and customs on goods entering and leaving Padua. Another judge, at the sign of the eagle (Aquila), heard cases concerning communal property and taxes, the *dacia*. The two other judges tried criminal cases, disputes between clergy and laity, and some cases of both a criminal and civil complexion. These two judges had specific jurisdictions: one heard cases arising in the quarters of Ponte Altinate and Ponte Molino and their parts of the contado; the other tried cases from the quarters of the Duomo and Torricelle and their jurisdictions in the Euganean Hills, Scodosia, Este, and Monselice.

The knights of the podestà were police officers whose duties paralleled those of the judges. One knight was deputed to the office of Vettovaglio and oversaw the administration of communal property. Another was in charge of public roads, bridges, and canals and made sure that the taxes due from the rural villages for their maintenance were forthcoming. A third worked with the criminal court judges to bring miscreants to justice, and the other two directed the policing of the city and countryside. The body concerned with the policing of the city was the *precones*, messengers of the commune.

The statutes provided for the election of twenty precones from their own guild every four months to serve directly under the podestà. Their duties were various. They accompanied the tax collectors to ensure the payment of the communal dacia and served as guards at the communal palace and the city jail. Most important, the precones served the warrants issued by the podestà or his judges for the arrest of debtors or criminals in the contado. Thus, the precones combined ordinary police duties with the obligation to arrest and transport to Padua for trial debtors and those wanted for other crimes. The most numerous ordinary communal officials were the twelve civil judges. Each held court for a term of four months at a distinctive sign, with a secretariat of five notaries, for a salary of £20 per term. Elected from the College of Judges, the ordinary judges had to be Paduan citizens, resident in the city, and inscribed on the tax roles, with at least five years of legal training. The other ordinary officials of the Paduan commune include the two heads and notaries of the chancery, which served mainly as a record depository. There all court decisions and lists of officials were kept. Communal treasurers, two *caniparii,* continued to serve until late in the Carrara period, though the collection of taxes increasingly came under the control of the lord. Serving as record keepers for all the ordinary communal officers were a number of notaries (as many as 110 at any time) elected from their own local guild.

A number of extraordinary officials served the commune on specific missions. These included ambassadors and proctors who represented the commune abroad to conclude treaties with foreign powers. In the second half of the Trecento, the commune typically appointed the lord's envoy as its own representative, thus simply affirming the lord's choice of personnel and policy. The communal lawyers, physicians, procurators, inspectors, and supervisors of public works oversaw the areas of food supply, public health, economic regulation, and public works, which the Carrara lords were willing to leave to the communal government. The most important task left to the commune was the regulation and collection of revenue.[25] The largest source of communal income continued to be rents from its property. The commune owned the public buildings of the city center as well as the shops, stores, and stalls they contained, and it rented these to guildsmen and retailers on long-term leases. In addition, the commune owned the thermal baths at Montogrotto, mills on the Battaglia Canal, and some land in the countryside. The commune also levied its own taxes, the dacia. Originally the dacia was foremost a direct personal tax, like the *lira* in Florence and Siena, levied on the basis of individual real and movable property as registered in the communal *liber extimorum.*[26] By the late Trecento, this tax, known as the *estimo,* was a percentage of the declared value of real estate,

TABLE 1.5
Ordinary Officials of the Communal Government of Padua, 1362

Office	Officer	Number of Notaries
Court of the Seal (Sigillo)	judge, knight	12
Court of Victualing and Unicorn	judge, knight	8
Court of Eagle (Aquila)	judge, knight	6
Criminal court	2 judges, 1 knight	16
Police force	2 knights, 20 precones, 60 berroverii	
12 civil courts	12 judges	60
Chancery	2 heads	4
Treasury	2 caniparii	4
Total	107	110

Source: *Stat. Car.*, Liber 1.

leases, merchandise held with partners, bank deposits, animals, personal property, and debts owed by others. The term *dacia* was later applied to excise taxes on a number of commodities and services and to custom duties, also known as *gabelle*, collected at the *officium bulletarum*. The excise taxes on such necessities as grain, meat, salt, and wine were typically farmed to local entrepreneurs, who paid a lump sum for the right to collect the dacia. In the second half of the Trecento, these tax farmers were increasingly Carrara favorites. Thus, the communal institutions were adapted to meet the needs of the Carrara lords, just as the Paduan church came increasingly under lay influence and signorial control.

The Paduan Church

In the late Middle Ages the Diocese of Padua largely, but imperfectly, duplicated the area under the jurisdiction of the lord and commune of Padua. The two had the same boundaries on the south (Adige River), east (lagoon and Musone River), and most of the western border with the Vicentino, but the towns and parishes of the northwestern part of the Oltrebrenta, including Cittadella, Fontaniva, and Carturo, came under the jurisdiction of the bishop of Vicenza. This loss was compensated by an enclave of the Paduan diocese in the foothills of the Alps, the region of the Sette Comuni, with parishes and religious houses at Marostica, Solagna, and S. Eulalia coming under at least the nominal sway of the bishop of Padua.

At the heart of the diocese was the ancient "Mother Church," the Cathedral of Padua, dedicated to the Virgin Mary, located near the center of the city at the intersection of the Strà Maggiore and Via Patriarcato. By 1308, when the parochial organization of chapels and baptismal churches was defined, the city and its *borghi* contained twenty-eight parishes. By the fifteenth century the bishop of Padua enjoyed the right of collation (authority to appoint the parish priest) for nearly half (twelve) of these parishes; the papal curia held collation for five parishes, the Benedictine abbey of S. Giustina, and the cathedral chapter and nunnery of S. Pietro for two each, with various monasteries holding patronage for the rest, often small urban parishes they had founded.[27] Within the walls of Trecento Padua were some forty religious houses, mainly Benedictine monasteries and nunneries. By the end of the thirteenth century, however, the mendicant orders had established churches in Padua. The most famous and powerful was the Basilica of S. Antonio, founded as a Franciscan convent in 1240 and dedicated to Padua's thaumaturgic friar and messenger of St. Francis, who brought the teachings of the Friars Minor north of the Apennines. On the spot where St. Anthony died in Arcella, just north of Padua, the Poor Clares erected a convent dedicated to the Virgin Mary, which soon became a focus of Franciscan spirituality. In 1226 the Dominican order founded its own convent, dedicated to S. Agostino, just outside the first western walls of the city. By the end of the century, the Augustinian Hermits had constructed their huge preaching church near the Arena northeast of the first walls, while the Carmelites founded their church dedicated to the Virgin Mary, north of the gate at Ponte Molino.

The definition of the Paduan church and its relation with secular authority in the fourteenth century owed much to the precedents and regulations that emerged from the fierce struggles between bishop and commune at the end of the Duecento.[28] When the Paduan commune curtailed clerical privileges, the pope placed the city under an interdict, which ended in August 1290 when Pope Nicholas IV issued a bull that lifted the ban of excommunication and defined the rights and corrected the errors of Padua's clergy.[29] Clauses from the bull which pertained to the morals, status, and rights of the clergy were incorporated in the reforming synods and the Carrara statutes of the next century, thus delineating the problems that continued to face the church in Carrara Padua. In general, the clergy came more and more under communal authority. For example, the bishop could not interfere with the podestà in cases in which the secular arm had jurisdiction, and clergy had to contribute, just as laity, to the repair of roads and dikes in the contado. In cases of debts, suits, and contracts with laymen and serious crimes (such as homicide), clergy were to be tried and punished in the communal courts. Episcopal tithes came increasingly under the power of their lay proprietors, since the bishop could no longer transfer to another party tithes held for at least twenty years. Finally, the Carrara statutes incorporated the commune's longstanding commitment to fight heresy: the detailed bulls of Pope Alexander IV from the 1260s were repeated verbatim in the statutes, as were the provisions from 1297 for using the podestà as the secular arm to combat heretics.[30] In these statutes Padua stood out as a Guelf city committed to uphold papal authority and Christian orthodoxy in the extirpation of heresy.

In the first half of the Trecento, the day-to-day administration of the diocese devolved upon a variety of vicars and notaries, since the bishops, Pagano della Torre of Milan (1302–19) and Ildebrandino Conti from Valmontone (1319–52), were often absentee officials. An important official and diplomat at the papal court at Avignon, Conti visited Padua for the first time only in November 1332, instead administering the diocese through his household of vicars, officials, and notaries, who were often kinsmen or compatriots from southern Latium. In all, twenty-one vicars served in Padua during Conti's long tenure, with all but three coming from outside the diocese. These officials were divided into two groups, those with legal knowledge and administrative skills, who oversaw matters "in temporalibus," and those concerned with spiritual matters.[31] During his visits to Padua, Conti demonstrated a zeal for reforming diocesan administration and the morals of his clergy. In 1333 he oversaw the reform of the cathedral chapter, with the creation of a single code of statutes. Here the number of canons was reduced to twenty, with the commune no longer required to pay for these canons who were absent for motive of study.[32] Thus, though an absentee bishop himself, Conti stressed the importance of continuous residence for the archpriest and canons of the Paduan cathedral. In the 1330s the canons of the Paduan church emerged as the privileged clerics of the growing Carrara elite, with Bartolomeo Capodivacca serving as archpriest and Leonardo and Perenzano da Carrara as canons.[33]

Among the many powers of the bishop of Padua was the granting of tithes to churches, religious houses, and especially lay proprietors. Originating as the gift of a tenth of the laity's income, the tithe became divided into two portions, with one-fourth (the *quartese*) assigned for the use of the local parish clergy, while three-fourths remained under the control of the bishop. By the thirteenth century, the episcopal tithes of Padua and other north Italian dioceses came increasingly under the control of powerful members of the local laity, as the bishop granted fiefs of tithes in the countryside to his vassals, who were often lay proprietors of rural villages.[34] Lay tithes began as simply the grant of the usufruct of the episcopal tithes for a limited period. Thus, with these infeudated tithes, also called decimal fiefs, the bishop granted the tithes of a district, or village, to a local landowner for a term of years. The transaction was simple; no oath of fealty was required, although the vassal was forbidden to alienate any of the grant. In late medieval Padua the decimal fiefs increasingly became hereditary, with a new vassal renewing the grant upon the death of his kinsman, usually his father. Obviously the heritability of these fiefs of tithes promoted the interests of local lineages. Losers in the struggle for political power were often exiled and, in effect, had to renounce their tithes to the bishop. Thus, the winners in the political conflict of the early Trecento, the Carrara family and its supporters, increasingly came into possession of the infeudated tithes of the Paduan contado.[35]

The laicization of the bishop's tithes was one result of the long-term interest of the Paduan commune in placing legal questions about tithes under its own jurisdiction. From the early thirteenth century, the commune decreed that its podestà would protect the rights of anyone holding tithes for more than thirty years (later twenty years), at the same time regulating the collection of the tithe.[36] Under this statute, the owner's rights were well protected, since the peasant had to notify the tithe holder of his intention to harvest. If the owner did not have his own collector in the area, the peasant had to set aside the owner's portion with two neighbors as witnesses, while delivering the *quartese* to the parish priest. Ultimately the right to collect tithes in the city and campanea of Padua was restricted to the bishop, monastic houses, and longtime lay proprietors, so tithes simply became an additional tax levied on the peasants of the Padovano. Tithes could be paid in cash or in kind, and for the bishop, cathedral chapter, religious houses, and the Carrara and their wealthiest followers, they became a considerable source of income and provisions. For example, in 1355 the cathedral chapter of Padua collected more than 400 *moggi* of wheat and other grain as its tithes in the campanea.[37] Not surprisingly, such wealth became a frequent source of litigation in which the Carrara lord was increasingly involved. In 1345 Giacomo II convened arbiters in the Reggia to settle a dispute over tithes between S. Giustina and the monasteries of S. Stefano and S. Teche in Este.[38] Gaining a voice in the appointment of the dispenser of tithes, the bishop of Padua, became a preoccupation of the Carrara lords of Padua.

The laicization of tithes was accompanied by the politicization of the ecclesiastical hierarchy of Padua, especially its bishops and canons.[39] The Roman nobleman Giovanni Orsini was the last absentee bishop, with Francesco il Vecchio often taking a direct hand in the appointment of his successors. The next bishop, Pileo da Prata, a canon at the Duomo since 1350 and the ruling lord's first cousin, was instrumental in monastic and university reform, using his influence at Avignon to confirm Padua's status as a *studium generale*.[40] The next bishop, Giovanni Piacentini, fell out of favor

Late Medieval Padua

TABLE 1.6
Bishops of Padua in the Carrara Period, 1319–1406

Term of Office	Name and Homeland
27 June 1319–2 Nov. 1352	Ildebrandino Conti, Valmontone, Latium
14 Jan. 1353–early 1359	Giovanni Orsini, Rome
12 June 1359–Jan. 1369	Pileo, count of Prata, Friuli
13 Jan. 1369–early 1371	Giovanni Piacentini, Parma
28 Apr. 1371–1372	Elias de Beaufort, Ventadour, France
23 Jan. 1374–late 1386	Raimondo Ganimberti, Friuli
Apr. 1388–Feb. 1392	Giovanni Enselmini, Padua
7 May 1392–1396	Ugone Roberti, Abruzzi
10 Apr. 1402–Jan. 1406	Stefano da Carrara, Padua

Source: Montobbio, *Splendore e utopia nella Padova dei Carraresi*, 353.

with the ruling lord and was translated to another see, at which time Pope Gregory XI named the French prelate Elias de Beaufort as an "interim" bishop. Perhaps the most effective of the "political" bishops was the papal diplomat and Benedictine prelate Raimondo Ganimberti, who first visited the city as a papal envoy to help end the border war in 1373 and settled there the next year as its bishop, being very active in monastic reform. Signorial influence in appointment to high ecclesiastical office culminated in 1402 with the election of Francesco Novello's illegitimate son, Stefano, as bishop of Padua.

Following the widespread mortality caused by the Black Death, consolidation, retrenchment, and reform were the norm for the religious orders in Padua, often aided by monks of the Camaldolensian and other Benedictine reform movements, especially under the leadership of Bishop Raimondo Ganimberti.[41] The fortunes of many monasteries were favored by the intervention of the lord of Padua, who frequently facilitated the purchase and exchange of property by dispensing with communal statutes against religious persons and houses acquiring real estate in Padua and its district. As early as 1350, Giacomo II da Carrara issued a decree allowing the abbot of S. Giustina to acquire property in Padua. Francesco il Vecchio made frequent dispensations to the Eremitani, the Benedictine nuns of S. Francesco, S. Pietro, and S. Agnese, the monks of S. Giovanni Battista del Venda, and the Dominicans of S. Agostino to acquire property by exchange, gift, or purchase.[42] Through patronage, gifts, and favors, the Carrara developed the control of the ecclesiastical system which extended in the second half of the century to filling religious office with illegitimate or less favored members of the family. Thus, the Paduan church joined the commune as inherited

FIG. 3. *Church of S. Stefano da Carrara. The principal church of the family's country seat, to which the Carrara lord had the* ius patronatus. *Photograph courtesy of Tracy Cooper*

institutions that were adapted to enhance the power and prestige of the Carrara dynasty.

Guilds and the University

Although Padua, unlike Florence, never required guild membership for political participation in the life of the commune, by the end of the Duecento the guilds of Padua had achieved considerable influence in the smaller, policymaking councils of the communal government. By legislation in the 1290s, the Council of Elders (Anziani) was to have members from both the community (*communancia*) and the guilds, with the latter's lower property and tax qualification betokening their status as artisans and tradesmen. To membership on the Anziani was added a committee of fifteen *gastaldi* (heads) of the guilds, charged with specific responsibility to ensure that the interests of trade guilds were met.[43] The institution of the Carrara regime greatly reduced the direct political participation of the guilds, but they remained the bedrock entities of Paduan economic life. The thirty-six guilds recognized by the commune in 1287 attest to the essentially artisanal and service character of the Paduan economy (see table 1.7).

The largest and most powerful guild was the notaries, which had been organized at the beginning of the thirteenth century. This was followed by the merchants who mainly dealt in textiles (*mercatores*) and entrepreneurs in the woolen industry (*lanarii*), which grew enormously under Carrara patronage. But the vast majority of the guilds were organized to provide the goods and services required in the local urban economy. Here artisans dominated, with the building trades of masons, carpenters, and bricklayers, the textile and clothing trades, and metal- and leatherworkers accounting for half of all guilds. In addition, a large portion of the working population was employed in the distribution and sale of agricultural products of the contado. The victualing guilds of butchers and bakers, grocers and greengrocers, spice and salt merchants, millers and fishmongers dominated the commercial city center surrounding the Padua's civic buildings. The rural character of much of Padua and its campanea was underscored by the inclusion of guilds of gardeners and reapers. Transport was handled by the guilds of wagoners and wine porters and by the boatmen, who were responsible for shipborne transportation of cargoes landing at the city's two major ports: the termini at Ognissanti on the east and at S. Giovanni delle Navi on the southwest. Completely lacking were commercial guilds of banking and international trade, such as Cambio and Calimala in Florence. The organization of Padua's moneylenders and pawnbrokers (*campsores*) was quite primitive, though regulated by the communal government to protect

TABLE 1.7
Guilds in Carrara Padua

Services	*Construction*
Notaries	Carpenters
Physicians	Masons and bricklayers
Barbers	Coopers
Textiles	*Clothing*
Merchants	Tailors
Woolen manufacturers	Doublet makers
Linen makers	Secondhand clothing
Weavers	Retailers
Dyers	
	Leather
Victualers	Skinners
Spice merchants	Tanners
Millers	Saddlers
Bakers	Shoemakers
Grocers	Cobblers
Greengrocers	
Butchers	*Transport*
Salt merchants	Wagoners
Fishmongers	Wine porters
Taverners	Boatmen of S. Giovanni delle Navi
	Boatmen of Ognissanti
Metalworkers	
Smiths	*Agricultural*
Goldsmiths	Reapers
	Gardeners

Source: Stat. Car., fol. 47rv, eds. in Roberti, *Corporazioni padovane*, 122, and Hyde, *Padua in the Age of Dante*, 311.

the debtor's goods given as securities.[44] Most loans were made by individuals or temporary partnerships on short-term contract, usually to the commune or leading families. Although the *campsores* were organized in a guild by the 1330s, only with the influx of Tuscan bankers and Jewish merchants in the second half of the Trecento did commercial banking come to Padua.

Perhaps the most prestigious occupational group, the judges of the Paduan court system, was never recognized as a guild but since about 1270 had been organized as the Collegio dei Giudici di Palazzo.[45] Like other Paduan guilds, the Giudici di Palazzo had their statutes approved by the podestà and his staff. These regulations provided for the spiritual and earthly welfare of the members and set the terms of their recruitment and employment. The judges had to be natives of Padua or its contado, with a tax assessment of at least £100, have six years of legal training, and possess the basic texts of Roman law, the *Code, Institutes,* and *Old Digest.* Admission to the college was gained upon recommendation of its officers and upon public examination by the podestà's vicar in the presence of the four gastaldi and a quorum of two-thirds of its members. From a membership of perhaps one hundred in the early Trecento, the college had fallen to sixty-eight in the census of 1320 and probably no more than forty-one in February 1347. But as the authority of the Carrara grew, the college became populated with favorites of the regime. A list of forty-eight judges matriculated in the college in 1361 reveals a membership of many distinguished jurists, who served the Carrara regime as envoys and councillors, including Francesco Beningrado, Tebaldo Cortellerio, Francesco Conselve, Guglielmo Cortusi, Guglielmo Curtarolo, Ottonello Descalzi, Alessandro Dottori, Enrico Gallo, Bartolomeo Piacentini, and Giacomo da Santa Croce.[46] Thus, the local college of judges was a prime source of many well-trained servants of the Carrara regime.

The largest of all the Paduan guilds was the notaries, those public officials whose validated instruments became, by the late Middle Ages, binding in courts throughout the Mediterranean world. The notary was indispensable to the conduct of government and diplomacy, commerce and agriculture, and the private law of dowry and testament. At its height, the Paduan guild had been composed of 500 members, of whom (as we have seen) more than 100 were, at a given time, employed in the communal government. Between 130 and 188 members attended chapter meetings in the 1330s, and on the eve of the Black Death, the membership stood at 328. By 1355 the meetings of the chapter were attended by 55 to 64 notaries, indicating a membership of no more than 150.[47] Even more than other Paduan guilds, the notaries guild privileged kinship relations, with membership and work assignments passed down from father to son. For example, the required rotation from service in the communal government was canceled if the office was given to a close kinsman—brother, father, or son.

Like other guilds, that of the notaries functioned as a mutual-aid and burial society; its statutes were marked by an explicit concern for the spiritual welfare and ethical behavior of its members.[48] The officers of the guild consisted of the *sindico,* who directed the day-to-day operation of the guild and oversaw its ceremonial and liturgical responsibilities, and four gastaldi, one elected from each quarter for a term of six months. The gastaldi had to be Paduan citizens, at least thirty years old, resident in the city, and inscribed in the communal dacia for an assessment of £200. Their principal task was to oversee admission to the guild and ensure the rotation of the notaries among the various offices of the communal government. Those nominated to the guild had to be native Paduans, twenty years of age, and supported by two gastaldi and the *sindico*. On nomination the candidate underwent a public examination by the guild officers and representatives of the podestà to demonstrate evidence of knowledge of types of instruments and clear handwriting. Each new notary was eventually confirmed in his office, as *tabelio et iudex ordinarius*, by the local count palatine, thus becoming a "public person."

Beginning with employment in the communal judiciary, the new notary followed a *cursus honorum* (career path), progressing to service in the more demanding offices in the chancery and on the podestà's staff. Since employment in the communal government, at a salary of £20 for a term of four months, often constituted a large part of a notary's income, rotation through the various secretariats was the norm. The gastaldi were responsible for keeping lists of vacant offices and eligible notaries, with two young boys making appointments by lot; one picked the notary's name from one sack, and the other chose the office from another bag. Notaries typically supplemented income in local government and the bishop's curia by redacting instruments for private clients at home. For example, early in 1371, Zilberto dagli Statuti earned £25 and £13 a month working at home but in March increased his income to £33, serving as notary at Vettovaglio while continuing to redact instruments for clients.[49] The massive reliance on written materials promoted detailed regulations on record keeping, for both the guild and commune required individual notaries to preserve written copies of private instruments, thus creating archives for many communal offices.[50] These requirements only served to enhance the importance of the notary in governing Trecento Padua.

The manufacturing and sale of textiles, mainly woolen and linen cloth, was the most conspicuous "growth" industry in Trecento Padua.[51] In the communal period, the nascent textile industry was organized into three guilds for making woolen cloth, entrepreneurs (*lanarii*), weavers and dyers, and a guild of linen makers (*linaroli*), underscoring the artisanal nature of this industry, in which monks and nuns as well as laity were often employed. Well into the Trecento, foreign cloth was freely imported to supplement the limited local production. Padua's extensive network of rivers and canals, however, permitted the construction of fulling mills and dyeing vats needed in textile manufacturing, while sheep herding in the Oltrebrenta and neighboring Vicenza, Verona, and Friuli provided the raw wool for manufacturing. In the second half of the Trecento, a trained labor force was created through the policy of encouraging the immigration of woolen workers of every sort: spinners, weavers, fullers, dyers, combers, shearers, and finishers. At the center of production stood the *lanaro,* who acquired the raw wool and oversaw its manufacturing into cloth, often employing his own "team" of spinners and weavers on long-term contracts. Textile manufacturing was spread throughout Padua, utilizing fulling mills at a number of locations, especially at Torricelle, Ponte Molino, and Ponte Corvo, with the dyers concentrated near Prato della Valle. Consuming after midcentury from 6,500 to 10,000 pounds (3,185–4,900 kilos) of local wool a year, the *lanari* were increasingly able to meet local demand for cloth. Minute regulations of the activities of spinners, weavers, and dyers, largely redacted in 1368, aimed at producing cloth of good quality, ultimately driving foreign competitors from the market. As we shall see, the Carrara lords early took an active interest in the textile industry. Ubertino da Carrara brought skilled fullers and wool workers from Tuscany, and Francesco il Vecchio promoted immigration and centralized the production and distribution of woolen cloth in his own warehouse. Thus, the wool guild (Arte della Lana) became a special object of Carrara patronage, with the creation its own court system in which disputes were adjudicated by the guild's three elected gastaldi and its rector, who was handpicked by the Carrara lord. Linking manufacturing closely to distribution and sale, the textile industry was dominated by entrepreneurs who functioned as merchants, earning the binomial *mercatores lanarii* in the late Trecento.

The guilds atrophied in power and independence in the course of the Trecento. The longstanding capacity of the Paduan commune to interfere in guild affairs and change guild statutes became even more explicit in the second half of the century. In 1360, the notaries guild recognized that the Carrara lord had the right to alter any guild regulation and that his vicar could pardon and reinstate members recently expelled. Exercising this right in 1373, Francesco il Vecchio restored to guild membership a notary once condemned by the commune and enrolled a foreign notary from Segni.[52] The lord's growing interference in guild affairs was accompanied by the blanket assertion in legislation of 1366 that the handpicked podestà of Padua could dispatch one of his knights to rescind any guild ordinance that was made "*contra publicam utilitatem.*"[53] With the costly wars of the 1370s and 1380s, guilds became subject to a lump-sum assessment to pay for military campaigns and acquisition of territory.

Created, according to tradition, by the migration of dissident students from Bologna in 1222, the University of Padua was nourished by a constant stream of foreign professors and students and protected by local public authority—communal and signorial—throughout the later Middle Ages. Scholarly privileges to attract teachers and scholars to Padua were adopted in a spate of legislation in the 1260s which was maintained and expanded in the Trecento.⁵⁴ These privileges aimed to protect the rights of foreign scholars, freeing them from payment of most local taxes, arrest for debt, and service in the Paduan army. Scholars were to be accorded clerical status in case of trial and enjoyed a limit on the interest exacted by moneylenders. During term lodgings were rented at a fixed and predetermined rate but had to be vacated when the university was out of session. The effect was to confer on foreign students and teachers the benefits but not the burdens of Paduan citizenship and thus to attract a large academic community to Padua with its obvious economic and cultural rewards.

The Paduan *studium* was organized in the late Middle Ages into five academic corporations: two universities of law, one of arts and medicine, and two doctoral colleges, one for doctors of law, the other for doctors of arts and medicine.⁵⁵ Throughout the Trecento, the *studium* was dominated by the two jurist universities, which were composed of ultramontane (north European) and cismontane (Italian) students. The statutes of the jurist universities, adopted in 1331, were largely inspired by the model of Bologna, although student power in certain particulars, such as the right to name professors, was limited from the outset.⁵⁶ By the early Trecento the universities, each governed by its own elected rector, were organized into nine ultramontane and ten cismontane nations. The rector was responsible for settling quarrels among students and enforcing the statutes governing terms and methods of instruction. Four students were selected to notify the rector of any lecturers failing to fulfill their statutory obligations. The rector was ultimately responsible to the students acting through their representatives (*consiliarii*) elected, one per nation, to the university congregations, over which he presided. Specifically charged with convoking the congregations for discussion of faculty appointments and salary, the rector also oversaw the election of most university officials: the treasurers, syndics, lawyers, and *peciarii* and stationers, who were responsible for providing texts and paper.

Thus, for the first half of the Trecento, Padua's legal faculty was kept under close student supervision. All teachers were to remain in Padua when the university was in session, and no teaching doctor could absent himself for more than one lecture without permission of the students. In addition to the oversight of the professoriate, the quality of legal education was maintained by a series of statutes governing curriculum and requirements for the doctorate. Eight years of study were required for the degree in civil law and six years for canon law. But the time spent studying one law could be applied toward the other: "if a student will have studied civil law for five years or more, and would like to transfer to canon law, it is sufficient for him to have studied canon law for only three years."⁵⁷ Although the statutes of the jurist universities prescribed rules for the examinations for the doctorate, their control was in the hands of the College of Jurist Doctors.

This college included both foreign and native professors teaching law in the universities and nonteaching doctors resident in Padua, who were often judges in the communal court system.[58] The doctorate was awarded on the successful completion of two examinations, one private, the second public. Often law students ended their education with the license gained with the private examination, thus avoiding the expensive fees and gifts required by the doctorate. But the prestige of the doctorate was great, especially in both canon and civil law, earning the title of *doctor utriusque iuris*. Those who obtained the doctorate were, on the payment of a stiff fee, admitted to the College of Jurist Doctors. The progressive increase in the size of the college documents the growing popularity of legal studies at Padua. In 1348 the membership was limited to twelve, later enlarged to twenty, twenty-five, and thirty, until in 1382 it was decreed that the college could admit as many doctors as it pleased its members. Moreover, the college enjoyed considerable prestige and influence in Padua, numbering among its priors such important Carrara officials as Giacomo da Santa Croce, Bartolomeo Capodivacca, Francesco Conselve, and Ottonello Descalzi.

For much of the Trecento, the University of Arts and Medicine and its corresponding college of doctors was considerably smaller and subordinate to the jurist universities and more closely controlled by public authority. In 1321 the Paduan commune agreed to pay the salaries of three professors of medicine and of one each in surgery, philosophy, logic, and grammar, in return for the commune's control of appointments. Only in 1360, after a sharp conflict that brought the mediation of the bishop of Padua, did the jurist universities reluctantly allow the University of Arts and Medicine to choose its own rector and professors. But the professors and scholars in arts and medicine still had to swear obedience to the jurist statutes, accept their courts as the final source of appeals, and pay fees to the officers of jurist universities at graduation. Only with the intervention of Francesco Novello in 1399 was the University of Arts and Medicine completely separated from the schools of law, depriving them of a large source of income, which was compensated by the lord's grant of a building to the jurist universities.[59] The professoriate of the school of medicine became staffed by some of the most famous physicians and scientists of fourteenth-century Italy, often native Paduans or immigrants from nearby cities. The smaller school of logic and philosophy had its professors housed in the College of Doctors of Arts and Medicine. Its teachers and students, recruited mainly from Padua and its contado and northeast Italy, lacked the international stature of the universities of law and medicine.

The major innovation in the academic life of Trecento Padua was the establishment of the college system for the housing and maintenance of indigent scholars. Here Francesco il Vecchio da Carrara led the way with the endowment in 1362 of a college for twelve poor students in civil law.[60] His example was followed by the medical professor Bartolomeo Campo, who, by his testament in 1369, endowed a college for students of medicine, donating his library for their use. Other endowments followed, founding colleges for students of canon law and other disciplines. Toward the end of the century provisions were made for foreign students from definite localities, reflecting the nations of the jurist universities, with instruction and lodging first given to four students from Cyprus. The former bishop of Padua Pileo da Prata established his Collegio Pratense in a dwelling donated by Francesco Novello for students from Ravenna, where he was currently bishop, and governed by the Carrara favorites Francesco Zabarella and Giovanni Lodovico Lambertazzi. The college system thus grew directly as a result of the philanthropy of the Carrara dynasty and its affinity.

Padua's status as a *studium generale*, attractive scholarly privileges, colleges for poor students, its distinguished professoriate, and the Carrara's notable patronage and extensive use of the professors and doctors in governing all had an impact on the size and nature of the university.[61] The number of professors, degrees awarded, and students in the jurist universities, where civil and canon law were taught, dwarfed the other parts of the *studium*. Although Paduan citizens were technically barred from publicly funded teaching positions, this prohibition proved difficult to enforce. In the second half of the Trecento, many Paduans were trained in civil law and went on to hold teaching posts in the *studium*, as the careers of Giacomo da Santa Croce, Francesco Dotti, and Alvarotto Alvarotti attest. Students, doctors, and professors of canon law tended to come more from outside Padua's domains, with a number of doctors and students coming from northern and central Italy and from German-speaking Europe. The teachers and doctors of medicine and arts were, by contrast, markedly local; nearly half of all the professors of medicine came from the city and its district, reflecting the powerful local dynasties of physicians practicing and teaching in Padua. The student body was predominately foreign, with 87 percent coming from outside Padua and its contado. Thus, the *studium* was a remarkably cosmopolitan community, mixing scholars from every region of Italy with those from the rest of Europe, especially German-speaking lands. Placed under the special protection of Giacomo il Grande da Carrara at his election in 1318, the *studium* was a major resource to the dynasty as it transformed the government of Padua from a commune to a signory.

Late Medieval Padua

From Commune to Signory

As a commune Padua enjoyed status as an independent city-state whose sovereignty was sometimes limited by the claims of a distant Holy Roman Emperor. These claims became a real, even traumatic, challenge to medieval Padua's own independence during the brutal lordship imposed in the second quarter of the thirteenth century by Ezzelino III da Romano (1194–1259). Scion of one of the most powerful feudal families of the Trevisan March, as imperial vicar for the Hohenstaufen emperor, Frederick II, Ezzelino quashed the Guelf (pro-papal) regimes in the eastern Veneto and established multiple lordship over the communes of Verona, Vicenza, Treviso, and Padua from 1236 until the 1250s. Even before the death of Frederick II in 1250, local feudal families, including the Carraresi, led the Paduan *popolo* in a struggle against Ezzelino and his Ghibelline (pro-imperial) supporters to wrest back control of the city. During the quarter century of Ezzelino's tyrannical rule over Padua, many Guelf party leaders, including the early Carrara lord Giacomo (d. 1240), lost their lives in opposition to da Romano rule. Although Giacomo was actually executed for treason after he deserted Ezzelino's cause, later apologists for the Carrara regime were quick to develop Giacomo's death into a hero's martyrdom for upholding the Guelf traditions of Padua.

After the fall of Ezzelino da Romano in 1259, the Carraresi were not numbered among the most powerful feudal families of Paduan society. The earliest Carrara lords, who later traditions claimed were German knights who migrated to the Padovano in the tenth century, held allods in the villages of Arquà, Bertipaglia, Bovolenta, Conselve, Gorgo, and Montegrotto, all near the ancestral village of Carrara. Two centuries later, the family gained by imperial grants comital jurisdiction over the region around Carrara and outlying villages in the southern Padovano, including Agna, Anguillara, Bagnoli, Cesso, Montagnana, S. Siro, Solesino, which later were held by its junior branch, the Papafava dei Carraresi.[62] With holdings in the two historical centers, the Carrara and the Papafava were only two of more than twenty magnate families granted by statute in 1278 the responsibility to arrest criminals caught within their jurisdictions. Thus, in the heyday of the Paduan commune, little indicated the future destiny of the Carrara as lords of Padua.[63]

Of the four cities that returned to independence following the extermination of the da Romano clan and the wreckage of their state, only Padua maintained a popular republican regime for very long. Verona remained in the Ghibelline camp under the lordship of the Della Scala family, while

FIG. 4. *Giacomo da Carrara beheaded on orders of Ezzelino da Romano in 1240. Source: Biblioteca Nazionale Marciana, Venice, MS lat. X, 381 (= 2808), fol. 1v of* Gesta magnifica domus carrariensis *(MS written in 1390). Reproduced with permission of the Biblioteca Nazionale Marciana, Venice*

the most potent feudal family of the Trevisan March, the da Camino, were elected lords of Treviso. To the south, the election of Obizzo d'Este as signore, with the help of Paduan allies, marked the beginning of papal and Guelf influence and the vanquishing of imperial forces in Ferrara. At the same time, the Este family continued to be the most powerful family in the southern Padovano. In the competition for power in the Veneto, the commune of Padua made alliances with Bassano and Vicenza and soon expelled the Veronese Ghibelline governors from office there. Thus, these two cities were brought into the Paduan orbit as political domination followed commercial investment. Vicenza was effectively Padua's satellite in the second half of the thirteenth century, during the height of its territorial expansion. Shielded on the north by the friendly regime of the Caminese *signoria*, or lordship, in Treviso and protected on the west by the buffer cities of

Vicenza and Bassano, by 1300 Padua had reached the height of its medieval prosperity under a broadly based communal regime.

During this period, Venice generally kept aloof from mainland affairs, developing its role as the major entrepôt in Mediterranean commerce. Claiming the lordship of the gulf, Venice also sought to control commerce on the Po and protect its right to the staple, or monopoly to act as middleman for all goods traded in the area of the northern Adriatic. In the first decade of the Trecento, Venice waged a brief war on Padua to maintain its salt monopoly and increasingly attempted to bring Ferrara, strategic in maintaining its staple rights, under its own political as well as commercial subjection. In 1308 Venice departed from its traditional policy of aloofness and seized a dispute over lordship of Ferrara as a pretext to annex Ferrara. As Ferrara's overlord, the papacy intervened and demanded surrender of the city. In the disastrous war that followed, Venice was placed under interdict and eventually forced to make a humiliating peace. Pope Clement V conveyed the lordship of Ferrara briefly to his ally, King Robert of Naples, though by 1313 Ferrara was again within Venice's orbit.

Meanwhile, the Carraresi had begun to emerge as one of the most prestigious families of communal Padua. Through a series of marriage alliances the Carraresi tied themselves to Guelf lords of Milan, the Della Torre, the Fieschi of Genoa, and the Gradenigo of Venice. By the early fourteenth century the Carraresi enjoyed international connections perhaps unmatched in Paduan society. In addition, death and feuds within the lineage served to reconcentrate landed and liquid wealth within the hands of a few members of the family, notably Giacomo il Grande and his nephew Marsilio. Papal intervention in Ferrara was but a prelude to the descent of Henry VII into Italy in 1310. The emperor's presence in Italy, supported by his vicar Cangrande della Scala, polarized the political sympathies and allegiances of the leaders of the Paduan commune. Hostile to the interests of Guelf Padua, Henry threatened invasion. Cangrande's later plans to conquer Padua further undermined reliance upon older political structures and brought new communal leaders to the fore.

The loss of Vicenza to Cangrande in 1311 and his continued threat to Padua crystallized local leadership. From the old Guelf party of the Trevisan March, the *pars Marchionis,* five men now emerged to lead Padua in its struggle with the lord of Verona: Francesco d'Este, Tiso Camposampiero, Niccolò da Lozzo, Guecello da Camino, and Giacomo il Grande da Carrara. Murder and death removed the first two lords the next year, and Guecello da Camino soon departed to assume the lordship of Treviso. Niccolò da Lozzo, whose feudal strongholds in the western Padovano were exposed on the Veronese attack, defected to Cangrande's camp, accompanied by his kinsmen, the Maltraversi of Castelnuovo and the Schinelli of Rovolon. Outbreak of sharp civil conflict in the streets of Padua in April 1314 led to the murder of several potential Carrara rivals of the Altichini and Ronchi families and to the exile of Maccaruffo Maccaruffi and Albertino Mussato, who had been advocates of all-out war with the Della Scala.

Within this context, many of the moderate Guelfs looked to the leadership of Giacomo il Grande, who seemed powerful enough to withstand Cangrande's attacks and astute enough to know when to make peace.[64] As the disintegration of communal authority placed greater reliance on the older structures of kinship and clientage, the Carrara lord's status as a wealthy landowner with a large peasant following and authority as patron of judges and notaries in the city made him the obvious leader. The vertical organization of urban patronage combined with a formidable territorial base and prestigious marriage alliances gave Giacomo the advantage over other candidates in gaining the post of captain general. After the loss of Vicenza to Cangrande, Giacomo followed a policy of reconciliation, helping Padua to make peace with the lord of Verona in 1314. This peace was broken when Veronese exiles, with their Paduan allies under Vinciguerra da Sambonifacio, attacked and briefly occupied Vicenza in the spring of 1317. This affront caused Cangrande to retaliate, renewing his strategy of attacking rural areas and minor strongholds, which resulted in his capture of Montagnana, Monselice, and Este in the southern Padovano. A second truce with Cangrande della Scala led to an attempt at reconciliation of the factions in Padua in the spring of 1318. When reconciliation failed early that summer, the most extreme opponents of Carrara rule, Maccaruffo Maccaruffi and Albertino Mussato, departed the city. Still torn by faction within and by Cangrande's renewed threat of conquest, late in June 1318 the commune's leaders took the momentous step of conferring the office of defender, protector, and captain general of Padua on Giacomo il Grande da Carrara. Giacomo alone of all party leaders was most likely to rally his fellow Paduans to preserve the commune, defend the city, and somehow resist Cangrande della Scala's conquest of Padua.

Chapter 2

Under Foreign Domination, 1318–1337

> Quod nobilis vir Dominus Jacobus de Carraria, natus quondam nobilis viri domini Marsilii de Carraria, sit et esse debeat, et esse intelligatur auctoritate presentis legis et statuti, et omni modo et iure quo melius esse poterit, Defensor, Protector et Gubernator populi paduani, et civitatis et districtus, et in eis habitantium Capitaneus generalis.
>
> [That the nobleman Lord Giacomo da Carrara, son of the late nobleman Lord Marsilio da Carrara, be and ought to be and is understood to be by the authority of the present law and statute, and with every measure and right by which he best can be the Defender, Protector and Governor of the Paduan people, and of the City and District, and Captain General of their inhabitants.]
>
> —Statute of election of 25 July 1318, ed. in Colle, *Storia scientifico-letteraria dello Studio di Padova* (1824–25)

The Election of Giacomo il Grande, Lord of Padua

On the morning of Tuesday, 25 July 1318, the feast of St. James the More, Giacomo il Grande da Carrara rode surrounded by friends and bodyguards from his palace in *contrada* S. Lorenzo to the city hall, the Salone, to become the first *signore* of Padua. His election had been brought about by the successes of his rival the lord of Verona, Cangrande della Scala. For most Paduan citizens, the choice was frankly a compromise, the best solution to war and chaos in a time of crisis. The alternatives were conquest and domination by Verona under the rule of Cangrande della Scala or the continued violence of factions run wild. The preamble of the statute of election provides the rationale for conferring the lordship on Giacomo: to return Padua and its people to a state of peace and tranquillity, to put an end to murder, robbery, and violence in the streets, and to ensure that each Paduan could now live independently (*ut quilibet possit vivere de suo*). To carry out these tasks, Giacomo was granted full jurisdiction in criminal and civil cases (*merum et mixtum imperium*), command of the Paduan army, and authority

FIG. 5. *Giacomo il Grande da Carrara receives lordship of Padua in 1318. Note that the podestà is conferring upon him the communal banner. Source: Biblioteca Nazionale Marciana, Venice, MS lat. X, 381 (= 2808), fol. 3v of Gesta magnifica domus carrariensis (MS written in 1390). Reproduced with permission of the Biblioteca Nazionale Marciana, Venice*

over the chief communal magistrates, the *podestà* and his staff, who were to execute and enforce the statutes of Padua and to obey his commands. In short: "to him and in him all authority and power of the people and commune of Padua are conceded and invested" [et ei, et in eum omne imperium et omnis potestas Populi et Comunis Padue concessa et translata sint]. Along with these powers, Giacomo could now make new statutes and ordinances and change or abrogate old ones as conditions required. The statute of election was to last in perpetuity, and even discussion of its revocation was forbidden in the Council of the Anziani or elsewhere. But there was an exception: the statute was to be treated as *"precisum"* and thus be revoked only by a two-thirds vote of the Maggior Consiglio, apparently at the instigation of Giacomo himself. There were other safeguards of communal rights: Giacomo was to swear to uphold these duties in a public assembly and his salary set and limited by a board of eight experts (*sapientes*), composed in this instance of the legal fraternity of the city, all respected judges and jurists.

Under Foreign Domination

Once the statute of election had been drawn up, Giacomo entered into the great hall of the Salone, and the description of his rights and duties was read aloud. Then, in the presence of the current podestà, Giovanni Molin of Venice, the Council of the Anziani, the fifteen *gastaldi* of the guilds, and many of the Paduan people, the statute was ratified. On behalf of the commune and people of Padua, the judge of the Anziani, Rolando de Piazzola, administered the oath of office, by which Giacomo, hand resting on the Gospels, swore to uphold his new duties. Rolando exchanged with Giacomo the kiss of peace and on behalf of the Anziani, gastaldi, the Paduan people, and himself bestowed on the newly elected lord the symbol of his office and responsibilities, the banner of the commune of Padua: a red cross on a white field. There followed the formality of the election of the board of eight to set Giacomo's salary and to establish his specific duties and obligations; the board was composed of civic leaders, judges, and lawyers who were to figure prominently in Paduan affairs in the next decade: the judges Paolo da Teolo, Giacomo Alvarotti, Domenico Agrapati, Antonio da Lio, Pietro da Campagnola, and Schinella de Doto, and the doctors of law Becaro Brugnacchi and Manfredo Manfredi.

Finally, the provisions of Giacomo's duties as captain general were spelled out in detail, providing a sense of both the extent of the crisis and his powers. Giacomo's first duty was the defense of the city, then under threat of conquest by Cangrande della Scala, and its provisioning with foodstuffs and other supplies. He was also to protect the university, whose faculty and students were to be treated "just like sons" [tamquam filios]. Giacomo was to have a free hand in the selection of the podestà and his staff, setting their salaries, overseeing the administration of justice, and dismissing these officials as he saw fit. The lord also had full control over the communal treasury, raising funds from fines, rents, and excise taxes and disbursing moneys as necessary. He had full authority over the treasurer and purser (*massarius et caniparius*), who were to make payments or remit money only with his express approval and seal (*bulla*). To Giacomo was conveyed also authority over the lesser officials of the communal government: the choice of the Anziani, gastaldi, communal judges, and podestà or vicars of the towns and strongholds of the *contado* was in his gift. No laws could be proposed before the Maggior Consiglio or lesser councils without his knowledge and consent, and any laws passed were subject to his ultimate approval.

To facilitate the execution of his duties he was given a number of perquisites and powers. If Giacomo so desired, the commune was to construct at its own expense a residence and palace near the seat of government, the legal basis for the Carrara Reggia later built between S. Clemente and Ponte dei Tadi. For his needs and expenses Giacomo was to have an annual salary of £12,000 and a staff of judges, police, squires, and bodyguards, paid with salaries as he determined. Most important, he was to hire knights and infantry in sufficient quantity for the defense and security of Padua. Finally, Giacomo was empowered to require all citizens to participate in Padua's defense and punish those who might opposed the exercise of his powers as set forth in this statute. A week later, on Tuesday, 1 August, the election was celebrated with a great feast. Soon a statute was enacted to commemorate Giacomo's election with a horse race (*palio*) on the Feast of St. James.[1]

Giacomo's Lordship of Padua, 1318–1320

But the commemorative *palio* probably did not take place for the next two decades, for, beset with problems and challenges, the reign of Giacomo il Grande lasted only eighteen months. Acting alone, Giacomo could do little to stop or even slow down the juggernaut of Scaliger conquest. By late 1318 Cangrande had laid siege to the neighboring city of Treviso, so the commune submitted to Frederick the Handsome of Habsburg, duke of Austria and king of the Romans and one of the claimants (with Lewis of Bavaria) to the crown of the Holy Roman Empire. Frederick promptly placed that city under the imperial vicariate of Enrico II, count of Gorizia. Deprived of Treviso as an object of conquest, Cangrande turned his full attention to Padua, making impossible demands for a truce or peace. In an attempt to cement relations with Cangrande in December 1318, Giacomo betrothed his own young daughter, Taddea da Carrara, to Mastino II della Scala, one of Cangrande's nephews and heir to the lordship of Verona. But the proposed marriage alliance had little immediate effect.

By the summer of 1319, the situation was desperate. The extreme Guelfs, such as Bartolomeo detto Maccaruffo da Maccaruffi, initially opponents of Giacomo's conciliatory policies toward Cangrande, had left Padua for the friendship and support of the Este lords of Ferrara, their kinsmen by marriage. The election of Giacomo as lord of Padua had driven Paduan Ghibellines, such as Marco Forzatè and Traverso Dalesmanini, into the arms of the Della Scala. With Cangrande in control of the southern Paduan strongholds of Monselice, Montagnana, and Este and the rulers of Ferrara adopting a policy of hostile neutrality, Padua was cut off from its traditional Guelf allies of Bologna and Florence.[2]

Cangrande settled in for the final conquest, establishing his field headquarters at Bassanello in the newly constructed fortress, the Isola della Scala, enrolling exiles from Padua in his army, so that in the words of one of the besiegers, "the defenders of Padua were like prisoners in their own city."[3]

Under Foreign Domination

By August 1319 Cangrande's army was at the gates of Padua, encamped in the Borgo S. Croce, threatening assault from a new wooden fortress. By diverting the Bacchiglione at Bassanello, Cangrande hoped to cut off the water supply in the city and stop the mills at Torricelle. Meanwhile, bands of armed men ravaged the Paduan contado, burning and looting as far as Mestre and the villages of the Oltrebrenta. Rural properties of the defenders of Padua were confiscated and given to the exiles fighting in the Scaligeri army. Giacomo sent a secret embassy to Treviso promising Bassano, Cittadella, and money to Enrico II, count of Gorizia, if he would come to Padua's aid. But Enrico also claimed friendship with Cangrande and turned a deaf ear to Giacomo's request. In vain, ambassadors from Venice tried to negotiate a peace between the Carrara and Scaliger lords, but Cangrande's terms were too drastic. He demanded that Giacomo da Carrara renounce the lordship of Padua, that the soldiers defending the city be dismissed, and that the exiles be restored with all their property. For the Carrara lord, the demands amounted to unconditional surrender and "placing wolves among defenseless sheep."[4] His terms rejected, Cangrande laid siege to the walled town of Cittadella, which was forced to surrender on 1 November.

Three days later, Giacomo and the leaders of Padua appealed again for protection from Enrico II, count of Gorizia, and Frederick of Habsburg, duke of Austria, whose intervention had saved Treviso from conquest by Cangrande a year earlier. Meeting in the great hall of the Salone on 4 November, Giacomo with the Venetian podestà, Marco Gradenigo, and his vicar, Bernardo da Cremona, proposed to the Maggior Consiglio that the commune send ambassadors to Frederick submitting to him and placing Padua and its contado under the protection of the Holy Roman Empire and his vicar Enrico of Gorizia. By a vote of 533 to 75, the motion was adopted, and a statute detailing the conditions of the dedication of Padua to Frederick and Enrico was drawn up for approval by Giacomo da Carrara. Then the statute was announced to the Paduan citizen body assembled in *arengo* by the notary of the Anziani, Rolando da Piazzola.[5] That same day two veteran statesmen, Dusio Buzzacarini and Aleardo Basilio, were appointed to negotiate with Frederick and Enrico II, count of Gorizia, for the protection of the empire and Enrico's appointment as imperial vicar in Padua. By December, this legation had arrived at Judenburg in Austria, where Duke Frederick appointed one of his vassals, Ulrich von Walsee, captain of Styria, as his representative to negotiate with Cangrande della Scala and other lords and cities to bring peace to northern Italy.[6]

The Early Carrara

Under German Vicars, 1320–1325

On 4 January 1320, Ulrich reached Padua, and on the next day, in an elaborate ceremony in the great hall of the Salone reminiscent of the election of Giacomo il Grande a year and half earlier, he became the vicar general of Padua.[7] The outgoing lord, Giacomo da Carrara, conveyed the keys to the gates of the city and banner of the commune and people of Padua to his German successor, who swore to defend the city against the Paduan rebels, Cangrande della Scala, and all its enemies. The new judge of the Anziani, Giovanni da Partinopeo, read aloud the detailed provisions of Ulrich's new duties. In general, the Paduan commune preserved more of its own powers under the imperial vicar than it had eighteen months earlier under Giacomo il Grande. Like his predecessor, Giacomo da Carrara, Ulrich was to govern Padua, reform the statutes, and provide for the defense of the city and the strongholds of the contado. He was specifically charged with the recovery of towns in the hands of the Este and Scaligeri: Rovigo, Lendinara, Castelbaldo, Torre, Este, Montagnana, Monselice, and Cittadella. He was also instructed to drive the rebels and exiles from the Padovano and confiscate their property, real and personal. At the same time he was to preserve the communal regime, its councils and organs intact, and enforce the usual election to six-month terms of podestà and vicars of the town and villages of the countryside. His power over the appointment of the podestà was limited to confirming one of three candidates nominated by the Maggior Consiglio for his approval. In general, the vicar's service was to be at the pleasure of Frederick of Habsburg, duke of Austria, and Heinrich, duke of Carinthia and titular king of Bohemia and Poland. In short, Ulrich's appointment was only a military solution to the military problem of Cangrande's design to conquer Padua.

The next month a truce was arranged to last until the third Sunday in Lent (4 March 1320) between Cangrande and Padua, now under the protection of the empire. Duke Frederick of Austria wrote to the Paduans on 27 February calling on them to send ambassadors to a *parlamentum* at Bolzano in the spring and observe the extension of the truce until the octave of Easter.[8] The much touted conference at Bolzano, to which the Paduans had sent their best diplomats, including Niccolò da Carrara, Rolando da Piazzola, Giovanni Camposampiero, and Aleardo Basilio, to meet with representatives of Treviso and the Della Scala, accomplished nothing. By early spring the truce had been broken, and the Scaligeri army composed of Veronese soldiers and Paduan exiles was again threatening Padua. Frederick of Habsburg responded by revoking on 29 May 1320 the old ban that

Henry VII had placed on Padua in 1311 and now received the commune and city as a friend, ally, and vassal of the empire, specifically according the *studium* the same standing as Paris, Bologna, Orlèans, and Montpellier.[9] At the same time, the Paduans begged for troops and military aid from their German protectors, Frederick of Habsburg and his vicar. The impending arrival of German reinforcements for the besieged Paduans prompted Cangrande to attempt to take the city by storm and stealth. In this attack, the Veronese troops and Paduan exiles were repulsed; Cangrande returned to his usual tactic of trying to starve the defenders of Padua into submission.

In July the Paduan defenders routed the exiles and Cangrande's prized contingent of French knights outside the walls. On 25 August, Enrico of Gorizia arrived with eight hundred German knights, attacked the Veronese forces, and captured their headquarters at Bassanello. Wounded in the sharp conflict, Cangrande fled for his life to his stronghold at Monselice and soon retired to Verona for the rest of the year. A number of Paduan rebels had been taken prisoner in these encounters, including the hated traitor Maccaruffo Maccaruffi, who was taken back to Padua, wounded by Marsilio da Carrara, and killed off by Rizzardo detto Tartaro da Lendinara and his accomplices. In September Count Enrico of Gorizia with Ulrich von Walsee besieged the Scaliger garrisons at Este and Monselice but soon withdrew to Padua. Both sides were exhausted by the conflict and willingly entered into negotiations that resulted in the proclamation of peace on 26 October. In due course, Padua and its vicar, Ulrich von Walsee, received back Cittadella, while Frederick of Habsburg was to gain the strongholds of Este, Torre, and Montagnana.[10] Prisoners were exchanged, but many rebels remained in exile with their goods confiscated.

On 30 December 1320, in the palace in contrada S. Niccolò of the imperial vicar, Ulrich von Walsee, the best legal minds of Padua gathered to draw up a statute that created a board of judges to oversee the final confiscation and distribution of the property of the now-vanquished rebels. As early as November 1319, in a desperate act of reprisal Giacomo da Carrara had exiled forever rebels in Cangrande's army and their kin to the third degree.[11] During the height of Cangrande's siege the next summer, the Council of Anziani assigned property near the Salone belonging to the rebels Giovanni Caligine and Antonio Engleschi to the nuns of S. Anna, whose church and convent near the western walls had been confiscated and demolished by the Paduan defenders during the recent siege.[12] Now a committee composed of four jurists — Giovanni da Piove di Sacco, Paolo da Teolo, Pantaleone Buzzacarini, and Aleardo Basilio — met to draw up a statute identifying the rebels and establishing procedures for confiscating their property.

With the capture of the Scaliger field headquarters at Bassanello that August, the Paduans had seized several ledgers defining the obligations of the Paduan exiles toward their new chief, Cangrande.

These records became the basis for the legal definition of rebels to the communal regime; one ledger contained the names of exiled Paduans to whom Cangrande has assigned horses, another the oaths and securities of those Paduans who had recently joined the Scaligeri army, and a third the names of all Paduan taxpayers for the past five years who had entered Cangrande's service at Bassanello and elsewhere in the Padovano.[13] All these Paduans were judged guilty of the crime of high treason (*laese maiestatis*) against their native city, and all their property, real and personal, was confiscated by the vicar, Ulrich von Walsee, and the Paduan commune. To carry out the confiscations a judge was to be appointed with full powers to seize property, levy fines, and even use torture to discover the rebels' hidden goods. Creditors with claims against rebels' goods were to register their claims within twenty days after the beginning of litigation unless there was some just impediment. A second group were defined as "good citizens," comprising those Paduans who had remained loyal to the commune during the recent struggles with Cangrande, and these were to be inscribed in a ledger of those who had defended the city. A third group comprised the "lukewarm or timid," taxpayers and citizens who had fled Padua when the city had recently come under siege but had not joined Cangrande's army. These were to be fully exonerated if they appeared before the judge within two months, posting a security of £100 and paying any back taxes. Known rebels who were not listed in the accounts seized at Bassanello were also subject to prosecution and confiscation; their names were to be given to the podestà for arrest. Cases of secret accusation had to be corroborated by the oaths of four citizens.

The entire procedure of identification, confiscation, and assignment of the rebels' property was valid until Christmas 1321. Ulrich von Walsee appointed two judges, aided by two assistants, for identifying and receiving the confiscated property. Five citizens from the Maggior Consiglio were to be elected to oversee the auctioning of rebels' goods brought to the communal treasury (*camera cataverorum*) located near the court of the Sigillo. Special guidelines were developed for ferreting out rebels' property that was hidden in the homes of citizens, with half the £100 fine going to the accuser. Anyone discovered harboring rebels or giving them aid and comfort was liable to a £300 fine. The requirement that anyone holding rebels' property was to appear before the podestà and list the goods in writing was announced three times at five-day intervals early in 1321. To encourage compliance accusers were to receive one-fourth of the value of unreported property, and the guilty were also liable to fines of £100.

Scant record remains of the success of this campaign to enrich the loyal Paduans through the confiscation of the property of their errant brothers. The property of the more powerful opponents of Carrara rule was confiscated and distributed to Marsilio da Carrara and his supporters. By the autumn of 1323, Marsilio had garnered enough wealth from these confiscations and other sources to deposit £12,800 in Venice's Grain Office as a precaution against any sudden change in political fortune.[14] Rebel property granted to the nuns of the convent of S. Anna continued to generate court litigation as late as 1326.[15] Attempts to recover dowries and goods by the Maccaruffi exiled in Venice received the support of the doge and council against the claims of the Paduan commune as late as 1326.[16] But much of the confiscated property was restored by the terms of the general peace of May 1323, so that if its provisions were observed, there would be little ground for disputes with all but the most intransigent rebels against Padua.

In February 1321 the Paduan *intrinseci* (defenders) enjoyed a rare moment of relative calm and sent an embassy to present their case against Cangrande to their new protector, Frederick of Habsburg. The duke of Austria knighted the three Paduan ambassadors, Niccolò da Carrara, Giovanni Camposampiero, and Schinella de Doto, much to the pleasure of their fellow citizens. But Cangrande's repeated threats of conquest and the loss of several strongholds in the Padovano made the peace reached in late 1320 increasingly precarious. On 19 July the Maggior Consiglio elected six seasoned diplomats, Niccolò da Carrara, Giovanni da Vigonza, Schinella de Doto, Giovanni Camposampiero, Aleardo Basilio, and Albertino Mussato, to appear before Frederick asking for the appointment of a new vicar to secure the return of fortresses of the contado and further aid against Padua's enemies and rebels. Realizing the weakness of his own position, the imperial vicar, Ulrich von Walsee, accompanied the Paduans north of the Alps.[17] When the Paduan delegation reached Frederick's court, they discovered that an embassy from Cangrande had already arrived and was arguing for the appointment of the lord of Verona as imperial vicar in Padua. The Paduan envoys were reluctant to oppose Cangrande directly, and von Walsee refused to return to Padua.

After some discussion, on 5 September 1321 Frederick was able to persuade his brother Heinrich, duke of Carinthia, count of the Tyrol and Gorizia and former king of Bohemia and Poland, to accept the vicariate of Padua in the stead of Enrico II of Gorizia, who remained vicar in Treviso. The next day, Frederick appointed fifteen German knights to assist Duke

Heinrich in the governing and defense of Padua. Early in November, one of these, the Tyrolian soldier Konrad von Aufenstein, arrived in Padua at the head of two hundred German cavalry and assumed the post of vicar for his superior, Duke Heinrich.[18] One of the first tasks of the new vicar was to revise the norms for the leasing of the rebels' confiscated property and to appoint a new board of four overseers, one chosen per quarter of Padua, who would impartially assign the property to be leased without respect to the wishes of the previous vicar, Ulrich von Walsee. In order to generate more income for the commune of Padua, the rents on confiscated properties were raised by 10 percent, minor dues in kind (*onori*) were commuted to money rent, and rents were now due twice yearly. In drawing up these new provisions on 18 November 1321, von Aufenstein received the advice of the Paduan leaders of the Carrara faction: Rolando da Piazzola, judge of the Anziani, Pantaleone Buzzacarini, Giovanni Camposampiero, Schinella de Doto, and Giovanni da Vigonza.[19]

The appointment of Heinrich of Carinthia as imperial vicar and the arrival in Padua of his deputy, Konrad von Aufenstein, with a strong contingent of knights initially dealt a severe blow to Cangrande's design to control northeastern Italy. But the departure of the deputy and some of his troops late in 1321 opened the way for a renewed campaign by Scaligeri forces and Paduan exiles in the southern Padovano in the spring of 1322. These troops occupied strongholds at Este and Vighizzolo and the rich villages of Arquà, Pernumia, Tribano, and Conselve that summer. The arrival of German reinforcements failed to dislodge the rebels at Este that fall. With a stalemate in the offing, peace negotiations reopened in the spring of 1323. Moreover, the mysterious sudden death on 24 April 1323 of Enrico II of Gorizia, vicar of Treviso, who had often supported the Paduan exiles and made plans for the conquest of Padua himself, opened the way for a general peace. Under the good offices of the papal inquisitor, the Franciscan friar Paolino, rebel chiefs met with three Paduan envoys, Marsilio da Carrara, Albertino Mussato, and Rolando da Piazzola, at the border village of Tencarola and reached an agreement on the Feast of St. Peter Martyr, 29 April. This treaty was unanimously ratified by the Maggior Consiglio in Padua on 19 May and later approved by Cangrande and the imperial vicar Heinrich, duke of Carinthia.[20]

Jubilation was widespread. On 4 May 1323 communal leaders met in the Palace of the Anziani and with the approval of the vicar Konrad von Aufenstein and the bishop's representative, Guidone, abbot of S. Maria in Vanzo, voted to establish the Feast of St. Peter Martyr as a major civic festival.[21] A month later, on 2 June, at a meeting of the Maggior Consiglio in the Salone, the vicar Konrad von Aufenstein set forth detailed procedures for the procession that was to be held in commemoration of the peace. Every year on the Feast of St. Peter Martyr, the vicar and the podestà, the Anziani, the gastaldi, the guildsmen, and all the communal officials of Padua were to assemble in the central square and march in solemn procession to the altar of St. Peter Martyr's chapel in the Dominican church of S. Agostino, there to hear Mass and make an oblation to the church.[22] With the proper civic ceremonies defined, on 7 July Paduan leaders met in the great hall of the episcopal palace to carry out specific clauses of the terms of the peace treaty. In the presence of the knights Marsilio da Carrara and Giovanni da Vigonza and the judge Giacomo Alvarroti, the vicar Konrad von Aufenstein ordered that all fines owed by the rebels would be canceled if partial payment was made to the Benedictine nuns of S. Anna. Except for those convicted of homicide or counterfeiting, all former rebels would be exonerated if those owing more than £100 paid one-sixth and those owing less than £100 one-fifth of their total fines by 29 June 1324. In this way, the exiles helped to compensate the nuns, whose convent had been demolished in the recent conflict, and the Paduan commune was relieved of a heavy obligation for rebuilding a major religious house.[23] The convent of S. Anna, filled with the daughters of the Paduan nobility, continued to benefit from the concern of Paduan leaders. On 27 June 1325, Marsilio da Carrara, in the courtyard of his palace in contrada S. Lorenzo, conveyed to Daria, the prioress of the convent, houses at the Porta S. Giovanni delle Navi, near the convent, in exchange for 10 *campi* of meadow near the Porta S. Croce.[24] After five years of constant strife, some rebels had rejoined the community, but the commune's future success was far from certain.

Civil Strife between Factions, 1325–1328

Over the next years, the Paduan commune again faced three difficult options: continued independence under the harsh rule of the German vicars and their garrison, local rule under a strongman such as one of the Carrara lords, or cession of the city to Cangrande della Scala. For the quinennium 1323–28, Padua followed the first course out of fear of consequences of Cangrande's rule on his Paduan opponents and the horrors of the civil war the ascendancy of the Carrara party would entail. But the German vicars and garrison often caused as much violence as they brought order, while the Carrara faction increasingly imposed a reign of terror on the citizens of Padua.

The death of the enigmatic Giacomo il Grande da Carrara without legitimate male heirs on 22 November 1324 removed a stabilizing influence on the headstrong, violent, and arrogant younger generation. Marsilio da

The Early Carrara

TABLE 2.1
The Carrara I. Branch of Giacomo il Grande and Marsilio il Grande

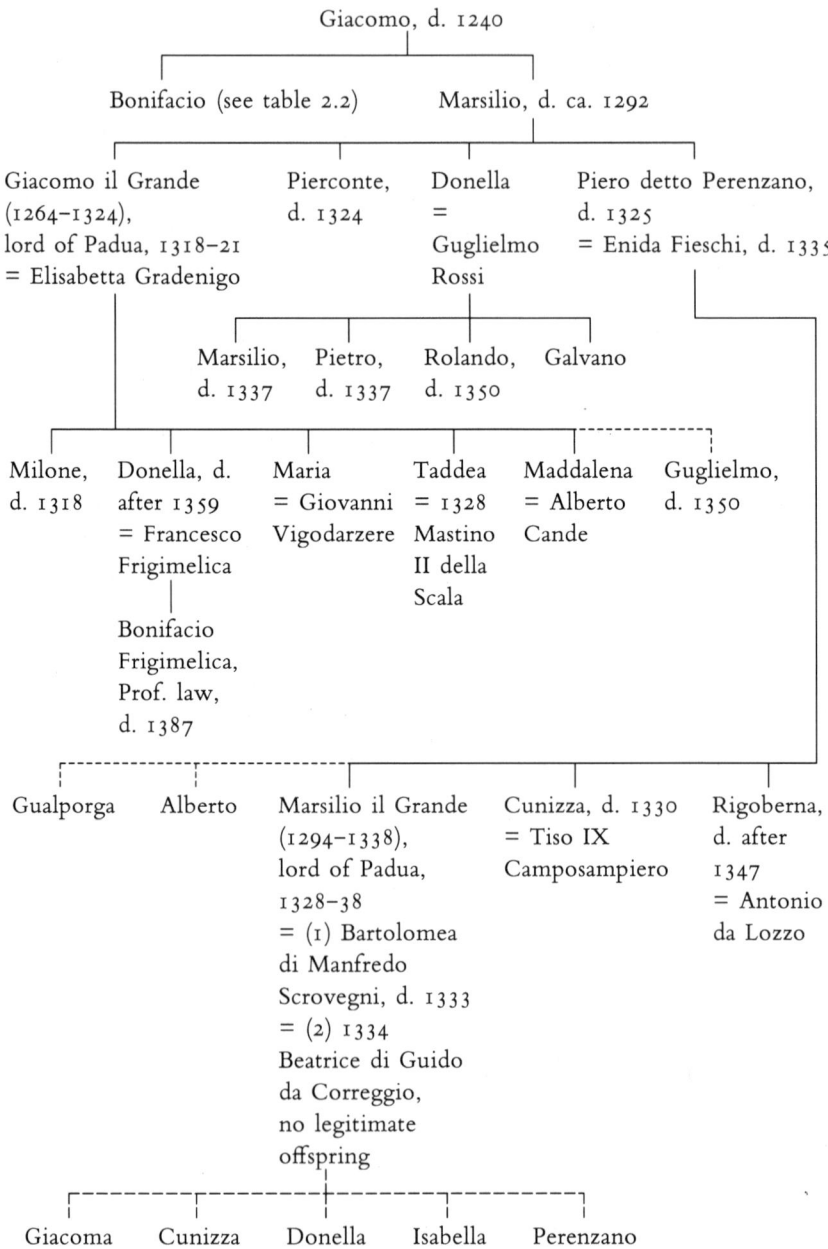

Under Foreign Domination

Carrara's uncle Pierconte died the same year and his father, Pietro detto Perenzano, the next. These deaths concentrated Carrara wealth and power in the hands of Marsilio, who assumed nominal leadership of his house and the Paduan commune. But his younger cousins, Niccolò qd. (qd. = *quondam*, "deceased") Ubertino il Vecchio and Ubertino qd. Giacomino, proved intractable to any moderating influence and prone to crimes of sex and violence, leading street gangs that terrorized the Paduan people for several years. The Carrara family's archenemy, the historian, poet, and communal leader Albertino Mussato, complained bitterly of their ruthless and libidinous behavior. Writing at the end of the century, even humanist apologists for the regime Pier Paolo Vergerio and Giovanni Conversini had to acknowledge Ubertino's violent ways until his conversion to a regime of law and order after he became lord of Padua in 1338.[25]

In early 1324 the continuing attacks of Cangrande della Scala and his allies among the exiles, especially the Lemici and Maccaruffi, posed the greatest threat to the communal regime. Marsilio and Niccolò da Carrara, Albertino Mussato, and Giovanni Camposampiero met secretly with the imperial vicar Konrad von Aufenstein to request military aid from the duke of Carinthia against the Della Scala forces. Von Aufenstein returned to Padua in May with a force of four hundred cavalry, soon followed by the duke of Carinthia himself at the head of a large army. Reaching Friuli in May, the German forces entered Treviso on 3 June and advanced to Curtarolo on the Brenta by 11 June. Contemporary chronicles greatly exaggerated the size of Duke Heinrich's army, putting the number of soldiers as high as fifteen thousand. Analysis of surviving accounts and contracts shows the forces comprised about fourteen hundred cavalry and three hundred archers. But the cost of this army to the Paduan commune was enormous: £48,000 for the month of June 1324, including about £30,000 for mercenaries' salaries, with the rest going for foodstuffs, horses, equipment, and gifts and bonuses to German captains and local notables. Among the latter, Duke Heinrich made gifts of £1,200 to Giovanni Camposampiero, frequent envoy at the Austrian court, and £300 to Guidone, abbot of S. Maria in Vanzo, a major church official in Padua.[26]

The German forces entered Padua briefly on 21 June before departing for an encampment near Monselice the next day. Pillaging and raping as they went, these troops brought more destruction than security to the Paduan countryside. The peasants of the Pedevenda fought back, killing German stragglers, claiming that the wars with Cangrande were preferable to visits from their nominal German allies. Rumors that the soldiers intended to besiege Padua brought the spirited attack of Paduan forces against German knights camped at Vigodarzere. Several Paduan soldiers were captured and

The Early Carrara

TABLE 2.2

The Carrara II. Branch of Niccolò and Ubertino

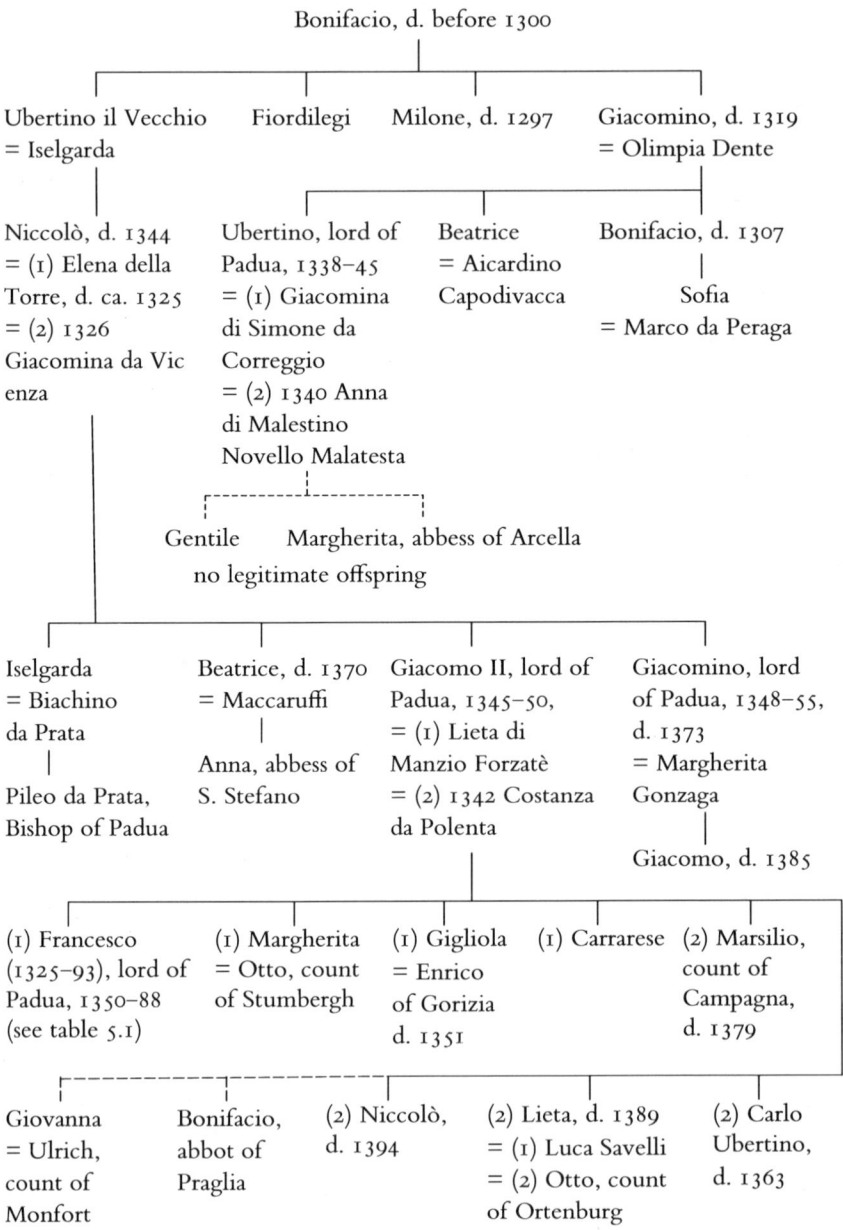

hanged in reprisal. At the end of July 1324 the duke of Carinthia made a six-month truce with Cangrande and departed with his hated soldiers. He left behind some officials, a small garrison, and Ulrich von Walsee as his vicar and the captain general of Padua.[27]

The small German staff proved more than merely a government of military occupation. On 20 January 1325 in the bishop's curia, Ulrich von Walsee, sitting with his vicar and treasurer, Siegfried von Rottenburg, and two German knights, one serving as the standard-bearer of Padua, confirmed the new statutes of the notaries guild.[28] Since 1320 Padua had been a royal city (*civitas regia*), and to collect taxes to pay for defense and government, a royal treasury was established alongside the communal one. Thus, when on 18 April 1326 the Anziani and gastaldi finally determined the amount due the Dominicans at S. Agostino on the feast of St. Peter Martyr, the gift of £100 was to be paid from money that was either "in the treasury of the Lord King [Heinrich] or in the *canipe* of the communal government."[29] Conscious of the great symbolic power of new coinage, several of Duke Heinrich's vicars, including Ulrich von Walsee, Konrad von Aufenstein, and Engelmar von Villanders, oversaw the minting, beginning in 1323, of a penny groat (*grosso aquilino*) that bore the inscription "PADVA REGIA CIVITAS." The imperial vicar's authority extended, most of all, to diplomatic relations. In a letter of 15 June 1325 to the Trevisan commune, Paduan ambassadors reported, "We have made known [this matter] to our lord the Duke of Carinthia without whose consent we can do nothing."[30] Although they controlled taxation, coinage, diplomacy, the introduction of new statutes, and guild regulations, the German vicars were unable or unwilling to curb the growing violence of the Carrara lords and their followers.

Remaining in Padua was the Lemici (Dente) clan, which headed the opposition to Carrara dominance in the city. When other communal leaders, including Pietro da Campagnola and Albertino Mussato, were sent to Innsbruck as ambassadors to Heinrich, duke of Carinthia, Ubertino da Carrara and his henchman, Tartaro da Lendinara, seized the opportunity to strike at their hated rival, Guglielmo Dente.[31] The pair murdered Dente in the streets of Padua on 17 June 1325. With the consent of Marsilio da Carrara, the current podestà, Napoleone Beccadello of Bologna, exiled the two assassins to Chioggia, and for a time peace was secured. Paolo Dente, Guglielmo's illegitimate half brother, plotted revenge for the murder and by the end of the summer had collected a band of supporters ready to exterminate the Carrara and their allies remaining in Padua. On 17 September, with the aid of Giovanni Camposampiero, who had become intimate with the Mussato faction during embassies to Germany, and Albertino's brother Gualpertino, abbot of S. Giustina, Paolo Dente led a force of one hundred followers into the central squares shouting: "Death to the House of Carrara." Marsilio da Carrara just managed to escape to the nearby home of his friend Schinella de Doto, who provided him with a warhorse and arms to return to the fray. The Dente faction, however, gathered momentum and attacked a large body of Carraresi and their allies in Piazza delle Biave. There Marsilietto Papafava dei Carraresi received a blow to the mouth which removed several teeth. Marsilio had two horses killed under him and sustained a wound on his thigh. Niccolò da Carrara was gravely wounded on his nose and arms and wanted to withdraw. But his young son Giacomo (the future lord of Padua) shouted: "If you quit this fight, you will never return to Padua. We must return to the battle."

Niccolò and Giacomo, reinforced by their friend Giacomino da Peraga and his men-at-arms, did return to the fray and eventually put the Dente partisans to flight. Paolo Dente went into hiding on Camposampiero estates at Treville, while the rest of the survivors escaped to Venetian dominions. The abbot Gualpertino Mussato fled with his two bastard sons to Chioggia, soon joined by his brother Albertino, who had reached Vicenza on his way home from Innsbruck when the civil strife broke out. Aicardini Malizia and his sons were exiled to Venice along with Giovanni Camposampiero and Corrado da Vigonza. On 24 September Ubertino da Carrara and Tartaro da Lendinara returned to Padua in triumph and found the podestà, Napoleone Beccadello, whom they held responsible for their exile, hiding in the Palace of the Anziani. They chased him to the roof of the building, where, despairing of escape, he plunged to the pavement below. There, Carrara thugs administered the *coup de grâce* to the podestà's crumpled body.[32]

Padua now belonged to Ubertino and his retainers. Armed with spears and swords, they swaggered through the streets of the city while honest citizens peered out of their doorways and trembled behind the walls of their houses. Dressed in the livery of the Carrara house, these thugs daily visited the people with assaults, violence, robbery, and murder—all according to the report of Albertino Mussato.[33] Much of the violence was vengeance taken against their enemies: three of the judges who had sentenced Ubertino and Tartaro to exile were executed and their court records burned. With the aid of the German vice-captain, the turbulent Engelmar von Villanders, Ubertino and his accomplices planned a special revenge on Pera, daughter of Vinciguerra di Sambonifacio and wife of Marino Maccaruffi, who had been exiled from the city. Smitten with the wealthy matron, Ubertino with his German knights made a forced entry into her home. While the sound of street music played by retainers hid her screams, Ubertino satisfied his burning lust for Pera as the crowd of cronies looked on.[34] Meanwhile, many Paduans departed for voluntary exile in Venice or Ferrara, leaving the troubled city to the Carrara, the German soldiers, and their supporters.

With the support of Engelmar von Villanders, Ubertino da Carrara and his ruffians terrorized the clergy of Padua as well as their political opponents. In a bull of 23 March 1327, Pope John XXII asserted that under the protection of the German vice-captain, Ubertino and his partisans and German mercenaries had broken into the bishop's storehouses and stolen grain, vegetables, wine, horses, tools, and, worst of all, the rents from episcopal property for an entire year. The pope directed his deputy in the region, the bishop of Feltre, to cite Ubertino da Carrara and his German and Paduan accomplices before a church tribunal to answer for their crimes. But apparently these attacks on ecclesiastical persons and property went unpunished.[35] Ubertino da Carrara and Tartaro da Lendinara were also accused of breaking into the convent of S. Agata and raping the nuns, kidnapping a priest named Tomeo on his way to the Duomo, and robbing and murdering the prior of S. Maria in Vanzo. At the same time, according to papal officials, the Carrara had illegally taken income from S. Stefano da Carrara, S. Maria in Vanzo, and S. Giustina, which had come into their hands after the flight of the abbot, Gualpertino Mussato.[36]

During these difficult times, Marsilio kept aloof, staying within his palace, looking after his own interests and those of the Papafava branch, his favored distant cousins. Members of the Carrara party openly enlisted the support of armed retainers, as did Niccolò qd. Antonio Capodivacca when, in May 1326, he enrolled the Buti brothers of Urbana, Uberto and Buto, as his vassals, in a contract made near the Salone.[37] Meanwhile, enemies of the regime were hunted down and executed. When, in February 1326, Corrado da Vigonza crossed the frontier with a hundred foot soldiers to seize the Paduan fort at Torre, Niccolò da Carrara counterattacked with a company of German knights. Corrado was captured, taken back to Padua for trial for treason, and publicly beheaded outside the Salone on 3 March. Many of his rebel allies simply had their throats cut.[38] Increasingly, Niccolò da Carrara aspired to form his own following, surpass Marsilio in prestige and power, and secure the lordship of Padua for himself. In 1326 he began to form alliances with those whom many considered the leading Ghibellines of Padua, entertaining them at banquets and holding secret meetings. Enlisted in this cause were Marco Forzatè, his nephew Giordano, Prosdocimo Caligine, Francesco da Vigonza, Francesco Sanguinacci, and Ruzierio Fabriano. Condemned along with Niccolò to exile in Venice in December 1326, by the next year this formidable group was in open revolt in the eastern Padovano.[39] Seen as more amenable than Marsilio to Cangrande's policies, Niccolò was disliked and distrusted by many Paduans. When he appeared before the walls of Padua with Cangrande's besieging army in the summer of 1327, Marsilio reacted by arresting Niccolò's two sons, Giacomo and Giacomino, and later sent them into exile in Germany. Niccolò's residence in contrada S. Egidio was sacked and then razed to the ground.

That autumn, however, Niccolò had gathered a large armed force. Supported by Rizzardo da Camino with two thousand knights from Bassano and Paduan exiles from Venice and the Vicentino, Niccolò camped at Bovolenta to the southeast of the city. He burned Abano and attacked the Porta S. Croce, while Cangrande besieged Monselice. The rebel forces burned and pillaged at will in the southern half of the Padovano, from the Brenta to the Adige. In late November Konrad von Aufenstein arrived with four hundred German knights sent by Duke Heinrich of Carinthia to save the day. Von Aufenstein with Marsilio's captains, Filippo da Peraga and Aicardino da Capodivacca, drove the exile army from the field into winter quarters in Verona. Having earned the undying hatred of his cousin, Marsilio, Niccolò had lost forever his opportunity to rule Padua and ended his days in exile in Chioggia. No admirer, certainly, but a shrewd judge of character, Albertino Mussato provided a vivid portrait of Niccolò's contradictory character: "A man of enormous genius, with great powers of mind and of body, fretful and active, from boyhood he had despised the commune of the city and the restrictions of laws and statutes. Daring, terrifying, always restless, avid for power, arrogant, not very eloquent, [Niccolò] was endowed more with craftiness than with wisdom."[40] From him were to descend the last three generations of the Carrara rulers of Padua.

Marsilio now ruled unchallenged, supported by the German vicars eager to milk Padua's finances for themselves and their master, Duke Heinrich. On 8 April 1327, in the presence of the vicar, Konrad von Aufenstein, his vice-captain Engelmar von Villanders, and Marsilio da Carrara, the Maggior Consiglio voted to bestow on Duke Heinrich and his representative, the judge Gottschalk von Neumarkt-Enn, the gift of £20,000 "because of the many services and benefits that the Lord Heinrich had provided to the commune of Padua."[41] Pretending to be neutral, Marsilio had allowed the vice-captain Villanders to remove his cousin, Marsilietto Papafava dei Carraresi, from his post as warden of the city jail on a trumped-up charge. German soldiers promptly looted the Papafava palace as Marsilietto fled from the city. While citizens complained of the high taxes and the unruly German garrison, Villanders was obsessed with selling communal property and the goods of the rebels at bargain prices and returning to Germany a rich man. In July 1328 the current podestà, Gherardo Morosini of Venice, fled to Vicenza, claiming that Ubertino da Carrara was plotting to murder him.⁴² Marsilio soon replaced him with the hated German knight Griffo von Villanders.

The Rule of Marsilio da Carrara, Vicar for the Della Scala

With the city torn by strife at home and besieged by enemies in the contado, Padua's only solution, preached Marsilio, lay in his election as lord and placing the city under the protection of a powerful neighbor. On 1 September at Venice Marsilio sealed the Carrara–Della Scala alliance by secretly betrothing Giacomo il Grande's daughter Taddea to Cangrande's nephew Mastino II. Two days later, Padua's Maggior Consiglio with the common consent of the citizens meeting in arengo elected Marsilio "captain, protector and general defender of Padua."⁴³ Marsilio dismissed his former allies and companions, the German vicars, including Engelmar von Villanders and his brother, Griffo, who had been made podestà, and installed his friend and kinsman Marsilio Rossi of Parma as the new chief magistrate. But Marsilio's independent rule was short lived. On 7 September Mastino della Scala arrived in Padua at the head of a force of two hundred knights and overawed the local populace. Marsilio made a speech stressing the need to seek the protection of the Scaligeri in place of the inadequate government of the German captain. Pledging his own efforts and those of the House of Carrara to bring about a lasting peace, Marsilio mentioned the recent betrothal of his niece to Mastino della Scala as an example of his willingness to bring peace to Padua. On the 8th Marsilio traveled to Vicenza to greet Cangrande, who was waiting there, and on the 10th the two triumphantly entered Padua. The next day Cangrande formally accepted the lordship of Padua and appointed Marsilio da Carrara his vicar.⁴⁴ Thus, ironically a decade after the election of the first Carrara lord as an alternative to Scaligeri conquest, a second Carrara lord had become vicar of Padua precisely as Cangrande's friend and client.

Padua fell under Della Scala domination as part of Cangrande's great expansionist designs to rule northeast Italy. With the descent into Italy of King Lewis of Bavaria the year before, Cangrande had assumed a major role accepting Lewis's policies set forth at the parliament held at Trent in February. A little later, on 13 March 1327, Lewis arranged a truce between Cangrande and the forces of Heinrich, duke of Carinthia, which was to last until 23 April 132, providing for the exchange of captured strongholds and to be enforced by three of the king's own councillors.⁴⁵ As King Lewis progressed to Rome, Cangrande kept the pressure on the Paduans to accept his rule over the city. The rapacity and corruption of the German vicars made the regime of Marsilio and Cangrande a welcome alternative. Meanwhile,

Carrara supporters had gained wealth and prestige through advantageous marriages and the confiscated property of the Paduan exiles. Rizzardo da Lendinara had received some of the estates of the Sambonifacio and married his son to the daughter of Renaldo II Scrovegni, whose dowry, according to Mussato, yielded the unbelievable annual income of £8,000. One of Aicardino da Capodivacca's sons was married to the daughter of Gaboardo Scrovegni. Marsilio himself enjoyed the confiscated goods of the Dente, Maccaruffi, Terradura, and Giovanni Camposampiero.[46]

Most of all, Cangrande's rule promised internal peace for Paduan society torn by discord and faction. In a letter of congratulations drafted on 20 September, only nine days after Cangrande had assumed rule over Padua, the Florentine *signoria* viewed Cangrande's election as an opportunity to impose peace on warring factions and bring well-being to the citizen body. With the death of the Lucchese signore, Castruccio Castracani, on 3 September, Florence itself had just emerged from a difficult period of war. It could afford to be magnanimous in its praise for Padua's new ruler, paraphrasing Ps. 119:165 to the effect that "great peace will have those who love your law and nothing can make them stumble." Dwelling on Cangrande's own growth as a leader and ruler, the Florentines asserted their great delight with the happy future of the Paduan people, analogous to the good fortune of the Israelites when God committed them to King David's rule. Concluding with a plea for Cangrande's good relations with ecclesiastical authority and respect for the faithful, Psalm 72:7 is quoted: "In our days may justice flourish and may peace abound." Within the clear constraints of diplomatic language, Florence's government expressed the belief that Cangrande's rule represented a chance for peace, security, and justice for the Paduan people.[47]

Cangrande acted promptly to confirm his commitment to several cherished Paduan institutions. From Verona on 17 September he confirmed the special privilege of great autumn fairs held at the feasts of S. Giustina and S. Prosdocimo in October and November, granting the usual suspension against reprisals to encourage an influx of foreign merchants. On 16 October, Cangrande's new podestà, the Veronese Bernardo Ervari and his vicars, reconfirmed the Paduan commune's contribution to the Chapel of St. Thomas Aquinas which had been authorized for the Dominican church of S. Agostino four years earlier. The next April his officials reconfirmed the civic processions on the Feast of St. Peter Martyr, which had been established to celebrate the general peace of 1323.[48]

Most of all Cangrande worked at cementing good relations with the major Carrara supporters. At the end of November he brought his new Paduan allies to Verona to celebrate his triumph and the marriage of Taddea da Carrara and his nephew Mastino della Scala. There, on 29 November

1328, he knighted twenty-nine of his friends and followers, including at least eleven Paduans. The names of new knights read like a roster of the Carrara ruling elite at the end of the commune: Marsilio il Grande, his brother-in-law Tiso da Camposampiero, husband of Cunizza da Carrara, and Ubertino da Carrara; three nobles from the Papafava branch, Marsilietto, the future lord of Padua in 1345, his nephew Jacopo, and his cousin Obizzo; and soldiers Filippo da Peraga, Aicardino and Francesco da Capodivacca, and Tartaro da Lendinara.[49] At the same time Cangrande confirmed Marsilio in possession of the confiscated property of the Paduan exiles, including the estates of the Maccaruffi, Dente, Ronchi, Terradura, Altichini, Scrovegni, and others.[50] Several of the exiles, including Albertino Mussato, Enrico Scrovegni, and Niccolò da Carrara, had returned to Padua hoping for amnesty following Cangrande's election as lord, but they were sent back into exile in Venice on Marsilio's express orders.

The next spring, Cangrande embarked on his last campaign, the conquest of Treviso, still under the control of German vicars. After sending Marsilio to Parma to help the Correggio faction defend that city from a besieging papal army, Cangrande appointed him captain in the Paduan contingents in the army that laid siege to Treviso in July. Concerned with his own interests until the end, on 27 June 1329 Cangrande directed the canons and chapter of S. Giustina of Monselice to elect one of his favorites to a benefice as archpriest of that church. The next month Cangrande added Treviso to his domains, dying in his newly conquered city on 22 July 1329. His nephews Alberto and Mastino succeeded to the lordship of his vast state, which now included the cities of Belluno, Feltre, Treviso, Brescia, and Padua as well as the traditional centers of Verona and Vicenza. The Scaliger brothers oversaw extensive additions to the communal statutes that fall, making important revisions in laws governing justice, inheritance, crime and violence, peace and prosperity in the countryside, the conduct of business, and weights and measures. In general, the new statutes aimed at curbing abuses that had developed during the near anarchy of the rule of German vicars, sometimes using Veronese customs to modify Paduan institutions, as in important new statutes on the inheritance of women.[51]

Using the native "strongman" Marsilio da Carrara as vicar, the Della Scala lords completed the reduction of the communal government to organs of daily administration. While a series of handpicked Veronese nobles served as podestà overseeing the dispensing of justice and collection of taxes, the citizen councils, especially the Anziani and the Sixty, were reduced to silence. Indicative of this change, the room in the podestà's palace which in 1328 was called "Chamber of the Sixty" became in 1337 "the Chamber that used to be called of the Sixty (*camera que consuevit appellari de sexaginta*)."[52] With the

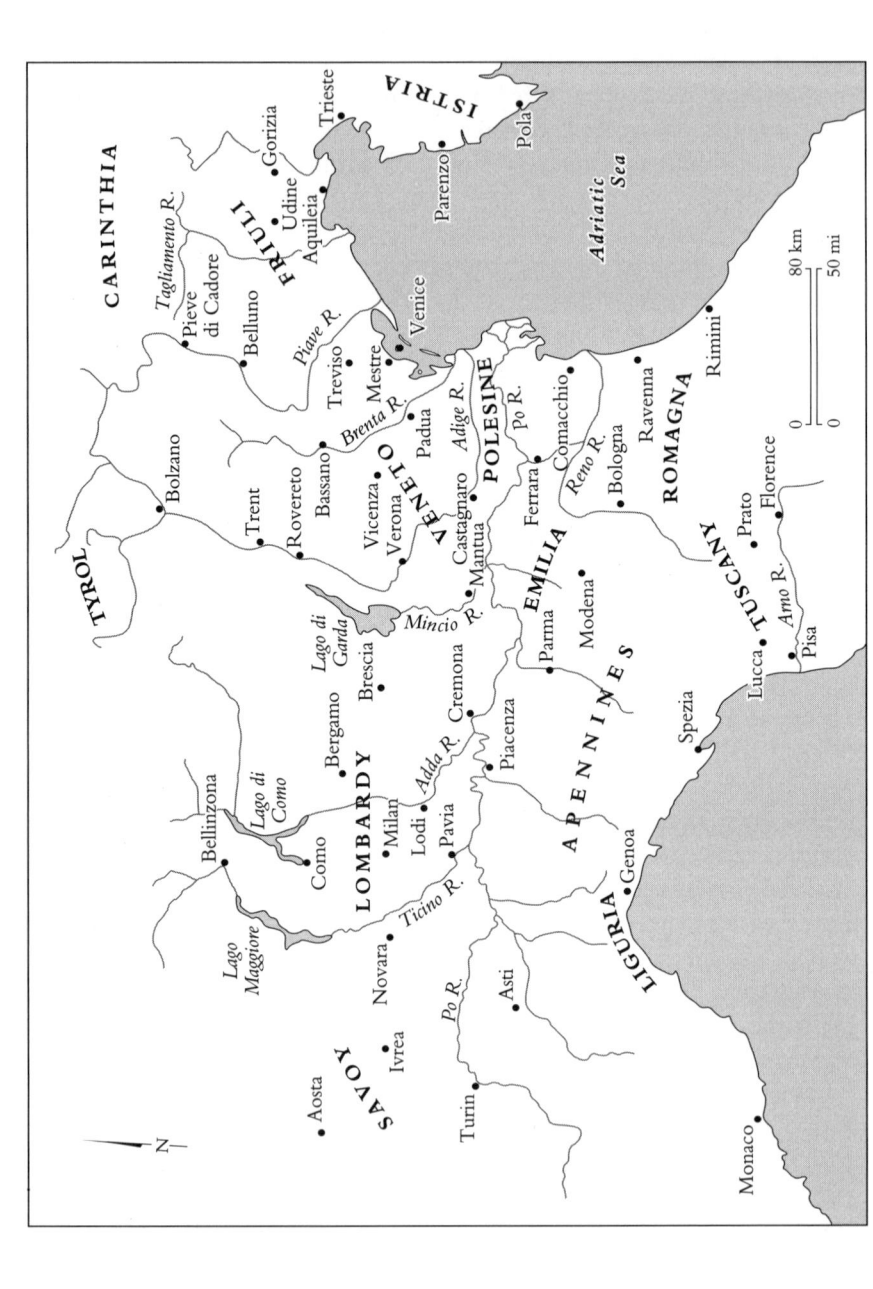

murder of Cunizza da Carrara and subsequent confiscation of Camposampiero estates, Marsilio da Carrara was bent on taming the unruly magnates of the Oltrebrenta, bringing rural villages throughout the Padovano more directly under the control of the central government. Pacification of the countryside was aided by the extinction of many magnate families and the destruction of their castles after decades of civil strife. Now Marsilio acted as a sort of intermediary between his own following of noble and powerful men and the Scaliger lords and their officials. Textile merchants, such as the Veronese Bevilacqua brothers and the Florentine Spinetta Malaspina, no doubt stimulated the local economy with a fresh influx of goods and capital. For example, in 1329 there appeared for the first time in Padua a guild of moneychangers (*campsores*), and new judicial procedures for mercantile cases were instituted. But, in general, the Scaliger rulers merely modified, rather than completely transformed, Paduan law and customs, promulgating new statutes only to solve specific problems and relying on existing communal offices to govern Padua.

However, the immediate effect of the death of Cangrande was to bring the Scaligeri brothers more direct participation in Paduan affairs. In August 1329 Alberto della Scala took up nearly continuous residence in Padua and began construction of a palace on the site of the future Carrara Reggia, clearing a space at the cost of demolishing several homes, as Mussato complained.[53] Marsilio da Carrara was, in effect, demoted and charged with several tasks governing the large Scaliger state. His first office in Scaligeri domains was a term as podestà of Vicenza, which ended in May 1330. Later he was given command of a Scaliger army that laid siege to Brescia early in 1332 and was made governor there after the fall of the city that summer. Shortly after the death of his first wife, Bartolomea Scrovegni (perhaps by poisoning), Marsilio was married to Beatrice da Correggio, a cousin of the Scaliger lords. Marsilio doubtless found this second marriage, on 13 July 1334, politically advantageous; he enjoyed as well lavish wedding gifts from the cities and rulers of the Scaliger state, including a donation of 600 florins from Treviso.[54] Later Marsilio served in the forces besieging Parma and Lucca, whose fall in 1335 brought the Scaliger dominions to their greatest extent.

In February 1336, the chronicler Guglielmo Cortusi visited the Scaliger court at Verona as an ambassador from the Paduan commune seeking relief from high taxes and forced loans. At the end of the Carnival season he beheld brilliant festivities that filled the Scaliger court with a host of notables from northern Italy, including Marsilio da Carrara with his new wife,

MAP 3 (*opposite*). *Northern Italy in the Fourteenth Century*

Beatrice, and Ubertino da Carrara from Padua; the three Rossi brothers from Parma, Rolando, Marsilio, and Pietro; the Della Scala lords' maternal uncles, Azzo and Guido da Correggio; the advocate of Treviso, Guecillo Tempesta; and nobles from the subject cities of Vicenza, Brescia, Novara, and Reggio. Stretching from the Alps to the Arno, from Friuli to Tuscany, the Scaligeri state had reached in less than seven years of rule under Alberto and Mastino an extent of which Cangrande himself had only dreamed. With this great wealth and power came, according to Cortusi, the seeds of the destruction of the Della Scala empire. Within six months the lords of Verona would be locked in a desperate struggle with Florence and Venice which would result in the ultimate downfall of their fragile dynastic state.[55]

The Coming of War with Venice

Relations with Venice had been amicable enough at the beginning of the Scaliger rule over the neighboring cities of Padua and Treviso. On 12 March 1329, the Venetian government had awarded the privilege of citizenship to Cangrande della Scala and his heirs with a golden bull.[56] To be sure, the Della Scala had exploited their new domains as much as possible, doubling tax revenues from Treviso between 1329 and 1335, so that Treviso contributed more than one-tenth of the revenues of the Scaligeri state in the early 1330s.[57] Alberto and Mastino exploited, as did all signori, tithes from the local bishops. For example, on 4 August 1333 they had the vicar of the bishop of Padua invest their offspring, Rainaldo and Fregnano della Scala, with extensive fiefs of tithes in the Vicentino and Veronese.[58] Next year, the Della Scala lords agreed to a Venetian request for arbitration that would force Ubertino da Carrara to restore tithes he had usurped from certain Venetian citizens on lands in the Padovano. At the same time, the Veronese ambassadors insisted that the business of tithes be settled amicably in a determined meeting place.[59]

The main source of contention lay in the Scaligers' challenging traditional Venetian prerogatives concerning the income of its citizens and monasteries in the Veneto and freedom of trade generally. As early as 1332, the Scaligeri had demanded new tithes from Venetian monastic houses in Piove di Sacco which had been by custom immune from local taxation. These actions prompted the Venetian Senate to discuss prohibiting the export of salt to Verona in retaliation, but this measure was rejected because it was thought that the Scaligeri might retaliate, in turn, by suspending the exportation of grain from the mainland to Venice. But the next year, invoking an old privilege as imperial vicars, the Della Scala brothers ordered a chain placed across the Po at Ostiglia, stopping river traffic and exacting tolls on goods shipped by water from Lombardy. This affront brought a sharp protest from Venice, which sent ambassadors demanding that the Scaligeri respect prior agreements and the tradition of free commerce of the Po River.[60] Early in January 1336, the Senate complained that the Scaligeri diplomats had responded to their protests only in the most general terms, but still instructed the Serenissima's ambassadors to seek a negotiated settlement and stress Venice's desire to peace and friendship with the Della Scala lords. But ten days later the Senate elected three new envoys to treat with the Della Scala and demand that they cease their hostile activities and observe all their prior treaties with Venice.[61]

The Scaliger lords' continued intransigence eventually provoked the predictable Venetian response of suspending the exportation of salt to their dominions. On 22 March 1336 the Senate appointed three of Venice's best diplomats, Giustinian Giustinian, Marco Morosini, and Giacomo Gradenigo, to bring the Della Scala lords to their senses. At the same time, the Senate voted 57 to 16 with 5 abstentions to restrict completely the exportation of salt to Veronese dominions. On 6 April, the prohibition was extended to the import or export of all foodstuffs, textiles, and manufactured goods between Venice and Scaligeri domains, with any goods traded in violation of the embargo to be confiscated.[62] An effort made by envoys of the Gonzaga lord to negotiate the differences later that month at Venice failed, since the Scaligeri were unyielding on the question of tithes, control of navigation on the Piave, and imposing tolls on goods transported on the Po. On 14 May the Venetian Senate reconfirmed its decision to demand full compliance from the Scaligeri, while the Veronese lords sought to create their own supply of salt. Their troops and artisans began construction of a saltworks guarded by a castle on the lagoon opposite Chioggia. War was now inevitable.

By late April the Venetians had already entered into negotiations for an alliance with Florence, which was alarmed by the Scaligeri occupation of Lucca and its contado the previous year. In May Florence had persuaded its primary Guelf ally, Bologna, to forbid the passage of Scaliger or Estense troops through the Romagna to reinforce Veronese garrisons in Tuscany. In the final treaty signed on 22 June, both states agreed to fight until the Della Scala were defeated, with Florence agreeing to bear two-thirds of the costs of the war.[63] The choice of a commander fell on Pietro Rossi, who with his brothers Rolando and Marsilio had just lost a lengthy struggle to rule Parma to the Scaligeri and their kinsmen, Azzo and Guido da Correggio. All three Rossi brothers had been the unwilling guests of the Della Scala at Verona during Carnival in 1336. Pietro returned to family estates in the Parmese, while his brothers secretly departed for Venice. The Scaligeri and their vicars in Parma, the da Correggio brothers, had earned the Rossi's undying hatred by confiscating much of the Rossi family's extensive property in that city and its district. By May Pietro Rossi was already a captain in the Florentine army in the Lucchese. Settling affairs in Tuscany, Pietro marched over the Apennines and took a ship on the Po which brought him to Venice by August.

In the approaching conflict, the continuing control of Padua was the main objective of the Della Scala lords, just as its conquest was of prime importance for the allied cities of Venice and Florence. A major assumption in the Scaliger war plans was the continued support of Marsilio da Carrara and his important following in Padua. On 2 April, the Della Scala lords had sought to maintain their cities' good will by making two major concessions. In an effort to stockpile provisions in the city in case of Venetian attack, they permitted the Trevisan commune to purchase 2,000 *staia* of wheat (at the price of 54½ *soldi* per *staio*) from Marsilio at Camposampiero and transport the grain into the Trevisano free of the usual taxes.[64] The Scaliger lords also ordered the bishop of Treviso to invest Marsilio da Carrara with extensive tithes in the Trevisano which had previously belonged to the husband and son, Tiso and Tiso Novello da Camposampiero, of his sister Cunizza da Carrara. The property included seven farmsteads (*mansi*) and thirty parcels near the Trevisan border at Rustega and Loreggia as well as two large woods on the Musone River.[65] But Venice also courted Marsilio da Carrara's favor. On 30 April 1336, the Senate appointed three *savi* (officials) to meet with Marsilio and keep him informed of Venice's policies, especially of its negotiations under the auspices of the Gonzaga and Este to maintain peace with the Scaligeri. The Venetian envoys reassured Marsilio that no secret treaties were being made with the Scaligeri and that the Serenissima was acting always in his own best interests.[66] Even the selection of the Rossi brothers as military captains was calculated to win Marsilio's eventual good will. Their mother, Donzella Rossi, née Carrara, was Marsilio's favorite aunt, who had often visited Perenzano da Carrara's palace in Padua with her sons in their youth.

Venice's first act of war preparations was to garrison villages and fortify Montalbano and Stalimbecco near the Scaligeri saltworks on the edge of the lagoon. This was followed by the election in the Maggior Consiglio of a war board of twenty-five with full powers to raise a militia and conduct the campaign. Troops were raised from all men between ages twenty and sixty in each *sestiere* of Venice. To create this militia, one soldier in twelve was selected in each contrada, with the *sestieri* of S. Polo, S. Croce, and Dorsodoro contributing the first troops. This force, which amounted to perhaps 1,250 conscripts, was charged with local defense and an assault on the

Scaliger Castello di Saline. All other military operations were entrusted to mercenaries, knights, and infantry, under the command of Pietro Rossi.[67]

Late in the summer of 1336, the Venetians began collecting their army at Motta under the temporary command of Pietro's brother, Marsilio Rossi. When Pietro Rossi finally reached Venice in September, the entire populace turned out to see him take the baton of command from the doge and enter the service of Florence and Venice. By 5 October Pietro Rossi reached the allied camp at Motta and began final preparations for the autumn campaign. Venetian officials had collected supplies, horses, arms, and money for the large force of German and Italian mercenaries they were enlisting. By September, they had assembled a force of 4,200 lances and 3,000 infantry for the war, paying 9 ducats per month for each knight furnished with warhorse and rouncy, 7 ducats with warhorse alone. The Venetians agreed to indemnify soldiers for horses lost, and the mercenaries were to keep any booty taken, while land and prisoners in general went to Venice. In certain cases, however, the mercenaries got both booty and prisoners, with Venice agreeing to pay 3 ducats for each knight captured and 50 ducats apiece for constables and captains. In the case of prisoners taken in pitched battles, Venice was to pay double the rate for enemy taken or indemnify any loss of horses with the captured enemy sent to Venice to be held for ransom. The mercenary captains and knights swore an oath of allegiance to Venice and agreed to serve for the duration of the conflict.[68]

On 23 October 1336, the allied army, drawn up in three squadrons, crossed the Piave into the Trevisano. The advance force under Marsilio Rossi consisted of 1,000 knights and an equal number of infantry; the main force under Pietro Rossi, 2,800 knights and 800 foot; the rear guard under Golfard Steinberg, 400 knights and 300 foot. In addition, peasants had been drafted into a force of sappers equipped with hoes and shovels. The Veronese forces fell back, leaving scorched earth before the invading army. Mastino and Alberto della Scala decided not to make a stand at the Brenta, allowing the allied forces to reach Piove di Sacco on 1 November, thus securing direct communication with Venice via Pontelongo. A week later Rossi and his army set up winter field headquarters at Bovolenta some 12 kilometers south of Padua. Almost immediately a force was dispatched to lay siege to the Scaliger garrison of about 100 men at Castello di Saline, which fell on 22 November. Throughout the winter the allied forces pillaged the southeast Padovano, fighting a sharp encounter on 26 December with Veronese knights who had sallied forth from their stronghold at Este. The allies captured 26 Veronese constables and more than 150 knights, who were taken to the camp at Bovolenta.[69]

In the spring of 1337 Pietro Rossi foraged in the Oltrebrenta, collecting

The Early Carrara

animals and provisions and forcing the Scaliger ally Guglielmo Camposampiero to surrender the town of Curtarolo and the fortress at Treville to a small garrison of allied forces. That same month ambassadors of the so-called Lombard lords, Azzo Visconti of Milan, Obizzo II and Niccolò I d'Este of Ferrara and Modena, and Ludovico Gonzaga of Mantua and Reggio, came to Venice to arrange peace. Instead the lords were persuaded to make a treaty with Florence and Venice to fight the Scaligeri to their final destruction. News of this new alliance in favor of Venice precipitated rebellions in the towns of the northern Veneto—Conegliano, Asolo, S. Zenone, Cittadella, and Camposampiero—against Scaliger rule. The allies then besieged Treviso, still under Scaliger control. Meanwhile, the Lombard lords began a campaign against Verona itself in the western theater of the war. Mastino responded by placing the bulk of his troops in his capital, leaving only a force of five hundred German knights and some local conscripts under Alberto's command in Padua. In June Mastino della Scala, with a large army, met forces under Luchino Visconti and Marsilio Rossi in open country south of Verona. Threatened by the larger Scaliger force, the Visconti lord quietly withdrew, leaving Marsilio Rossi alone with a small squadron. But Mastino did not press his advantage, and the allied force was able to withdraw in good order under cover of darkness. Next, Mastino resolved to attack the besieging army from the south, moved his forces to Este, and cut the lines with Venice at Pontelongo, capturing a number of ships and supplies intended for the allied forces. But again Mastino declined to meet the allied army in open battle and, harried by relieving forces under the command of Marsilio Rossi, retreated into Veronese territory.[70]

Meanwhile Alberto della Scala's situation in Padua was becoming desperate. With barely enough troops to man the walls of the city, much less repel a determined attack, the Scaliger lord was forced to rely on Marsilio and Ubertino da Carrara for support. To meet the costs of defending Padua, he demanded large forced loans from each of the Carrara, 22,000 ducats from Marsilio and 4,000 ducats from Ubertino. These heavy demands, the hopelessness of the Scaliger cause, and many personal affronts, including Alberto's seduction of Ubertino's wife, prompted the Carraresi to switch sides. When Alberto della Scala sent Marsilio on an embassy to Venice, the Carrara lord negotiated a secret treaty with the Venetian government, promising to hand over Padua to the allied forces in return for a number of concessions and assurances.

On 14 July the treaty was signed at Venice with the following provisions: Marsilio da Carrara was to be captain general and lord of Padua and its fortresses, including Monselice, Este, Montagnana, Castelbaldo, Cittadella, and Bassano, while the Polesine, Lendinara, and Badia were to remain under Este control. Florence and Venice and their allies were to aid Marsilio in conquering these towns and especially Padua. If Marsilio was killed in the assault, he was to be succeeded by Ubertino da Carrara in the lordship of Padua. If peace was made before Padua was captured, Venice and Florence promised to use all their powers to force the Scaligeri to return the forced loans and secure the Carraresi in their private property. Venice and Florence agreed to place Padua, its district, and the Carrara lords under their protection, and Marsilio and the Paduans were to defend and aid Venice in all future conflicts on land and sea. The dispute over the Camposampiero inheritance between Marsilio da Carrara and Guglielmo Dente was to be adjudicated by the doge. No taxes were to be levied on Venetian goods transported through Paduan territories and foreign goods brought from other places to Venice. Likewise, there were to be no imposts on goods imported from Florence to Padua and its district. Finally, harking back to one of the main causes of the war, Marsilio agreed that Venetian monasteries, corporations, and citizens could transport goods, produce, and rents to Venice free of any tariff. The Paduan guarantors of the treaty were intimates of Marsilio da Carrara's circle: Marsilietto and Giacomo Papafava dei Carraresi, Antonio da Lozzo, Tartaro da Lendinara, Dusio Buzzacarini, Francesco Frassalasta, Jacopo Capodivacca, Giacomino and Marco da Peraga, and Bonfrancesco Negri.[71]

On 24 July Pietro Rossi prepared for the final assault against the Veronese forces in Padua, moving his forces to Noventa, a few kilometers to the east of the city. Arrangements were made with Marsilio da Carrara for entry into Padua. On 3 August, some Venetian forces feinted an attack on the Porta S. Croce to the south, drawing there the German garrison, while the Carraresi opened the gate of Ponte Corvo to Pietro Rossi and his knights. These troops rushed to the central piazza and captured a dazed Alberto della Scala and his attendants. The German mercenaries soon surrendered on the promise that they would be given safe passage to their homelands. On the 6th, Marsilio duly received the lordship of Padua, elected captain and lord of Padua by the Maggior Consiglio, in the presence of Florentine and Venetian officials.[72] The stalemate had been broken. After ten months of siege and pillaging, Padua had fallen to the allies by treachery and not by open conquest. As the chronicler Jacopo Piacentino, scarcely a Carrara partisan, was forced to admit: "without [the betrayal of] Padua, the Venetians and Florentines would have struggled in vain. For it was the rebellion within this city which effectively destroyed the Della Scala and forced them to negotiate the end of the present war."[73]

Chapter 3

Venice's *Status Noster,* 1337–1355

> Non debet intelligi quod civitas Padue sit ad conditionem tyrampnorum, quia potest dici quod est nostrum statum proprium.
>
> [The city of Padua ought not to be considered under the rule of tyrants, because it can be said that it is our own state.]
>
> —Maggior Consiglio, 8 July 1339

Marsilio da Carrara Becomes Lord of Padua

In August 1337 Padua was liberated with a minimum of bloodshed, Alberto della Scala captured and sent to Venice under guard of Tartaro da Lendinara, and the German mercenaries discharged and repatriated with safe-conduct through Venetian territories. The Paduan populace enthusiastically greeted the return of the Carrara; citizens thronged the streets with genuine expressions of joy and approval. The next month the leaders of the notaries guild had painted on the walls and gates of the church of the communal palace the insignia of the allies, the winged lion of St. Mark and Florence's white lily as well as the red cross of the Paduan commune; to these arms the notaries added the four-wheeled cart (the red *carro*) of the Carrara dynasty in acknowledgment of the permanence of the new regime.[1]

It remained for Marsilio da Carrara to be formally invested with the lordship of Padua, which had been promised to him in the secret treaty of 14 July. Thus, on 6 August, the Florentine and Venetian ambassadors met with Marsilio and representatives of the Paduan commune in the great hall of the Salone. Speaking for the doge and commune of Venice, Marco Loredan greeted the Carrara lord and officials of the Paduan commune and expressed his joy at the liberation of Padua. Then he went on to convey this message:

> The Lord Doge, with the communes of Venice and Florence, wants Lord Marsilio to guide the city of Padua on the Venetian model [civitati Padue

FIG. 6. *Painted* carro *stemma and cross of Paduan commune, walls of Cittadella. Photograph courtesy of Tracy Cooper*

providere Venetiarum exemplo]. For the citizens of Venice are ruled by their fellow citizen, the Doge, who, by reason of blood and from love of country, has preserved Venice in a good and peaceful state for a very long time. In the same way, may it please Marsilio to treat the Paduan people with fatherly affection, deriving pleasure from all that has been said, may he indeed attain perpetual praise in this world and glory in the next.[2]

Marsilio da Carrara then ascended the podium and, as the crowd fell silent, responded with deep thanks to Venice and Florence for the liberation of Padua. He documented his claim to the lordship from recent Paduan history: the election of his uncle Giacomo il Grande as first Carrara lord, the protection of Frederick of Austria and Heinrich of Carinthia, the oppression and eventual expulsion of the German vicars, the necessity of his handing over Padua to Cangrande della Scala, the betrayal of this trust by the nephews Mastino and Alberto, the expulsion of the Veronese with the help of Venice and Florence. Now Marsilio swore to bring peace and justice to Padua and prosperity to the Paduan people; only the reconquest of Monselice remained to be accomplished. Those present shouted: "May the Lord preserve you. You are our hope; in your life is our salvation."[3]

After his installation as the new leader of Padua, Marsilio sent his general, Pietro Rossi, with Ubertino da Carrara and Marsilietto Papafava, at

FIG. 7. *Marsilio da Carrara receives lordship of Padua in 1337. Source: Biblioteca Nazionale Marciana, Venice, MS lat. X, 381 (= 2808), fol. 5v of Gesta magnifica domus carrariensis (MS written in 1390). Reproduced with permission of the Biblioteca Nazionale Marciana, Venice*

the head of a large contingent of German mercenaries to lay siege to the fortress at Monselice, which had been in the hands of the Della Scala for two decades. The very next day, Pietro Rossi was mortally wounded before the walls of Monselice. His death at the age of thirty-four on Friday evening, 8 August, thrust Padua into deep mourning, for he was the most beloved of all the military captains in the liberating army. The next week his older brother, Marsilio, died of fever and exhaustion at the age of fifty, leaving the allied army under the command of Rolando Rossi, the least respected and competent of the three brothers. First Pietro and then Marsilio were buried in great pomp in a side chapel of the Basilica of S. Antonio, in tombs bearing inscriptions attesting to the universal grief for and great martial accomplishments of the deceased.[4]

While the force of German and Paduan knights continued to lay siege to Monselice, other allied contingents carried the war to other fronts. In September the Veronese garrison at the Scaliger castle at Mestre ran out of provisions and surrendered when two constables handed over the keys to Venetian officials in return for a large bribe. In October Azzo Visconti occupied the Scaliger city of Brescia with the help of Ludovico Gonzaga. That same month, Mastino della Scala sent ambassadors to Venice offering Lucca to Florence for 80,000 florins and Treviso to Venice in return for peace. In December Veronese negotiators also offered Monselice and Bassano to Venice on the condition that these cities were not given to a third party, that is, to the turncoat Marsilio da Carrara, as had been stipulated in the treaty of 14 July. That same month ambassadors from the Visconti and Este, and Ludovico Gonzaga in person, arrived in Venice ready to negotiate a settlement. But the Veronese legates set too many conditions; the conference adjourned on 22 December without results. That winter Mastino della Scala tried another approach; he received imperial legates at Verona and agreed to cede Veronese strongholds at Peschiera sul Garda and passes in the Alto Adige in return for imperial protection from Lewis of Bavaria. In February German ambassadors appeared in Venice bearing letters from Lewis of Bavaria requesting a truce of one month, but Venice rejected Lewis's request and instead sent allied forces under Rolando Rossi and Guecello Tempesta on a large foraging expedition into Veronese territory. Discovering a ford over the Adige at Albaredo, the allied cavalry ravaged the countryside up to the gates of Vicenza, capturing a number of Veronese troops and returning home with cattle, horses, swine, goats, sheep, and hundreds of carts filled with grain, hay, and wine.[5]

On 1 March 1338, the future doge Marino Falier arrived in Padua to begin a six-month term as *podestà* to find Marsilio da Carrara gravely ill. From his deathbed, Marsilio reconfirmed his cousin Ubertino as his successor, "always with the approval of the Lord Doge of Venice and the commune of Florence." Marsilio died on 21 March, and his body was conveyed in a sumptuous funeral procession to lie in state in the south transept of the Basilica of S. Antonio next to the tombs of Pietro and Marsilio Rossi before burial in the family church of S. Stefano at Carrara.[6] Ubertino succeeded to the lordship of Padua and promptly saw to the reconfirmation of the treaty of July 1337. On 5 May, Paduan jurists, Pietro da Campagnola and Aldrigetto da Montagnana, appeared in the Ducal Palace before Venetian officials and Florentine legates as ambassadors from Ubertino and the Paduan commune to agree to the revised treaty. Four clauses treating the terms of the capture of Padua were omitted, while nine others were reconfirmed merely substituting Ubertino for Marsilio. Among these were two clauses that were to affect Paduan-Venetian relations for the next half century. One provided for the transport of goods from Venice into Padua and its district or transshipment of goods through Padua into Venice free of any customs (*gabelle*), beyond what had been normal in the time of the commune. Now goods from Florence were also to be imported into Padua free of duty. Further, no local taxes, or *dazii,* could be levied on the possessions of Venetian citizens or religious corporations or their workers. Venice (and to a certain extent, Florence) had won very important economic concessions. In return for guaranteeing Padua's territorial integrity and the security of the Carrara dynasty, the exorbitant custom duties charged by the Scaligeri were reduced to an ordinary level, defined as six *denari* per lira of value (or 2.5 percent). More important, Venetian citizens and monasteries could export grain, meat, and raw materials back to the city free of any Paduan taxes, treating the Padovano in effect as their own *contado,* the ready source of foodstuffs and income for Venetian religious communities and urban households. To these concessions was added on 5 May the provision that the lord and commune of Padua were now required to aid Florence against all its enemies, as had previously applied only to Venice. Thus, the fortunes of Padua were linked to the foreign policies of two of the most powerful city-states in Italy. This accomplished, there was still a war to be won.[7]

Indeed, the campaign to reduce Monselice and bring Mastino della Scala to terms had turned brutal. In March 1338 Ubertino summarily hanged eight Veronese soldiers trying to enter Monselice as reinforcements; in retaliation the Scaliger commander Pietro dal Verme hanged seven natives suspected of treason. Ubertino executed thirteen prisoners captured from the Scaliger garrison and slit the noses of starving local women found stealing foodstuffs in the Paduan camp.[8] In April, elements of the Venetian-Florentine forces under Rolando Rossi and Paduan troops under Tartaro da Lendinara entered Veronese territory at Monteforte and advanced to the walls of Verona, where the allied army staged a *palio* to taunt the defenders. Under the eyes of Mastino della Scala and his garrison, the enemy knights held a horse race for a prize worth 50 ducats. The flaunting of military prowess proved unbearable, and a number of Veronese knights sallied forth to attack the allied camp, only to have three killed, five captured, and the rest retreat in disorder.

In the meantime, Mastino was seeking new allies. In February he concluded a secret treaty with Luigi Gonzaga and began recruiting a new army. By May, when he took the field to recover Montecchio and relieve Monselice, Mastino could muster a force of two thousand cavalry and six thousand infantry. With these troops he invested the allied garrison at Montecchio, but the besieging army was routed by a company of German knights under Rolando Rossi. Mastino regrouped and on 17 June attacked the small allied

FIG. 8. *Tomb of Marsilio da Carrara (1339), S. Stefano da Carrara. Photograph courtesy of Tracy Cooper*

garrison under Ubertino da Carrara and Raimondino Lupi at Longare. The Scaliger forces were repulsed, and many were drowned attempting to recross the Bacchiglione River. Meanwhile, the German mercenaries went on strike until 1 August, claiming their contracts provided for a bonus of double pay for their action in the rout at Montecchio. The Venetian army commissaries promised a generous future settlement and placed a reward of £10,000 on Mastino's head. But the campaign in the Veronese came to a halt as the mercenaries refused to take the field. An appeal to the Holy Roman Emperor, Lewis of Bavaria, brought a decision favorable to the German mercenaries. But the Florentines refused to accept this arbitration, claiming that as Guelfs their religious scruples prevented them from obeying Lewis, a heretic and rebel against the church.[9]

Terms of Peace, 1338–1339

With its mercenary army in disarray, the allied command concentrated on the final capture of the Veronese stronghold at Monselice. At a conference at Venice in July, the allies had agreed that Ubertino da Carrara would pay a bonus of 8,000 ducats for the German and Italian mercenaries under Scaliger command to surrender all fortifications, except the Rocca

FIG. 9. *Carrara Castello, Monselice. Photograph courtesy of Tracy Cooper*

at Monselice. The garrison, including the commander Pietro dal Verme, was to be given safe-conduct to Verona. Fifteen hostages, eight from the garrison and seven from Ubertino's forces, including the pride of Paduan knighthood, Albertino Papafava, Giacomino da Peraga, Bonfrancesco Negri, and Paradiso Capodivacca, were to remain sequestered in the monastery of S. Giorgio Maggiore in Venice until the peace was made. On 19 August 1338, the Scaliger forces evacuated Monselice, much to the joy of the Paduan people and relief of their leaders.[10] The *gastaldi* of the notaries guild reacted by appointing a board of *savi,* who, on 21 August, proposed an annual celebration commemorating the liberation of Monselice to the assembled leaders of all the Paduan guilds. By a vote of 102 to 52, the leaders of the several guilds voted to honor the event, which fell on the feast of St. Louis of Toulouse, with a procession of the podestà and his officials, with the clergy and guildsmen of Padua, from the Duomo to the Basilica of S. Antonio. The proposal was approved by the current podestà, Marino Falier, and, thus, another civic procession was instituted to mark the victory of Carrara arms.[11] With the consigning of Treviso to Venice and surrender of the Rocca at Monselice to Paduan forces in November, the allies' major objectives had been accomplished, except for Florence's taking Lucca.

Peace negotiations, begun in October under the good offices of Luigi Gonzaga, who had been a lukewarm ally of Venice and secret friend of the Della Scala, finally bore fruit in January 1339. The stalemate of recent months meant that the Della Scala were able to retain more of their dominions than promised by the allied commitment to a struggle aimed at the extinction of the enemy. Florence, in particular, felt betrayed by Venice's insistence on an early peace, for the much sought prize of Lucca was to remain in the possession of the Della Scala, while the Florentine commune received only the towns and fortresses at Buggiano, Pescia, Altopascio, and Colle on its western frontier.[12] In fact, the Scaligeri remained a major force in Italian affairs, retaining possession of Verona, Vicenza, and Parma as well as Lucca. As might be expected, from the terms of the treaty ratified in the Basilica of S. Marco on 24 January, Venice was the major beneficiary: the Scaliger challenge had been contained, a friendly buffer state of Padua under the Carrara had been established, and Venice itself took possession of Treviso and its district, while the frontier strongholds of Bassano and Castelbaldo went to the new Carrara lord of Padua. Scaliger troops and garrisons in Treviso and other strongholds were given safe-conduct back to Verona, and Alberto della Scala and his entourage of hostages were released after eighteen months of captivity. The chain at Ostiglia was destroyed, and freedom of commerce on the Po was guaranteed. The Della Scala agreed to observe fully older pacts granting Venice extensive trading rights in their territories. War damages of up to 10,000 ducats were to be paid on property of Venetian churches, monasteries, and citizens in the eastern Veneto, based on a survey conducted by Venetian officials within six months and paid from new tariffs on cheese, salt meat, and salt sent to the Scaliger domains. In general, property rights of Venetian citizens in Scaliger lands were to be respected, as were those of Veronese citizens in Venetian and Paduan dominions. Other allies agreed to the terms of the treaty. Azzo Visconti, lord of Milan; Obizzo II and Niccolò I d'Este, lords of Ferrara and Modena; Luigi Gonzaga and his sons, lords of Mantua and Reggio; and Ostasio da Polenta, lord of Ravenna, as well as Scaliger adherents, confirmed the pact, bringing peace to northern Italy.

Florence and Venice soon began to carry out the articles of the treaty. On 14 January 1339 the Venetian official Stefano de Franchino assigned Bassano and its castle to Dusio Buzzacarini, acting as proctor for Ubertino da Carrara and the commune of Padua. On the 17th Dusio also received Castelbaldo.[13] Meanwhile, Ubertino had already begun the process of establishing his rule in Padua. In the late summer of 1338, the Paduan clergy and people had received from Pope Benedict XII a letter lifting the papal interdict that had been imposed on Padua when it was under the control of the hated Ghibelline tyrants, Mastino and Alberto della Scala. Now, in return for the Paduans' agreement never to invade papal lands nor give aid to Lewis of Bavaria and his followers or any heretics and enemies of the

FIG. 10. *Portrait of Ubertino da Carrara, with banner of Paduan commune and winged, horned Moor (late fourteenth century). Source: Biblioteca Civica, Padua, MS B.P. 158, fol. 26v. Pier Paolo Vergerio the Elder,* De principibus Carrariensibus. *Reproduced with permission of the Biblioteca Civica, Padua*

church, the pope promised to send to the commune of Padua within four months a sealed letter confirming the end of the interdict and restoration as faithful followers of the Holy Mother Church.[14] Ubertino cemented his relations with Venice, requesting and receiving a grant of Venetian citizenship soon after Marsilio's death.

As a Venetian citizen and lord of Venice's most favored client state, early in 1339 Ubertino worked closely with the podestà, Marino Falier, on extensive reform of the Paduan statutes.[15] The main thrust was to ensure that the communal government maintained a stable civil society. The massive legislation against treason, conspiracy, and civil disorder aimed at promoting the security of Padua, its ruling family, and contado. Other statutes attempted a new definition of the Paduan citizen, permitting the return of "reliable" exiles to the city and setting forth the criteria for membership in Padua's Maggior Consiglio. Seats on the council now became hereditary, with a member bequeathing his place to whoever met the general requirements of Paduan citizenship. In short, Falier's legislation provided for a "closing" of Padua's Maggior Consiglio, similar to the restrictions developing in contemporary Venice, with membership more limited and clearly defined than in the past and now largely hereditary. Although the powers of the council diminished with the years under Carrara rule, its membership, whose quorum was one hundred, continued to enjoy legal rights in the appointment of the new podestà, election of certain officials, and ratification of new legislation.

Punishing Old Enemies: The Camposampiero and Dente

Throughout the spring and early summer of 1339, Ubertino and the commune of Padua worked out with the Venetian government the terms of the recent treaties of alliance and peace. On 28 February, the Venetian Senate agreed that the commune of Pirano had to repay within two months an earlier loan made by Marsilio and Ubertino at Venice's request, under penalty of a fine of £1,000.[16] In March 1339 the Senate turned its attention to the settlement of the disputed inheritance of Tisone (IX) Camposampiero. The roots of the dispute went back to troubled Scaligeri rule in Padua. Tisone (VIII) Camposampiero had taken as his second wife Cunizza di Perenzano da Carrara, Marsilio's sister, by whom he had one son, Tisone IX. Cunizza had earned her brother's wrath by siding with the rival claimant to the lordship of Padua, Niccolò da Carrara. As a widow she took a Burgundian soldier as her lover, defying convention and infuriating her brother and son. At the instigation of Marsilio da Carrara, the son Tisone IX was able to discover his mother with her lover in Verona in 1330 and murdered the two on the spot. When Tisone IX died young without heirs, he left his entire inheritance to Marsilio da Carrara, who in turn willed it to Ubertino at his own death in March 1338. The rival claimant to the huge Camposampiero legacy in the Oltrebrenta was Guglielmo, son of Giacomo, who had been Tisone VIII's son by his first marriage to Engelinda da Camino. Giacomo had predeceased both his mother and his half brother, Tisone IX, leaving the young Guglielmo nearly powerless to defend his claim to half the Camposampiero properties made through the testament of his grandfather, Tisone VIII. Venice's Senate decided that litigation between two of most powerful families in nearby Padua was grave enough to warrant the promise of direct arbitration of the dispute.[17]

On 6 March 1339, the Venetian Senate ordered Guglielmo da Camposampiero to present promptly his arguments for receiving the inheritance, and on 18 March it appointed a board of three savi to handle the case and render their opinion by 15 April. In the event, the board took more than a year to arrive at its judgment. On 24 March 1340, the savi divided the inheritance between the two parties. Ubertino as heir of Marsilio da Carrara received the village and castle of Camposampiero with property in the Oltrebrenta; Guglielmo got extensive holdings in the eastern Padovano and the Trevisano. Since Guglielmo's property yielded rents of nearly £3,500 per annum, while Ubertino's annual income amounted to about £3,600, the legacy was divided about equally between the two litigants.[18] Disgruntled with receiving only a portion of the legacy, Guglielmo retired to his castle and estates at Treville, where he died in February 1342, honored a year earlier with the bestowal of Venetian citizenship for his service to the republic during the recent Scaligeri war.[19]

From his marriage to Caterina Dente, daughter of the Carrara archenemy Vitaliano Dente, Guglielmo da Camposampiero left only a daughter, Sara, who married Meliaduse di Guecello Tempesta, advocate of Treviso, against her father's wishes. Soon after the death of her father, Sara appeared before the Venetian podestà of Castelfranco presenting an inventory of her inheritance and requesting release of the property. In a decision of 7 March 1342, the Senate decreed that Sara could receive the moveables only if she posted a security equal to their value, since there were still many outstanding claims against Guglielmo's estate. In fact, ten days earlier, the *signoria* had ordered its *provveditore,* or civil commissioner, in Treviso to proceed with a contingent of foot soldiers to Camposampiero to secure Guglielmo's property there after his death.[20] On 6 September 1342, Meliaduse died at Padua under mysterious circumstances, and Sara was summoned there by a letter purportedly sent by her husband. Instead of Meliaduse, Sara found at Padua the *condottiere* (mercenary captain) Rolando Rossi proposing that she marry his son, Beltrando. Sara apparently did marry Beltrando Rossi the next day, much to the anger of her mother, Caterina Camposampiero née Dente, and her former affines, the Tempesta of Treviso, who stood to lose control over Camposampiero estates in the Trevisano and the stronghold at Treville. On 14 September Sara's mother complained to the Venetian government that her daughter had been abducted by the Rossi and brought to Padua against her will and requested that the Venetians investigate the matter. Two days later the Senate warned ambassadors of Ubertino da Carrara in Venice that the alleged abduction of Sara da Camposampiero from Venetian dominions in the Trevisano was an affront to the Serenissima's honor and prestige.[21]

Meanwhile, the castellan and gastaldo of Meliaduse Tempesta's infant brother, son of the sister of the powerful Paduan noble Enrico da Lozzo, rode to secure the Camposampiero stronghold at Noale. In July 1343, Sara publicly confirmed her marriage to Beltrando in a ceremony at Padua attended by both Ubertino da Carrara and the current podestà, the Venetian Giovanni Gradenigo. But Venice still feared the consequences of the stronghold at Treville coming into the hands of Rolando Rossi and offered £6,000 to the Tempesta castellan to raze the castle to the ground. Only months later did the castellan surrender the stronghold after receiving permission from Enrico da Lozzo. When the castellan turned over Noale to the knights of the podestà at Treviso, he was promptly arrested for his obstinacy and sent in chains to Venice, where he died in prison. Rolando Rossi's efforts to obtain the Camposampiero legacy in the Trevisano were also thwarted. Replying to Rolando Rossi's request in the summer of 1343 to take over Camposampiero properties there on behalf of his son Beltrando, the Senate refused to permit the transfer of land, citing longstanding Trevisan statutes against foreigners acquiring real estate in the Trevisano.[22] Apparently Ubertino da Carrara was able to help his kinsmen the Rossi acquire part of the Camposampiero inheritance in the eastern Padovano, but the villages of the Trevisano remained in the hands of those more amenable to Venetian interests.

In the busy spring of 1339 Paduan and Venetian representatives set about to define more precisely the clause from the treaty of July 1337 which allowed Paduans to impose on Venetians and their peasants only those *gabelle* "which they were accustomed to pay in the times when the city of Padua was a commune." On 8 April the Senate decreed that Venetians could transport their goods through Paduan territory free of any impost, denying the right of Padua to place any duties on goods imported from Venice. But Venetian citizens and religious corporations had to pay the usual duties on crops sold within Padua and its district as well as a small impost of 2.5 percent (6 pence per lira) on certain commodities—wood, charcoal, honey, wax, linen cloth, and hemp rope—exported to Venice. There were to be no duties on poultry and game imported to Venice, and only the usual tax of 2 percent of value on horses, mules, and donkeys. On salt imported from Chioggia to Padua, the Paduans could levy only the usual duty of £12 per each 100 *moggi* of salt. These provisions were ratified in a pact in the Ducal Palace on 17 April, confirming Venetian citizens and monasteries in their privileged position in the Padovano and serving as an invitation for them to continue investment in estates and property there.[23]

Several issues of unjust Paduan taxation of peasants working lands of Venetians remained outstanding. On 19 August the Senate appointed three savi to examine and make recommendations on these problems. On 20 September the savi reported back to the Senate on three abuses Ubertino and the Paduan government were visiting on locals working for Venetian persons and corporations. First, Paduan tax officials were exacting unjust duties on moveables and household goods of peasants working for Venetian employers. Second, peasants were forced to pay an excise tax of 16 pence per *staio* of grain ground in the mills of Padua, in addition to the usual miller's portion. Third, Paduan tax officials were exacting a tariff of 8 pence per lira on all farm animals sold by peasants working for Venetian landowners in the Padovano. The savi recommended the abolition of the first two exactions as unjust and unprecedented and the lowering of the dazio on animals to the customary 4 pence per lira. But the recommendations had little immediate effect. On 30 December, the Senate voted to continue to study the problem, while other clauses of the treaty were implemented.[24]

Ubertino da Carrara and Venice

On 8 June 1339, the lord and commune of Padua fulfilled for the first time their obligation to come to Venice's defense by sending a contingent of two hundred knights into the Trevisano, as requested.[25] That same day, Venice's Maggior Consiglio debated legislation affecting the participation of Venetian citizens in governing mainland tyrannies. Recalling the precedent of a law of 1312, the Senate voted that for five years no Venetian citizen could serve as podestà, captain, councillor, or employee of any tyrant under penalty of a fine of £500. Now the Maggior Consiglio agreed to ratify this prohibition for two reasons: Venice should not be deprived of its best magistrates by allowing them to serve in foreign lands, and through service in such governments, Venetians might become too familiar with foreign tyrants. A month later, the Maggior Consiglio debated whether this prohibition applied to Padua under the lordship of Ubertino da Carrara. In the end, the Venetian government decided that it could allow its nobles to serve as podestà in Padua for several reasons. First, the pact between Venice and the lord and commune of Padua provided for mutual defense of both cities. Second, Venetian citizens and monasteries enjoyed enormous prerogatives on their real and moveable property in Padua and its district. Third, Venice was obliged by treaty to defend and uphold the present regime, and this requirement was more readily met if a Venetian, rather than a foreigner, served as podestà keeping watch over events there. Considering all these factors, the Maggior Consiglio voted 263 to 70 with 26 abstentions: "The city of Padua ought not to be understood under the rule of tyrants, because it can be said that it is our own state." Thus, Venetians were allowed to serve as rectors in Padua, notwithstanding the law against service in the lands of tyrants. The law had its desired effect. Over the next two decades, Venice held a monopoly over the podestaship of Padua, with thirteen Venetian nobles, including three future doges, Marino Falier, Giovanni Gradenigo, and Marco Corner, serving as podestà.[26]

The settlement of disputes over inheritance, such as the Camposampiero case, and the presence in Padua of talented Venetian administrators as podestà did not end all friction between the restored Carrara regime and its powerful neighbor. For years, Venice and its lagoon had harbored many of the most intractable enemies of the Carrara dynasty, including Vitaliano Dente, whom Ubertino had driven into exile after killing his father, Guglielmo, in the civil strife of the summer of 1325. In Venice, Dente had prospered as a merchant and banker, gaining in late 1339 a pardon by vote of the Maggior Consiglio from charges of usury on a loan of some 2,500 ducats.[27] Hearing in summer 1340 that Ubertino da Carrara lay ill in Padua, Dente sought to kill off his hated enemy with poisoned sweets. With the help of Francesco Scrovegni, Dente bribed the servant of the Venetian physician attending Ubertino in the Reggia in Padua to deliver the gift of poisoned confections. But the Carrara lord was too ill to receive the servant, who became very nervous after waiting several days in Padua. Eventually he admitted his crime and was arrested and sent back to Venice. On 4 August 1340 the Council of Forty passed down its decision in the case, banning Vitaliano Dente and Francesco Scrovegni from Venice and its dominions and sentencing the would-be poisoner to three years in prison, followed by perpetual exile from Venice. Vitaliano Dente went into exile in Verona, protected by his kinsmen, the Scaliger lords, while his palace, Ca' Giustinian in *contrada* S. Pantaleone, was occupied and moveables confiscated. But by August 1343, Vitaliano Dente was permitted to return to Venetian domains in Capodistria, though he still had to remain outside the *dogado* and mainland territories of Treviso and Ceneda. On 7 February 1345, out of consideration for his poverty, the Maggior Consiglio appointed Vitaliano Dente constable of a troop of cavalry in Capodistria, perhaps also moved by pleas of his family and Venice's increasing tensions with Ubertino da Carrara. By May 1349 Vitaliano's ban of exile had been completely lifted, since he again was residing in Venice, this time in contrada S. Moisè.

Ubertino da Carrara, however, bided his time and three years after the attempted poisoning exacted his vengeance in his ongoing vendetta with the Dente. In May 1343 in broad daylight in Piazza S. Marco, three of Ubertino's hired assassins struck down Lemezio Dente, natural half brother of Guglielmo and uncle of Vitaliano. The three Paduan assassins—Giovanni Cavosio, a vagabond from Sarmeola; Giovanni Cestario of Piove di Sacco, and Lorenzo, a barber from Camponogara—were arrested and brought to trial before the Council of Forty. Charged with killing Lemizio at the instance of Ubertino da Carrara, each was sentenced to blinding and perpetual exile from Venice and its dominions. Ubertino was cited by ducal letter to answer for this crime, but he refused to come to Venice. Aware that tact and diplomacy were required to bring an ally and neighboring head of state to justice, the Council of Forty debated various solutions. Discussed and rejected were several proposals, including the imposition of a large fine, the deprivation of Venetian citizenship, and the prohibition of allowing Venetian nobles to serve as podestà or captains in Padua as a *terra tyrannorum*. Finally, it was decided to ban Ubertino from Venice and its domains from Grado to Cavarzere. Thus, the Forty arrived at a politically acceptable solution to Ubertino's affront to the dignity of the republic. Perpetual banishment seemed severe, but it affected Ubertino very little. Justice was served, and the way was kept open for reconciliation.[28]

Ubertino's Foreign Policy

Ubertino's most implacable foes remained, however, not Paduan rivals, but the Scaligeri lords of Verona. At least one late chronicle records that among the several offenses that drove the Carraresi to form the alliance with Venice and Florence in July 1337 was Alberto della Scala's repeated seduction of Ubertino da Carrara's first wife, Giacomina da Correggio. While Alberto was living in Padua as vicar at the outbreak of the war, he repeatedly mocked Ubertino, vowing on one occasion that he would made him a cuckold three times that night. According to the anonymous writer, Ubertino simply smiled and planned his revenge.[29] As is well known, with the liberation of Padua, Ubertino personally arrested Alberto della Scala and had him packed off to prison in Venice. Ubertino then took as part of his personal arms the image of a horned Saracen, perhaps as a reminder of his humiliation. In any case, soon after the conquest of Padua, Ubertino sent Giacomina da Correggio back to Verona and obtained dissolution of the marriage, vowing that it had been forced upon him and was never consummated. As we have seen, Ubertino was brutal in his treatment of Scaliger troops and officials in the siege of Monselice and the final stages of the war. Whatever the motive, the early years of Ubertino's rule were marked by continuing quarrels and often open conflict with the Della Scala lords.

The initial stage of Ubertino's "grand design" was to form a league to retake the city of Vicenza, which had been taken by Cangrande della Scala a generation earlier in 1311. At the border town of Lendinara on the Adige on Palm Sunday, 9 April 1340, Ubertino concluded a pact with the lord of Ferrara, Obizzo d'Este; the lord of Bologna, Taddeo Pepoli; and Florence, aimed at the recovery of Vicenza and destruction of the Scaligeri. This alliance was promptly countered by a league of Mastino della Scala, Luchino Visconti, and Luigi Gonzaga aimed against Bologna. Ubertino's plans to take Vicenza were thus thwarted, and instead he had to send a contingent of troops under the German mercenary Engelmar von Villanders to the defense of Bologna.[30] The allies were able to keep Bologna only by placing it under the protection of the papacy, with Taddeo Pepoli taking the title of papal vicar and conservator of the church.

Closer to home Ubertino sought Venice's aid in carrying out the provisions for the restoration of confiscated property detailed in the peace of January 1339. In October the Venetian Senate elected two nobles, Niccolò Morosini and Dordi Dolfin, to investigate and settle these claims and, in general, enforce peace between the Carrara and the Scaligeri. Early the next year the two ambassadors reported back to the Senate, where they were given free rein to proceed as they considered just in passing sentences and making the peace treaty effective.[31] In the meantime, Ubertino's hostile moves against Vicenza had brought retaliation from Mastino della Scala in the form of cutting dikes on the Adige, thus flooding the area near the Carrara stronghold at Castelbaldo. The Scaligeri had also placed pilings across the canal between Este and Montagnana, impeding commerce in the southern Padovano. On 6 July the Senate received the ambassadors' reports on the restoration of property and Scaligeri damages to Paduan waterways and voted to require the Scaligeri to observe the terms of the peace treaty and repair dikes and remove impediments on rivers and canals in the Padovano. Four days later the doge accepted these recommendations favorable to Ubertino's rights and placed Venice's authority behind the Carrara dynasty in Padua.[32] Tensions remained high, however, between the lords of Verona and Padua. In October the Venetian Senate agreed to send out new envoys to make inventories of property that the Della Scala should continue to hold in Padua and the Padovano, "because the disputes between the Della Scala and their followers and Ubertino and his have not ceased, and, thus they vex us greatly and bring scandal and uncertainty between the parties."[33] The ambassadors meet with some success, since in response to Ubertino's ambassadors petitioning the Senate for a speedy resolution to differences between Padua and Verona, the Senate voted: "Since we desire the honor and quiet state of lord Ubertino as our own, . . . we will do all that we can in the matter of the property to protect Ubertino's honor."[34]

Ubertino's actions belied his protestations of peace. On 11 February 1341, Ubertino met at Ferrara with Giovanni and Luchino Visconti, Obizzo II and Niccolò I d'Este, Taddeo Pepoli, and Luigi Gonzaga to form a league directed against all enemies but mainly designed to wrest Parma from Mastino della Scala.[35] The Della Scala lords informed the Venetian Senate that they had sent ambassadors asking the Carrara, Estensi, Gonzaga, and Visconti lords not to disturb the peace and that they hoped Venice would act to prevent war in Lombardy. When Ubertino began to move troops up the Brenta against the Della Scala dominions that summer, the Senate appointed two ambassadors to inform him that Venice deplored these troop movements and any bellicose acts against the lords of Verona, hoping instead for peace in the Veneto.[36] But Ubertino and his allies continued their campaign against the Della Scala, with Azzo da Correggio seizing Parma that summer and both Pisa and Florence threatening Lucca. In July 1341 the Florentines, in fact, asked Ubertino for troops in their siege of Lucca as required by the treaty renewed in 1338. But preoccupied with his own campaigns, in a letter of 1 August Ubertino refused to honor Florence's request, stating that all his troops were already engaged, with four companies defending Bologna, others at Bassano on the Veronese border, and the rest garrisoning Padua.[37] Later that summer Paduan troops pillaged enemy territory up to the walls of Verona, threatening a new siege of Vicenza. But the sudden withdrawal of Gonzaga and his Mantuan troops, laden with booty from the campaign, doomed Ubertino's effort to retake Vicenza.

Late in summer of 1341, Venice began diplomatic maneuvers aimed at bringing peace to the Veneto. Responding on 20 August 1341 to the roseate report from Paduan ambassadors of Ubertino's peaceful intentions, the Senate asserted, "We hope from him [Ubertino] in all matters just as he does for us, because his good is ours and ours is his."[38] Stressing mutuality of interests, in October the Senate appointed a board of three savi to negotiate a lasting peace between Ubertino da Carrara and Mastino della Scala.[39] Venetian diplomats worked throughout 1342 to settle grievances between the two parties and ensure observance of the peace of January 1339. The question of the restitution of confiscated property remained difficult: three new savi were elected in March 1343 to hear complaints and hand down final sentences by the end of April.[40] In late April, the decisions on property rights had been accepted, and the Senate informed ambassadors from both Padua and Verona how delighted the Venetian government was that peace was at hand. On 25 May the two parties reached a general peace at Montagnana, celebrated by the marriage of Gentile da Carrara, one of Ubertino's illegitimate daughters, to one of Mastino's natural sons.[41]

Venetian interests in the Carrara dynasty extended beyond questions of war and peace in northeast Italy. A major problem was the siltation of the mouth of the Brenta opposite Venice, threatening stoppage of river commerce and in the long run silting up of the lagoon itself. In 1339, the Venetians appointed a board of twelve to make sure dikes were in good repair and riverbeds kept open.[42] Early in 1340, dikes on the Brenta were cut at Oriago, causing the Venetians to appoint a board of three savi to investigate. Late the next year, the Venetians asked Ubertino to improve the course of the Brenta Canal cut at Strà toward Chioggia. The Paduans were to plant trees, build up dikes, and enlarge the mouth of the canal as it flowed into the southern part of the lagoon. Because the bed of this new cut of the Brenta often changed course, trees and dikes were needed to hold it in place, while the periodic excavation of its mouth would keep the canal open and navigable near Chioggia.[43] Heavy rains and flooding early in 1343 brought massive destruction to dikes, roads, and bridges in the eastern Padovano. Local peasants and villagers were so overwhelmed by the task of rebuilding that Ubertino da Carrara petitioned the Venetian government to share in the responsibility for repairs. On 10 February the Senate agreed to permit the Venetian landowners in the area, who were by treaty exempt from any tax for public works, to have their peasants contribute to the corvées for the repairs. Five days later, Doge Andrea Dandolo acceded to the Paduan request for help, stressing that the aid was for this time only and could not serve as a precedent for future claims for assistance and did not alter treaty obligations between the two states.[44]

Such caution was needed, for as we have seen, Ubertino da Carrara's expansionist ambitions in the Veneto often made Venice wary of Paduan cooperation and friendship. The attempt of the bishop of Padua, Ildebrandino Conti, in the spring of 1342 to take over tithes in the Trevisano, which had been the traditional prerogatives of the bishop of Treviso, now under Venetian control, brought a sharp rebuke from the Senate. Venice sent a notary to Ubertino and the bishop's curia reminding them that these tithes had long been in the gift of the bishop of Treviso and warning them to desist from these illegal actions.[45] But that same year, Ubertino honored one of his most conspicuous treaty obligations by sending two hundred knights to aid Venice in putting down the revolt at Candia. Venice reciprocated in December by permitting Ubertino to transport 5,000 *staia* of grain from Venice to Paduan garrisons low on foodstuffs. In January 1343, the Maggior Consiglio agreed to exonerate one of Ubertino's messengers caught carrying a concealed knife in Venice; apparently, Ubertino's good will was more important than strict enforcement of laws against concealed weapons.[46] Two years later the Senate voted to allow Ubertino to bring to Padua three hundred crossbowmen for his own defense.[47]

The continuing questions of boundaries near the lagoon and taxes on Venetian goods in the Padovano increased tensions in the last years of Ubertino's rule. Early in 1344 Ubertino sent Paduan officials to occupy S. Ilario, near the ferry station at Fusina, to collect customs from merchants traveling through the area. This infringement of Venetian prerogatives caused the Senate to elect three savi to investigate. The savi reported that the Paduan guards were causing unprecedented disruption of shipborne trade into Venice, so the Senate ordered Ubertino to desist in this behavior and remove his officials.[48] In response to his rebuke, Ubertino moved his guards a little farther inland but continued to exact the tolls. A new board of five savi was then elected to inform Ubertino that he had to remove all his guards.[49] The border dispute dragged on without resolution until early 1345, when Paduan and Venetian arbitrators met to set the boundaries between the two states.[50] A more serious problem was caused by the settling of exiles from both Padua and Venice at S. Martino di Lupari, on the Trevisan border, forming what the podestà at Castelfranco called "robbers' dens," which preyed on citizens from both states. Lacking any formal treaty of extradition with Padua, the Venetian Senate called for the informal exchange of criminals arrested in the two jurisdictions.[51] This provisional solution led to negotiations for a treaty of extradition eventually approved late in 1345.

The Brief Lordship of Marsilietto Papafava dei Carraresi

By early 1345 Ubertino was gravely sick, probably of venereal disease, since Vergerio describes a chronic illness caused by "excessive use of his genital member."[52] On 9 March he died without legitimate offspring, having provided for his succession by naming his distant cousin Marsilietto, from the Papafava branch of the Carrara family, to the lordship of Padua. Thus, Ubertino was able to thwart the ambitions of Giacomino and Giacomo II, sons of the hated rival Niccolò da Carrara, who had died in exile in Chioggia the previous year. Marsilietto, the middle son of Albertino Papafava and Adelaida Scrovegni, daughter of the usurer Rinaldo, had suffered at the hands of Marsilio da Carrara and had been briefly exiled to Venice in 1328. But he had become a loyal follower of Ubertino, serving several terms as podestà of Piove di Sacco and as warden of the city prison as well as a knight in the Paduan army, active in the siege of Monselice during the Scaliger war.[53] Earlier in May 1338, Marsilietto had been awarded Venetian citizenship in recognition of the services that he and his father, Albertino, had given the republic.[54] Elected lord on 27 March 1345, Marsilietto received the banner of the commune of Padua in public *arengo* and took up residence in the Carrara Reggia, appointing as his vicar the jurist Pietro da Campanola, who had recommended his succession to Ubertino. On 29 March Marsilietto arranged an elaborate funeral for Ubertino, who was buried in a chapel of S. Agostino.

Wary of the claims of his distant cousins Giacomo and Giacomino to the lordship of Padua, Marsilietto moved promptly to reconfirm the treaty of 1337, thus placing himself under Venice's protection. On 13 April Marsilietto appointed Sachetto da Campagnola proctor for himself and the commune of Padua to renew the treaty with Venice. Among the witnesses to this act were his future assassin, Giacomo qd. Niccolò da Carrara, and his supporter, Dusio Buzzacarini, along with Marsilietto's son-in-law, Enrico qd. Guido da Lozzo, Giordano Forzatè, and his vicar, Pietro da Campagnola. On 16 April the Senate elected three savi as ambassadors to meet with Paduan officials to confirm the earlier pacts of July 1337, March 1338, and April 1339 made with Marsilio and Ubertino da Carrara.[55] The Senate also expressed the hope that the Paduans would, at a later date, approve the treaty of extradition which Ubertino had been negotiating. On 20 April Venice's chancellor, Benintendi dei Ravignani, proclaimed a new alliance between Venice and the lord and commune of Padua. Besides changing Ubertino to Marsilietto throughout, the treaty removed the clause requiring Padua's aid of Florence against all enemies and added a stipulation: "The commune of Venice will have and hold the same lord Marsilio [i.e., Marsilietto] and commune of Padua and its district in its protection and defense against any person in the world."[56] There followed chapters on exiles and on the rights of Venetian persons and monasteries in the Padovano on the import, export, and use of goods, largely free of duty, as defined in the accords of 17 April 1339. Thus, Venice reconfirmed its economic hegemony in the Padovano and its special responsibility for the defense of Padua and the Carrara dynasty. Significantly that very week, the Maggior Consiglio overturned a motion to prohibit Venetians from acquiring property in the Trevisan March and Ferrara, thus removing the last obstacle to widespread Venetian investment in real estate in the neighboring *terraferma*.[57]

While, on 3 May, the Senate continued its negotiation with Marsilietto on the treaty of extradition of fugitives and criminals for debt, plans were afoot in Padua to remove the new lord from his office.[58] Quietly gathering support from the leading families of Padua and bribing the guards to

FIG. 11. *Andriolo de' Santi, tomb of Ubertino da Carrara. Church of the Eremitani, Padua, 1345. Reproduced with permission of Alinari/Art Resource, New York*

leave unlocked the doors of the Reggia, Giacomo II da Carrara entered Marsilietto's chambers on the night of 6 May and murdered him with a sword. Aided by supporters among the Paduan people and nobility, Giacomo hounded Marsilietto's nephew and great-nephew, Jacopo qd. Rinaldo and his son, Albertino Papafava dei Carraresi, into exile. Marsilietto's body was secretly buried and soldiers sent to secure the strongholds at Cittadella and Monselice. Giacomo had arrested and later executed three of the late lord's trusted advisers, Pietro and Marco da Campagnola and Albertino Gottola. Other followers were sent to confiscate Papafava estates in the southern Padovano. Giacomo then exacted an oath of allegiance and loyalty from knights at the Carrara palaces, declared a general amnesty for dozens of citizens and clergy recently imprisoned, and recalled from exile enemies of Ubertino and friends of the late Niccolò, such as Bonfrancesco Negri. Finally, Giacomo courted approval for his violent deed by bestowing lavish gifts of gold and clothes, horses and arms, houses and lands on would-be supporters. The day after the assassination Giacomo married his eldest son, Francesco, to Fina Buzzacarini, daughter of Pataro and granddaughter of Dusio, lawyers and magistrates, loyal servants of the Carrara and of Padua.[59]

The Lordship of Giacomo II da Carrara, 1345–1350

Giacomo promptly dispatched three ambassadors, Dusio Buzzacarini, Niccolò da Lozzo, and Giordano Forzatè, to Venice to complete work on the treaty of extradition and assure the Venetian government of his good will and continued friendship.[60] To these last sentiments, the Senate voted this rather cool reply: "Let us respond to the ambassadors of the Lord of Padua with appropriate words that we would hold as good what the same Lord told us, and we believe that his response is correct for the good and peaceful state of the city of Padua, which we desire at all times."[61] The diplomats from the two states then completed the treaty, which was ratified on 21 June by the Maggior Consiglio of Padua, in the presence of the Venetian podestà, Bernardo Giustinian, following the prior agreement of Giacomo II da Carrara and Doge Andrea Dandolo. The treaty addressed two major concerns: one economic, the other political. The first clause provided for the return of all fugitives who had fled from Venice since 1337 for debts or taking goods of other persons. These fugitives, who were to be named in ducal letters or by special envoys, were to be arrested, jailed, and transported back to Venice for trial. The second part provided for the extradition of criminals and traitors who had fled from Venice into Paduan domains or from Padua to Venice, including in the latter case traitors who might plot against Giacomo da Carrara and the commune of Padua. But

Venice reserved the right to judge the validity of Carrara demands for the extradition of criminals and traitors, while Padua had to extradite all persons demanded by Venice. Thus, anyone Venice declared a fugitive had to be arrested by Paduan authorities and escorted back to the Venetian border, whereas Venetian authorities could harbor Paduans who were accused of treason and deny their extradition to Padua.[62]

Giacomo II also continued discussions concerning the disputed border at S. Ilario. On 25 June 1345, the Senate requested the Paduan lord send to Venice ambassadors fully empowered to complete agreements on the boundaries of the two states to their mutual satisfaction. Four days later the Senate informed the lord of Padua that Venice intended to use the same savi who had been in negotiation with Ubertino so the border settlement could be accomplished more efficiently. Finally on 25 July, the Venetian savi received permission to proceed as they saw fit in negotiations with the Paduan envoys so that an agreement could be reached.[63] The Carrara lord made accommodations with Venice in other ways, sending a large shipment of grain to the city in time of scarcity and honoring treaty obligations of mutual defense by sending troops to the defense of Zara under siege by Louis of Hungary late that year. When Giacomo da Carrara attempted to change border markers near Asolo, encroaching on Scaligeri territories, the Senate warned him that Padua should live at peace with its neighbors, Mastino della Scala of Verona and the Este lords of Ferrara.[64] Despite the Estense occupation of Vighizzolo near the Adige and tensions with Mastino, Pope Clement VI obtained a truce of two years between the Carrara, Estensi, and Scaligeri, to begin in June 1346.[65]

The greatest challenge to Giacomo's authority came early in his rule from the Lozzi brothers, members of the ancient Maltraversi family. To assuage any bitterness caused by his murder of Marsilietto, Giacomo II heaped gifts on the three brothers, Francesco, Niccolò, and especially Enrico, who was the husband of the murdered lord's only daughter, Lieta. But these gifts generated only jealousy and a desire for vengeance, as the Lozzi plotted to kill Giacomo and seize control of Padua. Servants revealed the conspiracy; Francesco Lozzo was arrested and disclosed under torture the names of his accomplices, Azzo Dalesmanini, Francesco da Monselice, and Giacomo Grosso. Giacomo da Carrara, then, invited Enrico da Lozzo to dinner, where he was arrested and forced to acknowledge his role in the conspiracy. The Carrara regime imposed a reign of terror in Padua, with a public execution of Francesco and Enrico on 14 November 1345 and the beheading of a number of conspirators the next week. Only Niccolò, who went into hiding in the monastery at Praglia when the conspiracy was discovered, was able to escape, first to the family castle at Lozzo and later outside Paduan territory. The property of the Lozzi and their allies was confiscated and distributed among Carrara supporters. On 7 January 1346, the podestà of Padua tried Niccolò da Lozzo *in absentia,* condemned him to death, confiscated his property, and declared him enemy of Padua and its lord. The Venetian government acted swiftly to support the Paduans during this conspiracy. On 8 December 1345, the Senate sent three ambassadors to Padua to express condolences and thanks for keeping the government informed of recent events. At the same time, the Senate agreed to send a company of one hundred crossbowmen for one month to keep order in Padua.[66]

Earlier, in October 1345, the Maggior Consiglio, on recommendation of the Council of Forty, had awarded Venetian citizenship to Giacomo II da Carrara and to his son, Francesco, and their heirs, for the good and faithful service to the Serenissima.[67] That same autumn Giacomo sent at Venice's request a contingent of Paduan troops for the Zara campaign, and on 6 December a Venetian envoy in Padua agreed to pay the amount owed for their services.[68] In January 1346, Giacomo II and Francesco traveled to Venice to receive their grant of citizenship. Met at Oriago by a throng of Venetian nobles and conducted to the city, they were received by Doge Andrea Dandolo and his councillors aboard the *Bucintoro*. On the 16th Giacomo received from the Venetian government gifts of gold and silver vases and luxury clothes valued at 1,000 ducats, in return for his fealty as a loyal new citizen of Venice. On the 24th, he returned in triumph to Padua, where he pardoned servants and retainers of the Lozzo, who had been imprisoned because of the conspiracy. At that time, Giacomo ordered a *palio* to be run every 7 May in honor of his assumption of the lordship of Padua.[69]

Throughout 1346, Giacomo II continued his aid of Venice in its struggle to retake Zara from Hungarian forces. In May the Paduan lord dispatched a force of two hundred horsemen and one hundred crossbowmen for the renewed fighting in Zara, and in recognition of this aid he was summoned to Venice to participate in the festivities marking the successful end of that war. That autumn Giacomo stepped in to arbitrate the dispute between Engelmar von Villanders, Lewis of Bavaria's imperial vicar in Feltre and Belluno, and Sicco di Caldonazzo, competing for the same title. In resolving this discord, Giacomo was able to gain possession of Covolo, a stronghold on the Tesino River. In the contest between Charles of Bohemia and Lewis of Bavaria, Giacomo followed the policies of Pope Clement VI and sided with Charles, sending him reinforcements at Trent early in 1347.

The entry of Venice's rival in Dalmatia, King Louis of Hungary, into Italian affairs early in 1347 caused strains between Giacomo and the Venetian government. Proposing to march to Naples to avenge the murder of his brother Andrew, King Louis sent ambassadors asking Giacomo's permission to cross Paduan territory in his descent into Italy. Giacomo was disposed to grant the safe-conduct requested and sent one of his best diplomats, the jurist Giacomo da Santa Croce, to Venice to make his case. In a sharp rebuke drafted on 21 April 1347, the Senate reminded the Carrara lord

> that he should consider the pact we have had with the commune of Padua and with his predecessors, and that we have at present, namely, that our enemies are his enemies, and his enemies are our enemies. Therefore, we require and beseech his magnificence, that, acknowledging the agreements he has made, he is to abstain from granting safe-conduct or permission to the troops of the said king by letter or otherwise, and, if he has already given these, he must strive for his own good and ours to revoke these in any way that will seem to work.[70]

The Venetian government had every right to be alarmed, for the growing friendship of the Carrara lord of Padua and King Louis of Hungary was to be the undoing of the Serenissima's domination of the eastern Veneto. But for the moment, Giacomo II rejected Louis's request and remained subservient to Venetian interests. In March 1347, he lavishly entertained at Padua Isabella del Fiesco, the wife of Luchino Visconti, who was making a pilgrimage to the tomb of St. Mark in Venice. Meeting the large Visconti entourage at the western border, Giacomo conducted them to Padua for sumptuous banquets, before escorting the Lombards to Venetian domains at S. Ilario, whence Francesco da Carrara brought them into Venice itself.[71] That spring, the Carrara lord donated 8,000 *staia* of grain to Venice in time of famine, asking to be repaid when foodstuffs reached Venice by sea. In May Venice repaid Paduan generosity by donating to Padua 1,500 *staia* each of wheat and millet.[72] Still acting in Venice's interest, in June, Giacomo kept the Senate apprised of the return of King Charles of Bohemia to northern Italy, receiving secret instruction to report all of the king's doings and sayings. Summoned by Charles to Feltre the next month, Giacomo sent an envoy to Venice reporting on interviews with Charles, receiving back instructions to respond "with general words of love and good wishes."[73] When Giacomo accompanied Charles on his way back to Prague, the king of Bohemia placed Belluno and Feltre under the protection of the Carrara lord.[74] In August Giacomo II requested and received Venice's permission to join in a defensive league of mainland lords, proposed by Luchino Visconti and including Taddeo Pepoli of Bologna and the Este lords of Ferrara.[75]

The death of Lewis of Bavaria on 11 October 1347 and the expedition of Louis of Hungary to Naples that same fall threatened to change the balance of power throughout Italy. On 23 October Pope Clement VI wrote Giacomo II da Carrara and a dozen other lords and cities in Italy ordering them not to give aid to King Louis in his invasion of Naples.[76] But when Louis appeared in Friuli in December, Giacomo II rode out to receive him at Cittadella and escorted his forces across the Padovano, much to the chagrin of the Venetian government. The next year the lord of Padua gained support from another source, King Charles of Bohemia. At his residence in Moravia, Charles received the Paduan ambassador Bernardo da Castiglione and issued a diploma on 4 June revoking the sentence against Padua of his grandfather, Emperor Henry VII, and confirming the privileges of earlier emperors to the Carrara. The next day Charles appointed Giacomo II da Carrara imperial vicar over Padua and its district, explicitly placing the strongholds of Bassano, Monselice, Solagna, and Fontaniva under control of the Carrara lord. More than simply a token of Charles' friendship or symbol of prestige, the imperial vicariate brought legitimation of Carrara rule over Padua, broader authority in the affairs of northeast Italy, and the possibility of greater independence from Venice.[77]

The vicariate and friendship with Charles soon thrust the Carrara lord into the contested ground of Friuli and the Tyrol. Late in 1348, after the death of Bishop Niccolò Alreim di Bruni, the canons of the Diocese of Trent, alarmed at the aggressive policies of the marquis of Brandenburg, son of Lewis of Bavaria, asked Giacomo II da Carrara to come to their defense. By January 1349 Giacomo II had taken the fortress at Pergine and gained through bribery several other strongholds of the Valsugana, including Selva, Roccabruna, and Levico. Thus began Padua's attempt to dominate the south Tyrol, often putting the Carrara lords in conflict with the marquis of Brandenburg and later the Habsburg dukes of Austria.[78] In April Giacomo II further aided imperial control in the region by sending troops to Belluno to suppress a rebellion there. New responsibilities also brought new income, as when, in July 1350, Giacomo II and Giacomino da Carrara appointed their vicar, Giacomo da Santa Croce, to collect rents of fiefs and tithes in the Diocese of Belluno.[79] In the spring of 1350 Giacomo II attempted to strengthen his alliance in Friuli by betrothing his daughter Gigliola to Enrico, the count of Gorizia, who was then in open conflict with the patriarch of Aquileia, lord of much of the region. On 25 May Venice granted safe-conduct across the Trevisano to the bridal entourage, composed of four companies of knights, with the dire warning to the lord of Padua not to allow any of the soldiers to bring damage to the area.[80] But the wedding had to be delayed because of the assassination of the patriarch by Enrico's own men. Venice sent out ambassadors to investigate and restore peace to Friuli, but Giacomo's hopes to bring influence to the area through a marriage alliance were dashed by the count of Gorizia's early death without heirs.[81]

Padua's recognition of Venice's superiority continued, however, in prompt fulfillment of obligations of mutual defense. When in September 1348 Capodistria revolted against Venetian rule, the Senate at once asked the Carrara lord for troops to help quell the rebellion. Giacomo II da Carrara sent a force of cavalry and infantry to the siege at Capodistria, which surrendered in early October. By November, informed of the large garrison in that city, the Senate ordered the fifty Paduan troops to return to Venice. But Giacomo's support was not forgotten; he was invited in February to the great feast held in Venice to celebrate the victory and granted a palace on Campo S. Polo, reputedly worth 5,000 ducats.[82]

Venice's greatest concerns for the alliance with Padua were caused by the Carrara lords' growing independence in mainland affairs. As early as May 1348 Giacomo II had made his much younger brother, Giacomino, his partner in governing Padua, and both are styled the lords of Padua in diplomatic correspondence, especially with Venice, until the elder brother's death two and a half years later. As war clouds gathered in May 1348, the Carrara brothers sent Giacomo da Santa Croce to Venice to seek the confidential opinion of the Senate on several questions of policy. Responding to the question whether the Carrara ought to grant aid to the Gonzaga, who were under imminent attack by Mastino della Scala, the Senate counseled that a policy of delay and neutrality would avoid conflict. On joining a league with Bologna and Florence, Venice advised against the utility of such an alliance. On the issue of serving as mediator between Louis of Hungary and Charles of Bohemia, Venice saw no need for intercessions by Paduan envoys but hoped to be kept informed on Charles' movements. Venice still hoped that Padua would (like itself) remain aloof from Italian entanglements.[83] In the long run such neutrality proved impossible for both states.

As we have seen, the bestowal of the imperial vicariate soon brought the lord of Padua into the affairs of Friuli and the Tyrol. The efforts of Pope Clement VI in early 1349 to establish a general truce in order to promote the free passage of pilgrims to Rome for the Jubilee directly affected Padua when the papal legate and diplomat Cardinal Gui de Boulogne visited the Carrara court on his way to Germany and Hungary to promote papal policy. The cardinal legate returned twice to Padua: first, for the translation of San Antonio's body to a new tomb in February 1350 and, second, to preside over a synod of clergy from the cities of northern Italy to bring peace to the area and define the jurisdictions of the patriarch of Aquileia and the count of Gorizia that April. In the event, the papal legate failed to bring peace to northeast Italy.[84] But in late November 1349, Giacomo II and Giacomino da Carrara did agree to join for ten years a defensive league, comprising the Visconti of Milan, Taddeo Pepoli of Bologna, the Gonzaga of Mantua, the Malatesta of Rimini, the Della Scala of Verona, the Este of Ferrara, and the Polenta of Ravenna. The next month, the league was formally concluded in Milan, against all enemies, with the Carraresi, Scaligeri, and Estensi excepting Venice.[85] But that summer Giovanni Visconti took the offensive against papal dominions, occupying Bologna in October, causing Pope Clement VI to issue an appeal to the league to form a new alliance directed against the Visconti lord.[86]

Giacomino and Francesco da Carrara Share the Lordship of Padua

By the time the papal request arrived in Padua, Giacomo II was already dead. While warming his feet after dinner on 19 December, the lord of Padua was stabbed to death by Giacomo il Grande's illegitimate son, Guglielmo da Carrara. The assassin was promptly killed by loyal household retainers, who sent Pataro Buzzacarini to fetch back to Padua the heirs apparent, brother Giacomino and son Francesco, who were hunting hares on family estates near Camposampiero. In the meantime, to calm an anxious populace, family supporters placed the murdered lord's young son, Marsilio, on a horse bedecked with the red *carro* and paraded him through the central squares of Padua, to shouts of "Viva, viva, a la casa di Carrara." The new lords arrived back in the city late that night after a hard ride. Three days later in public arengo, Giacomino and Francesco were duly elected to the lordship of Padua and received the acclamation of the Paduan citizen body.[87]

In February 1351, during the second *podestaria* of Marino Falier, a statute confirming the powers of the new lords was enacted. Since the only surviving copy dates from September 1357, only Francesco il Vecchio is mentioned, but the text explicitly validated the provisions from the day of Giacomo II's murder. These well-defined prerogatives formed the legal basis for the rule of the Carrara dynasty over Padua during the second half of the Trecento. The most general power conferred was that of "merum et mixtum imperium et iurisdictionem et liberam bayliam et potestatem in omnibus." Along with these broad powers of life and death in criminal cases came the responsibility to govern and defend the city and district of Padua. The next power enumerated was the right of appointment of certain government officials, including the podestà and vicars of the towns of the contado, constables and soldiers, and other officials, appointing and removing them at will. Third was the ability to legislate, enact, modify, and abrogate statutes of the commune of Padua, which led in 1362 to a completely new redaction of the statutes of the city of Padua. The Carrara lord also gained the power to create new citizens. Using this prerogative, he often awarded the citizenship to those who came to Padua to ply a trade or engage in commerce in the city and enlarged his local following by naturalizing loyal foreigners. Under powers of justice, the lord could condemn, pardon, and sentence as he saw fit. This prerogative meant that the Carrara lord was the highest source of justice, the final court of appeal, but these decisions in practice were usually delegated to trained jurists of the Carrara circle, rendered according to established legal procedures. The lord also received the right to levy and collect taxes and to administer the property of the commune, selling, renting, and alienating it at his pleasure. This mandate placed the officials of Padua, whether named by the *signore* or by the commune, in personal obedience to the lord and made his orders inviolable and irrevocable. Finally, the lord had the right to make treaties and enter into agreements with other lords and communes, thus granting the Carrara lord wide powers in the conduct of foreign affairs. To the powers of the statute of 1351, which was broader and more sweeping than the earlier statutes of 1318 and 1328, was soon added the office of imperial vicar, which provided the basis of Francesco il Vecchio's designs for a regional state.[88]

The newly elected lords inherited an enormous responsibility toward Venice. The outbreak of the Third Genoese War prompted the Senate in September 1350 to send ambassadors to Padua to confirm the old pacts of mutual defense. Working through the current Venetian podestà of Padua, Marino Falier, these envoys renewed the prior agreements and made sure that Padua supplied troops and support as the treaties stipulated. On the day after Giacomo's assassination, three experts in *terraferma* affairs, Fantin Morosini, Pietro Giustinian, and Giovanni Zorzi, appeared at the Carrara Reggia to offer condolences and pledge support of the new lords.[89] In fact, the Carrara lords both sent troops and lent money to support Venice's struggle with Genoa. At the conclusion of the conflict, in June 1353, the lords of Padua acknowledged receipt of reimbursement of 12,000 ducats and £25,000 of loans made to Venice.[90] For its part, Venice ostensibly remained the Carrara's friendly ally. In May 1351 the Senate provided ships and a large galley to transport the wedding party of Lieta da Carrara, daughter of the late Giacomo II, to Germany after her marriage to Count Otto of Ortenburg, even appropriating an additional £600 because of the size of the entourage.[91]

More crucial for Padua was Venice's continuing interest in peace in the Veneto. Venetian diplomats fixed the southern border between Este and Carrara territories and arranged the exchange of frontier castles and a pact of perpetual friendship between the two dynasties, which was confirmed in the Ducal Palace in January 1354. At the same time Venice oversaw the settlement of boundaries disputes in the Vicentine with Cangrande II and Giovanni della Scala, paving the way for a treaty of alliance between the two powers.[92] Thus, Francesco da Carrara promptly came to the aid of the legitimate Scaligeri lords during the rebellion of Fregnano della Scala in February 1354. Later that year, at Venice's instigation, Francesco da Carrara was elected the head of a new league composed of Venice, Verona, Ferrara, and Padua, directed against Giovanni Visconti and Genoa. At the request of the allies, King Charles of Bohemia came into Italy to end the conflict and to receive the Iron Crown of the Regnum Italicum and the imperial crown in Rome. In November 1354, Francesco and Giacomino da Carrara met the imperial party at Bassano and escorted King Charles to Padua, where he was received by throngs of Paduans and sumptuously entertained by the Carrara in the Reggia. After several days of feasting, visiting the city's shrines, and distributing alms to the poor, Charles continued his journey. When the retinue was stopped at Cremona on 31 December 1354, King Charles dubbed Francesco da Carrara knight and vassal of the empire, while German knights in the party gave him new silver spurs. The Carrara lord, in turn, knighted his closest Paduan followers, including his father-in-law, Pataro da Buzzacarini; his maternal uncle, Alvise Forzatè; and his paternal aunt's husband, Zanino da Peraga, as well as Guidone Castronovo, Ugolino Scrovegni, Gerardo Negri, and Zambon Dotti. Elated with this signal honor, the new Paduan knights returned home, while Charles proceeded to receive the Iron Crown in Milan in January and the imperial crown in Rome in April 1355.[93]

Francesco's popularity and success aroused the envy of his uncle, Giacomino, who had married a daughter of the lord of Mantua, Margherita Gonzaga. In June 1354 Margherita bore Giacomino a son, named Giacomo after the beloved older brother. The wives of the two Carrara lords soon started quarreling, with Margherita claiming priority in succession for her infant son, Giacomo, since Francesco's wife, Fina, had borne only daughters at that time. Jealous of his nephew's popularity as a commander in the field and eager to rule alone, Giacomino secretly engaged Zambon Dotti to assassinate Francesco. Learning of the uncle's intentions from one of his advisers, Paolo Dotti, Francesco confronted Giacomino with his plot, arrested him, and, confiscating Giacomino's property, imprisoned him in the Rocca at Monselice, where he lived in gilded captivity with a few retainers until dying of natural causes in 1372. Margherita Gonzaga and young Giacomo were sent back to Mantua. The would-be assassin was arrested and eventually strangled to death by his kinsmen, Paolo and Giacomo Dotti, as a test of their own loyalty.[94]

THE EARLY CARRARA

In neighboring Venice the newly elected doge Marino Falier also plotted to make himself the supreme head of state. His conspiracy was discovered, and the doge who would be lord was executed and his extensive property, real and personal, confiscated by the Venetian government. Francesco da Carrara occupied Falier estates in the eastern Padovano at Corte and Camponogara as tempting additions to his own possessions, but Venice ruled that these estates should be confiscated along with the rest. After some negotiations through his vicar, Giacomo da Santa Croce, Francesco acceded to the Venetian decision. As the document states, the lord of Padua surrendered the Falier property "in a courteous fashion" to the procurator for the new doge, Giovanni Gradenigo, the Ducal Council, and the Council of Ten.[95]

Francesco da Carrara's authority was greater, however, further from home. After the return of the Charles IV to Bohemia in the spring of 1355, Francesco became good friends with the emperor's natural brother, Nicholas of Luxembourg, the new patriarch of Aquileia, who had remained behind in Padua. Soon after the emperor awarded the cities of Feltre and Belluno to his half brother, renewed conflict broke out between the patriarch and the other claimant for authority in Friuli, the count of Gorizia. Francesco agreed to mediate the dispute, but his settlement was so favorable to the patriarch that the count of Gorizia refused to recognize the terms of the agreement. Thus, conflict dragged on until a general peace was reached in Friuli in March 1356.[96] In the meantime, Francesco was presented with a much greater challenge with the threat of a Hungarian invasion of the Veneto. Seeking to make good his claims to Dalmatia, Louis now proposed to attack Venice nearer home, threatening to invade the Trevisano. Aware of Francesco da Carrara's wavering loyalties, the Senate responded to the Carrara lord's proposal of friendship with Louis of Hungary with a sharp admonition: "Although [the lord of Padua] may wish and may have wished for the good-will and love of the Lord King of Hungary, still he has wished and should wish to live for the good and honor with our Venetian government, which considers his state its own and always will consider it to be its own, just as, conversely, the Venetian government has acted and will act toward him."[97]

This was, in fact, the last time the Venetian government officially called Padua "status noster." On 13 June 1356 the emperor affirmed Francesco da Carrara in the imperial vicariate and confirmed the gift by his predecessor, Frederick II, in 1239 of the strongholds of Treville and Castelfranco, the River Sile, and other property in the Trevisan March, which Venice had occupied since 1339, to the lord and commune of Padua. Now the Carrara lord had ample reason to contemplate the repudiation of the Venetian alliance.[98] Two decades after Venice engineered the restoration of Marsilio da Carrara as lord of Padua, Francesco il Vecchio rejected the "Venetian model" of government and abandoned his alliance with Venice. Instead he placed his hopes in the distant authority of the Holy Roman Emperor in Prague and the promised support of the king of Hungary in Buda.

Part II

Francesco il Vecchio, 1356–1388

Chapter 4

Seeking Other Allies, 1356–1376

> Memor
>
> [Remember]
>
> —Motto taken by Francesco il Vecchio da Carrara, September 1373

King Louis of Hungary's invasion of Friuli and the Trevisano as part of his renewed campaign to wrest the Dalmatian provinces from Venice in the summer of 1356 imposed on Francesco il Vecchio a crucial choice for Paduan foreign policy. In July Francesco convened a council of leading Paduans to decide how to handle the Hungarian invasion. The Carrara lord and his councillors decided to seek friendship with King Louis, sending a legation laden with gifts to the Hungarian camp. Early in August the Collegio of the Venetian government reacted by sending an embassy, composed of two Procurators of San Marco, Simeone Dandolo and Niccolò Lion, and the chancellor Benintendi dei Ravignani, to Padua to make certain of the Carrara lord's good intentions and solicit his aid in bringing about peace with Louis.[1] But by the end of the summer, Louis's forces had occupied Conegliano and Asolo and were besieging Treviso. Amid the stresses of invasion, the aged Doge Giovanni Gradenigo died, on 8 August 1356. Thus, the proposals of peace made the next day by the papal nuncio Pietro di Pati, bishop of Fermo, providing for the cession of Venice's Dalmatian cities to the king of Hungary, fell on deaf ears. Ten days later, the newly elected Doge Giovanni Dolfin was found besieged in Treviso. When King Louis refused him safe-conduct to return to Venice, Dolfin broke out of the besieged city as the head of a body of cavalry to assume the office of doge.[2] During that autumn, the king of Hungary's successes in the field and the Carrara lord's ever greater aid and friendship with the invading army led the Venetian government to reconsider its "special relationship" with the lord and commune of Padua.

Padua Turns to the King of Hungary

Meeting on Sunday, 27 November 1356, the Maggior Consiglio voted on the recommendation of the heads of the Quarantia to forbid service of Venetian patricians as magistrates in Padua, now defined as a *terra tyrampnorum*. The preamble recalled the law of 2 August 1327, which enunciated Venice's policy against service in the government of foreign lords: "Our forebears recognized that it would be useful and healthy for the preservation of our state that our citizens were not permitted to accept or fill the post of rectors in the lands of tyrants." Since the ordinance had been disregarded, much to the harm of Venice's honor, henceforth no Venetian was allowed to hold any office in any city or locality not subject to Venetian rule under fine of 2,000 ducats. Any Venetian holding such an office had to resign it within six months, and those having loans or goods in such territories had to liquidate them promptly, except for Venetians holding ancestral lands. The prohibition did not, however, extend to offices held beyond the gulf in the Oltremar, in the dominions of Galeotto Malatesta of Rimini, or in territories where a Venetian had lived for more than twenty-five years. The intent was clearly to serve notice to Francesco il Vecchio for his disloyalty toward Venice and keep Venetians from serving in the government of a hostile Padua. The law was scrupulously observed, with only one Venetian, Marino Memmo, appointed in 1383 to oversee implementation of the Peace of Turin, serving as *podestà* of Padua until Francesco Novello's restoration.[3]

But Francesco il Vecchio continued to play the role of mediator between his former patron and new friend. In October a truce of five months had been imposed on the two parties. Now in Padua at the end of December, Francesco il Vecchio pledged to enforce the terms of the truce in the Veneto and to oversee the restitutions and compensations required. Witnesses to the truce included the most powerful men in Padua at the time: Pataro Buzzacarini, the lord's father-in-law; Zanino da Peraga, the lord's uncle; Giacomo Rossi of Parma and Manno Donati of Florence; the outgoing podestà, Marino Morosini, of Venice, and the incoming one, Giovanni Manfredi of Reggio; the lord's vicars, Bartolomeo Piacentini and Giacomo da Santa Croce; Federico Manthelor; and Enrico Valcherich of Hungary. Francesco il Vecchio agreed to hear and settle the dispute between Henverardo Aspermont, the king of Hungary's vicar general in Conegliano, and Pietro Michele, Venice's ambassador. The specific clauses provided for the release of twelve carts of Louis's wine in exchange for restoration of Venetian provisions held by the Hungarians in Conegliano, the transport of goods through captured territories subject to the payment of proper custom duties, and freedom of villages from pillaging and destruction. Compensa-

FIG. 12. *Portrait of Francesco il Vecchio da Carrara, with motto "Memor" (late fourteenth century). Source: Biblioteca Civica, Padua, MS B.P. 158, fol. 44v. Pier Paolo Vergerio the Elder,* De principibus Carrariensibus. *Reproduced with permission of the Biblioteca Civica, Padua*

tion was to be paid for locals in Venetian territory decapitated by Hungarian soldiers or those of Louis's ally, the patriarch of Aquileia. Cattle seized and soldiers made prisoner at Motta were to be restored to the Venetians, and in general damages in Istria, Treviso, and Ceneda were to be compensated according to the Carrara lord's best judgment. Finally, Francesco il Vecchio pledged to enforce the observation of the truce, counting on the prestige of his office as lord of Padua.[4]

When the truce expired the next spring, hostilities were renewed with the Paduan lord firmly in Louis's camp. The Hungarians besieged Serravalle, which was starved into surrender in June, and tightened the sieges at Castelfranco and Treviso that summer. As early as 25 May the heads of the Quarantia proposed to the Senate a retreat from Treviso by extricating Venetian forces from the besieged city and counseled negotiation with anyone, "except the lord of Padua, with the least harm and most advantage to our soldiers that we can." But that proposal failed to gain the necessary two-thirds majority, with only 54 votes in favor, 36 opposed, and 14 abstaining. Other proposals made in the Collegio—to enlist the help of Duke Rudolf of Austria, Cangrande II della Scala of Verona, or the Holy Roman Emperor Charles IV—also failed to gain the needed majorities, even after repeated balloting.[5] Continued Hungarian successes and Padua's support of the besieging army led in July to the reopening of peace talks in Padua. The next month the Collegio appointed three ambassadors to treat for peace with the king of Hungary, traveling by way of Padua to inform the Carrara lord of their plans.[6] At the same time, the Venetian government protested strongly against war damages caused by Paduan troops in the Trevisano and the new policy of impeding or taxing exportations from Venetian landowners in the Padovano. On 20 September Francesco il Vecchio asserted that his new alliance with Louis of Hungary invalidated existing treaties with Venice and he was bound by new orders to suspend any exportation of provisions to Venice or its dominions.[7] That same month, Zara fell to the besieging Hungarian army, which included a contingent of Paduan troops. In a desperate counterattack in the Veneto theater of war, Venice sent a strong contingent of its German mercenaries against the Hungarian forces at Nervesa on the Piave. The Hungarian garrison from Conegliano countered the thrust, sending the Venetian forces in retreat. According to the chroniclers, the Hungarians killed two hundred of the Venetian force, taking many prisoners, while the rest fled back to Treviso. Fifty cartloads of arms were seized and sent back to Padua. Venice faced a humiliating peace.[8]

Late in November, the Venetian Senate sent three seasoned diplomats, Pietro Trevisan, Giovanni Gradenigo, and Chancellor Benintendi dei Ravig-

Seeking Other Allies

nani, to Louis's court at Zara to hammer out terms for peace. Finally in February 1358, Venice made peace with Hungary, agreeing to cede all its cities and dominions on the Dalmatian coast south of Istria to King Louis. Thus, at one stroke, Hungary received the cities of Dubrovnik, Split, and Zara, with many smaller towns. The doge renounced his title as "Dux of Dalmatia and Croatia," and the Venetians promised to hand over all places not already in Hungarian hands and withdraw their garrisons from the strongholds there. In return, boundaries and possessions in the Veneto and Istria remained as before the war, with Venice retaining control of Treviso and its *contado* and recovering Conegliano, Serravalle, and Asolo. The peace was a great setback for Venetian claims on the Dalmatian coast. Venice's authority in the Veneto was compromised, with Francesco il Vecchio da Carrara and the patriarch of Aquileia named specifically as Hungarian allies immune from Venetian reprisals.[9]

In May 1358 Louis of Hungary rewarded Francesco il Vecchio with an official grant of protection against Venice or any other enemy, thereby guaranteeing the lord and commune of Padua the defense of a powerful, if distant, protector.[10] At the same time, Venice began to cultivate the goodwill of its former client and recent enemy. On 26 May the Collegio debated the question whether Francesco il Vecchio and his Paduan state could continue to receive salt from Chioggia, especially in view of the recent loss of Dalmatian saltworks to Hungary. At first, it was proposed to limit Padua to 40,000 *moggi* of Chioggian salt per annum, but after more discussion it was agreed that "the lord and commune of Padua and their successors may purchase as much salt of Chioggia as is needed for their own use in the city and district." Clearly Venice intended to use its near monopoly of the indispensable salt as a means to court Paduan friendship once again. In the negotiations, the Venetian ambassadors were charged with assuring Francesco il Vecchio that Venice "intended to live with him in all love and charity just as with a brother."[11] Then Francesco il Vecchio, with a large retinue, proceeded to Venice, where he ratified the peace treaty in the Ducal Palace on 7 June. Staying at his own palace on Campo S. Polo, the Carrara lord received the plaudits of the Venetian nobility (at least according to Cortusi's account) before returning to Padua, where he treated the city's notables to lavish banquets, announcing the general peace with Venice on 18 June amid celebrations of the entire Paduan populace.[12] Late that year Francesco il Vecchio further cemented friendly relations with Venice, selling in time of scarcity 2,000 *moggi* of grain to Venice for a total of £12,800.[13]

Disputes with Venice, 1358–1365

Over the next decades, Padua's disputes with Venice arose from the complex politics of northeastern Italy. Following the death of the patriarch of Aquileia, Nicholas of Luxembourg, who was the emperor's half brother, in the summer of 1358, a power struggle ensued for control of the Friuli and the cities of Feltre and Belluno in the foothills of the Italian Alps. The election of Lodovico della Torre as the new patriarch increased Louis of Hungary's influence in the region at the expense of Charles IV, who the next year ceded the Alpine cities to Louis of Hungary. Probably out of obligations arising from the recent war with Venice, the king of Hungary invited Francesco il Vecchio to take control of Belluno and Feltre and their strongholds. In early November 1360, the Carrara lord sent his father-in-law, Pataro Buzzacarini, to receive the keys to the cities from Hungarian and imperial representatives, thus fulfilling his aim of gaining a foothold in the Alps and control over passes on the Piave into Italy. Venice soon became apprehensive of Padua's new strategic advantage, with garrisons now ready to threaten Treviso and its district from the north as well as the west.[14] Two years later the citizen councils of the two cities formally voted approval of the statute submitted by Francesco il Vecchio which bestowed on him "merum et mixtum imperium" and other broad powers.[15]

Many issues between Venice and Padua arising in the recent war, however, remained unresolved. In August 1358 a dispute arose when a Carrara favorite, Manfredo qd. Guecellone Monfumo, confiscated property in Padua and S. Bruson which belonged to the Venetian patricians Pirano and Angelberto Contarini. The Venetian government asserted that Monfumo had acted against the Contarini brothers in violation of treaties between the two states, while Francesco il Vecchio claimed that this was a matter for internal Paduan adjudication. Rejecting his claim, the Senate appointed Leonardo Caronelli as legate to Padua to require enforcement of the treaty of 1337 in deciding the case. The Carrara lord repeated his view that the dispute was a local Paduan matter, but he promised that if Paduan judges agreed it was a dispute of international law, then he would permit the case to come before a board of three Venetian *savi* as the Senate proposed on 11 April 1359. By June 1360, however, the case had already been decided in Padua. Replying to a further embassy by Caronelli, Francesco il Vecchio asserted that Paduan judges had handled the cases correctly without violating any treaty. But he remained ready to submit the issue of jurisdiction to impartial arbiters as he had already proposed in November 1358.[16] Thus, Francesco il Vecchio tried to treat disputes with Venetian proprietors in the Padovano as coming strictly under his jurisdiction, explicitly denying

Venetians any special standing in such cases. His policy of limiting Venetian privileges in the Padovano soon extended to other issues.

Among the constant points of friction were related issues of boundaries and extradition. In June 1358, days after the peace treaty guaranteeing the monopoly of Chioggian salt in Padua, the Senate found it necessary to appoint a board of three savi "to investigate diligently the differences of boundaries that have arisen between the commune of Chioggia and the lord of Padua."[17] The next March the Senate sent an ambassador to Padua to discuss the extradition of criminals that were fleeing into the Padovano. By October the list of issues had grown: the Senate appointed a legate to the Carrara court to settle a dispute between the monastery of S. Giustina and a Venetian proprietor at Cavarzere, discuss a complaint of the abbot and monks of S. Trinità at Brondolo over illegal taxation, and determine the correct frontiers at Chioggia.[18] Questions of Venetian economic privileges loomed large. In October 1360, the Senate accused Francesco il Vecchio of refusing to carry out sentences against debtors who had sought sanctuary in the Padovano, and it appointed three savi to clarify treaty obligations for extradition of debtors to Venice. The next April, the savi developed elaborate new rules for sentencing Venetian debtors residing in Padua. In general, the accused debtors had to post in Padua a security equal to the amount of the debt before extradition to Venice; the deposit was returned if the debtor proved his innocence, confiscated and sent to Venice if found guilty. After negotiations, however, only Venetians and those named in ducal letters could be extradited from Padua; foreign merchants not domiciled in Venice were to be immune from such extradition.[19] Thus, the Carrara lord succeeded in limiting arbitrary extradition for trial by the Venetian Consoli dei Mercanti.

For a time, goodwill between the two cities was restored. During a time of scarcity in May 1362, Francesco il Vecchio agreed to deliver to the Venetian grain office 30,000 *staia* of grain and 6,000 of flour, which his agents would be permitted to sell in shops there. At the same time, he supplied another 6,000 *staia* of grain and legumes to Venetian dominions, thus helping to alleviate the short supply. The next week, the Senate agreed to supply a boat for the passage of Francesco il Vecchio's sister, Lieta, spouse of Otto, count of Ortenburg, to Capodistria, on return to her home in the Drava Valley.[20] But Venetian criminals seeking asylum in Paduan territory placed strains on the recent treaty of extradition. That same May the Senate voted to send a sharp letter to Francesco il Vecchio protesting his refusal to extradite Venetian fugitives on demand. The Carrara lord claimed that he and the Paduan judiciary had the right to determine the guilt of Venetians who had entered his domains. But Venice claimed that the treaty of extradition

FIG. 13. *Rocca degli Alberi, with walls of Montagnana, constructed by Francesco il Vecchio da Carrara, 1372. Photograph courtesy of Tracy Cooper*

of 1345 as amended in 1360 gave its government broad powers to demand extradition of any persons named in ducal letters.[21]

To this intransigence against Venice's legal right of extradition the Carrara lord added an extensive program of frontier fortifications, especially at the new stronghold of Castelcarro on the Bacchiglione opposite Chioggia and at Oriago on the Brenta near the lagoon. He constructed two towers in Padua at the gates of Saracinesca and S. Croce, rebuilt the castle at Bovolenta, and erected two fortresses at Piove di Sacco. In only two years he was able to complete under the direction of Francesco Schici a 2-kilometer curtain of walls at Montagnana, where he also transformed the castle of S. Zeno at the west gate into an up-to-date stronghold, the Rocca degli Alberi.[22] His intentions of girding Padua for war seemed confirmed by the fortification of the Casa Mace on the Trevisan border in the summer of 1362. The Senate promptly dispatched to Padua a notary-legate demanding an explanation for these hostile acts, but he received no acceptable reply.[23] Tensions increased when Venice fortified part of the island of S. Ilario, which Padua had always claimed as part of its own territory. In September a Venetian posse headed by a husband in hot pursuit of a laborer who had run off with his wife and part of his household goods arrested the couple, who had claimed sanctuary in the church at S. Ilario. The posse escorted the couple back to

Venice. Francesco il Vecchio fumed at this affront to Paduan sovereignty and had the Paduan podestà pronounce a capital ban against the enraged husband and his gang.[24] Reviewing the incident, the Senate found that the husband, Bartolomeo, had in fact made the arrest with the permission of the Venetian *signori di notte* and voted to have the Maggior Consiglio elect five savi to conduct an inquiry. On 3 October 1362 the Senate created a special junta of twenty-five noblemen, elected one per Casa, to help the savi to investigate the affair and propose a solution by the end of the month.[25]

The case soon become the focus of international attention. Through his adherence in April 1362 to Pope Urban V's league directed against the rebel-heretic lord of Milan, Bernabò Visconti, Francesco il Vecchio confirmed his position as one of the principal Guelf leaders in northern Italy.[26] This role later brought him in conflict with Duke Rudolf IV of Habsburg, who was attempting to extend his influence in Friuli at the expense of the papal ally, the patriarch of Aquileia. As early as 1361 these incursions had forced the patriarch to ask for armed help from the Holy Roman Emperor, the Carrara lord, and even Venice. The patriarch's principal ally became Francesco il Vecchio, who from his newly acquired cities of Belluno and Feltre sent troops into Friuli to protect the patriarch's property and lands. In the meantime, the duke of Austria cultivated Venice's support: in July 1361 Rudolf had made an elaborate state visit to Venice, promising to live at peace with the patriarch. Content to play the role of peacemaker, Venice maintained a policy of benevolent neutrality in Friuli, while secretly supporting Rudolf's aggression. In December 1362 the Senate flatly denied the patriarch's request for military aid and special Venetian protection, citing the need to garrison its own strongholds and Venice's longstanding neutrality.[27]

In February 1363, Rudolf was able to document for the Venetian government the Carrara lord's incursions against Habsburg possessions in the Tyrol and Friuli and asked for Venice's aid to make Louis of Hungary curb the actions of his ally, the Paduan lord.[28] By spring, Francesco il Vecchio began in earnest his policy to dominate Friuli and, at the same time, stymie Venice's efforts to impinge upon Paduan sovereignty in the S. Ilario affair, enrolling a number of German mercenary captains with their companies for the campaign in Friuli (and potentially against Venice).[29] Early in March Pope Urban V directed Venice not to harm Francesco il Vecchio nor to favor in any way the excommunicated Bernabò Visconti; the pope also ordered Duke Rudolf not to allow any of his subjects to aid the Visconti lord.[30] Alarmed at the size of the Carrara forces, both in Friuli and on its own frontier, the Venetian Collegio desperately began recruitment of its own mercenary army in the late spring. Concerned that the Carrara lord was hiring away its best troops, on 7 June Venice ordered the captains and vicars of its mainland cities and fortresses to exile perpetually any soldiers leaving Venetian service for the growing enemy force. The next day the Collegio wrote to the count of Spilimbergo to enlist four companies of his troops in the Venetian forces and warned an embassy from Niccolò II of Ferrara that he was exaggerating any threat Venice posed to Francesco il Vecchio or the league of the cardinal legate, Egidio Albornoz. By the next week Venetian commissioners (*provveditori*) had raised a large number of troops in a very short time: 1,100 were assigned to Treviso, 268 to Asolo, 216 to Mestre, 270 to Castelfranco, 100 to Serravalle, 150 to Noale, and 85 at Valmareno, with more mercenaries and provisions on the way.[31]

Elated with the rapid buildup of its garrisons and enlistment of more than thirty companies of German cavalry from Gorizia and Friuli, on 27 June the Collegio instructed its ambassadors to negotiate with Rudolf of Habsburg, offering him 25,000 ducats to attack the Padovano for four months with a force of at least a thousand lances. Any Paduan strongholds captured were to be handed over to Venice for safekeeping, while the Austrian forces could keep any booty taken in the field. The hope was the overthrow of the Carrara regime itself: "in the event that the city of Padua is taken from the hands of the said [Carrara] lord, and he is deprived of his state, Padua, its towns and fortresses ought to be set free and ruled *per commune.*" In return, Rudolf was promised rule over Feltre and Cividale if these cities fell to his army. With such massive forces now threatening Padua, Francesco il Vecchio promptly accepted Venetian terms for settling the boundary dispute at S. Ilario.[32]

On 6 July 1363 a treaty was signed at Venice by which the island of S. Ilario was divided between the two states with each forbidden to construct fortresses on its half. Observance of the pact was required under penalty of a fine of 30,000 ducats.[33] The next day Doge Lorenzo Celsi wrote to the podestà of Treviso announcing that an accord had been reached with the lord of Padua and that hostilities were over.[34] Despite Venice's peace with the Carrara lord, Rudolf of Habsburg continued to attack the men and possessions of the patriarch in Friuli through the summer. When in September the patriarch's ambassador asked Venice to intercede between the two parties, the Senate agreed to send two ambassadors to urge the duke of Austria to seek peace. The next month, distancing itself from its recent ally, Venice denied Rudolf's request for armed intervention against the patriarch, citing its ancient treaties with the patriarchate of Aquileia and tradition of nonintervention in Friulian affairs. In response to a request from the count of Spilimbergo, the Senate ordered another embassy to Friuli to bring peace between the parties.[35] By December the Venetian government was prepared to forget its recent tensions with the Carrara dy-

Seeking Other Allies

nasty in Padua when the Maggior Consiglio voted to bestow citizenship on Francesco il Vecchio's consort, Fina, and her brother, the noble knight Arcoano Buzzacarini, out of consideration for the devotion and love the two had felt for Venice.[36] True to its attempt to keep Padua firmly in its camp and concerned with the growing rebellion in Crete, the Venetian government dangled the allure of its friendship and support, once the disputed borders had, for the moment, been settled.

Early in 1364 the lord of Padua was still obligated to serve as commander of in the Guelf league against Bernabò Visconti's threat to Bologna, but at the same time he hoped to help the patriarch of Aquileia to gain the upper hand over Rudolf of Habsburg in Friuli. Peace made with Bernabò Visconti in March 1364 freed the Carrara lord to concentrate on the campaign in Friuli.[37] Though called in papal letters a loyal son of the church, Francesco il Vecchio was scarcely an ideal ally of the papacy: on 10 April, Pope Urban V sent a sharp note to the Este lord of Ferrara and Carrara lord of Padua reminding them to repatriate the Visconti soldiers recently captured at Bologna, and on 3 August he appointed Agapito, bishop of Asolo, papal envoy to make peace between Francesco il Vecchio and Rudolf, Albert, and Leopold of Habsburg, dukes of Austria.[38] Francesco il Vecchio persisted, however, in his policy of aggrandizement in northeast Italy, forming on 13 August a defensive alliance with Lodovico della Torre, patriarch of Aquileia, directed against the dukes of Austria and anyone hostile to the patriarch. Requiring a contribution of two hundred armed knights from Padua, the league was to last until 25 April 1367, with a fine of 10,000 ducats levied if the agreement was broken.[39] Meanwhile, Pope Urban continued in his efforts to bring peace to Friuli, sending on 11 September two letters to Louis of Hungary, one asking help in bringing peace between the dukes of Austria and the patriarch, the other between the dukes and the Carrara lord.[40] But Friuli proved for the Carrara lord too tempting a prize to resist. When Doge Lorenzo Celsi denied free passage for Francesco il Vecchio's troops through the Trevisano that fall, the Carrara lord retaliated by permitting the circulation of false ducats made in Padua, prompting the Senate to send two ambassadors to Padua to remind the lord of his treaty obligations.[41] But Venice's instructions were difficult to enforce: by early 1365 Paduan forces were moving with impunity through Venice's mainland possessions. When the Austrian captain at Pordenone asked for an explanation of the free passage of Carrara troops in Friuli, the Venetian government lamely replied that these troops movements were contrary to Venice's express wishes but the area was too large to police properly.[42] Clearly the effort involved in putting down the rebellion that had broken out in Crete in 1364 made protecting its mainland possessions a difficult, even impossible, task for Venice.

When his military situation in Friuli became hazardous, Rudolf of Habsburg turned to diplomacy. A year earlier, in 1364, Rudolf had made an unsuccessful attempt to form a league with the Visconti and Scaligeri directed against Francesco il Vecchio and negotiated to receive the cities of Belluno and Feltre as fiefs from his father-in-law, Charles IV, Holy Roman Emperor. Early in 1365 he arranged the marriage of his younger brother, Leopold, with Verde Visconti, one of Bernabò's daughters. At the same time Rudolf proposed the marriage of another brother, Albert, to Elisabeth, daughter of King Louis of Hungary, who had at that time no legitimate male heir. Such a marriage, which threatened to deprive the Carrara lord of his principal ally in central Europe, also alarmed Florence, which viewed it as dangerous to the Guelf powers of Italy. In March a Paduan ambassador arrived in Florence, asking the *signoria* to use its influence with the pope to prevent such a union. After considerable debate, the Florentine government voted to send an ambassador to Avignon requesting Pope Urban V to ban the marriage on the grounds that it might enable the Habsburgs to become heirs to the kingdom of Naples, thus imperiling the power of the papacy and the Guelfs in Italy.[43] That same spring the pope forbade the marriage.

Thwarted in the Hungarian marriage alliance, Rudolf continued to threaten Friuli and Padua itself, traveling with a large party through the Trentino to Brescia on his way to Milan for his brother's wedding. Alarmed at the proximity of Austrian forces and the possibility of war with Milan, the Carrara lord requested and received that summer a contingent of two hundred knights from Florence to help defend Padua. On 27 July 1365 Rudolf died in Milan at an early age, leaving the duchy of Austria to his younger brothers, Leopold and Albert. Three days later, Lodovico della Torre died, leaving vacant the patriarchate of Aquileia. With the sudden departure of the chief protagonists in the struggle for Friuli, a strange peace settled over northeast Italy. The Florentines promptly withdrew their unneeded troops from Padua. The late Rudolf's principal follower, Walterpertold of Spilimbergo, renounced his fidelity to the Habsburgs and pledged himself and his followers to Francesco da Carrara; Meynard, count of Gorizia; and the new patriarch, Marquardo of Randek, even agreeing to pay back 3,300 ducats the count of Spilimbergo owed to the lord of Padua.[44] For the next fifteen years, as the Habsburg threat diminished, Friuli remained relatively peaceful under the shared rule of its communes, its feudatories, and the patriarch of Aquileia. Francesco il Vecchio turned his resources and military capacity to extend his influence and develop new allies among the states of Italy.

Seeking Other Allies

The Carrara Lord's Relations with Florence, the Pope, and the Emperor, 1364–1370

The common policy of the Carrara lord and the commune of Florence against the proposed marriage of Albert of Habsburg and Elisabeth of Hungary demonstrated how close the outlook of the two Guelf powers had become. Both opposed Visconti expansion beyond the Apennines, both stood for the integrity of the patriarch of Aquileia's rule in Friuli against the Habsburg dukes, and both wanted to minimize the authority of Charles of Bohemia in Italian affairs. In June 1364, at the height of its war with Pisa, Florence received an interest-free loan of 27,000 ducats from the lord of Padua.[45] The loan was gradually repaid, with a payment of 3,400 ducats promised in a letter from the signoria to the lord of Padua on 25 October 1365, an installment of 8,000 ducats repaid in Padua on 15 August 1366, and the final payment of 5,000 ducats made on 10 January 1367, which canceled the entire debt of 27,000.[46] In a letter of 6 October 1365 to Francesco il Vecchio recommending Scolaio Cavalcanti for a term as podestà of Padua, the Florentine signoria stressed not only Cavalcanti's abilities as a magistrate but also Padua's need to employ officials dedicated to the Guelf cause in Italy. Somewhat later Florence reminded the Carrara lord of the customary freedom of imposts on Florentine goods imported into Padua following the treaty of 1337 and its renewals.[47] Thus, Florence sought to utilize its friendship with the lord of Padua in foreign policy, economic privileges, and employment of its best magistrates. At the end of 1370, Francesco il Vecchio lent Florence's ally, newly independent Lucca, 10,000 florins to help meet payments to the emperor for the commune's freedom—a loan that was repaid in full only in 1384.[48] The signoria rewarded the Carrara with the bestowal of Florentine citizenship on Francesco il Vecchio, his consort, Fina, and their male heirs in February 1370.[49] Nearer home Francesco il Vecchio used his influence and wealth to aid his friends, potential and actual. In the spring of 1366, acting out of friendship for Louis of Hungary, Francesco il Vecchio made an interest-free loan for two years of 2,000 ducats to representatives of the commune of Zara for defense of the city against its enemies. That fall, in the presence of two influential Carrara officials—his vicar Giovanni Salgardi and his factor Giovanni Naseri of Montagnana—a Paduan *campsor*, Brocardo qd. Pietrobuono of *contrada* Fallaroti, made a short-term loan of £2,800 to procurators from the city of Feltre.[50]

At the same time the lord of Padua sought to maintain good relations with the most powerful of his potential adversaries, Venice and the Holy Roman Emperor. On 1 August 1366, perhaps mindful of his impending descent into Italy, the emperor Charles conferred on Francesco il Vecchio's vicar Giacomo da Santa Croce the title of count palatine, thus empowering the Carrara favorite to create notaries and legitimate bastards in Padua.[51] That December the Venetian Senate agreed to permit Francesco il Vecchio's newly wedded daughter, Gigliola, to cross the Trevisano with her husband, Wenceslaus, duke of Saxony, and a retinue of three hundred guests and soldiers. The next February the Senate honored the request of a Paduan ambassador to allow Francesco il Vecchio to charter a ship in Venice to transport at his own expense three hundred Paduan troops requested by the king of Hungary for service at Segni on the Dalmatian coast.[52] From Prague on 1 August 1367, Charles IV confirmed Francesco il Vecchio, his heir apparent, Francesco Novello, and their successors as "the duke of Carrara" with jurisdiction over all the castles and towns of the Padovano, a title that was revived in the early 1390s.[53]

Early in 1367 Pope Urban V began his long-awaited return to Rome from Avignon. That spring as well the emperor Charles IV instructed his ambassador in Italy to join a league proposed by the pope with Queen Joanna of Naples, the Carrara lord of Padua, the Este lords of Ferrara, the Gonzaga lords of Mantua, and the communes of Genoa and Florence for the general defense of northern and central Italy. On 4 April, the Paduan ambassador Giacomo da Santa Croce reached Bologna, where he met with the papal cardinal vicars Androin de la Roche and Egidio Albornoz and announced Francesco il Vecchio's intention to join the proposed league.[54] In May Pope Urban V sailed from Marseilles, disembarked at Corneto, and proceeded to the papal residence at Viterbo. There that summer, legates of the interested parties met to hammer out terms of the proposed alliance, which was now directed against Bernabò Visconti and Cansignorio della Scala. The Carrara lord was represented by Bartolomeo Piacentini, his trusted vicar and jurist, and his noble friend Bonifacio Lupi, exiled Marchese of Soragna, both originally from Parma. In the short term, from Italy only the lords of Padua, Ferrara, and Mantua adhered to the league with pope, emperor, and king of Hungary. In Florence partisan passions and endless debate in the communal councils immobilized decision making. Of the three north Italian lords, the Gonzaga were the most exposed to Visconti retaliation and, therefore, the least enthusiastic. They were offered special concessions: thus, the Gonzaga were not required to deploy any troops outside their own territories, and they were to receive at Mantua, for their own safety, four companies (*bannerias*) of knights from the papal forces. In event of war with the lords of Milan and Verona, the Este and Carrara lords were to provide armed ships to defend Borgoforte at the Mantuan frontier on the Po from enemy attack. Mirandola and any lands of Cremona or Brescia taken in war were to become the possession of the Gonzaga lords without dissent from other mem-

Seeking Other Allies

bers of the league. In general, Pope Urban V sought to protect the northern frontier of the papal states against his principal Ghibelline enemies, the Visconti and Scaligeri, by catering to the special interests of his new allies.[55]

Soon after the death of the ruthless papal vicar Egidio Albornoz, late in August, Urban moved on to Rome at the head of a large retinue of curialists and Italian lords and legates, including Marquis Niccolò II d'Este of Ferrara and Count Amadeus VI of Savoy. Greeted by a joyous populace in Rome, Urban set about to pacify the papal state and renew war with the Visconti, making his own brother Anglic Grimoard his vicar general in place of the lethargic Androin de la Roche. By early 1368, Francesco il Vecchio had arrived in Bologna at the head of a contingent of Paduan troops ready to take the field with the papal army. But as often happened, Bernabò Visconti had seized the initiative, attacking Mantua and taking the stronghold of Borgoforte on the Po. The descent of the emperor Charles at the head of a large army this spring did little to reverse the Visconti lord's advantage. Received in Udine on 1 May 1368 by Francesco il Vecchio da Carrara, Pileo da Prata, bishop of Padua, and Francesco Petrarca, the emperor and his retinue proceeded at a leisurely pace through the Veneto, reaching Curtarolo on 16 May and entering Padua two days later. There Francesco il Vecchio lavishly entertained his imperial guest for several days as he had on the first descent into Italy fourteen years earlier.[56] That summer the north Italian lords made a truce with Bernabò Visconti, while Charles advanced down the peninsula, entering Rome on 21 October. Through the winter emperor and pope worked together to bring peace to Italy, eventually negotiating a treaty between the papal allies and Bernabò Visconti which was signed at Bologna on 11 February 1369. The next month Francesco il Vecchio da Carrara and the Este lords of Ferrara joined a new league with their former enemies, the Visconti and Scaligeri, negotiated by the papal vicar Anglic Grimoard and aimed at destroying the mercenary companies then ravaging Italy.[57] The problem of lawless and dangerous *condottieri* remained intractable, however, with the Visconti hiring Sir John Hawkwood to harass papal allies in the Romagna and Tuscany. That summer the emperor Charles IV returned home to Prague, taking ship at Venice after lavish entertainment by the doge. Pope Urban V stayed only another year in Italy, making another peace with the Visconti in the summer of 1370, before embarking at Corneto for Avignon on 5 September.[58] With the two rulers claiming ecumenical authority safely back in their respective capitals on the Rhone and the Vltava, the Carrara lord of Padua turned to the perennial question of boundaries and prerogatives of his powerful neighbor, Venice.

Tensions with Venice, 1368–1371

Venetian attempts to limit Paduan sovereignty on the mainland by extraditing accused criminals at will were met with increasingly stiff opposition from the Carrara lord. When a murder occurred near the Trevisan border late in 1366, Paduan ambassadors demanded the return of the culprits from Venetian Asolo to Paduan Bassano, only to receive a flat refusal from the Venetian Senate. When some months later the Paduan podestà tried to extradite a peasant named Domenico from Castelfranco for a violent crime, he was informed by the Venetian Senate that "Domenico had lived and worked for more than thirty years paying taxes in the Trevisan district" and thus was under Venetian jurisdiction.[59] Later that summer a rancorous dispute broke out at the border near Chioggia. On 9 June the Venetian envoy Niccolò Falier informed Francesco il Vecchio of the illegal actions taken by the Paduan podestà at Piove di Sacco against certain Venetian subjects seized near Chioggia. Apparently the Paduan captain at Abbà di Brenta had discovered a certain Chioggiote Prosdocimo and his sons stealing materials for an oven being built in Chioggia, placed them under arrest, and sent them to the podestà at Piove di Sacco for trial. There the podestà, Boscarino Buzzacarini, whipped the boys illegally. Next armed Paduans entered Venetian territory at the mills near Chioggia cutting down valuable trees along a canal. Following a further exchange of ambassadors, Francesco il Vecchio accepted some of the Venetian charges and demands but wanted more information on the alleged sentencing of fifteen Chioggiotes *in absentia* to a perpetual ban from the Padovano. The Senate voted to demand that the Carrara lord rescind the sentence of confiscation and ban made by his podestà at Piove di Sacco, since he had clearly overstepped the limits of his jurisdiction and authority.[60] The record is silent on the outcome of the matter.

Just a few months later trouble broke out on the Trevisan border, with Venice claiming that the Paduan vicar at Cesana had led several hundred men on raids into the Trevisano, moving border markers and thus violating the treaty of July 1363. From the Carrara palace on Campo S. Polo, Paduan ambassadors Arsendino Arsendi and Paganino Sala denied the charges, asserting that Paduan rights had been violated instead.[61] Later that year, Francesco il Vecchio began to despair of peaceful settlement of his differences with Venice: on 29 December 1369, he appointed Giovanni Naseri his proctor to receive "all quantities of moneys that any merchants and inhabitants of Venice owed him."[62] Mindful of the Venetian ploy of confiscating the assets of potential enemies and belligerents, the Carrara lord decided to settle accounts before the Venetian government acted.

Tensions continued along the borders of the two states. In September 1370, the Venetian captain at Noale warned the doge that Francesco il Vecchio was attempting to dam up the Musone River and divert water into the Tergola near Camposampiero. In October the Senate complained that the Paduan authorities were again taxing the produce of Chioggian subjects, which by treaty ought to enter the *dogado* free of duty. In November the Carrara lord ordered Ugolino Scrovegni, his podestà at Belluno, to report on Austrian troop movements against Venice in the region of Conegliano and Serravalle. In December Venice finally forced Padua to sign a treaty calling for the excavation and maintenance of canals near the borders, especially at S. Ilario.[63] In the late winter of 1371 the Venetians complained that the Paduan lord was again cutting dikes and diverting water at Noale. But Francesco il Vecchio replied that the dikes were ruptured by violent flooding, not on his orders. The Senate remained skeptical, asserting that the breaks must have been intentional because they happened not just once but several times, and it asked the Paduan lord "to punish his subjects in such a way that it will be an example to others not to commit such acts, which are an affront to our honor."[64] That autumn Venice accused the Paduan lord of an even greater threat to Venetian economic well-being, the diverting of timber cut in the foothills of the Alps from Venetian markets for sale instead in Belluno and transportation to Padua. In a sharp note, the Senate reminded Francesco il Vecchio of the earlier agreements allowing export of Alpine timber directly to Venice for use in shipbuilding and other industries and enjoined him to stop his officials from impeding Venetian merchants from conveying the needed timber to Venice. From Monselice three days later the Carrara lord responded, denying that his officials had sequestered any timber at Belluno and asserting that the missing wood was now in Treviso, not in Padua, as unjustly charged.[65] At the end of the year, Venetian officials had a new worry that the Paduans were fortifying the frontier near the lagoon and building saltworks near Chioggia. In a letter dated 31 December 1371, Doge Andrea Contarini ordered his podestà at Treviso to investigate rumors of new Paduan fortifications in the area of Mestre and Oriago and send at once a report back to Venice.[66]

The Border War with Venice, 1372–1373

In fact, Francesco il Vecchio had built a fort named Villanova on reclaimed land near Oriago which he had received in an exchange with the Venetian monastery of S. Giovanni Evangelista, in which the monks got better land to the south near Liettoli. He had also fortified the border strongholds at S. Boldo near Mel, Castelcarro near Chioggia, and Portonuovo. Venice demanded that all these forts be razed to the ground, threatening to close the border to Paduan goods if the Carrara lord did not oblige. An investigative committee of five Venetian nobles appointed on 30 December apparently found cause for concern, for on 6 February 1372 Venice recalled its citizens from Paduan territories and for a few days suspended any Venetian commerce in the area.[67] Francesco sent ambassadors to Venice justifying his need for frontier fortification and others to Bologna and Tuscany seeking help from potential allies. In March Venice dispatched its envoy Pantaleone Barbo to request the aid of the lord of Verona, Cansignorio della Scala, against Padua. Cansignorio would have preferred to remain neutral, but he did allow troops from his domains to be enrolled in the Venetian forces, perhaps motivated by Venice's payment of some of the 275,000 ducats he had deposited in Venice's Grain Office.[68] By late March the Senate was concerned enough about the outbreak of war to forbid the employment of subjects of the Carrara lord from Feltre and Belluno as judges, notaries, or soldiers in Treviso and the towns of its district, thus limiting the possibility of treason from within.[69]

The threat of conflict between Padua and Venice alarmed several of the powers of Christendom.[70] On 19 March Pope Gregory XI sent a letter to Venice urging peace with the Carrara lord through the mediation of the local papal legate. Two weeks later the pope wrote to his nuncio Enrico, bishop of Como, asking him to make peace or at least arrange a truce between the two states.[71] By early April ambassadors from Pope Gregory XI, King Louis of Hungary, Florence, and Pisa arrived in Venice, attempting to arrange a truce and avert hostilities. On 12 April, these ambassadors got Francesco il Vecchio to agree to demolish his tower at S. Boldo and other recent fortifications, restoring the frontier to its original state.[72] On the first of May the two states arranged a truce of two months, dating from 24 April, during which a commission of ten men, five from each state, was to investigate the disputed boundaries and arbitrate all quarrels. The Venetians included Jacopo Moro, Procurator of San Marco, Lorenzo Dandolo, Jacopo Priuli, Taddeo Giustinian, and Pantaleone Barbo; Padua was represented by the Carrara lord's uncle Alvise Forzatè, the knight Fruzerino Capodivacca, the jurist Arsendino Arsendi, the medical professor Giovanni Dondi dall'Orologio, and the lord's treasurer, Jacopino Gaffarello. But at the very moment that the Carrara lord was agreeing to mediation and a peaceful settlement, he was plotting espionage against the Venetian government and the assassination of his staunchest enemies among the Venetian patriciate, including several members of the border commission itself.

That same spring, to gather intelligence in Venice, Carrara agents were able to enlist as spies four nobles highly placed in the Serenissima's government: an Avogador di Comun, Alvise Molin; his son-in-law Leonardo Morosini; a ducal councillor, Piero di Bernardo; and one of the heads of the Quarantia, Francesco Barbarigo.[73] The principal agent, a certain Friar Benedetto, came under suspicion of the Council of Ten, was arrested, and under torture confessed the names of the four traitors. The nobles were brought to trial and convicted: Molin and his son-in-law were condemned to life imprisonment for trading state secrets, and the other two were sentenced to a year in prison for failing to report possible espionage against the republic. When the attempt at espionage failed, Francesco il Vecchio resolved to murder his political opponents in Venice. By early June, when it became clear that the Venetian commissioners were never going to agree to what the Carrara lord believed were Padua's just claims to territory, assassins were sent to Venice to murder his enemies. This plot, too, was discovered, thanks to a prostitute named Cateruzza, who, taking one of the Carrara agents as her customer, learned of the plans to assassinate the nobles. She promptly informed one of the intended victims, Lorenzo Zano, of his fate. Zano notified the *signori di notte,* who arrested the agents and had them brought to trial. Forced confessions revealed that among the intended victims were two of the most accomplished members of the commission, Taddeo Giustinian and Pantaleone Barbo, who had rejected the Carrara border claims and sought to thwart any accommodation with the lord of Padua. To provide a stern reminder to the Carrara lord, his convicted agents were subjected to a ritual execution, beginning with dragging the assassins from the Rialto to the Piazzetta by the tail of a horse, dismemberment and execution at S. Marco, and finally hanging the bodies from the columns at the Bacino. The mutilated corpses were then allowed to rot at the edge of the lagoon, where passersby from Padua would witness that justice had been done. Rumors were rampant that Carrara agents had poisoned the wells of Venice as well as attempting to murder leaders of the government. Venice made much of Paduan terrorism: in a letter of 8 July Doge Andrea Contarini complained to Niccolò II d'Este of Francesco il Vecchio's attempts to assassinate members of the commission and called upon the lord of Ferrara to seal his border with Padua.[74]

That spring, before war broke out, Venice had permitted transit through its territories of Stefan, count of Veglia, Louis of Hungary's handpicked groom for Francesco il Vecchio's middle daughter, Caterina. The marriage took place in May at Padua as war clouds gathered.[75] On 19 June, despairing that any agreement could be reached, Doge Contarini ordered his podestà at Treviso to prepare to close the frontiers with Padua on the 24th, when the two-month truce was due to expire. A state of war now existed between the two states.[76] Earlier Louis of Hungary had maintained a policy of benevolent neutrality, listening patiently to embassies from both parties, having been reminded in a letter of 14 May from Pope Gregory XI that it was the duty of Christian rulers, such as himself, to take the cross against the infidel Turk or exterminate depraved heretics, not promote war among Christian nations.[77] But in early July Louis offered to send troops to aid Padua, perhaps spurred by the instructions from Pope Gregory XI to work to thwart any alliance of Cansignorio della Scala and the dukes of Austria with Venice directed against the Carrara lord.[78] Venice dispatched an embassy to Buda to argue against Hungarian intervention.

In Padua Francesco il Vecchio convened twenty-five of his most trusted advisers—knights, jurists, diplomats, courtiers—to plan strategy for the upcoming struggle with Venice. Paduans exiled for debt and lesser crimes were recalled to aid in the war. Bonifacio Lupi, whose abilities had already been proven in embassies to Louis of Hungary and Pope Urban V, was sent with Arsendino Arsendi to Bologna to enlist support from the papal legate and then to Tuscany with instructions to enroll Hawkwood's White Company. Household officers Marsilio Turchetto and the chronicler Galeazzo Gatari were sent to Ferrara, Florence, Pisa, and Genoa to secure free passage of goods and provisions to Padua. In September, raising cash for the war effort, Francesco il Vecchio had demanded from the Anziani of Lucca repayment of 10,000 florins lent a year earlier to Lucchese merchants resident in Venice.[79] Military captains were deployed to frontier strongholds: the lord's trusted brother-in-law Arcoano Buzzacarini was made commander of the garrison at Bassano, and Francesco Casteltealdo was posted to Solagna farther north on the Brenta. Zanino de Peraga was given command of the forces at Mirano, Simone Lupi the garrison at Camposampiero, and Antonio Lupi troops at Gambarare near the border at S. Ilario.[80] Venice enlisted a leading condottiere of the day, Rainiero Vasco of Siena, who eventually took command of Venetian forces at Treviso early in October.

In the meantime Pope Gregory XI worked feverishly to preserve the peace. On 19 July he appointed the Franciscan prelate Tommaso da Frignano, the patriarch of Grado with residence in Venice, to bring a seasoned diplomat to the Adriatic region. The pope hoped his able friend would be able to mount the long-delayed crusade against the Turks, turning the Genoese from war against the king of Cyprus to fight the infidel instead. He also expected that Tommaso would be able to reconcile Padua with Venice before the conflict became too bloody and irreversible. Finally, he wanted the patriarch to prevent troops from the dukes of Austria from aiding Bernabò Visconti in Lombardy that autumn.[81] In September the pope was still hopeful of an amicable settlement, urging King Louis of Hungary to arrange peace between the two states or at least negotiate a truce

Seeking Other Allies

of two or three years, so that a permanent settlement could be reached.[82] Indeed, a negotiated peace still seemed possible, since the fall campaigns consisted mainly of foraging raids across the Musone and Brenta. Venice's attempt late in October to take Borgoforte on the Adige with a naval expedition from Chioggia and Cavarzere ended in disaster, with the capture of the Venetian commander, Moretto da Canale, and the loss of ships and men. When Rainiero Vasco's descent down the Brenta to invest Padua from the Brentelle was repulsed at Limena, the Venetian forces retired to winter quarters at Treviso.

Late that autumn a large force of Hungarian troops under the command of King Louis's nephew Stephen, voivode of Transylvania, reached the Veneto. A surprise attack on 9 December on the Venetian camp at Nervesa on the Piave garnered many prisoners, including the Venetian *governatore*, Taddeo Giustinian. But Venice continued to construct stockades on the eastern frontier at Lova and occupied the Paduan fort at Curan near S. Bruson. Thus, despite the victory at Nervesa, the Carrara lord felt compelled to seek peace with Venice. But in discussion that January, the Serenissima set impossibly harsh terms, including the cession of Bassano, Belluno, and Feltre, an indemnity of 300,000 ducats, and duty-free importation of all goods from the Padovano in return for the end of hostilities. In February, to gain the support of the dukes of Austria against Venice, the Carrara lord conveyed Belluno and Feltre and the whole of the Valsugana to the Habsburg dukes. Applying economic pressure, King Louis offered free trade with all his Dalmatian cities to any state that would inflict damage on Venetian forces and shipping, outfitting ships in his Adriatic ports to prey on Venetian commerce. But the Austrian dukes proved lukewarm allies, more concerned with garrisoning their new possessions and occupying the Valsugana than opposing Venetian forces in the field. Raids and skirmishes across the borders were inconclusive, as Venice continued its fortification of the Paduan frontier under a new commander, Giberto da Correggio.

On 14 May 1373 at the frontier fort at Lova, the combined Hungarian and Paduan forces won their finest victory.[83] The Venetians with three thousand horsemen and one thousand archers under the command of Giberto da Correggio began the battle, crossing the Brenta Canal at Lova, burning their bridges behind them. Hungarian troops led by the voivode wielding a giant lance charged the Venetian ranks, cutting a swath through the enemy. As the Venetians began to waver, the Paduan forces charged under the command of Francesco Novello da Carrara dressed in a white surcoat covered with vermilion *carri*. The flower of the Paduan nobility led its soldiers into the fray, shouting fierce battle cries. As the Venetian forces began to break, Gilberto sounded the retreat, which soon became a rout. Perhaps as many as three hundred Venetians were slain in battle; nearly as many were crushed to death or drowned as they scrambled to escape, falling into the Brenta Canal. The Hungarian voivode knighted several Paduan nobles for bravery on the field of battle: Francesco Novello, then age fourteen; Niccolò da Carrara, the lord's half brother; Giacomo and Enrico Scrovegni; Boscarino Buzzacarini; Francesco Dotti; and Negro de' Negri. More than thirty Venetian nobles, over fifty *popolani,* and as many mercenaries were captured and taken back to Padua to be held for ransom. But the signal victory at Lova counted for very little. In June a contingent of five thousand troops reached Venice from the Levant, and on 1 July the allies suffered a disastrous defeat at the battle at Buonconforto.

Venice seized the war as an opportunity to drive a wedge between Francesco il Vecchio and his younger half brothers, who had already shown a desire to wrest the lordship of Padua from their older brother. At the beginning of his rule Francesco had been willing to share the Carrara patrimony but not political power with his half brothers, Marsilio, Niccolò, and Carlo Ubertino, sons from his father's second marriage, to Costanza da Polenta of the ruling house of Ravenna. For example, in October 1354, when the three were still minors under the guardianship of their uncle Giacomino da Carrara, all four brothers rented extensive property held *pro indiviso* in Faedo in the Euganean Hills.[84] In August 1363 Francesco, with Marsilio and Niccolò, appointed Francesco Pizzegoti proctor to receive from the bishop of Vicenza tithes that their father Giacomo II da Carrara had held earlier, but with the premature death of the canon Carlo Ubertino that same year, Francesco il Vecchio divided their joint inheritance, settling two-thirds on the two surviving half brothers, who resided with their mother, Costanza, in a palace in contrada S. Andrea.[85] In 1368 young Marsilio's ambition led him to support a plot to overthrow his half brother fomented by Count Toberto da Prata, kinsmen of both the Carrara and the bishop of Padua, Pileo da Prata. Although only the ringleader was executed for this conspiracy, Marsilio found it prudent to leave Padua. On 16 September, with a retinue of perhaps twenty knights and their servants, including Vitaliano and Bicco Vitaliani, Giovanni de' Negri, and Fruzerino da Capodivacca, Marsilio left the family palace in contrada S. Andrea for the Carrara residence in Campo S. Polo in Venice and, thence, for service in Cyprus and Rhodes.[86] There Marsilio received a knighthood from the king of Cyprus before returning to Italy and traveling to Avignon, where, early in 1371, the new pope, Gregory XI, enlisted him in the papal army, conferring on him the title of "Conte della Campagna e della Marittima."

While the older brother, Marsilio, was abroad in the service of Venice or the pope, Niccolò continued to reside in the palace near S. Andrea looking after their common patrimony, selling some property to meet his brother's expenses, but usually leasing extensive holdings in the southern Padovano for rents in cash and kind. For example, in October 1368, Niccolò, acting for himself and his brother, sold for £2,000 a house with courtyard, garden, and orchard near the Basilica di S. Antonio, perhaps to provide funds for the voyage to Cyprus.[87] The next summer, in the *spenderia* (counting room) in the family palace near S. Andrea, Niccolò leased property in Camposampiero, Monselice, and Valsanzibio, as well as extensive fiefs and arable in the villages of Agna, Cona, Borgoforte, Anguillara, Pernumia, and Conselve, bringing in an annual income of more than £2,000.[88] When the purchase of houses in Padua and the Euganean Hills for £5,000 and the sale of parcels of land in the Paduan *campanea* for £2,000 are added, the brothers emerge by 1370 as very wealthy young men in Paduan society.[89] Their fortune increased considerably when, in August 1371, the brothers received a large inheritance amounting to one-half of the estate of their maternal uncle Ostasio da Polenta. A few months later, in the family's country home at Monselice, Niccolò da Carrara appointed Marsilio proctor to take possession of these extensive holdings in the Ravenna district and receive investiture of *livelli,* fiefs, and other property rights.[90]

The brothers retained possession of the huge Ravenna inheritance until early in 1373. At that time Marsilio da Carrara was still in the Roman Campagna with his friend the Paduan jurist Pietro Paolo Crivelli, who was serving as *iudex generalis* for that province.[91] But on 15 January 1373, at his residence at S. Andrea, Niccolò appointed a new proctor, one Giovanni da Portogruaro, to receive from their cousin Guidone III da Polenta, *signore* of Ravenna, a payment of 1,500 ducats, thus completing payment of 3,000 ducats for the sale of the Carrara brothers' interests in the Polenta patrimony in the Ravenna region. This sum was supplemented on 19 March by the rental of all property in certain villages in the Ferrarese for £270 a year.[92] Now supplied with ample funds to reward friends and retainers, in April Marsilio traveled north to Padua, ostensibly to help his half brother in the border war with Venice. Marsilio fought well in the battles at Lova and Buonconforto and, at the same time, laid plans with Pietro Paolo Crivelli, at the urging of Doge Andrea Contarini, to overthrow Francesco il Vecchio and become the new lord of Padua. But the plot was uncovered and those captured condemned to death.[93] Marsilio fled to Venice, and Niccolò took sanctuary in the bishop's palace.

Making Peace with Venice, 1373–1376

The Venetian victory at Buonconforto, with the capture of many Paduans and Hungarians held for ransom in Venice, made peace imperative. Among the prisoners were King Louis's own nephew Stephen, voivode of Transylvania, and thirty Hungarian nobles; the Paduans included the knights Bonzanello da Vignoza and Negro de' Negri.[94] With the Hungarians threatening mutiny and demanding the release of the voivode, Francesco il Vecchio moved swiftly to come to terms with Venetian demands. The terms of peace were only slightly better than those offered six months earlier.[95] A commission of five Venetian nobles was empowered to determine boundary disputes within three months. It was finally agreed not to include within Venetian domains the traditional Paduan strongholds at Cittadella, Solagna, and Camposampiero to the north, Stiano, Mirano, and Castelcarro on the eastern frontier, and Borgoforte and Anguillara on the Adige. The tower at Curan, however, was to remain in Venetian hands, and Francesco il Vecchio was forbidden to construct any fortifications within 7 miles of the lagoon and ordered to raze strongholds at Oriago, Portonuovo, and Castelcarro and forts at Bassano, Camposampiero, Stiano, Mirano, and elsewhere on the frontier. The older pacts on Venice's salt monopoly and freedom of commerce in the Padovano were to be observed, and Francesco il Vecchio was charged with bringing Louis of Hungary to the peace negotiations. The dukes of Austria had already agreed to peace with Venice, retaining their newly acquired towns and strongholds in the Valsugana and the upper Piave. The commune and lord of Padua had to pay reparations of 250,000 ducats, with 40,000 due immediately and the rest paid over fifteen years at the rate of 14,000 ducats per annum. Most humiliating were the requirement of admission of war guilt before the doge in Venice and guaranteeing the Paduan property of the traitor Marsilio da Carrara. On 21 September peace was proclaimed, and ten days later Francesco Novello, accompanied by an ailing and frail Francesco Petrarca, went to Venice to acknowledge the Carrara lord's guilt for the recent war. On 2 October before doge and Maggior Consiglio, Petrarch made in a trembling voice a brief speech, praising the recent peace and calling for the reestablishment of friendship between the two states. Taking as his text the tag from Terence "the quarrels of lovers are the renewal of love," Petrarch preached the identity of interests of the two cities and the need for peace in Christendom.[96]

Several of the peace terms were difficult to fulfill. With his treasury exhausted by the costs of war, Francesco il Vecchio turned to his old allies, Florence, Hungary, and the papacy, for aid in paying the indemnity Venice had exacted. On 19 October, the Florentine government voted "to pay and to return to the magnificent and outstanding knight lord Francesco qd. Giacomo da Carrara, dominator of the city of Padua, or to lend and have lent to him up to 20,000 gold florins." The loan, which was to be interest-free, was apparently to be repaid by the Carrara lord at his earliest convenience.[97] The next spring, the border commission, made up of five Venetian patricians, established the new boundaries between the two states in a detailed report, largely setting frontiers at some distance from the lagoon as stipulated in the treaty of September 1373.[98] In April, Francesco il Vecchio's vicar Antonio Zecchi appointed two proctors to collect all debts owed the lord of Padua in Friuli and all other parts of the world, no doubt to help replenish a depleted treasury.[99] That summer the king of Hungary lent Francesco il Vecchio and the commune of Padua 14,000 ducats for the first installment of the annual indemnity owed to Venice as set forth in the treaty. The bulk of the loan came through the Paduan merchant Giacomo Saraceno, resident in Buda, as an official of King Louis.[100] On 1 August, Pope Gregory XI ordered his vicar general to return to Francesco il Vecchio a loan of 15,000 ducats, probably to help the Carrara lord meet payment of the huge indemnity.[101]

The Carrara regime had to prepare for demobilization and dismissal of contingents of its mercenary army. The sudden end of hostilities left virtually stranded in Padua a group of English knights under the leadership of Hugh qd. Edward Despencer, thus probably the grandson of Hugh Despencer the Younger (d. 1326). Staying at the Hospicium Angeli in contrada S. Lucia near the Carrara Reggia in late October, six knights received advances for a total of 900 ducats from a Pisan agent of Sir John Hawkwood, which enabled them to settle their debts in Padua before joining the English mercenary company in papal service that autumn. The six soldiers, identified in the documents by name, surname, and diocese, were John Haveringen of Lincoln, William Howard of Wincester, Guillaume de Brabant of Cambresis, John Atwood of Exeter, John Sherman of York, and William Norduç (perhaps Northwood) of Norwich. The advances enabled the six unemployed knights to pay off their debts for room and board in Padua, thus escaping threat of a term in debtors' prison, before joining Hawkwood in his campaigns against the Visconti.[102] The next March, the group was apparently still in Hawkwood's employ, since Hugh Despencer, temporarily back in Padua at the Hospicium Angeli, received another advance, this one for 1,700 ducats, from Andrea qd. Pace da Arezzo, Hawkwood's proctor at Bologna, to be repaid at Michaelmas (29 September 1374) in Venice.[103] As late as August 1374, Francesco il Vecchio was still trying to collect debts from Italian mercenaries employed in the recent war. In his residence in the presence of Zanino da Peraga, Arsendino Arsendi of Forlì, and Gugli-

Seeking Other Allies

elmo Curtarolo, the Carrara lord appointed Giacomo Magneto of Imola his proctor to collect loans of 100 ducats and more than £150 advanced to mercenaries mainly from Bologna and Emilia.[104] That autumn Francesco il Vecchio improved relations with Cansignorio della Scala, lord of Verona and Vicenza, by agreeing to a treaty of extradition between the two states.[105]

In the winter of 1373, Francesco il Vecchio's half brothers again plotted to seize the lordship of Padua. From his sanctuary in the Duomo in November, gathering followers for the conspiracy, Niccolò da Carrara granted life income on properties in Valbona and Guzzi to a certain Fiora Poliavolo and her husband, Pariano, for services to be rendered in the future.[106] After Christmas that year, Niccolò and his illegitimate half brother Bonifacio da Carrara, abbot of Praglia, together with Alvise Forzatè and his son Filippino, made another unsuccessful attempt on Francesco il Vecchio's life. This time the Forzatè were captured and executed, and Niccolò and Bonifacio were imprisoned for life in the Rocca at Monselice. Marsilio da Carrara and a few conspirators escaped to the relative security of his residence in Venice.[107] Feeling horror and dread at the attempted assassination, Francesco il Vecchio complained to Petrarch of the existence of such evil in the world. Dwelling on a favorite theme of Heraclitean flux, in a brief letter Petrarch mused on the ironies of life, including evil in a universe ruled by a benevolent God. Crediting evil to the working of the devil and the perversity of men, Petrarch reminded the Carrara lord of the many times brother had risen up against brother, son against father, servant against master, forgetful of past favors and benefits. Petrarch warned Francesco to be watchful over his courtiers and subjects but to stand before his people unfrightened and unbowed, committed only to those whose fidelity was proven. Assuring the lord of Padua that God kept watch over righteous men, Petrarch expressed the wish that he had been helpful not just with his prayers but also with his advice.[108]

More useful still in overcoming the memory of defeat in war and near death from conspiracy were public tournaments held early in 1374 in Padua between teams bearing the Paduan and Carrara colors of red and white. Competing for prizes of plumed caps gilded with gold or silver bestowed by Donzella da Carrara, Arcoano da Buzzacarini, the lord's brother-in-law and champion for the Reds, won the gold cap, while Giovanni da Rodi got the silver.[109] In March, Carrara favorites, including Boscarino Buzzacarini and Negro de' Negri, welcomed Francesco il Vecchio's candidate for

FIG. 14 *(opposite)*. Altichiero, Portrait of the Aged Petrarch in His Study. *Sala dei Giganti, Carrara Reggia, Padua, 1375. Reproduced with permission of the Biblioteca Civica, Padua*

bishop of Padua, Raimondo Ganimberti, to the city. Early in April Francesco il Vecchio attempted to exact vengeance against his treacherous half brother, sending into Venice Carrara agents instructed to murder Marsilio. The principal would-be assassin, Gherardo da Trambacche, was arrested, tried before the Quarantia, and sentenced to three years in prison. The Carrara official behind the plot, Francesco Turchetto, escaped, but he was tried *in absentia* and sentenced to perpetual exile from Venice and blinding if seized in Venetian dominions.[110] Shortly thereafter, Francesco il Vecchio lodged before the Senate a complaint of mistreatment by members of Marsilio's household, which was referred by a close vote to the Avogadori di Comun for investigation.[111] The traitor Marsilio da Carrara continued to enjoy the income from his Paduan properties as provided in the treaty of September 1373, much to the consternation of his half brother and sworn enemy Francesco il Vecchio.[112]

The next year, as Florence led a rebellion against the pope, Francesco il Vecchio was forced to chose sides between his Guelf ally, Florence, Pope Gregory XI, and, ultimately, his sometime protector and sometime enemy Venice. In a sharply worded letter of 25 January 1375, Pope Gregory damned the Florentines for their new alliance with the perfidious tyrant Bernabò Visconti and demanded that the Carrara lord send troops to aid the papal vicar Guillaume Noellet in the defense of Bologna and surrounding territory.[113] Padua remained neutral in the burgeoning conflict, scarcely responding to Florence's request in September to help enlist the aid of Louis of Hungary in the newly forged Florentine-Visconti alliance.[114] Rather, Francesco il Vecchio was intent on forging a marriage alliance of his own, informing in August the lord of Verona, Cansignorio della Scala, of negotiations to marry his only legitimate son, Francesco Novello, to Taddea d'Este, daughter of the ruler of Ferrara, Niccolò II.[115] The ambitions of the dukes of Austria to control Friuli and the Veneto soon, however, brought the Carrara lord to Venice's defense for the last time as a reluctant ally.

In the spring of 1376, at the head of a force of three thousand lances, Duke Leopold descended the Piave, penetrating the pass at Quero and causing damage to Venetian dominions in the Trevisano. Venice responded by sending troops to defend its *terraferma* possessions and, in May, ambassadors to Padua to demand more energetic opposition of Leopold's raids as required in the peace of September 1373. The Senate also dispatched Pietro qd. Marco Giustinian and Francesco Corner to the Carrara court to remind the Paduan lord and commune of their treaty obligations against the dukes, thanking Francesco il Vecchio for keeping provisions out of Austrian hands, detailing hostile actions in the Trevisano, informing him of an embassy to Verona to procure more troops, requesting intelligence on Austrian troop movements, and assuring him of Venetian successes against the enemy. Later that month, in response to the duke of Austria's threat that Padua should remain neutral or suffer dire consequences, the Senate instructed its envoys to inform Francesco il Vecchio of its effort to enlist Sir John Hawkwood and his company in the Venetian forces, thus assuring Venice of success in arms.[116] Eventually Venice was able to persuade Francesco il Vecchio, lukewarm at best in his opposition to the dukes of Austria, to join the Venetian cause: on 9 July the Carrara lord responded to the doge's demands by appointing three of his most trusted officials, Bonifacio Lupi, Arsendino Arsendi, and Antonio Zecchi, as ambassadors to conclude a league with Venice against the dukes of Austria. Ten days later the Great Council of the commune of Padua, acting through the podestà, Rizzardo da Sambonifacio, confirmed the appointment of the same three envoys to conclude the league.[117]

On 6 August, after tough negotiations, a league was formed between the lord and commune of Padua and the doge and commune of Venice. As it happened, after several months of discussion, Sir John Hawkwood, who was in the pay of Florence, refused to enter Venetian service.[118] Only a few mercenary companies from the Romagna enlisted in the Venetian forces; instead, the Carrara lord was required to provide four hundred lances and three hundred infantry to join Venetian troops in the conflict in the Trevisano. In addition, the Paduans were to guard the passages at Quero and Scalon against Austrian attack. Padua could retain any strongholds recovered in the Valsugana, while Venice was to have Belluno and Feltre, if these towns were won back from the Austrians. Since the closure of the pass at Scalon had cut Padua off from its usual supplies of animals, timber, iron, and pitch, Venice agreed to provide these at a fair price with only nominal duties levied. Padua agreed to make no separate peace, and Venice promised to prevent its troops from inflicting any damages on Paduan territory. Finally, the doge and commune of Venice pledged "to hold and regard the said lord of Padua, and his son and state as intimate sons, true and pure friends, and as their good neighbors, and [treat them] favorably, benignly, and without any rancor."[119] This was virtually the last time the Venetian government would address the lord of Padua with such condescension. Through the mediation of Louis of Hungary a truce was arranged in November, and peace came briefly to the Veneto.[120] Soon Padua joined a coalition of states which dealt Venice its severest test in the conflict that came to be known as the War of Chioggia.

Chapter 5

Signorial Government and Carrara Wealth

Haud verebor . . . senioris Francisci urbanas laudes supponere qui, suscepto Padue sceptro, menis urbis supplevit, vacua spatia domibus constructis ornavit, artes auxit, lanificinam induxit, civium facultates promovit, studia literarum unice excoluit.

[I do not hesitate to add . . . the urban accomplishments of Francesco il Vecchio, who after taking over the rule of Padua completed the city's walls, adorned the empty spaces with houses, encouraged the guilds, promoted the woolen industry, increased the prosperity of the citizens, and fostered the study of literature to a great degree.]

—Giovanni Conversini, *Dragmalogia*

In the years following the advent of the Black Death in July 1348 and the assassination of Giacomo II da Carrara in December 1350, the lord of Padua faced two large sets of problems: one economic, the other administrative. He had to rebuild the local economy, especially the woolen industry, consolidate his own holdings in land and interests in manufacturing and banking, and, at the same time, create an efficient household government to rule at home and further his relations abroad with the pope, the emperor, the king of Hungary, and the states of Italy. An important first step toward restoring Padua as a commercial center was the promulgation of a series of statutes in 1352 defining the relation between foreign and local merchants and providing speedy, impartial justice in case of litigation. To ensure speedier trials, suits among merchants were moved from the judge at Vetteveglia to the vicar of the *podestà*, where sworn testimony would be held as valid and cases settled summarily, as the legal formula had it, "sine strepitu et figura iudicii." These new statutes gave foreign merchants in Padua greater rights. Now foreign merchants could sue Paduan debtors in the local courts with the same standing as native citizens. Any controversies arising from such suits were to be settled by consultation with two or three local merchants, expert in such questions. To prevent frivolous or malicious suits, any merchants falsely bringing actions had to pay all court costs. Final interpretation of these procedures was reserved for the Carrara lord or those appointed by him.[1] In general, the streamlined procedures worked: foreign merchants, especially from Florence, Lucca, Parma, and the cities of Emilia, settled in great numbers in Padua during the next decades, bringing new capital, complex commercial networks, and advanced techniques to the business life of the city.

The Early Carrara Household

In 1350 the brother and eldest son of Giacomo II inherited a complex of buildings, the Reggia, and small staff of household officials near the city center. In the 1350s, Francesco il Vecchio moved his consort, Fina Buzzacarini, into a new palace for women of the court, the Palazzo di Levante on the eastern edge of the complex. Here were born three daughters, Gigliola, Caterina, and Lieta, whose marriages brought alliances with several ruling houses of central Europe: the duke of Saxony, the count of Veglia, and the count of Ortenburg, respectively. On 29 May 1359 was born the heir apparent, Francesco Junior, who was soon groomed for the lordship of Padua. At the age of four the young Francesco began the study of Italian and Latin grammar under Simone di Maceri of Parma and was later instructed in German, the language of his father's mercenary captains, by one Lunardo Rothegnanz. Education in arms and chivalry was provided by famous knights of the Carrara court, especially Simon Lupi of Parma and Bernardo Scolari of Florence, while Niccolò Beccari of Ferrara tutored the young heir in Italian verse and Provençal literature.[2] Thus, the young Carrara lord received instruction in languages, literature, and war, to fit him for success at court and on the field of battle.

Newcomers as well as natives were important in staffing the household government that was being elaborated in the Carrara Reggia early in the regime of Giacomino and Francesco da Carrara. The chief officers serving the Carrara lords were a pair of vicars, both trained in law and skillful diplomats, the native Paduan Giacomo da Santa Croce and Bartolomeo Piacentini of Parma. The son of a local notary, Giacomo da Santa Croce was admitted to the College of Judges in 1338 and served in the communal judiciary and as adviser to Giacomo II before assuming the post of vicar by February 1351. In this role, the jurist became a fixture in the Carrara chancery, witnessing, for example, the lords' bestowal of Paduan citizenship on Leonizio Piacentini, brother of the other vicar, Bartolomeo, and serving as judge delegate to settle suits among members of the ruling elite. By 1353, Giacomo da Santa Croce had emerged as one of the most influential and

Francesco il Vecchio

FIG. 15. *Loggia of Carrara Reggia, Padua. The First Carrara Palace constructed by Ubertino da Carrara. Reproduced with permission of Alinari/Art Resource, New York*

prestigious jurists and statesmen in Padua, earning the privilege of Venetian citizenship for himself and his heirs. Until his death in 1372, Giacomo da Santa Croce often served the lord and commune of Padua as an envoy to Venice, the king of Hungary, and the pope.

Bartolomeo Piacentini was one of several immigrants with legal training who came from Parma to Padua to serve in the communal government, working in the court of the podestà Giovanni Gradenigo of Venice from

Signorial Government and Carrara Wealth

TABLE 5.1
The Carrara III. Francesco il Vecchio's Legitimate Offspring

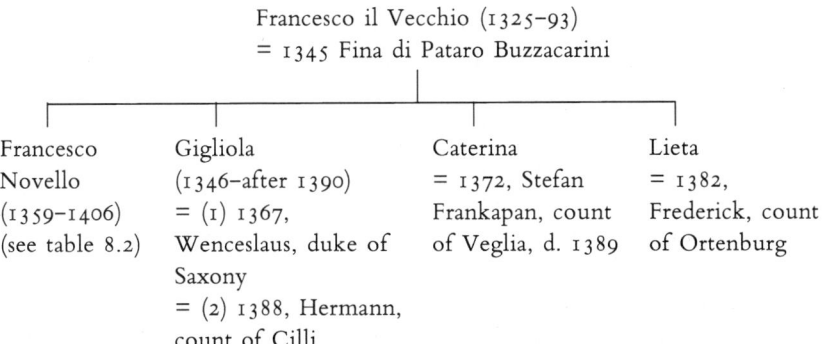

March 1342 to August 1343. Thereafter he gravitated to university circles, serving as witness and sponsor in several examinations for the doctorate in civil law. As early as 1347 he appeared as vicar in the Carrara household, witnessing in the Camera Nerone in the Reggia Giacomo II's grant to a member of the Lion family and serving as his adviser in settling the dispute between the rectors and doctors of the university. Piacentini also served the dynasty as a diplomat on embassies to Venice, Louis of Hungary, Bernabò Visconti, and Pope Urban V until he left Carrara service shortly after 1373.[3] Neither vicar handled the daily paperwork of the nascent Carrara chancery. In the early 1350s that task fell to Nicoletto d'Alessio from Capodistria, in the post of scribe. Born in 1320 and trained as a notary, Nicoletto worked in the ducal chancery until he was implicated in plotting his native city's uprising against Venice. On 29 December 1349 he was sentenced to eight years in prison for his part in the rebellion, but through the intercession of Cardinal Gui de Boulogne, he was released and went to Padua six months later.[4] By 1354 he was listed as a scribe in the Carrara court. Later promoted to the post of prothonotary in 1360, he served the regime until his death in 1393.

To these judicial and administrative positions were soon added financial posts. A brief, ambiguous notice from October 1351 names a merchant from Lucca, Guidone di Collacio Paganelli, as "residing in Padua in contrada S. Bartolomeo, to bring into being a fund of the Carrara lords" [ad faciendum facere montam [sic] dominorum de Carraria].[5] This is perhaps a reference to the establishment of a funded debt of the Carrara regime. As we shall see, by the time of the Border War of 1372–73 forced loans (*prestiti*) became a standard method of financing military conflict. The office handling contracts with mercenaries (*camera stipendiariorum*) was staffed by local notable Nascimbene Grompo in October 1354.[6] Grompo, who died only three years later and left two young sons, Pietro and Ubertino, who became soldiers in the Carrara army, had extensive holdings in the southwest of the Padovano, including farms in Villa Estense and Urbana, as well as seven houses in Padua.[7] Hence, the first curial official to enlist and supervise the mercenaries of the Carrara army was himself a man of substance, perhaps skilled in military affairs. Soon joining the Carrara household were a treasurer, Jacopino Gaffarello, comptroller (*massaro*) Solimano da Ponte, and three economic officials, usually called factors, who oversaw Carrara landed and business interests: Giovanni Naseri of Montagnana, Luca da Casale, and Paolo Dotti. The articulation of departments and accounts became complex enough to call for, in 1357, the first known annual accounting of the household government, drawn up by a notary in the Carrara chancery, Pietro Saraceno.

Here the notary Saraceno redacted a balance sheet compiled by the Carrara treasurer, Jacopino Gaffarello, for the Carrara lord's revenues and expenditures for the year 1357. This account provides a rare glimpse into the composition and offices of the Carrara household and relative cost of various departments and activities only two years after Francesco il Vecchio assumed sole control of the *signoria* of Padua. The budget is analyzed according to the categories employed by Gaffarello and other financial officers of the Carrara household.

Expenditures were divided into three major groups. Extraordinary expenses for diplomacy, war, and mercenaries, both in outlays and gifts (*largiti*), came to £29,000. Provisioning of the household totaled £13,500 in payments and gifts. Payments to individual accounts, which included the household departments of consumption, for wine from the cellarer, woolens, linen and silk cloth, leather goods, and goldwork came to nearly £13,500, and expenditures for armor, horses, and falcons amounted to nearly £2,700. In addition, £4,500 was paid to the "account of the ladies," the expenses of the household maintained by the lord's consort, Fina, with her ladies-in-waiting, children, and servants in the Palazzo di Levante. In all likelihood, Francesco il Vecchio had chosen to remain in Ubertino's old palace while his consort set up her own household on the eastern side of the complex.

Under income the first item was lump payments of twelve *bullete* (probably administrative orders-to-pay) made at £3,000 each month by the lord's *massaro*, a druggist and banker named Solimano da Ponte, for a total of £36,000. From the account of extraordinary income came an equal amount of just over £36,000, while another £14,000 came from accounts of different persons. Nearly £1,000 of income came from interest on deposits

TABLE 5.2
Balance Sheet of the Carrara Household, 1357

	£ s. d.	Ducats
Expenditures		
Sum of money paid out by Lord Jacopino	21,024. 3. 4	1,765
For purveyance	2,444. 5. 8	
Sum of grants for extraordinary items	4,954. 7. 4	1,115
Sum of grants for the lord's purveyance	11,054. 6. 6	
Sum of outlay to the extraordinary account	587. 5. 8	
Sum of outlay to the account of the cellarers	1,501. 7. 0	
Individual consumption accounts		
For woolen cloth (*pannorum de lana*)	4,725.12. 8	
For account of linen cloth (*pannorum de lino*)	502. 1. 2	
For account of leather and furs (*pellium et varorum*)	2,151.10.10	
For account of silk and fabrics (*sete et cendati*)	1,649.19. 0	
For the goldsmiths' account (*aurificum*)	1,971. 0. 5	
For the ladies' account [Fina's household]	4,585. 5. 4	
For the account of arms (*armorum*)	1,216. 5. 8	
For the account of falcons (*falconum*)	595.15. 0	
For the account of horses (*equorum*)	887.12. 3	
Total	59,852. 7.10	2,880
Revenues		
Cash on hand at beginning of year	2,948.17. 4	145
From Ser Solimano, Carrara *massaro*, 12 *bullete*	36,000. 0. 0	
From Ser Solimano, *de extraordinariis*	36,279.18. 0	496
From several other persons	14,119. 8. 8	1,207
From interest on loans	986.13. 6	
Total Revenue	90,334.17. 6	1,848
Balance: Revenue over expenditures	30,482. 9. 8	(1,031)
Loss in ducats expressed in lire (70s. per ducat)	−3,612	
Net receipts for 1357	26,870. 9. 8	

Source: AN, 256, fols. 61–62 = Papafava, 4:124–27, for 1357

the Carrara lord had with various bankers (*campsores*). The precise source of much of the income is hard to interpret. As the lord's massaro, Solimano was probably responsible for receiving income from the vast Carrara estates and interests in the woolen industry, which he conveyed for household expenses in monthly chits of £3,000. In any case, Solimano prospered in his banking house in *contrada* S. Andrea until his death about 1373. His

FIG. 16. Guariento, Angel Blessing Pilgrim and Poor Beggar. *Chapel, Carrara Reggia, Padua. Reproduced with permission of the Museo Civico, Padua*

Signorial Government and Carrara Wealth

TABLE 5.3
Assets and Cash on Hand, Carrara Household, 1357

	£ s. d.	Ducats
Interest income from bank deposits	7,300. 0. 0	710
Income assigned from the account for 1356	4,760.10.10	420
Income assigned from the account for 1357	23,464.19. 0	1,765
Surplus in cash from balance sheet of 1357	26,870. 9. 8	
Sum of all money in possession of Jacopino in cash and debts (*in denariis et debitoribus*)	62,395.19. 6	2,895
Sum of ducats expressed in lire (70s. per ducat)	10,132.10. 0	
Grand total in lire	72,528. 9. 6	

Source: AN, 256, fol. 262r, 1357.

son Arimondo married Jacopa, daughter of famed scientist Giovanni Dondi dall'Orologio. When Arimondo died intestate in 1393, the required inventory showed him to be one of the wealthiest bankers in Padua, with houses and extensive property in the city, Este, and the Euganean Hills as well as more than nine hundred accounts with local citizens.[8] Thus, very early the Carrara lord employed successful entrepreneurs from Padua's merchant class to oversee his financial interests.

In 1357, the Carrara signoria was clearly solvent. An annual income of £90,000, with £63,000 in expenditures, produced a hefty surplus of nearly £27,000. The treasurer went beyond these accounts to calculate the sum of all money in possession of the regime's treasurer at the end of 1357. These resources fall into four categories. First was "the interest from balances and debtors consigned" [pro restis sive debitoribus consignatis] to the treasurer, Jacopino Gaffarello. Second was the income assigned to the treasurer from the accounting for 1357, and third, the income for 1357. Finally, from the balance sheet analyzed above (from table 5.2), the sum of nearly £27,000 was assigned as cash on hand. The total assets of the regime from these four sources came to just over £72,500, counting both cash and credit for debts owed to the lord of Padua.

Carrara Investments

Among the sources of income noted above was interest from a number of deposits that the Carrara lord had with *campsores* in Padua and occasionally in Venice. In the shifting alliances of the second half of the Trecento, Francesco il Vecchio often bought allies and sweetened friendships by making interest-free loans to foreign powers, such as Louis of Hungary, Florence, Lucca, Zara, Belluno, and Trieste. Closer to home the Carrara lord made money from interest by depositing cash with local bankers. The interest payments were usually disguised in the form of a penalty to be paid when there was no prompt restitution of the loan. Occasionally interest charges were hidden by falsifying the amount of the loan, with the amount stated in the contract to be repaid larger than the amount of money actually deposited.[9] During the first two decades of his regime Francesco il Vecchio deposited more than £140,000 with various Paduan moneylenders and bankers, with the largest single deposit, £90,000, made with the local Jewish banker Padovano da Pozzoveggiano early in 1372.[10] Although Francesco il Vecchio did business with both Christian and Jewish bankers, he was particularly welcoming to the local Jewish business community, which resided largely in contrada S. Canziano. In time of plague in 1384 he permitted local Jews to establish a cemetery in nearby contrada S. Leonardo.[11] The latter half of Francesco il Vecchio's rule saw few loans, except for political purposes, since almost all liquid revenues went toward payment of the indemnities imposed by Venice at the conclusion of the Border War of 1372–73 and the Peace of Turin in 1381.

The Carrara lord made other investments that were more profitable and stimulating to the Paduan economy than short-term deposits with moneylenders. One of his overriding concerns, typical of the age, was to ensure the economic autarky of the city and district of Padua, expressed in sufficiency of foodstuffs, especially grain for the urban population, and of raw materials for the textile industry for internal consumption as well as export. As early as 1346 the Carrara lord had established his grain warehouse (Fondaco delle Biave) in contrada S. Canziano to the east of the Salone, under the direction of Francesco qd. Giacomo Salgeri, who was later to become prior of the Casa di Dio.[12] The Fondaco delle Biave is mentioned at the same location in documents from 1365, 1369, 1377, and 1379, when the notary Salimbene Zennari is listed as the head official.[13] Here the Carrara lord stockpiled grain, especially wheat, which was used to feed the local populace and sold to friendly powers in time of famine to win alliances to the political arena.

The lord of Padua's principal economic interest was in textiles, especially in promoting the manufacturing and sale of woolen cloth. As we have seen, Ubertino da Carrara brought Florentine engineers to Padua in the 1340s to construct fulling mills at Ponte Corvo and Torricelle. At that time, most of the woolens traded in Padua were imported from Florence and north of the Alps, with finished woolens from Flanders and serge from Scotland especially prized. Paduan textile manufacturing was limited to linens and mixed woolen and hemp cloths (*panni greggi*). In 1346, Giacomo II was already encouraging local manufacturing, appointing a Paduan merchant, Giacomo di Ser Niccolò detto Terrazzo, to advance capital, partly in wool, partly in cash, of £800 to a woolen entrepreneur, one Alberto qd. Francesco a Lana.[14] Ten years later, the woolen cloth warehouse of the Lord of Padua (Fondaco dei Panni del Signore) was established in contrada Duomo just south of the Reggia, under the direction of Marco qd. Francesco Resta of Milan. There in July 1356 three major local merchants and sometime Carrara officials, Giovanni qd. Ansedesio da Casale, Gualperto Cetto, and Giovanni Naseri of Montagnana, acknowledged having received a loan of £3,000 made by the *fondacario* Marco Resta in the name of Francesco il Vecchio, of which £2,669 5s. had already been received in cash and wool from the recently deceased *fondacario*, one Giacomo Torlone.[15] More than two years later, the Carrara factor Paolo Dotti acknowledged receipt from Gualperto Cetto of the final £1,000 due on this loan, which had been made to promote woolen manufacturing.[16] Later in the summer of 1356, the lord of Padua helped a recent Veronese immigrant, a *lanaro* named Fioremonte di Benasuti, acquire a fulling mill at Terranegra outside Ponte Corvo with a loan of £140 made through his *fondacario*, Marco Resta.[17] In addition to lending capital to woolen entrepreneurs, the Carrara lord provided housing for favored immigrants. For example, in 1358 he bestowed in perpetuity by fief a house in contrada Duomo on the Tuscan wool merchant Giovanni detto Vannozzo, father of the future court poet Francesco di Vannozzo, for faithful services rendered to the Carrara regime.[18]

In the next few years, the lord of Padua made even more concerted efforts in support of the industry to attract workers and artisans to his city. At Christmas in 1359, in order to replenish the population of the city and district of Padua diminished by the plague, the Carrara lord granted amnesty to all exiles who would present themselves at the Court of Aquila by the end of April, promise to remain in the city or *contado* for at least three years, and pay a nominal amount (5 percent) of any outstanding fine.[19] The next year, Francesco il Vecchio named one Francesco qd. Panino Spinelli da Terranegra and his heirs for life to the position of broker for the wool guild of Padua. This official was charged with inspecting and recording all sales and purchases of textiles in the city. After posting a security in the communal treasury (*canipa*) and being registered in the communal chancery, the broker had to record all transactions concerning textiles, both finished cloth and raw materials, within three days of the sale. Thus, every textile sale or purchase was to be registered so costs would be verified in case merchandise was returned or a foreign merchant bought cloth for future retail sale. Any fraud by the broker was subject to a fine of £50, and any sale of cloth not registered with the broker resulted in a fine of one lira for the merchant.[20]

Rates set for the broker document the types of textiles manufactured in Padua in 1360. Along with cloth of pure wool, half-wool and coarse cloths (*panni greggi*) were also produced, as well as cotton and linen cloths.

Still concerned with attracting skilled workers for the Paduan textile industries, on 25 October 1362 the lord of Padua extended and defined privileges for wool merchants and workers, including weavers, spinners (both male and female), fullers, and shearers, who would come to ply their trades.[21] Since these rights had been explicitly granted to all who had migrated to Padua during the past sixteen years, the decree was probably only a confirmation of existing statutes. In any case, benefits conferred on immigrants in the textile industry were great, including exemption from taxes, duty-free importation of raw wool and materials, such as dyes used in manufacturing, and exportation of finished cloth free of any customs, provided it had been inspected and tagged in the lord's Fondaco dei Panni. Immigrants were granted the privileges of Paduan citizenship, which enabled them to make purchases, sales, and contracts and enjoy immunity from arrest for debts contracted in other jurisdictions, except for treaties of extradition between Venice and Padua. Legal disputes were to be decided swiftly before the rector of the wool guild, Francesco Falconetti of Florence, "lest [the immigrants] be troubled with hardships and expenses" [ut expensis et laboribus non graventur]. This clearly enlarged the jurisdiction of the wool guild, though difficult cases could be settled by appeal to a Carrara official, Francesco detto Checcho Lion or Bartolomeo Piacentini. To ensure cheap housing for immigrants, landlords were forbidden to evict tenants for any reason, except nonpayment of rent and use of the dwelling as their own residence.

The strategy of privileges for immigrants, loans to entrepreneurs, and quality production of textiles for the local market had its desired effect: the membership of the wool guild grew, as did the profits the Carrara lord derived from his central warehouse.[22] The earliest surviving matriculation list of the wool guild, made a generation later in 1393, shows 122 members, of whom half (61) are from Padua and at least 16 from the towns of the contado. Of the remaining 45 members, 10 came from Florence, 5 each from Milan and Vicenza, and 4 each from Parma, Treviso, and Venice. Thus, six cities account for two-thirds of the matriculants of foreign origin, while the remaining 13 foreigners hailed from other cities of northeast Italy: Bergamo, Cremona, Feltre, Mantua, Udine, and Verona.[23] By 1375 the Fondaco dei Panni had been removed from near the Duomo to contrada S. Martino, surrounded by other commercial property owned by the Carrara lord.

Francesco il Vecchio's concern for the economic well-being of Paduan guildsmen extended to retail merchants, such as the butchers' guild. Meeting in chapter in early July 1361, the butchers of Padua voted 49 to 13 to appoint one of their number, Antonio detto Radico Becari qd. Zordano, to petition Luca da Casale, acting as factor for Francesco il Vecchio, to lease them a large slaughterhouse abutting the city walls in contrada S. Andrea. Two weeks later in the Carrara chancery, with Solimano da Ponte, Simeone dagli Statuti, and Luca da Casale looking on as witnesses, Giovanni Naseri, acting as agent for Francesco il Vecchio, rented the butchers' guild a slaughterhouse for dressing and selling meat for £420 a year.[24] Four years later, Giovanni Naseri, again acting as factor for the Carrara lord, renewed the lease on the Beccaria Nova in contrada S. Andrea for an annual rent of £410 and 200 pounds of tallow at Christmas.[25] At the same time, Francesco il Vecchio leased half of the old slaughterhouse (now vacant) to a grocer in contrada S. Clemente for £40 a year. But a few years later the Carrara lord found a new favorite tenant for the old slaughterhouse, forcing the grocer to renounce his lease and renting the property to a weaver for the same rent, thus promoting the manufacture of woolens at the expense of a local retailer.[26] Finally, in 1376, to protect his monopoly and perhaps limit pollution from the refuse of slaughtering draining into the canals surrounding Padua, Francesco il Vecchio decreed that there could be no butcher shops except in the Beccaria Nova at S. Andrea and ten other locations near the gates of the city walls.[27] The Carrara lord also promoted the sale of other products, such as skins, furs, and hides, and the manufacturing of other goods, such as ironware, through favorable decrees and generous leases.[28]

Flax, Fish, and Agriculture

Early in his rule, Francesco il Vecchio promoted the production of linen as well as the woolen industry and retail trades. As ruler of Padua and its imperial vicar, the Carrara lord had jurisdiction over the waterways of the Padovano, including the authority to grant licenses (expressed in the form of fiefs) to fish the streams and to ret and scutch flax. Throughout the summer of 1357, Paolo Dotti, as factor for the Carrara lord, granted to some seventeen landowners and eight linen makers fiefs to soak and beat flax in the branches of the Bacchiglione surrounding Padua at Ponte S. Niccolò and on the Vigenzone and Brenta Canals in the southeast part of the Padovano.[29] The local landowners, who included such Carrara favorites as Fulcone, Gian Enrico and Niccolò Capodivacca, Gualperto Cetto, Tebaldo Engleschi, Alvise Forzatè, Giovanni Andrea Sanguinacci, and Corrado Zacchi, usually held their fief of a *vadum maserandum* (soaking pit) in return for a pledge of fealty and nominal dues in game, a brace of partridges in August or quail at Christmas. These notables, important members of the Carrara affinity, enjoyed the right to charge flax growers for the privilege of using the *vadum* to soak sheaves of flax preparatory to beating them to separate the linen fibers from the woody core.[30] About ten grants were made to Paduan linen makers, usually residing at Terranegra, Ponte Corvo, and Ponte S. Niccolò, with the right to charge others "one bundle of flax for each sheaf" [una faglia lini pro quolibet faxo] in return for cash rents.[31] Francesco il Vecchio also invested in the nascent linseed oil industry: for £900 on 8 May 1360 the lord of Padua, through his factor Paolo Dotti, sold 192 *moggi*, 8 *staia* of flaxseed to one Rizzardo qd. Giacomo of contrada S. Massimo.[32]

Beginning in the summer of 1367, Francesco il Vecchio used his status as imperial vicar to grant commercial fishermen the right to fish the streams and rivers of the Padovano. That August Emperor Charles IV granted to Francesco il Vecchio and his son all imperial possessions in the Padovano, and at that time the lords of Padua bestowed in thirty fiefs the right to fish in specific localities.[33] Most of the grants were made in the center of Carrara influence on the Vigenzone and Bacchiglione in return for the annual gift of a large trout or carp delivered to the Carrara Reggia during Lent, and especially at Holy Week, and a pair of kid gloves at Christmas. In a grant of July 1368, when the Carrara lord's factor Giovanni Naseri invested a certain fisherman of contrada Ponte Peochioso to fish the Vigenzone from Battaglia to the salt point, the imperial basis for the authority was made explicit: "by virtue of the law and right given by the Most Serene Lord Emperor and his predecessors to the aforesaid Lord and the forebears of his house."[34] At least eight other fiefs were granted or renewed to fishermen over the next few years, each grant requiring the delivery of a large trout to the Carrara refectory during Lent.[35] Although most fiefs of fishing rights required payment in kind, perhaps sufficient to feed the Reggia's staff during Lent, on one occasion the right to fish the Bacchiglione from Gorgo to the lagoon was granted for money rent of £135.[36]

This minute concern over fishing rights demonstrates just how dependent the Carrara regime was on local agriculture and the products of field and stream. Despite his deposits with bankers and interests in the woolen industry and commercial property in Padua, Francesco il Vecchio remained essentially a landed nobleman, feeding his urban household with the products of his rural villages. An analysis of the leases and purchases of farmland, vineyards, and homesteads made between 1356 and 1372 demonstrates that although Francesco il Vecchio owned property throughout the Padovano and beyond, his landed wealth was concentrated in the family's country seat south of Padua.[37] Initially Carrara investment stretched even into the Vicentino, where, in 1362, Francesco il Vecchio and his three half brothers leased nearly two hundred homesteads and parcels of farmland to sharecroppers in the village of S. Giovanni Ilarione west of Vicenza for about £500 in cash and much produce, with the tithes in the same village sold to the Florentine merchant resident in Vicenza, Filippo qd. Nero Pegolotti.[38] But typically leases to sharecroppers were closer to home. That same summer the Carrara lord and his half brothers leased nearly three hundred parcels scattered in dozens of villages throughout the northern Padovano to scores of sharecroppers for perhaps £1,000 in money rent and half of the crops delivered in Padua.[39] In 1367, the Carrara lord leased seventeen parcels at Lozzo and the frontier castle of Valbona to local peasants for money rent and half of the grain crop and chickens.[40] And his land could yield more than grain, vegetables, and poultry. In October 1368, the lord of Padua, through his factor Giovanni Naseri, leased a forest on seventy *campi* for £1,020 per annum with the stipulation that all timbering had to be completed by the next April and the cutters had to practice basic conservation by leaving standing four trees per *campo*.[41]

Typical of exploitation of peasants in the Carrara lord's villages was a series of *livelli* made to peasants in Bovolenta, 12 kilometers southeast of Padua.[42] The lord's manager (*gastaldo*) in Bovolenta made some twenty-three separate contracts with local peasants for plots of about 1 hectare each for average annual rents of £10–15, with gifts (*onori*) of hens due at Shrovetide or ducks at All Saints. This typical village of thatched wooden houses lining the main village street practiced an intensive mixed agriculture of grain, vineyards, gardening, and poultry raising. In the year 1372 the Carrara lord earned nearly £300 in cash as well as hens, ducks, and cockerels for his household from the rents in Bovolenta.

The lord's consort, Fina Buzzacarini, joined her husband in investing heavily in agriculture in the Padovano. Utilizing her father's deathbed *donatio inter vivos* of nearly £6,000 made in January 1361, Fina purchased fourteen parcels of mainly arable land, hedged with vines and fruit trees, in Arzercavalli and nearby Ponte Casale from Manfredino Conti and his son Engolfo. The purchase also included seven farmhouses with sheds and barns on more than 150 *campi*. In this small village near Piove di Sacco, Fina already held considerable land and often used her father's gift to buy parcels contiguous with her own to develop large blocks that could be cultivated more efficiently.[43] Fina's farming interests continued to be centered in three villages to the east and south of Padua: Noventa, Brugine, and Arzercavalli. Fina increased and consolidated her holdings through purchases or exchanges with her husband or brother. For example, in 1368 she received from Francesco il Vecchio nearly 1,000 *campi* in 156 parcels and a mill in Noventa in return for granting him 2,000 ducats and 1,014 *campi* in 158 parcels in Ar-

zercavalli and Braida.⁴⁴ Additional purchases were made in 1370: on 8 June Fina bought for £503 more than 25 *campi* in three parcels in Noventa, and that same day she acquired two large parcels in Noventa, granting in exchange four plots in Villa Rosta to her brother, Arcoano Buzzacarini.⁴⁵ On 4 July Fina bought two parcels in Noventa from Bartolomeo, *preco* of the communal government, and at Christmas in 1370 lent nearly £150 to her sharecroppers in Arquà for seed for spring planting of legumes and barley.⁴⁶ In January 1371 she leased for five years a house in Padua near the Benedictine convent of S. Agata to the linen worker Biagio Scadelato and his son for an annual rent of £40 and a pound each of wax and pepper at Christmas.⁴⁷ That spring she enlarged her holdings in Noventa by exchanging parcels with her husband and purchased more than 40 *campi* from one Simone da Noventa, taking possession of these properties through her agent Alberto Figario that May.⁴⁸ That June Fina bought for £2,410 sixteen parcels of arable in Piove di Sacco from Anna, daughter of Bonaventura Pasini, and her husband, Francesco Corte, and in March 1372, she filled in some blocks in Brugine buying for £200 4 *campi* from Caterina, wife of Giovanni di Prato, residing in contrada S. Giuliana.⁴⁹ But the outbreak of war between Venice and Padua that summer brought an end to Fina's acquisitions of land, as it did her husband's. Indeed, the war and subsequent indemnity demanded by Venice nearly bankrupted the Carrara regime in Padua.

Household Government after 1373

At the conclusion of the Border War on 14 September 1373, the financial situation was grave enough to require an accounting of the indebtedness caused by the costs of the conflict. Gone was the surplus of nearly £27,000 of 1357. Expenditures driven by the war with Venice had increased more than tenfold, from £60,000 to well over £800,000 per annum.

Thus, this account of 17 September 1373 closed with the unbalanced entry called "Old and New Prestiti in the hands of the Treasurer" for £1,802,911 plus 1,244 ducats. Subtracting £750,000 for total loans outstanding on 25 December 1372 means that £1,062,389 (or 295,108 ducats) of new in-

FIG. 17 (*opposite, top*). *Castello Carrarese, Valbona. Constructed by Francesco il Vecchio to guard the Vicentine frontier of the Padovano, located just to the west of the Euganean Hills. Photograph courtesy of Tracy Cooper*

FIG. 18 (*opposite, bottom*). *Tower of Carrara Castle at S. Pelagio. Francesco il Vecchio built strongholds like this one at S. Pelagio, a few kilometers from the family seat at Carrara. Photograph courtesy of Tracy Cooper*

TABLE 5.4
Extraordinary Borrowing and Expenditures of the Carrara Regime in 1373
(25 December 1372–14 September 1373, in lire)

State of Debt Administration on 25 December 1372	
Cash on hand	82,808
Borrowing	
Old *prestiti*	547,351
Other *prestiti*	197,802
Total	827,961
Expenditures	
Purchases of real estate	3,202
Gifts	1,085
Other expenses (mainly for war)	815,816
Total	820,103
State of Debt Administration on 14 September 1373	
Balance (entered as cash on hand)	7,858
Old and new *prestiti*	1,802,911 plus 1,244 ducats (£4,478 at 72s. per ducat), or 1,807,389 total.

Source: AN, 33, fols. 424r–25r, 14, 17 Sept. 1373.

debtedness was contracted during the nine intervening months. The total indebtedness of the regime at the end of the Border War (the last figure in table 5.4) stood at just over 1.8 million lire, or over half a million ducats. By way of comparison, Venice's public debt in 1373 has been estimated at 6 million lire a grossi, or about 2.3 million ducats, and Florence's indebtedness in 1367 has been estimated at 1.25 million florins (roughly equal to ducats). By contrast, Lucca's public debt in 1375 stood at only 90,000 florins.[50] For the rest of the century, the reality of crushing indebtedness would be a constant in Padua under the Carrara lords. One method of reducing indebtedness and meeting the indemnity required by Venice was to levy an annual lump-sum assessment on major guilds in Padua. A memorandum inserted in the notarial cartulary of Giovanni della Stuva lists several guilds with annual payments in ducats due to the Carrara lord, probably in 1375. The assessments, in descending order, were on the following guilds: wool, 700 ducats; notaries, 600; priests of the cathedral, 500; College of Judges, Lawyers, and Jurist Doctors, 450; merchants, 200; druggists, 125; parish priests (*fratalea cappellanorum*), 100; and town criers (*precones*), 27, for a total levy of 2,702 ducats.[51]

By the end of the Border War with Venice, the Carrara household government had grown enormously. Like other Italian *signori,* the Carrara regime saw the rise of a class of professional administrators, continued lavish building in the Reggia, and the melding of private and public office and finances, as we have seen in Carrara accounts plotting the costs of war and diplomacy. Alongside the informal Carrara affinity composed of kin, affines, and close friends, both natives and newcomers, carrying out the duties of war and diplomacy, a household staff of professional administrators headed the chief offices of the signorial regime.[52] The most important of these were the lord's legal advisers, his vicars. As we have seen, Francesco il Vecchio had inherited from his father's regime a pair of loyal and learned law professors, Giacomo da Santa Croce, who died in 1372, and Bartolomeo Piacentini, who left Padua about the same time. The lord of Padua replaced these men with another skilled jurist, Giovanni Salgardi, who had migrated from Feltre to serve first as assessor and then vicar to the podestà in the late 1350s and then stayed to oversee the massive task of revising the communal statutes in 1362.[53] Serving often as vice-podestà during the next decades, Salgardi had an intimate knowledge of Paduan law and experience serving on embassies for the Carrara lord, which made him a natural successor as vicar. Even after fifteen years in Padua, Salgardi continued to acquire property in the Feltrino, buying several farmsteads there for £800 in 1372.[54] Francesco il Vecchio put his vicar's standing in the Alpine towns to good stead the next year, appointing Salgardi his proctor to consign Belluno and Feltre to the dukes of Austria at the conclusion of the war with Venice. Just three years later Salgardi undertook an even more dangerous mission that was to cost him his life: in 1376 he was decapitated on the orders of the dukes of Austria for attempting to bribe local notables in Belluno to return the city to Carrara rule.

Succeeding Salgardi was another foreign jurist, Antonio Zecchi, who had migrated from Moncalieri in Piedmont to receive Paduan citizenship from the lord of Padua in May 1371 before he joined the staff of the new podestà, Federico Lavellongo, that fall.[55] Zecchi served the lord and commune of Padua often as an ambassador during the War of Chioggia, returning to his native region as one of three Paduan envoys to negotiate the Peace of Turin in the summer of 1381. Following his father, Manuele, as count palatine, Zecchi appears often in Paduan records from 1374 to 1386 creating notaries and legitimating bastards, no doubt often extending these privileges at the Carrara lord's command. Distinguished service brought its rewards: soon after arriving in Padua, Antonio Zecchi had accumulated enough capital to make several loans in places as distant as Genoa, Lucca, and Bassano, and by 1380 his elder son, Grisolfo, had been appointed to a canonry at the Duomo.[56] Shortly before the first fall of the Carrara, Antonio Zecchi dropped from the records, and he had definitely died by August 1392.[57]

After the vicar, the most constant fixture at the court of Francesco il Vecchio was Nicoletto d'Alessio, variously called scribe, protoscribe, or prothonotary, who functioned as head of the chancery. Many important documents survive in his own hand, suggesting that he personally redacted much of the correspondence and acts of appointment, procuration, and privileges of the regime. His major vernacular chronicle on the Border War with Venice is full, detailed, and accurate, based on many official documents, now lost, and contains dialect versions of the lord's letters and field orders. By early 1371, Nicoletto was residing in contrada Pozzo Mendoso, and two of his sons, Pandolfo Guidone and Carlo, were already enrolled as students of canon law in the *studium*. By October 1378, his son Carlo, though still a minor under his father's *potestas,* had become prior of the Hospital of S. Daniele in Padua.[58] In 1382, Nicoletto leased for five years a rich farmstead of 22 *campi* of arable and vineyard in the Paduan *campanea* at Brusegana, yielding annually hens and chickens as *onori,* five *moggi* of wheat, and cash rent of £45. Two years later Nicoletto finally severed his ties with Capodistria, appointing on 20 June 1384 his brother Giovanni to rent all his property there, consisting of farms, houses, woods, and meadows.[59] The next year, Nicoletto's long and faithful service to the Carrara lord was rewarded with the grant of a large two-story stone house, with well, court, and garden in contrada Pozzo Mendoso, leased for the nominal dues of a pair of gloves at Christmas.[60] By this time several scribes had formed Nicoletto d'Alessio's staff in the work of redacting documents in the Carrara chancery.

A document from the summer of 1374 lists three scribes, all notaries, employed in the Carrara chancery—Enrico qd. Antonio Rabatta, Marco qd. Niccolò Guarnerini, and Pasquale qd. Bernardo Berini.[61] The most important notary in the chancery in the early years of Francesco il Vecchio's rule was Pietro Saraceno of contrada Pozzo Campione, who redacted many of the contracts of purchase, lease, and sale affecting Carrara landed wealth from 1349 until his death in about 1371.[62] He was succeeded by the notary Giovanni da Campolongo, resident in contrada S. Margherita, who joined the Carrara chancery in 1369 and redacted two stout volumes of acts over the next decade.[63] The major chancery notary for the final third of the century was the native Paduan Bandino Brazzi, son of the notary Angelo, who first appeared in the communal judiciary in 1364, moved to the Carrara chancery in 1370, and served the regime as ambassador in 1383 and perhaps

Signorial Government and Carrara Wealth

as chancellor in 1395.[64] By 1369 Marco Guarnerini, resident in nearby contrada S. Lucia, was employed in the chancery and within the next decade had acquired farmland in Este and made a *soceda* contract for five years with a peasant from Corte.[65] Another major Carrara notary was Zilio Calvi, son of the notary Facino from Montagnana, who began working in 1370 in the commune's Officio della Bolleta before moving to the Carrara chancery a decade later.[66]

Our knowledge of Carrara business interests and household organization largely rests on the surviving records of these five notaries, since the records kept by each household unit have unfortunately been lost or destroyed. But notarial documents mention several account books, once in use, which provide some sense of the record-keeping practices of the Carrara household. For example, in March 1364, reference was made to a "Liber catasti possessionis Domini," which was a survey of all Carrara real estate, and in 1370, Pietro Saraceno noted that he had recorded Fina da Carrara's purchases from Engolfo qd. Manfredino Conti in a "Liber imbreviturarum Domini," which contained in a single volume Carrara rents and business transactions.[67] That same year, in the Carrara chancery, in a document involving a widow's wardship, there appears the phrase "ad substinendum honera dicte custodie sicut in dicto libro apparet"—thus referring to a Book of Wards probably kept there.[68] In February 1375, the general factor Giacomo Turchetto ordered Bandino Brazzi to record payments of grain from Carrara estates in a "liber descriptionis bladorum," apparently a master list of grain deliveries to the Fondaco delle Biave in Padua.[69] Finally, the Carrara lords maintained careful records of one of their chief prerogatives, the creation of new Paduan citizens, in a volume (now lost) kept by Nicoletto d'Alessio in the chancery.

Also serving in the household government was the treasurer, Jacopino Gaffarello, residing by 1358 on the north side of the Reggia in contrada S. Niccolò. Gaffarello compiled annual accounts redacted by court notaries on two occasions: in 1357 by Pietro Saraceno and at the conclusion of the Border War in September 1373 by Bandino Brazzi. In addition, during that war he served on several embassies and was even held as a hostage in Venice in 1373, a guarantor for the safety of Taddeo Giustinian, captive in Hungary.[70] But during his absence, the task of overseeing vast sums proved too tempting for Gaffarello's associate, Giacomo dall'Olio, "olim thesaurius et massarius domini" [the lord's former treasurer and comptroller], who absconded that May with £67,975, "which money said Giacomo had received over what he paid out according to the accountings of the Treasury of the said magnificent lord." In June 1374, three Carrara officials, Francesco Turchetto, Luca da Casale, and Baldo Bacanzani, caught up with Giacomo and his brother Francesco in exile in the home of the captain of Vicenza, Nicola Cavalli, and demanded the Dall'Olio brothers return the embezzled funds.[71] Although the brothers admitted they had received a large overpayment from the Carrara gastaldo at Camposampiero, it took nearly three years to recover a portion of the missing funds. Meeting at the Della Scala palace in Verona, a new Paduan envoy, the law professor Valerano Lambardi of Cetona (who was later to serve as podestà of Padua, in 1385), got the two brothers to pay back 22,187 in lire and 10,000 in ducats.[72] Jacopino Gaffarello continued to be a trusted member of the Carrara household. In June 1374, he bought from a Venetian noble, Pietro Lando, for under 400 ducats more than 400 *campi* of arable, pasture, and woodland near the Brenta.[73] Acquiring property in the eastern Padovano at Torre in 1371 and at Villa Estense in 1380, Gaffarello lived near the Reggia as a rentier, enjoying income in kind and cash from his farms and dabbling in moneylending until the end of his life in 1387.[74]

Life in the Carrara Reggia

Life in the Carrara court was divided between the great public functions held in the Hall of the Illustrious Men, the daily administration carried out in Ubertino's palace, the quarters of soldiers and servants with stables for their horses, and a segregated consort's household, a "gendered" space to ensure the safety of the women of the court. In her later years, Fina Buzzacarini created a miniature female court in the Palazzo di Levante on the eastern edge of the complex. There she entertained in a grand chamber decorated with personifications of the four virtues—Justice, Wisdom, Temperance, and Courage—and there in September 1378 she dictated her last testament, a revealing document of the values and affection of the Carrara lord's consort. Fina was a woman of great piety, and her interests in death, as in life, centered on three concerns: family, friends and servants, and religion.[75] In her testament she provided handsomely (with endowments of 6,000 ducats each) for her married daughters, consorts of the duke of Saxony and count of Veglia, and an equal amount for the still unmarried third daughter, Lieta. Other largess in the form of gifts for dowries went to the young ladies-in-waiting she had assembled in her household. She bequeathed more than £8,000 in dowries to young women of the Arsendi, Capodivacca, Dotti, Festucci, Costabile, and Zabarella families, as well as lesser sums as pensions for her servants. Other grants of £200 were made for marrying daughters of the managers (gastaldi) of her villages of Noventa, Brugine, and Arzercavalli. Pious endowments were made for decorating the Chapel of S. Lodovico in the convent of S. Benedetto, where her sis-

FIG. 19. *Carrara stemma representing the four cardinal virtues. From a treatise of moral philosophy by Francesco Caronelli,* De curru carrariensi, *composed at Padua in the 1370s and dedicated to Francesco il Vecchio. Source: Bibliothèque Nationale, Paris, MS Latin 6468, fol. 9v. Reproduced with permission of the Bibliothèque Nationale, Paris*

ter Anna Buzzacarini was abbess, and for the churches of S. Michele and S. Maria dei Servi and the Baptistery, where she was to be buried. Her universal heir was her son, the heir apparent to the lordship of Padua, Francesco Novello. Although her husband, Francesco il Vecchio, was named executor, he received nothing from Fina's estate. His callous philandering had apparently cost Fina much mental anguish, even to the point of forcing her to rear one of his own illegitimate daughters, a Margherita da Carrara, who received in the will the modest bequest of £100 for the good of her own soul. Besides her patronage of family and religion, Fina earned her own immortality in Paduan art. In the Baptistery where she was buried, Fina commissioned Giusto de' Menabuoi to depict her both in a votive portrait and with her three daughters as onlookers in a scene of the birth of John the Baptist. Here she was buried with great pomp in October 1378.

As we have seen, Francesco il Vecchio supplied part of the foodstuffs for the Reggia from the produce of his rural holdings, especially grain stored in his *fondaco*, and legumes, poultry, game, and fish delivered as *onori* on holidays. The growth of bureaucratic and military staff in the 1370s required greater and more reliable sources of provisions. In the spring of 1375 factor general Naimiero Conti contracted for three years with two local butchers to provide annually to the Reggia's kitchens 6,000 pounds of salt meat and lard and 5,000 pounds of soft cheese at the price of 3s. 4d. per pound. Thus, each year the Carrara staff consumed about 5,357 kilograms (nearly 6 tons) of this food. The same day, Conti made another contract for food, engaging two butchers in contrada S. Lucia to provide three types of "fresh meat from the Beccaria for the lord's court" [carnem frischam a Becaria pro curia domini] at 22d. per pound. One-third was to be milk-fed veal (presumably for the lord's table), one-third was called (vaguely) "meat sufficient for soldiers" [carnem sufficientem a milite], and the last third was "coarse meat, fat or lean, for the household" [carnem grossam, grassam et magram, pro familia]. The Carrara factor promised to buy at least £1,000 of these provisions annually, delivered in lots of 500 pounds (233 kilograms), costing about £45 per lot. To ensure the ready supply of this fresh meat, the butchers were permitted to graze their herds just outside the southwest walls of the city between Porta Trinità and Saracinesca and at Porta S. Croce.[76] Later that summer near the Salone at his *dazio* office for wine on tap, Naimiero Conti contracted for provisioning the Carrara household with a poulterer named Femerina Pinarollo, who agreed to supply a reasonable quantity of fowl for the next two years, delivered in lots of forty pairs of hens at 14s. a pair and sixty pairs of chickens at 5s. a pair. The Carrara officials were to give her eight days' notice prior to each delivery, and Femerina readily agreed to deliver another hundred pairs of hens each year at the Carrara palace on

FIG. 20. *Giusto de' Menabuoi, portraits of Fina da Carrara and her daughters. Baptistery, west wall. Photograph courtesy of the Soprintendenza di Belle Arti per il Veneto*

Campo S. Polo in Venice. Significantly, Femerina was free to move about the Reggia "without armed guards" [asenta a costodibus], suggesting that outsiders were normally escorted within the complex.[77]

As the staff and size of the Reggia grew, so did the hazards of court life, as Giovanni Conversini da Ravenna revealed in his treatise on life at the Carrara court a few years later. Discharged from his teaching post in Belluno, Conversini arrived in Padua at the height of the Chioggia war in the summer of 1379. Here he struck up a friendship with the Latin teacher Carletto Galmarelli, who resided just to the north of the Reggia in contrada S. Agnese, and was soon introduced to the lord of Padua himself. The intermediary was another immigrant to Padua, Montorso qd. Guglielmo Montorso, who in 1374 had acted as the Carrara lord's proctor for a loan of 300 ducats to Andrea qd. Francesco of Cittadella and his brother, Francesco, archpriest of Ferrara. Three years later Montorso began to acquire farmland in the contado, with the lord's backing, and by 1380 Montorso was a significant figure in the eastern Padovano, where he was appointed in the Carrara chancery to settle disputes arising from injurious words and blows between men of Fiesso near the lagoon.[78] An inscription, placed in S. Niccolò in 1383, records the Carrara lord's grant of a nearby residence to Montorso, described as "an attendant nurtured from a tender age in the same [lord's] court."[79]

As Conversini records in his intimate account of his first stay at the Carrara court, Francesco il Vecchio took an instant liking to the young scholar, insisting that he accompany him everywhere. Trying to explain why he eventually left the Carrara court, Conversini emphasized the humiliating aspects of such personal service to the lord: often at court he would be required to explain passages of the Bible and the meaning of Mass heard in the Reggia's chapel, fan the lord in the heat of the siesta and massage his feet and thighs, read to him and listen to his innermost thoughts, dress and undress him, attend him while he played at dice in the evening, and eventually, exhausted from the day's toil, put the lord of Padua to bed.[80] In compensation for such service, Conversini received the use of a house leased by the lord, annual allotments of wine, salt pork, provisions, and firewood, biannual gifts of clothing and money, and 10 ducats a month salary. In addition, he was entitled to two meals at the lord's *mensa*: fowl or boiled meat with sauce, loaves, and two flasks of wine at dinner in late morning, and the same meal with roast meat for supper at sundown.[81]

But the lord's familiarity and generosity evoked jealousy from the other courtiers, and, through their machinations, Conversini's rations were at times reduced or canceled. Even taking into account the author's biases and special pleading, there emerges a disturbing portrait of corruption and abuse at the Carrara court. The chief villain was the majordomo, Niccolò Curtarolo, who, as the general factor for the lord, oversaw the acquisition and distribution of foodstuffs, provisions, and money from Carrara estates and contracts. His chief assistant was Manfredo Crescenzio, who, as head of the *camera massarie,* supervised household accounts and expenditures. Crescenzio first appeared during the Chioggia war, when he purchased for 18 ducats a small boat, equipped with sails and oars, from three infantry captains, probably to transport soldiers and supplies to the front. By March 1382, he was already in the *camera massarie,* witnessing the transfer of 70 marks to the mint, and later that summer bestowed a dowry of £800 on Agnese Crescenzio, daughter of his recently deceased brother, Antonio.[82] Other courtiers who attempted to help Conversini through the confusing maze of court politics included Marsilio da Brescia, Antonio Polastro, and Biagio Ovetari, all subsequently economic officials for Francesco il Vecchio or his son.[83] In their attempts to mollify Conversini's complaints, Curtarolo and the other courtiers offered several type of rewards. Conversini's friends at court pleaded for fair treatment from the butcher Gaiardo of Ponte dei Tadi, who served as purveyor of meat to the Carrara refectory.[84] But Gaiardo blamed his superior, the majordomo, for the orders suspending the rations. When complaints of mistreatment reached the Carrara lord, Niccolò Curtarolo attempted to make amends, dangling typical rewards for courtiers before Conversini: appointment of his young son, Israele, then five, to a canonry; the offer of a dilapidated house on the Piazza dei Signori, extorted from a Paduan named Papino on his deathbed, and, shortly after the death of Conversini's second wife, the offer of a new wealthy bride handpicked by Francesco il Vecchio himself.[85] In the end Conversini rejected all compensations the Carrara court could offer—meals in the refectory, provisions and salary, an ecclesiastical living for his son, a home for his family, even a woman for himself—and left Padua for Venice, vowing to celebrate the Carrara dynasty in his future works.

The household that Conversini left behind in 1382 was complex, elaborated and articulated as a result of the demands of the Chioggia war. A number of distinct offices had now emerged. At the top stood the vicar, a jurist steeped in issues of international law and diplomacy, aided by the chancellor, Nicoletto d'Alessio, who employed several scribes trained to redact various types of letters and instruments of diplomacy. In fact, at precisely this period the Carrara regime developed a formulary, which contained nearly one hundred form letters for use in every possible occasion.[86] The treasury, headed by the *referendario* (treasurer) Francesco Turchetto, included specialized officials to staff the lord's loan office, enroll mercenaries for the army, and oversee and audit the accounts. Chief of the several economic

TABLE 5.5
Organization of the Carrara Household, 1380

Legal	Diplomatic	Financial	Economic
Vicar	Chancery	Treasury	Factors general
Antonio	Nicoletto d'Alessio	Francesco	Niccolò Curtarolo and
Zecchi	and scribes	Turchetto	Manfredino Conti
	Curial notaries	Referendario	Fondaco dei Panni
		Accountants	Camera Massarie
		Camera Expendarie	Camera laboreriorum
		Office of Merce-	Grain Office
		naries	Mint
		Loan Office notaries	notaries

officers was Niccolò Curtarolo, often styled factor general, who with Manfredo Crescenzio supervised the household accounts in the *camera massarie;* other officials headed the Grain Office, the cloth warehouse, and the mint.

The Mint under Francesco il Vecchio

At the beginning of the War of Chioggia, Francesco il Vecchio asserted his sovereignty and dominion by minting a series of coins, from a gold ducat to the penny, but he concentrated on the production of two silver coins, the *carrarese* and *carrarino,* worth 4 and 2 *soldi,* respectively. Supplied with a great quantity of bullion by King Louis of Hungary in the autumn of 1378, the Carrara lord flooded Venice and the eastern Veneto with his new coins, the *soldino* with a *carro,* the symbol of the dynasty, on the obverse and a cross and PADVA on the reverse. In addition, he minted the *carrarino,* with the *carro* framed by the legend FRANCISCVS DE CARARIA on the obverse, bearing the effigy of one of two patron saints, with the legend of either S. PROSDOCIMVS or SANCTVS DANIEL on the reverse.

An assay of the coins issued for the Carrara mint, located in contrada S. Lorenzo near other commercial establishments including the Fondaco dei Panni, shows production in January 1379 of 1,300 marks of *carrarini* made by the moneyer Giovanni qd. Canzelerio Malempensa. Each mark was to yield *carrarini* valued at £23 7s. of 0.946 fineness, since a mark of silver used contained 62 carats of dross (*tenet caratos sexaginta duos pejus fine pro Marcho*), and each mark weighed 1,152 carats (1,152 − 1,090/1,152 = 0.946). Next, samples of 1,000 marks of pennies of 75 percent fineness were assayed, and both coins were approved as "sound, legal and sufficient" [bonas, legales, et sufficientes] by the examining committee of six, composed of two rep-

Signorial Government and Carrara Wealth

FIG. 21. Carrarini *of* 2 soldi, *minted by Francesco il Vecchio. Obverse, cart (*carro*) in circle flanked on each side by an* F, *and surrounded by legend* FRANCISCI. DE. CARRARIA. *Reverse,* S. Prosdocimo *standing with miter and nimbus, with right hand raised in act of benediction and left hand holding crozier, surrounded by legend* S. PROS–DOCIMUS. *Reproduced with permission of the Museo Bottacin of the Musei Civici, Padua*

resentatives from the moneychangers guild (*fratalea campsorum*), two from the goldsmiths guild, and two "good men" representing the commune of Padua.[87] The new Paduan coins that flooded Venice at the beginning of the war drew a prompt reaction from the Senate, which on 18 January decreed that all coins bearing the *carro* circulating in the city had to be exchanged at the mint within one month for sound local coins; thereafter, all Paduan coins still in circulation would be confiscated, with the holder suffering the loss. The reason for the Senate's action is readily explained. At the height of the Chioggia war, the debased *carrarino* (of 0.946 fineness) competed with various issues of the Venetian *soldini* (0.958 fine for the *soldino da leone* and 0.955 for the *vecchi*) and threatened to drive the somewhat "heavier" Venetian coins from the marketplace.[88] In May Venice countered by minting a new *soldino* of reduced weight and reintroduced the *grosso*. But the Carrara lord continued to mint coins, creating during the next decade sufficient coinage for his expanded dominions and gaining additional income from seigniorage at his mint.

Early in 1381, the lord's economic officials, headed by his *gestor* (agent), Lodovico Paradisi da Capodivacca, contracted with a Florentine moneyer, Niccolò qd. Bartolomeo Compagni, to manufacture *carrarini* at the rate of 1,000 marks per month, melting down and recoining Hungarian and Venetian *soldi* from the Carrara dominions. Permitting dross of 64 carats per mark (with tolerance of 4 carats), each mark contained 1,088 carats of pure silver (thus 0.944 fineness). For each mark the minters were to pay £21 12s. and produce coins valued at £23 8s., with a margin of 36s. per mark for seigniorage and manufacturing costs. Profit of 24s. 6d. per mark was specified as the lord of Padua's seigniorage, while Niccolò Compagni and his staff received 11s. 6d. per mark as brassage for their labor. Thus, seigniorage per month for Francesco il Vecchio came to £1,225 (1,000 × 24.5s.); the mo-

FIG. 22. *Two views of upper die for striking* carrarini *in Francesco il Vecchio's mint. The upper die, called the punch die or* borsello, *was used in the Carrara mint in the 1380s to make* carrarini da due soldi. *The view of the top shows the obverse of the* carrarino, *which is also pictured in figure 21. Reproduced with permission of the Museo Bottacin of the Musei Civici, Padua*

neyers received for their labor £575 per month (1,000 × 11.5s.), and total monthly production amounted to £21,600 (1,000 × £21 12s.). Since the contract was to run for the next twelve months, the annual value of coins produced was to be £259,200, with the Carrara lord receiving £14,700 in seigniorage and Niccolò Compagni £6,900 in brassage. In addition, Compagni, his family, and craftsmen were to work and reside rent-free in the large house designated as the mint in contrada S. Lorenzo, enjoying exemption from local taxes, while agreeing to make coins exclusively for the Carrara lord. The next March, Lodovico Paradisi, as factor for the lord of Padua, renewed the contract for minting *carrarini*, with Niccolò Compagni now involving his brother Nerio in the work. The two brothers agreed to manufacture 700 marks of *carrarini* (at fineness of 0.944) per month, again acquiring the silver at £21 12s. per mark and producing *carrarini* valued at £23 8s., thus assuring a profit of 36s. per mark. This time Francesco il Vecchio received only 21s. per mark in seigniorage, while the Compagni brothers got 15s. per mark in brassage. Thus, the *carrarini* made each month were worth £15,200, while the lord's seigniorage came to £735 and the

Signorial Government and Carrara Wealth

TABLE 5.6
Output of the Carrara Mint, 1381–1383

Year	Marks (per month)	Value of Carrarini (£ per annum)	Seigniorage (£ per annum)	Moneyer's Income (£ per annum)
1381–82	1,000	259,200	14,700	6,900
1382–83	700	181,440	8,820	6,300

moneyers' income to £525 a month.[89] The output of the Carrara mint for the biennium February 1381 to March 1383 is shown in table 5.6.

Records of later assays of the weight and fineness of coins produced at the Carrara mint show changes in personnel: on 8 January 1384, in contrada S. Lorenzo, "in domo ubi fabricatur moneta," Lodovico Paradisi, now styled factor general for Francesco il Vecchio, made an assay of 1,400 marks, valued at £23 8s. per mark, of new *carrarini*—of these, Nerio Compagni had made *carrarini* from 1,343 marks, while Carlo da Genova had manufactured coins from the remaining 57 marks—showing the usual 1,088 carats of silver per mark (or 0.944 fineness). An assay of 619 marks of new *carrarini* taken that summer showed that now Carlo da Genova had turned 600 marks into *carrarini*, while the Compagni brothers had made *carrarini* from only 19 marks. At both assays were present the six representatives of guilds of moneylenders and goldsmiths and the commune with a host of local merchants as well as Benedetto Girlandi da Siena, vicar for the new podestà, Marino Memmo of Venice, and the Carrara lord's officials, the factor general Lodovico Paradisi da Capodivacca, the mintmaster, Bartolomeo di Salvo Malacri of Piacenza, and the lord's purveyor (*spenditore*) Antonio Pavanello.[90] The entire business and political community had a stake in the creation of reliable Paduan coinage.

Francesco il Vecchio's expansion of his dominions with the purchase of Treviso in 1384 and later acquisition of Belluno, Ceneda, and towns in Friuli meant a wider scope for circulation of coins produced by the Carrara mint. In August 1384, he proclaimed a monopoly for Paduan coinage, especially *carrarini, carraresi,* and *soldini* in the Trevisano, banning Hungarian issues from circulation, requiring the sale of the Venetian *soldino* at 10 Paduan *denari*, and setting the value of the ducat at 73 *soldi*. The next March Francesco directed his officials in the new territories to announce the issue of a new *carrarese* valued at 4 *soldi*, which was to circulate with the established Paduan coinage.[91] Throughout 1386, Francesco refined his monetary policy in the new dominions. On 18 June he proclaimed a monopoly for Paduan coinage in

Belluno, offering to acquire the banned foreign issues at a fair rate, and on 27 June decreed that only Paduan silver coinage could be used in Belluno, except that foreign merchants could use in trade Hungarian and Venetian *soldi,* which were then to be exchanged at 10 *denari* for the Venetian and 8 for the Hungarian *soldino.* Responding in July to petitions for representatives from Belluno, the Carrara lord declared that Hungarian coins could not circulate in the area, while setting the value of the Venetian *soldino* at 10 *denari* and the ducat at 73 *soldi.*[92] The creation of a currency monopoly in the new dominions had its desired effect: immense quantities of Hungarian and Venetian silver coins came to Padua to be recoined at the Carrara mint, with the lord of Padua taking a hefty seigniorage of 5 percent with each issue.

Early in 1386 Francesco il Vecchio appointed the merchant entrepreneur Milano di Jacomelli Malabarba as governor of the Carrara mint. A summary of accounts drawn up late in 1388, the last year of Carrara domination in the Trevisano, by the regime's head accountant, Matteo da Ferrara, provides details of mint operations for the two years of Milano's tenure. The account shows that the mint's chief function was recoinage: to assay and melt down Venetian and Hungarian silver coins, mainly *soldini* and *grossi,* and even the *Friesacher* from Friuli, and to mint new silver coins in Paduan denominations.[93] The first task was to mint large numbers of *carrarini:* between July 1386 and March 1387, the Carrara mint received from the Paduan lord's Citadel near S. Tommaso 20,869 marks of pure silver, which were minted as *carrarini* valued at £520,000. But most of the old coinage to be reissued came from the Carrara treasury located in the Stuveta in the Reggia, while some quantities of silver came from the Carrara lord's vault (simply called "Volto" in the account). In all, 47,276 marks of silver, worth £24 each, were issued as *carrarini,* for a total value of £1,137,824, while the total value of *carraresi* minted was given as £2,110,858. Issues of billon coins, *quattrini* worth 4 pence each, amounted to £183,526, for a grand total of more than £3.4 million in coins. If Francesco il Vecchio continued to take seigniorage of about 5 percent as he had in the contracts with the Compagni moneyers, his income from the mint for these two years was more than £175,000.

Changes in Government: Padua and the Case of Cittadella

The capital event in the definition of the communal government of Padua under the Carrara was the compilation of the revised code of municipal statutes ordered by Francesco il Vecchio in 1362. As we have seen, in 1339 extensive new legislation under the podestà Marino Falier redefined the formal communal government at the beginning of Ubertino da Carrara's lordship over Padua. Only two decades later Francesco il Vecchio commissioned his learned vicar from Feltre, the jurist Giovanni Salgardi, to issue a thoroughly revised statutory code, incorporating the most useful legislation from the early Trecento (including Falier's) and reflecting the realities of communal government under an increasingly powerful lord. In some respects, however, the new code was conservative, adhering to the established format of four books used in communal statutes throughout the cities of northern Italy. Thus, the first book defined the structure of government, the powers of the podestà and his "family," and the nature of communal offices. The second book provided detailed rules for the administration of civil justice, procedures, and contract, and the third treated criminal justice and the regulation of industry, guilds, and commerce. The fourth book encompassed public works in the city and gave in detail the obligations of the villages of the contado for the maintenance of roads, canals, dikes, and bridges, as well as legislation on taxes, citizenship, and scholarly privileges.[94] The greater authority of the Carrara lord in these statutes was manifested in several ways, but nowhere more clearly than in the hierarchy of the sources defining the podestà's responsibility to dispense justice. The podestà had to render justice first "according to the form of the statutes and ordinances of the commune of Padua, and where they are lacking according to the form of the Roman law, and the good and ancient customs of the city of Padua." To this hierarchy of written statutes, Roman law, and local customs was added at once the qualification: "And more or less with changes and exceptions according to the pleasure and will of the lord himself."[95] Thus, the Carrara lord could intervene to alter the administration of justice even of his handpicked podestà. But in practice this rarely happened, though as focus of final appeal, the lord, his vicars, or judges delegate did render judgments above the system of communal courts. And, as we have seen, Francesco il Vecchio often dispensed communal statutes, for example, to permit foreigners or religious houses to acquire property in Padua or allow wives and husbands in dire necessity to spend dowries. Another sign of signorial authority was a new statute that provided that ambassadors chosen by the lord could also legally represent the commune, thus placing the conduct of diplomacy more firmly under the control of the lord and his chancery.[96]

Despite the arduous undertaking of compiling a new, up-to-date code, additional legislation and modifications of existing statutes continued to be enacted after 1362, especially under the podestà Simone Lupi in 1366, Federico Lavellongo in 1372, and Jacopo Rangoni in 1375. Many of the new statutes corrected problems in civil procedure or modified rules governing taxes, measures, landownership, and citizenship, no doubt adjustments made in response to new needs and opportunities. In 1372 the crisis of an impending border war with Venice prompted creation of a new set of communal officials: four *deputati ad utilia,* who were charged to work with the podestà to ensure that wells were kept safe, streets and walls maintained, and derelict houses repaired or torn down. Because of the possibility of fire and attack, the *deputati* had to see that ladders, hooks, and axes were available, requiring the massaro of each *centenari* to keep inventories of these tools. Thus, the Carrara created a group of citizen leaders to aid in the defense of the city, perhaps creating for the first time the *deputati ad utilia* that became a standard office early in the Quattrocento.[97] But the Carrara lord's requirements of defense and cooperation extended most of all to the walled towns of the Padovano.

Constructed in the early thirteenth century as a walled bastion guarding the Trevisan frontier, Cittadella was the largest town of the Oltrebrenta, assessed in the 1362 statutes at 225 hearths for the road, bridge, and canal repairs. Although the commune of Cittadella received its first written statutes only in 1387, adapting those of Montagnana composed twenty years earlier, the communal government was already in place by the middle of the Trecento.[98] Since the late Duecento the chief magistrate had been the podestà, a Paduan knight or jurist, originally appointed by the commune of Padua and now by the Carrara lord. But much of the responsibility for local government was in the hands of the town council, composed of at least forty men, and officials elected by and from it.[99] These officials were typical of the rural communes of the Veneto in the late Middle Ages, including the *sindico,* who was in charge of renting communal property; the massaro (communal accountant); and the *cavatore,* who investigated the misconduct of officials, peasants, and their animals, aided by his rural police, the *saltuarii.* The budget for 1353 shows the nature and extent of the commune's income, which totaled £417 that year.[100] The major sources were the rent of communal grazing rights, which forty-seven men shared, and of houses in the town and fields in nearby villages. This was supplemented by tithes for £44, the duty on meat (*dacium becarie*) for £16, and fines and charges. Among standard expenses were the employment of a schoolmaster (*doctor grammatice*), who received a free residence in addition to his salary, and the wages of the other communal officials and the podestà.

Handpicked by the Carrara lord were the podestà, usually soldiers from the Paduan nobility, such as Prosdocimo Brazolo in 1362, Ilario Sanguinacci in 1368, Jacopo Enselmini in 1374 and 1379, and Lanzarotto Lanzarotti in 1387.[101] While his vicar administered justice, the podestà's main duties were the defense of Cittadella, aided by a small garrison, and maintenance of its walls, citadel, and the podestà's residence, which was the property of the Carrara lord. An inventory of April 1371 provides a glimpse of the podestà's household, which was furnished with five beds, several tables, and benches

FIG. 23. *Walls of Cittadella. Photograph courtesy of Judith C. Kohl*

for his soldiers, as well as chests for flour, work tables, and a cupboard with glass vases in the kitchen. The apartment of his vicar, who handled legal cases, was furnished with a bookcase and writing table as well as the usual tables, benches, chest, and bed. That autumn, on Francesco il Vecchio's order, the podestà's residence was enlarged, with a second-story bedroom and living room added, perhaps to accommodate visits from the lord. When another inventory was made in 1388, along with the usual beds, benches, barrels, and tables were listed flags of the Carrara lord and a torture tool (*sega magna a tormento*): sure signs of Carrara presence in the Padovano.[102]

The main task of Cittadella's podestà was to provide for the defense of the northern Padovano, though for much of Francesco il Vecchio's rule Bassano and Belluno defined the northern frontier. In response to the raids of Rudolf of Habsburg in 1376, £530 was expended for timber, nails, and arms for Solanga on the Brenta above Bassano. As war with Venice became imminent in 1377, more than £800 was appropriated for the construction of a large wooden bridge at the town walls, with nearly half (£358) going for labor, a third for materials, and the rest for supervision, customs on materials, and guards to convey from Padua money to pay for the construction. At the same time, the Carrara lord strove to keep the inhabitants of

Cittadella content. When it turned out that during the Chioggia war mercenaries had stolen beds from locals, Arcoano Buzzacarini wrote a sharp note to the podestà, Jacopo Enselmini, warning him "to have the beds returned without delay, before the matter comes to the ear of our magnificent lord." Months later, when the Carrara lord planned a parley in Cittadella, his vicar, Antonio Zecchi, assessed the commune and ten villages "to provide entertainment and lodging," while six villages were exonerated from the tax.[103] Fortifying Cittadella in haste in May 1386, Francesco il Vecchio had the head of his *fondaco,* one Bartolomeo detto Guastopane, simply borrow £500 from the communal massaro, with seven local citizens standing as sureties.[104] Among these, pledging £100, was Giovanni Ovetari, whose brother Biagio was a rising figure at the Carrara court in Padua. The Carrara lord's policy of creating a loyal affinity, coupled with his growing presence in the towns of the contado, was paying off.

Chapter 6

Creating the Carrara Affinity

Amor

[Love]

—Personal motto of Bonifacio Lupi, marchese of Soragna

In 1355 Francesco il Vecchio inherited a regime wracked by violence and assassination. A decade earlier he had seen his father, Giacomo II, murder his distant cousin Marsilietto Papafava to seize the lordship of Padua, five years later Giacomo II was murdered by a crazed kinsman hoping to gain rule over the city, and in 1354 Francesco himself narrowly escaped assassination by one of his own captains hired by his own uncle. Thus, his most pressing need was to build a following of the best men in Padua, recruiting supporters from his wife Fina's family, the Buzzacarini, and soldiers and advisers from the remnants of the feudal nobility that had proven their loyalty to the House of Carrara: the Forzatè, Capodivacca, Negri, and da Peraga clans. Reconciliation with the Scrovegni, led by Ugolino, and the presence of the powerful Lupi clan provided men of experience and international reputation for the tasks of war, government, and diplomacy. Foreign knights and nobles, who had often come to Padua as *podestà* or political exiles, were persuaded to stay, beneficiaries of Carrara patronage in land and offices. Professors from the *studium,* especially its legal faculty, were recruited to administer justice, undertake diplomatic missions, and provide legal advice. Finally, "new men" from the Paduan merchant class, such as the Lion, Turchetto, and Curtarolo, and from the towns of the *contado,* such as the Naseri from Montagnana, became officials of the household government, providing the lord of Padua with some of his ablest and most loyal supporters. Out of this group the Carrara lord especially cultivated Paolo Dotti, who had warned him of the recent plot on his life. But other members of the elite, particularly the Papafava dei Carraresi, who had suffered greatly under his father, stood apart, waiting to be drawn into the affinity. These two families,

Extremes of the Affinity: Paolo Dotti and Albertino Papafava

Serving in the Paduan army in 1354, Paolo Dotti earned Francesco il Vecchio's gratitude by warning him of the plot on his life hatched by his uncle Giacomino and his would-be assassin, Zambon Dotti, and proving his loyalty by executing Zambon with his own hands. After serving a term as podestà of Piove di Sacco in 1351, a few years later Paolo became the lord's factor general, responsible for administration of the dynasty's wealth.[1] Along with this high office, Paolo Dotti's wealth also grew: in 1356 Dotti bought several cows from peasants in the contado, leasing them back for five years in *soceda*, and also bought a farm at Ponte S. Niccolò.[2] The next January, the Paduan Maggior Consiglio confirmed Paolo Dotti in possession of all property, real and moveable, confiscated from the traitor Zambon Dotti, making him a rich man overnight. But not all Paduans approved of the confiscation. In her will of June 1360, India Mangiaspessa, widow of Pietro di Bartolomeo Zacco, looked after Zambon Dotti's widow, Bartolomea di Marco de Peraga, providing her with a life annuity of £25 in oil, cheese, and meat.[3] In December 1357, Paolo Dotti acquired from Alberto di Marsilio Bibi a large half-timbered house in contrada S. Andrea for £1,200, and in August 1358, he deposited 300 ducats with a local banker.[4] In June 1362, Dotti exchanged 9 *campi* of farmland in Villa Casale with his fellow courtier Giovanni Naseri.[5] By 1363 Paolo Dotti's interests had extended to Venice: in September he appointed an agent to recover debts there; in November he was awarded Venetian citizenship *de intus*, and five years later he was appointed a proctor to recover investments at the Grain Office.[6]

Paolo Dotti made two wills, one early in 1365, the other early in 1368, which reveal him as a man of great, but not enormous, wealth. The first will shows much more interest in pious causes, with £300 to the Eremitani for weekly Masses and grants to Padua's mendicant houses and monasteries and to the poor. A major concern was his heirs, his adolescent sons, Francesco and Antonio, who were to be placed under the tutelage of the Carrara lord himself and fined 1,000 ducats if they failed to administer the will exactly as specified. In the second will, deposed three years later, many of these con-

FIG. 24 *(opposite). Altichiero, Dotti votive painting with Madonna Enthroned. Church of the Eremitani, Padua. Reproduced with permission of Alinari/Art Resource, New York*

Francesco il Vecchio

TABLE 6.1
The Dotti

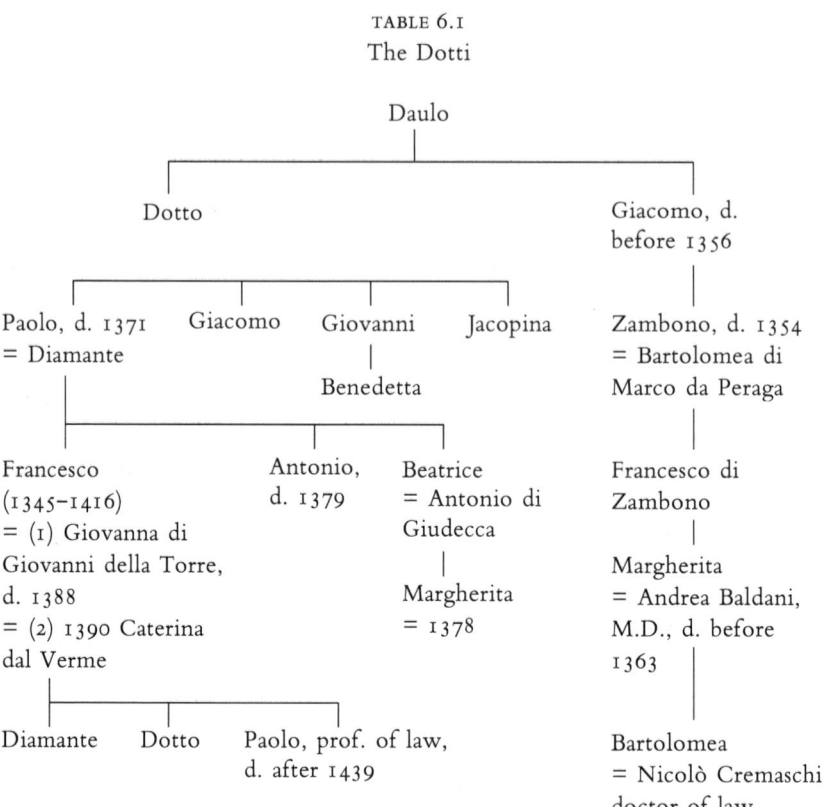

cerns had disappeared. Now, instead of an annuity of £100, his only daughter, Beatrice, was to receive a dowry of £1,300, while his wife, Diamante, was restored her dowry of £700, with an inheritance of £1,000 and an annual allowance for food and clothing. Two nieces, Giovanna and Ginota, were allotted grants of £300 each toward their dowries, while serving girls received dowries of £50 each. The executors were three friars, Matteo, Bonsembiente, and Bonaventura Badoer, from the Eremitani, where, two years later, Paolo was buried in a chapel decorated with frescoes by Altichiero. The universal heirs, no longer threatened with fines or in need of Francesco il Vecchio's guardianship, were still his sons, Antonio (d. 1379) and the jurist Francesco (1345–1416), who became a major official for the last two Carrara lords.[7]

Part of the process of building the affinity was a policy of reconciliation with members of the Carrara *domus*. As we have seen, in 1345 Giacomo II murdered his distant cousin Marsilietto Papafava dei Carraresi to seize the lordship of Padua, drove Marsilietto's young nephew, Jacopino,

Creating the Carrara Affinity

and his son Albertino into exile, and confiscated their property. During his exile, Albertino married Caterina, daughter of Ansedisio di Michele Schinelli and Antonia di Giovanni da Peraga.[8] The Schinelli, a feudal family from Rovolon, had long been out of favor with the Carrara regime, and in 1360 their lay tithes were conferred on the new Carrara favorite, Francesco detto Checcho Lion.[9] But in 1364, after Jacopino's death, Francesco il Vecchio came to terms with his grandnephew Albertino, restoring to him vast Papafava holdings in the southern part of the Padovano.[10] On 29 July 1364, in the sacristy of the Duomo, Albertino conveyed by a *donatio inter vivos* a large portion of these lands valued at 30,000 ducats to the Venetian noble Andriolo di Stefano Badoer, who was a kinsman of Zanino da Peraga, one of the witnesses to the act. At the same time, the Carrara lord countervened statutes that prohibited foreigners from acquiring real estate in Padua and its district, thus permitting Albertino to sell to Badoer for 20,000 ducats a complex of houses in contrada S. Martino and farmland in Agna, Cona, and S. Siro, retaining right of usufruct of these properties.[11] But these were only a portion of the lands restored to Albertino. A survey of his properties in 1364 showed that he owned virtually entire villages, with tithes and grazing rights, in the southeast Padovano, including forty-four parcels in S. Siro, thirty in Borgoforte, sixty in Agna, and twenty-three in Cona, with his sharecroppers paying rent of one-third of the grain crop, plus legumes and cash.[12] Although enriched by the restoration of the Papafava patrimony, Albertino did not participate in the public life of Padua. He passed his time as a rentier, overseeing his rural estates and urban properties in Prato della Valle and administering his wife's dowry, which consisted of land and tithes in Costa, Carbonara, and Rovolon on the northern edge of the Euganean Hills. His life as a large landowner was complicated, beginning with efforts in 1374 to recover the dowry of his sister Caterina, widow of Marco Resta of Milan, who had been, as we have seen, head of the Carrara Fondaco dei Panni. After Resta's death, his brothers resident in Venice refused to restore fully Caterina's dowry, leading Albertino to seek a sentence of contumacy against them, which was pronounced in July by the Paduan podestà's vicar, Cortesia Lambertini.[13]

The Affinity Crystallizes: The War Council of 1372

As Francesco il Vecchio worked to promote harmony among the leading families of Padua, he offered special privileges to those soldiers and diplomats who would help him in creating a major state in northeastern Italy, independent of Venice and dominating the *terraferma,* as had the Scaligers a generation earlier. Together these men formed the Carrara affinity, crys-

Francesco il Vecchio

TABLE 6.2
The Papafava dei Carraresi

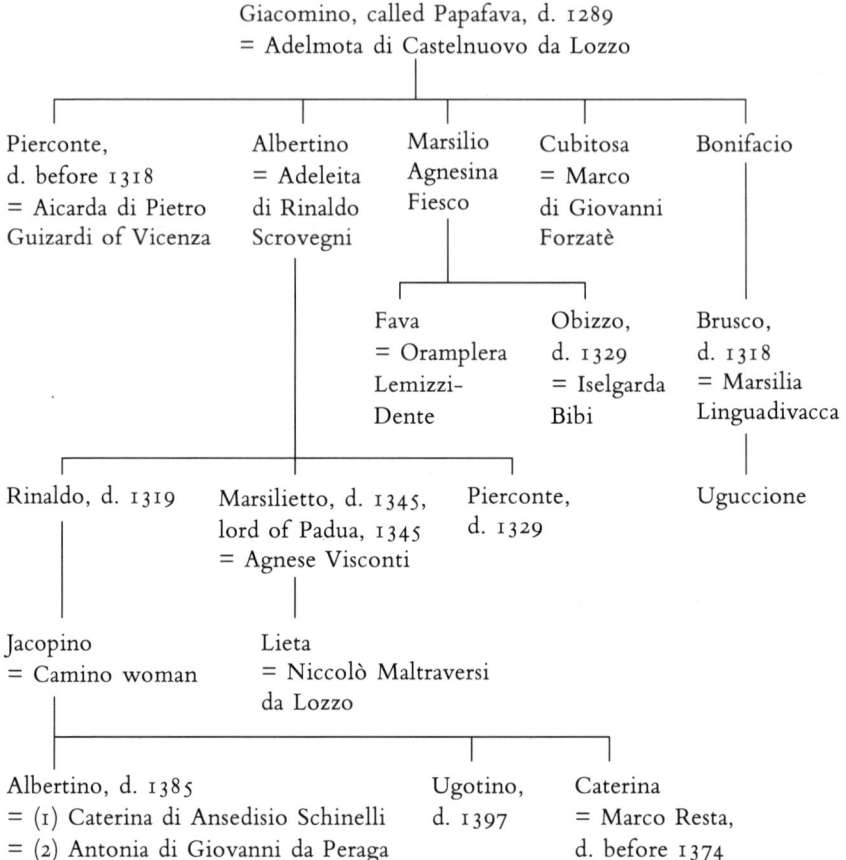

tallized in the early 1370s by the policy of Paduan independence and the subsequent rupture with Venice. Summoned to the war council in July 1372 were twenty-five of the most powerful, able, and important men in Padua, mainly knights or councillors, including the lord's brother-in-law, the city's chief magistrate, the podestà, three members of the wealthy Scrovegni family, three soldiers from the Lupi clan from Parma, three Florentine knights, and four leaders from Padua's feudal nobility, the most distinguished jurist and most famous scientist from the *studium,* and a half dozen trusted officials of the Carrara household government.

The affinity was the product of mutual trust and benefit. Many of the men who served as councillors were affines and kinsmen to the Carrara

Creating the Carrara Affinity

TABLE 6.3
Members of the War Council of July 1372

Name	City	Status	Date of Death
Arcoano Buzzacarini	Padua	knight	1402
Federico Lavellongo	Brescia	knight	1373, wounds
Rizzardo Sambonficio	Verona	count	1394
Ugolino Scrovegni	Padua	knight	1404
Giacomo Scrovegni	Padua	knight	1435
Enrico Scrovegni	Padua	knight	after 1429
Simone Lupi	Parma	knight	Jan. 1385
Antonio Lupi	Parma	knight	after 1385
Bonifacio Lupi	Parma	knight	Mar. 1391
Manno Donati	Florence	knight	1374
Bernardo Scolari	Florence	knight	1387
Rainiero Scolari	Florence	knight	after 1387
Alvise Forzatè	Padua	knight	1374, executed
Zanino da Peraga	Padua	knight	1374, of wounds
Fruzerino Capodivacca	Padua	knight	after 1387
Negro de' Negri	Padua	knight	1387
Arsendino Arsendi	Forlì	jurist	prob. 1387
Giovanni Dondi dall'Orologio	Padua	physician	1389
Checcho Lion	Padua	soldier	after 1382
Francesco detto Checcho Lion	Padua	rentier	prob. 1387
Niccolò Curtarolo	Padua	banker	1390
Jacopino Gaffarello	Padua	treasurer	after 1387
Bonacorso Naseri	Montagnana	jurist	1390, executed
Paganino Sala	Padua	jurist	1390, executed
Giacomo Turchetto	Padua	jurist	1394

Source: Gatari, *Cronaca carrarese*, 63–64.

lord. For others he was a patron, who bestowed houses and offices, or served as executor of their testaments or guardian to their children. As table 6.3 shows, these men were among the wealthiest in Padua, connected to the lord by their interests in wool manufacturing and trade; they were often holders of extensive lay tithes, and almost all owned considerable real estate, often gained from the confiscation of the property of the Carrara's enemies a generation earlier. The contracts, dowries, and wills analyzed here reveal how much the members of the council of 1372 profited from their service to the lord of Padua. Together they formed the "inner circle" of the Carrara regime under Francesco il Vecchio.

Affines: The Buzzacarini

Arcoano Buzzacarini fought as a valiant soldier in all of the elder Carrara's wars, starting with commands in the Border War, followed by service in Chioggia and Friuli.[14] He became a wealthy man, holding well over 1,000 *campi* of decimal fiefs in the eastern Padovano at Brentasecca, Sabbioncello, Saonara, and Piove di Sacco, building on tithes he and his sister Fina had received earlier in the Vicentino.[15] Following the rural depopulation caused by the Black Death, Arcoano worked at building blocks of farmland in Noventa. A survey of his possessions in Arquà shows him holding eleven small parcels of vineyards with houses on 17 *campi,* valued at £2,502 (or about £150 per *campo*).[16] At the death of his sister Fina in 1378, Arcoano received her interest in the family complex in contrada S. Urbano, where he had established his household with his wife, Nobilia Manfredi, daughter of the lord of Faenza.[17]

There Arcoano fathered a large family of seven children: four sons and three daughters. His sons bore names resonant with the Buzzacarini's high status: Pataro after his father; Francesco after his brother-in-law, the ruling lord of Padua; Lodovico Ungaro, commemorating a knighthood bestowed by the king of Hungary; and Venceslao for the future Holy Roman Emperor and son of Charles IV, Carrara patron and guest during the descents of 1354 and 1368. As well as serving as a military captain, Arcoano was a tutor and adviser to his nephew Francesco Novello and with his sons Francesco, Pataro, and Ludovico was a soldier for the Carrara regime at the end of the century.

Two Powerful Clans: The Scrovegni and Lupi

The Scrovegni had been exiled during the early years of the Carrara regime, suffering confiscation of their property at the hands of Marsilio and Ubertino da Carrara. When Enrico di Rinaldo made his will in Venice in March 1336, he complained bitterly of the Carrara usurpation of his lands and holdings in the Padovano, estimating that during the past eight harvests they had taken crops, rents, and animals worth more than 25,000 ducats. In his testament Enrico made numerous bequests to the religious houses of Padua, especially the Arena Chapel, where he was to be buried, and the friars of the nearby Eremitani. His survivors included his widow, Giacomina, from the Este dynasty of Ferrara, two minor sons, and four daughters. Capellina was to marry twice into noble families of the Veneto, first Guido di Niccolò da Lozzo and second Vinciguerra Sambonifacio, while two other daughters had already married into the Venetian aristocracy, Caterina, wife of Paolo Morosini, and Giovanna, wife of the future doge Marco Corner; Orsina became the wife of Bertolozzo Parzili. Of the two sons, Bartolomeo died prematurely before 1353, and Ugolino became the leader of the clan, taking as his wife Lusia, daughter of Pietro Rossi of Parma, the heroic savior of Padua in 1337.[18] Perhaps as part of the policy of reconciliation, Giacomo II and Francesco made some settlement with Enrico's heirs, since in 1352 Ugolino and his aged widowed mother, Giacomina, were back in Padua residing at the Scrovegni palace near the Arena, where they received their kinsmen, Francesco and Rinaldo d'Este, in flight from Obizzo, who had just usurped the lordship of Ferrara.[19]

In Padua the Scrovegni worked at recovering land and tithes: in May 1358, in an act of procuration in the bishop's chancery, Ugolino was called "patron of the church of S. Tomà of the Arena," and eighteen months later his mother, Giacomina, appointed Zinello, priest of the Scrovegni chapel in the Arena, proctor to receive from the bishop decimal fiefs in more than one hundred parcels in Sermazza. A survey made in 1362 showed her holding many parcels of farmland and vineyards in the Euganean Hills at Monselice, Montericco, and Arquà.[20] In January 1360, Ugolino Scrovegni purchased extensive vineyards in Montagnana, before accompanying Pataro Buzzacarini, Simone Lupi, and others to receive Belluno for the Carrara lord from representatives of the king of Hungary.[21] As part of a practice of accommodation, in 1370 Scrovegni sold to the Carrara lord land on the Brenta near Strà, where he constructed Castro Bellaguarda, a stronghold to defend the border with Venice.[22] Over the next decades, Ugolino spent much time outside Padua, serving as the Carrara podestà in Belluno in 1361, 1369, and 1371 and three terms as *capitano del popolo* in Florence, from February 1374 to June 1375. Also present at the war council of July 1372 were his two sons, Enrico and Giacomo, who received commands in the Paduan army in both the Border War and the War of Chioggia.

In 1376 Ugolino made an advantageous marriage for his only daughter, Maddalena (1356–1429), to the noble knight Francesco Manfredi, son of a former podestà of Padua, Giovanni Manfredi, whose family were at some time the *signori* of Bagnacavallo and Faenza. Widowed early, Maddalena had returned to Padua by 1381, residing in the family complex in the Arena.[23] There Ugolino worked at building a block of property, acquiring in 1380 a house at S. Tomà, bordered on two sides by Scrovegni land, and the next year entering a suit against a neighbor, Giovanni di Daniele dagli Statuti, for building a house abutting the wall of his own palace. The judges whom Francesco il Vecchio delegated to hear the case—Paganino Sala, Benedetto Girlandi da Siena, and Ludovico Paradisi da Capodivacca—found for the defendant, permitting Statuti's house to stand, though the Scrovegni clearly

TABLE 6.4
The Scrovegni

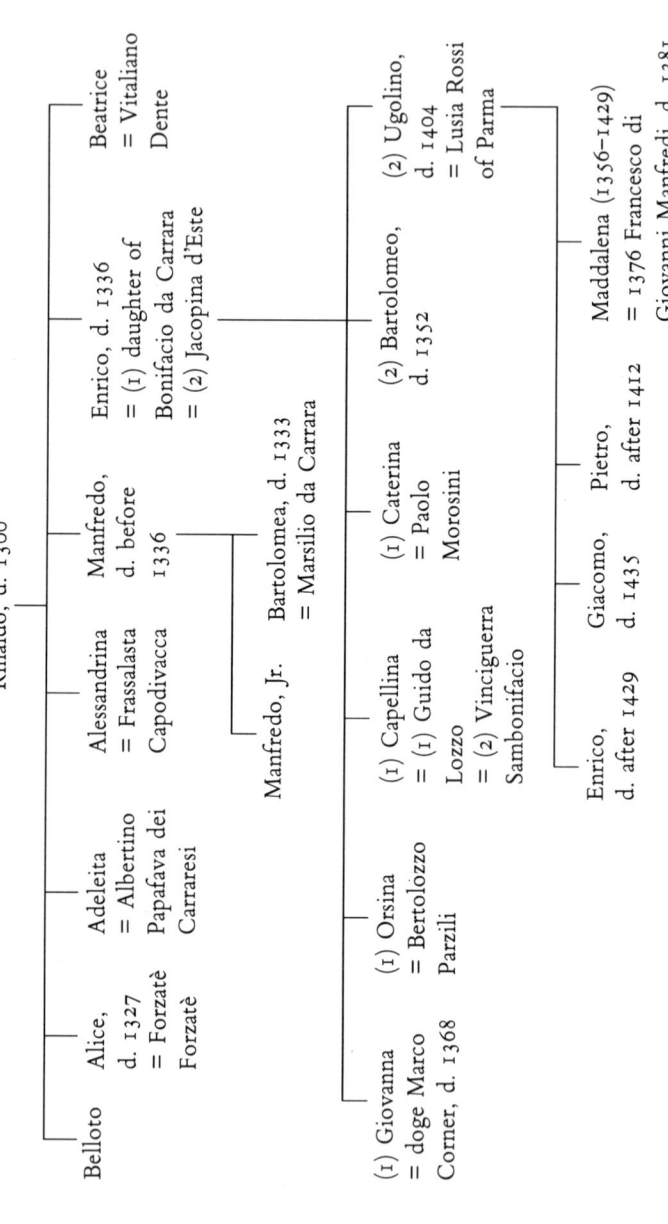

dominated this part of the city.²⁴ Although the available evidence suggests that Ugolino had little interest in the family profession of banking, at the end of the Chioggia war, both his sister Caterina and daughter Maddalena invested in Venice: in March 1382 the Senate allowed Caterina, wife of Paolo Morosini, to reinvest 200 ducats just earned in the Grain Office. That same month at her home in the Arena, Maddalena appointed a Venetian noblewoman, Maria Corner, her agent to collect a deposit of 150 ducats made with a banker at the Rialto, Rigo qd. Giovanni Caresino. Maria was, in fact, Maddalena's cousin, the daughter of her aunt Giovanna Scrovegni and the deceased doge Marco Corner (d. 1368). In 1386 Maddalena made a Venetian notary her agent to recover money invested in the Monte and deposits from the same banker.²⁵

As the Scrovegni were the richest and most powerful native family that supported the Carrara regime under Francesco il Vecchio, so the Lupi were the most distinguished newcomers to Padua in that period. Originally from Parma, allies and kinsmen of the Rossi, who had been instrumental in the restoration of the Carrara, the Lupi had been exiled from their native city in the early Trecento. Winning support of King Charles of Bohemia in 1347, the Lupi cousins Ugolotto di Bonifacio and Raimondino di Rolandino were restored as marchesi of Soragna. By midcentury Bonifacio had succeeded his father, Ugolotto, as head of his branch, and Raimondino served as imperial ambassador to Venice to form a league against Giovanni Visconti. At the time of his first descent Charles bestowed his patronage on Bonifacio, granting him castles at Crema, Pizzighetto, and Castelnuovo of Boccadella in June 1354 and an annual pension of 300 florins to be paid from the Florentine treasury. Accompanying Charles to Pisa in the spring of 1355 and then back toward Prague, Bonifacio Lupi had his international stature confirmed by Venice's grant of citizenship "for meritorious service" late that year. As a supporter of the same anti-Visconti league, composed of Francesco Gonzaga and Niccolò II d'Este and headed by Francesco il Vecchio, Bonifacio Lupi soon settled in Padua, where the ruling lord took advantage of his friendship with the emperor and skill as a diplomat to dispatch him to the court at Prague. There Bonifacio secured for the Carrara lord Charles' annulment of an earlier sentence of Henry VII against Padua and confirmation of certain rights in the Trevisano.²⁶

Back in Padua, Bonifacio Lupi translated his wealth and standing into an active program of land acquisition in the city and district. Employing as his agents Francesco il Vecchio's own factors, Giovanni Naseri of Montagnana and Antonio da Casale, Bonifacio soon acquired at bargain prices property in Campagnola and Rosta from the estate of one Domenico di Guido Checcho.²⁷ Before Bonifacio Lupi departed from Padua to aid Florence in its war with Pisa, he made a massive exchange with the five Dondi brothers, who gained extensive parcels near Bovolenta and Piove di Sacco.[28] Establishing his household in the parish of S. Fermo in the northern part of the old city, Lupi surrounded himself with Tuscan and Parmesan merchants and bankers, only a few meters from Ugolino Scrovegni's residence in the Arena. Here in May 1368 Bonifacio Lupi came to terms with his childless second marriage (made during the Pisan campaign) to the Tuscan banking heiress Caterina di Antonio Franzesi da Staggia, and he made a codicil to his will, in which he lavished legacies on his wife, his niece Agnese Biancardo, his wife's niece Isabetta, and a goddaughter and ward in Mantua, one Bartolomea Lupi.[29] At the same time Bonifacio Lupi maintained his interests in Florence and the family estates at Soragna. For example, in late December 1370, he appointed the Florentine bankers Franceschino del Bene and his brother Betto his proctors to collect the annual pension of 300 florins owed him by Florence from the imperial grant of some fifteen years earlier, requiring the same proctors to collect other unspecified debts and rents in Florence.[30] A few years later he served as executor of the estate of a Parmesan friend and familiar, one Niccolò di Spado, who was residing in Padua in nearby contrada S. Andrea. In the summer of 1376, Lupi continued to make loans abroad through his banker Franceschino del Bene, this time a deposit of 2,000 ducats to a *campsor* in Genoa.[31]

A soldier and diplomat of international repute, Bonifacio Lupi was soon drawn into the Carrara affinity, appearing as early as July 1363 as witness to important notarial acts drawn up in the chancery of the Reggia.[32] When war clouds gathered between Venice and Padua in the spring of 1372, Francesco il Vecchio appointed Bonifacio Lupi along with his councillor Checcho Lion as ambassadors to King Louis of Hungary in Buda to secure support in the event of war with Venice. Returning that summer with a promise of armed intervention from the King of Hungary, Bonifacio Lupi and his cousins Simone and Antonio were included among the inner circle that was summoned to the war council that July. Employed as both soldier and diplomat during the Border War with Venice, Bonifacio Lupi was captured at the disastrous rout at Buonconforte and held prisoner in Venice until his ransom was paid. Granted Paduan citizenship by the Carrara lord,[33] Bonifacio Lupi was sent as one of the ambassadors to negotiate a league with Venice against the dukes of Austria in July 1376 and again to discover Venice's intentions at the beginning of hostilities in May 1378. During the Chioggia war, Lupi was appointed one of the ambassadors representing the lord of Padua at a preliminary discussion at Cittadella in 1380 and was summoned to the council in Padua to consider terms for peace the next year. In the summer of 1383, Francesco il Vecchio appointed Bonifacio his envoy,

Creating the Carrara Affinity

TABLE 6.5
The Lupi, Bonifacio's Branch

Unknown Lupi, fl. 13th c.
- Bonifacio, d. 1301
  - Ugolotto, marchese of Soragna = Legarda Rossi
    - Caterina = Antonio Biancardo
      - Ugolotto Biancardo, condottiere, d. 1408, heir of Bonifacio Lupi
    - Donatella
    - Bonifacio, marchese of Soragna, d. 1391
      = (1) woman from Parma
      = (2) Caterina di Antonio Franzesi da Staggia, Tuscany, d. 1405
      no legitimate offspring
    - Donnina = 1330 Manfredino Pallavicini
    - Giovanni, canon
- Rolandino (see table 6.6)

along with Paganino Sala, to negotiate terms for receiving Treviso from Duke Leopold of Austria.[34]

This turned out to be the last mission Bonifacio Lupi undertook on behalf of the Carrara lord. Lupi's main preoccupation of his later life was ensuring his own immortality: overseeing the construction and decoration of his funerary chapel of S. Giacomo in the Santo, completing the nearby chapel of S. Giorgio for his cousin Raimondino, and later endowing the Hospital of S. Giovanni Battista in Florence, which was to be his principal beneficiary, according to his will of 1377.[35] As early as 1372 Bonifacio had engaged the best sculptor in Padua, the aged Andriolo de' Santi, and his son Giovanni as architects for a new chapel in the Santo. In a contract drawn up by Petrarch's amanuensis, Lombardo della Seta, Bonifacio specified in detail the design, columns, sculpture, and dimensions of his funerary chapel, incorporating the tombs of his kinsmen from Parma, Pietro and Marsilio Rossi. The chapel was dedicated to St. James the More, patron saint of Spain and of soldiers, whose intervention on behalf of warrior kings, including Charlemagne and Ramiro of Oviedo, was only part of the many stories detailing his life and miracles. Bonifacio commissioned Altichiero da Zeno to paint the frescoes of the Chapel of S. Giacomo and later the Oratory of

Creating the Carrara Affinity

S. Giorgio, which was to serve as a mausoleum for the branch of the clan headed by Raimondino Lupi.[36]

As the research of Margaret Plant and others has shown, the frescoes painted by Altichiero in these two chapels are a virtual portrait gallery of the Carrara affinity.[37] In the Council of the Crown in S. Giacomo, King Louis of Hungary appears with his forked beard, as King Ramiro, holding the symbols of his power, orb and scepter, gazing benevolently at his client, Francesco il Vecchio, and his son Novello. Seated below the lords nearer the throne are Petrarch and his secretary Lombardo della Seta, emblems of the richness of Paduan culture and of the friendships forged between king, lord, and poet and the Lupi patrons. To the left of King Ramiro, the council contains portraits of members of the Lupi clan. In the middle of the group, as a stout man with sparsely bearded jowls, is depicted Giovanni Lupi, canon at the Duomo and the patron's younger brother. In the lower left corner stand Bonifacio and his wife. The patron is in profile wearing a heavy dark beard with his motto, AMOR, stitched around his cap. Next to him is his wife, Caterina Franzesi, shown in three-quarter view, wearing a cape with a hood covering her luxuriant dark hair. The portraiture was extended to the nearby Oratory of S. Giorgio, tomb for Raimondino Lupi and his family, decorated with scenes from the lives of St. Lucy and St. Catherine of Alexandria as well as St. George. Here again are depicted members of the Carrara elite, Petrarch, Lombardo della Seta, and Marsilio da Santa Sofia, as well as Giovanni Lupi and other family members. On the north wall Raimondino's forebears and immediate family are depicted as votaries, each kneeling in a file before the Virgin and Child protected by his own patron saint. With these precocious examples of "patronage within patronage" (in Margaret Plant's felicitous phrase), Bonifacio Lupi memorialized himself, his family, and the Carrara elite, while he retained connections with friends and clients in Parma and Tuscany.

Bonifacio continued to use his property in Parma as a source of income as his agents there collected rents from both clergy and laymen, renewed leases and *livelli,* and pleaded court cases regarding disputed property.[38] Bonifacio also emerged as a leader and mediator among Parmesan and Tuscan bankers, soldiers, and merchants in Padua. For example, on 5 April 1380, he adjudicated a dispute over inheritance between two brothers from Cortecelle near

FIG. 25 *(opposite). Altichiero,* The Council of King Ramiro. *Chapel of S. Felice (formerly S. Giacomo), Basilica of S. Antonio, ca. 1378. Portraits of King Louis of Hungary, Bonifacio and Caterina Lupi, Francesco il Vecchio and Francesco Novello da Carrara, Francesco Petrarca and Lombardo della Seta hidden in fresco depicting Council of King Ramiro. Reproduced with permission of Alinari/Art Resource, New York*

Parma, Pietro qd. Franceschino Petroni, residing in contrada S. Urbano, and Bernardo, who was castellan at Gallivelle, temporarily lodged at S. Fermo.[39] On 19 February 1381, Bonifacio Lupi had the lord's vicar, Antonio Zecchi, in his office as count palatine, legitimate another son of the deceased Franceschino (of the disputed legacy), the Parmesan moneylender Maffeo Petroni, whose mother was the late countess of Cortecelle, Sibilia di Pietro Rossi, and thus the sister of Ugolino Scrovegni's wife, Lusia. This was followed the next day by the count palatine's legitimation of Maffeo's own son, Bartolomeo, whose mother was also from Cortecelle; thus, Maffeo and his family became eligible to ply their trade of moneylending in Padua.[40] In fact, early in March, a kinsman of Bonifacio's wife, a Tuscan pawnbroker named Aloisio Franzesi, rented from Maffeo Petroni a pawnshop (*stacio mutui*) in contrada S. Urbano for £100 a year and a percentage on the capital of pledges, moveables, and cash, valued at £13,866. Maffeo found the arrangement profitable, for two years later he renewed the lease for an annual rent of 100 ducats, after Aloisio had restored all the capital and paid Maffeo the profit of £2,000 made on the loans.[41]

Bonifacio's leadership of the large Tuscan and Parmesan community was strengthened by the presence in Padua of two cousins from the collateral branch of the Lupi, the military captains Simone and Antonio, both sons of Guido di Rolandino. Simone Lupi first appeared in Carrara service as one of the local notables sent to receive Belluno from the king of Hungary in 1360 and then served an unprecedented eight terms as podestà, from September 1364 to February 1368. Largely ignorant of the law, he was greatly aided in this capacity by his vicar, the learned jurist Giovanni Salgardi, who rendered the more important court decisions.[42] Simone remained in Padua as one of the preceptors for the heir apparent, Francesco Novello, before being appointed captain general of Paduan forces during the Border War with Venice. Simone also served in the Chioggia war and was wounded at Mestre early in the conflict before he assumed command of cavalry raiding the Trevisano. Serving as captain general of Carrara forces left in the area after the Peace of Turin, Simone had the honor of leading the triumphal procession that took possession of Treviso soon after Francesco il Vecchio purchased it early in 1384, staying until October to serve as the first Carrara podestà.[43] The Carrara lord then recalled Simone to Padua, where he was again appointed podestà early in November, following the departure of the Venetian incumbent, Marino Memmo. He died in office only two months later, after a quarter century of service to the Carrara regime.

Simone Lupi received rewards appropriate to his station, a salary of £12,000 per annum for the nearly four years he served as podestà, and tithes in Piove di Sacco and farms in the Paduan *campanea* at Volta Brusegana,

Creating the Carrara Affinity

TABLE 6.6
The Lupi, Simone's and Antonio's Branch

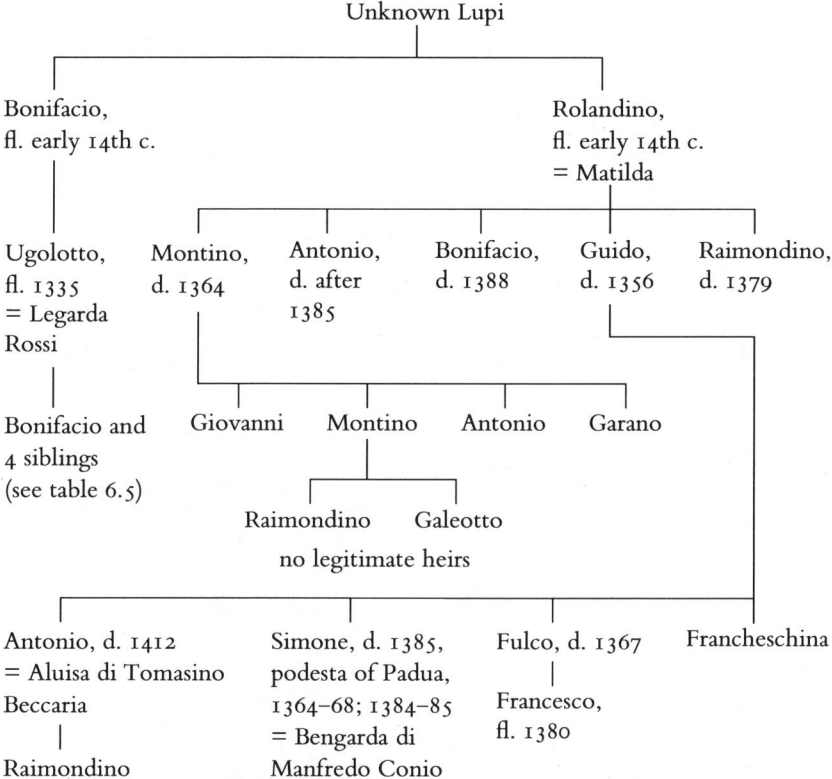

while he retained some land and fiefs in the Parmese.[44] Dying childless in January 1385 in the house acquired near the Duomo fifteen year earlier, Simone Lupi left the bulk of his estate to his brother Antonio, appointing as his executors the priors of S. Maria di Monteoliveto and S. Giovanni del Venda. His widow, Bengarda, daughter of Count Manfredo Conio, received some lands and lifetime right to a house in Ponte dei Tadi, with Francesco il Vecchio dispensing statutes against inheritance by those who were not Paduan citizens or taxpayers holding property in the city.[45] His brother Antonio Lupi served as a captain in the Border War, first securing the fortress at S. Ilario before leading raids in the Trevisano. The next spring Antonio was captured at the Battle of Lova, sent to Venice, and released in time to be taken prisoner again at the Battle of Buonconforte in July. While in Padua Antonio Lupi resided in contrada S. Lorenzo, where in August 1371 he witnessed his wife, Aluisa di Tomasino Beccaria of Pavia, as she made

her will, leaving him the bulk of her estate, and where a year later she appointed an agent in Pavia.[46] Antonio fought briefly in 1379 in the Chioggia war but resided mainly in Mantua, where his uncle Raimondino appointed him and Bonifacio Lupi rectors of the hospital he had endowed there.[47]

After the departure of Antonio and death of Simone Lupi, Bonifacio had few close colleagues in the Carrara regime; he and his wife, Caterina, spent more time outside the city at their country estate at Mandria near Abano. There Bonifacio had acquired extensive property from Carrara favorites, buying parcels from Margherita qd. Niccolò Porcellini, wife of Piombiolo Piombioli, in 1365 and from Negro di Gherardo de' Negri in 1375. To these properties he added other parcels, purchasing a large block for £2,050 in 1381.[48] Here in March 1382 Bonifacio sold to the captain of the Castello in Este, Scanuzzi Rossi of Parma, a house for £650, and in November Bonifacio's wife appointed two Florentine merchants her agents to look after certain interests in Tuscany.[49] The next spring Bonifacio appointed Petruccio Lariolo of Parma, who had settled as a druggist in Venice, his agent to acquire shares in the Venetian Monte and make other investments. Since 1355 Bonifacio had enjoyed Venetian citizenship, and late in 1385 his wife appointed the same Petruccio Lariolo one of her two proctors instructed to obtain for her Venetian citizenship and, with it, the right to acquire property there. In March 1387 Bonifacio named two agents, one of whom was Petruccio Lariolo, with orders to purchase a residence in the parish of S. Giovanni Decollato and take possession of it as soon as possible. That May Caterina, named a Venetian citizen in the document, bought her own home in the same parish.[50]

Bonifacio saw to other family matters as well. Following the death of Caterina's only brother, Rainiero, in 1382, Bonifacio supervised the awarding of the inheritance to his three young nieces by their guardian, the Florentine merchant Betto di Tano del Bene, taking a particular liking to Rainiero's natural son, Stefano, who came to live with his aunt and uncle at the palace in contrada S. Fermo. Early in 1384, with Caterina's approval, the eldest niece, Verde, married Tommaso di Biancardo Masini, a Florentine worker in the Carrara mint.[51] Most of all, Bonifacio lavished his affection on his sister's only son, the young *condottiere* Ugolotto Biancardo of Parma, who was to serve the Carrara in the Scaliger War. After the early death of Ugolotto's father, Antonio, Bonifacio came to regard his nephew almost as

FIG. 26 (*opposite*). Altichiero, Soldiers of Lupi Family of Parma. *Chapel of S. Giorgio, near the Basilica of S. Antonio. Votive painting with Lupi of Raimondino's branch kneeling before St. George and St. Lucy, Padua, 1384. Reproduced with permission of the Museo Civico, Padua* his own son. In a ceremony in the Lupi palace on 25 January 1386, witnessed by Enrico and Pietro Scrovegni, Lombardo della Seta, and Gabreotto Palma from Parma, Bonifacio bestowed on Ugolotto his own personal coat of arms, to be inscribed on banner, surcoat, and helmet and carried on his lance.[52] When Ugolotto left Padua for the employ of Giangaleazzo the next year and Carrara fortunes worsened thereafter, Bonifacio and Caterina Lupi were able to contemplate a move to the security of their new residences in Venice.

Foreign Notables in 1372

Several other foreign knights and nobles were called to the war council of July 1372. An obvious choice was the current podestà, the knight Federico Lavellongo of Brescia, who had taken up his office in September of the previous year. In January 1372, the podestà's residence became the setting of the Carrara lord's efforts to recruit soldiers when Francesco il Vecchio advanced a loan of 200 ducats to the mercenary Niccolò Filippo di Brancaleone of Casteldurante, with Rainiero Scolari, Pazzino Donati, and Federico himself standing as sureties and the podestà's staff, composed of knights from Mantua, Brescia, and Forlì, serving as witnesses.[53] That fall Lavellongo took the field against the Venetians, leading raids into the Treviso and helping to defend the frontier forts at Lova and Boion that spring. The rigors of war proved too arduous for the aged podestà, who died of wounds and exhaustion in August 1373 and was buried surrounded by mourners from the Carrara elite on 1 September.[54] Also present at the council was the future podestà, Rizzardo di Vinciguerra, count of Sambonifacio, of Verona. As opponents of the Scaliger lords, the Sambonifacio lords had been exiled from their native city and soon settled in Padua. During the Border War, Rizzardo had commanded a third of the Carrara forces, a company of 2,600 cavalry fighting at Piove di Sacco, and helped to plan the disastrous attack on the Venetian fortress at Buonconforte, when he and many other Paduan captains were captured. He returned to the conflict at the end of July, taking part in the assault against the Venetian fortress called Medicina, only to be wounded in the leg by mortar fire.[55]

At the conclusion of the Border War, Rizzardo remained in Padua to recuperate at the family palace in contrada Pozzo Mendoso, where he had resided with his brothers, Manfredo and the canon Bonifacio, as early as 1372, leasing land in Lendinara and Carmignano in the Oltrebrenta.[56] During the early 1370s, Rizzardo became a fixture in the Carrara chancery, earning Francesco il Vecchio's trust and continuous appointment as podestà of Padua for seven years, from May 1375 to May 1382. With Rizzardo living in the podestà's palace in contrada S. Martino while Manfredo continued to reside in the family home at Pozzo Mendoso, the two brothers leased farmland and collected rents in their country seat in Carmignano di Brenta.[57] Their relations with the Carrara lord remained close: when Manfredo made his testament in February 1378, he left the bulk of his estate to Rizzardo, but if his brother should predecease him without legitimate heir, the estate was to go to Francesco il Vecchio himself.[58] In fact, Rizzardo did succeed Manfredo. At his residence in contrada Salone, in 1386 Rizzardo appointed an agent to lease property and collect rent in Lendinara.[59] He survived the Visconti occupation of Padua to serve Francesco Novello as his podestà from August 1390 to April 1392.

The most distinguished foreign soldier at the council was the Florentine Manno di Apardi Donati, who had been knighted by his commune thirty-five years earlier on the recommendation of Pietro Rossi shortly after he took command of the Venetian and Florentine forces backing the Carrara restoration in Padua.[60] A leader in the expulsion of Walter of Brienne from Florence, Manno and his family were unpopular with the new regime and fled the city after brief imprisonment. By 1354 Manno Donati was a captain in the Carrara army, where he commanded a troop of two hundred lances sent to help Cangrande II della Scala retake Verona from the upstart Fregnano. Two years later Manno was sent with Nascimbene Grompo to Levico in the Trentino to curb the depredations of Sicco da Caldonazzo under the command of the marquis of Brandenburg in the Valsugana.[61] Returning briefly to take a command in Florence's army, by 1361 Manno and his younger brother Pazzino had been again banned by the commune and soon returned to serve the Carrara regime. A seasoned diplomat and able commander, in 1362 Manno represented the Carrara lord in forming a league against Bernabò Visconti before Francesco il Vecchio allowed him to return to Florence, with Bonifacio Lupi, to serve in the war against Pisa.

Returning to Padua to command Carrara forces aiding the patriarch of Aquileia against enemies in Friuli, Manno Donati became a major figure in Carrara court life, leading a troop of Paduan knights (organized as the Reds against the Whites) in tourneys held to celebrate the wedding in January 1367 of Francesco il Vecchio's eldest daughter, Gigliola, and Wenceslaus, duke of Saxony. Recalled once more by Florence, Manno took command of six hundred lances in the summer of 1370 against Bernabò Visconti in Lombardy. In several accounts (including an epitaph written by Petrarch), Manno's death is given wrongly as 31 August 1370, but from Galeazzo Gatari's report and Florentine tax records it seems certain that he died in 1374.[62] His death probably came fighting against Visconti lords, Bernabò and Galeazzo II, who were at war with the papacy in 1374, as suggested in

FIG. 27. *Tomb of Manno Donati, Basilica of S. Antonio, Padua. Reproduced with permission of Alinari/Art Resource, New York*

a letter that Coluccio Salutati wrote to Gregory XI on behalf of Florence on 19 May 1375: "that noble and outstanding deceased knight, lord Manno Donati, whose memory we recall with grief, ended his last day in the service of the Holy Mother Church, fighting against the lords of Milan."[63] After Manno's death, his brother Pazzino and young son Manno remained

Creating the Carrara Affinity

in Padua, major figures in the Tuscan business community and sometime diplomats for the Carrara regime. For example, at the first rumors of war in January 1378, Pazzino Donati and Bonifacio Lupi appointed Simone Allegro and Pietro Simeone their proctors to collect debts in Venice, while in September 1382, attempting to pay off war debts, Francesco il Vecchio made Pazzino Donati his agent to sell a large house in Florence.[64] In December 1386, the Carrara lord appointed Pazzino his proctor to recover a debt of 600 ducats owed him in Florence.[65] Manno's widow, Giacoma, daughter of Guido Alberto, count of Modigliano in the Romagna, remained in Padua in contrada S. Lucia with her son, Manno, who was destined to serve Francesco Novello.[66]

The other Florentine knights on the council were Bernardo and Rainiero di Zuppo Scolari. Bernardo had arrived in Padua by September 1371, when he witnessed Albertobono Ovetari making his testament, and stayed on to fight in the Border War with Venice, in the Trevisano against Leopold of Austria and in Friuli.[67] This service created trust, for in June 1385 Francesco il Vecchio appointed Bernardo, along with Francesco Turchetto and Valerano Lambardi, his envoy to conclude a league with the rulers of Milan, Mantua, and Ferrara—Giangaleazzo Visconti, Francesco Gonzaga, and Niccolò II d'Este—against the mercenary companies. Bernardo Scolari returned to Padua to take the field with Sir John Hawkwood and Francesco Novello against the Scaligeri in 1386. A year later, he was badly wounded while besieging the Veronese garrison at Torre Bernice near Vicenza and was carried back to Padua to make his will.[68] His brother Rainiero had left Padua after fighting in the Border War for service in Cyprus, so Bernardo appointed as executors two major members of the Carrara affinity, Bonifacio Lupi and Pazzino Donati, who with his widow, Caterina, were to establish the size of dowries for the two young daughters, Mabilla and Giovanna. After setting aside £200 for any misdeeds (*pro maleablatis*), he made his two sons, Taddeo and Filippo, his principal heirs under the guardianship of wife Caterina. Filippo, who became a famous condottiere better known by his nickname, Pippo Spano, continued the family tradition of service in the Carrara army into the early Quattrocento.

Paduan Knights and Nobles in the Affinity

The local feudal nobility contributed four members of the war council: Alvise Forzatè, Zanino da Peraga, Fruzerino Capodivacca, and Negro de' Negri. The most powerful magnate family to survive in Carrara Padua was the Forzatè, represented on the council by Lodovico di Marco (also Marzio), called Alvise, who was the ruling lord's maternal uncle. His grandfather

TABLE 6.7
The Forzatè

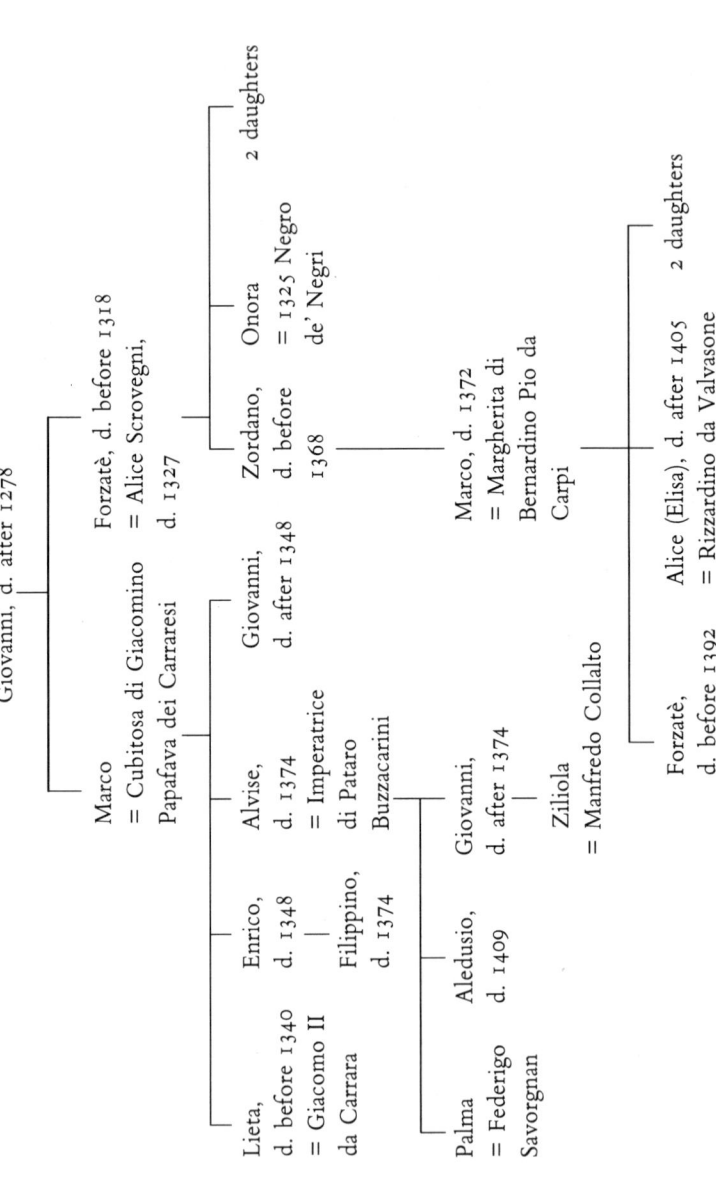

Creating the Carrara Affinity

Giovanni Forzatè had been reputed late in the last century to be among the most powerful nobles of the Padovano. During the civil strife of the early Trecento, the Forzatè kept to family estates near the Venetian lagoon at Vallonga, Rosara, Codevigo, and Melara. Giovanni's two sons married well: Forzatè took as his wife one of the richest women in Padua, Alice di Rinaldo Scrovegni, and Marco married Cubitosa di Jacobino Papafava dei Carraresi. To Marco and Cubitosa were born three sons and a daughter, Lieta, who in 1318 married the future lord of Padua Giacomo II di Niccolò da Carrara.[69] Marco's branch of the Forzatè settled in a large palace in contrada S. Niccolò, where in 1337, his son Alvise welcomed the conquering heroes Marsilio il Grande and Ubertino da Carrara back to Padua. The next year the vicar of the bishop of Padua restored to the Forzatè decimal fiefs in Solagna in the Oltrebrenta taken from the da Romano in the previous century. Alvise and his brothers Giovanni and Enrico, sons of Marco, were to hold the tithes *pro indiviso* with their cousin Zordano qd. Forzatè Forzatè.[70] By the early 1350s, after the first visit of the Black Death, the brother Enrico Forzatè and their cousin Zordano had died, leaving Alvise and his minor nephew Filippino di Enrico in possession of extensive fiefs of tithes and other property in Solagna, Piove di Sacco, Lova, and S. Marzaro as well as the large townhouse at S. Niccolò.[71]

By now Alvise Forzatè was a major member of the Carrara affinity, winning his knighthood from Francesco il Vecchio in December 1354 during the celebrations attending Emperor Charles IV's first descent into Italy.[72] In 1369 Alvise attended to both official Carrara and private Forzatè affairs: on 2 March he witnessed in the Carrara chancery the appointment of an ambassador to the pope and on 30 June oversaw the restitution of the dowry of his daughter Palma, recent widow of the Friulian noble Federigo Savorgnan.[73] The next year on behalf of the Carrara lord he undertook an embassy to Belluno with Fruzerino Capodivacca and Giovanni Dondi dall'Orologio, among others, and then served as a key member of the Paduan commission attempting to resolve the border dispute with Venice. In June 1372 Alvise accompanied Francesco il Vecchio's middle daughter, Caterina, recent bride of Stefan Frankapan, to her new home on the Dalmatian coast at Veglia, promptly returning to attend the war council the next month.[74] During the Border War, Alvise Forzatè served with conspicuous valor at encounters at Brentelle, Lova, and Boion before the end of hostilities in September 1373.[75]

The Forzatè clan sometimes acted as rivals to the ruling family and supporters of their enemies. For example, Alvise Forzatè was close friends with the Mantuan lawyer Niccolò Cremaschi, who by October 1363 had married Bartolomea Baldani, descendant of the would-be Carrara assassin Zambon Dotti, herself dowered with £2,000 from her maternal grandfather, Francesco Dotti, Zambon's only surviving son. A few years later, after Cremaschi had moved to Ferrara, Alvise's home was the setting for Cremaschi's business transactions in Padua. The Mantuan lawyer even dictated his last will there in 1370.[76] Alvise, along with his nephew Filippino and his cousin Zordano and his son Marco, continued to hold extensive tithes in the Padovano, renewing fiefs of the vast holdings near the lagoon at Lova, Codevigo, Rosara, Vallonga, and Cambroso and in the Oltrebrenta at Bosco di Sacco, Curtarolo, Camposampiero, Arsego, Marsango, and Solagna on 21 December 1371.[77] When Alvise's cousin Marco di Zordano Forzatè made his will in the family complex in contrada S. Niccolò the next spring, he named the future traitor, the lord's half brother Marsilio da Carrara, one of his executors.[78] At the conclusion of the Border War that fall, Alvise, his son Giovanni, and nephew Filippino joined with other disgruntled members of the inner circle, attempting to overthrow Francesco il Vecchio and bestow the lordship of Padua on Marsilio instead. As we have seen, the plot was discovered; Alvise and Filippino confessed their part under torture and were turned over to the podestà, Giacomo Rangoni, for trial and eventual execution. Giovanni was sentenced to confinement in prison at Castelbaldo, which ended with his death a few years later.[79] But Francesco il Vecchio was lenient with other surviving members of the family, perhaps because Alvise's widow, Imperatrice di Pataro Buzzacarini, was Fina's younger sister. Alvise's granddaughter, Ziliola di Giovanni, who had married Manfredo di Toberto Collalto, of one of the great magnate families of Treviso, continued to reside in contrada S. Leonardo, enjoying a life annuity of £200 from her late husband's estate.[80] Alvise's minor son Aledusio received favorable treatment. For example, in 1386 Francesco Novello handed down a court decision that granted him possession of more than 80 *campi* in Tribano.[81] Kinship and the Forzatè's great popularity with the common people of Padua softened vengeance on the next generation. Still current in the Quattrocento was the opinion that Francesco il Vecchio had ordered Alvise's death under a false pretext.[82]

An offshoot of the Venetian Badoers, the da Peraga took their name in the late thirteenth century from their family seat at Peraga in the Oltrebrenta, which belonged to Balzanella, wife of Marco Zeno Badoer. At the turn of the century Marco da Peraga had married Sofia di Bonifacio da Carrara, who as a widow in 1325 and 1327 bought land and leased property in Arzergrande and Piove di Sacco.[83] From this marriage three children survived to maturity: Albertino, who married Jacopa Malatesta of Rimini; Bartolomea, who, as we have seen, married Zambon Dotti, the would-be assassin of Francesco il Vecchio; and Filippo, who married Margherita di Antonio Castelnuovo. At his residence in contrada Duomo, Filippo had been a staunch ally of the Carrara. He accompanied Marsilio il Grande to negotiate with the dukes of Austria and Carinthia in 1327 and helped to arrange the putative marriage of Taddea da Carrara with Mastino della Scala the next year.[84] Filippo had five children who survived to adulthood: two sons, Marino and Zanino, and three daughters, Albertina, Ursula, and Filippa. In June 1352, Filippo further cemented his close ties with the Carrara by marrying his son Zanino to Bonfemina di Pataro Buzzacarini, who was another sister of the ruling lord's wife, Fina.[85]

Four years later, the da Peraga brothers, residing in a joint household in the family palace in contrada Duomo, oversaw the sale of property that Albertino's wife, Jacopa, had inherited from her mother, Polentesia Malatesta, in Rimini.[86] But Filippo also turned out to be a liability to Padua's peaceful relations with Venice. One day after sundown in the spring of 1361, crossing the lagoon by boat from Venice with Rizzardo da Sambonifacio and four male servants, Filippo's party was hailed by three *signori di notte*. When the Paduans refused to stop, the Venetian police declared them under arrest, only to have their barque attacked by the noblemen and their henchmen, brandishing drawn swords. One guard was thrown overboard, another was allowed to escape when he declared he could not swim, and the third got off by swearing he was from Padua. The Venetian government fumed at this affront, and the Forty tried the Paduans *in absentia*, sentencing the nobles to fines and their servants to fines, jail terms, and exile from Venetian dominions.[87] Although it is unclear whether the sentences were ever carried out, the incident surely served to heighten tensions between Venetian authorities and members of the Carrara affinity.

In the summer of 1360 Zanino da Peraga entered Padua's public life, serving as one of the commissioners appointed to establish the border with Venice at S. Ilario and as ambassador to Venice a decade later. During the Border War Zanino commanded a garrison of two hundred cavalry and three hundred infantry at Mirano, frequently led raids into the Trevisano, and emerged as one of the heroes of the conflict.[88] Probably exhausted by the campaigns, Zanino da Peraga made his testament shortly after the end of the war in the autumn of 1373. Surrounded by neighbors in his own palace in contrada S. Sofia, the testator directed that his body was to be buried in the family chapel in the Eremitani, providing the friars with £100 for services and £50 per annum for commemorative Masses. Settling £500 on the Franciscans, £100 each on the Dominicans and Carmelites, and £10 on each parish in Padua, Zanino reserved the bulk of his legacies for his family and servants. He conferred life annuities of £200 each on his sisters, Albertina, wife of Federico della Torre, and Filippa, who was unmarried. His mother, Margherita Castelnuovo, was to receive back her dowry of £3,000, while his wife, Bonfemina, was to receive £500 in addition to restitution of her unspecified dowry. Childless, Zanino awarded legacies to kin of the next generation: his grandniece Polentesia di Albertino da Peraga, wife of Negro de' Negri, was to receive life income from his property in Brenta and Codevigo; the brothers Giovanni and Guido di Bonfrancesco de' Negri (called his *nepti*) got £200 each; and another niece, Alice, received life interest in all Zanino's property in Villa Caltana. Zanino's universal heirs were his five nephews, Giovanni, Geremia, Albertino, Bartolomeo, and Giacomino, all sons of his deceased older brother, Marino. Executors included the distant kinsman and powerful cleric Friar Bonaventura Badoer of the Eremitani, Checcho di Pietro Lion, and Giacomo di Corrado Zacchi, while Zanino asked Francesco il Vecchio to make sure "that all the aforesaid legacies and debts of this his last will would be executed by his aforesaid executors."[89]

Zanino, however, recovered from the stresses of war, only to make a second will two years later shortly before his death in August 1375. Dictating the second testament before several witnesses, including Giovanni Dondi dall'Orologio, Checcho di Pietro Lion, Giacomo and Bartolomeo di Corrado Zacchi, and Ludovico di Giovanni Cortusi, Zanino made only a few changes, mainly adding several new legacies. This time his youngest sister, Ursula, received £1,000 for her dowry, while sister Filippa got life interest in his property in Ronchi Morelli. His wife, Bonfemina, now got a life annuity of £200, while his sister's sons, Martino and Geremia della Torre, received all his property just south of Padua at Abano, Mandria, Monterosso, and Montortone. One Francesco da Peraga was to receive the property in Villa Pionche, while the Carrara lord got "the two forts, great and small, he had built at Mirano during the recent war with Venice, and all houses existing within the stockades." Zanino's principal heirs remained his five nephews, while now Francesco il Vecchio was named executor of the estate, with full powers to alienate property to satisfy debts and settle disputes.[90] Thus, the Carrara lord assumed another responsibility toward members of his affinity, overseeing distribution of their legacies.[91] Throughout the 1370s Zanino and his clan were major powers in the Padovano, where they consolidated estates inherited from the Della Torre affines, received tithes from the bishop of Padua, and even enlisted peasants as armed retainers on estates in the Oltrebrenta at Borgoricco and Desmano.[92] Over the next decade Zanino's nephews and heirs, especially Giovanni, Geremia, and Bartolomeo detto Peraghino, loyally served the lord of Padua as knights and military captains, though Albertino was executed for attempting to betray Padua to the Visconti in 1388.

Another noble family at the council was the Capodivacca, represented by Fruzerino. The son of Aicardino di Marco Capodivacca and Beatrice di Fava

Creating the Carrara Affinity

Papafava, Fruzerino, named after a favorite uncle who died childless after 1331, was, like several other members of the council, distantly related to the ruling lord.[93] Aicardino had accompanied Marsilio il Grande da Carrara to negotiate a treaty of friendship with the dukes of Austria and Carinthia in 1327 and the next year was one of the Carrara supporters knighted by Cangrande della Scala to celebrate his acquisition of Padua. In May 1336, Aicardino appointed one of his kinsmen, the archpriest at the Duomo, Bartolomeo Capodivacca, to receive from the vicars of the bishop of Padua fiefs of tithes in Saletto, Urbana, and Cagnola in Scodosia. These tithes were probably part of a settlement made earlier that winter, when Niccolò qd. Antonio Capodivacca had to secure enough capital to restore half of the huge dowry of £3,500 due the heirs of his recently deceased wife, Francesca di Pietro Altichini.[94] By 1350 the son had married into another major Paduan banking family, taking as his bride Ailetta di Gaboardo Scrovegni, and five years later was plying the family trade of moneylending.[95] In the summer of 1360, Fruzerino entered public life in Padua when Francesco il Vecchio appointed him one of six ambassadors sent to Venice to discuss construction of a fortress at S. Ilario. Fruzerino returned to Venice on an embassy in 1371 and as a member of the commission to settle boundaries the next year.[96]

During the Border War, Fruzerino Capodivacca served as podestà and captain of Bassano, using armed force to prevent betrayal of the city to the Venetians. At the same time, Fruzerino kept up good relations with the bishop of Padua, receiving a grant of all tithes in Urbana and Campolongo Maggiore in June 1373, which was renewed by the new bishop, Raimondo Ganimberti, at his accession less than two years later.[97] Enriched from his wife's dowry and other Scrovegni property in Creola, Selvazzano, Saccolongo, and Trambacche, after a term as podestà of Castelfranco at the end of the Chioggia war, Fruzerino settled down as a rural landowner, leasing land in Vigonovo and parcels of arable and vineyards to peasants from Trambacche in return for grain, millet, and capons.[98] Indeed, Trambacche became the focus of his rural holdings, with Francesco Novello conveying the Carrara fortress there, bounded by the Bacchiglione and Tesino Rivers, to Fruzerino Capodivacca at the fall of the regime in November 1388.[99] Fruzerino served as one of the ambassadors elected to negotiate the submission of Padua to Giangaleazzo Visconti, but he prospered under the restored Carrara, residing at the family palace in contrada S. Canciano, where he made his will in the fall of 1392.[100]

Negro de' Negri was also a kinsman of the ruling lord, since his mother, Buzzacarina di Dusio Buzzacarini, was the aunt of Francesco's consort, Fina. In the census of 1320, Negro's great-grandparents, Negro di Guido de' Negri and his wife, Lina di Vince Sambonifacio, resided at the family's urban residence at S. Giuliana near contrada S. Martino.[101] Negro's father, Gherardo di Guglielmo de' Negri (1314–ca. 1370), received his knighthood in December 1354 from Francesco il Vecchio during Emperor Charles IV's Italian journey and served as podestà of Belluno in 1361–63, but for a time he was imprisoned for trying to turn over the city to Duke Rudolf of Habsburg the next year.[102] Returning to Padua by 1365, Gherardo leased extensive wetlands (*valle*) between Anguillara and Tribano for £180 a year. This was followed by leases of many farms in the Oltrebrenta at Campo S. Martino, Curtarolo, and S. Giorgio di Bosco for £600 a year.[103] Following his father's death, Negro de' Negri entered Carrara service as a member of the council of July 1372, fought in the Border War, and earned a knighthood for valor at the Battle of Lova early in 1373, only to be captured at Buonconforte later that summer.[104] Repatriated to Padua that autumn, by the spring of 1375 Negro, with his younger brother Prosdocimo, leased farmland to peasants in Bassano in return for money rents delivered to the family residence in Padua. At this time Negro's cousin Giovanni di Bonfrancesco was residing in the family complex called "Volta illorum de Negris" and oversaw transactions occasioned by the death of his brother Guido, selling for £340 a small house Guido had owned to a widow from Bologna and conveying for £300, with the approval of Negro and Prosdocimo, parcels to a peasant in Carpanedo.[105]

Negro and Prosdocimo fared better as woolen merchants and rentiers than did their cousin Giovanni since they acquired additional property in Carpanedo from him in 1382, became his heirs at his death in 1384, and later restored her dowry to his childless widow, Beatrice Capodivacca, daughter of another member of the war council, Fruzerino.[106] Some years earlier Negro had married Polentesia di Albertino da Peraga, cousin of another Carrara favorite, Zanino da Peraga. Early in 1383, summoning woolen manufacturers from Belluno and Ravenna as witnesses, Negro made his testament, in which he bequeathed the bulk of his estate to his brother Prosdocimo, settled a dowry of 1,000 ducats on his only child, Jacopa, and restored her dowry and other property to his wife, Polentesia.[107] Prosdocimo, in fact, became the more active brother over the next few years, appointing the Venetian noble Lorenzo di Bernardo Giustinian proctor to appear before the abbot of S. Giorgio Maggiore to receive tithes that the Negri traditionally held in the Padovano. In a final act, Negro advanced his brother Prosdocimo a loan of £10,000, which was not to be repaid if Negro died without a male heir, with all but £2,000 to be paid back if he had a son. When Negro died late that year survived only by wife and daughter, most of his estate went to Prosdocimo and his son, Daniele.[108]

Creating the Carrara Affinity

TABLE 6.8
The Negri

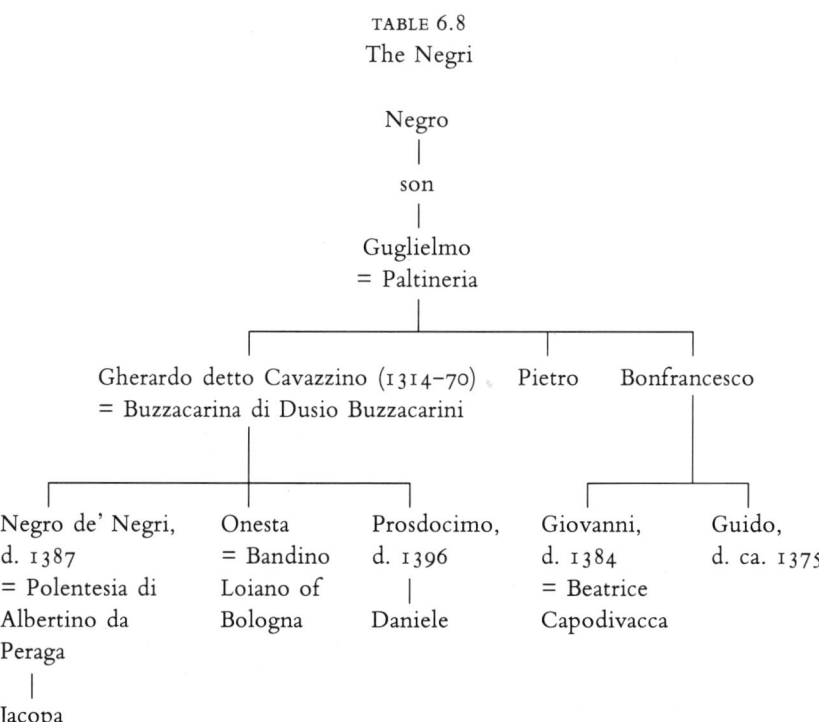

Of the two men named Francesco detto Checcho Lion, one was an obscure soldier, the other one of the Carrara lord's most trusted advisers. The soldier, Checcho di Donati Lion, who probably served in both the Border War and the War of Chioggia, appeared early in 1381 as captain of the Castello of Padua and two years later made his will in his home in contrada Duomo, bestowing dowries of £600 on each of four daughters and naming his two sons, Antonio and Giacomo, his universal heirs. Since he was to be buried in S. Antonio, he is perhaps to be identified with the "Chechus ipse Leonius heros," commemorated in an inscription near the altar.[109] One son, Antonio, remained in Carrara service, serving as *spenditore* (bookkeeper) in the regime's counting house. At the restoration, the family had fallen from favor, and Antonio was forced to sell to Francesco Novello his house near the Duomo and land in Faedo for 1,300 ducats. Three years later, Antonio di Ser Checcho, a resident of the monastery of S. Giustina, renounced to Luca Lion, acting as Carrara agent, his lease on land in the campanea, which was rented that very day to a tailor from S. Clemente near the Reggia.[110]

The notable Checcho Lion, son of Pietro and father of Giovanni, seneschal in the Carrara household in 1375, and of Luca and Paolo, major agents for the last two Carrara lords, owned mills at Torricelle as early as 1347. He went on to become a wealthy landowner in Padua and its district in the early 1360s, dying there in 1387. Checcho di Pietro Lion's rise to wealth and power demonstrates vividly the importance of Francesco il Vecchio's favoritism and largess. Following the murder of Marsilietto Papafava, his factor Albertino Gottola was executed, and his two sons sent into exile in Venice. There they sold more than 410 *campi* of farms and urban lots for £12,000 to a priest, Giovanni di Pietro, who was rector of S. Andrea, where the Gottola family used to live. By February 1359 Francesco il Vecchio had granted the priest Paduan citizenship, and two months later he became a member of Padua's Maggior Consiglio. After the sale was completed, the priest took legal possession of the properties acquired from the Gottola brothers and held them for about a year, before he sold them in six transactions for a total of £19,768 to Checcho di Pietro Lion. The properties were mainly farmsteads and parcels of vineyards and arable located to the south of Padua in the villages of Maserà, Pernumia, Polverara, Casalserugo, and Albignasego, surrounding the family's country seat at Lion. While the priest realized a profit of nearly £8,000, Checcho Lion was able to add considerably to his rural holdings, creating blocks of farmland that could be efficiently cultivated. At the same time he acquired for £3,730 from peasant landowners more than 95 *campi* of grazing land in the Patriarcati, a large pasture stretching north from Bovolenta through the villages of Bertipaglia and Cornegliana. In 1362 Checcho emerged as the patron of S. Giacomo in Lion, having the right to appoint the local priest at a salary of £100 per annum.[111] In nine different transactions from 1350 to 1375, Checcho bought more than 20 *campi* of farmland, vineyards, orchards, and olive groves in Arquà for £2,668 (or £124 a *campo*), while in April 1361 he acquired, for £600, 15 *campi* of arable with vineyards and olive trees in Bassano, renting for £36 per annum (yielding a return of 6 percent on his investment).[112] Though outside the ancestral village of Lion, these were acquisitions of valuable orchards and vineyards, which would yield major cash crops. Early in the 1360s, Checcho di Pietro Lion acquired numerous tithes in Montagnana which had been renounced by Ansedisio Schinelli da Rovolon and which were augmented by new grants by Bishop Pileo da Prata in 1371.[113] Checcho was rich enough to provide his daughters, Aleta and Jacoba, with handsome dowries of £2,000 each at their marriages in 1364 and 1366.[114] In December 1366, Francesco il Vecchio, with Marsilio and Niccolò da Carrara, donated to Checcho 217 *campi* of farmland in Lion with another 83 *campi* in nearby Chiosure, making him clearly the most powerful landowner in the area.[115] When Checcho Lion was chosen to accompany Bonifacio Lupi on an embassy to Hungary in 1372, he had become one of the richest and most respected members of the affinity.

Scholars in the Carrara Affinity

Gracing the council were perhaps the two most famous scholars in law and medicine in Padua, Arsendino Arsendi and Giovanni Dondi dall'Orologio. Arsendino Arsendi arrived in Padua in 1344 with his father, the distinguished jurist Rainiero, whom Ubertino da Carrara had appointed professor of civil law at the *studium* at the enormous salary of 600 ducats per annum. Probably educated at Bologna, where his father taught law before coming to Padua, Arsendino emerged in the third quarter of the Trecento as the most trusted legal adviser and diplomat for the Carrara lords.[116] Professor at the *studium* and author of several legal opinions, Arsendino often served as examiner and promoter on the doctoral boards of some of the best law students in Padua. But he made his mark as a diplomat. In the spring of 1369, Emperor Charles IV employed Arsendi and Bartolomeo Piacentini, both called "vicars" of the lord of Padua, as appellant judges to settle a dispute over an annual pension of 250 florins he had awarded.[117] The next year Francesco il Vecchio appointed Arsendi ambassador to conclude a league with Florence, the Este lord of Ferrara, and Pope Urban V. Throughout the 1370s, Arsendi served the lord of Padua as envoy to Venice, first to try to avert and then to settle the Border War and again to negotiate peace ending the War of Chioggia. At the same time, he appeared often as a witness in the Carrara chancery and adviser on foreign policy until his death in 1387. From his first marriage, to Caterina della Bonelda, Arsendi had a son, named Ubertino, no doubt in honor of his father's benefactor. After Caterina's death, Arsendi married into the Tuscan nobility, taking as his second wife Parte, daughter of Petrarch's friend Guido, count of Battifolle, and widow of Count Lodovico Zazoni of S. Miniato.

As Arsendi was the most distinguished jurist at the Padua *studium* in the 1370s, so Giovanni Dondi dall'Orologio (1318–89) was its most famous scientist. Giovanni's father, Jacopo (1290–1359), was also a physician, practicing in Chioggia, when Ubertino da Carrara appointed him professor of medicine at Padua in 1342.[118] There Jacopo won considerable acclaim for his text *Aggregator,* which harmonized the conflicting opinions of physicians on medicinal cures for various diseases, while working, at Ubertino's behest, on the design and construction of a great astrological clock. Jacopo also investigated methods for the extraction of salt, earning from Francesco il Vecchio the perpetual right to extract salt from the thermal waters at Montegrotto and sell it in Padua free of taxes. At his death in 1359, Jacopo was proud of his achievements, alluding in his self-authored epitaph (preserved in the wall of the Baptistery) to his works in medicine and science but giving pride of place to his famous clock in the tower of the nearby Reggia.

Giovanni continued the family tradition of service to the Carrara dynasty, first appearing as professor of medicine at the *studium* in 1349. Lured to Florence to teach medicine for three years, Giovanni returned to Padua to serve on the border commission in 1371 and on the war council a year later. Under his father's tutelage, Giovanni composed his famous *Tractatus astrarii* and constructed his renowned planetary clock, which designed the movements of the sun, moon, and five known planets according to the Ptolemaic system. But Giovanni Dondi was soon attracted to the Visconti court at Pavia, first briefly as an attending doctor in 1372 and later in the 1380s as court physician for Giangaleazzo. Married twice and the father of three sons and three daughters, he left his grown offspring in Padua married into notable local families: Orsola wed Jacopo Camposampiero in 1379, and Jacopa married Arimondo di Solimano da Ponte the next year. A cherished ornament at the Visconti court, Giovanni died on a mission to Genoa in 1389. Leader of the university community, friend of Petrarch, wealthy landowner in Chioggia and the Padovano, and confidant of the lords of Padua and of Milan, Giovanni Dondi was also a scholar of wide learning, possessing at his death a library of some 120 volumes, mainly scientific texts but also including the works of Livy and Ovid, Dante and Petrarch.[119]

The New Men: Curtarolo, Gaffarello, Sala, Naseri, Turchetto

Niccolò Curtarolo was a member of the professional classes of Padua; his father, Enrico, was a notary, an older brother Guglielmo (d. before 1352) a judge, and another brother, Pietro, was the father of the notary and Carrara diplomat Guglielmo di Pietro.[120] Niccolò emerged in the public record as a member of the war council, serving in that war before becoming the tyrannical head of the Carrara household, well described by Giovanni Conversini. As Carrara factor general Niccolò oversaw Francesco il Vecchio's complex economic interests and served on several embassies as well: in February 1378, with Michele Rabatta, to the court of Louis of Hungary and to Genoa a year later. Active in collecting the heavy tax imposed for the purchase of Treviso, Niccolò fought against the Scaliger army at Brentelle in May 1386 and was knighted for valor following the battle. When, later that year, Francesco il Vecchio received from Leopold of Austria the castle at Mel on the Piave, he turned over the stronghold to Niccolò, bestowing on him

Creating the Carrara Affinity

the title of count of Zumelle and Cesana. In the summer of 1388 Niccolò Curtarolo followed the elder Carrara to Treviso, where he dictated his testament on 31 August. Providing small legacies for his sister India; his wife, Pantisilia, daughter of a distant kinsman, Alberto Curtarolo; and natural son Niccolò Junior, he left extensive real estate at Curtarolo in the Oltrebrenta to Francesco Novello, while the rest of his patrimony was divided between his nephew Pietro Piccinino qd. Pietro and kinsman Francesco qd. Matteo Curtarolo. His executors were members of the affinity: Paolo and Luca di Checcho Lion, Biagio Ovetari, and the jurist Giovanni Porcellini. But the legacy was shared differently in the event: instead of holding the estate *pro indiviso*, four heirs—Guglielmo, India, Pietro Piccinino, and Francesco—each got land in specific villages, mainly in the Euganean Hills, and they divided a large meadow at Montegrotto between them.[121] In any case, the inheritance caused disputes. Shortly after his death, the Visconti vicars confiscated much of Niccolò Curtarolo's property as ill-gotten gains from the churches, widows, and poor of Padua. Litigation continued between the legal heirs and his bastard son, Niccolò Junior.

Niccolò was not the only member of the family to profit from close association with the ruling lord. Maria di Almerico Curtarolo became Francesco il Vecchio's mistress even before the death of her husband, Bartolomeo Taddeo Cortelerio, in the summer of 1373. A respected member of the Padua judiciary, in May 1370 Taddeo had been freed by the Carrara lord from the onus of acting as guardian to his wife's five minor brothers, before undertaking an embassy to Venice the next year.[122] About this time Maria gave birth to Francesco il Vecchio's son, Pietro da Carrara, who as Francesco Novello's *fradello naturale* served the Carrara regime in war and peace until his death in 1404. Meanwhile, Maria continued to prosper in Padua, selling 4 *campi* of farmland in Polverara for 100 ducats in autumn 1376 and acquiring two houses in contrada S. Andrea some years later. Pietro accompanied his half brother into exile in the fall of 1388, while his mother remained in Padua and attempted to collect some debts during the Visconti interregnum. In 1395 Maria invested £600 as a partner in her brother Guglielmo's business as a druggist; she survived the fall of the Carrara dynasty, dying in July 1410.[123]

Close associates of Niccolò Curtarolo were the Carrara treasurer, Jacopino Gaffarello, diplomat Paganino Sala, and factor Bonacorso Naseri. Gaffarello had begun his career in Padua as a moneylender, married into the Basilio family of notaries and communal judges, and was soon appointed head of the Carrara treasury, where he worked for twenty years.[124] Residing near the Reggia in contrada S. Niccolò as early as 1366, Gaffarello developed landed interests in vineyards and small farmsteads in the Euganean

Hills at Teolo and Faedo.[125] He also had landed interests in Pontelongo and surrounding villages. For example, in the fall of 1375, he acted as a surety for one of his sharecroppers on a loan of £150 made by Naimiero Conti on behalf of Francesco il Vecchio, which was payable at the next wheat harvest in August 1376.[126] Gaffarello also acquired land in other areas, buying in the summer of 1374 the rights to the 400 *campi* of meadow, woods, and arable bordering the Brenta River near Vigonza. Sometimes he combined the business of landowning with banking, acquiring for 500 ducats many parcels in Torre, only to sell back the property to its owner when the ducats were restored the next month. Apparently, Gaffarello had simply made a short-term loan, holding the property at Torre as collateral until the loan was repaid. Gaffarello made outright loans to others, such as the rector of S. Daniele, who in December 1375 repaid the loan of £300 with 30 *moggi* of grain as interest. His fellow Paduans came to rely on Gaffarello to serve as executor for their estates, for example, paying out in 1379 small legacies to the Franciscans from ordinary citizens.[127] Thus, Gaffarello combined his duties as treasurer and statesman with moneylending, living largely from his rural estates.

Like so many officials of the Carrara household, Paganino Sala descended from members of the Paduan judiciary. Following his father, Corrado, into the College of Judges in 1361 after earning his doctorate at the *studium*, Sala served Francesco il Vecchio often as an ambassador, especially during the Chioggia war. Earning the reputation of a "mellifluous orator," Paganino served in negotiation with Leopold of Austria for Treviso in 1383 and to protest the Visconti occupation of Vicenza in 1387.[128] With landed interests in Sala near Mirano, during much of the 1380s Sala taught law in the *studium* and served as councillor to Francesco Novello in the crisis of 1388.[129] Paganino married twice into families of the Carrara circle: his first wife was Biancafiore da Casale and the second Agnese di Francesco Capodivacca.

Like Sala, Bonacorso Naseri was a lawyer, drawn into the Carrara affinity through his father, Giovanni, who emigrated from Montagnana to become a factor for Francesco il Vecchio early in his rule.[130] Trained in law at the *studium*, along with his brother Antonio, who was to become, through his father's influence, bishop of Belluno and Feltre, Bonacorso married Sibilia, daughter of the Carrara factor Gualperto Cetto. After service to the Carrara regime as councillor for Francesco il Vecchio in 1370 and ambassador to Venice in 1372, Bonacorso spent much of his career as a judge and professor at the *studium*. Along with his father, Giovanni, Bonacorso was a leader and property owner in contrada Rudena, near S. Margherita, where his wife's family also resided. Like other members of his family, Bonacorso combined interest in land with banking. Obtaining Venetian citizenship, in 1382 he purchased on behalf of Francesco il Vecchio shares in the Monte. Becoming a servant of the Visconti during the interregnum, Bonacorso was hunted down during the retaking of Padua in 1390, his house in contrada S. Margherita was sacked, and he was captured and executed. His father enjoyed a better fate. After being exiled along with many enemies of the regime in 1390, Giovanni was pardoned two years later, while Bonacorso's widow, Sibilia, who had already married the Carrara *referendario* Baldo Bonafari, received much of the Naseri's wealth.

The jurist Giacomo Turchetto, son of the notary Antonio, originally from Arquà, received his legal training, including the doctorate, at the *studium* and served in the communal judiciary, starting in 1365, before entering the service of the Carrara lord as an ambassador. Giacomo was one of five *savi* appointed to resolve the border dispute with Venice in 1372, and during the Chioggia war he explored various peace initiatives: with Charles of Durazzo in 1379, with representatives of the belligerents at Cittadella in 1380, and as envoy to negotiate peace at Turin in 1381. In 1387 Giacomo represented the Carrara lords in negotiating various alliances with Giangaleazzo Visconti and late in 1388 was one of the diplomats named by Florence and Bologna to negotiate a settlement, hoping to avert war between Padua and Venice.[131]

However, both in importance to the Carrara regime and as guardian of the family's wealth, Giacomo was overshadowed by his elder brother Francesco, who served as referendario for the signorial regime from 1365 to 1382. Like Giacomo, Francesco Turchetto served often as an ambassador: for example, in 1373 to consign Belluno and Feltre to the dukes of Austria and in 1387 to conclude a league with Giangaleazzo Visconti against the Scaligeri. He profited early from his service: on 23 August 1368, Francesco il Vecchio bestowed on Turchetto fiefs earlier held by Niccolò Cane, and later many other properties held "at the pleasure of the lord."[132] An inventory compiled in the early Quattrocento shows that by the fall of the Carrara in 1388, Francesco Turchetto had become a wealthy rentier and merchant, with property in Padua, its campanea, and the district. Although several of the purchases were made at bargain prices from peasants in lieu of the full payment of debts, the inventory shows the process of the landed acquisitions of a major Carrara favorite.[133] The richest rural holdings were located in the family's home town of Arquà, where Turchetto had acquired about 30 *campi* of vineyards and olive and fruit trees in many small parcels for £3,000 (or £100 a *campo*). At Solesino and S. Elena to the south, he bought 57 *campi* of farmland at £1,200 (or £22 a *campo*) and at Merlara near Montagnana 67 *campi* of arable and meadows for £1,850 (or £28 a *campo*). At S. Maria di Non on the Brenta, Turchetto purchased 42 *campi* of farmland for £1,720 (or £40 a *campo*). In the campanea he acquired several farmsteads and parcels of arable land and vineyards in four locations, Ponte S. Niccolò, Volta Barozzo, outside Pontecorvo, and "near the walls," totaling 106 *campi* for £8,506 (or about £80 a campo). Within the city, his holdings were concentrated in three areas, at the main family residence near the Duomo, another family complex where his brother Giacomo lived in contrada S. Giovanni delle Navi, and shops near the Salone. A contract of 24 April 1387 indicates the source of some of Turchetto's wealth: at brother Giacomo Turchetto's home at S. Giovanni delle Navi, with Drudone da Ravenna and two recent immigrants from Monselice as witnesses, Francesco advanced £6,000 for the purchase of warp, dyes, and cotton to three textile workers, who promised to repay the loan at the rate of £1,000 each month, beginning in October, with a penalty of £100 for missing the deadline. Later that day, Turchetto advanced another £3,000 to the same men, thus lending £9,000 in capital for textile manufacturing in Padua.[134] These business interests, coupled with the acquisition of hundreds of *campi* of rich farmland, made the Turchetto brothers among the most conspicuous newly rich of Carrara Padua.

Sophisticated, well educated, wealthy, and ambitious, the men called to the war council of 1372 often became the servants of the Carrara lord in his wars against Venice, the Scaligers, and the Visconti fought between 1378 and 1388. As Francesco il Vecchio changed from Venice's favorite client to its mortal enemy, members of Padua's elite had to choose between loyalty and treason during this decade when the Carrara regime faced its greatest tests.

Chapter 7

Venice's Mortal Enemy, 1377–1388

> Informati sumus quod ipse dominus Padue publicus hostis noster.
> [We are informed that the lord of Padua is our public enemy.]
> —Senato, Secreta, 16 August 1388

When the truce arranged by King Louis of Hungary in the fall of 1376 extended into a stalemate and, for a time, peace with the dukes of Austria, Francesco il Vecchio turned to cementing his friendship with his most reliable and loyal neighboring *signore*, Niccolò II d'Este, lord of Ferrara. As we have seen, in 1375 he undertook negotiations for the marriage of Francesco Novello and Taddea d'Este. On 31 May 1377, the young couple (Francesco had turned eighteen just two days earlier) was wed in Ferrara, amid jubilant celebration, crowned by jousts in the city square on 1 June. Even Venice, scarcely a close friend of the Carrara, sent four ambassadors to the ceremony in Ferrara, bearing a scarlet robe and other gifts. That week Francesco took his bride home, reaching Monselice on 5 June and making a festive entry into Padua on the 7th.[1] Thus was solidified a friendship between the two Guelf dynasties which was to endure, with some strains, for the next decade.

The Outbreak of the War of Chioggia

Even before peace came to the Veneto in the fall of 1376, King Louis of Hungary had concluded a defensive alliance of fifty years with the patriarch of Aquileia on 21 June 1376. The king promised aid to the patriarch against any enemy, except the pope and emperor, at his request or that of his *vice dominus* or, in their absence, the Parliament of Friuli. Joining the league was Francesco il Vecchio, who also agreed to defend the patriarch and restore to him any of his cities taken in war. Otherwise, the signatories were to share plunder and ransom of prisoners. For his part, the patriarch pledged to aid the king of Hungary and his successors in wars, within and outside

Friuli, against any enemy, except pope and emperor, to close passes and stop commerce at the king's request, and never to make a separate peace. Confirmed by the Parliament at Udine on 27 July, the league became the basis, along with the continued alliance with the Carrara lord, for Louis's interests in the affairs of northeast Italy.[2] Venice countered by concluding in November 1377 a league with Bernabò Visconti, lord of Milan, directed against Genoa, to last four years beginning on 1 March 1378. The Visconti lord was to provide at least four hundred lances and two thousand crossbowmen to attack Genoa and its possession from the land, while Venice was to man twenty galleys to conduct the war at sea. Bernabò promised to enlist the forces of his brother-in-law, King Peter II of Cyprus, to prosecute the conflict in the Levant with subsidies from the Venetian treasury.[3] Venice was now ready to face the inevitable challenge from Genoa for control of commerce in the eastern Mediterranean.

The Fourth Genoese War, or the War of Chioggia, broke out from the dispute between Venice and Genoa over the small island of Tenedos, located just south of the Dardenelles, from which a garrison and fleet could control trade with Constantinople and ports on the Black Sea. At the beginning of hostilities, the king of Hungary concluded on 16 February 1378 a secret treaty with Genoa, directed against their traditional enemy, Venice. In March Venice attempted to keep its mainland dominions secure by extending the peace with the dukes of Austria, requiring Francesco il Vecchio da Carrara and the commune of Padua to send ambassadors to Venice affirming their participation in the truce.[4] But through the spring, as tensions heightened, Genoa and Venice began to enlist other allies. By the time full-scale hostilities opened in June, Venice could count only on the lukewarm support of Bernabò Visconti, lord of Milan, one of Genoa's traditional enemies, and King Peter II of Cyprus, who signed a treaty of defense with Venetian envoys at Nicosia.[5]

Genoa, on the other hand, had amassed a formidable array of allies, including the lord of Padua, the dukes of Austria, the Scaligeri lord of Verona, Queen Joanna of Naples, and the city of Ancona, as well as King Louis of Hungary, who continued to hold the cities of the Dalmatian coast opposite Venice. In May, when Francesco il Vecchio began to enlist troops for the impending conflict, Venice dispatched ambassadors to Padua to learn of the lord's intentions. Francesco reminded the envoys of the many past wrongs done by Venice: causing the loss of the towns of Belluno and Feltre, fomenting two attempts on his life by his own brothers, trying to remove him from the lordship of Padua and place his city under Venetian rule, and, most recently, sending mercenaries under Sir John Hawkwood and Count Landau to ravage the Padovano. The Paduan ambassadors were sent to inform Venice of the Carrara lord's intentions to fortify his own frontiers at Oriago, Castelcarro, and Borgoforte. At the same time, Francesco il Vecchio dispatched his trusted diplomat Michele Rabatta to the Hungarian court to assure Louis of Padua's loyalty and need for support.[6] On 28 May at Buda Louis issued letters patent to be delivered to the Venetian government and doge, informing them of his renunciation of friendship (*diffidatio*) and that a state of war would exist between the two states fifteen days after receipt of the letters.[7] The Venetian government had already elected Vettor Pisani captain general of the sea and sent him, with fourteen armed galleys, to harass enemy shipping in the Adriatic and eventually in Genoa's home waters.

In late June war began in earnest in the Veneto. A force of five thousand Hungarian troops crossed the Piave under the king's nephew Stephen, voivode of Transylvania, and Janos Chur, while Paduan cavalry raided the Trevisano from the west.[8] In July Giovanni degli Obizzi assumed command of the Carrara forces, setting up camp at Carpenedo near Mestre. That summer Paduan troops raided and burned suburbs at Mestre and defeated a Venetian force at Castelcarro, while Hungarian troops under the voivode aided Bartolomeo and Antonio della Scala against Visconti incursions near Brescia. By late August, Venice had already begun to feel the pinch of the Paduan-Hungarian control of the frontier when Florentine merchants complained to the Maggior Consiglio of Francesco il Vecchio's refusal to permit the shipment of merchandise from Padua to Venice.[9] Early in September King Louis sent six hundred additional Hungarian troops with three wagons of gold and silver to Padua to aid the war effort. Francesco il Vecchio immediately appointed four of his economic officials, Checcho Lion, Francesco Turchetto, Galeazzo Gatari, and the moneylender Giovanni Brocardo, to oversee the minting of the precious metals into coins to meet the expenses of the war, even coining gold half-ducats as well as silver *carrarini* and *carraresi*.[10] Within a few months, new undervalued *carrarini* were flooding Venice. As we have seen, the Senate sought to remedy this monetary warfare by promising to redeem each mark of *carrarini* with 24 silver groats turned in to the mint by the end of January 1379. Any Paduan coins, including the new *carrarini,* found in circulation after that date would be confiscated, with the holders losing the value of the coins and subject to a fine of £1,000.[11] In September 1378 a truce between the Scaligers and Bernabò Visconti brought peace to the Veronese frontier, allowing allies to concentrate on attacks in the Trevisano and the *dogado*. To ensure the Della Scala lords' participation in the allies' cause, Francesco il Vecchio made an interest-free loan of 5,000 ducats to the Scaliger brothers in October 1378, to be repaid in June of the next year.[12] At the end of the year, Vettor Pisani was ordered to take up winter quarters at Pola in Istria, where he could more readily protect convoys bringing supplies to Venice, while Carlo Zen, with the other fleet, cruised the eastern Mediterranean, far from the action developing in the Gulf of Venice.

In the spring of 1379 a Genoese fleet under Pietro and Luciano Doria sailed the northern Adriatic setting fire to Grado, Caorle, and towns in Istria and the *dogado*. In April Pisani returned to Pola from a voyage to Apulia, whence he had escorted grain ships to Venice and raided some Genoese shipping. While Pisani had laid up part of his fleet, cleaning and careening some of his vessels, a Genoese fleet appeared flying the insignia (a sword pointing downward) inviting battle. Although several of his twenty-four galleys were in poor repair and his crews depleted by disease and desertion, Pisani decided to give battle, since the Genoese had only sixteen vessels in view, though another six were hidden behind a headland. Sounding the call to battle, Pisani collected his crews, enlisted Slavic soldiers and other mercenaries garrisoned at the fortress at Pola, and sailed forth to meet the enemy. At first the Genoese fleet retreated, luring the Venetians some 5 kilometers out to sea. While engaging the main Genoese fleet, Pisani's forces were set upon from the rear by the hidden enemy galleys. Although the Genoese admiral Luciano Doria had been killed and the Venetians appeared victorious, the surprise attack turned the tide of battle against Pisani's fleet. When defeat seemed imminent, Pisani retreated with five or six galleys, leaving the rest of his fleet to the Genoese. The other Venetian vessels soon surrendered to the more powerful Genoese force, which took over twenty-four hundred prisoners, including twenty-four Venetian nobles. More than eight hundred foreign mercenaries in Venetian service were massacred and their bodies thrown into the sea. The Venetian prisoners were transported back to Genoa, where they remained in prison for more than eighteen months. Pisani escaped to Parenzo with the remnants of his fleet and was recalled to Venice to stand trial for the disaster. Tried for the defeat at Pola before the Senate, augmented by the Quarantia and a war board, Pisani had to answer to two charges: leading his fleet into battle unprepared and in disorder and, more serious, deserting the battle before the outcome was certain. By a vote of 70 to 48, with 14 abstentions, Pisani was condemned on 12 July 1379 to six months in prison and deprived of all offices for five years. The Venetian Senate put a most favorable construction on the second charge, which could have carried the death penalty, by asserting that Pisani had left the scene of battle in order to save the few galleys not already in Genoese hands.[13]

The Capture of Chioggia

The defeat of the legendary Pisani at Pola had done much for the morale of the allied forces. On 6 May Francesco il Vecchio ordered a feast and procession of thanksgiving for the victory and a solemn requiem in the Duomo for the fallen Genoese admiral Luciano Doria.[14] By the end of the month, Genoese and Paduan forces had sealed off Chioggia at the bottom of the lagoon, while Hungarian troops besieged Treviso and plundered the Trevisano threatening Noale, Bassano, and Mestre. The victorious Genoese fleet attacked at will, setting fire to Malamocco and Pellestrina on the Lido, with the smoke of the burning villages visible from S. Marco itself. While the Genoese fleet interdicted any reinforcements from Venice, Francesco il Vecchio brought up his forces in three columns from the south. Joining forces with Genoese soldiers from the fleet, the allied army launched its final attack on Chioggia on 16 August. In the words of the Paduan chronicler, Galeazzo Gatari,

> Our own Paduans were also fighting towards the bridge of Chioggia, where they engaged the Venetians in a fierce battle; thus it became clear to us that victory would not be possible because of the tenacious defense of the bridge. Messer Gherardo [Manthelor] and Messer Arcoano [Buzzacarini] cried to the men in the field that if any could fire the bridge he would be rewarded with 150 gold ducats. On hearing this, a Genoese soldier immediately stripped off his armor, got into a boat which he filled with straw and powder from our cannon, and began to row toward the bridge. When he was almost there, he set the straw on fire and jumped into the water, pushing the boat toward the bridge, so that it caught and held under the bridge, engulfing it in flames so that the Venetians could no longer hold it.[15]

The Venetians retreated into the center of Chioggia, pursued by Paduan and Genoese soldiers who had breached the last defenses. The rout turned into a massacre as the Piazza of Chioggia turned red with the blood of slain Venetians and Chioggiotes. In the end more than 860 defenders were killed and many prisoners were taken, including the Venetian *podestà* of Chioggia, Pietro Emo, the Venetian captain of the troops, Taddeo Giustinian, and the governor of the fort, Niccolò Contarini.[16] The banner of the commune of Genoa was raised above the Piazza, the *carro* of the lord of Padua hung above the door of the communal palace, and the Hungarian flag flew from the Tower of Chioggia. A few defenders fled south to Brondolo, where they were rounded up by Paduan soldiers. Pietro Emo was handed over to Gherardo Manthelor, who promptly ransomed him for 3,000 ducats and seized in Chioggia his personal property and arms, valued at more than 2,000 ducats. The Venetian mercenary captains Balbo di Gallucci and Niccolò da Gallicano, taken by the Genoese, were sold to Francesco il Vecchio, who took them to Padua and had them hanged in the Piazza delle Biave. Venetian ambassadors sent to Chioggia to negotiate a peace settlement received this brusque reply: "Return to the Signoria and tell your government that we will not entertain your pleas until we have bridled the horses that stand above San Marco."[17]

Two days later, forces under Pietro Doria tried to establish a bridgehead on the southern tip of the Lido but were repulsed by Venetian defenders after hours of intense hand-to-hand combat. The next day Vettor Pisani was released from prison and given a minor command at Torcello. In Venice itself, the aged Doge Andrea Contarini collected all available galleys and personally instructed artisans and shopkeepers drafted into service in the rowing of the vessels from the Giudecca to the Lido and back. Chains were placed across the entrance to the lagoon at S. Niccolò di Lido to prevent Genoese galleys from making a frontal attack on Venice. On 24 August, Genoese ambassadors offered to sell Chioggia to Francesco il Vecchio for the bargain price of 50,000 ducats. But while this offer was being considered, the Genoese had second thoughts about the income that Chioggia's salt and commerce would generate and raised the asking price to 200,000 ducats. This opportunism was too much for Francesco il Vecchio, who left Chioggia in disgust, retiring with many of his troops to Padua.[18] Except for Pietro Doria's vain attempt to occupy the Lido, the allies failed to follow up on their major victory at Chioggia. Venice gained some time to prepare its defenses and eventually plan a counterattack.

Charles of Durazzo and Preliminary Negotiations for Peace

In late summer of 1379 King Louis of Hungary sent his nephew Charles of Durazzo at the head of an army of perhaps ten thousand soldiers into Italy to conclude a favorable peace with Venice and depose Queen Joanna of Naples, who had years earlier been charged with the assassination of Louis's brother and her consort, Andrew of Hungary. By the middle of August the Hungarian forces had reached Udine, entered the Trevisano, and joined the allied army, composed mainly of Paduan troops and mercenaries, besieging Treviso. At the same time, Charles was ready to entertain ambassadors from the allied powers, including Genoa, the lord of Padua, and the patriarch of Aquileia, as well as three seasoned Venetian diplomats, Giovanni Gradenigo, Niccolò Morosini, and Zaccaria Contarini, in an effort to forge the peace.[19] From the beginning of the negotiations, Charles of Durazzo was conciliatory toward the Venetian envoys, asserting on 24 August that King Louis would be very displeased with the destruction of Venice and hoped that it could maintain the integrity of its own institutions and government. But it soon became apparent that Louis set a very high price for peace: the Hungarians demanded from Venice annual tribute of 100,000 ducats or, as an alternative, the cession of the salt monopoly at Chioggia, immediate payment of an indemnity of 1 million (later reduced to half a million) ducats, cession of Trieste, recognition by Venice of the king of Hungary and his descendants as feudal overlord, and the delivery of Treviso, Conegliano, Castelfranco, Noale, and Mestre as security that these terms would be met. The Venetian ambassadors were astonished at the harshness of the terms and suggested in a letter to the doge that secret agents be sent to negotiate a separate peace with Genoa and the lord of Padua rather than accept these impossible demands. In fact, for the next month, discussions between Charles of Durazzo and his Hungarian barons and the Venetian ambassadors consisted of little more than endless restatement of earlier positions. In general, the Venetian tactic of delay worked, for while negotiations went on through the month of September, the siege of Venice itself came to a virtual standstill.

The Venetian envoys were careful rarely to provide clear or definite responses to the terms set by the Hungarians and, when asked for specific proposals, pleaded that consultation with the doge and the *signoria* was necessary before any concrete counterproposals could be advanced. Under these conditions, what came to be called the search for "an honorable and reasonable peace" [pax honesta et rationabilis] dragged on for several weeks. Disgusted and dismayed with the lack of progress, the more bellicose allies, the lord of Padua and envoys from Genoa, arranged separate discussions with the Venetian diplomats, no doubt hoping to negotiate a settlement highly favorable to their own cause. On 9 September Francesco il Vecchio da Carrara provided detailed terms for peace with Venice, which anticipated in many respects the peace terms that were to be agreed to at the Peace of Turin nearly two years later.[20] While offering some accommodations, the Venetian diplomats rejected most Paduan proposals point by point. To the first demand that Venice cede Treviso and its district to Padua, the envoys replied that that part of the *terraferma* had been under Venice's dominion for some time and the Carrara lord had never before pretended to the lordship of Treviso; hence, Venice was ready to submit to the judgment of Louis of Hungary its obvious right to that city. To the demand that Chioggia and S. Ilario be ceded to Padua, the Venetians asserted that they had held these areas for centuries and any adjustments of boundaries must be submitted to the adjudication of two Paduans and two Venetians. The Venetians also turned down Francesco il Vecchio's proposal to tax the rents and products of Venetian proprietors in the Padovano, as well as his demand for the cession of Torre Curano near the lagoon.

Reciting a litany of the Carrara lord's past crimes against Venice, including attempted assassination of members of the nobility, the Venetian envoys systematically rejected the rest of the Carrara lord's peace terms. These included the cancellation of indemnities still owed for the peace of September 1373, with restitution of those already paid, and the cancellation of the traitor Marsilio da Carrara's right to collect rents and income in Padua. Venice also turned down Francesco il Vecchio's request for aid in regaining Feltre and Belluno, which he had ceded to the dukes of Austria, and refused to restore shares in the Monte and return investments at the Grain Office owned by Francesco's consort, Fina, which the Venice government had "frozen" at the time of her death a year earlier. In addition, Venice refused Paduan demands to alter several provisions from the settlement of the Border War of 1373, including freedom for Venetian nobles convicted of treason as spies for the Carrara and full pardon of the harsh sentence for the Carrara agent Francesco Turchetto. Finally, Venice turned a deaf ear to the lord of Padua's territorial demands, refusing to hand over Cavarzere to the south or Treviso to the north or to pay an indemnity of 100,000 ducats for Padua's war expenses. A little later, the other main belligerent, Genoa, made even more excessive requirements for peace, demanding an indemnity of 1 million florins, cession of Crete and other Levantine possessions, and exclusion of Venetian shipping from the Mediterranean except in ports designated by Genoa.

The Venetian ambassadors rightly identified these terms as unreasonable, dangerous, and prejudicial to their city's very existence.[21] Capitalizing on dissension between the allies, Charles of Durazzo and the Hungarian barons advanced King Louis as an "honest broker" in bringing peace, reiterating the promise that in return for the cession of Tenedos and Treviso and its district, an indemnity of 1 million florins, and recognition of Louis as overlord, the king of Hungary would force peace on his recalcitrant and difficult allies.[22] The Venetian envoys would have nothing of this offer; two of them, Zaccaria Contarini and Giovanni Gradenigo, claimed sickness and withdrew to Venice. By the end of October, Charles of Durazzo and his army broke camp and moved down the peninsula, leaving Venice still at war with formidable Paduan and Genoese forces.

Venice Takes the Offensive

While peace negotiations dragged on, both sides planned for victory in the continuing conflict. The policy of the Genoese commander, Pietro Doria, was to starve Venice into submission. After failing to capture the southern end of the Lido in late August, Doria took Malamocco and the island of Poveglia early in September, blockading Venetian shipping and threatening to dig a canal across the Lido to bring galleys and *garzanroli* into the lagoon. At the same time, the Genoese planned to break the chain at the entrance of S. Niccolò, thus penetrating Venetian defenses opposite the city itself.[23] But these ambitious projects were never realized. In early October, Doge Andrea Contarini began to arm a fleet at Venice to take the counteroffensive, imposing a fine of 2,000 ducats on any noble who dared even to dissent from this decision. The doge himself took the title of captain general of the sea and appointed the popular Vettor Pisani as his chief of staff. Each of the ducal councillors undertook to arm a galley at his own expense, and captains of each galley were charged with enrolling crews and crossbowmen. Initially, crews were to serve without salary, but owing to the difficulty of arming all the thirty-four galleys required, the Senate decided to pay most seamen and soldiers for the upcoming campaign. On 1 December, Zaccaria Contarini, back from negotiations at Treviso, proposed to admit to the Maggior Consiglio those thirty citizens who contributed the most for the Venetian war effort. The promise of this reward, along with Venetian citizenship for meritorious foreigners and annual pensions of 5,000 ducats for war heroes, brought Venetian war preparedness to a fever pitch. In the middle of December, the well-armed fleet under command of Taddeo Giustinian and Vettor Pisani moved off to blockade Chioggia, led by the aged Doge Contarini, who vowed never to return to Venice until Chioggia had been retaken by his forces.[24]

Meanwhile, all that autumn in Milan, the Venetian envoy Pietro Corner had been trying to promote Bernabò Visconti's armed intervention against Genoa and purchase foodstuffs and arms for the Venetian war effort. Furnished with a grant of 14,000 ducats for the expenses of diplomacy and residence, Corner established his household in Milan, where, in November, he finally presented his credentials to the Visconti lord. At a meeting in mid-December, Corner attempted to persuade Bernabò and his adviser Pasquino Capelli to mount a campaign against Genoa from the rear or, at least, to close the border above the Ligurian coast. The Visconti lord refused to consider a military campaign, citing the lack of troops and supplies, but a month later, the Milanese did close routes through Lombardy to Genoese troops being sent as reinforcements to Chioggia. In general, the Visconti lord hoped to limit his involvement in the conflict; he expressly denied Corner's request to send soldiers to aid Venice in Chioggia and promised no material aid to the Venetian cause.[25] In the long run, Corner would have to purchase provisions in Lombardy for the Venetian war effort. But the struggle for Chioggia was not the only conflict in Italy. Florence was pitted against the papacy for the control of Tuscany.

Francesco il Vecchio's Role in the Chioggia War

While engaged in his own war against Venice, Francesco il Vecchio had been able to remain aloof from Florence's War of the Eight Saints against the papacy in Italy. Responding to requests for aid from Pope Urban VI, the Carrara lord had remained neutral in this conflict, which ended late in June 1378. The Ciompi rebellion that summer and the subsequent exile of the most conservative oligarch, Lapo da Castiglionchio, to Padua brought the new Florentine regime in conflict with the Carrara lord. On several occasions the Florentine signoria requested the extradition of the hated traitor, who had been sentenced to death with confiscation of his property. When the Carrara lord responded that he would not expel Lapo da Castiglionchio from the safety of exile in Padua, Coluccio Salutati composed a letter explaining the evil crimes and dangerous plots the traitor had perpetrated against the Florentine state.[26] When Francesco il Vecchio refused extradition, the signoria asked that Lapo be arrested and punished in Padua, averring that rebels against the Florentine regime were now flocking to Padua and Lapo's plots had brought nothing but violence to their city.[27] Later that autumn, Florence discovered that Benedetto di Simone Peruzzi, outlawed in perpetuity by the regime, was hiding in Padua and asked the Carrara lord to bring the traitor to justice lest his accomplices flee to Padua.[28] To all these entreaties, Francesco il Vecchio turned a deaf ear, unsympathetic with the more radical Florentine regime and preoccupied with bringing about a successful conclusion to the Chioggia war.

Returning to Padua shortly after the fall of Chioggia, Francesco il Vecchio both sought a favorable peace with Venice and, failing that, an allied victory over his mortal enemy. Early in the conflict the Carrara lord had made loans to his principal allies: 84,000 ducats to the patriarch of Aquileia and 50,000 ducats to Louis of Hungary to gain support for the war effort. Now in late September 1379, the Carrara lord aided the Genoese war efforts by making an interest-free loan of 25,000 ducats to procurators for the doge and commune of Genoa, which was to be repaid within one year.[29] That same autumn, Francesco il Vecchio supported another ally, the Hungarian client state of Ragusa (Dubrovnik), by making the small loan of 150 ducats to two ambassadors to be repaid within one month.[30] Early in December, Francesco il Vecchio adjudicated a dispute over booty taken in a skirmish at Cavarzere by some of his leading captains, Giovanni da Carpi against Conradino and Ugolino di Manfredino Lupi and the German

FIG. 28. Altichiero, Soldiers Casting Lots for Garments of Christ, *detail of Crucifixion.* Chapel of S. Felice (formerly S. Giacomo), Basilica of S. Antonio, ca. 1378. *The armor, clothing, and weapons depicted in this fresco would have been very similar to those worn by soldiers and civilians in the War of Chioggia. Reproduced with permission of Osvaldo Böhm, Venice*

mercenary Hermann.³¹ Later that month, marshaling resources for the continuing struggle, Francesco il Vecchio appointed Simeone dagli Statuti his proctor to collect a loan of £3,000 owed from the estate of Bonzanello da Vigonza, who had recently died in the conflict.³² On 20 December, as the Venetian siege of Chioggia grew ever tighter, Francesco il Vecchio allowed the Genoese representative in Padua, Lorenzo Gentile, to enlist a band of twenty-five German mercenaries for three months' service in Chioggia, "against all cities and lands, except the lord of Padua."³³ Such troops would be sorely needed, for on 1 January 1380 Carlo Zen's long-awaited Levantine fleet appeared at Chioggia destined to alter the outcome of the war.

Shifting Fortunes of War: Venice Recovers Chioggia

Taking council with Pisani and the doge, Zen at once sailed for Brondolo to shore up the weakest point in the Venetian blockade of Chioggia and captured the stronghold at Loreo in the Po Delta, facilitating the delivery of supplies and provisions sent down the Adige from Milanese territories. Armed with bombards, the Venetian forces then invested the enemy garrison at Brondolo, killing on 25 January the Genoese commander Pietro Doria, when the campanile hit by cannon fire fell on him. The fighting was promptly suspended while the Genoese soldier was buried with great ceremony in the Duomo at Chioggia. Meanwhile, both sides strove to provide supplies and fresh troops for the siege of Chioggia. On 13 January the head of the Paduan grain warehouse (Fondaco delle Biave) sold to Lorenzo Gentile, Genoese proctor for the garrison at Chioggia, more than 216 *moggi* of grain for £5,591 13s. 4d., at top price of £26 per *moggio*.³⁴ Ten days later, three English mercenary captains, Roger qd. John Littell, "Zanichinus" qd. William Brock, and one John qd. John, appeared in the Carrara chancery enlisted as soldiers in the Genoese army.³⁵ On 3 February, a Genoese agent enlisted a company of twenty-seven soldiers under the command of one Leone da Brescia for a term of three months' service in Chioggia, paying 16 ducats a month for the captain, his squire, and drummer, 6 ducats a month for each crossbowman, and 4 ducats a month for each foot soldier.³⁶ Meanwhile, in Lombardy, the Venetian ambassador and agent Pietro Corner was busy collecting military hardware for the Venetian war effort. By the end of January, Corner had assembled hundreds of breastplates and helmets and 12,500 darts for transport down the Po eventually to Venice. In March, through agents in eastern Lombardy, Corner purchased many casks of saltpeter, totaling hundreds of pounds, for shipment to Venice for use in gunpowder in the siege of Chioggia.³⁷ Throughout the spring, Corner continued to purchase arms, saltpeter, and especially quantities of grain, mainly through the good offices of Regina della Scala, Bernabò's consort, whose implacable hatred of the Carraresi made her disposed to favor the Venetian cause. In May, vast quantities of grain were shipped from Pavia, Crema, and Cremona down the Po for final destination at Chioggia, as Venice tightened the noose around the beleaguered Paduan and Genoese forces.[38]

Meanwhile, a Genoese fleet under Marco Maruffo, which had just captured Taddeo Giustinian and twelve ships sent to collect grain from Sicily, arrived off Chioggia in April, causing great alarm to the besiegers. But Pisani and Zen were able to avoid open sea battle with Maruffo's forces while they reduced the Paduan and Genoese garrison to near starvation. The Paduan chronicler Galeazzo Gatari reported that the garrison at Chioggia "was in such an extreme condition that perforce the men . . . had to resort to eating their own horses to stay alive, and even to eating dogs and cats; even more there were those who caught rats to eat; there was no bread and no wine left."[39]

Given the need for money for the war effort, Francesco il Vecchio was forced to confiscate the goods of Florentine merchants in Padua to help pay the enormous cost of the struggle, which brought a sharp rebuke from the Florentine signoria.[40] Throughout May, the allies put out feelers to bring about a peaceful solution to the conflict, and on 8 June ambassadors from the lord and commune of Padua, Genoa, the king of Hungary, and the patriarch of Aquileia met with the Venetian legates, Zaccaria Contarini and Andrea Gradenigo, at Cittadella to discuss terms for peace. Representing the lord of Padua were his most trusted councillors, Antonio Zecchi, Bonifacio Lupi, Giacomo Scrovegni, and Paganino Sala, while ambassadors from the commune of Padua were other Carrara favorites, Guglielmo Curtarolo and Giacomo Turchetto. Perhaps sensing the impending surrender of the allied forces in Chioggia, the Venetian ambassadors began to temporize and on 13 June broke off the negotiations.

Early that summer the Genoese fleet was forced to retire to Istria, depriving the forces at Chioggia of their last hope for salvation. Finally, on 24 June 1380 the starving garrison at Chioggia surrendered to the besieging army. As many as five thousand Paduan and Genoese troops and mercenaries fell into the hands of the jubilant Venetian forces. The entire populace of Venice turned out to welcome the fleet and army that returned in triumph to the city with the aged Doge Andrea Contarini at its head. The *Bucintoro* sailed out in state to greet at the Molo the doge and his triumphal procession, which brought in train the remnants of Pietro Doria's fleet, seventeen battered galleys, and their abject crews. The soldiers captured at Chioggia were consigned to prison to await ransoming, while many of Venice's mercenaries were paid in full, as promised, for their loyalty in the last campaign.⁴¹ But with the northern Adriatic still to be cleared of Genoese naval forces and Paduan forces investing the Trevisano, Venice's victory was far from certain.

Earlier that spring Pietro Corner had finally persuaded the Venetian ally Bernabò Visconti to mount an attack on Genoa from the north at Gavi and Serravalle and, at the same time, hinder Genoese reinforcements from reaching Chioggia. Charles of Durazzo's descent into Italy the previous year on his way to claim the Neapolitan throne, however, had caused Bernabò Visconti to redeploy his troops from action against Genoa to defend his eastern frontier. At this moment, the old Guelf entente between Padua and the Florentine signoria was weakened by the War of the Eight Saints against the papacy and by the rivalry for the throne of Naples between Louis of Anjou, nephew of King Charles VI of France, and Charles of Durazzo, nephew of King Louis of Hungary. Thus, while welcoming the Carrara favorite Francesco Dotti as the new podestà of Florence in April 1380, the Florentine government demanded that the lord of Padua report on Charles of Durazzo's movements, the status of rebels against the regime, and the hostile activities of Alberico da Barbiano's Company of St. George. Later that year, certain of Charles' continuing opposition to the Ghibelline Visconti lord of Milan, Florence thanked Francesco il Vecchio for gifts and intelligence sent through Francesco Dotti as podestà.⁴²

The End of the Conflict: Peace of Turin

Returning to the Adriatic in July 1380, the Genoese fleet aided the forces of the patriarch of Aquileia to occupy Venice's ally, Trieste, while it continued to raid Venetian shipping and ports in Istria. On 13 August the popular Venetian naval hero Vettor Pisani died at Manfredonia on the Apulian coast from exhaustion of his summer campaign against enemy forces in Istria. On the mainland, Francesco il Vecchio tightened his siege of Treviso, bribing contingents of English mercenaries employed by Venice at Mestre to join his forces. In December, after a long siege, Castelfranco surrendered to Paduan forces, and two months later, the Paduans occupied the Venetian stronghold at Noale. New meetings begun at Cittadella on 12 February 1381 lasted for two months, helping to pave the way for a general peace conference convened at Turin by Amadeus VI, the count of Savoy. Concerned by the unsettled conditions produced by prolonged warfare in northern Italy, in early May Florence sent letters to the chief protagonists—Venice, Genoa, the Visconti lord of Milan, and the Carrara lord of Padua—urging peace.⁴³ After Treviso had been consigned in May to Leopold, duke of Austria, to prevent it from falling into the hands of the Carrara lord, Venice was ready to open negotiations in Turin. Louis of Hungary wrote in June urging Francesco il Vecchio to accept Leopold's occupation of Treviso and not let contention for that city cause dissension between the two allies.[44]

On 8 August 1381, after long and arduous negotiations, the peace ending the War of Chioggia was finally signed at Turin. In many respects, the provisions of peace between Venice and the lord and commune of Padua called for a return to the status quo ante bellum.[45] Hostilities were immediately suspended, prisoners exchanged, and the frontiers established in the peace of 21 September 1373 observed, though Francesco il Vecchio could keep strongholds and towns captured in the Trevisano. The fortresses at Cavarzere and Moranzane were to be returned to Venice, while the Carrara lord retained his stronghold at Curan and the right to maintain fortifications at Castelcarro and Oriago. River traffic was reopened, the trade in salt reestablished, and property seized during the conflict restored to the original owners. In general, the older treaties governing extradition and Venetians' property rights in the Padovano were to be observed, though peasants of Venetian proprietors now had to pay the same taxes as Paduan leaseholders. Venice was accommodating on a few personal matters: the 20,000 ducats that the lord's recently deceased consort, Fina da Carrara, had invested in the Monte at Venice was to be "unfrozen" and restored to her heir, Francesco Novello; goods and money already paid from Paduan estates to the lord's traitorous half brother Marsilio da Carrara were not to be returned, but no future payments need be made. The indemnities required in the peace of 1373 were canceled, but a stiff new war reparation was exacted from the lord and commune of Padua: 50,000 ducats to be paid in three equal installments. Deprived once more of its mainland possessions, Venice agreed that Padua would be allowed to occupy Belluno, Feltre, the pass at Quero, and S. Boldo on the Piave, if the Carrara lord was able to gain these territories in the future. At first Venice stood firm in its condemnation of the Carrara favorite Francesco Turchetto, who had been convicted *in absentia* of attempting to murder Venetian noblemen in 1373, and refused to pay the indemnity of 4,000 ducats the Carrara lord was demanding for the unjust sentence of his valued henchman. But later that autumn, at the instance of the count of Savoy, the Maggior Consiglio agreed to revoke the sentence passed in the Council of Forty against Turchetto, thus removing the threat of the death penalty if he was found in Venetian domains.[46] On the larger issues, Venice agreed to hand over to the Green Count its fortresses on the island of Tenedos—the immediate cause of the conflict—acknowledge Genoa's special rights in Cyprus, and pay an annual indemnity of 7,000 ducats to the king of Hungary in recognition of his lordship of the Adriatic.

These pacts were then ratified in the capitals of the belligerents, marked by solemn celebrations of peace, ending this most bitter and costly conflict. On 20 August Francesco il Vecchio ordered a Mass of thanksgiving held in the Duomo, followed by a procession through the neighboring squares of the clergy, guildsmen, and people of Padua, featuring in the line of march seventy-two Venetian nobles who had been captured in the recent war. On the 22th the chief notary of the Carrara chancery, Bandino Brazzi, redacted confirmation of the peace made at Turin on the 8th between Zaccaria Contarini, Giovanni Gradenigo, and Michele Morosini, proctors for Venice, and Taddeo Azzoguido, Antonio Zecchi, and Giacomo Turchetto, ambassadors for the lord and commune of Padua.[47] On 31 August, in the Camera Lucrezia of the Carrara palace, Francesco il Vecchio appointed Bonacorso Naseri and Bartolomeo Vanzerio his proctors to ratify the peace in Venice, and on the same day the Maggior Consiglio of Padua confirmed the same men as ambassadors to represent the commune of Padua at the ratification.[48] The next day, on behalf of both lord and commune of Padua, the young canon lawyer Francesco Zabarella made a stirring speech before the doge and signoria of Venice praising peace between the two great cities. Peace was formally proclaimed in both cities.[49] With the exchange of prisoners on 2 September 1381, the main issues outstanding were the adjudication of borders and Padua's payment of the indemnity of 50,000 ducats.

Francesco il Vecchio's occupation of certain towns of the Trevisano, which had been ceded to Leopold of Austria, continued to cause grounds of contention between Padua and Venice. In general, the Carrara lord sought to placate Venetian demands while retaining control of the towns he had captured in the recent war. For example, responding to a ducal letter early in October, the Carrara lord agreed that he would permit the Venetians Niccolò and Jacopo Dandolo to hold property their father, Francesco, owned in Castelfranco, which Padua had occupied since December 1380.[50] But other problems proved more intractable. Within a month after the proclamation of the Peace of Turin, the Venetian Senate appointed a legate to notify the Carrara lord of the necessity of razing his fortress at S. Ilario near the lagoon, thus having him conform to earlier pacts and the recent peace, which forbade fortification in this area.[51] Several weeks later Doge Morosini had the Senate draw up instructions for the embassy of Luca Contarini to settle disputes arising from certain terms of the peace. The envoy was to confirm Venice's fishing rights at Cavarzere and Cona, which had recently been conveyed to Venice, as well as the illegality of any forts built at S. Ilario. The Venetian ambassador was also to warn the lord of Padua that he could not demand labor services and taxes from peasants leasing land from the monastery at S. Ilario, which remained under Venice's protection and jurisdiction. Finally, money that the lord of Padua had taken as taxes from Venetian citizens during the recent conflict was to be restored, as provided by treaty. In short, Venice was eager to see the terms of the Peace of Turin carried out and expected the lord and commune of Padua to fulfill their obligations.[52]

The precise definition of boundaries between the two states was, in the long run, left to arbitration by Niccolò II d'Este, as had been agreed at Turin. On 21 October, the Senate provided for the election of three nobles as *savi* on the matter of confines. Of those nominated, four noblemen refused election; only Giovanni Bembo and Pantaleone Giustinian accepted the post. In the event, the boundary settlement took nearly a year to complete: in December the Senate appropriated another 50 ducats for the expenses of the savi, beyond the per diem already provided. The next March the Maggior Consiglio of Padua voted to appoint its envoy Giacomo Turchetto to extend negotiations on disputed borders to the feast of Pentecost (25 May 1382). Early that June at Cona near the lagoon, the envoys of the lord and commune of Padua, Simone Lupi, Antonio Zecchi, and Giacomo Turchetto, met with the Venetian savi and agreed to the terms set by Niccolò II d'Este. Only in August, after the audit of the agreement by notary of Venice's Great Council, was the question of borders finally settled.[53]

Border settlement was not the only matter that required careful and wary negotiation between the lord of Padua and the government of Venice. During the Chioggia war, Francesco il Vecchio had made an interest-free loan of 50,000 ducats to Louis of Hungary, and by the Peace of Turin, the lord of Padua was required to pay an indemnity of 50,000 ducats to Venice, while Venice had to pay annual tribute of 7,000 ducats to the king of Hungary. With exhausted treasuries and crushing indebtedness heightening the need for cooperation among the former belligerents, in late December Louis of Hungary sent a letter to Venice proposing that since he owed 50,000 ducats to the lord of Padua, at least 49,000 of the indemnity Francesco il Vecchio owed Venice should be paid from the first seven years' tribute that Venice owed him. Meeting in late January 1382, the Senate debated the question and decided against Louis's request, since the lord of Padua had paid a third of the indemnity and the second third, due that Easter (6 April 1382), had already been assigned to settle urgent outstanding debts. But Venice was happy to allow the Carrara lord to make payment of the final third from the first three years of the annual tribute Venice owed Hungary.[54] On 1 April the representative of the king of Hungary acknowledged payment of 21,000 ducats from three years of tribute owed from Venice, which sum was then to be assigned to the lord and commune of Padua, deducting the final payment of 16,666⅔ ducats owed to Venice. On 15 May both Carrara lords, Francesco il Vecchio and Francesco Novello, appointed Guglielmo Curtarolo their proctor to receive from Doge Andrea Contarini receipt for the final payment. The next day Venice's grand chancellor, Raffaino Caresini, made receipt to Curtarolo for the final third, promising to pay to the Carrara the difference of 4,333⅓ ducats from the 21,000 ducats owed to Louis of Hungary only in August 1384, when the third year of tribute would fall due.[55] Thus, scarcity of specie compelled former enemies to juggle obligations and devise ingenious solutions to the payment of the indemnities required by the Peace of Turin.

Padua's Offensive for Treviso and Friuli

In the mind of Francesco il Vecchio the Peace of Turin left unresolved two large issues: who was to rule Treviso and control Friuli. Venice's cession of Treviso to Duke Leopold of Austria had infuriated the lord of Padua because it cheated him of one of his main objectives in the Chioggia war. At the end of August 1381, Francesco il Vecchio sent heralds throughout the Trevisano up to the Piave River to warn peasants against sending any supplies to the beleaguered city of Treviso, thus hoping to starve out the populace there. The Trevisans sent repeated requests for aid to Duke Leopold, who in May finally entered his new city, which lay destitute after sixteen years of intermittent warfare. Leopold soon turned over the government of Treviso to Hugh, count of Duino, as captain general and Bertold Spilimbergo as podestà and retired to his residence at Graz. Into the next spring, the struggle continued between Carrara forces and besieged Treviso. Already in control of major strongholds of the Trevisano at Castelfranco, Noale, Asolo, and the pass on the Piave at Quero, the Carrara lord now constructed a series of forts on the Sile River south of Treviso from which to mount his final attack.[56] In January, Trevisan ambassadors beseeched the duke for aid and protection: Leopold reminded the Venetian government that it was to pay its debts to individual citizens of Treviso and restore records taken from the chancery when Venetian officials had left the city. The ambassadors repeated the plea for military aid against the forces of the lord of Padua, who preyed on local workers and interdicted supplies to the city from their forts on the Sile.[57] Throughout the spring and summer the Trevisans sent legations to the duke informing him of the worsening conditions and begging for help against the Paduan invaders.

Elated by his initial successes in the war for Treviso, Francesco il Vecchio continued his diplomacy farther afield for control of Trieste. During the Chioggia war the patriarch of Aquileia had finally wrested dominion over Trieste from Venice when in August 1380 his grand marshal received the keys to the city and the banner of S. Giusto from the citizens of Trieste. The patriarch's control of Trieste was ratified in the Peace of Turin, but the appointment of the French cardinal Philippe d'Alençon *in commenda* to the patriarchate of Aquileia caused widespread rebellion among the nobles and communes of Friuli. Disposed to stand by the new patriarch but uncertain that d'Alençon would actually be able to keep Trieste against the rebellious nobles or the menaces of Leopold of Austria, Francesco il Vecchio arranged a loan of 1,000 ducats to the commune of Trieste. On 1 April 1382, the proctor for Trieste, Adelmo de' Petazzi, appeared in the Carrara chancery to receive the sum to cover urgent expenses, promising to repay the debt within one year. But the Carrara lord's generosity had little effect: on 9 August, Trieste came under the dominion of Leopold of Austria when Hugh, count of Duino, received the oath of fealty from its citizens. The next month, the same Adelmo de' Petazzi who had received the loan in Padua traveled to Graz to receive from Leopold the charter of Habsburg possession of Trieste.[58]

Deprived of influence in Trieste, the lord of Padua found it, for the moment, expedient to accommodate his old enemy, Venice. Earlier in January, the Carrara lord, through his factor Niccolò Curtarolo, sold for 900 ducats 800 *staia* of grain to Donato Maresa acting for the commune of Chioggia and its current podestà, Pietro di Marco Giustinian. The other Carrara agent in the deal was Antonio Meneghini, resident in the Carrara palace on Campo S. Polo in Venice, who undertook the final collection of the payment from the commune of Chioggia. Thus, Francesco il Vecchio provided needed foodstuffs to Chioggia at a high price, £5 per *staio*, employing his best spy in Venice to make the deal favored by the podestà of Chioggia, who was perhaps already a Carrara agent in the heart of the Venetian government. Only three years later both Meneghini and the podestà Giustinian were executed in Venice for trading state secrets to the lord of Padua.[59]

Reluctant to evacuate Tenedos and destroy its fortifications, as provided for in the Peace of Turin, Venice's government invented reasons to delay consigning the island, while making certain of the neutrality of Genoa's former allies. Thus, on the touchy issue of confines with Padua, Venice had accepted the mediation of Niccolò II d'Este and had been conciliatory toward Padua's occupation of strongholds of the Trevisano. At the height of the debate over the fate of Tenedos in April 1382, the Senate sent Leonardo Dandolo as ambassador to Padua to profess love for the Carrara lord, like that which "obtained between his forebears and magnificent house and us [the doge] and our commune, just as in times past," promoting good will and cooperation between the two states.[60] That same month, Francesco il Vecchio favored Venetian interests in the Trevisano, appointing envoys to permit Roberto Morosini to take possession of his inheritance at Noale.[61] Wanting to ensure Paduan benevolence, Venice became increasingly hostile to Leopold of Austria, who now controlled both Treviso and Trieste and threatened to tax and interrupt Venetian commerce with Germany. Grateful for a virtually free hand in his attempt to conquer Treviso, Francesco il Vecchio was pleased to appoint the splendid legation composed of the current podestà, Roberto Mario Camporini, Simone Lupi, Antonio Zecchi, Bonacorso Naseri, and Boscarino Buzzacarini to congratulate the new doge, Michele Morosini, elected on 10 June 1382.[62]

Marriage Alliances and Diplomacy

In the late spring of 1382, to increase his influence near the Habsburg domains, Francesco il Vecchio turned to a favorite instrument of diplomacy, the marriage alliance. In January 1367 the Carrara lord had married his eldest daughter, Gigliola, to Wenceslaus, duke of Saxony, with a dowry of 60,000 ducats and trousseau of 30,000 in precious stones, clothes, and jewelry. This daughter, who was to have three sons by the duke, outlived her first husband and in 1388 married the widower Hermann, count of Cilli (Celji), in eastern Croatia. In 1372, at the urging of King Louis of Hungary, the second Carrara daughter, Caterina, was married to Stefan Frankapan, the count of Veglia and lord of Segni on the Dalmatian coast. The Frankapan domains were a virtual client state of the Hungarian Crown, and Stefan was made even more amenable to the policies of the Carrara-Magyar alliance by having Francesco il Vecchio's daughter as his consort.[63] Now a decade later Francesco il Vecchio negotiated the marriage of his youngest daughter, Lieta, to Frederick IV, count of Ortenburg, who ruled territories in the upper Drava River valley to the west of Habsburg domains. Agreeing by proxy in June 1382 to a dowry of 16,000 ducats, augmented by a trousseau of jewels and precious metals valued at 4,000 ducats, Frederick later married his bride in Padua amidst the usual celebrations and brought her back to lower Austria. There she probably met her paternal aunt, Francesco il Vecchio's sister, also named Lieta, who had some years earlier taken Frederick's father, the widowed Otto IV of Ortenburg, as her husband.[64] Thus, one Lieta da Carrara succeeded another as countess of Ortenburg in the lord of Padua's efforts to secure a powerful ally against the hostile Habsburg dynasty.

The Trevisan War

In the late summer and autumn of 1382, Francesco il Vecchio renewed his efforts to occupy Treviso. Early in August, the Carrara lord's success continued: his forces bribed the Trevisan captain to hand over the Serra Carrarese on the Trevisan border, while he persuaded the lord of Ferrara, Niccolò II d'Este, to contribute one hundred cavalry and forty archers to the Trevisan campaign.[65] By the middle of September Paduan forces were at the gates of Treviso, freely pillaging the farms and villages of the *contado*. In their attacks, Paduan soldiers sometimes harmed the property of Venetian landholders in the area, bringing a sharp rebuke from the doge. In August Carrara troops from Castelfranco had inflicted violence on Venetian citizens at Zero near Mestre, mistaking them for subjects of Leopold of Austria. Complaints from the Venetian government brought an instant apology from Francesco il Vecchio, who averred that the offenses were committed without knowledge of their superiors and that the damages had now been repaired.[66]

The Carrara policy of conciliation and recognition of Venetian rights had its rewards. After the death of Louis of Hungary on 11 September 1382, the queen regent Elisabeth joined Leopold of Austria in sending an embassy to enlist Venice in a defensive league. But the Senate flatly refused, citing its recent treaty with Genoa and Padua and affirming its desire to remain at peace with all states in the world.[67] That same month, Venice permitted the Carrara lord to authorize his agent Antonio Meneghini to purchase from individuals in Venice shares in the Monte, which were then selling at about 40 percent of par. Thus, the lord of Padua joined other favored mainland signori, Bernabò Visconti, Niccolò II d'Este, and Francesco Gonzaga, who were permitted to invest money from grain sales to Venice in the Monte at bargain prices per share. Aware of the good value of the shares, Francesco il Vecchio gave Meneghini carte blanche "to acquire in Venice from any person or persons, one or several, lay or clerical, and from any commune, college, and organization any quantity of shares at whatever sum, in whatever market, and for whatever price, as he will deem appropriate."[68]

Besides allowing investment in the Monte and denying help to Duke Leopold and his garrison at Treviso, late in 1382 the Venetian government honored the Carrara lord's request to permit transportation of material up the Sile River for the construction of his siege towers outside the walls of Treviso. By a vote of 62 to 19 with 2 abstentions, the Senate agreed that the lord of Padua could send "on Venetian waters to his *bastita* on the Sile, paying the usual tolls" quantities of lumber, beams, and nails for the tower as well as salt meat, wine, and clothing for his men.[69] Thus, Venice opened to its recent enemy a direct river route starting in the *dogado* at Musestre, enabling Francesco il Vecchio to supply his army besieging Treviso. That winter hostilities came to a standstill with both sides agreeing to a truce to last until the feast of the Annunciation (25 March) in 1383. In fact, both armies had been devastated by the plague that ravaged Italy that autumn, causing very high mortality in Venice. Although Carrara forces under Simone Lupi had seized the vital junction at Nervesa on the Piave to cut off reinforcements from the north, enough provisions and fresh German troops had reached Treviso in November to keep the populace supplied into the spring. Duke Leopold alternated attempts at diplomatic settlement with promises to lead a large force into Italy to relieve Treviso the next summer. In the meantime, the Carrara lord continued to construct his fortress under the walls of Treviso, securing permission from Venice in February to transport up the river five hundred oaken planks, thirty thousand bricks, twelve barrels of nails, and timber and other hardware as well as a quantity of bread and flour for his men and oats for their horses.[70]

The presence of numerous Paduan troops in the Trevisano, where Venetians owned extensive property, caused inevitable tensions. In early March 1383, in reply to a complaint that he was building forts in the *dogado* itself, Francesco il Vecchio pointed out that his new fortifications were not, in fact, in Venetian territory. A little later he had to promise not to harass Venetian officials and landowners in Povegliano, north of Treviso. Apparently raids and construction of forts infringed on Venice's interests, prerogatives, and property.[71] But through the spring of 1383, Venice permitted the buildup of Paduan arms and forces outside Treviso. At the end of March the Carrara lord sent up the Sile foodstuffs, tents, and timbers and especially bombards, gunpowder, and cannon balls as well as arrows and darts for a final assault. By the middle of May, the lord of Padua had deployed a large army besieging Treviso, supplied with nearly forty cannon.[72] Just at that moment, Leopold of Austria fulfilled his longstanding pledge to relieve Treviso, arriving at the ford of the Piave at Nervesa at the head of an army of more than eight hundred knights and a large contingent of infantry. Part of his troops immediately attacked the Paduan camp at Musestre, taking quantities of supplies back to Treviso. At the end of May, Leopold led his garrison from Treviso in a frontal attack on the Paduan tower outside the walls.[73] But the duke's successes were limited, and soon a truce was declared, ending with a fruitless parley between Francesco Novello and Austrian envoys at Noale. By the middle of July, Leopold perceived that the situation was hopeless and left Treviso for Austria, vainly vowing to return. Late that summer, Paduan forces attacked at will in the Trevisano, capturing Oderzo and Motta and besieging Conegliano. Writing on 14 August to the Trevisans, Francesco il Vecchio could claim, "All the [Trevisan] territory this side of the Piave River is mine, . . . acquired by me not without great labor and expense."[74] Treviso was isolated, awaiting its fate.

Throughout the late summer and autumn of 1383, Paduan forces tightened the noose around Treviso. In July, the Venetian Senate approved

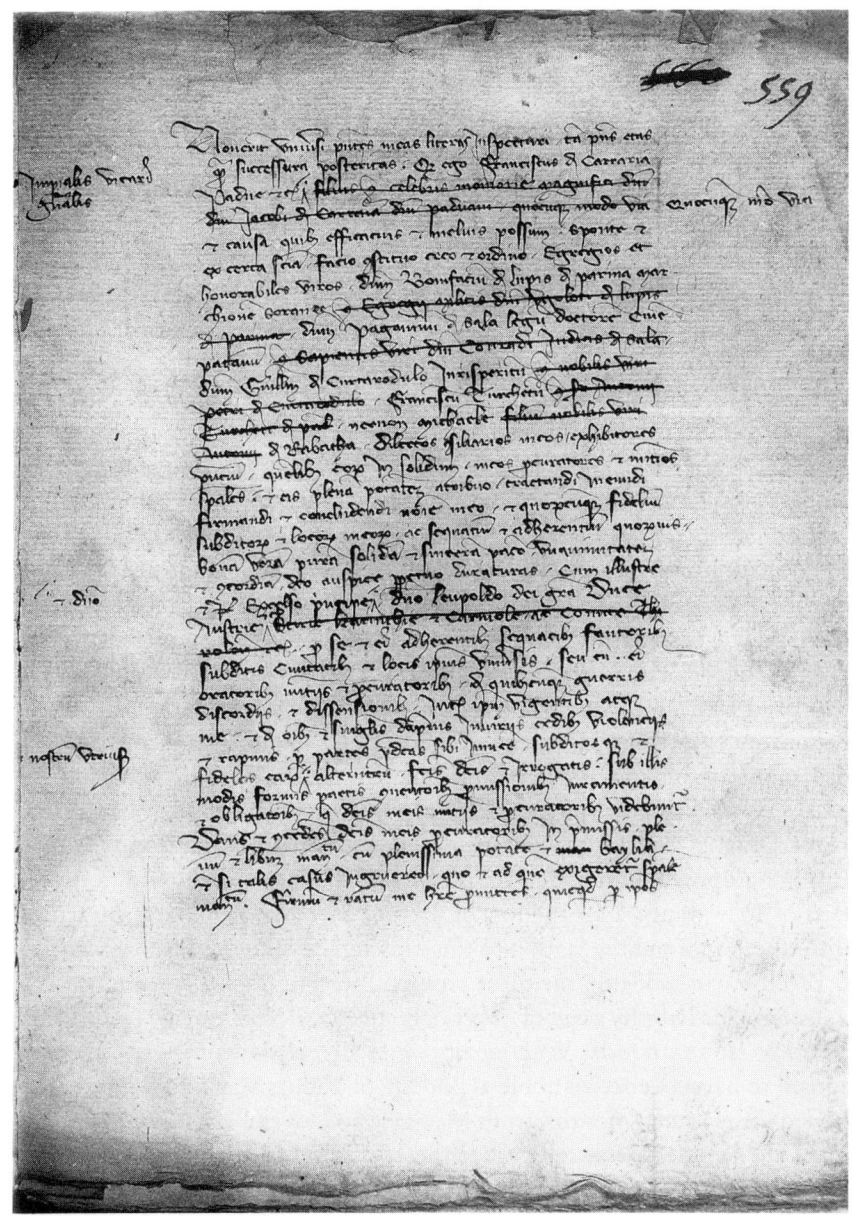

FIG. 29. *Notarial act appointing Carrara envoys. Draft of an act of procuration drawn up by court notary Bandino Brazzi, in which Francesco il Vecchio, styled lord and imperial vicar of Padua, named Bonifacio Lupi, Paganino Sala, Guglielmo Curtarolo, Francesco Turchetto, and Michele Rabatta* nuncios speciales *to make peace with Duke Leopold of Austria in the spring of 1383.* Source: Archivio di Stato, Padua, AN, 38, fol. 559r, 1 May 1383. Reproduced with permission of the Archivio di Stato, Studio Fotografico, Padua

another shipment up the Sile of cannon and tons of gunpowder as well as flour, salt meat, cheese, and wine for the soldiers. By the end of September, three more tons of munitions and fifty cannon had arrived at the Paduan fort outside Treviso, supplying the bombardment of the walls of the city which had begun on 1 August.[75] In the middle of October, the Trevisans wrote to Leopold stressing the gravity of the situation: no provisions were coming from Friuli because of the conflict between the patriarch and the Udinesi nor through Paduan lines from Venice, causing great scarcity of grain, wine, and meat.[76] Abandoned by Leopold and under heavy bombardment from the Carrara forces, Treviso was a doomed city. Leopold broke his promise never to convey Treviso to the lord of Padua and early in January 1384 agreed to sell Treviso and its district to Francesco il Vecchio for 100,000 ducats, adding Ceneda, Serravalle, and Conegliano for another 17,000. On 4 February the lord of Padua made his triumphant entry into Treviso at the head of his conquering army, accompanied by Simone Lupi, captain general of the Carrara forces, with Bartolomeo Cermisone leading a thousand *provisionati* and Paolo da Bologna two thousand infantry, each bearing a pennon of the Carrara arms. To win the hearts of his new Trevisan subjects, Francesco il Vecchio made large loans to local merchants and exempted from taxes craftsmen who would come to ply their trades in the desolated city.[77] He even proposed to cement the peace with the duke of Austria by betrothing his young granddaughter Gigliola da Carrara to one of Leopold's sons and informed the Venetian government by letter in February "of the betrothal of the daughter of his son with the son of the lord Duke Leopold, and of the peace and concord that he made with him."[78] But the proposed marriage never took place. Habsburg influence in the affairs of Italy waned after the loss of Treviso. Possessing domains stretching from the Adige and the lagoon to the Alps and beyond the Piave, Francesco il Vecchio was suddenly the most powerful lord in northeastern Italy.

During the lengthy siege of Treviso, Francesco il Vecchio had made every effort to accommodate Venetian interests in his domains. He had even agreed to have a Venetian noble as podestà of Padua, Marino Memmo, who served for eighteen months, from May 1383 to November 1384, an appointment the Senate saw as critical for the execution of the provisions of the Peace of Turin.[79] During the recent war, peasants farming in the *dogado* had sometimes paid taxes and rents to Paduan officials who oversaw the occupied territories. Now when the Benedictine house at S. Ilario claimed dues for three years from one of its tenants, who had paid rents to the Carrara officials, a Paduan court decided that the Benedictines could not expel their leaseholder for unpaid dues but had to accept him as their current tenant.[80] Shortly after the Paduan occupation of Treviso, Venice permitted Francesco il Vecchio to send up the Sile huge quantities of foodstuffs for the destitute population.[81] Even a few months later, Venice continued to allow the Paduans to transport duty-free two millions bricks and two hundred wagonloads of lime for the construction of fortifications at Treviso and at Motta on the Livenza River.[82]

However, as the Carrara occupation of the Trevisano continued, tensions with the Venetian proprietors there grew. In order to pay for the purchase of the city, Francesco il Vecchio had levied an inheritance tax of 10 percent on property of deceased subjects and exacted a large forced loan, appointing four curialists to carry out the task.[83] In February a special tax of 300 ducats was levied on the Druggist Guild, doubtless applied to other Paduan guilds at the same time.[84] Sending his main economic official, Francesco Dotti, to replace Simone Lupi as podestà of Treviso in October 1384, the Carrara lord levied taxes on landowners in his new territories, including Venetian proprietors who were by earlier treaties exempt from such exactions. The Senate was quick to send ambassadors, reminding Francesco il Vecchio of the privileged position of Venetian landowners in the Trevisano, guaranteed by the pacts of 1318 and 1322, which Leopold of Austria had promised to observe when he received the city. In early June the ambassadors were instructed to reprimand the lord of Padua for his repudiation of Venetian privileges in the Trevisano and read aloud to him relevant portions of the earlier treaties, even giving him copies of the texts so that he would be aware of his obligations.[85] Perhaps the Carrara lord curtailed his illegal exactions from Venetian landowners in the Trevisano, for on 8 August the Senate granted permission to the Paduans to transport another 10,000 *staia* of grain up to Sile, paying the usual customs.[86] But very soon the Carrara lord's designs on Friuli would end any special considerations from Venice.

Paduan Interests in Friuli

Control of Friuli, in alliance with the patriarch of Aquileia, had for several years been a prime objective of Paduan foreign policy.[87] Early in 1383 Francesco il Vecchio offered armed support to the new patriarch of Aquileia against the rebellion of the Udinese feudatories led by Federigo Savorgnan, who had favored the appointment of Louis of Halfinstaign. For the moment, Philippe d'Alençon, who held the patriarchate *in commenda* following the death of Marguardo di Randek, declined the offer. Encouraged to arbitrate a settlement by Queen Elisabeth of Hungary, that fall Francesco pressed on the commune of Udine his proposal to mediate any disputes with the patriarch.[88] Perhaps encouraged by a letter of January 1384 from the commune of Udine praising his services to peace and the Holy Mother

Church in Friuli, Francesco il Vecchio decided to expand his authority there. That spring the lord of Padua petitioned Pope Urban VI to have his natural son Conte da Carrara named abbot of the Benedictine house of Rosazzo.[89] When this request was rejected, the Carrara lord began to fortify Conegliano and insist on his right to arbitrate the disputes between the patriarch of Aquileia and the Friulian rebels, rejecting Queen Elisabeth of Hungary's accusation that he was collecting troops to conquer Friuli. Rumors were rife. In July Venice's ally, the patriarch of Grado, reported to the Collegio that the lord of Padua through Niccolò da Spilimbergo had offered to pacify Friuli on the condition that d'Alençon accept Conte da Carrara as his vicar and then convey to him after a few months the patriarchate, sealing the agreement with a gift of 35,000 florins.[90] In the event Conte da Carrara was not made patriarch, but his father's alternation of threats and blandishments persuaded the Udinese rebels to accept his arbitration. At the end of July, the Carrara lord handed down his judgment: all rebels were to swear their allegiance to the patriarch of Aquileia within six days. In return, the patriarch was to suspend all legal actions against the rebels. Both sides were to restore lands and castles taken, free prisoners, and allow exiles six months to return home. Difficult cases were to be referred to the lord of Padua for final arbitration.[91] Several Carrara favorites were immediately installed in the patriarch's regime: Guglielmo Curtarolo as temporal vicar; Giovanni, abbot of S. Benedetto, as spiritual vicar; Michele Rabatta as the patriarch's marshal; and Gherardo Manthelor as the captain of Udine. For the moment the lord of Padua dominated Friuli. At the end of August the Collegio at Venice had the report that "the lord Cardinal and Patriarch [d'Alençon] says clearly for all to hear that he considers the lord of Padua to be the Patriarch of Aquileia."[92]

Mindful that Venice was likely to retaliate for his attempt to control Friuli, the Carrara lord began to liquidate deposits in Venetian banks and the Monte. As early as February 1384, he had insisted on the prompt payment of 12,000 ducats Venice owed from a large grain sale, appointing the manager of his grain warehouse, Paolo qd. Ture di San Giovanni, proctor to receive the first installment of 4,000 ducats in Venice, along with the Carrara agent there, Antonio Meneghini. At the end of March, Paolo was appointed to receive the second installment, but apparently the whole amount was not received, for on 14 September, the Carrara lord made Antonio Meneghini his proctor to get a final payment of 4,000 ducats from the Grain Office.[93] Early in 1384, the Carrara lord appointed Meneghini his envoy to appear before the doge and other Venetian officials to collect the shares that his late wife held in the Monte, as had been provided for in the Peace of Turin.[94] As the costs for a Friuli campaign loomed large, Francesco il Vecchio sold interests in partnerships and collected deposits. On 17 June he appointed the Florentine merchant Francesco Allegro to sell his interests in the estate of Bartolomeo qd. Coluccio Seta to the heirs for 1,800 ducats, and on 30 September he made Antonio Meneghini his proctor to collect all deposits the Carrara lord had with any Venetian *campsores* through the Florentine banking firm of Vieri de' Medici and Jacopo di Francesco Venturi.[95]

Meanwhile, Venice cultivated support of its allies in Friuli, the patriarch of Grado, Federigo Savorgnan, and the commune of Udine, while threatening to protest to Pope Urban VI the secret accords of the Carrarese-Aquileia alliance. Responding to a letter from Francesco il Vecchio on the question of borders, in late September the Senate counseled patience, suggesting that each side send arbiters to determine the true boundaries.[96] A month later, pleading that he was deeply involved in protecting the patriarch of Aquileia in Friuli, the lord of Padua declined to join a league or make a loan of 25,000 ducats, requested by Florentine ambassadors Roberto Aldobrandino and Lorenzo Fracassini during the crisis caused by the descent into Tuscany of Enguerrand, sire de Coucy, on his way to support the duke of Anjou's claims to the Kingdom of Naples.[97] By the end of the year, Francesco il Vecchio probably came to view renewed conflict with Venice as inevitable and appointed his *spenditore* Antonio Pavanello as his proctor to sell all his shares in Venice's Monte for whatever price he could get.[98]

Padua's Relations with Venice Worsen, 1385–1386

Early the next February, Venice continued to disguise its true intentions. The Senate voted to give a guarded response to questions from Carrara agents whether Venice intended to join the league forming in Friuli directed against the patriarch of Aquileia and the lord of Padua, asserting that revealing the negotiations would provide Francesco il Vecchio with grounds for breaking the peace.[99] Five days later, Venice joined at Grado the "Felice Unione" of anti-Carrara forces in Friuli, composed of Federigo Savorgnan, Venceslao da Spilimbergo, Doimo and Nicoletto da Castello, Francesco Prampero, the counts of Colloredo and of Maniago, and the communes of Udine, Venzone, Sacile, and Marano, all dedicated to preserve the liberties of Friuli and the Aquileian church and the welfare of Venice.[100]

Faced with an uneasy peace and secret negotiations, Francesco il Vecchio turned to his best spies to discover Venice's real intentions. Resident in the Carrara palace on Campo S. Polo, the Chioggiote Antonio Meneghini had long served as Francesco il Vecchio's principal agent in Venice and now negotiated with the state attorney, Pietro di Marco Giustinian, to trade state secrets to Padua. Giustinian, a fixture in *terraferma* politics for several decades, turned out to be the sort of nobleman the Venetian government dreaded most—one readily corrupted by the goals and gold of a great mainland lord. As early as 1356, Pietro Giustinian had represented Scaligeri interests in Venice, before accepting the posts of proctor to the Abbey of Rosazzo in Friuli in 1370 and podestà of Conegliano in 1372. Three years later he served a term as one of the Provveditori alle Biave, before accepting appointment in the spring of 1376 as Venetian envoy to the Della Scala court in Verona to attempt to conclude a league against Leopold of Austria.[101] At the outbreak of the Chioggia war, Giustinian served as ambassador to Genoa before becoming ducal councillor in 1378.[102]

As we have seen, he was the podestà of Chioggia in 1382 who reorganized the commune's government while negotiating the purchase of grain from Antonio Meneghini as agent for the lord of Padua. On 3 June 1384, Pietro Giustinian appeared among the Avogadori di Comun, but by the next March his treason was suspected, for the Avogadori ordered an investigation of all trials and condemnations made during his term of office. The next week Giustinian was dismissed from his office and arrested with his accomplice, Antonio Meneghini, for revealing the Venetian state secrets to the lord of Padua. On 20 March 1385 Francesco il Vecchio sent ambassadors to Venice asking for clemency for Meneghini, insisting that he had given his agent no commission to warrant the death sentence and demanding to know the exact charges. The Senate voted to inform the Carrara lord that a careful examination of Meneghini's confession showed him guilty of the death penalty. The charges would not, however, be revealed because "all matters of the Council of Ten must be held and are held in the greatest secrecy nor can they be revealed to anyone in any fashion." Guilty or not, on 5 May 1385 Pietro Giustinian and Antonio Meneghini were executed, condemned to death by the Council of Ten.[103]

In the spring of 1385, both Venice and Padua scrambled to enlist new allies. Antonio della Scala's record of animosity toward the Carrara made him an eager candidate for alliance with Venice, which responded favorably to the Veronese overtures. On 22 April the Collegio, acting in secrecy, drew up terms for a treaty, entrusting to Giovanni Gradenigo final negotiations in Verona.[104] The league was defensive, lasting to the end of 1389, with the Della Scala contributing 5,000 ducats a month to the war effort if the lord of Padua made war on Venice, and any territory taken in a war was to go to the Scaligers, except for strongholds near the *dogado* at Castelcarro, Gambarare, Oriago, Torre, and Motta, which were to go to Venice. If Venice chose to adopt a defensive posture, the lord of Verona had to contribute two hundred infantry at the cost of 600 ducats a month for the duration of the conflict. Similar obligations applied to Venice if the Carrara lord made war on Verona. Any union of forces for more effective action was to be negotiated as the need arose. From the pact it is clear that Venice wished to remain a maritime power, taking only frontier strongholds in the event of victory. The treaty's purpose was to maintain the lord of Verona as an enemy of Padua and provide a counterpoise to the west which would draw off Carrara forces from the conflict in Friuli. In both these policies, Venice, in the long run, succeeded admirably. Venice hindered Paduan operations in the Friuli in other ways. On 6 April the Senate refused the lord of Padua's request for free passage of matériel up the Sile to Treviso and the Livenza to Motta and, in effect, sealed its border with Carrara domains.[105]

The War against the Scaligeri and in Friuli, 1385–1386

While Venice cemented its relations with Verona, the Carrara lord found a new ally in Giangaleazzo Visconti, who since the deposition of his uncle Bernabò had ruled all of Lombardy. On 24 June 1385 Francesco il Vecchio and his son appointed Valeriano Lombardo, Bernardo Scolari, and Francesco Turchetto their ambassadors to conclude a league with the Visconti of Milan, the Este of Ferrara, and the Gonzaga of Mantua against the mercenary companies ravishing northern Italy. At Pavia in August the treaty was made, providing Padua with the assurance of Milan's benevolent neutrality in its struggle in Friuli and a counterpoise to the Scaliger threat on its western frontier.[106] That May the Carrara lord improved relations with the marquis d'Este, sending troops to his defense, when a tax revolt broke out in Ferrara causing looting and destruction and costing the life of his chief minister, Tommaso da Tortona. Now the two lords cooperated to promote the security of Lombardy and the Veneto.[107] Venice still hoped to avert full-scale war with Padua, sending an embassy in June to insist on the Carrara lord's observance of the treaties guaranteeing the privileges of Venetian landowners in the Trevisano. At the same time, Antonio della Scala sent his own embassy to Padua urging the Carrara lord to desist from the use of arms in Friuli. The embassies only succeeded in proving the lord of Padua's intransigence and determination to assert his authority in northeastern Italy.[108]

As war with the Scaligers and in Friuli became certain, feverish preparations were made in Padua, with the enlistment of several mercenary companies and the brilliant soldier Giovanni Azzo degli Ubaldini for the Carraresi. Throughout the summer as the Carrara lord sought to strengthen his authority in the Trevisano, his relations with Venice deteriorated. Francesco il Vecchio openly taxed the property and products of Venetian landowners in the district, even confiscating timber and grain being shipped to Venice.

At the end of June, the Senate sent ambassadors with instructions to require the lord of Padua to observe earlier treaties guaranteeing free transport of goods to Venice. If the Carrara lord failed to permit the customary duty-free export of Venetian goods, the envoys were to warn him: "Our government will be very surprised and troubled by such a response because it did not consider that the lord of Padua ought to respond in such a manner and because we shall not be able to make do with less than is required for the honor of our state and for the welfare of our [citizens]."[109] A last-minute plea for peace before the Senate from envoys of Niccolò II d'Este failed.[110] Venice's demands for its rights in the Trevisano met with stony silence from Padua, as Francesco il Vecchio marshaled troops for the invasion of Friuli, commanded by his best captains, Giovanni da Barbiano, Bernardo Scolari, Ugolotto Biancardo, Arcoano Buzzacarini, and Giovanni Azzo degli Ubaldini. That fall Paduan forces entered Friuli to aid the beleaguered patriarch of Aquileia, while Francesco il Vecchio appointed Giovanni Francesco qd. Salvatore, his servant at the palace on Campo S. Polo in Venice, proctor to collect interest on his remaining shares in the Monte.[111] That same month Antonio della Scala collected forces at Marostica to mount an attack on the western Padovano. Shortly before Christmas Carrara troops skirmished with Scaligeri forces in the Vicentine, bringing back much booty and prisoners to Padua. Named by Cardinal d'Alençon advocate for the church of Aquileia, Francesco il Vecchio now began in earnest his effort to dominate northeast Italy.[112]

The year 1386 started badly for the Paduan cause: in January Udinese troops captured a body of Carrara forces besieging Brugnera, including the commanders Michele Rabatta and Count Morando da Porcia. Despite the intervention of Queen Elisabeth of Hungary and the archbishop of Pecs attempting to secure his release, Rabatta remained imprisoned in Friuli for almost two years.[113] In February, the forces of Antonio della Scala pillaged the western Padovano, even for a time laying siege to Montagnana, defended by Perugian mercenaries under the command of Tommaso Cerdolini, who died of wounds received in the encounter.[114] At that time German mercenaries in the pay of the "Felice Unione" also captured two constables, Guglielmo Lischi and Daniele da Valle, with the Carrara army in Friuli, releasing them only when they promised not to fight again in that campaign. Antonio della Scala dispatched to Friuli as reinforcements six hundred troops paid for with Venetian money.[115] Relations with Venice worsened in the Trevisano, as Paduan troops harassed peasants near the border of the *dogado* and Carrara officials taxed and sometimes confiscated Venetian property there. At the end of March, Francesco il Vecchio prudently ordered his agent Paolo qd. Ture to liquidate all his shares in the Monte at Venice, recovering funds before they could be confiscated and securing capital for the purchase of Belluno and Feltre from Duke Albert of Habsburg achieved that May.[116] Meanwhile, the lord of Verona was collecting a large army, under the command of Ostasio da Polenta, Giovanni degli Ordelaffi, and Cortesia da Serego, to threaten Padua itself.

In late winter, Veronese forces dammed and diverted water from the Bacchiglione, stopping the mills in Padua. An elated Antonio della Scala dispatched an envoy challenging Francesco il Vecchio to personal combat to decide the conflict between the two states. When Francesco Novello offered to fight for his father, the elder lord counseled, in the presence of the Veronese ambassador, "Son, it's neither right nor honorable, that you and I, who are born of noble and legitimate matrimony, should fight with a most vile bastard, born from the stomach of a wretched baker woman."[117] Soon after the lord of Verona received that reply, he sent a army of eighteen hundred lances and five thousand foot soldiers with many bombards and an enormous quantity of supplies to attack the Padovano at several points. But Paduan forces were able to parry each of these thrusts: the Carrara commander Giovanni Azzo degli Ubaldini beat back the attempt to cross the Brenta at Curtarolo, forcing the Veronese army to try to enter the Padovano at the southwest, investing Montagnana. Here expert marksmen manning the bombards on the walls of Montagnana shot down the Scaliger standard-bearer and several knights in the besieging army, causing it to withdraw toward Este. At the Serraglio of Este, the Scaliger army met a similar fate, repulsed with heavy losses in a frontal assault. Part of the Paduan army under Bernardo Scolari even followed the Veronese force in its own territory, pillaging and burning villages around Schio.[118] Regrouping the Veronese forces, Cortesia found the main Paduan army under Giovanni Azzo degli Ubaldini encamped at Tencarola a few kilometers to the west of the city, where the Bacchiglione joins the Brentelle, while one of the ruling lord's natural sons, Giacomo, guarded the ford over the Bacchiglione. Feinting to the north, on 23 May Cortesia deployed his main force to the south, crossing a ford of the Brentelle at Brusegana. Now only open country lay between the Veronese army and the walls of Padua. But here the Veronese commander halted for two days, allowing the Paduans to collect their forces while he brought up supplies in forty barques on the Brenta River.

On the morning of 25 June, a brilliantly clear and sunny day as Andrea Gatari notes, the two armies first observed all the formalities of war, exchanging challenges and drawing up contingents to the beating of drums and the blaring of bugles, before battle was joined.[119] Both armies were confident of success: the Veronese had the larger force, while the distinguished professor of astrological medicine at the Paduan *studium,* Biagio

Pelacani, had made it known to the Carrara lord and his commanders that all the signs were right for a great victory over the enemy. The Veronese army enjoyed initial success, driving back a large body of armed peasants to the gates of Padua. Elated with this easy victory, Cortesia sent word to Antonio della Scala waiting in Vicenza to hurry to enter the captured city. But as the lord of Verona approached Padua, he found a different situation. Just as the Veronese forces stopped to slaughter the peasants outside Padua, Giovanni Azzo degli Ubaldini ordered his troops to attack the pursuers. The Paduan army fell upon the main force of the enemy. Shouting "Carro! Carro!" the unit commanders led their companies into battle, cutting down several of the Scaliger standard-bearers and killing a number of Veronese commanders. Cortesia da Serego was himself soon unhorsed. Now completely demoralized, the Veronese force was routed. More than 800 of the enemy were killed, many of whom drowned desperately trying to recross the Brentelle. More than 8,000 men—virtually the entire army—were taken prisoner, including every one of the Veronese commanders. More than 6,000 horses were captured along with 38 bombards and 240 wagons of gunpowder, weapons, and provisions. Among the stranger profits of war paraded back to Padua were 211 prostitutes, who had accompanied the Veronese soldiers on the campaign. The Scaliger army had been destroyed. The lord of Padua ordered that the great victory of the Paduan forces at Brentelle on the feast of Sant'Alò be commemorated annually by a solemn procession to the altar at S. Clemente, where Mass would be heard.[120]

Despite this stunning victory, Francesco il Vecchio could not force the lord of Verona to accept peace. Fortified in his resolve by a subsidy of 60,000 ducats from Venice, Antonio della Scala refused any offer of peace and set about to raise another army, hiring the dreaded German mercenary Count Lucius von Landau as his new commander and enlisting troops from Friuli and the Veronese countryside. Meanwhile, the Carrara lord repatriated almost all the private soldiers, only demanding the promise of never taking up arms against Padua again. Ostasio da Polenta, son of the lord of Ravenna, was released because he was a kinsman of both Francesco il Vecchio's stepmother and Francesco Novello's wife. But several of the other commanders were held for large ransoms: 9,000 ducats was demanded for Cortesia's freedom, which occurred only after he had spent a year broken in spirit and gravely ill in prison in Padua. But within a few months, some sixty captains taken prisoner, including such famous mercenaries as Facino Cane and Antonio da Castelbarco, were released.[121]

While defending his homeland from the Scaliger threat, the Carrara lord had designs on the island of Corfu, which had been nominally under control of Charles of Durazzo until his murder in February 1386. Seizing the opportunity to expand his influence on the Adriatic coast, that May the Carrara lord sent Giacomo Scrovegni to Corfu with a body of troops to wrest control from local notables. But this effort to extend the Paduan sphere of influence to the Adriatic coast was too little and too late. For some years, Venice had waged a propaganda campaign to persuade leading Corfiotes to accept Venetian control of Corfu's harbor and fortresses. Spurred by the Paduan interest, Venice sent its captain of the gulf to establish a protectorate over the island, after securing agreement from the local leaders.[122]

Secure at home but thwarted in his ambitions to control Corfu, the lord of Padua now turned his attention to the conquest of Friuli. Distressed by the continuing conflict in northeast Italy, Pope Urban VI appointed as his vicar in Friuli Ferdinand, patriarch of Jerusalem, who in August 1386 arranged a truce for one year. But Venice, its allies, and the lord of Padua disregarded the call for peace and continued their struggle for dominance. Francesco il Vecchio strengthened his position by bribing the *condottiere* Count Landau to quit the theater of war for six months, taking his company into the Romagna. Late that autumn Giangaleazzo Visconti began negotiations with Francesco il Vecchio for a league aimed at the destruction of the Scaliger regime. The lord of Padua favored the lord of Milan by allowing in November his best condottiere, Giovanni Azzo degli Ubaldini, to accept an advance of 12,000 florins to enter Visconti service the next year. On 14 January 1387, acting together as the lords of Padua, Francesco il Vecchio and Francesco Novello appointed Francesco Turchetto their ambassador to Pavia to conclude the pact against the lord of Verona.[123] After a series of skirmishes on his eastern frontier, Antonio della Scala raised an enormous army to invade the Padovano from the south. The Carrara lords countered by sending Giovanni Azzo degli Ubaldini to Faenza to enlist the English mercenary captain Sir John Hawkwood with his company of five hundred mounted men-at-arms and six hundred archers. Accompanied by Francesco Novello as nominal commander, the two experienced captains invaded the Veronese, pillaging the countryside with impunity. In response, the lord of Verona placed in the field an army of nine thousand cavalry, one thousand infantry, and sixteen hundred archers and crossbowmen under the command of Giovanni degli Ordelaffi. This army marched down the west bank of the Adige threatening to cut off the Carrara army from its supplies. Hawkwood beat a hasty retreat toward Padua's border fortress at Castelbaldo on the north bank of the Adige, where there was a great store of provisions. The Veronese force in pursuit was composed of sixteen thousand men, armed peasants as well as cavalry, archers, and infantry, thus perhaps four times the size of the Paduan army. After holding a council of war with his main commanders, Hawkwood decided to make his stand on the south side of the Adige at the village of Castagnaro with the river at his back and his flanks protected by marshes and irrigation canals.[124]

On the morning of 11 March, Hawkwood arrayed his cavalry of eight companies each under the standard of its commander in three divisions. He placed his own English archers with Ubaldini's company in the first rank, Francesco Novello and his Paduan troops and the *provisionati* under Bartolomeo Cermisone in the second, with two companies of sixteen hundred lances held in reserve. Just before the battle, Francesco Novello knighted five of his closest comrades in arms, his two half brothers Conte and Giacomo da Carrara, his two cousins Francesco and Pataro Buzzacarini, and Bernardo Scolari, each receiving golden spurs from Hawkwood himself. Paduan skirmishers drew the Veronese army to the attack, lured on by the prize of Francesco Novello, who stood conspicuously surrounded by his bodyguards. Instructed to give no quarter and shouting, "Scala, Scala, Carne, Carne," the Veronese cavalry mounted its attack, slowed and confused by a hidden ditch before the Paduan defenders. As the Paduan forces fell back, the Veronese troops pressed forward, exposing their flank to English archers and Italian crossbowmen. At the moment the Veronese army was fully engaged, Hawkwood directed his English men-at-arms on the enemy's flank and charged with all his forces into the left wing of the Scaliger army as the archers rained arrows from the bank. The Veronese army collapsed under the onslaught, and their reserve under Ordelaffi and Ostasio da Polenta advanced only to be driven back upon their own standards. The major captains, nearly eighty in all, were captured. Several squadrons of cavalry fled toward Legnaro but were soon captured by their pursuers. Only a unit of Veronese infantry and armed peasants under Giovanni da Isola remained effective. When these rejected Hawkwood's call to surrender, they were cut to pieces. In all nearly five thousand prisoners were taken, while more than seven hundred of the enemy were killed and nearly nine hundred wounded.

A few days later Francesco il Vecchio welcomed the triumphant army, laden with bombards, munitions, and prisoners of war. But for a second time the lord of Padua was unable to capitalize on his victory. Backed with subsidies from Venice, Antonio della Scala again rejected all overtures for peace. Later that spring, Padua's finest condottieri found other masters: Giovanni Azzo degli Ubaldini and Ugolotto Biancardo entered the service of Giangaleazzo Visconti, and Sir John Hawkwood took his company to Tuscany in the pay of Florence.[125] As in the aftermath of the battle of Brentelle, Francesco il Vecchio freed many prisoners on their own parole not to take up arms against Padua again, as with the Veronese mercenaries Francesco dei Galluzzi, Antonio da Siena, Franceschino da Alessandria, and Giovanni da Milano, or granted complete freedom for friends of the regime, as in the case of Antonio Obizi of Lucca.[126] As prisoners were ransomed and the victorious army disbanded, the lords of Padua still faced two unfinished matters: the destruction of Antonio della Scala's regime in Verona and achieving domination in Friuli.

To accomplish the first task, on 19 April 1387 the Carrara lords entered into a league with Giangaleazzo Visconti aimed at overthrowing the Scaliger lord and dividing his domains between them: the Visconti lord was to receive Verona, while the Carrara lords were to have Vicenza.[127] The next day Giangaleazzo also secured the support of Francesco Gonzaga of Mantua and soon made a pact with Duke Albert of Austria to close the Alpine passes to any troops coming from Germany to aid the Scaligers. The count of Virtù took the field that summer advancing on Verona from the east, taking the Rocca di Garda on 19 June, while the Carrara forces raided the Vicentino, retaking a few border towns. Wenceslaus of Bohemia attempted to save the Scaliger regime by sending envoys to Italy twice that summer to urge Giangaleazzo Visconti and Francesco il Vecchio to make peace with the lord of Verona, said to be under imperial protection. These demands for peace were rejected, as the Visconti army, harboring a number of the powerful Veronese exiles, including Spinetta Malaspina and Guglielmo Bevilacqua, approached Verona.

Since Giangaleazzo Visconti had assumed command of the campaign against the Della Scala, Francesco il Vecchio decided to concentrate on Friuli. Already possessing the cities of Belluno and Feltre, the lord of Padua had at first hoped for a negotiated settlement, answering a call for discussions by Ferdinand, patriarch of Jerusalem, in July by sending three diplomats, Francesco Dotti, Guglielmo Curtarolo, and Tisone di San Angelo, to parley at Cordovado. But the Paduan envoys soon learned that the lords and towns of the "Felice Unione" were asking too stiff a price for peace: virtually the complete withdrawal of the lord of Padua and his allies from all strongholds and towns held in Friuli.[128] Despairing of a peaceful solution, in August the lord of Padua sent an army into Friuli to reduce the towns of Sacile, Aviano, and Caneva to obedience, thus providing a secure route for trade with Germany. Troops under the command of Conte da Carrara assisted by the *provisionati* of Bartolomeo Cermisone, who had fought so valiantly at Castagnaro, besieged Sacile, which fell on 12 September. The smaller towns of Aviano and Caneva capitulated the next day. From Padua Francesco il Vecchio appointed Paganino Sala his proctor to confirm the agreements made between Conte da Carrara and the communes of Sacile and Caneva, while Francesco Dotti was to ratify the pact with Aviano. In general, the lord of Padua was lenient with his new possessions: he promised to allow no reprisals for injuries done in battle or past wrongs to the patriarch. Conte da Carrara swore to observe all terms of the treaty, assuring the citizens peaceful possession of their lands and property as before the conquests.[129] In return, Francesco il Vecchio promised "that the citizens of Aviano will be treated gently and benignly in his lands and districts, as are treated his other subjects, Paduans as well as Trevisans."[130] The Carrara lord was intent on incorporating these towns in his domains, where citizens enjoyed their usual property rights and followed local customs while being seen as subjects of a larger dynastic state. There was some profit in the new possessions; that same autumn Belluno paid into the treasury of the lord of Padua annual taxes totaling £24,000.[131] Further advances in Friuli were soon stymied, as Francesco il Vecchio turned his attention to the imminent fall of Verona.

The Visconti Lord and Venice Oppose the Carrara Lords, 1387–1388

While the lord of Padua gained three towns in Friuli, the lord of Milan planned the conquest of all the Scaligeri dominions. At Pavia Giangaleazzo entertained pleas for peace from ambassadors of Antonio della Scala and his protector Wenceslaus of Bohemia while his army approached the gates of Verona. Veronese exiles made contact with discontents within the city, who on 18 October arranged to open the gates to Milanese troops. Repudiated by his own populace, Antonio della Scala collected what treasure he could and with his family and a few loyal servants took ship down the Adige, eventually reaching Venice.[132] Three days later, Milanese agents received Vicenza in the name of Caterina Visconti as heir of her mother, Regina della Scala, much to the consternation of the lords of Carrara, who had been promised that prize. While the Carraresi fumed at the trickery and duplicity of their sometime ally, Giangaleazzo infuriated them further by laying claim to the Paduan border towns of Noale and Montegalda. Convinced of the danger the Visconti conquests held for northeast Italy, late in December Niccolò II d'Este convened a general meeting of all interested parties in Ferrara.

Cardinal d'Alençon resigned his post as the patriarch of Aquileia and retired to Rome, and on 27 November 1387 Pope Urban VI named in his place John Sobieslaw of Moravia, nephew of the late Emperor Charles and, thus, cousin of Sigismund of Hungary and Wenceslaus of Bohemia. The grave dangers posed by Visconti control of the old Scaliger dominions prompted most parties to send envoys to the Este court. On 30 December 1387, Francesco il Vecchio named four of his best diplomats—Paganino Sala, Francesco Dotti, Giacomo Turchetto, and Guglielmo Curtarolo—to represent him at the peace conference, and in Venice on 2 January 1388 the doge and his council dispatched three statesmen.[133] But convinced of the rightfulness of his claims to Friuli, the Carrara lord would not listen to pleas for accommodation from his Guelf allies, Florence and Bologna. Thus Florentine mediation failed at the meeting at Ferrara, but the lord of Padua did cement ties with Bologna by having one of its leading jurists, Ugolino de' Preti, reappointed podestà of Padua for a term of six months beginning on 27 February 1388.[134]

Meanwhile, Venice and the count of Virtù were working to form an alliance dedicated to the conquest of Padua.[135] The death of the Carraresi's staunch friend Niccolò II d'Este at the end of March placed his brother Alberto in control of Ferrara, prey to Visconti blandishments of friendship and pressure for support. At the very moment that the Florentine government was urging the lord of Padua to make peace at almost any cost, Venice and Milan were secretly exchanging envoys to hammer out an agreement.[136] In early April Venetian envoys heard Giangaleazzo's proposals at Pavia, and in a closed meeting of the Senate on the 19th Venice agreed to enter the league, demanding as its spoils Treviso, the Trevisano, and Ceneda as well as several strongholds on the Paduan frontier.[137] After another round of discussions, the treaty to partition the Carrara state between the lord of Milan and Venice was concluded on 29 May.[138] To the war effort Giangaleazzo Visconti was to contribute at least fifteen hundred cavalry, one thousand infantry, four hundred crossbowmen, and one thousand sappers and engineers, while Venice would field a smaller force supported by a fleet on the Adige. In addition, Venice was to pay a subsidy of 100,000 ducats for the first year and 8,000 ducats a month thereafter. As previously agreed, the lord of Milan would receive Padua and the hill towns of Belluno and Feltre, while Venice was to recover the Trevisano and its border fortifications. Venice insisted that its ancient privileges in the Padovano be observed, explicitly requiring the Visconti regime to respect the rights of Venetian proprietors to export their crops and rents duty-free to Venice, fulfill the earlier treaties of extradition, and even buy all salt for Padua from the monopoly at Chioggia. In short, though agreeing to install the Visconti lord as its neighbor, Venice required the new regime to respect the privileges won from the lord and commune of Padua in the 1330s.

On 12 May 1388 Florence made a final bid for peace, sending a letter to Venice which pressed for a settlement with the lord of Padua, announcing that the signoria would send an envoy who would mediate the conflict.[139] But the Venetian government did not listen; the two powers enlisted Francesco Gonzaga of Mantua and Alberto d'Este of Ferrara in their league and on 8 June concluded a pact assuring Genoa's neutrality. Francesco il Vecchio's desperate effort in late May to convince Florence and Bologna to mediate his differences with Venice was doomed to failure.[140] On 21 June, Giangaleazzo Visconti sent the elder Carrara a formal challenge (*diffidatio*), charging him with perfidy and plotting the destruction of the Visconti state.[141] Faced with an overwhelming coalition and uncertain of the support of his subjects, Francesco il Vecchio called together his leading advisers to consider his best course of action. After emotional, often brutal discussions, the elder Carrara decided to abdicate in favor of Francesco Novello. On 23 June Francesco il Vecchio legally emancipated his son from his *patria potestas,* two days later he had drawn up an instrument of *donatio inter vivos* conveying to him all his property, and on the morning of the 29th he renounced the lordship of Padua to the Paduan commune, which in turn conferred it on Francesco Novello.[142] Sick and worn down from the years of conflict and hoping no doubt to appease Venice by removing himself from rule over Padua, Francesco il Vecchio retired to Treviso to await his fate.

Part III

Francesco Novello, 1388–1405

Chapter 8

Exile and Restoration, 1388–1392

> Civitatis ipsius introitus et obventus, quorum ex perceptione ipsa sumptibus debitis suspirabat, minorati sunt (et quasi totaliter defecere). . . . Et tamen expedit militie ipsi solvi.
>
> [The income and revenue of that city have been so diminished (and are now almost totally lacking) that it seems to be groaning under the debts assumed. . . . And yet the soldiery must be paid.]
>
> —Court notary Zilio Calvi's rationale for sale of Carrara property

The Fall of the Regime

The desperate attempt to save the Carrara regime by transferring the lordship of Padua from Francesco il Vecchio to his son was accomplished with all the legal niceties that the perilous times would allow. The emancipation of and gift to the son of all of the elder Carrara's property were standard procedures under the *ius commune* and the communal statutes, but the transfer of public power required the reinstitution of at least some of the organs of the communal regime. Padua's Great Council had maintained a shadowy existence, convened in order to nominate a new *podestà* and occasionally elect a board of syndicators at the end of a podestà's term of office. But the election of a new lord was a signal event in the precarious life of the Paduan commune. On the morning of 29 June 1388 in the Great Hall of the Salone, Paganino Sala, acting as proctor for Francesco il Vecchio, renounced the lordship of the city and district to the *sindico* and Anziani of the commune, and these, in turn, together with the podestà, confirmed Francesco Novello in his office.

The representatives of the commune had been well chosen for the occasion. The syndic, whose duty it was to confer the communal banner on the new lord, was perhaps the most distinguished jurist in the city, Alvarotto di Pietro Alvarotti, who had enjoyed a long career as a judge, a law pro-

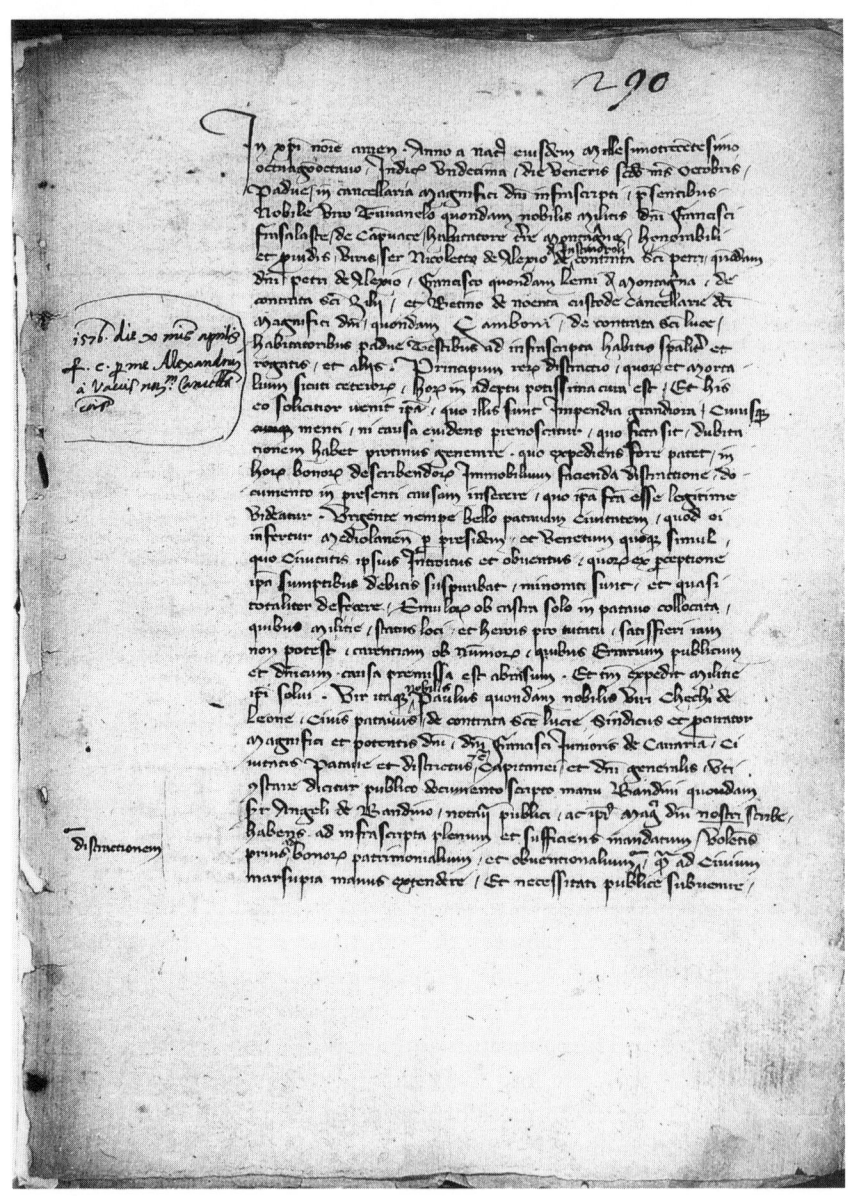

FIG. 30. *Rationale for Carrara sales, fall 1388*. Zilio Calvi, scribe in the Carrara chancery, on 2 October 1388 record of sales to Carrara favorites. Source: Archivio di Stato, Padua, AN, 5, fol. 290r. Reproduced with permission of the Archivio di Stato, Studio Fotografico, Padua

fessor, and, a few years earlier, a term as vicar to the podestà of Bologna. The four Anziani, each representing one of the city's quarters, were likewise local notables. Giacomo Zacchi was a merchant and judge, connected by marriage to both the university dynasty of the Dondi dall'Orologio and the da Ponte banking family. Galeazzo Gatari, by profession a druggist, was better known as the chronicler of the Carrara house. Antonio Torcoli was a banker from *contrada* S. Croce, who for the past few years had run a pawn shop for the Carrara in Treviso, and Domenichino Descalzi was a merchant originally hailing from Este, whose brother Ottonello had served the regime often as consulting judge and, with the Carrara lord's blessing, a term as vicar at Zara.[1]

The statute of election concluded with an enumeration of the powers of the new lord, based, with a few changes, on the statute of election of Francesco il Vecchio from February 1351. Francesco Novello was made only lord of Padua and its district, since the lordship of Treviso, Belluno, Feltre, and the recently acquired cities in Friuli remained with his father. But in the new listing of powers were a major omission and an important addition, both of which gave more authority to the new lord. In the earlier statute, communal officials and magistrates had to obey all the lord's commands, except for those contrary to the communal law of Padua and laws common to other cities or pacts concluded by the commune of Padua with foreign states and lords. But this second exception was omitted from the statute of 1388, so that Padua's earlier pacts that had guaranteed Venice's right in the Padovano no longer bound the new lord, his officials, or the commune of Padua. To this step toward greater signorial authority were added new titles. From now on all Carrara lords, present and future, were to enjoy the titles of lord, captain, and imperial vicar, making them "free of any communal or municipal law and bestowing on them all imperial privileges, prerogatives, favors and honors." As a practical benefit of these new imperial prerogatives, Carrara lords could buy and sell, acquire and alienate communal and other property in Padua, its district, and all other places subject to their rule.[2] At the end of the ceremony Francesco Novello received the popular acclamation of his subjects, crowning the event with banquets, festivals, and jousts.

The political realities in Padua, however, were far from joyful. Before leaving on the day of his son's election, Francesco il Vecchio had appointed Enrico Gallo proctor to enlist two soldiers, Antonio qd. Gerardo of Modena and Cristoforo qd. Jacopo of Padua, as his vassals, promising service, fealty, and a gold ring at Christmas, in return for extensive fiefs; one received more than 100 *campi* in twenty-one parcels in Caselle di Bagoto, the other a house and 60 *campi* in six parcels in Sabbioncello.[3] That summer the Carrara also resorted to the old ploy of the marriage alliance to cement existing friendships or to enlist new allies. Earlier Francesco il Vecchio had tried without success to betroth his recently widowed daughter Gigliola, duchess of Saxony, to one of the Este and later proposed her marriage to the count of Gorizia. Now in a letter of 12 July to his brother Enrico Rabatta in Friuli, Michele Rabatta reported that the elder Carrara had finally betrothed the widowed Gigliola to Hermann, count of Cilli, enlisting a friendly power near Hungarian domains.[4] But the gravity of the situation was best indicated by the obsequious replies to the declarations of war (*diffidationes*) sent from Venice and Milan. On 30 June Francesco Novello sent a fawning apology to the doge, saying that his father had renounced the lordship of Padua to please Venice and entreating the *signoria* to allow him to keep his state, promising "always to be a son and friend of the illustrious Ducal Dominion." Meanwhile, from Serravalle on his way to Treviso, Francesco il Vecchio dispatched a detailed, point-by-point rebuttal of Giangaleazzo Visconti's accusations of treason and betrayal, ending with abject apology for any unintended harm done to the lord of Milan and beseeching him to be merciful to his innocent son and successor.[5] Probably aware that mere words would not halt the impending war, Francesco Novello prepared to oppose his enemies with diplomacy and with force.

On 4 July 1388 the lord of Padua appointed his ablest Florentine adviser, Francesco Allegro, longtime resident and merchant in Padua, his envoy to convince Florence and Bologna to negotiate a peaceful settlement with Milan and Venice on behalf of the Carrara. Two days later the Florentine signoria sent a letter congratulating Francesco Novello on his recent election by the Paduan people and wishing him a happy rule over his homeland in both war and peace.[6] Thus, Florence remained guarded in its support of the Carrara, though in the middle of July both Florence and Bologna sent ambassadors to the Visconti court at Pavia to plead for peace. The Florentine ambassador at Venice suggested that perhaps peace could be gained through a change of government in Padua; "for the happy state of Italy" Florence and Bologna would "arrange that the city of Padua would be governed as a commune, that the lord of Padua would be content to live in peace as a private person."[7] Venice did not accept the offer because it contradicted accords already made with the lord of Milan. Besides, the Venetians now held that the "lord of Padua had become its public enemy," worthy only of overthrow and destruction, so its ambassadors were to persuade Florence and Bologna to remain neutral.[8] At the same time, Venice sought to reduce Carrara influence in Friuli, encouraging the new patriarch of Aquileia, John Sobieslaw of Moravia, and Wenceslaus of Bohemia to recover the towns the Carrara forces had taken there. Perhaps already convinced of the hopelessness of the Paduan cause, Florence turned cool toward Francesco

Exile and Restoration

Novello's pleas for help. In a letter to Giangaleazzo Visconti, Salutati denied that his government ever contemplated sending troops or lending money to the lord of Padua.[9]

Augmenting diplomacy, Milan and Venice turned to force in the summer of 1388 to bring about the final destruction of the Carrara.[10] Giangaleazzo Visconti appointed his ablest general, Jacopo dal Verme, as commander of his forces and employed two troops of cavalry of the *condottieri* Giovanni Azzo degli Ubaldini and Ugolotto Biancardo, both recruited from the Carrara army a year earlier and possessing intimate knowledge of Paduan topography and resources. Visconti forces crossed the Paduan frontiers in July, raided in the Oltrebrenta, seized the stronghold at Limena, and threatened to divert water from Padua by damming the Bacchiglione. Francesco Novello fielded a force commanded by members of his own family: his two half brothers Conte and Giacomo da Carrara and cousins Francesco and Pataro di Arcoano Buzzacarini. The most seasoned commander, Conte, launched a counterattack against the Visconti camp at Limena, killing several of the enemy, including the son of one of the commanders, Giovanni Azzo degli Ubaldini. But discouragement pervaded the Carrara councils, heightened by the success of the Venetian fleet, which took the frontier fort at Borgoforte on the Adige and occupied Conselve in September. With the Visconti army camped on the Brenta just outside the walls of Padua, the marshal of the Carrara forces, Albertino da Peraga, treated with Ugolotto Biancardo to hand over the suburb of Ognissanti to the enemy. Francesco Novello heard rumors of the plot and confronted Albertino, who confessed under torture. Observing the legal niceties, the Carrara lord turned over the would-be traitor to his podestà, Ugolino Preti, for trial. Found guilty of treason, Albertino da Peraga and a kinsman were executed in Piazza delle Biave, while another accomplice was hanged outside Porte di Porciglia, where the Visconti troops had expected to enter Padua—actions that served only to increase the anxiety of the Paduan people and unpopularity of their lord. With the city surrounded, Francesco Novello dispatched an embassy to Albert, duke of Austria, promising Treviso and Carrara dominions in Friuli in return for armed intervention. But once again Giangaleazzo Visconti proved the shrewder diplomat, enlisting the duke of Austria as his own ally and paying a subsidy of 50,000 ducats in return for his renouncing in favor of Venice any claims to Treviso and Ceneda.

As the war of attrition continued, the resources of the Carrara regime were severely strained. By the autumn, Francesco Novello and his advisers came to the decision that the only way to pay for the defense of Padua was to sell off Carrara property at bargain prices to friends and supporters. Beginning in the summer with gifts and rewards to household officials,

TABLE 8.1
Carrara Sales of Summer–Fall 1388

Month	Amount (lire)	Amount (ducats)
July–August	8,800	4,500
September	19,700	5,926
October	28,250	606
1–19 November	15,250	3,300
20 November	130,537	37,410
21–24 November	67,300	14,000
Total	269,837	65,742 (or £289,265)
Total in lire 559,102		

Source: Appendix 3.

by November the alienation of Carrara property reached gigantic proportions, with major members of the affinity contributing huge amounts to the war effort.[11] Arcoano Buzzacarini bought all Carrara lands in Polverara and Saonara for £20,000, Bonifacio Lupi acquired property in Bovolenta and Brugine for 16,000 ducats, and Giovanni Parisino Mezzoconti purchased the city's butcher shops, the Carrara bank (*domus mutui domini*), and other commercial properties as well as pastures and wetlands for £30,000. Michele Rabatta bought all of Conte da Carrara's real estate for £30,000, with other members of the affinity and household contributing thousands of lire for various properties. For example, Guglielmo Ongarelli got land in Noventa and Biagio Ovetari all Carrara holdings in his native Cittadella. Giovanni Savonarola, Zilio Calvi, Simeone dagli Statuti, Guglielmo Curtarolo, and Giovanni and Paganino Sala all made major purchases. In the end, as table 8.1 shows, the Carrara lord earned more than half a million lire from these sales, with the bulk of the revenue gained in the final five days of the regime.

Early in November the duke of Austria, now firmly in the Visconti and Venetian camp, closed the Alpine passes to any aid from allies in Germany and Hungary and forbade recruitment of any soldiers from their domains into the Carrara forces.[12] When Visconti forces occupied major strongholds in the *contado*, at Bovolenta, Piove di Sacco, and Castelcarro, peasants and townsmen alike called for the end of the Carrara regime. Even though the sales had not directly burdened the Paduan *popolo*, Francesco Novello's war had been so destructive and unpopular that he was in fear for his life. Calling a meeting of his closest advisers late in November, the Carrara lord listened to conflicting advice. Bonifacio Lupi and Paganino Sala (who were perhaps already in the pay of the Visconti) emphasized the hopelessness of the

Exile and Restoration

situation and advised abdication. In the end, Francesco Novello accepted this counsel of despair. In the words of a Florentine chronicler, writing two decades later, "The councillors, who were traitors, advised him to throw himself on the mercy of Giangaleazzo Visconti and give him Padua and its strongholds, and go with his wife and children to see him in Pavia, and when he had done this, the Visconti lord would laden him with gifts and treat him grandly. And [Francesco Novello], who was very foolish, with very little sense, did just what he was advised (though he did not inform his father, who was in Treviso, anything about it)."[13]

Having decided to place himself at Giangaleazzo's mercy, Francesco Novello dispatched Paolo Lion and Guglielmo Curtarolo as envoys to discuss terms of surrender with the Visconti commanders, Jacopo dal Verme, Giovanni Azzo degli Ubaldini, and Spinetta Malaspina. The Carrara lord agreed to surrender his dynasty's dominions, including Padua, Treviso, Ceneda, Feltre, and Belluno, to the lord of Milan in return for Giangaleazzo's pledge not to sell off any part of Padua and its district, to safeguard the city and his subjects' property against sack and reprisal, and to provide safe-conduct to Pavia for the Carrara lord and his family.[14] In the grim, chaotic days of transition as Francesco Novello turned over Padua to local authorities, the Carrara Grain Office, chancery, and other properties were looted and sacked, records destroyed, and much treasure stolen. Departing from the city on 24 November from Porta Saracinesca with his wife, family, and a few favorites, Francesco Novello proceeded by boat to the Carrara stronghold at Monselice and thence to Lombardy. Amid the chaos, the remnants of the Carrara affinity in Padua jockeyed for power while awaiting the new regime.

Transition to Visconti Rule

The change of regime brought out into the open the grievances felt by many former members of the affinity. On the morning of 22 November in the Carrara chancery in the presence of Bonifacio Lupi, Paganino Sala, Alvarotto Alvarotti, Giacomo Turchetto, and others, Ugolino Scrovegni ratified documents dated June 1388 concerning the purchase by Manno di Manno Donati, for 2,500 ducats, of Carrara property, including a mill, in the villages of Creola and Saccolongo. Declaring that he was not acting under coercion, Ugolino also promised not to contest the rights of Donati, in whose favor he renounced any rights of his own. But that same day, back in the family palace in the Arena and before different witnesses, Ugolino stated that he was under intimidation from Francesco Novello to confirm the sale to Manno Donati of property that rightly belonged to the

Scrovegni but had been usurped years back with Francesco il Vecchio's approval. Now he swore that his apparent consent was due to "his fear and the tyranny of the Carraresi" and that "Manno and his aforesaid parent were by bad faith in possession of the property and held it without any legal right."[15] Immediately after this statement Ugolino made a *donatio inter vivos* bestowing the property and rights at Creola on his sons, Enrico and Giacomo Scrovegni.[16] Like the Scrovegni, many other apparent supporters of the regime were biding their time and saw the coming of the new Visconti rulers as an occasion to take vengeance for past wrongs.

When Francesco il Vecchio in Treviso heard of his son's capitulation in Padua, he flew into a rage and "shouted that [Francesco Novello] was not his son, but only a really stupid bastard."[17] He marshaled what forces he still possessed and prepared for the inevitable conquest, as Jacopo dal Verme led a Visconti army from conquered Padua toward Treviso. On 29 November, the Trevisans, who deeply hated the Carrara dynasty and its rule, rose up against Francesco il Vecchio and ransacked his bank and offices, stealing huge quantities of money and supplies. Shorn of any support in Treviso, the elder Carrara broke off the negotiations he had begun with dal Verme and chose to surrender to his former captain Ugolotto Biancardo as he entered Treviso at the head of other Visconti troops. On 15 December Visconti representatives turned over Treviso and its territory to Venetian vicars, as had been provided for by treaty, and Francesco il Vecchio, now a captive under guard, began his sad journey toward Verona and eventual imprisonment in several strongholds in Lombardy. The next January the Venetian Senate eventually responded to his protest that the cash and goods taken in the uprising should be returned to him as stolen property. The Senate's interpretation went against restitution of Carrara property, since "the Trevisan people for its own safety and security took up arms and seized control of the city, so that in this fury the Carrara pawnshop and houses and those of some of his followers were sacked.... And afterward [the Trevisans] gave their city to our rectors, but it is clear to us this was an allowable uprising that the Trevisan people made for their own safety and the salvation of their city."[18]

Thus, the Venetian government came to terms with the new situation, counting on the bad government and hatred of the Carrara to justify destruction of their property and confiscation of their goods. Certain that Francesco il Vecchio would never return from captivity and his son's future existence was at best precarious, Florence, too, accepted the Visconti conquest, sending the lord of Milan a note of congratulations, praising his bloodless conquest of Padua, and hoping for peace in the future.[19] The native Paduan leadership was left alone to cope with the fact of Visconti conquest.

Exile and Restoration

During the three weeks between the frantic flight of Francesco Novello and his retinue on 24 November and the triumphant entry of the new Visconti officials on 18 December 1388, local leaders worked feverishly, often employing the older organs of the communal government, to create order and arrange favorable articles of surrender to the Visconti lord.[20] Informed by the Visconti rector Jacopo dal Verme of the terms of Francesco Novello's surrender of Padua, four of the ablest commanders of the former regime were assigned to secure order within the city, one for each quarter: Fredo Malizia for the Duomo, Gherardo de' Negri for Torricelle, Geremia da Peraga for Ponte Altinati, and Lion Lenguazzo for Ponte Molino. These men confronted the Carrara podestà, Ugolino Preti, and removed him from office in favor of the jurist and law professor Giovanni Porcellini. Then was created a small board of eight Anziani, elected one noble and one commoner per quarter, which was charged with formulating policy to deal with Visconti rule. First, the Anziani named Bonifacio Lupi *capitano del popolo* in command of the four captains of the quarters and charged with Padua's security and defense. Then, on the recommendation of the Anziani, the Paduan citizen council elected a board of nine notables, composed of jurists, nobles, and merchants and charged with drawing the *capitoli* of surrender to its new lord and selecting a delegation of twelve ambassadors to present the proposals to Giangaleazzo Visconti in Pavia. These groups included several opponents of the Carrara, such as Bonacorso Naseri and Fruzerino Capodivacca on the board of Nine and Enrico Scrovegni among the ambassadors. But the Paduans also elected Carrara favorites known for political and legal talents, such as the jurists Alessandro Dottori and Alberto Aproino on the Nine and Giovanni Lodovico Lambertazzi, Alvarotto Alvarotti, the soldier Africano Enselmini, and the chronicler Galeazzo Gatari as ambassadors. Thus, the citizen boards that greeted the Visconti rectors in December represented the best talent the university and the commune could offer, pleased to cooperate with the new podestà, Bertetto Visconti; the captain, Luchino Rusconi; and the commander of the Castello, Andrea Tolomei of Siena.

One of the first duties of the new regime was to carry out the audit of the old podestà, Ugolino Preti, who had been handpicked by Francesco il Vecchio and was leaving the office in a shambles.[21] Following procedures set forth in the communal statutes, five Paduan citizens were elected to investigate the podestà, his vicar and staff of judges, knights, and police constables, finding, in this case, no evidence of "barratry and extortion (*baratarias et extorsiones*)" but instead unpaid debts and unsettled accounts. In the desperate last days of the regime, Ugolino Preti had failed to pay the salaries of several of his staff, and these, in turn, had run up some large bills with local tradesmen. The podestà, who received a monthly stipend for his own salary and his staff's, had not paid the full salaries to four associates, owing his vicar 11 ducats, a criminal court judge 12 ducats, his judge at Aquila more than £90 for nearly four months' work, and the judge at Vettoveglie more than £27. In addition, he was in debt to several local tradesmen: more than £78 to a draper for cloth and linens, £30 for the rent of beds and mattresses, £3 for candles, and 85 ducats and £37 to two Jewish pawnbrokers. No doubt, the commune, so strapped for funds, had simply failed to pay the podestà's salary, and he was forced to live on credit. A knight and constable on the staff were also deeply in debt, owing the local baker for bread, butcher for meat, and taverner for wine and incidentals. Now these officials, dismissed in the middle of their term, had to settle accounts before they could leave Padua.

However, the most important problem was negotiating the most favorable possible terms of surrender with the count of Virtù.[22] In fact, after making obsequious remarks about the "immense joy" caused by the coming of Visconti rule and "citizens of Padua faithful in heart and mind," the ambassadors were to outline two options: delegated authority to the Paduan commune or direct Visconti rule over Padua and its district. Under the first scheme, all Paduan customs and institutions would be preserved, with local citizens filling the major offices of the commune, while the Visconti lord retained appointment of the podestà and the captains of the fortresses of the city and district. The Paduan commune would pay the salaries of all these officials, the cost of the garrisons, and all other necessary expenses; in addition, each year the commune would pay a lump sum (*taglio*) directly to Milan, while one of Giangaleazzo's councillors would be appointed governor of the city. If Giangaleazzo Visconti decided "to retain for himself rule and administration of Padua and its district," the ambassadors were to request the following conditions. Communal property sold or donated by the Carrara lord was to be restored, and most private sales made "to the great damage and prejudice of the communes and individuals" were to be declared null and void. Padua and its strongholds were to be placed under the direct protection of the lord of Milan, while the local system of taxation, government, and justice was to be preserved unchanged, with the podestà's decisions seen as binding.

Under the articles of surrender, a primary concern was the removal of the old ruling clique—"the bad seed, which had corrupted the whole city" under the Carrara. Thus, the ambassadors were to demand the banishment of those closest to the Carrara regime, about thirty men in all, under various charges and with varying penalties. The first object of exile was the

Carrara clan itself: both Francesco Senior and Junior and their ascendants, descendants, and collaterals were to be exiled in perpetuity with their property confiscated, except Albertino Papafava dei Carraresi and his family, who were judged innocent and could remain in Padua so long as they did not display the hated *carro*. Also subject to sweeping penalties of perpetual exile and confiscation of property were the Carrara affines, the Buzzacarini up to the fourth degree of consanguinity. To these despised families was added a corpse, the deceased Niccolò Curtarolo, damned for his extortions of the widows, wards, monasteries, churches, and citizens of Padua. Other Carrara officials were condemned to similar harsh sentences, including the priors of S. Giovanni di Verdara and S. Maria in Vanzo, the chief scribe, Enrico Gallo, the regime's accountants, Matteo da Ferrara and Bartolomeo d'Altegrado da Lendinara, and Giovanni Parisino Mezzoconti, all charged with crimes against the Paduan people.

Placed in a different category and given more lenient sentences were other Carrara favorites. Naimiero Conti and his offspring were to be exiled but were permitted to sell for cash one-third of his property, if the remainder was handed over to the Paduan commune. The three Turchetto brothers—Giacomo, Francesco, and Giovanni—called "rapacious wolves," were likewise permitted to convert a third of their goods into cash before going into exile. Even lighter penalties were asked for other Carrara councillors: Paganino Sala, Francesco Dotti, Guglielmo Curtarolo, and three Lion brothers, Paolo, Luca, and Niccolò, were to be banished, but their families could retain all their patrimonies. Those whose reputations for greed and extortion had made them unpopular with their fellow Paduans were, however, subject to stiff penalties: the Carrara *spenditore* Antonio Pavanello, the agent Montorso Montorsi, and foreign financiers Francesco Allegro of Florence and Milano Jacomelli of Milan were all subject to exile and confiscation of goods for their crimes and extortions. But in the event, most of these harsh penalties were never imposed. In January Giangaleazzo Visconti greeted the Paduan embassy with his usual disarming affability, accepted in general the *capitoli,* and promised to send able rectors to defend and rule Padua. Regarding "all Paduans as his children," Giangaleazzo agreed to handle the issue of exiles "in a way that [would] be useful to the whole city of Padua." Thus, the lord of Milan flattered the Paduan envoys, calling their city the equal of Venice, while endeavoring to secure allies from within the Carrara ruling elite who would be willing servants of the new regime.[23]

Francesco Novello's Exile

As former Carrara supporters flocked to serve the new regime, early in December Francesco Novello and his family began from Monselice their fateful journey of exile.[24] Stopping in Verona in December, the Carrara retinue found hospitality in the home of Guglielmo Bevilacqua, where Francesco Novello met briefly with his father, now a captive under a Visconti guard. Proceeding to Brescia and Bergamo, the party arrived in Milan for the Christmas season at the Visconti court. Treated with indifference bordering on contempt by Giangaleazzo Visconti and his courtiers, Francesco Novello confessed his anger and plot to murder the lord of Milan to his secretary and confidant Arturo Conti. When the Visconti lord learned of Francesco Novello's hatred, his own attitude changed from contempt to a quest for vengeance. In January 1389, Giangaleazzo exiled the Carrara lord from Milan, rewarding him with a dilapidated castle of Cortesone west of Asti and a pension of 500 ducats a month. Urged by secret communication from his father, now in custody in Cremona, to escape Visconti dominions, Francesco Novello left behind several of his retinue, who took service with the Visconti in Milan, and traveled with wife, children, kinsmen, and small escort through Alessandria to Asti, where he was greeted by the local governor. After viewing the ruined castle, unfit for habitation, and now certain of Giangaleazzo's plans for vengeance, Francesco Novello asked permission to make a pilgrimage to the shrine of St. Anthony of Vienne near Grenoble, concocting the story of a solemn vow made to this revered figure of Paduan hagiology.

That winter, leaving several members of the family and household in Asti, the Carrara party, including his wife, Taddea, natural brother Rodolfo, several children, servants, and retainers, set out through Savoy, crossing the Alps into the Dauphiné, and traveling up the Isère Valley to Grenoble. After visiting the shrine of St. Anthony of Vienne in the abbey at Motta, the party turned south. Heading down the Rhone, the Carrara entourage stopped briefly at Avignon, meeting the antipope Clement VII, before traveling to Marseilles. Destitute and desperate for food and money, Francesco Novello was there befriended by the former bishop of Padua Raimondo Ganimberti, who received him in his home and helped procure a ship to Monaco. Thence, the Carrara party went down the Ligurian coast to Savona, where they took ship to Pisa. After enduring many hardships, including dangerous storms at sea, Francesco Novello, his wife, their children, and retinue entered Florence in early April 1389.

There Francesco Novello was greeted by his Florentine friends from

Exile and Restoration

better days in Padua, Pazzino Donati and Francesco Allegro, who had tried without much success to transfer moneys from the recent sales of property in Padua. Though he was perhaps popular with the Florentine people, the Carrara lord's official reception from the signoria was distinctly cool. Not wanting to upset the fragile standoff with Giangaleazzo Visconti, the Florentines at best tolerated Milan's greatest enemy in their midst, refusing to pay money Francesco Novello insisted had been sent to Florence from the enormous sales of the previous autumn. But gradually his situation improved. His half brother Conte was already in Florence's pay, commanding troops in the field against Siena. In discussions with the priorate, Francesco Novello reminded the Florentines of his house's ancient allegiance to the Guelf cause. Determined to reconquer Padua, Francesco Novello dispatched two advisers, Baldo Bonafari da Piombino and Pazzino Donati, as envoys seeking subsidies from his brother-in-law Stefan Frankapan, count of Veglia, while at the same time reuniting in Florence almost all his family, including several members who had been left behind in Asti. Those reunited included his legitimate offspring, Francesco III, Giacomo, Marsilio, and Gigliola, and Novello's four illegitimate half brothers, Conte, Giacomo, Pietro, and Rodolfo, who were all potential military captains in any attempt to reconquer Padua. Probably at this time his wife conceived their youngest son, named Ubertino Fiorentino after the family's city of sanctuary and born on 24 January 1390, just over nine months after the destitute Carrara retinue reached Florence. Also with Francesco Novello were two of his own natural offspring, a daughter, Gionata, and the future bishop of Padua, Stefano, as well as Andrea, abbot of S. Giustina, and a certain Servio, who are probably to be included among Francesco il Vecchio's numerous bastards.[25] Best of all, Francesco Novello was able to recover valuables and funds worth from 60,000 to 80,000 ducats left at Asti and bring them to Florence, thus obtaining the war chest needed for the reconquest of Padua.

Most encouraging was the tough and realistic advice that his father, Francesco il Vecchio, sent via the faithful courtier Enrico Gallo from captivity in Como.[26] The elder Carrara, resigned to living out his days in a Visconti prison, forbade his son to pay ransom or exchange property for his freedom. Rather, Francesco Novello was to look for help from the next generation, employing as commanders in his army all the able bastards of the house, while forcing the weaker ones to enter religious life (*metere a vitta chattolica*). The young men of the Carrara family were to marry as soon as possible so that the house could multiply and grow (*a ciò che la caxa moltipichi e cresse*). The son, in effect, took the father's advice. Despite various negotiations for the elder Carrara's release, he was to die in the Visconti stronghold at

TABLE 8.2
The Carrara IV. Francesco Novello's Offspring

Francesco Novello (1359–1406), executed
= May 1377 Taddea d'Este, d. 1404

| Gigliola (ca. 1379–1416) = Niccolò III d'Este | Francesco III (1383–1406), executed = 1397 Alda di Francesco Gonzaga | Giacomo (ca. 1385–1406), executed = 1403 Belfiore di Rodolfo da Varano, lord of Camerino | Niccolò, d. infant | Marsilio, soldier (ca. 1386–1435), executed | Ubertino (1390–1407), poisoned | Valpurga, OSB abbess of S. Agata, d. 1405 |

| Stilio Gionata no legitimate offspring | Stefano (ca. 1375–1449), bishop of Padua, 1402–5, of Nicosia, of Teramo, archbishop of Rossano | Milone (ca. 1380–before 1416), legitimated in 1400 | Agnese = 1399 Ognibene Scola, d. after 1429 | Gionata (?) |

Exile and Restoration

Monza some four years later. But his counsel was fulfilled. Over the next fifteen years almost all of the males of the house, legitimate and natural, served the Carrara cause in war, politics, and religion.

After promising, but inconclusive, discussions with members of the Florentine government, including Donato Acciaiuoli and Niccolò Niccoli, then serving on the Ten of War, the Carrara lord decided to pursue the liberation of Padua in earnest. Heartened by a spontaneous but abortive revolt against Visconti rule in Padua in May 1389, Francesco Novello decided to seek aid from his sister Caterina and her consort, Stefan Frankapan, count of Veglia and lord of Segna. Traveling to the Romagna, where he was threatened with capture by Carlo Malatesta, Francesco Novello found his way blocked by Venetian officials in Chioggia. Instead he turned back to Bologna, where he sought support from its communal government and met the young Pier Paolo Vergerio before returning to Florence. In an enthusiastic letter to a friend, Vergerio commented on their discussion, shrewdly assessing Francesco Novello's situation as he embarked on his campaign of reconquest.[27] Sometime pupil at the Paduan *studium* and partisan of the Carrara regime, Vergerio praised Francesco Novello's skill at governing and love of justice, comparing him to Priam in having the bearing and presence of a great leader who would be loved and respected by his Paduan subjects.

Although it seems unlikely that the words of encouragement of the young humanist had any direct effect on Carrara policy, at the end of August 1389 Francesco Novello with his half brother Rodolfo left Florence for Pisa on the first leg of his journey to Germany seeking aid from family, affines, and, most of all, Stephen, duke of Bavaria, who, as a son-in-law of the deposed and murdered Bernabò, was viewed as a "natural enemy" of Giangaleazzo Visconti. Because the easy route to Munich across the peninsula and up the Adriatic by ship was cut off by Venice and the Visconti, the Carrara lord retraced his recent journey from Provence.[28] After a sumptuous reception by the lord of Pisa, Pietro Gambacorta, the Carrara lord took ship at Livorno for Monaco and proceeded through Piedmont, furnished with a safe-conduct from Count Amadeus. Arriving in Switzerland at Geneva, the Carrara retinue traveled through Bern and Zurich and rested for a few days at Constance before reaching the court of Duke Stephen of Bavaria in Munich late in September. There, dwelling on the need to destroy Giangaleazzo in vengeance for Bernabò's murder, Francesco Novello joined envoys from Florence and Bologna in urging the duke of Bavaria to invade Italy and restore the Carrara to rule over Padua. Although these negotiations in Munich had little immediate effect, the relations between the Guelf powers and the Visconti were worsening in a fatal drift toward war.

Throughout the summer of 1389, Bologna and Florence had maintained ambassadors at the Visconti court at Pavia, hoping to negotiate a nonaggression pact among the principal states of north and central Italy.[29] With the Gonzaga of Mantua and Este of Ferrara now included among Giangaleazzo's satellites, Florence and Bologna looked outside Italy to the king of France and the antipope Clement VII at Avignon for support, and, as we have seen, to Duke Stephen of Bavaria as a potential ally. Within Italy Florence sought to demarcate spheres of influence, ceding to the Visconti lord domination to the north of the Secchia River and west of Modena, while hoping to maintain its dominance over Tuscany. Thus, Florence eventually accepted Pietro Gambacorta's call to a new peace conference to convene at Pisa early in August to carve out alliances and spheres in Italy. Giangaleazzo hoped to increase through diplomacy his influence in central Italy, insisting on his right to provide troops for his friends in Tuscany, such as Siena. The negotiations at Pisa dragged on into the autumn, as both sides prepared for war. Finally, on 9 October 1389 the pact of Pisa was signed, little more than a testament to the tenacity of the lord of Pisa, Pietro Gambacorta. The pact provided for Florentine and Milanese spheres of influence, common action against mercenary companies in Italy, and settlement of any future disputes through arbitration.

The pact of Pisa of October 1389 only provided a breathing space for war preparations.[30] The day after the pact was concluded, Florence entered into its own league with Bologna, Pisa, Lucca, and Perugia, gathering allies to preserve the peace in Tuscany and the Romagna, while Giangaleazzo increasingly manifested his hostility. Later that month, claiming a Florentine plot on his life, the lord of Milan expelled all citizens of Florence and Bologna from his dominions. The discovery later that fall of a Visconti plot to foment a rebellion against the communal government of Bologna served only to exacerbate tensions. The growing Visconti influence in Siena and Perugia and the waning authority of Florence's ally in Pisa, Pietro Gambacorta, intensified the frantic search for allies and troops. Early in 1390 Florence and Bologna reopened negotiations with Stephen of Bavaria in Munich, who now supported Francesco Novello's plans to restore his rule over Padua. Some eighteen months after the Visconti had occupied Padua, a new struggle for the lordship of the city became inevitable.

Life in Visconti Padua

As we have seen, the Visconti conquest of Padua had been openly and joyfully hailed by some members of the former Carrara elite. The entry of Jacopo dal Verme to take control of the city in December 1388 had elicited an extravagant letter from Maddalena di Ugolino Scrovegni, praising the

Exile and Restoration

Visconti conquest of Padua and rejoicing in the downfall of the hated Carraresi.[31] Praise was followed by loyal allegiance to the new Visconti regime, with Bonifacio Lupi, Ugolino Scrovegni, Ubertino Grompo, and Bonacorso Naseri emerging as the local leaders. As *capitano del popolo* of Visconti Padua, Bonifacio Lupi continued business as usual. He invested his spare cash making short-term deposits with favorite local bankers, increased his urban property by purchasing a large house near the Duomo which had previously belonged to a Carrara favorite, and approved the collection of rents as well as grants to several Franciscans by the rector of his hospital of S. Giovanni Battista in Florence.[32]

The best portrait of the community of Carrara opponents in Padua is provided by the act of nomination of a proctor drawn up in Bonifacio Lupi's palace at S. Fermo on 30 July 1389.[33] There in the presence of Bonifacio, Fra Giovanni, prior of the monastery of S. Benedetto of Padua, Ugolino qd. Enrico Scrovegni, Petrarch's son-in-law Francescuolo da Brossano, and Ubertino qd. Nascimbene Grompo of contrada S. Cecilia, Lombardo della Seta permitted his illegitimate son, Pellegrino — note the resonance of Petrarch's "peregrinus ubique" — to appoint Bonifacio's nephew the *condottiere* Ugolotto Biancardo as his proctor to appear before the count palatine Antonino of Langusco to secure his legitimation. With Francesco il Vecchio safely in prison and Francesco Novello in exile in Florence, this group of soldiers and men of letters doubtless saw themselves as the new leaders of Padua.

Ubertino Grompo, whose father, Nascimbene, had headed the regime's office of mercenaries early in Francesco il Vecchio's rule, hailed from an old noble and feudal family with estates in the southern Padovano. Division of property among the surviving sons in 1357 revealed the Grompo as wealthy landowners, with seven houses in Padua and extensive farms and tithes in Villa Estense, Urbana, and Casale north of the Adige.[34] Some two decades later, Ubertino remained one of the richest men in the area, owning one-quarter of extensive marshlands in Ponso held *pro indiviso* with the Carrara lord and the marquis of Este.[35] Ubertino served his lord in the Chioggia war with a term as the podestà of Noale in 1381, before returning to the life of rentier residing in contrada S. Cecilia and sometime courtier in the Carrara Reggia. The early death of two brothers, Rolando and Gombertino, permitted Ubertino to share the large Grompo estates with his sole surviving brother, Pietro, a knight and captain in the Carrara campaign in Friuli.[36] A final division of their property early in 1388 shows Ubertino with large holdings in Casale, Villa Estense, and Montagnana, while Pietro received land in the ancestral home, Villa Grompo.[37] Thereafter, one brother, Pietro, remained loyal to the House of Carrara, contributed to the defense of Padua in the autumn of 1388 by purchasing all Carrara land in Borgoricco for £3,000, and later joined Francesco Novello in Friuli on the eve of the reconquest of Padua.³⁸ But the other brother, Ubertino, took the collapse of the Carrara regime as the opportunity to cultivate friendships with the local notables of Visconti Padua.

Ugolino Scrovegni and his sons used their family's longstanding enmity against the Carrara to their own political and economic advantage. With daughter Maddalena's warm speech of welcome to Jacopo dal Verme attesting to her family's enthusiasm for the new rulers, her father and brothers wasted no time in distancing themselves from the Carrara clique and harvesting the rewards that service to the Visconti regime could bring. After the fall of the Carrara the Venetian government had been quick to sequester Paduans' property and goods and "freeze" shares of the funded public debt. Long-term servants of the Carrara regime from Florence suffered for their service to the exiled family. In denying the request of a Florentine ambassador for the return of the property of Francesco Allegro, the Senate replied that, despite Venice's friendship for Florence, Allegro's property would remain sequestered because "for many years he served lord Francesco da Carrara, the former lord of Padua, [who is] our natural and perfidious enemy."³⁹ Thus, Venice joined the Visconti in punishing those loyal to the Carrara, but it also rewarded those who turned against the regime. Three months later, the Senate, noting that Venice had sequestered property of all subjects of the deposed Carrara lord, made an exception in the case of the Monte holdings of the Scrovegni family, including Ugolino, Maddalena, and Enrico, because "everyone knows that the said lord Ugolino at every time and situation, both favorable and adverse, has always conducted himself laudably for the honor of our state."⁴⁰ Indeed, Ugolino used his privileged position in Visconti Padua to collect extensive income from tithes in several villages in the Diocese of Vicenza. The next April he appointed two proctors to appear before Visconti officials in Padua to plead a suit concerning disputed property there.⁴¹

Among others who made accommodation with the Visconti conquest was the brilliant mercenary captain Bartolomeo Cermisone, who had entered the service of the Carrara during the Chioggia war, helped to defeat a larger Veronese army at Brentelle, and later taken Sacile in the Friuli campaign. By the summer of 1387 Cermisone had settled in Borgo Novo Patriarcato, probably in a house leased from the Carrara lord, where he appointed proctors to recover debts owed in Parma.⁴² Charged with the internal security of the city during the siege of 1388, Cermisone had advised resistance to Visconti forces and even offered to execute with his own hands Paduans plotting a coup d'état against the Carrara regime. In return for his service

Francesco Novello made Cermisone a gift of the houses in Borgo Novo. He also contributed to the Carrara cause by purchasing for £2,000 some 110 *campi* of farmland in Spassano. But disgusted with Francesco Novello's decision to flee and ask for Giangaleazzo's mercy, Cermisone remained in Padua, accepting the reality of the new regime. When the legality of the Carrara gift and sale was called into question, Cermisone produced a letter from Giangaleazzo Visconti, validating his possession of the former Carrara property, thus confirming his rights to his Paduan holdings.[43] Other former notable supporters of the Carrara dynasty, such as Paganino Sala and Giovanni, Antonio, and Bonacorso Naseri, became warm adherents of the new regime, perhaps believing (as Silvana Collodo has speculated) in "the definitive eclipse of the Carrara."[44]

Although the military and civil leadership of Padua changed radically under the Visconti, ecclesiastical officialdom remained much the same. Beginning with Petrarch himself, the Carrara lords used the post of canons of the cathedral as reward and compensation for officials of their regime. A meeting of the chapter held in December 1387 shows that among the canons were numbered such Carrara stalwarts as Ludovico and Francesco Buzzacarini and Prosdocimo Conti, as well as such foreigners as Matteo Cavalcanti of Florence, Filippo Melzi of Milan, and Domenico of Bergamo.[45] One of the most experienced and respected canons was Giovanni di Bartolomeo Enselmini, from an old feudal family once dominant in the eastern Padovano. Perhaps a canon as early as 1365, Giovanni purchased extensive property in Brusegana and Galzignano, and in 1379 he rented for 54 ducats a year tithes held in nearby Rubano to one Jacobo da Ferrara, rector of the suburban church of S. Fidone in Sarmeola.[46] Enselmini earned his doctorate in canon law at the *studium* in November 1385, with his future vicar, Filippo Melzi, a witness at his public examination. When Bishop Raimondo was translated to Marseilles early in 1387, the See of Padua lay vacant for perhaps a year, until Pope Urban VI provided Giovanni Enselmini to the bishopric of Padua in the spring of 1388. Enselmini was already active as bishop that June when he promoted some twenty-six men to clerical orders. He presided over an examination in canon law on 20 November, just before the fall of the Carrara regime.[47]

Thus, Enselmini was not a Visconti candidate for the office, and, more important, he exhibited little discrimination against members of the Carrara elite or favoritism toward Visconti followers. To be sure, he took as his vicar the longtime Milanese canon of Padua Filippo Melzi, who played a large role in the day-to-day administration of the diocese. But there was no great change in the composition of the chapter of cathedral canons or much prejudice shown in the awarding of decimal fiefs. Bishop Enselmini continued the practice of investing tithes with the heirs upon the death of the incumbent, thus usually passing the tithes on from father to son, with little concern for their standing with the new local regime. In this fashion, the bishop invested fiefs of tithes with the minor branch of the Buzzacarini, sons of Salione and Bartolomeo detto Priore.[48] During his term, other tithes were invested with such leading families of Carrara Padua as the Lion, Piombioli, Rio, Turchetto, and Vitaliani.[49] Other members of the Paduan elite awarded decimal fiefs during the interregnum included Matteo and Padovano qd. Pizzacomino Pizzacomini in Carmignano di Brenta and Ludovico Cortusi, who was invested with fiefs of tithes in S. Eufemia di Borgoricco.[50] Giovanni Enselmini even invested Anna da Carrara, abbess of S. Stefano of Padua, with extensive decimal fiefs in Bovolenta.[51] Certainly, Visconti supporters also profited: Giangaleazzo's new ally the lord of Ferrara, Alberto d'Este, received extensive fiefs in Solesino di Scodosia as well as renewal of his right of patronage over the nunnery of S. Giovanni Battista di Zemola.[52] Sometimes Carrara supporters were penalized: Naimiero Conti was forced to renounce his decimal fiefs in Pernumia in favor of the Paduan notary Ser Oliviero di Enrico Gallo.[53] But, in general, the system of the control of powerful local families over fiefs of tithes in their villages was left undisturbed.

Although a few clerics from Lombardy were added to the bishop's staff, the daily administration of the diocese changed little. In January 1390 and again in June, Bishop Enselmini promoted seven men to the clerical order of the first tonsure; one came from Piacenza, the rest from Padua or the nearby cities of Belluno and Ferrara.[54] By February 1390, the Lombard jurist Paolo da Dugnano, *ordinarius* of the Duomo in Milan, had become one of the bishop's vicars as well as a canon of the Paduan cathedral. That spring a certain Paolino Gabatori of Milan was numbered among the clergy of Padua.[55] This laissez-faire policy extended to the bishop's own brother, the knight Africano Enselmini, who had been a valiant soldier in the Carrara wars: commander of archers at Piove di Sacco in 1373, captain at Chioggia in 1379 and in Friuli in 1387.[56] One of Padua's ambassadors sent to the Visconti court in 1388, Africano became a fixture in the episcopal curia the next year, where he continued to oversee his interests developed earlier in his rural estates located in the eastern Padovano at Brentasecca, Fiesso, Villanova, and Strà.[57] For example, on 10 September 1389 in the bishop's palace Africano rented a house near the Strazaria Nova to the artisan Jacobino qd. Vivano, and on 20 December he granted a lease of twenty-nine years to a peasant in Fiesso.[58] In May 1390 Africano was at his home in contrada Salone, where he served as a witness to an act of sale.[59] His presence in his own home and in the curia of his brother Giovanni during 1389 and

1390 makes it difficult to believe the report made to Francesco Novello in the court of Frederick, count of Ortenburg, early in 1390 that Africano Enselmini and his brother Giacomo were among those Carrara supporters already imprisoned by the Visconti rulers of Padua.[60] Although there was unrest among the Paduan elite and some repression by Visconti officials, most of the former Carrara elite remained free in Padua, scarcely aware of plans for Francesco Novello's triumphant return.

Francesco Novello's Reconquest of Padua

After visiting his sister Caterina at Veglia late in 1389, that spring Francesco Novello set up his household at the court of Frederick, count of Ortenburg, husband of his sister Lieta, recruiting support among friends in Germany and Friuli and actively enlisting Duke Stephen of Bavaria in his cause of reconquest.[61] Meanwhile, Giangaleazzo sought additional troops, sending Ugolotto Biancardo into the Romagna to enroll as many as two thousand lances. On 5 April Florence and Bologna finally succeeded in enlisting the duke of Bavaria into a league against the Visconti lord, agreeing to a monthly stipend of 21,000 florins for an army of two thousand lances (or about six thousand horsemen at three soldiers per lance) to take the field that May. Supplemented by additional German cavalry and the forces raised by Francesco Novello and his allies in Friuli, a sizable army had been recruited for the reconquest of Padua. Angered by Florence's obvious meddling in the affairs of his Tuscan allies, including taking Montepulciano under its direct protection, on 19 April 1390 Giangaleazzo declared war, accusing a small and vicious clique of Archguelfs of breaking the peace and tyrannizing Italy.[62] In a counterdeclaration sent on 2 May followed by a circular letter to all Italian powers on the 25th, Salutati identified the Visconti lord as the real enemy of peace, who had repeatedly broken his word and meddled in the affairs of central Italy. Rehearsing every deception, conflict, and plot that the lord of Milan had fomented in recent years, Salutati emphasized that the only hope for the peace of Italy was a union of the states of the peninsula to wipe out this monster, their common enemy.[63]

Giangaleazzo Visconti opened the conflict in the field by besieging Bologna. Meanwhile, Francesco Novello concluded an alliance with his old enemy the patriarch of Aquileia, John Sobieslaw of Moravia, and moved his small army of perhaps five hundred lances and two thousand infantry into Friuli. Composed of Paduan and Veronese exiles, friends and allies from Friuli, and some contingents of German mercenaries, the Carrara forces first stopped at Cividale to receive reinforcements and intelligence before crossing the Talgiamento, to set up a temporary headquarters at the castle of Valvasone, seat of two Friulian commanders, Counts Rizzardo and Giacomo. Though officially neutral, the Venetian government had watched apprehensively as the Visconti rulers often challenged and infringed on the rights of its proprietors in the Padovano.[64] Scarcely pleased with the alliance between the Carrara lord and the patriarch of Aquileia, Venice had to face the new realities. As Francesco Novello's army approached the Trevisano, the Venetian government permitted his forces to cross their domains unchallenged.[65]

By the middle of June the Carrara lord encamped his forces north of Padua at Camposampiero and sent a herald to Padua demanding surrender. Meeting in the Hall of Illustrious Men in the Reggia, the Visconti rectors and their Paduan supporters counseled resistance, calling out the garrison to man the walls. The Carrara army crossed the Brenta and invested the northern suburbs. At dawn on 19 June, shouting "San Antonio" and "Carro," the Paduan forces attacked the walls at Ponte Molino and Porciglia and soon penetrated the outer defenses of the city. Carrara forces regrouped at the Eremitani, where Francesco Novello attempted to bolster the morale of his soldiers by knighting six of his commanders: his half brother Rodolfo, the marshal of the patriarch of Aquileia, Nicholas Trincher, two captains from Friuli, Febo della Torre and Rizzardo da Valvasone, and two Paduan knights, Missio da Castelnuovo and Pietro Grompo. His troops then set fire to and sacked Ugolino Scrovegni's palace in the Arena, prompting Francesco Novello to appoint his *spenditore* Antonio Pavanello and Pietro Grompo, who had only recently left Padua, to identify the homes of loyal citizens and safeguard them from sack. Investing the eastern half of the city, the attacking army regrouped at the Santo before taking control of the quarter of Torricelle.

Thus, with the Carrara army in control of much of Padua, the Visconti defenders were gradually pushed into the old center of the city. For the final assault, Francesco Novello organized his forces into three divisions; Missio and his half brother Rodolfo were placed in charge of a force of one thousand Paduan citizens and peasants; Febo della Torre, aided by his half brother Giacomo da Carrara and Rizzardo da Valvasone, commanded the troops from Friuli; and Hermann Spisser took charge of the German mercenaries. In the course of the attack Francesco Novello spied Bonifacio Lupi near his home at S. Fermo and called on him to open the city walls. Now identified as a turncoat, Lupi refused, declaring: "I have never been a traitor. When I was in the service of the house of Carrara, I was loyal to them, and now I intend to be [loyal] to the Visconti house, and especially to the Count of Virtù."[66] The attacking forces soon forced entrance at the gate of S. Matteo, precipitating the flight of the Visconti rectors and

Exile and Restoration

their soldiers and supporters from the Reggia via the *traghetto* and city walls to the Castello in the southwest corner of Padua. On the 21st, the Carrara lord and his forces took control of the central *piazze* flanking the Salone and soon entered the Reggia, freeing political prisoners found there. By evening almost all of Padua was again in Carrara hands. The next day all the strongholds and towns of the Padovano surrendered to the conquering forces. Only the sizable remnant of the Visconti garrison occupying the Castello gave cause for concern.

The success of the reconquest of Padua had depended on rapid movement, surprise, and coordination among the forces opposing the Visconti. At just the moment the Carrara army was investing Padua, Sir John Hawkwood directed his troops to attack Jacopo dal Verme's forces besieging Bologna, preventing any aid from being sent to the beleaguered garrison at Padua. The news of the reconquest of Padua had prompted a spontaneous uprising against the Visconti garrison in Verona, which was brutally suppressed by troops under the command of Ugolotto Biancardo. Now dal Verme lifted his siege at Bologna and started a forced march toward Pavia, intending to enlist other Milanese troops to join Biancardo's small force in the Veneto. With the Visconti armies on the counterattack, the situation in Padua became grave. Writing from Venice on 29 June, Sienese merchants emphasized the weakness of the Carrara lord's position, predicting that Biancardo's forces would soon retake Padua, because "almost all the Carrara troops were unarmed peasants, who are not accustomed to war and very fearful of the coming of Lord Ugolotto, to whom they are not expected to offer resistance."[67] The salvation of Padua lay in the timely arrival of Duke Stephen's army of more than six thousand cavalry, which, according to Venetian officials in Treviso, had reached Friuli only on 30 June. But on 3 July the German advance guard of three hundred lances under command of Count Duino had reached the Trevisano, when Venetian officials complained of damages to crops and slaughtered livestock.[68] By forced marches, the main body of Duke Stephen's army entered Padua a week later to a joyous reception. Soon deployed in the field, the duke of Bavaria's army effectively blocked Biancardo's forces coming from Verona.

Padua was now securely in Carrara hands. The death of the able Visconti commander Giovanni Azzo degli Ubaldini at the end of June and the presence of Stephen's large force in the Padovano permitted the allies to go on the offensive. From Florence on 11 July, Salutati wrote to the lord of Padua, rejoicing with him on the arrival of Duke Stephen's army and urging him to make common cause to defeat Giangaleazzo and bring security to Italy: "For unless that serpent [Giangaleazzo], who had hoped with his gaping jaws to devour us and all of Italy, is manfully destroyed, unless his unimpaired power is crushed in such a fashion that instead of seeking the heights he walks in humility, we will not be able to sleep safely."[69]

Rather than taking the field against Giangaleazzo, however, the Carrara lord remained concerned with wreaking vengeance on the traitors found in Padua and starving out the Visconti garrison in his citadel. Stephen of Bavaria proved even less prone to engage in further conflict with Visconti forces. Susceptible to Giangaleazzo's bribes and blandishments, the duke of Bavaria was soon accused of treason, dismissed by his employers, Florence and Bologna, and sent back to Germany that fall.[70] At the end of August, the Visconti garrison trapped in the Castello finally surrendered and was soon paroled and repatriated to Lombardy. With the whole city now safely in his hands, on 8 September Francesco Novello was formally reelected lord of Padua by the Anziani in a stately ceremony held in the Great Hall of the Salone. The Anziani elected for the occasion formed the nucleus of Carrara supporters, drawn from the professional and merchant classes of Paduan society, including the jurists Francesco dalle Ave, Bartolomeo Capodivacca, Lodovico Cortusi, and Ottonello Descalzi and the apothecary Andrea Bazaleri. Placed in command of the Paduan army, Conte da Carrara was ordered again into the field to attack the forces of Alberto d'Este at Rovigo. By the end of October the Este army had been defeated, eventually forcing Alberto to make a separate peace with Francesco Novello and his allies. Now the Carrara lord was free to oversee the restoration of his regime in Padua.

To commemorate the signal victory and conquest of Padua on 19 June 1390, Francesco Novello later commissioned the design and striking of two medals, one bearing his own portrait and the other that of his father, Francesco il Vecchio, still in Visconti captivity. Modeled on the bronze sesterce of the early emperors, especially of Vitellius, the Carrara lords' portraits were highly classicized, depicted in profile with shaven faces. On the obverse, the bust of Francesco Novello in right profile is surrounded by the legend "EFFIGIES DNI.FRANCISCI.IVNIORIS. D. CARARIA. PAD." The reverse bears the heraldic *carro* used in Paduan coinage with the legend "1390 DIE. 19. IVNII. RECVP-ERAVIT:PADVAM:ETCETA. The obverse of the other medal shows the bust of il Vecchio in left profile, with the legend "FRANCISCI. DE CARRARIA"; the reverse, with the *carro,* bears the same legend commemorating the reconquest. The distribution and use of those medals is unknown. But they were doubtless part of several attempts, including issuing the biographical history of the Carrara clan in the elaborate *Gesta magnifica domus Carrariensis,* which were meant to bolster the prestige and restore the authority of the dynasty and its regime.[71] Harking back to the founding of the family by Lotolfo in the early eleventh century, the author of the *Gesta* took pains to show how the fortunes of Padua and the Carrara were inter-

FIG. 31. *Portrait medal of Francesco Novello, 1390. Struck to commemorate the conquest of Padua in the summer of 1390. This portrait head of the last Carrara lord on the obverse was modeled on bronze sesterces of imperial Rome, especially those of Vitellius. The reverse shows a* carro *similar to those on Paduan coins of the period. Reproduced with permission of the Museo Bottacin of the Musei Civici, Padua*

twined. In his lives of early Carrara, he emphasized the importance of the Carraresi as Guelf leaders against Ezzolino da Romano, which had led to the execution of the heroic Giacomo da Carrara at the hands of the hated Ghibelline tyrant.

Reestablishing Carrara Rule

Having secured his control over Padua by the end of the summer of 1390, Francesco Novello set about to restore his regime, calling on two of his father's most trusted officials, Giovanni Porcellini and Count Rizzardo Sambonifacio of Verona, to serve as his new vice-podestà and podestà, respectively. One of Sambonifacio's first duties was to draw up new statutes to punish rebels against the regime and, with the assistance of the criminal judge, bring the most infamous traitors of the Visconti interregnum to trial. Against any claim that those who were in exile might make on income from their property in Padua and to replenish a population decimated by war and disorder, a statute was enacted in November 1390 stating that foreigners settling in Padua could enjoy all property rights that citizens customarily enjoyed but no one living outside the city and its district could possess property there or derive income from it.[72] A related statute of that same autumn decreed that no one could acquire land or fiefs and enjoy income from these unless he was a Paduan citizen subject to the temporal jurisdiction of Padua and paying *onera et factiones* on such property.[73] Clearly both statutes were aimed at cutting the flow of income from Paduan properties to those in exile because of their previous treason against the Carrara regime.

That same autumn the podestà tried *in contumacia* fifteen of the most notorious rebels against the Carrara regime.[74] Working according to the statutes through the *giudice dei malefici,* Rizzardo di Sambonifacio sentenced each of the group to perpetual banishment from Padua, with heirs and kin up to the fourth degree of consanguinity, and confiscated their property. Further, each traitor was to be condemned to public decapitation in the communal square if he was ever arrested and brought under Paduan jurisdiction. The traitors so banished and condemned to death *in absentia* were Ubertino qd. Nascimbene Grompo; Ugolino Scrovegni and his sons Enrico and Pietro; Nascimbene qd. Alberto della Ricca from Cittadella; Giovanni Naseri of Montagnana; Paganino Sala; Giovanni qd. Guglielmo Camposampiero and his brother Giacomo; Milano Jacomelli; Daniele Lenguazzi; Giovanni di Saltimberto da Cremona; Antonio da Cartura; and Giovanni da Cremona, Francesco il Vecchio's captain at Monselice. The charges of treason fell into several categories: Pietro Scrovegni, Antonio da Cartura, Daniele Lenguazzi, and Milano Jacomelli were convicted of conspiring with the Visconti captains to betray the city during the siege of the fall of 1388; Paganino Sala of trading state secrets from the Carrara council to Giangaleazzo Visconti; Giacomo and Giovanni Camposampiero for refusal to defend the lord; Ugolino Scrovegni and Nascimbene della Ricca of vituperation of the Carrara lord and his honor. Most were also charged and convicted of giving aid and comfort to the enemy. All of these charges were based on the statutes defining treason promulgated during the *podestaria* of Marino Falier a half century earlier. Even the penalties were consistent with those specified in the statutes of 1339. Thus, the Carrara lord was upholding the letter of the law in his quest for vengeance against the traitors of the Visconti period.

The next year these traitors were still viewed as a major threat to the restored Carrara rule. In February 1391 a statute was enacted which forbade communication between the rebels and residents of Padua. No native Paduan or foreigner living in the city or district could send or receive any message, letter, or messenger to or from the rebels, now called public enemies, or anyone acting on their behalf. Anyone detecting and denouncing to the authorities such treasonable activities was to have half of the property confiscated, and no one, except Venetians, was now permitted to leave Padua and its district without a passport issued by the podestà or his vicar.[75]

Other statutes dealt with disruptions caused by the recent reconquest or attempted to promote the economic self-sufficiency of Padua. One provided that foreign creditors could in no way lay claim to real estate, livestock, or moveables in the settlement of debts arising from the recent war. And if the property was pawned or otherwise alienated to settle debts, the transaction was declared invalid. The lord of Padua also promoted the repair of churches damaged in war and now excluded foreigners from holding benefices in the diocese, with the podestà charged with making certain that only native Paduans were admitted to enjoy ecclesiastical livings. Finally, in order to encourage foreigners to study in the several faculties of the *studium*, depopulated because of the recent war, the rules licensing renting houses to foreign scholars enrolled in the university were relaxed. Now anyone who owned a house in the city of Padua was free to rent it to students on both long- and short-term leases, thus considerably enlarging the local housing market.[76]

Utilizing a statute promulgated by podestà Simone Lupi in 1376, the Carrara lord further actively encouraged the immigration of artisans to replenish a population reduced by war, plague, and disorder. From late in 1390 to early 1392, the Carrara curial notary Marco Guarnerini recorded the bestowal of Paduan citizenship on more than twenty men, with ten coming from nearby Vicenza and Treviso and their districts and the rest from the cities of Romagna, Lombardy, the Veneto, and Friuli. Where the occupations of the new immigrants are given, they are usually textile workers, needed in an enterprise of vital interest to the Carrara lord.[77] The nature of this influx of skilled foreign labor is confirmed by the geographic origins of members of the wool guild in the matriculation list for 1393.

Besides punishing his opponents and encouraging industry, trade, and the university, Francesco Novello saw to the staffing of the communal judiciary and the policing of the city. The Visconti regime had appointed a number of its supporters as judges and notaries in the judiciary, including Ubertino Grompo, Enrico Scrovegni, and Nascimbene della Ricca, while still permitting such Carrara favorites as Alessandro Dottori, Ottonello Descalzi, and Giovanni Porcellini to continue to hold office.[78] During the biennium after his restoration, Francesco Novello purged his enemies and appointed jurists to the thirteen civil courts of the communal government; this list reads like a roster of Carrara supporters from the legal profession. The ten jurists who most frequently held office in 1390 and 1391 as communal judges were Francesco Beningrado, Bartolomeo Capodivacca, Francesco Conselve, Lodovico Cortusi, Ottonello Descalzi, Alessandro Dottori, Giovanni Francesco Lambertazzi, Mezzoconte Mezzoconti, Giovanni Porcellini, and Antonio di San Angelo.[79] Likewise was revived the appointment of the volunteer police serving as the *capi* of the twenty wards (*centenarii*), which were distributed five per quarter throughout the city. Aided by an assistant, called *menevallo*, and a notary to record the names and deeds of miscreants, the *capi* served to deter crime, violence, and damage to property. The lists for the two years after the restoration show several gaps, suggesting that it was sometimes difficult to fill the office, though enrollment of officials for the quarters of Ponte Altinate, Torricelle, and Ponte Molino was more complete than for the Duomo.

In order to govern effectively the Carrara lord needed money. As we have seen, in October 1390, his handpicked podestà decreed the confiscation of the property of the regime's rebels. Early in November, Francesco Novello began to sell off confiscated property taken from his enemies, conveying to two local textile merchants, Bartolomeo detto Scrivano qd. Jacobo and Gerardo qd. Antonio, for 1,000 ducats (or £3,250) some twenty-two houses or lots located in the city in contrade S. Bartolomeo, S. Fermo, and Ognissanti as well as large holdings in the contado, especially in Este and the Euganean Hills. In a separate transaction the same merchants bought for £400 two more houses in contrada S. Bartolomeo, bringing the Carrara lords total income for the day to £3,650.[80] Ready cash was gained in another way: on 21 April for £4,000 the Carrara lord's proctor sold some forty parcels held *a livello* in Corte to Andrea di Daniele Zabarella, scion of a rising family from Piove di Sacco.[81] Francesco Novello also demanded additional payments for the bargain sales of the fall of 1388. Claiming that, under the pressure of the times, his factor had sold at £1,125, less than half the just price, a house in Padua and a few *campi* in the contado to a certain Bartolomeo Goffonario, the Carrara lord's agent now required a supplement of £1,100 to make up the real value of the properties. The next year, the Carrara lord received supplements of 1,100 ducats on a bargain sale of parcels in Gorgo and Gazzo to a Paduan merchant, Nascimbene di Zambono, and of 250 ducats on property sold to Michele Pignolati in Arquà in the fall of 1388. Thus, the bargain sales that had rewarded loyal supporters at the fall of the regime became a source of additional income at its restoration.[82]

The Carrara lord also raised his rents, when in October 1390 he appointed Bartolomeo di Benedetto his proctor to reinvest leases that had elapsed since his exile and generally collect rents and debts due on real property.[83] In addition, Francesco Novello cemented relations with the Jewish community, decreeing on 4 March 1392 that a Jewish moneylender named Abraham could set up a pawnshop in Piove di Sacco under agreement with the communal government there and upon an annual payment of £100 to the lord of Padua for the privilege.[84] Finally, as relations with the Este of Ferrara and Venice normalized, the Carrara lord looked after his interests in those two cities. On 6 May 1391, he appointed the jurist Pietro da Casale his proctor to handle court suits involving Carrara interests in Ferrara, and that same day he named four men, two Paduan lawyers, Giovanni Porcellini and Antonio di San Angelo, and two Venetian citizens, Marino and Leonardo Baldo, his proctors to appear before the Ducal Council and other bodies to pursue legal suits involving his property in Venice.[85]

Although restoring security, justice, and economic well-being was important, winning the war against Giangaleazzo Visconti was paramount.[86] In October Florence concluded an alliance with Count Jean d'Armagnac, who agreed to bring an army to fight in Italy against the Visconti. Early in 1391, an allied army gathered in Padua under the nominal command of Francesco Novello to mount the campaign from the east. The Paduan contingent was led by the ruling lord's half brother Conte da Carrara, and the commanders for Bologna and Florence were two legendary mercenary captains, Giovanni da Barbiano and Sir John Hawkwood. In a vivid letter of 22 January 1391 to his friend Giovanni da Bologna, Pier Paolo Vergerio describes the bustling activity of the soldiers of "the league of communes and princes" encamped in the Prato della Valle.[87] Estimates of the size of the allied force varied: Galeotto Malatesta calculated nine thousand cavalry and five thousand infantry, while a Bolognese chronicler counted only four hundred lances from Bologna, two hundred each from Florence and Padua, with fifty under the command of Astorre Manfredi of Faenza, for under three thousand calvary, at three horsemen per lance.[88] A Florentine contemporary claimed fourteen hundred lances in the service of Florence, with six hundred for Bologna and two hundred for Padua.[89]

After an attempt to retake Verona late that winter had been repulsed, the allied force reorganized under Hawkwood's command and set out in the middle of May for Milan. Its attack from the east was to be coordinated with the advance of the army under the count of Armagnac coming from France.[90] Destroying crops and cattle, Giangaleazzo's forces fell back before the invading army as it crossed the rivers of eastern Lombardy. Hawkwood halted at the Oglio, where his advance guard met and repulsed an attack by a force of seven hundred Visconti cavalry. By the feast of John the Baptist, 24 June, the allies had reached the banks of the Adda within 30 kilometers of Milan. There Florentine troops staged a *palio* to taunt Lombard soldiers on the opposite shore. But the Visconti scorched-earth policy had succeeded. In short supplies and unable to live off the country, Hawkwood now had to retreat, harried by Milanese cavalry as his army finally reached the safety of Castelbaldo on 10 July and entered Padua on the 12th. The Visconti army under the command of Jacopo dal Verme was now free to turn its full might on the French troops coming from the west. The French army was crushed in a battle before the walls of Alessandria, its commander slain and soldiers scattered, often cut down by peasants in their hasty retreat toward Piedmont. The initiative gained by the reconquest of Padua was lost with the defeat of the allied armies. In the wake of the disaster at Alessandria, Coluccio Salutati wrote from Florence on 4 August, promising to send a lion cub to Francesco Novello as "a gift befitting a fearless lord, who possesses the heart and boldness of a lion, and appropriate to a Guelf prince and the Paduan people."[91]

The cub never arrived. As the war dragged on to stalemate, Pope Boniface IX appointed a trusted papal diplomat, Riccardo Caracciolo, the grand master of the Hospitalers at Rhodes, to negotiate a peace among the belligerents, who were summoned to meet at Genoa under the auspices of Doge Antoniotto Adorno.[92] By late August envoys from the allies, with Michele Rabatta and Francesco Conselve representing the Carrara lord and the commune of Padua, reached Pisa. Though distrustful of Adorno's favoritism toward Giangaleazzo, the allies sought peace. Giangaleazzo was reluctant to abandon his claims to Padua but finally accepted the Carrara restoration in return for an indemnity of half a million florins, 10,000 to be paid annually for the next fifty years.[93] The peace signed at Genoa on 20 January satisfied none of the parties, least of all Francesco Novello. Both Florence and Venice lamented the harsh terms imposed on Padua. But in a letter written on 24 January, Coluccio Salutati valued the general peace brought to Italy above the hardship suffered by any one of the allies and advised Francesco Novello to swallow his pride and accept the indemnity. Meeting in secret on 3 February, the Senate responded to the Paduan envoy, Luca Lion, that Venice expected Florence and the other allies to support the peace settlement and do nothing to place additional burdens on Padua. With Padua now formally at peace with Giangaleazzo Visconti, Venice assured Francesco Novello that its government would always offer advice that promoted the well-being of his state.[94] The next month Venice honored Francesco Novello at a lavish ceremony held in the Ducal Palace.[95] With Padua safely restored as a buffer state on its border, Venice once again cultivated the Carrara dynasty as its most valued ally on the Italian mainland.

Chapter 9

Reconstituting the Carrara Regime

> E per parte del signor Veio pregò misser Francesco che volesse promuovere li bastardi dela caxa da Carara e puonergli ale arme, e gli altri non abilli a ciò metere a vitta chatolica e fare che tuti che sono ad età abiano con si una femina a ciò che caxa moltipichi e cresse.
>
> [The old Lord begged that Messer Francesco should promote the bastards of the House of Carrara and train them in arms, and the others less able should be placed in religious life, and he should make all those who were old enough settle down with a woman so that the House [of Carrara] will multiply and grow.]
>
> —Advice of Francesco il Vecchio to his son during the Carrara exile from Padua, summer 1389

At his restoration Francesco Novello faced a number of important tasks. First, he had to enhance his status as lord, ensuring his own economic well-being, maintaining his landed wealth, revitalizing his interests in Paduan industry, especially textiles, and reviving the Carrara mint. Second, he wanted to punish the traitors against the regime. Third, he needed to enhance his powers and prerogatives, creating a body of councillors to help guide policy and a chancery suited to the tasks of diplomacy. Finally, to ensure that his dynasty would continue to rule Padua, he adopted a policy of extreme nepotism, with his half brothers and sons serving as soldiers in his army and other members in important posts in the Paduan church.

Carrara Economic Interests

One of Francesco Novello's primary concerns at the restoration was to put order to the shambles that his economic interests had suffered. As we have seen, the abdication of his father, the massive sales of 1388, and his own hasty departure had left accounts unsettled and debts uncollected. One money-raising scheme was to require supplements to the bargain sales of November 1388. Another was to audit and settle the accounts of his own financial officials. Thus in March 1391, in the presence of Conte da Carrara; the *referendario,* Baldo Bonafari; and two factors, Luca Lion and Serafino di Benvenuto, Domenichino Descalzi settled accounts with the Carrara lord by the payment of a supplement of 1,125 ducats as head of several offices in the fall of 1388; Descalzi's offices included official in charge of income of the lord's property, *massaro* of his Fondaco delle Biave, overseer of custom duties and gate taxes of the city of Padua, and superintendent of *dazii* and *gabelle.*[1] In November 1392 in the Camera Camillo in the presence of his chief officials, including chief accountant Matteo da Ferrara, styled *superstes rationum,* his factor Galvano Lattuga, Giovanni Bassanello, and Prosdocimo di Dusio Maccaruffi, the Carrara lord recognized the faithful service of the notary Francesco Ton, who had worked in the Carrara bank and Grain Office at the fall of the regime, and remitted any and all debts in return for a lump payment of 1,400 ducats. At the audit the same day, Ton was identified as "the overseer and official deputed over [the lord's] bank of loans and moneys, and the goods and account of the said bank, and all the loans in the same." As such Ton dealt with a variety of officials, including Bartolomeo da Montagnana as head of the Fondaco delle Biave and *stuveta* (strong room), Montorso and Belengero, called Francesco il Vecchio's bodyguards, and Biagio Ovetari, *familiaris* of both lords.

Other economic officials at the fall of the regime included Matteo de Ferrara, head accountant, and the *campsor* Brocardo, who was called "the official over the lord's Pawn Shop for silver, coins and pledges" [officialis supra mutuum pignorum de argento et denariis ac pignoribus sibi consignatis]. Giovanni Turchetto was identified as "the official in charge of pawns consigned for student loans" [super mutuo scholarium in pignoribus sibi consignatis], while Milano Jacomelli was called Francesco Novello's official in charge of "credits from rents consigned from property and other accounts" [pro consignatione debiti in bona quam alia ratione].[2] Several of these officials, including Milano Jacomelli, were later exiled. The titles of the officials making settlements and their witnesses indicate what important sources of income were custom duties, excise taxes, and interest from the lord's bank and pawn shop at time of Francesco Novello's restoration. Six months later, the Carrara lord settled two other accounts with former officials: he permitted Francesco di S. Zilio, a notary at the "officium bladorum et officium bulletum," at the fall of regime to even accounts upon payment of 300 ducats and Matteo "de Buleis" of Monselice, described as official at the Fondaco delle Biave, to square accounts for 300 ducats.[3]

One of the restored Carrara lord's most vital sources of patronage was the awarding of communal property and offices to his supporters. For example, the Carrara favorite Naimiero Conti held such long-term control

Reconstituting the Carrara Regime

over certain of the communal dazi that he was called *dacarius* in the records. Evidence suggests that Francesco Novello determined who was permitted to lease communal property, while the Paduan *canipa* still received the rents. For example, in the fall of 1390, the Carrara factor Bartolomeo di Benedetto, a former apothecary, lauded the sale for £550 of a long-term lease on a shop in Piazza della Frutta to Nicola a Seta, who paid annual rent to the commune of £10. A year later, on the order of Francesco Novello an oil shop in the Androne dei Fabbri was leased to Andrea Assale of *contrada* S. Fermo for the annual rent of £12, payable every March to the communal *canipa*.[4] Carrara influence extended to communal property in the *contado*, when, in 1397, Bartolomeo Vanzerio, syndic for the commune of Padua, invested the Carrara *familiaris* Bernardo Lazera with *livelli* of *mansi*, farms, and woods in the Oltrebrenta for an annual rent of £60.[5] But appointment to certain offices remained nominally under communal control: for example, acting for the commune in 1395, Padovano Fantelli sold to a goldsmith, Nerio di Isacco Cagnoli da Cortona, "the right to inspect and validate all weights, measures, scales, balances and marks in Padua" for one year for £150.[6] The right to control the office of *dacarius*, however, was securely in Francesco Novello's hands. When one Tomeo qd. Luca of Piove di Sacco, who had collected tolls at the Gate of Ognissanti, died in office, the Carrara lord had the judge at Draco award him nearly £150 in debts still owed from the farm of the tolls. Toward the end of the regime, perhaps some real estate once owned by the commune came into Carrara hands: acting for Francesco Novello in 1403, Luca Lion rented for 28 ducats a year an apothecary shop bordering Piazza della Frutta, which was once communal property.[7] Deriving his authority over the property of the commune of Padua from the statute of election of July 1388, Francesco Novello usually leased communal property only to his own followers.

The nature of the Carrara lord's interests in the Paduan textile industry changed at his restoration.[8] Francesco Novello was never able to recover ownership of the Fondaco dei Panni, sold in the fall of 1388, which had been the focus of the Carrara interest in wool manufacturing in Padua under his father. Statutes were promulgated to attract textile workers and merchants to Padua, and a number of foreign textile workers were granted Paduan citizenship. As we have seen, the matriculation list of the wool guild, drawn up at Francesco Novello's instance in 1393, showed 122 men enrolled. Over the next decade between 1394 and 1405, the wool guild enrolled some 165 new members. Of these 120 came from Padua and the towns of the Padovano, mainly Este, Monselice, Montagnana, and Camposampiero. Of the some 50 immigrant members, at least 12 came from Florence, 6 from Verona, and 5 each from Parma and Vicenza. Thus, the geographic origins of textile workers under Francesco Novello closely paralleled that under his father, with more than two-thirds of the new members native and the rest immigrants from Tuscany and the Veneto.[9]

Even more important for woolen cloth manufacturing was the first redaction of the statutes of the Arte della Lana that same year. Now the production, quality, and distribution of woolen textiles was minutely regulated, with the guild having its own tribunal to hear cases and settle disputes. In 1393 Francesco Novello issued an edict forbidding the importation of foreign cloth into Padua and its district, thus providing, for the first time, the Paduan woolen manufacturers with a monopoly of textiles in Carrara domains. Perhaps most important was his promulgation two years later of separate statutes for the guild of woolen cloth retailers, *scavezzadori*, which was witnessed by eleven of the dynasty's elite: Michele Rabatta; the lord's nephew Francesco Buzzacarini; his vicar, Benedetto Girlandi da Siena; Morandi, count of Porcia; Daniele da Rio; Giovanni Porcellini; Francesco Beningrado; Luca and Paolo Lion; Enrico Gallo; and his referendario, Baldo Bonafari da Piombino.[10] These statutes provided for speedy justice in disputes between merchants and independent jurisdiction outside the purview of the *podestà*'s court.

Francesco Novello facilitated the construction of a new seat for the textile guilds in 1396, by donating land in contrada S. Martino (perhaps the site of the earlier *fondaco*) to the wool guild. The next year the construction of the Grazerie Nuove was far advanced, for when, for 600 ducats, he sold to one Benedetto, a carder from contrada Eremitani, a house in "contrada Fallaroti sive Portelli Johannis Francesci vel Sancti Martini," it was bounded by a public street, Carrara property, and "lodia garçararium novarum."[11] In June 1399, Francesco Novello aided in the completion of the building by the gift of a house (probably the property cited in the sale of 1397) near Palazzo Bo to enlarge the Garzerie's loggia. The Garzerie Nuove were, however, built mainly from contributions from guildsmen and loans made by the principals of the woolen industry, Domenichino Descalzi and Giacomo Manzone. Completed perhaps by 1400, the Garzerie Nuove were owned by the wool guild and contained the guild's office and courts as well as rooms for the display and sale of finished cloth, a cloth warehouse, and shops for sorting, carding, and spinning wool. Though relinquishing direct control over the sale of woolens, Francesco Novello continued to promote their manufacture, especially among his supporters, donating in 1399 communal property at Terranegra to Paolo Lion and Giovanni Savonarola for the construction of fulling mills. In February 1400 he took a hand in settling disputes affecting the wool guild and appointed Giovanni Porcellini arbiter in an appeal from the guild's rector, Colombano Rizollo da Piacenza, and himself serving as judge in April in a dispute between a wool worker's widow and her nephew.[12] In August 1400 the Carrara lord settled litigation between Bonjacopo qd. Ognibene da Mantova, a *gastaldo* in 1384, whose son Ognibene Scola had married his own illegitimate daughter, Agnese da Carrara, and other Carrara favorites, Prosdocimo and Francesco Brazolo.[13]

The Carrara lord and his associates supported other industries at Padua. In 1394 Francesco Novello promoted the brick-making industry by investing one Barto Brendoli with a large kiln with seven chambers and two small houses on 15 *campi* outside the city walls at contrada Saracinesca for 10 ducats annual rent.[14] Four years later his general factor Paolo Lion promoted silk making in Padua by advancing capital of 80 ducats to a silk maker (*artifex sete*) from Bologna as "a free loan made from pure love."[15] In 1404, another Carrara factor, Nascimbene da Rodi, provided capital of £1,000 to Venturino di Alessandro Venturino and Enrico di Pietro Curtarolo for the purchase of looms and thread.[16]

At his restoration the Carrara lord, acting through his factor Bartolomeo da Rio, leased a number of houses to ordinary subjects in Padua and its *campanea*. Since his property in the historical center of the city was often invested as fiefs or granted at nominal rents to close supporters, most of the urban livelli from the early 1390s were modest homes on the margins of the city. From November 1390 to February 1395, Francesco Novello leased twenty-five properties in the city and four small farmsteads in the campanea.[17] In the campanea, he rented a house with barn on 20 *campi* at Bosco for £6, a house on 2 *campi* at Terranegra renting for £5 5s., and a house on 4 *campi* at Brentelle with annual rent of £10. Within the city, most of the properties located on the periphery were very modest. Three small houses at Porta S. Croce rented for 5 *soldi* each with a ham and cakes due at the Reggia as *onori* at Christmas. Five properties in Borgo Todesco earned annual rents ranging from 14 *soldi* to £6 for a total income of £14. The two largest properties were lots with two houses each in contrada S. Urbano and at Ponte Corvo renting for £41 and £20, respectively. But the typical urban dwelling that Francesco Novello leased in the period rented for £1 to £4 per annum. One house valued at £50 rented for 14 *soldi* a year, while another worth 20 ducats (£90) rented for £4 due at Christmas. Thus, the first showed modest annual return of less than 2 percent, the second 4.5 percent on the property. Most rents were for cash, though the smallest properties, clustered at the gate at S. Croce, required only customary gifts of pork shoulder and cakes at Christmas. The total annual rent from these properties amounted to £170, scarcely a large part of the dynasty's income.

Carrara property in the contado leased during the same period was somewhat more extensive. About forty *livelli* survive from these years, showing, not surprisingly, concentration of Francesco Novello's rural interests in the historical center of Carrara lands in and near the Euganean Hills. The parcels leased were often small vineyards at Arquà, Faedo, Lozzo, Montericco, Monselice, S. Pelagio, and Valsanzibio, which sometimes yielded annual rents of £1 per *campo* of vineyard or olive orchard. A good vineyard of 2¾ *campi* at Montenuovo rented for £8 5s. (or £3 per *campo*), and the tithe yielded another £2 15s. (or £1 per *campo*). Typically the rents were a mixture of cash and kind, with a lump sum of cash due at St. Justina (7 October) and *onori* of hens, chickens, and pork shoulders. Sometimes payment was made in grain, usually wheat, though millet and rye are also mentioned. Two rents were to be paid in wine: 1 *campo* of vineyard in Montericco rented for 6 *mastelli* (430 liters) of wine, while a house with 2 *campi* of vineyards returned £3, two hens, and 1.5 *mastelli* (108 liters) of wine. The rate of return on property in the contado equaled that in the city: a house in Monselice renting for £10 per annum sold for £200, providing the buyer with an annual return of 5 percent on his investment.[18] These data suggest that the Carrara lord made few changes in his rural estates, seldom raising rents, content to derive customary dues in what was perhaps a depressed agricultural market.

The restoration did, however, bring a flurry of sales of Carrara property, mainly to reward followers and dispose of undesirable holdings. In November 1390 Francesco Novello sold to Antonia qd. Gerardo Raini for 220 ducats six parcels in Bertapaglia surrounded by her family's estates, and the next month for 114 ducats the Carrara lord sold to Bartolomeo di Giovanni Papino "omnia sua iura" in a tavern in contrada S. Martino, bounded by the cloth retailers guild.[19] Several urban properties were sold to newcomers and followers: in December a tailor from Ferrara named Alidosio bought for £400 a house with court and garden near Ponte dei Tadi; in January Bartolomeo di Giacomo Pasini purchased for £600 the Carrara lord's interest in two houses abutting the hospital of S. Giacomo; and in June for £950 Antonio Avalista acquired a house near the Duomo.[20] Thereafter, sales fell off. In May 1393, the Carrara lord exchanged with a boatman named Antonio a small house near Porta S. Croce for a lot in contrada Banzi, containing the "fovea prefati magnifici domini," probably part of the city's defenses. In April 1395 for £100 Francesco sold to Giovanni Savonarola, acting as proctor for Gregorio Cararia and his son Cristofano, *dominium perpetuum* on 13 *campi* in Boschi which the two had previously rented from the Carrara lord.[21] After 1392, instead of disposing of property, Francesco Novello became active in the acquisition of local real estate.

The Carrara lord was, however, a selective, shrewd buyer, acquiring mainly farmland and vineyards at bargain prices. For example, on September 1392, Francesco Novello acquired 26 *campi* of arable and vineyards in

Monselice for £600 (or £23 a *campo*). In two transactions on 29 May 1393 he bought, for £5,400, 75 *campi* in the campanea at Terranegra and Volta Barozzo, thus acquiring suburban farms with houses, ovens, and barns for £72 a *campo*.[22] The Carrara lord also acquired property in his southern frontier stronghold of Castelbaldo, adding three contiguous parcels and houses in 1393 and buying for £800 the next year lots and residences in the Castello itself. In January 1395, he created a block of property by buying for £650 several more houses and lots surrounded by his own holdings.[23] Francesco Novello was acquiring sites to house his garrison in this vital border town on the frontier of the dominions of Niccolò III d'Este, which he hoped to annex in the future.

Late in 1393, the aged Viride della Scala, daughter of the late Mastino and consort of the late Niccolò II d'Este, made her will at her residence in Campo S. Maria Formosa in Venice, appointing Giovanni Contarini and the wealthy banker Gabriele Soranzo her executors. After making many pious bequests to friends and churches, she made her daughter Taddea, consort of Francesco Novello, her universal heir, bequeathing her properties in Padua and its contado, Venice, Ferrara, and Verona.[24] In order to be permitted to acquire the Venetian portion of this inheritance, six months later, Taddea appointed a proctor to appear before the doge and his councillors to request bestowal of Venetian citizenship. With her husband contravening statutes against foreigners' acquiring property in Padua, in 1398 Taddea sold part of the property inherited at her mother's death to a professor of medicine at the *studium*, Gabriele Torcoli da Mantova.[25] Two years later Taddea exchanged another part of the inheritance with her husband, receiving lands in Campagnola and Brugine.[26] Thanks to her mother's generosity, Taddea d'Este emerged as a substantial landowner in Padua and other parts of northeast Italy at the end of the Trecento.

The Mint under Francesco Novello

The reestablishment of the Carrara mint in contrada S. Margherita in 1394 brought together several of the same men who had worked there a decade earlier, who contracted to mint coins on much of the same terms. On 31 July 1394, the local banker Rolando Curtivo entered into partnership with Pietro dall'Olio as moneyer, advancing him £600 to be delivered within eight days and another £302 within twenty days as well as utensils worth 130 ducats. That May Pietro, termed "olim campsor, nunc monatarius," had created his own capital, selling for 600 ducats nearly 50 *campi* of arable and vineyards in his native Monselice to Giovanni di Andrea Zabarella.[27] On 11 August 1394 in the Carrara curia "penes chameram a laboreriis sub Ecclesiola," witnessed by several of the lord's economic officials, Padovano Fantelli, Giovanni Mussato, Antonio Pavanello *spenditore,* and Pileo Pilei, the two partners contracted with Pagano Capodivacca and Guglielmo Ongarelli, serving as factors for Francesco Novello, to coin money at the mint for three years beginning on 1 September.[28] Rolando and Pietro agreed to manufacture *carrarini* on much the same terms as under Francesco il Vecchio, minting coins containing 1,088 carats of pure silver (thus 0.944 fineness) per mark, valued at £25 10s. per mark. The *carrarini* were to be stored in a locked chest in the tower of the mint, with keys held by the minters and the lord's vicar, until 1,000 marks of coins had been manufactured. Then the *carrarini* and other coins were to be assayed by an expert, appointed by Carrara officials and paid £4 for his work by the minters, before they were certified and distributed. Rolando and Piero agreed to mint at least 1,500 marks of coins at their own expense each year, paying £24 18s. for each mark, thus leaving 12s. for brassage. As in earlier contracts, the moneyer and his helpers were to reside at the mint free of rent, enjoy exemption from local taxes, and make coins only for the lord and commune of Padua. There were some differences from previous contracts: the moneyer was now required to purchase salt used in the process (for £3 per *staio*) from the Carrara lord's monopoly. For his part, the lord no longer took any seigniorage. For their precious metal, the moneyers were to rely on "free silver," since anyone could import silver and bronze for sale at the mint free of duties and taxes. But the partnership ran into difficulty, for the minting of coins halted within a year or two.

In October 1396, the Carrara factors Guglielmo Ongarelli and Nascimbene di Zambono, acting for both the lord and commune of Padua, entered into a contract with the Florentine moneyer Jacopo di Zero, with Bartolomeo da Rio standing as his surety, to mint *carrarini* and so-called black money, small coins of low silver content, *piccoli,* and, for the first time, *sestini neri*.[29] The contract for making *carrarini* was the same as two years earlier; Jacopo was to make coins of 0.944 fineness, containing silver valued at £25 10s. per mark. But the *sestino,* worth 6 *denari,* was much debased, containing only 1½ ounces of silver (thus, 0.185 fineness) worth only £6 4s. per mark. The contract called for the production of 200 marks of the "black money" per month, limited to 2,400 marks in any given year. Jacopo di Zero took over operation of the mint from the failed partnership of Rolando Curtivo and Pietro dall'Olio, since starting in 1399 he appears in a lawsuit between the aggrieved parties.[30] The suit involved the attempt of two *campsores,* Zanino Balarino and Antonio Bassanello, to recover loans advanced to Rolando Curtivo for his work at the mint. Apparently Pietro dall'Olio had pulled out of his partnership, leaving his brother Bartolomeo dall'Olio, his surety, owing £550 to Rolando as well as part of the security of 130 ducats posted for the utensils used in making coins. Most of this equipment had been given *in commenda* to Jacopo di Zero when he took over manufacturing, but according to testimony given by interested Carrara officials, Giovanni Renaldino of Este and Giovanni Mussato, these tools had to be consigned to Rolando Curtivo to help repay Pietro dall'Olio's debts. After depositions were taken from Renaldino and Jacopo de Zero in July, the whole matter was referred to members of Francesco Novello's council for judgement, who agreed with testimony that debts had already been settled with Carlo da Genova for making assays and to Berto d'Areolda for grinding silver shavings produced in manufacturing. The Carrara council, composed on this occasion of Francesco Zabarella, Naimiero Conti, Ottolino da Monselice, Giovanni Savonarola, and Giovanni da Montagnana, decided in favor of the plaintiffs and ordered a sword maker, one Guglielmo da Pernumia, *spatarius,* to release Rolando's sequestered goods to them to settle the debt.

Following the failure of the contracts of 1394 and 1396, Francesco Novello issued a third agreement in June 1398 to make coins at the Carrara mint. Acting through his "factores et generales administratores" Guglielmo Ongarelli and Nascimbene di Zambono, Francesco Novello rented his mint for two years to a moneyer, Giovanni di Simone dall'Argento da Bologna, who was then residing in Ferrara.[31] Giovanni agreed to manufacture as needed *carrarini* of the usual fineness and alloy. He also undertook to made a large quantity of *sestini neri,* containing 1½ ounces (0.185 fineness) of silver per mark of coinage, and *piccoli,* containing three-quarters of an ounce (0.093 fineness) of silver per mark. For his part, the Carrara lord agreed to provide the silver and bronze needed to manufacture £20,000 of *sestini* and £10,000 of *piccoli* over the two years of the contract. The moneyer agreed to respect the usual working conditions of the Carrara mint, paying for periodic assays to certify the coinage and buying salt needed in manufacturing for £3 per *staio* from the Carrara lord's monopoly, while residing in the mint free of rent and taxes.

However, Giovanni dall'Argento was able to fulfill the contract for less than a year: in March 1399 he and his two sons were murdered and robbed of 900 ducats that he had just borrowed from the banking partnership of Bono Leti of Florence and Manfredino Osio of Milan. Giovanni had intended to use the loan to purchase silver from one Bartolomeo Bertono, who instead murdered him and used the ducats for a huge shopping spree, buying clothes, jewels, furniture, and all sorts of goods from several vendors.[32] The two foreign bankers promptly appeared before the Carrara vicar Benedetto Girlandi of Siena and asked for help in recovering the 900 ducats. Owing to confusion concerning precise ownership of the precious metals stored in the mint following Giovanni dall'Argento's death, Benedetto ordered that

Giovanni's ledgers kept there were be considered the authentic record in any suit arising between the two bankers, Leti and Osio, and the sometime mintmaster Pietro Bovi and appointed a board of Paduan merchants to investigate the matter. In the end, the two bankers were required to turn over a quantity of silver to Pietro Bovi, who was found to own the bulk of the precious metals in the mint. A board of public merchants from the Carrara circle, including Giacomo Zacchi, Giovanni Savonarola, Giovanni Zabarella, Renaldino di Martino, called *campsor,* Giovanni Boto, Domenichino Descalzi, and the goldsmith and assayer Carlo da Genova, decided to aid Leti and Osio in recovering their lost ducats. The vicar and the merchant court decreed that the two bankers were entitled to the money that Bertono and his wife possessed, the goods they had brought, and any property pawned following the robbery and murder, up to the sum of the 900 ducats they had lost.

In 1402, the Carrara lord reopened the mint, contracting for three years to have three *campsores,* Giovanni Boto, Francesco dall'Olio, and Albertino Gotolla, manufacture *carrarini* and *soldi* of the same fineness as Venetian coinage, thus worth £27 2s. per mark of silver, for up to 1,500 marks a year.[33] The usual rights and duties were to obtain: free import of precious metals for coinage, monopoly on minting coins, freedom from Paduan taxes, and status in the merchants' court. The partners were also to mint 100 marks per month of *sestini,* with the fineness of 1 ounce, 12 *denari* (worth £6 16s.) per mark, *piccoli* and *quattrini* with fineness of 1 ounce (worth £4 18s.) per mark. But again the agreement was short lived, since in October 1403 Pietro Bovi challenged the validity of the contract of Giovanni Boto and Francesco dall'Olio, thus becoming the last governor of the Carrara mint.[34]

Rebels Become Exiles

Surely the most galling provision of the Peace of Genoa was the requirement that the Carrara lord permit traitors during Visconti rule to retain all property that they held in the city and district of Padua and enjoy income and profits from their estates. Thus privileged were some of the most conspicuous rebels, banned in November 1390, including the Scrovegni, Camposampiero, Lenguazzi, and Ubertino Grompo, to whom were added other traitors to the regime, the Sanguinacci, da Peraga, and the *condottiere* Bartolomeo Cermisone.[35] Further, all these rebels were now exempted from any sentences and personal condemnations and free from paying any fines. They could also freely alienate and dispose of any of their property in the city and contado, with the only restriction that they could not enter or reside in Paduan domains without the express permission of the Carrara lord.

Reconstituting the Carrara Regime

At the insistence of Giangaleazzo Visconti and his diplomats at the peace conference in Genoa, the former supporters of his short-lived regime in Padua, now living in exile, were to enjoy broad rights over their property in their former homeland.

However, in fact Francesco Novello never permitted the provisions protecting the property rights of the rebels to be carried out. From dispositions taken in Padua after the final fall of the regime, it is clear that Francesco Novello never intended the rebels to enjoy their property, which in any case had been confiscated and given to favorites following the sentences of the autumn of 1390.[36] Riccardo Lenguazzi, who had sought to procure the return of property confiscated from his paternal uncle Daniele, testified that he spoke first with the curial notary Enrico Gallo and then with Pietro Grompo. Grompo raised the question with Francesco Novello, who said to Lenguazzi "that he wanted those to whom he had given the said property to hold and possess it, and that he did not want that those living outside Padua and its district who were friends of the Count of Virtù should enjoy any of their property, notwithstanding the said ruling."[37]

Thereafter, Giangaleazzo Visconti sent his own envoy, Giovanni da Nono, to represent those claiming rights to property in Padua, including the Camposampiero and the da Peraga. When the envoy asked Francesco Novello about his taking possession of the confiscated property of the Camposampiero, the lord replied that he was happy to see the property of the exiles restored. But when Giovanni returned "to his lodgings in Padua, a certain Niccolò da Strassoldo approached him and said: 'You have come seeking permission to recover the property of the exiles. Upon my word, if you don't get out of Padua, I'm going to beat you to death with my whip.' When Giovanni heard this he left Padua in a great fright and returned to Lombardy, never daring to return [to Padua]."[38] A similar story of contempt and refusal to honor the treaty of 1392 was told by agents of Bonifacio Lupi's widow, Caterina, residing in Venice. According to their testimony, Francesco Novello had given the Lupi palace at S. Fermo and the country estate at Mandria to a new familiar, Giacomo Trambachino. Because of the Carrara lord's hatred for the Lupi, no one even dared to represent their interests in Padua, even though in the words of one witness, an old servant Armelina, she knew that Caterina had never alienated the property in Mandria because that belonged to both the lord Bonifacio Lupi and the hospital of S. Giovanni Battista in Florence.[39] Thus, Francesco Novello excluded the claims of the traitors of the Visconti interregnum from the Paduan property guaranteed to them by the Peace of Genoa. But in the end the exiles prevailed, and their claims were finally honored after the demise of the Carrara in 1405.

FIG. 32. *Tomb effigy of Caterina, widow of Bonifacio Lupi, cloister, Basilica of S. Antonio. Photograph courtesy of Robin Simon*

Reconstituting the Carrara Regime

Prerogatives and Powers

Francesco Novello used the broad powers deriving from his statute of election to adapt Paduan law and institutions to his own needs and those of his favorites. Among his prerogatives were the creation of new citizens, dispensation from communal statutes in cases of hardship or need, and standing as the final court of appeal in legal disputes among his subjects. From his own largess, he granted fiefs to supporters and henchmen as well as making outright gifts of property.

New Citizens

At his restoration, the Carrara lord promulgated several statutes designed to bring new workers and talents to Padua. As we have seen, in the first years of rule, Francesco Novello conferred citizenship on a number of newcomers. Thereafter, he continued to create new Paduan citizens, though at a slower rate. For example, in June 1392, the lord granted Paduan citizenship to a priest, Niccolò di Antonio da Faenza, who resided in contrada S. Agnese. The next year he permitted a local priest to inherit from his father land in Monselice valued at £200 free of any taxes and granted Giovanni Vercelli, a native of Monselice, the right to acquire and sell property in Padua.[40] To followers Francesco Novello sometimes granted citizenship with exemption from taxes: in October 1397 Paolo di Biagio da Bologna was granted Paduan citizenship with the right to acquire and hold property free of taxes because of "the vigil, zeal and care he exhibited incessantly for the magnificent lord."[41] Two years earlier a German knight, Ludwig of Dedech, was granted Paduan citizenship with the right to acquire land in the city and contado with the lofty rationale "that it ought to be a goal of the prince that his subjects multiply in virtues, for indeed, on the witness of Aristotle, 'when the subjects are improved, so is the prince.'"[42] The fragmentary sources do not permit exact figures on immigration to Padua. Despite Francesco Novello's best efforts, it seems likely that foreigners who became new citizens in the 1390s are to be numbered in the scores rather than the hundreds.

Dispensations

The hardships of the Visconti occupation and war of reconquest had impoverished many Paduan families, driving them into debt with local creditors and moneylenders, often placing a wife's dowry at risk to satisfy her husband's obligations. Early in 1393, Francesco Novello was petitioned to deal with several such cases, abrogating a statute enacted in 1380 which forbade the use of the wife's dowry to met her husband's debts. On 10 February the Carrara lord decreed that one Oliana could permit her husband, Vendranio di Antonio of contrada Ognissanti, to sell her dowry, consisting of a small farmstead of arable and vineyard in the campanea, to satisfy his debt to a local *campsor,* Niccolò da Rio. Since the moneylender was an active member of the Carrara regime, Francesco Novello's decree permitted the family to get out of debt and at the same time enriched one of his supporters. Two days later he allowed one Ricolda to have her husband sell for debts a house in contrada Calfara she had brought as her dowry. In April Francesco Novello extended the same right to alienate dotal property to an impoverished couple in Piove di Sacco.[43] In May the lord of Carrara intervened in a more desperate case, permitting one Marco Bello, who was threatened with jail for extensive debts, to sell his wife's dowry, a house near Porta S. Giovanni, to escape imprisonment and crushing poverty.[44] In a different context, Francesco Novello gave permission to Antonia di Francesco Pezzogoti, widow of his mother's distant kinsman Giacomo di Salione da Buzzacarini, to sell half interest in a house she held *pro indiviso* with the noble Antonio Salamone.[45] Here the favor derived more from the Carrara lord's desire to aid his affines than from alleviating great economic hardship. Sometimes statutes were dispensed to help ecclesiastical institutions, as when, in 1393, Francesco Novello allowed the Hospital of S. Massimo to inherit land in the contado from a local notary.[46]

Appeals for Justice

Among the Carrara lord's most significant powers was the right to dispense justice, serving as a court of final appeal, thereby supplementing and extending the work of the communal judiciary. Several of the appeals following the Carrara restoration were of a deeply personal character. A petition from a "faithful servant and familiar," Berto Strazzarolo from contrada S. Lucia, reveals the disruptions of the Visconti rule. For sixteen years, Berto had rented from Francesco il Vecchio a small house near the Reggia for £22 a year, with six years' rent remitted in return for the care Berto's wife had given to one of il Vecchio's illegitimate daughters. At the fall of the regime Gaiardo, the Carrara butcher, had acquired the property, raised the rent beyond Berto's ability to pay, and was now threatening eviction. The facts of the case were heard in the court of Aquila, and Gaiardo was ordered to reduce the annual rent as he had originally agreed. But Gaiardo protested that that sum was too low and he needed the house for other purposes and appealed to the Carrara lord for judgment. On the advice of his council Francesco Novello had his referendario, Baldo Bonafari da Piombino, appoint a local jurist to make a final decision.[47]

The next year Filippo Zerdo, who had served in the Carrara army in the recent Visconti war, appealed for justice in a dispute with a Jewish pawnbroker named Musetto. Before he left on the campaign, he had pawned his wife's mantle, valued at £70, for a mere £12 and returned to discover that the pawnbroker had sold the cloak. When questioned, Musetto replied that the Carrara lord himself had given him permission to sell all pawns worth less than £25. Filippo asserted that the cloak was worth much more than £25 and asked Francesco Novello to have the vicar of the podestà compel Musetto to restore the pawn upon payment of interest and capital, "considering what I have done for your state and that the same Jew had sold the pledges of many others." But after discussion with his council, the Carrara lord merely referred the case to Aquila for a decision.[48] The final decision on this appeal, based on patriotism tinged with anti-Semitism, is unknown.

Over the years, appeals from the communal judiciary to the lord's jurisdiction became somewhat regularized. Appeals were usually made first to Francesco's vicar Benedetto Girlandi of Siena, but the disposition of the case was often referred to the lord's council, which in the 1390s was becoming a formal body. For example, in a dispute on whether Guido Ruine da Reggio could inherit property in Padua, the question was first broached with the *consiliarii magnifici domini* assembled in the Camino Ercole: Antonio da San Angelo, Guglielmo Curtarolo, Francesco dalle Ave, Naimiero di Naimiero Conti, and Ugotone Casone, all of whom had some training in law.[49] Often there were several stages in the review, as in a dispute late in 1401 between Giovanni Parasino Mezzoconti and Reprandino dalle Calze, in which the dissatisfied parties appealed from the judge at Cavallo to Francesco Novello's vicar Jacobo Saliceto of Bologna, who referred the case to three of Francesco Novello's best legal experts, Pietro Paolo Crivelli, Lodovico Cortusi, and Prosdocimo Conti. These, in turn, appointed Benedetto Girlandi and Daniele da Rio to review the case and render summary justice.[50] But sometimes the lord's councillors themselves rendered the judgment. In a case involving a moneylender and his clients, Francesco Novello simply confirmed the sentence given by Francesco Zabarella, Naimiero Conti, Ottolino da Monselice, Giovanni Savonarola, and Giovanni da Montagnana.[51] The interested parties might also appeal from the judgment of the lord's vicar to a third party, as did the priest Biagio of Zara and the *campsor* Giovanni "a Pallata," electing the jurist Nicola Gloria to settle their dispute in 1395.[52] Although the system of appeal was largely utilized by members of the Carrara affinity and the business community of Padua, especially in cases involving dowries, inheritance, and banking, disputes among Paduan churchmen sometimes came under the lord's jurisdiction. In 1395 the Carrara vicar Benedetto Girlandi heard a case in which the canons of the cathedral chapter alleged wrongdoing by the Duomo's *custos*, Giovanni Andrea, "in his actions and administration of the goods, property and revenues of the said cathedral *canipa*" from 1389 to 1394. Eventually Girlandi ordered Giovanni Andrea to pay back nearly £500 and a quantity of grain to make right the accounts.[53]

The Carrara lord and his legal experts also undertook to ensure peace in the contado, settling disputes between villages and peasants' feuds arising from violations of person and honor. Early in 1394 a dispute broke out between the men of Teolo and Villa in the Euganean Hills on questions of boundaries, tax assessments, and the status of the vicar. Francesco Novello appointed a board of three of his closest advisers, Guglielmo Curtarolo, Giovanni Porcellini, and Enrico Trapolino, to hear the case; the three judges ordered a peaceful settlement under penalty of 100 ducats' fine, requiring adjustment of the *estimo* and hearth assessments and definition of borders between the two villages by four newly appointed police (*saltuarii*).[54] In the fall of 1399, Francesco Novello intervened to prevent further bloodshed among peasants in Campolongo Maggiore. Andrea and Giovanni had struck Martino, whose son Bartolomeo retaliated by attacking his father's assailants. Now all three were to forgive the wounds and reach "a good, tranquil, and perpetual peace, by kissing one another on the mouth, while holding hands."[55] In June 1403, the lord's *referendario*, Baldo Bonafari, intervened to prevent a blood feud following the murder of a peasant named Giovanni Strazzavacca in Campo S. Martino. Following the homicide Baldo assembled Giovanni's two brothers and three other local men in the Camino Ercole and required them to come to peace with the assailants from Campo S. Martino and nearby Tremignon under penalty of a fine of 100 ducats.[56]

Fiefs and Favors

Francesco Novello used both his private property, bestowed in the form of life fiefs, and his authority to abrogate statutes to reward followers and friends among natives and newcomers in Padua. Late in 1390, the Carrara lord granted a number of houses as fiefs for nominal dues to local artisans to gain skilled labor for the Paduan economy and provide housing for members of his household. For example, a mason named Berto received a house in contrada Rudena and Pietro Neve a house with courtyard in contrada Parenzi for dues of a pair of gloves at Christmas; Giacomo di Domenico da Ferrara, called "the lord's familiar," received a house in contrada S. Leonardo for a pledge of fealty.[57] Even more extensive was the award of fiefs of land in the countryside (often confiscated from the regime's rebels) to followers and friends. On 27 November 1390, Bartolomeo da Rio, acting as agent for Francesco Novello, invested one Silvestro detto Pengallo of contrada Duomo with fiefs of twenty parcels in Vallone in exchange for service as vassal and a pair of gloves at Christmas. In December Margherita, widow of Bartolomeo detto Bartolazzo, was invested with 100 *campi* of arable and vineyards in her native Este in return for a pair of falconry gloves at Christmas. The next February, the lord's favorite Niccolò Latuga was invested with twenty-nine parcels among Carrara holdings in Abano, Pernumia, Monterosso, and the Patriarcati in return for an "oath of homage and pledge of fealty against all others" and gloves at Christmas.[58] At the beginning of the campaign against the Visconti in the summer of 1391, fief of a house near Ponte dei Tadi was granted to a soldier from Parma, the count of Lavargna, who was serving in the Carrara army. In June 1392, Francesco Novello invested Alberto Goffo with more than 100 *campi* in the Paduan campanea in exchange for his oath of fealty and gift of a gold ring worth 2 ducats each Christmas. Years later as Padua came under attack from Venice, the Carrara lord made Alberto a gift of the same properties for services rendered.[59] Finally, Francesco Novello used grants of property to bring famous teachers to Padua, bestowing on Niccolò da Fano, professor of medicine at the *studium* from 1393 to 1405, twenty-nine parcels in Abano in return for the nominal rent of a ducat a year.[60]

Sometimes the statutes were abrogated and taxes remitted for services rendered. For example, in January 1393, Francesco Novello, "from his plenitude of power and all authority that he possesse[d]," exempted a notary from the Oltrebrenta village of Zumignana, now residing in contrada S. Lucia, from all local taxes that he owed on some twelve parcels of land in his native village.[61] In November 1394 in response to a petition from a peasant from Merlara, Albertino Zordani, who had been granted Paduan citizenship in 1388, Francesco Novello allowed the petitioner to pay taxes directly to the commune of Padua instead of the heavier village *onera et factiones* that local peasants (*villici*) were required to pay, "because of the numerous services" he had rendered, "day and night not without great anxiety of mind and bodily exertion to the same magnificent lord, his deceased father and the distinguished house of Carrara."[62]

In his effort to gain legitimacy Francesco Novello exercised drastic new powers and revived old titles. In October 1395 a soldier drunken and in high spirits, one Antonio da Friuli, insulted the guard at the city's citadel, the Castello, cursing the officers and demeaning the lord of Padua. For this crime Antonio was arrested, accused of treason, found guilty of lèse majesty, and in the presence of the three captains of the Castello had his arm severed from his shoulder.[63] At the same time, Francesco Novello enhanced his new powers by reviving titles Francesco il Vecchio had used in the 1380s. At the old lord's funeral in October 1393, the Carrara lord placed three horses, bearing three coats of arms, in the line of march: one horse was bedecked with the *carro,* another with his arms as "Dux" of Carrara, a third with his blazon as "Comes" of Anguillara.[64] The next spring when he conferred full Paduan citizenship on three noble Collalto brothers, the lord of Carrara styled himself "Franciscus de Carraria, Carrarie Dux et Comes Anguillarie, civitatis et districtus Padue dominus et capitaneus generalis."[65] Later he used the same title in a grant to the *scavezzadori* (cloth retailers) guild as well as on other occasions. Thus, a few years after his restoration, Francesco Novello had become a *dux* (duke) and a *comes* (count) as well as the *dominus* (lord) and *capitaneus generalis* (captain general) of Padua. He strove to match these grander titles with a more elaborate court and household.

The Carrara Household and Court

Soon after the reconquest of Padua in the summer of 1390, Francesco Novello reoccupied the Carrara Reggia, the lord's residence, which also contained offices for diplomacy, war, and administration. The most splendid hall in the complex was the Sala Virorum Illustrium, which was decorated with frescoes of illustrious men and used for grand state events, such as weddings of the dynasty's young women and receptions for visiting envoys. Under Francesco il Vecchio two chanceries developed, the first housed in Ubertino's original palace and the newer "camino Ercole," with its depictions of the labors of Hercules, probably located near the reception hall. There Francesco Novello reinstated as chancellor the aged Nicoletto d'Alessio, assisted by scribes and notaries from his father's time: Bandino Brazzi, Zilio Calvi, and Enrico Gallo. The return of Giovanni Conversini to Padua, after quitting his post of schoolmaster in Udine in the summer of 1393, provided potential new talent for the work of the restored chancery. Giovanni had originally intended to settle in Venice and sent ahead his books and moveables, asking his grown son Conversino to find him suitable employment. When employment in Venice proved impossible, Giovanni migrated to Padua, initially refusing the Carrara lord's invitation to rejoin his household, taking instead a *cathedra* at the *studium,* where he lectured on Latin grammar. The death of Nicoletto d'Alessio at the end of 1393 propelled Giovanni Conversini into the chancellorship when Francesco Novello made him a generous offer, praising his skills and appealing to his vanity. There he was to remain for the next eleven years, the chief of the chancery redacting the diplomatic correspondence of the regime. But Giovanni found the court of Francesco Novello even more beset by intrigue and faction than the one he had described a decade earlier in his account of his stay at Padua, *De primo eius introitu ad aulam.*[66]

In his most extensive treatment of the Carrara court under Francesco

Novello, *De fortuna aulica,* Giovanni Conversini divides the Carrara officials into four categories.[67] Of the highest rank is the prince and his family, who direct the policy of the Paduan state, followed by those officials who carry out public administration. The third group comprises those who execute the orders of the first two categories, and the lowest group includes the ordinary servants of the regime: chamberlains, butlers, cooks, stevedores, serving women, and nurses. The structure of Carrara court described by Conversini corresponds well to the contemporary Gonzaga court in Mantua, known from documentary sources. About 200 persons resided in the Gonzaga court, including 18 *familiares* of the lord, 20 chamberlains, 12 cooks, 5 nurses, 29 girls and ladies-in-waiting, and 10 boys, attending the Gonzaga *signora,* with 49 servants, 7 stevedores and 7 provisioners for the court as a whole. Added to these were about 60 courtiers, including scribes, notaries, councillors, factors, and administrators, perhaps 180 knights and 100 men-at-arms, for more than 500 persons on the payroll of the Gonzaga lord in 1384.[68] The number of salaried and other employees in the Carrara court was rather smaller. At Fina's death in 1378, perhaps a dozen ladies-in-waiting and ten servants resided in the consort's Palazzo di Levante. The number attending Francesco Novello's consort, Taddea d'Este, was probably no larger. Although no precise figures are available, it seems likely that the seneschal, chamberlains, tutors, barbers, cooks, servants (*famuli*), porters, and nurses of the Carrara household (Conversini's lowest category) numbered perhaps twenty. The numbers and individuals in Conversini's other categories, however, can be better defined.

The chief legal official under Francesco Novello continued to be the lord's vicar, whose main function was to handle legal cases appealed to the ruling lord or his council. This task was mainly handled by Benedetto Girlandi of Siena, who had migrated to Padua, where he served as the vicar of the podestà Rizzardo di Sambonifacio in 1375 and of the Venetian Marino Memmo in 1383. At the restoration, Girlandi became vicar of the lord's court, serving frequently as judge appellant or consultant in cases coming before the Carrara lord or his council. From 1395 to 1404, he also served as vicar or sometimes vice-podestà to several of the Venetian nobles, Pietro Pisano, Francesco Bembo, and Jacopo Gradenigo, who served as Padua's chief magistrate. In the first years of the Quattrocento, the vicar was Bartolomeo da Saliceto, a Bolognese jurist who taught in the Paduan *studium*.[69] Compared with the office under Francesco il Vecchio, the lord's vicar now led an intermittent existence; the post was reserved for distinguished jurists when they were called upon to adjudicate appeals made to the lord and his councillors.

In order to identify and reward his closest supporters, Francesco Novello created the office of *consiliarius*, reflecting greater specialization at court. This term was reserved for the lord's closest advisers, such as Francesco and Paolo Dotti, Naimiero and Prosdocimo Conti, Luca and Paolo Lion, Michele Rabatta, and Enrico Gallo. Usage at the Carrara court probably followed the practice of the contemporary Este court in Ferrara, where the title "denote[d] a new rank of administrator, interposed between the *signore* and the functionaries of chancellery and *camera* who executed his orders."[70] Thus, the Paduan lord's *consiliarii* corresponded to Giovanni Conversini's second category of policymakers, comprising (as at Ferrara) "a kind of personal general staff," who advised and aided the ruling lord and his family. But the lord's factors, agents, and familiars were also sometimes called his *consiliarii*, who served more in an economic than policymaking capacity. In any case, the office and duties of the *consiliarii* remained flexible and fluid until the end of the regime.

The economic recovery of Padua and its ruling dynasty was among Francesco Novello's most pressing concerns. Reduced in property and income, the Carrara lord was deeply distressed by the indemnity imposed at the Peace of Genoa and tried to avoid or suspend payment whenever possible. The regime's straitened circumstances placed special burdens on its financial officers, the treasurer (referendario), the accountant for household expenses and income (massaro), and bookkeeper (*spenditore*). The office of referendario was first held by the jurist Francesco Beningrado and later by the lawyer and merchant Baldo Bonafari. Formal training for the office varied, with Beningrado serving first on the bench in the communal judiciary before briefly holding the office of treasurer. Baldo Bonafari had some training in civil law, but his main experience was as a proprietor and businessman during his long tenure as referendario. Other economic officials were of humbler origins, often serving as the lord's factors or business agents before assuming the office of accountant or bookkeeper. The financial officers of the restored Carrara regime numbered no more than a score at any one time, including agents in Venice or abroad as well as factors, accountants, and gastaldi at home.

Of all the departments of the Carrara court, the best defined was the chancery, with its half dozen scribes or notaries. Giovanni Conversini assumed the office of chancellor late in 1393 and held it until dismissed for reason of economy during the final struggle with Venice. In his autobiography and other works, Giovanni complains of the great weight of the office and its manifold duties. The chancellor's chief task was overseeing the composition of the regime's correspondence, both letters in Latin to foreign powers and communications, usually in the vernacular, to members of the Carrara family and household and the podestà and vicars of the Padovano.

Reconstituting the Carrara Regime

Beyond this, the chancery was the center for the redacting of the notarial records of the regime. Literally thousands of legal documents of all sorts, from the appointment of ambassadors and proctors, to contracts for leases, rents, and sales of Carrara property, to pardons, exemptions, and privileges for members of the affinity, emanated from the chancery. Early in 1406 the Council of Ten confiscated and transported the documents of the Carrara chancery to Venice, where almost all were later lost or destroyed. From this large archive one invaluable source survives, a volume containing the diplomatic correspondence for 1402, the *Copialettere,* which provides a unique insight into the daily workings of the Carrara chancery.[71]

Each letter sent from the Carrara chancery went through at least three stages. First, someone in authority, the lord or his sons, the chamberlain (*camerarius*), the chancellor, one of his staff, or even a member of the lord's council decided that a letter needed to be written, that is, the letter was "commissioned." At the end of each letter, the "commissioner" is identified with the verb *comisit.* For example, a letter is signed *Franciscus tertius comisit, Camerarius domini comisit, Ludovicus comisit,* that is, "Francesco III [da Carrara] commissioned, the lord's chamberlain commissioned, Ludovico [Buzzacarini] commissioned [this letter]." Then the chancellor or one of his notaries composed, that is, dictated, that letter, with such an annotation as *Johannes dixit,* or *Zilius dixit,* meaning "Giovanni da Ravenna" or "Zilio Calvi dictated this letter." Finally, the letter was written out, with a similar record: *Xichus scripsit,* or *magister Jo. scripsit,* that is, "Sicco Polenton" or "Giovanni da Ravenna wrote this letter." Sometimes the same person both commissioned and composed the letter: *magister Jo. comisit et dictavit,* that is, "Maestro Giovanni commissioned and dictated [this]." At other times, one notary dictated, while another wrote: *Zilius dixit, Xicho scripsit.* Finally, very important letters were reviewed after they were commissioned, composed, and written. Thus, at the end of a letter was written: *omnes de consilio comiserunt et viderunt,* "the whole council commissioned and saw [this letter]."

Mainly responsible for composing the regime's correspondence in 1402 was the prothonotary Zilio Calvi, who wrote more than 350 of the letters contained in the letterbook. He was aided by Giovanni Conversini, noted as *magister Johannes,* Marco Guarnerini, Enrico Gallo, Pietro Zabarella, Antonio Beccari, Sicco Polenton, Ognibene Scola, Fantello Fantelli, and a certain Florio. At times of peak demand as many as six scribes were employed in the Carrara chancery at the beginning of the Quattrocento. In 1402 they composed and wrote 800 letters, half in Latin for the pope and emperor, the kings of France and Cyprus, cardinals and foreign princes, Italian states and lords, doctors of law, arts, and medicine, and sometimes Carrara favorites and officials. Letters in the vernacular were usually sent to military captains and podestà, friends, family, confidants, merchants, Carrara ambassadors, and women. A few of the letters were sent in cipher; almost all were sealed. Until early in 1402, Francesco Novello used the *carro* sealed in wax. After one set of seals had been lost, the seal was changed to his personal arms, the winged Saracen with horns.[72] Employing Giovanni Conversini and Sicco Polenton, with Pier Paolo Vergerio next door as a tutor at the Carrara court, the chancery was an informal center for the study of Latin literature and the liberal arts. Replying to criticism that he often neglected his duties at court, Giovanni Conversini admitted that he often composed treatises in his small cubicle near the "camino Ercole."[73] Although at the fall of the regime Giovanni Conversini had nothing but criticism for the failings of Francesco Novello and the viciousness of his courtiers, the Carrara chancery under his leadership was among the most advanced in Italy, indeed in Europe.[74]

Francesco Novello's Brothers and Sons

Perhaps doubtful about the loyalty of many of his regime's former adherents, at his restoration Francesco Novello followed his father's advice and relied heavily on members of his own family to carry out the tasks of governing. The Carrara lord employed his kin in three areas of government: diplomacy, war, and the church. Captains in the Carrara army included his half brothers, Conte, Giacomo, Rodolfo, and Pietro, and later his sons, Francesco III, Giacomo, and Ubertino Fiorentino, as well as his uncle Arcoano Buzzacarini and his sons Pataro and Francesco. Nephews who received military commands were Bonifacio and Niccolò da Carrara, sons of his half brother Giacomo and his wife, Lucia Contarini. In his chancery the lord employed a nephew, Ludovico Buzzacarini, and his son-in-law Ognibene Scola, husband of his own illegitimate daughter, Agnese. In the hierarchy of the Paduan church, one of Francesco il Vecchio's bastards, the Benedictine monk Andrea, served as abbot of S. Giustina from 1396 to 1405, and another Benedictine, Servio, was abbot of S. Stefano da Carrara. The highest church office was reserved for Francesco Novello's own bastard son Stefano, who served first as administrator of the diocese of Padua and after 1402 as its bishop. The success of this policy of extreme nepotism depended, as we shall see, on the reward of Carrara wealth, mainly in land to brothers and sons in return for service in moments of need or danger.

Francesco Novello's foremost captain in the First Visconti War was his half brother Conte da Carrara. Born about 1350 from the union of Francesco il Vecchio and Giustina Maconia, the daughter of Rinaldo Maconia and Capellina di Rinaldello Scrovegni, Conte was groomed for the priesthood, was early appointed a canon at the Duomo, and for a time even studied canon law at the *studium*.⁷⁵ In his campaign to dominate Friuli, Francesco il Vecchio advanced Conte's candidacy first as abbot of Rosazzo and later even as patriarch of Aquileia. But Conte's real vocation was war; he served his father and younger half brother as a commander of Carrara forces against the Scaligers in Friuli and defended Padua against the Visconti in the fall of 1388. To help pay for the final defense, Conte sold all his Paduan property to his fellow campaigner in Friuli Michele Rabatta and late in November accompanied Francesco Novello into exile.⁷⁶ Enlisted in the pay of Florence against the Visconti, early in 1390 Conte was taken prisoner at Bologna by Carlo Malatesta but released in time to aid in the reconquest of Padua in June. Rewarded for his service with the confiscated property of Ugolino Scrovegni, Conte established his residence in the Scrovegni palace in the Arena, which had been partially destroyed in the retaking of the city.⁷⁷ With the coming of peace in 1392, Conte entered the service of Pope Bonifacio IX as a condottiere but returned to help his half brother defend Niccolò III d'Este against Azzo's attempted coup in 1395 and remained in the Veneto to serve in the pay of Venice in the Mantuan War.

Thus, though mainly a military commander in the papal army, Conte retained a lively interest in his family's fortune and the welfare of his estates and offspring in Padua. Conte's trusted factor Ugolino da Prato oversaw the management of his rural estates, mainly confiscated from the Scrovegni. For example, in August 1395, Ugolino made a *soceda* contract with two peasants in Sarmazza near Camin; in February 1400, Ugolino lent £100 to a peasant from Mestrino to be repaid within five years and in March £155 to another peasant from Teggi, both villages northeast of Padua. The loans were probably advances to sharecroppers to buy seed and supplies for the spring planting.⁷⁸ That May, Conte's factor made loans of £64 and £319 to peasants on his farms in Roncon and Sarmazza, respectively, and in August Ugolino lent a peasant at Vanzo near Monselice 26 ducats to acquire a yoke of oxen and made a soceda contract on cows valued at £32.⁷⁹ Conte had extensive property in the Euganean Hills, since by 1400 there was a "canipa domini Contis de Carrara" in Valsanzibio, where an agent received repayment of a loan to local peasants.⁸⁰

Though often absent from his home in the Arena, Conte attempted to maintain his influence in the neighborhood, having his factor Ugolino da Prato witness the appointment of "Antonius de Plebis capellanus" as archpriest of S. Maria Arena in March 1399.⁸¹ That January in the sacristy of the Duomo, Conte's illegitimate son Ardizzone had been granted a benefice as canon of the cathedral chapter to fill the vacancy created by the "voluntary" resignation of Francesco Squarcialupi. Thus, the son came to occupy

TABLE 9.1
The Carrara V. Francesco il Vecchio's Illegitimate Offspring

Francesco il Vecchio (1325–93)

- Conte, condottiere (ca. 1350–1421), count of Ascoli, 1413–21, son of Giustina Maconia
  - Obizzo, condottiere, count of Ascoli, 1422, d. after 1439
- Andrea, OSB, d. 1405, abbot of S. Giustina, 1396–1405
- Giacomo (ca. 1350–1405), executed
  = Lucia di Bartolomeo Contarini
  - Bonifacio, d. 1425
    = 1398 Caterina Bocassi
  - Niccolò, knight, d. after 1425
  - Maria
    = (1) Niccolò Contarini
    = (2) Alvise Storlato
- Ugolino, d. 1398
- Rodolfo, knight, fl. 1390, d. after 1425 in Crete
- Pietro, fl. 1400
- Servio, OSB, abbot of S. Stefano da Carrara 1401, d. 1417 in Crete
- Paolo, knight (legitimated in 1401)
- Antonio, priest
- Ardizzone, condottiere (ca. 1370–after 1435)
  = 1418 Antonia di Muzio Attendolo Sforza
  - daughter
    = Giosio d'Acquaviva, duke of Adria

the post of canon which the father had renounced to follow his career as a soldier a decade earlier.[82] Presented to his canonry by Carrara favorites Matteo Cavalcanti and Pietro Rabatta, Ardizzone remained under the protection of his father, an influential figure in papal and Paduan politics. That December Conte appointed the Carrara *referendario*, Baldo Bonafari, his agent to have the priest Biagio Sclavio act in Ardizzone's interests.[83] Conte's son's benefice derived much of its income from tithes in Pernumia which Ugolino da Prato, acting for Conte da Carrara, rented for £1,200 in 1402. Two years later Ugolino, as Conte's factor, leased for £22 a year to local fullers tithes on mills in Pernumia "which belonged to the canonry of Ardizzone da Carrara."[84] Conte returned to Padua only in 1405 to aid Francesco Novello in the last defense of the city. Afterward, Conte da Carrara continued his career as a condottiere in the papal army.

Francesco il Vecchio's Illegitimate Offspring

Another of Francesco il Vecchio's bastards, Giacomo, followed the career of soldier in the Paduan army, fighting against the Scaligeri and Visconti, before following his half brother into exile in November 1388. Active in the reconquest of Padua, in the autumn of 1391 Giacomo was rewarded with Francesco Novello's *donatio inter vivos* of more than 1,000 *campi* of rebels' property confiscated in the Oltrebrenta at Piazzola, Carturo, Grantorto, and Trentamezzo.[85] Married to the Venetian noblewoman Lucia di Bartolomeo Contarini, by May 1392 Giacomo had settled in contrada Duomo, where he paid the salary of £176 of Agnese, wife of Domenico, who had served as a wet nurse to his children for the past six years.[86] Like his father, Giacomo sired several natural children, including two sons, Paolo and Antonio, by one Antonia "de Solutiis," who were legitimated by the count palatine only in June 1401.[87] Resident in Padua, Giacomo oversaw estates in Piazzola, where in 1394 he rented 30 *campi* to a peasant and in 1395 he leased to a local artisan a farmhouse on 12 *campi* for £12 a year.[88]

Rather more favored was Giacomo's legitimate son, the soldier Bonifacio, who had been captured while serving in his uncle Conte da Carrara's company in the Romagna. Ransomed back to Padua, in July 1395, with approval of his father, Bonifacio appointed another uncle, Rodolfo da Carrara, his proctor to redeem the pledge left with the German knight Gottard, who had taken him in combat.[89] By early 1399 Bonifacio had married Caterina, daughter of Gerardo and Orsola Bocassi and granddaughter of Simeone dagli Statuti. That summer young Caterina fell ill, perhaps of the plague, and made her testament leaving the bulk of her estate to her husband, Bonifacio, naming her father-in-law, Giacomo da Carrara, and her grandfather

Simeone dagli Statuti as executors.[90] Caterina's early death occasioned a lengthy lawsuit for the restitution of the dowry, which consisted of three houses and £500 in cash.[91] In February 1401 Simeone dagli Statuti named the jurist Giovanni Porcellini as his proctor to plead his case before the judge delegate, Prosdocimo Conti. That March Prosdocimo Conti set the cash value of the dowry at £4,333, though it is not clear when the property was returned to Caterina's family.[92] Bonifacio served with the Carrara army fighting against Giangaleazzo Visconti in 1402. When his father, Giacomo, secretly entered the pay of Venice in April 1405, Bonifacio and his brother Paolo denounced their father's treason to Francesco Novello, who seized and imprisoned his half brother, killing him with his own sword.[93] As a legitimate male heir, Bonifacio inherited much of Giacomo's land, selling more than 2,000 campi of woods and meadows at Piazzola, Cartura, and Campo S. Martino for 3,000 ducats to local merchants before he went into exile in Florence.[94] Because of their loyalty to Francesco Novello, Venice later confiscated what was left of Bonifacio's and Paolo's property and conveyed it to their sister Maria, who had also married into the Contarini family.

Francesco il Vecchio's other bastards more faithfully obeyed their father's advice, given in 1389, to serve the Carrara house. Rodolfo accompanied Francesco Novello during his exile and was knighted for his bravery during the reconquest of Padua. He fought with Sir John Hawkwood in the campaign against Milan the next year, chaperoned his nephews Francesco III and Giacomo at the installation of Giangaleazzo as duke of Milan in the spring of 1395, and accompanied Giacomo and his bride, Belfiore da Varano, home from their wedding in Camerino in 1403. By 1400 Rodolfo was a resident in S. Giustina, where his half brother Andrea was abbot, renting small parcels of arable in Piove di Sacco.[95] Another of Francesco il Vecchio's bastards, Pietro, also fought in Francesco Novello's wars: at Brescia in 1401, at Bologna in 1402, and in the final defense of Padua in 1405. His landed interests were centered in vineyards and farmland located in the Euganean Hills at Valsanzibio.[96] Another of the Vecchio's illegitimate sons, Andrea da Carrara, followed an ecclesiastical career. Francesco Novello had him made abbot of S. Giustina as early as June 1396, when, in that office, Andrea appointed a proctor to make collation of a benefice. Two years later he appointed an agent to recover rents and debts owed his monastery, especially from 1390 to 1393.[97] Under Andrea's leadership, the fortunes of S. Giustina declined precipitously, though Francesco Novello interceded for his half brother with Niccolò III d'Este, attempting to procure him a benefice in Ferrara in the summer of 1402. By the time of Andrea's death in July 1405, there were only three monks left in the once great Benedictine house.[98]

Reconstituting the Carrara Regime

The greatest Carrara churchman was Francesco Novello's illegitimate son Stefano, who was born about 1375, when his father was still a teen-aged bachelor. He accompanied the family into exile, first at Asti, later at Florence, and returned to Padua to begin his ecclesiastical career, at about age eighteen, as a canon of the cathedral chapter in June 1393.[99] The Carrara used collation to the canonries of the Duomo as a means of rewarding family and foreign supporters; sometimes future soldiers, such as Pietro Rabatta, Conte, and Ardizzone and Paolo da Carrara; and often jurists, such as Prosdocimo Conti, Francesco Zabarella, Francesco Beningrado, and Aicardino and Giacomo Alvarotti.[100] The size of the chapter was limited to fourteen or fifteen canons, headed by the archpriest, who usually lived in close proximity to the cathedral, assisting at services and living from benefices that usually consisted of tithes in villages of the Padovano. As Silvana Collodo has observed, the appointments to canonical benefices under the Carrara "did not simply favor friends of the dynasty, but corresponded with great precision to the need to recompense the service of men employed in the government or the administration of the state."[101] Thus, collation to the chapter of canons favored men of ability in public affairs but of small spiritual calling.

Such a person was Stefano da Carrara, who succeeded the departing bishop of Padua, Ugone Roberti, in June 1396, as "administrator and governor of goods, spiritual and temporal, of the Paduan Church," when he was a canon in minor orders. He and his uncle Andrea da Carrara, abbot of S. Giustina, were promoted to the subdiaconate in April 1398, with Stefano alone becoming a deacon that June.[102] In fact, Stefano turned over most spiritual duties to his vicars, especially Niccolò da Portogruaro, but was zealous in distributing the diocese's vast holdings in tithes to his father's family and favorites. For example, in January 1399, Stefano made a Paduan cloth merchant, Giovanni Maioli, his vassal, awarding him decimal fiefs in Villa Brazoli. A year later, Francesco Novello appointed Nascimbene Zamboni his factor to receive "investiture of every and all fiefs from the Paduan Church that the same magnificent lord claimed [as his]."[103] In the summer of 1402 while the Visconti War was raging, Stefano da Carrara finally became bishop of Padua, appointing Michele Dulcini his proctor to make the proper payments in Rome.[104] Probably to raise money for the purchase of his office, the next May, for 10,000 ducats, Stefano da Carrara rented to his legitimate half brothers Francesco III and Giacomo da Carrara all tithes in thirty-eight villages in the northeastern Padovano between the Brenta and the Trevisano border.[105]

Control over the Duomo, its chapter of canons, and the abbey of S. Giustina were not Francesco Novello's only ecclesiastical interests. For some time, the Carrara had enjoyed the right of appointment (*ius patronatus*) of the abbey of S. Stefano in their ancestral village. There a pontifical Mass was celebrated each year on the feast of St. Stephen (26 December). In 1395 it was attended by members of the ruling clique, including the archpriest Giovanni Enzegnerati, Baldo Bonafari, Serafino di Benvenuto, and Stefano and Servio da Carrara.[106] Soon after recovering Padua, the Carrara lord asserted his rights over the church of S. Maria dei Servi, which his mother, Fina, had constructed and endowed some fifteen years earlier. On 31 October 1392, Francesco Novello appointed Benedetto Girlandi his proctor to appear before the bishop of Padua to claim *ius patronatus* over Padua's Servite church. This Benedetto did at the Duomo the next day, with the final authority for the grant of patronage coming from the prior general of the Servite in Florence, Andrea da Faenza, who granted to the Domus Carrariensis "every right of patronage that belonged to and was due [it] by law and custom in that place and church."[107] That April the Carrara lord repaid the Servites by allowing them to acquire property valued at 1,000 ducats, contravening Paduan statutes that forbade such rights to religious house.[108] Francesco Novello's control of high church and political office in Padua, his claim of lofty new titles, his patronage of his affinity, and his nurturing of Padua's textile industries were part of a grand design to maintain and enhance his city's independence in the face of Venice's growing interest and authority in mainland affairs.

Chapter 10

Ambition and Destruction, 1392–1405

> Homo morto non fa guerra.
> [A dead man does not make war.]
>
> —Venetian proverb

At his restoration the Carrara lord of Padua had greater ambitions for his regime than existence as a mere client state of his powerful neighbor Venice. His most pressing need was to find money to pay the hated annual indemnity of 10,000 ducats imposed by the Peace of Genoa, while providing for his own military security and maintaining cordial relations with his recent enemies.[1] The need for mutual defense was satisfied by the signing of the Treaty of Bologna on 11 April 1392, which united the former Guelf allies of Florence, Bologna, and Padua with their former enemies in the Visconti war, Alberto d'Este, lord of Ferrara, and the ruler of Imola, Lodovico Alidosi, that of Faenza, Astorre Manfredi, and those of Ravenna, Pietro and Ostasio Polenta.[2] The treaty provided for protecting the two dynastic states nearest Lombardy, the Carrara and Este, against any future Visconti aggression and for the mutual defense of all signatories in event of attack. From his old allies Florence and Bologna, the Carrara lord received material aid in the form of a loan of 5,000 ducats to help pay his indemnity; this combined with sale of property in Padua and collection of debts in Genoa permitted full payment of the first installment to the count of Virtù in June 1392.[3]

Allies at the Restoration, 1392–1393

The return of Francesco Novello's wife and children from Florence that spring marked the resumption of normal family life. On the second anniversary of the reconquest of Padua, 19 June 1392, Pier Paolo Vergerio made a speech on behalf of the Paduan people, giving thanks to Francesco Novello for the end of the harsh Visconti rule.[4] Praising the Carrara lord's military skill that finally brought an end to bloodshed, Vergerio stressed the need to cultivate the arts of peace and the dependence of the Paduan people on Francesco Novello's just rulership. To help guarantee the security of the restored Carrara, Bologna and Florence sent to Padua a small troop of seventy lances under the mercenary captain Alberico da Barbiano, while promising to keep Francesco Novello informed of any negotiations with Giangaleazzo Visconti, both directly and through Paduan legates resident in Bologna.[5] Still, Francesco Novello rankled under the heavy indemnity and the continued captivity of his father in the Visconti stronghold at Monza, asking Florence to have its ambassadors at the Visconti court intervene to secure his father's release. Insisting that Florence's envoys were doing all they could, Salutati pleaded that while the Visconti lord mouthed sentiments of honor and friendship, there was little immediate hope of securing Francesco il Vecchio's freedom.[6]

Francesco Novello had better luck closer to home. Appointed peacemaker by Pope Boniface IX, in May the lord of Padua achieved a certain prestige by negotiating a truce between two major lords of the Papal States, Antonio Montefeltro of Urbino and Carlo Malatesta of Rimini, who would be subject to a fine of 10,000 florins for the resumption of hostilities.[7] Early in September Francesco Gonzaga was induced to join the League of Bologna, whose members agreed to guarantee his possessions and rights, while providing him with 18,000 ducats for constructing a bridge at Borgoforte, which could be used to close the Po to commerce and send troops into Lombardy. The next month, through the good offices of Alberto d'Este, Francesco III da Carrara (then nine years old) was betrothed to Alda, daughter of Francesco Gonzaga, amid celebrations in Ferrara capped by jousts and tourneys, with the Carrara lord himself in attendance.[8] That autumn, Francesco Novello received an honor already accorded the lords of Ferrara and Mantua, being admitted into the Venetian nobility with full citizenship by an overwhelming vote of the Maggior Consiglio. In this final act of reconciliation with the Carrara dynasty, the Maggior Consiglio decreed: "Francesco da Carrara, intimate friend of our dominions, . . . is assumed as our citizen and a Venetian noble in our Great Council, with his sons and heirs, by special privilege."[9] That December Doge Antonio Venier brought all three *terraferma* clients, Alberto d'Este, Francesco Gonzaga, and Francesco Novello, to Venice to celebrate the feast of S. Lucia, combining religious observance with political discussions. Venice also extended the rights of citizenship to other members of the Carrara family and affinity, granting status of *cives de intus* to Francesco Novello's widowed sister, Caterina Frankapan, and her daughter, Elisabeth, in March 1393, followed by grants of citizenship to his consort, Taddea d'Este, Bartolomeo Paradisi da Capo-

FIG. 33. *Portrait of Francesco Novello da Carrara (late fourteenth century). Source: Biblioteca Civica, Padua, MS B.P. 158, fol. 45v. Pier Paolo Vergerio the Elder,* De principibus Carrariensibus. *Reproduced with permission of the Biblioteca Civica, Padua*

divacca and his sons Rambaldo and Francesco, and Marsilio di Santa Sofia. Two exiled lords, potential pawns in Venetian diplomacy, awarded citizenship *de intus* were Guglielmo della Scala and Carlo di Bernabò Visconti, both then resident in Venice.[10]

The completion of the bridge at Borgoforte with its threat of invasion of Lombardy the next spring brought Giangaleazzo's wrath down on Francesco Gonzaga. The lord of Milan's damming and deviation of the Mincio at Borghetto into the Adige threatened to expose Mantua to attack and stop its mills. Ambassadors of the League of Bologna met in Ferrara to discuss the problem; Florence's sharp rebuke and the Gonzaga lord's promise not to use the bridge for aggression against the Visconti encouraged Giangaleazzo to stop work on his dam. The death of Alberto d'Este in late July caused a crisis in Ferrara, propelling his nine-year-old heir Niccolò III into the lordship with the backing of Pope Boniface IX. Niccolò was placed under the regency of a council of Ferrarese notables, advised by a board of Venetian nobles, representing Venice as guardian during his minority as provided for in his father's will. The unstable situation tempted the Carrara lord with territorial expansion, and he moved troops south into the Polesine di Rovigo, the northern part of the Ferrarese between the Adige and the Tartaro. Alarmed at the dangerous situation, Bologna and Florence sent contingents of cavalry to guard the young Este lord in Ferrara, while Venice dispatched 270 crossbowmen under two noble commanders.[11] Meeting secretly in early August the Senate instructed its ambassadors to express to the lord of Padua Venice's displeasure at any claim made on the Polesine as the inheritance of his consort, Taddea d'Este, or for debts owed for her dowry. Instead Francesco Novello was to consider the love and friendship he owed Venice and young Niccolò and the dire consequences for any aggression against the Este state.[12] The allies' show of force and Venice's strong language forced the Carrara lord to abandon, for the moment, his territorial ambitions in the Polesine.

Death and Funeral of Francesco il Vecchio, 1393

The death of Francesco il Vecchio on 7 October 1393 in captivity in the Visconti stronghold at Monza occasioned perhaps the most lavish ceremony in the history of the Carrara regime. According to stories circulated at the time and later collected by the court humanist Giovanni Conversini, the elder Francesco had spent his time in prison trying to outwit his cruel and wily captors. For example, when still captive at Como during the reconquest of Padua, Francesco il Vecchio was told that his son had died trying to recover the city. Perceiving his captors' lies, he responded, "Your bells have for some time been proclaiming this." The guards were dumbfounded, for the silence of the bells had indicated that no Visconti victory had occurred.[13] The body of Francesco il Vecchio, dead at the age of sixty-eight, probably of natural causes, was transported back to Padua for burial beside his consort, Fina, in the mausoleum she had prepared in the renovated Baptistery. To commemorate the great lord's passing, ambassadors were invited from all the neighboring states. Meeting on 23 October, the Venetian Senate voted to send a letter of condolence to the son and elected two nobles to serve as representatives at the funeral. Appointment was open to all nobles, without loss of office, except for those *savi* who were negotiating differences between the lords of Padua and Ferrara. The two "old *terraferma* hands" first elected, Paolo Morosini and Pietro Emo, promptly refused the office, leaving the embassy to lesser men. From Florence, Salutati sent a standard letter of consolation, stressing that history teaches that death comes to all leaders and averring that Francesco il Vecchio had now been released from both his earthly and bodily prisons.[14]

In Padua on 20 November, an impressive funeral cortege was arranged, beginning with the preparation of the body, which lay in state in the Carrara palace, surrounded by the noble matrons of the city, headed by the ruling lord's consort, Taddea d'Este.[15] Thence, it was removed in stately procession to the Duomo. The line of march began with all the monks and friars of the diocese, each in his own order, followed by the clergy of the parishes of the *contado* and the city, canons of the cathedral, higher clergy, and the bishop. Next came the beggars of the city, who had been given new clothes and wax tapers and paid a coin for the occasion, followed by a large number of prisoners just released from Padua's jail and peasants from the ancestral village of Carrara. Then followed the knighthood of Padua, dressed in black, each horse led by a squire, followed by knights from each town of the contado, displaying its name and coat of arms on the trappings. Some knights carried the red cross of the commune, others the family's red *carro,* others still the dynasty's arms superimposed on the commune's cross, always red on a white field. Leading the bier, covered with purple cloth worked with gems and gold, came two stalwarts of the regime, Michele Rabatta and Francesco Dotti, each carrying a baton of military command, and following the body came the son, Francesco Novello, and the grandsons, all shedding tears. After came ambassadors from Venice and Bologna and many other cities, followed by a great throng of the Paduan people. From the second-story windows of houses along the line of march watched young women and matrons, their cheeks moist with tears.

Converging at the cathedral, the cortege and its accompanying throng heard the funeral orations.[16] Speaking on behalf of the Paduan people, Pier

Paolo Vergerio stressed the deceased lord's great deeds and character, his patronage of churches, arts, and letters, his leadership in war, combined with his love of peace, and his mercy and moderation, concluding with advice to the son to carry on his father's greatness. The famed jurist and lawyer Giovanni Lodovico Lambertazzi took as his theme the Old Testament text "A great prince has fallen today" (2 Kings 3:38) and composed his oration around the four cardinal virtues, dwelling most on that one the Carrara lord had surely never lacked in life: courage. Both speeches were conventional expressions of condolence and lament, drawing on the precepts of Roman Stoicism and embellished with quotations from Scripture and classical authors. Both orations, and especially Vergerio's, presented a detailed portrait of Francesco il Vecchio's accomplishments as the ruler of Padua, while allowing for the rhetorical exaggeration that the occasion demanded. Thus, the elder Carrara's funeral provided a rare moment to express Paduan solidarity and enhance the prestige of Francesco Novello's regime.

Foreign Relations and Marriage Alliances

That same autumn Francesco Novello endeavored to steer a policy of independence from Florence and Venice, hoping to increase his influence at Ferrara, while coping with his own limited resources. The regime's lack of liquidity forced him to threaten to suspend his contribution to the league, which brought a sharp rebuke from Florence. Stressing the league's obligation to pay the recently enrolled mercenary companies of Conrad von Landau and Azzone Castello, Salutati expressed amazement of the Carrara lord's refusal to pay his share and help to keep the peace. When Francesco Novello responded pleading shortage of funds and the powerlessness (*impotencia*) of his regime, the chancellor assured the lord of Padua that his expenses were nothing compared with Florence's. Silence from Padua brought a short letter insisting that the Carrara lord honor his commitments to the league, both to keep evil men in check and to maintain peace in Italy.[17] Francesco did eventually contribute his allotment to the league, while turning his attention to events in Ferrara.

Intent on gathering forces to intervene in Ferrara, in December Francesco Novello asked Venice to secure the release of Conte da Carrara, who as a captain in the papal army had been captured by Gentile da Varano, lord of Camerino. Venice reluctantly agreed to intercede "in order to preserve the love and goodwill of the lord of Padua."[18] Although Conte did not immediately return to Padua, Francesco Novello did invite Azzone d'Este to the Carrara court, secretly agreeing to support his plot to seize the lordship of Ferrara with the help of the Romagnol *condottiere* Giovanni da Barbiano, count of Cunio. In June 1394, Azzone made his will in Padua, naming his only legitimate son, Taddeo, as his universal heir but leaving all his property to the Carrara lord's consort, Taddea d'Este, should the son predecease him.[19] Again complaining of lack of money, Francesco Novello threatened not to pay the indemnity to Giangaleazzo Visconti due that June, evoking a second sharp response from Florence, reminding the Carrara lord of his obligations as stipulated in the Peace of Genoa.[20] Desperate for cash to pay the indemnity, the Carrara lord demanded from young Niccolò III payment on loans made earlier to Niccolò II and Alberto d'Este as well as the portion still owed for Taddea's unpaid dowry. Vitally interested in harmony among the mainland lords, Doge Antonio Venier directly intervened to promote a settlement, lauding partial payment on Taddea's dowry made in June 1394.[21] That autumn Francesco Novello abandoned his plans of backing Azzone's rebellion against Niccolò. But Azzone, aided by Giovanni da Barbiano, continued to incite local peasants and lords against Niccolò's regime and led raids into the Ferrarese that winter.

At a pitched battle that April at Portomaggiore, southwest of Ferrara, Niccolò's troops, aided by contingents from Florence and Bologna, defeated Azzone's forces, killing perhaps one thousand rebels and capturing their leader, who was handed over to Astorre Manfredi to be held in prison at Faenza, before he was eventually exiled to Crete. Stationing crossbowmen and cavalry in Ferrara to guard against attack by the remnants of Azzone's forces, Venice was resolved to defend Niccolò's regime, while gaining ever greater influence in the region. The Este state came under Venice's direct protection, with a Venetian *vice dominus* appointed to oversee the affairs of the Council of Regency. At the end of April Venice rendered the Este regime solvent by granting an interest-free loan of 50,000 ducats in return for receiving the Polesine in pawn. Thus, Venice gained control of important towns on the northern estuaries of the Po, with all the strongholds of the district handed over to Venetian garrisons. The Venetian rectors were to disturb local government as little as possible and impose no new taxes, while the fortresses were to be garrisoned at Venice's expense. To encourage eventual repayment of the loan, any balance left unpaid after five years was subject to interest of 7 percent.[22] Venice continued to involve its nobles in the Council of Regents governing Ferrara, who were naturally interested in the identity of young marquis's future bride.

As we have seen, the eldest son of the lord of Padua, Francesco III da Carrara, was already betrothed to Alda Gonzaga, the eldest daughter of the lord of Mantua, much to the anger and chagrin of the lord of Milan, who had counted the Gonzaga among his loyal allies. According to chronicler Andrea Gatari, Giangaleazzo Visconti preyed upon Francesco Novello's ambitions and lack of cash by proposing to forgive the indemnity in return for the friendship of the lord of Padua and the betrothal of his daughter Gigliola da Carrara to his natural son Gabriele Visconti, designated to become lord of Verona and Vicenza, and Francesco's second son, Giacomo da Carrara, to a granddaughter of Bernabò Visconti.[23] But Francesco Novello finally rejected the offer, both out of basic mistrust felt toward Giangaleazzo and because of the Venetian government's strong disapproval of any marriage alliance between the Visconti and one of its mainland lords. From the start Venice favored a match between Gigliola da Carrara and Niccolò III d'Este. In September 1396, the Senate informed a Paduan envoy that the marriage "would please us greatly, because we recognize that it would serve to preserve the affection and states of both parties." To facilitate the union Venice offered to pay for the costs of obtaining Pope Boniface IX's dispensation from prohibited degrees of consanguinity (the future groom's father and the future bride's grandfather were brothers) and negotiated a lower dowry of only 20,000 ducats for the Carrara lord. The wedding finally took place in Padua in the midst of the Mantuan War on 2 June 1397, with the groom accompanied by four hundred knights from Ferrara. After a round of jousts and feasts, the groom, only fourteen years old, took his bride back to Ferrara, with two generations of the houses of Carrara and Este now closely intermarried.[24]

Meanwhile, Giangaleazzo Visconti's quest for power and prestige brought him into conflict with the League of Bologna, especially Florence, following a policy of courting support from the weak and impecunious king of the Romans Wenceslaus. Early in 1395 the count of Virtù negotiated with imperial officials for the bestowal of the title of duke of Milan, finally receiving the title on 11 May in return for payment of 100,000 ducats. That summer Giangaleazzo dispatched invitations to heads of state throughout Italy to attend his coronation at Milan set for early October. The ceremony caused some concern among Giangaleazzo's enemies, who wanted to observe diplomatic formalities without appearing too enthusiastic for his new title.[25] In the event only a few minor lords attended, Teodoro II, marquis of Montferrato, and Antonio da Montefeltro, count of Urbino, while most states sent two or three envoys. After discussion, the Carrara lord appointed his two eldest sons, Francesco III and Giacomo, as his representatives, and Venice sent three nobles as its representatives, Francesco Corner, Pietro Contarini, and the future doge Tommaso Mocenigo. After much debate, the Florentine *signoria* dispatched two seasoned statesmen as its ambassadors, Cristofano Spini and Maso degli Albizzi, who were empowered to enter into negotiations with the Visconti lord if the occasion should arise.[26] After an elaborate ceremony of installation, a rigid etiquette was observed at the seating at the banquet afterward, with the imperial representative seated at the duke's right, followed by the ambassadors of Venice, Florence, and Bologna and Giacomo da Carrara, with lesser lords and the envoy from Sicily on his left. The sumptuous feast of many courses was followed the next day by a tournament involving more than three hundred knights, all designed to impress the rulers of Italy with the wealth and grandeur of the new duke of Milan.

With Pisa and Siena his potential allies in Tuscany, Giangaleazzo next sought to gain access to the Mediterranean by bringing Genoa under his control, challenging the claims of the French crown to that city. As a result Florence intensified its search for additional allies, while Venice promoted ever greater control over its three "Lombard" lords, who were to serve as buffer states against Milanese expansion. Florence's weakness in papal Romagna, the very region where Venice was gaining strength, was demonstrated by two minor crises: the struggle for control of the fortress of Castrocaro near Forlì and the threat of an alliance of powerful mercenary companies. In order to help the impecunious Pope Boniface IX, in August 1394 Florence lent him 18,000 florins in return for receiving the stronghold of Castrocaro in pawn.[27] But the local castellan Tommaso Novi refused to surrender the fortress to Florentine forces. When Florence threatened siege, Bologna and the lords of the Romagna came to the castellan's defense. Faced with open hostility from its closest allies and the prospect of a long and difficult siege of an impregnable stronghold, Florence backed down and accepted Venice's offer to mediate a settlement. Late in 1396, the Florentine government had to accept the decision of the doge in Venice, who turned over control of Castrocaro to a small garrison of troops sent by the Carrara and Gonzaga lords, while Florence retained nominal jurisdiction and the obligation to pay and provision the soldiers billeted there.[28]

Florence's sense of impotence on its northern frontier was heightened in March 1396 by the threat of blackmail from mercenary companies in the Romagna, joined together under the leadership of Giovanni da Barbiano. The companies formed an army of more than twenty-five hundred lances and threatened to cause great harm to Florence and even attack its troops outside Castrocaro unless they were bought off. Alarmed, Florence asked Bologna to negotiate with these petty lords, who included Conte da Carrara fresh from service in the papal army. In a plaintive letter of 3 April, Salutati asked Francesco Novello to persuade his half brother to quit the league of mercenary captains and join Florentine service instead with his company of five hundred lances.[29] That spring Conte did leave the mercenary league to enter the papal army in the March of Ancona with orders to reduce Macerata and Fermo to obedience. In helping his half brother further papal policy, Francesco Novello played a decisive role by obtaining permission from the Senate to send bombards, arms, and munitions through Venetian domains to Conte's forces in the Marches.[30] Meanwhile, Florence had grander plans, concluding on 29 September a treaty with King Charles VI of France which aimed at placing the French crown in control of Genoa, as Salutati informed the allies of the League of Bologna in letters sent the next month.[31] The new Franco-Florentine alliance stirred Giangaleazzo Visconti to a renewed attack on the allies, making the Mantuan War inevitable.

As war clouds gathered late in 1396, Francesco Novello looked to marrying Francesco III and Alda Gonzaga, who had been betrothed some years back as children. Late in September the Carrara lord appointed Paolo Lion his proctor to oversee fortifications in Ferrara and then move on to Mantua to discuss the question of Alda's dowry.[32] By the next March the dowry had been set at 25,000 ducats, and meeting in secret, the Senate voted to stand surety for the sum "out of the paternal love for [Francesco Novello] and his state." By late May the Senate held an election of the ambassador to the wedding ceremony, and on 5 July, the Maggior Consiglio voted a wedding gift costing no more than 150 ducats.[33] With Mantua unsafe because of the war with the Visconti, the marriage was celebrated in Padua on 16 July 1397, when the groom had just turned fourteen. His bride was perhaps a year or two older. In August the dowry contact was stipulated, with Francesco Gonzaga's proctor agreeing to a dowry of 25,000 ducats in cash with 8,000 in jewels and goods. The provisions followed Paduan custom: if Francesco III first died without common heir, the entire dowry returned to the Gonzaga family; if Alda died first without heir, only half the dowry reverted to her family. Late that year, the Carrara lord appointed Naimiero Conti his agent to receive payment from the Venetian government of 5,000 ducats of Alda Gonzaga's dowry.[34] Thus, the Serenissima advanced dowry payments from its own funds to foster a marriage alliance between two of its major "Lombard" lords.

The Mantuan War

Francesco Gonzaga had been an enemy of the Visconti since he had caught his wife, Agnese, daughter of Bernabò Visconti, in a flagrant act of adultery in 1390 and had her beheaded. Recalling the execution of his kinswoman and wary of Florence's alliance with Francesco Gonzaga and other "Lombard" lords, Giangaleazzo ordered the invasion of Mantua in the spring of 1397. When the able Visconti captain Ugolotto Biancardo entered Mantuan territory in March, the members of the league rallied to Francesco Gonzaga's cause, electing Carlo Malatesta head of the allied army in

May.³⁵ At Padua Francesco Novello marshaled what forces he could, fulfilling Florence's request for aid by dispatching Conte with his 500 lances to Mantua and enlisting the company of Morando, count of Porcia, who had recently returned from a pilgrimage to the Holy Land.³⁶ Initial encounters went against the allied forces, with a Visconti fleet on the Po setting fire to Borgoforte in June and besieging the Serraglio at Mantua the next month. On 17 July Francesco Novello pleaded before the doge and council for aid from Venice, which abandoned its policy of neutrality and dispatched a fleet of seven armed galleys and many *barche* under command of Francesco Bembo. While Visconti forces under Jacopo dal Verme renewed their attack on the Serraglio, Carlo Malatesta received reinforcements from Florence and other allies. Several lords of the Romagna were enlisted as mercenaries to help with the war effort: Giovanni da Barbiano pledged 500 lances to Bologna, Count Ugo of Monfiore and Gherardo Obizzi 600 lances to Mantua, and Corrado Prosperi with 400 lances and an English company of 315 lances were enlisted by Florence. Now commanding an army of 6,000 foot and 2,000 horse, with 300 bombards, Carlo Malatesta coordinated his advance with Bembo's fleet, which had entered the Mincio from the Po. Investing the Visconti forces at its beachhead outside Mantua at Governolo, the two armies fought a pitched battle at the end of August. The allies were victorious, taking more than 6,000 prisoners, though they suffered a number of casualties, including the Carrara lord's cousin Pataro Buzzacarini, who was mortally wounded in combat with Facino Cane. The Visconti forces retreated, only to launch a renewed attack on Gonzaga's forces at Borgoforte at the end of October. Before hostilities were suspended for the winter, the five allies enlisted the service of the companies of Guido da Correggio and Giovanni Ordelaffi, with payments assigned to each city-state according to its wealth and importance in the league: Florence contributed 44 percent of the contract, Bologna 25 percent, the Carrara lord 12 percent, and Este and Gonzaga 10 percent each.³⁷

As the stalemate in the field made a truce likely, Boniface IX worked to reestablish his authority on the northern frontiers of the Papal States. As part of the policy of attempting to dominate Ferrara, Francesco Novello had received from Niccolò III d'Este control over papal fortresses at Bazzano, southwest of Bologna, and Nonantola, northeast of Modena. In a sharply worded letter threatening excommunication, late in 1397 Boniface IX ordered the Carrara lord to surrender the castles with all their possessions and rights to papal representatives. By the next May the two strongholds were back in papal hands, as Boniface strove to impose his will in the Romagna, while Francesco Novello retreated to a more defensive posture following the enormous outlays in men and matériel necessitated

FIG. 34. *Jacopo da Verona*, Adoration of Magi. *Like many Paduan frescoes of the period, this one contains "hidden" portraits. Francesco il Vecchio da Carrara appears as the first magus, Francesco Novello as the second, and Francesco III as the third, 1400. Oratorio of S. Michele, Padua. Reproduced with permission of the Museo Civico, Padua*

by the Mantuan War.[38] The war had caused Venice to compromise its policy of neutrality, supplying ships, troops, and arms to the conflict. On 1 March 1398 Salutati wrote the lord of Padua, urging him to enlist Venice formally in the League of Bologna to ensure their common safety and the destruction of Giangaleazzo Visconti. At the end of the month Venice agreed to join with the members of the League of Bologna for four years, promising to pay a fifth of the expenses, while Florence contributed a third, Bologna a fifth, and the Carrara, Este, and Gonzaga lords each 9 percent. But the defensive league was only preparatory to negotiating the Truce of Pavia, proclaimed on 11 May 1398, to last for ten years.[39] Francesco Novello was permitted to suspend payments of the indemnity for the duration of the truce, which was welcomed with great festivities in Padua and a speech by Francesco Zabarella praising peace.[40] With the cessation of war, Francesco Novello turned to solving issues of Paduan policy by diplomatic means.

Ambition and Destruction

Padua and Venice, 1398–1401

One of Francesco Novello's first acts following the truce was to dispatch Michele Rabatta to Tuscany to request Florentine citizenship for his two eldest sons, for both the prestige and the political support it brought. A few months later the Carrara lord appointed Rabatta his ambassador to Antonio Caetani, patriarch of Aquileia, to resign his office of advocate of the church of Aquileia, which he had received a decade earlier from Filippo d'Alençon, in favor of the counts of Gorizia, Enrico and Giovanni Mainardi, traditional allies of the patriarch, who had now achieved their majority.[41] Venice also demanded that its Carrara ally meddle less in the affairs of Friuli. Indeed, Francesco Novello was much more concerned in extending his influence in Este dominions, governed by his young son-in-law Niccolò III. Promoting peace between the lord of Ferrara and the Polenta lords of Ravenna in the summer of 1398, the Carrara lord tried to direct Este policy by placing a number of his own closest advisers on the marquis's council. Since at one time or another Michele Rabbata, Enrico Gallo, Guglielmo Curtarolo, and Giovanni Parisino Mezzoconti served in Ferrara, the Carrara lord was kept well informed of developments at the Este court.[42] Francesco Novello even attempted to gain influence among the Ferrarese nobility by agreeing to serve as godfather for the infant daughter of the soldier and courtier Gherardo Boiardo.[43] But despite his interest in Ferrara, the Carrara lord's main task remained cultivation of friendship with Venice.

The question of borders had already arisen in the spring of 1397 when Francesco Novello had asked the Senate permission to alter the course of the Musone, rebuild his fort at Oriago, repair dikes between Noale and Mestre, and generally to provide for his defense and control flooding in the lowlands near the lagoon. After careful consideration, Venice agreed to these requests, specifying that all improvements were to be carried at Paduan expense and not harm Venetian commerce or agriculture.[44] At the end of 1398, the Senate again reviewed its borders and treaties with the commune and lord of Padua, under the pretext of removing cause for recent abuses and reaching new agreements. As a result of a proposal from Michele Steno and others, Leonardo Dandolo was appointed as envoy to confer with the Carrara lord on the transport of goods between the two states and renewal of earlier pacts. Francesco Novello was pleased to revise the treaties, because he now wanted the right to levy taxes on products sent to Venice, estimating that realistic custom duties could bring in annual revenue of 20,000 ducats, sorely needed to repay debts incurred in the Mantuan War. The Senate was disposed at least to discuss higher levies on products imported from the estates of Venetian proprietors in the Padovano into Venice and the *dogado*.[45] By 14 March agreement was near. At his Venetian residence at Ca' Corner on the Grand Canal, Francesco Novello appointed Pietro Paolo Crivelli and Bonifacio Guarnerini his proctors to renew, confirm, and revise all treaties with the doge and Comune Veneciarum. More than three months later the new pacts were completed, ready to be approved and promulgated by the two parties.[46]

The new agreements, which incorporated most of the earlier treaties going back to 1337 and even to the time of the commune, continued to give Venetian citizens and religious houses large privileges in the Padovano. Thus, in many respects the Carrara dynasty and Paduan people remained subservient to Venice's political and economic interests. First came a pledge of mutual defense: Venice promised to keep the Carrara lord under its protection, "against any person in the world," while Francesco Novello repeated the ancient formula of defending the Comune Veneciarum with all his might, both on land and sea. Second, rents and crops from land owned by Venetian churches and monasteries in the Padovano were to be imported into the city duty-free, as provided for by treaty sixty years earlier. No customs were to be imposed on goods shipped from Venice to Padua, although customary dues could be imposed on Paduan materials, such as wax, wood, charcoal, leather, and linen cloth, imported to Venice. But to augment his own revenues the Carrara lord was now permitted to impose duties on a number of products that Venetian proprietors, lay and ecclesiastical, shipped into Venice. The new charges were usually levied as a fraction of estimated value (usually 1 or 2 *soldi* per lira, or 5–10 percent of worth), but sometimes as a set sum per hundredweight or length of cloth. The imports to be taxed included materials for the shipbuilding industry, such as timber, poplar, oak and fir logs, oakum, cordage, and hemp; products for the household, such as wood, charcoal, honey, and wax; and raw materials for manufacturing, such as leather and hides for shoes and flax and linen for clothing. In general, Venice permitted modest levies on the most valuable Paduan products used in shipbuilding and in the shops of its own artisans. Thus, Venice allowed the Carrara lord to raise new taxes on its citizens owning land in the Padovano, providing badly needed revenue for his regime. Almost all the other older privileges remained in effect. The pact continued to provide for the extradition of fugitives, especially those fleeing debts in Venice, maintained the monopoly of Chioggia salt in Paduan domains, and kept the same frontiers at Mestre and Curano as set by Niccolò II d'Este following the Peace of Turin and the borders with the Trevisano as determined in 1374. Venice tried to accommodate the need of the Carrara dynasty for new sources of income. The treaty of August 1399 represents the high point of cooperation between the two states.

While keeping on good terms with Venice, the Carrara lord sought new allies in the Romagna and Friuli, using both the older policy of the marriage alliance and a newer one of spiritual kinship. As we have seen, in the autumn of 1398 Francesco Novello (through a proctor) stood as godfather to the infant daughter of a potential Ferrarese ally, Gherardo Boiardo. In January 1400, he appointed another agent to be godfather to the infant son of Aimerico di Giovanni Manfredi, the grandson of the *podestà* of Padua in the 1350s and newest member of the collateral branch of the ruling family of Faenza. That May the lord of Padua honored the exiled lord of Verona, Guglielmo della Scala, by serving as godfather to his infant son, through the proctorship of his son-in-law Ognibene Scola.[47] At the same time, Francesco Novello tried to find a politically useful wife for his second son, Giacomo. In July 1399, he dispatched his seneschal, the Gascon knight Dorde de Gaubert, to negotiate Giacomo's betrothal with Sveva Caetani, daughter of Jacobello and thus niece of the patriarch of Aquileia, Antonio Caetani. The mission apparently failed, since in April 1401, Francesco Novello appointed his half brother Conte to renew negotiations for Sveva's hand. This round of talks also failed, for in March 1402 the lord sent Francesco Buzzacarini and Bonifacio Guarnerini as his envoys to discuss Giacomo's marriage to Belfiore da Varano, daughter of Rodolfo, lord of Camerino in the Marches. In the meantime, the Carrara lord tried to marry his third son, Marsilio, to a daughter of Andrea Matteo, the duke of Atri and count of Flaviano.[48] Of all these attempts at matchmaking, only the wedding of Belfiore and Giacomo actually occurred, taking place in Camerino in February 1403.

On the Italian scene Giangaleazzo Visconti presented a great danger to Florence and its ally the Carrara lord of Padua as he controlled Verona, Vicenza, Feltre, and Belluno in the Veneto and had gained new client states in Tuscany. In February 1399 the duke of Milan became lord of Pisa, in September of Siena, and in January 1400 he even occupied Perugia. Florence desperately tried to keep the League of Bologna alive, but that cause was hopeless. Francesco Gonzaga had already returned to the Visconti camp, while Niccolò III d'Este was increasingly removed from the Florentine orbit. The Venetian government turned a deaf ear to Florence's pleas to maintain the truce and made peace with Giangaleazzo Visconti at Venice for itself and Francesco Novello on 21 March 1400. Among the conditions agreed to was the reduction of the annual indemnity the lord of Padua owed the duke of Milan to 7,000 ducats. Thus, while payment of the hated tribute had to be renewed with the end of the truce, the yearly burden was set at a more acceptable level. Late in April the lord and commune of Padua ratified the treaty.⁴⁹ Florence continued to receive from Padua intelligence on affairs in Germany and France, with Salutati thanking Francesco Novello for his communications sent that fall.⁵⁰ But the plague that struck Italy that summer brought governments to a standstill in most of the peninsula. To escape the pestilence Taddea had removed her own household with her daughter Gigliola, consort of the Este lord, to Gorizia. Now as autumn approached, the Venetian Senate voted to allow the Carrara women to come to Chioggia, setting up residence there until the plague subsided, importing provisions from Padua, free of the usual customs. Such privilege of duty-free provisioning was repeated the next spring when Francesco Novello took up residence in Ca' Corner, on the occasion of the visit of the Byzantine emperor, Manuel II.⁵¹

The Visconti War, 1401–1403

The deposition of the weak, intemperate, and capricious Wenceslaus in August 1400 and the election of Rupert of Bavaria as king of the Romans provided the remnants of the Guelf league with a new savior. Among the reasons the imperial electors gave for deposing Wenceslaus was his subservience to Giangaleazzo Visconti, especially his bestowing the title of the duke of Milan without any consultation with the German princes. Florence was overjoyed at the prospect of a new German ally who would oppose the duke of Milan coming soon to Italy to receive the imperial crown in Rome. Late in 1400 Francesco Novello dispatched his seneschal, the Gascon knight Dorde de Gaubert, as ambassador to Rupert's court, where negotiations for his descent into Italy were already taking place with Florentine envoys. Receiving a report on Dorde's visit on 17 June 1401, the Venetian Senate assured the Carrara lord of its esteem for Rupert and belief that his coming could bring peace and honor to Italy.⁵² In the same report, the Paduan envoy complained of the renewal of Giangaleazzo's efforts to divert the Brenta and Bacchiglione Rivers and submitted that such hostile actions entitled the Carrara lord to suspend payment of the annual tribute of 7,000 ducats. The Venetians replied that they were not yet certain of the Visconti lord's intentions, but in any case payment of indemnity was required by the treaty signed the year before. Dissatisfied with Venice's tepid response, the Carrara lord decided to strengthen his alliance with Florence while staking his hopes on Rupert's Italian expedition.

To aid in its planning Francesco Novello dispatched two of his ablest younger diplomats, both trained in law and letters, his cousin Francesco Buzzacarini and his son-in-law Ognibene Scola, to Rupert's court at Nuremberg. There the king of the Romans made an agreement with Florence's ambassadors to make his descent into Italy, starting from Augsburg that September, in return for a subsidy of 200,000 florins. But the threat of Giangaleazzo's army on his border working on the diversion of the Brenta made Francesco Novello impatient for action. In April the Carrara envoys again insisted before the Senate that the duke of Milan's bellicose acts made it reasonable for the lord of Padua to suspend payment of the indemnity, but Venice reiterated that observance of the recent peace obliged him to pay the tribute. In the summer Francesco Novello had written to the Florentine *signoria,* asking for help against the Visconti forces on his western frontier. Salutati replied that though the count of Virtù was working night and day to harm his neighbor, Florence had just committed three hundred lances to Pisa and could send no aid.[53] Deprived of any aid from Florence, the Carrara regime greeted the approach of Rupert's army with great enthusiasm that September.

Crossing into Italy at Trent, the king of the Romans and his forces were greeted by Francesco Novello, captain of a force of two thousand horsemen.[54] It was soon decided to attack Brescia, where friendly Guelf nobles had been allies with Florence and Padua since the Mantuan War. Hoping that an attack in eastern Lombardy would trigger uprisings against the Visconti regime, the large but poorly trained German army, supported by nine hundred Paduan *provisionati* and a thousand mounted men-at-arms under the command of Giacomo da Carrara, crossed into Lombardy in October. At Brescia, Giangaleazzo had marshaled his best troops, six thousand strong, under his ablest commanders, Facino Cane and Jacopo dal Verme. With the end of the campaigning season at hand, several German commanders had deserted the cause before reaching Brescia, while others complained of the lack of supplies and support. Finding Brescia heavily fortified and well manned, after a brief skirmish on 21 October, Rupert's forces withdrew to Trent, leaving the Visconti territories completely unharmed. Meanwhile, at Venice, Milanese envoys complained of the enormous costs of defending Lombardy from the German hordes, insisting that the Visconti lord had to impose new taxes of 375,000 ducats, of which only 200,000 had been paid. Asserting that the Carrara lord was the hostile party in this dispute, Milan asked Venice's support in bringing peace to northern Italy.[55]

Rupert's Italian expedition proved expensive, not only to his enemies but also for the military expenditures and costs of entertainment borne by his friends. After the embarrassing defeat at Brescia, some of the German captains returned home, while the remnants of Rupert's forces retreated to Trent, whence they made a long detour via Lienz and Friuli, reaching Padua on 18 November. There Rupert's army was received with great courtesy.

Francesco Novello

The royal party was greeted by Francesco Novello and lodged in the Reggia; other captains stayed with leading families of the Carrara affinity. The next day the king of the Romans was welcomed with great ceremony by Stefano da Carrara, acting as bishop of Padua, and on the 20th was received by the professors and students of the university, where Pietro Alvarotti made a speech in his honor.[56] Pietro lauded Rupert as the savior of Italy, that historical source of kings, dukes, even emperors, which long awaited his coming to bring peace and justice to the Roman state. Praising Rupert as the embodiment of the four cardinal virtues, Alvarotti concluded that the king of the Romans was especially welcomed by the learned men of the *studium* in this royal city of Padua, ruled by his imperial vicar Francesco da Carrara. On 10 December, Rupert and his retinue went on to Venice, greeted by the doge and council and sumptuously entertained. Meanwhile, the Florentine government sought news of the reasons for the disgrace at Brescia and of Rupert's future intentions.[57] Initially hopeful that Rupert would again attack the duke of Milan, as the months passed the Florentine *signoria* became aware of his uselessness, doling out meager subsidies to the remnants of his army left in winter quarters in Venice and Padua. When in March 1401 Florence refused requests for further aid, Rupert finally departed, in the words of a Milanese chronicler, "compelled to return empty-handed and shamefaced to Germany."[58] Short of funds and still under pressure from Giangaleazzo Visconti, Florence and the Carrara lord sought to shore up their old alliance with Bologna, the next target of Visconti aggression.

Divided by faction and on the verge of civil war at the end of the Trecento, Bologna was among the last of the Guelf cities to elude Giangaleazzo Visconti's grasp.[59] The Guelf and Ghibelline feuds of the early Trecento had crystallized into two factions: the Scacchesi, headed by Nanni Gozzadini and Giovanni Bentivoglio, drew their support from the guildsmen and artisans; the Maltraversi represented the more intractable magnates. Nominally under papal lordship, Bologna had achieved practical independence when Pope Boniface IX conferred the office of papal vicar on the chief magistrates of the communal government, the Gonfaloniere and Anziani. Early in 1399 both Scacchesi leaders, Nanni Gozzadini and Giovanni Bentivoglio, were exiled for their attempt to depose the ruling Gonfaloniere, Carlo Zambeccari, who was to die of the plague that summer. Returning to Bologna late in 1399, Nanni Gozzadini and Giovanni Bentivoglio became members of the Council of Sedici, competing for control of the city's government. Winning support of both the guildsmen and some of the Maltraversi and forging an alliance with Bologna's sometime enemy the lord of Faenza, Astorre Manfredi, Bentivoglio was able to drive Gozzadini from the city and was elected *Gonfaloniere perpetuo* and proclaimed lord in March

1401. Though aided by troops and subsidies from Giangaleazzo Visconti in becoming lord of the city, Bentivoglio maintained a policy of friendship with Venice and listened to Florence's overtures to renew the old Guelf alliance. By the summer of 1401, Bentivoglio was gravitating toward Florence, while asking Venice for help against the condottiere Alberico da Barbiano, the Visconti captain in Emilia. Though alarmed by Rupert's descent that autumn, after his victory at Brescia the Visconti lord could turn his full attention to defeating his two most powerful foes, Giovanni Bentivoglio, lord of Bologna, and Francesco da Carrara, lord of Padua.

Throughout the autumn of 1401, Giangaleazzo threatened Padua with raids on its western border and the project of damming the Brenta near Bassano. Venice repeatedly promised to aid the Carrara lord against Visconti incursions and permitted the transport of grain and munitions across its domains from the Romagna into the Padovano.[60] Preoccupied with Visconti threats on his frontier and the expensive, increasingly fruitless stay of the king of the Romans, Francesco Novello paid little heed to pleas from his allies Florence and Bologna. As we have seen, in 1396 Florence was forced to turn over Castrocaro near Forlì to garrisons supplied by the lords of Mantua and Padua but maintained at Florence's expense. Pressing military needs coupled with the disruption of the plague caused Florence to beseech the Gonzaga and Carrara lords to reduce the size of their garrison in Castrocaro, or, better still, hand the stronghold over to Florence.[61] This the lord of Padua refused to do, until its garrison was paid in full, as stipulated in the original agreement. Alarmed that the fortress was held by Francesco Gonzaga, now a Visconti ally, late in 1401 Florence insisted that the soldiers' stipends had been paid and the garrison should evacuate Castrocaro. But early in January 1402, the Paduans still garrisoned the fortress under command of Bernardo Valvasone, who was instructed not to leave Castrocaro until Florence had paid its debts.[62]

Threatened by a growing army of Bolognese exiles under Visconti captains, in January 1402 Giovanni Bentivoglio requested that Padua's *provisionati* be sent to Bologna. But Francesco Novello refused, citing the presence of Visconti troops under Alberico da Barbiano on his own border. At the end of January, Francesco ordered Giacomo Scaltanigo, his commander at the frontier fortress at Castelbaldo on the Veronese frontier, to bring in men and stockpile supplies, bracing for a Visconti attack. At the same time, he commanded his podestà at Monselice and Montagnana, Giovanni Parisino Mezzoconti and Tommaso da Mantova, to prepare for hostilities by removing flammables, such as straw and thatch, from their citadels and bringing in more supplies. Dissatisfied with the poor quality of mercenaries under Muzio Attendolo Sforza which Florence had enrolled to guard Lendinara,

Francesco Novello demanded repeatedly that Florence pay off and transfer these troops, who had been foraging the western Padovano for provisions while awaiting their back pay.[63] Aware of his own perilous status, in the middle of January Francesco Novello appeared in person before the doge and council to ask for more troops and a month later received the promise that Venice would hire three hundred lances for his defense. Hiring companies totaling four hundred lances under Filippo da Pisa and Gherardo Boiardo at 15 ducats per lance per month, Venice sent the new troops to defend the Paduan frontier at Montagnana and Castelbaldo and its own strongholds in the Polesine.[64]

The Carrara lord's state of mind as he prepared for an attack from Giangaleazzo early in February can be gauged from a letter to his sister Caterina, the widowed countess of Veglia, occasioned by the betrothal of her daughter Elisabeth to Frederick, count of Cilli, partisan of the deposed Wenceslaus. Francesco would clearly have had his niece marry a political ally, but he had no say in the matter. He stressed the dangers presented by the duke of Milan, with his work at Bassano of diverting the Brenta and raids into the Padovano, and the help he expected from King Rupert and his ally Henry IV of England, who was rumored to be sending four thousand knights and four thousand archers to help the Guelf cause in Italy.[65] While the dangers were real, the solutions were fanciful, consistent with the mistaken hope the lord of Padua continued to place in the chimaera of Rupert's power. A more sensible response to Visconti aggression was the order issued on 1 March that all subjects must return within the Paduan frontiers for their own protection, followed the next day by refusal to send saltpeter and bombards requested by Giovanni Bentivoglio for the defense of Bologna, citing his own needs against the Visconti threat.[66] On 4 March, Francesco Novello ordered his factor Donato Linaroli to liquidate all debts in Venice and appointed Paolo Lion his proctor even to sell his Venetian palace on the Grand Canal, the Ca' Corner, to raise money for the war effort.[67] Strapped for cash, the Carrara lord had to look after his own security before he could fulfill obligations to allies, much less his own dreams of territorial aggrandizement.

The spring of 1402 was spent trying to juggle those competing goals. The arrival in March at Mestre of the three hundred lances hired by Venice bolstered the lord of Padua's spirits, as did the pillaging of Visconti domains by Guelfs from Brescia later that month. As Rupert's return to Germany became certain at the end of March, the Carrara lord withdrew his two ambassadors, Enrico Gallo and Luca Lion, from the papal court in Rome. Indeed, Rupert's departure freed Visconti troops on the Paduan frontier for transfer to Bologna. With Bolognese exiles swelling the Milanese army encamped outside Bologna, on 16 April their commander, Francesco Gonzaga, issued a declaration of war to Giovanni Bentivoglio, accusing him of crimes against his own people. The lord of Bologna responded in kind, preparing for the final struggle.[68] Besought by Florence to honor his commitment to the league and send troops to Bologna, Francesco Novello turned to the Venetian Senate for permission and advice. In its deliberations on the 18th, the Senate stressed that Venice was always dedicated to the preservation of the Carrara lord's state but advised caution in breaking the peace with the duke of Milan. Five days later, Paduan ambassadors again asked permission to dispatch four hundred *provisionati* to the defense of Bologna. After much deliberation and three ballots, the Senate finally granted permission to send aid to Bologna by the narrow margin of 60 to 42 with 16 abstentions.[69] Advised by his Venetian agent Ermanno of the Senate's vote, the Carrara lord wrote to his son-in-law Niccolò III d'Este, demanding safe-conduct for the troops and supplies that he was sending to Bologna, and informed Giovanni Bentivoglio of his support, stressing the ability of the Breton mercenary Bernardon de Serres, recently enlisted by Florence to head the defense of the city.[70]

Several events undermined the Carrara lord's capacity to act in defense of Bologna. Giangaleazzo Visconti had already removed Francesco Gonzaga from the league, while he extended his influence in the Romagna, enlisting the Malatesta and Polenta as his allies. Thus, when the Carrara envoys, returning by ship from their mission to Rome, were blown ashore by storms on the Adriatic, they were detained by Obizzo da Polenta, lord of Ravenna. Efforts by Venice to free these valued advisers, Enrico Gallo and Luca Lion, were ignored for several months by the lord of Ravenna, who was loath to offend Giangaleazzo Visconti. That spring the duke of Milan renewed the construction of the dam on the Brenta at Bassano, designed to divert the river, stopping commerce to Padua. Finally, Giangaleazzo cultivated the friendship of the young marquis of Ferrara, attempting to wean him from his dependence on Padua and Venice, which tried without success to stop Niccolò III from allowing provisions to cross his domain for Visconti forces at Bologna.[71] Early in May the cream of Padua's nobility, perhaps fifteen hundred knights, accompanied by the four hundred *provisionati*, left for Bologna under the nominal command of the heir apparent, Francesco III da Carrara. Aware of the dangers posed by the large Visconti army, Francesco Novello tried to augment those forces and instructed his ambassadors in Venice to argue for service in Bologna of two hundred of the lances the Serenissima had contributed for the defense of Padua.

Early in June Venice's threat of war with the lord of Ravenna finally secured release of the hostages Enrico Gallo and Luca Lion, who were dispatched for service in Bologna. Meanwhile, Francesco Novello kept alive the hope that Rupert would return to save his Italian allies and asked his nephew Rudolf III, duke of Saxony, son of his widowed eldest sister, Duchess Gigliola, to intercede to enlist the aid of the king of the Romans.[72] Alerted on 13 June by an agent of the need for more troops to defend Bologna, now encircled by the Visconti army, the next day Francesco Novello presented his case for sending two hundred crossbowmen to Bologna before the Senate. Venice continued to refuse direct aid against the Visconti lord, which would have broken its nominal neutrality. Francesco Novello was very anxious for the safety of his sons trapped in Bologna, ordering them in letters sent in the middle of June to stay protected by their own troops, near the commander Bernardon de Serres, no matter what happened, and promising to send additional soldiers under the command of Ludovico Buzzacarini.[73]

A week later Francesco Novello wrote to Doge Michele Steno full of news, good and bad. A report that Niccolò d'Este's first minister, Uguccione Contrari, was threatening to close the frontiers and seize the strongholds of Ferrara as a Visconti ally turned out to be false, as did the belief that the king of the Romans was returning to Italy. More accurate was the Carrara lord's report that marriage negotiations with the lord of Camerino were proceeding smoothly and that he had sent his councillor Enrico Gallo to Bologna.[74] But only a week later, the lord of Padua's worse fears proved justified. Low on supplies and cut off from water, on 26 June the allied forces marched from Bologna and gave battle to the Milanese army at Casalecchio, a beachhead on the Reno outside the walls. The Visconti forces under Jacopo dal Verme, aided by troops under Francesco Gonzaga and Pandolfo Malatesta and Bolognese exiles under Bente Bentivoglio, were completely victorious, taking more than two thousand prisoners and entering Bologna the next day. Giovanni Bentivoglio was hunted down, captured, and later executed by his enemies; his body was stripped naked and lay for three days before the altar of S. Giacomo.[75] Informed of the disaster, including the capture of his sons and the whole Paduan contingent, Francesco Novello instructed the podestà of his strongholds at Montagnana and Castelbaldo to stockpile provisions and increase their garrisons.

Fearful of the execution of his sons and an impending attack on Padua, the Carrara lord sought aid from any quarter, sending pleas for help to King Rupert; Stephen, duke of Bavaria; Rodolfo da Varano, lord of Camerino; and the doge at Venice.[76] Writing to the doge on 2 July, Francesco Novello remarked grimly (with only some exaggeration) "that the city of Bologna has changed regimes three times in two days: because after the murder of the lord of Bologna, the people made the Anziani rulers, and after that the soldiers of the Duke of Milan dismissed the Anziani, and claimed the city in the name of the Duke himself."⁷⁷ Broken in spirit and fearful of defeat, the lord of Padua willingly entered negotiations for peace at Venice and named his three best diplomats, Michele Rabatta, Pietro Alvarotti, and Paolo Lion, as envoys to appear before the doge and Senate "to treat for peace or alliance or truce or agreement with the illustrious and mighty lord, Giangaleazzo Visconti."⁷⁸ At the same time, Venice abandoned its policy of neutrality and openly aided the Paduan cause, releasing Conte da Carrara's *brigata* of three hundred lances for service in defense of his half brother's state and enlisting several smaller mercenary companies. But the attack on Padua or Tuscany expected after the fall of Bologna never materialized. The Visconti commanders were happy to go their separate ways, more concerned with ransoming wealthy captives than prosecuting the war.

The famed condottiere Facino Cane took under his personal custody a number of Paduans, including Enrico Gallo, Luca and Francesco Lion, Ludovico Buzzacarini, and Francesco III da Carrara, whom he transported first to Modena and then to Parma. Poorly guarded at Parma, young Francesco da Carrara made his escape and, after a series of adventures, arrived safe in Padua on 13 July. Greeted joyfully by his father, after a few days of recuperation, the young lord was sent to join in the peace talks being held in Venice. By the end of the month Francesco III was well enough to write a cheeky letter to his aunt Caterina, widowed countess of Veglia, asking for the gift of a horse, claiming, "All my horses and those of my magnificent father have been lost in the battle [of Casalecchio]."⁷⁹ Another of Francesco Novello's sons, Stefano, prospered, gaining papal approval as administrator of the Diocese of Padua and on 2 September election as bishop after his agent in Rome had agreed to pay 2,500 florins to the Apostolic Camera and the College of Cardinals and another 2,500 florins owed by his two predecessors.⁸⁰ Francesco III's escape and Stefano's success in Rome were followed by the news of the rupture of Giangaleazzo's dam across the Brenta at Bassano early in August, destroying much property and killing many of the workers.

A more closely guarded secret was Giangaleazzo's fever, contracted in Bologna in the middle of August, which was to cause his death on 3 September. At first incredulous and then overjoyed at the news of the demise of his archenemy, Francesco Novello overworked his chancery dispatching news of the event to friends and rulers, far and wide, on the 6th to Florence, Venice, and the king of the Romans and a few days later to the patriarch of Aquileia, the archbishop of Salzburg, and a dozen German princes.⁸¹ From Florence on the 13th, Salutati wrote in a sobering letter: "Indeed it is true that since the Duke of Milan has paid his debt to nature, we now hope for peace in Italy for many years. But we recognize that we must work for this, lest when the Viper's seed will have matured, we fall into the same danger."[82] The fighting halted for a month to allow for Giangaleazzo's elaborate funeral in Milan.

There a Council of Regency, composed of leading captains and statesmen, was established to advise his widow, Caterina Visconti, and two young sons, Giovanni Maria and Filippo Maria. The Visconti state was under great pressure, with rivalries among the mercenary companies, heavy taxes for war, and the restive populations of Lombard cities all undermining the authority of Giangaleazzo's widow and the Regents. Florence worked at expelling the Visconti regimes from Tuscany, hoping by diplomacy to oust Milanese rulers from Pisa, Siena, and Perugia. The Carrara lord sought to gain control of eastern Lombardy and in September launched an attack on Brescia which was repulsed by the rapid deployment of troops under Jacopo dal Verme. With Florence preoccupied with Tuscan affairs and Vicenza and Verona still under Visconti rule, at the urging of Venice, the Carrara lord decided to negotiate peace. According to the chronicler Galeazzo Gatari, Francesco Novello's initial demands were very high: cession of the cities of Vicenza, Bassano, Belluno, and Feltre, canceling of the annual tribute, and payment of an indemnity of 80,000 florins. But in the negotiations that took place that autumn between Caterina Visconti and the Regents with Paduan representatives Enrico Gallo and Ognibene Scola, these demands were reduced to a more modest settlement.[83] The peace treaty reached in Pavia on 7 December 1402 provided for an immediate end to hostilities and the forgiveness of any past injuries, especially those committed by Francesco Gonzaga while in Visconti service. The annual indemnity was not eliminated but reduced to 3,000 ducats, while prisoners were to be exchanged, exiles returned, and trade resumed as before. Other pacts with Wenceslaus, Rupert, and Venice were still valid, and the entire treaty was to be ratified within a month. Since there were no provisions for the cession of territory or stoppage of Visconti work on the Brenta, the treaty marked more a truce than peace, destined to be broken within the next year.

As we have seen, many prisoners taken at Casalecchio were ransomed or escaped before the end of hostilities. Giacomo da Carrara, who was closely guarded in captivity under Francesco Gonzaga at Mantua, managed to escape that autumn, reaching Padua at the end of November. His departure without his captor's permission brought a torrent of abuse from the lord of Mantua, which the Carrara chancery returned in kind, accusing Gonzaga and his councillors of acting like clothmongers (*revenditrices*), market women (*treche*), and foot soldiers (*pedites*).[84] Francesco Gonzaga's demand that Giacomo honor his word and return to captivity in Mantua went unheeded, as the Carrara lord sought to cement an alliance with Rodolfo da Varano, lord of Camerino, by finally marrying Giacomo to his daughter Belfiore. Working through the good offices of Conte da Carrara, Francesco Novello had been negotiating the marriage alliance since early in 1402. The wedding, which was to have taken place in the summer of 1402, was delayed only because of Giacomo's service in Bologna. On 18 June the Maggior Consiglio had authorized the use of a large ship to transport Giacomo and his retinue to Camerino; on the 23th Francesco Novello had notified the bride's father, Rodolfo, that Giacomo was preparing to leave Bologna for Padua, accompanied by Francesco Buzzacarini; and on the 26th the Venetian Senate appointed two envoys to attend the ceremony, bearing wedding gifts of luxury clothes and jewels, worth 130 ducats.[85] But on that very day Giacomo was captured at Casalecchio, prompting Francesco Novello to send Rodolfo news of the disaster. Later, in the middle of August, a plea for help in securing his son's release was sent.[86] With Giacomo's safe return to Padua at the end of 1402, plans could now go forward for the long-awaited wedding, which took place in Camerino early in February. Thence, the wedding party traveled north on a galley provided by Venice to Chioggia, where the bride and groom were greeted by Francesco III da Carrara and Niccolò III d'Este. Proceeding by ship through Bovolenta to Ponte S. Niccolò, the couple was greeted at the gates of Padua by the notables of the Carrara affinity, who celebrated the marriage with feasts and jousts.[87] Since Francesco Novello had lost all influence over his eldest son's father-in-law, Francesco Gonzaga, he hoped that Giacomo's marriage to Belfiore da Varano would secure an ally in the Marches, as he planned to attack Visconti garrisons in the Veneto.

That April a new anti-Visconti league was formed, comprising France, Florence, Pope Boniface IX, and the lords of Padua and Ferrara, with young Niccolò III d'Este serving as the captain general of its armed forces. Francesco Novello now seized the opportunity to realize his dream of creating a large territorial state stretching from the Adige to the Alps, from the Mincio to the lagoon, and he began to assemble a force of mercenaries and native soldiers to accomplish the task.[88] In the meantime, Venice's government grew alarmed at the Carrara lord's reckless use of his new power. Meeting on 17 June 1403, the Maggior Consiglio decided to issue a warning to Francesco Novello, voting to withdraw all Venetian officials from Padua, now declared a land of tyrants, repeating the 1356 statute, which had marked the beginning of Venice's hostility toward the Carrara dynasty nearly half a century earlier.[89] In this act Venice forbade any of its citizens to receive gifts, lands, or fiefs from any mainland lord, limiting contact with the Carrara and the possibility of corruption. Thus, Antonio Bembo became the last Venetian podestà of Carrara Padua, with Andrea Vettore of Florence assuming the office in October. Venice hoped to curb the ambitions of the Carrara lord by having him follow its own policy of peace and accommodation of Visconti interests. But the threats posed by the Genoese fleet in the Levant under the command of Marshal Boucicault limited, for the moment, Venice's capacity to act in the *terraferma*. Aware of Venice's distractions and hoping to enlist the Carrara lord's aid, Salutati sent a letter on 6 June 1403 calling for the extinction of Ghibelline power and (using a favorite metaphor) checking the Viper's ambition.[90] Empowered by his league with Florence and Ferrara and encouraged by Rupert writing from Heidelberg, the lord of Padua acted on his desire for revenge.[91] On 11 August 1403 he declared war on the duchess of Milan.

Francesco Novello's claims of past wrongs and present dangers posed by the Visconti were set forth in an arrogant letter composed by Pier Paolo Vergerio, then tutor at the Carrara court.[92] The lord of Padua assured Caterina Visconti that the uprisings against her rule that summer in several Lombard cities—Lodi, Cremona, and Parma—would destroy her regime, and he went on to claim that she had repeatedly broken the terms of the recent peace, continuing to dam the Brenta at Bassano and inflicting other wrongs. Since the duchess of Milan had refused to convey the cities of Belluno, Feltre, and Bassano, which everyone knew belonged to the Carrara dynasty, the lord of Padua had no recourse but to go to war to protect his legitimate rights and interests. The next day Francesco Novello left Padua with his son-in-law Niccolò III d'Este at the head of an army of four hundred lances and hundreds of *provisionati,* entering the Veronese on the 16th and investing Brescia on the 21st.[93] Within a few days, the allied forces had driven the small garrison into the citadel of Brescia, only to face a large relieving army from Milan of more than four thousand lances, under command of Jacopo dal Verme. The Paduan forces withdrew in hasty retreat, while Francesco Novello sent Bonifacio Guarnerini on a futile embassy to Bolzano to enlist aid from Duke Albert of Austria.

Upset by the sudden reversal of fortune, the Carrara lord called for a brief truce, regrouped his demoralized troops in Padua, and early in October even contemplated peace, appointing Enrico Gallo and Luca Lion his envoys to negotiate with Caterina Visconti and her sons in Milan.[94] Meanwhile, Venice continued to caution the Carrara lord to live at peace with the duchess of Milan. At the end of the year, Salutati, writing for Florence, assured Francesco Novello of its continuing cooperation and asked his support in bringing about the ruin of the Visconti state.[95] Now bent on territorial aggrandizement in the Veneto, the Carrara lord was on a collision course with Venice. As border skirmishes with Visconti garrisons in the Veronese matured into plans to seize Vicenza and Verona the next spring, war with Venice had become inevitable.

The Final Struggle with Venice, 1403–1405

Elated with news of the victory of its forces over the Genoese fleet off Modone in the autumn of 1403, the Venetian government was now free to wage war in the *terraferma*.[96] Still, the *signoria* would have preferred a peaceful settlement. Early in 1404 the Senate dispatched two envoys, Carlo Zen and Gabriele Emo, to the lord of Padua, offering to mediate peace with the duchess of Milan, especially in view of the four thousand cavalry she had sent into the Veronese under the command of Pandolfo Malatesta and Facino Cane. But hopeful of support from Florence and King Rupert, Francesco Novello continued preparing to conquer Verona and Vicenza, creating a league with Niccolò III d'Este and recalling from Venice the pretender to the lordship of Verona, Guglielmo della Scala, who had served a term as the podestà of Padua the year before. The illegitimate son of Cangrande II, Guglielmo was the logical candidate for the restoration of Scaliger rule in Verona, since he had two sons, Antonio and Brunoro, to carry on his line.[97] On 27 March a pact was concluded with Francesco Novello at Padua for the dismemberment of the Visconti dominions in eastern Lombardy: Verona was to go to the Della Scala lords, and the Carrara lord was to receive Vicenza and its contado and the land near Legnago. On 30 March 1403, Easter Sunday, the combined Paduan and Ferrarese forces, with some Veronese exiles, marched out of Padua, with Guglielmo della Scala, gravely ill with fever, following behind in a cart.

The campaign to conquer Verona was short, swift, and very successful.[98] The city was garrisoned by only a few Milanese troops under Ugolotto Biancardo, and its populace was tired of Visconti rule and eager for change. A week after leaving Padua the allied army arrived outside Verona, where under cover of darkness a few troops scaled the city walls near the Campo Marzo and opened the gates to the forces outside. On the morning of 8 April the city fell to the allied army, with Ugolotto Biancardo and his garrison retreating to the Cittadella. Two days later, the ailing Guglielmo della Scala was proclaimed lord of the city but died a week later amid rumors that the Carraresi had poisoned him. But since Guglielmo was very sick even before the start of the campaign, that charge seems unlikely. He was succeeded by his sons, Brunoro and Antonio, though the effective control of Verona was in the hands of the Paduan commander, Francesco III da Carrara. Leaving the Della Scala brothers to starve out the Visconti troops trapped in the Cittadella, the Paduan army marched out to take Vicenza.

Fearful of just these events, early in March the duchess of Milan had sent Jacopo dal Verme and the exiled Paduan Enrico Scrovegni as envoys to ask Venice to mediate peace with the lord of Padua or, failing that, to convey the cities of Verona and Vicenza to the Serenissima for a price. The Venetian Senate temporized, debating the merits of different courses of action, reluctant to become involved in mainland wars. The Carrara conquest of Verona, however, had alarmed the rulers of Venice, and the clear interest of the people of Vicenza in submitting to Venice, rather than the hated Carraresi, flattered Venetian political sensibility.[99] As the fall of Verona became certain, the Senate toyed with the duchess's offer to sell Vicenza for 60,000 ducats. But the purchase proved unnecessary, since on 12 April Vicentine envoys offered to surrender their city to Venice in return for protection against the would-be Carrara lords. While, at the end of April, the Venetian Senate was forestalling Paduan envoys with words of peace and fatherly affection, Venice's envoys were also negotiating the surrender of Vicenza to its chosen representatives. On 25 April 250 Venetian crossbowmen under the command of Giacomo Suriano entered Vicenza, raising the banner of S. Marco and claiming the city for the Serenissima. On 1 May representatives of the commune of Vicenza swore fealty to Venice and two weeks later conveyed its terms of dedition, receiving confirmation of its rights and privileges in return. Outside the walls of Vicenza, Francesco III fumed at the loss of the promised city, ordering the execution of the herald who bore news of Venice's lordship under a flag of truce. Paduan demands for justice in the matter of Vicenza received replies of icy condescension from the Venetian Senate, reminding the Carrara lord's ambassadors that the Vicentines were happy under Venetian rule and had freely given their city to Venice, warning him to lift his siege and trouble them no more.[100] Looking for a scapegoat, Francesco Novello ordered the arrest of Antonio and Brunoro della Scala for refusing to release their forces to help in the siege of Vicenza. Giacomo da Carrara invited the Scaliger brothers to dinner on the feast of Pentecost (18 May) and had them seized and conveyed for confinement in the Rocca at Monselice. Four days later, Francesco Novello arrived to accept the lordship of Verona, having to be content with taking only a fraction of the former Visconti dominions on his borders.

Meanwhile, Venice took over from Caterina Visconti control of Bassano on the Brenta and Belluno and Feltre on the Piave, which at once protected its trade routes into Germany and deprived the Carrara lord of three coveted towns on his northern frontier. As tensions rose, Niccolò III d'Este offered to serve as mediator between Venice and the lord of Padua. While Francesco Novello scrambled to find allies in Florence, Genoa, and Germany, Venice resolved to fight its upstart neighbor to the finish, equipping the Po fleet and raising an army to bring the war to Padua. Since Venice had made peace with Genoa earlier in April, it was at last free to turn its full might against Padua. In its reply of 2 June 1404 to a Florentine legation sent to ask for peace, the Senate drew up a lengthy rationale for war. The Venetian government now accused Francesco Novello of ingratitude and duplicity and underlined how much treasure and blood Venice had expended in the past on the preservation of Carrara rule in Padua. The Senate argued for the justice of its dominion over Vicenza and against the lord of Padua's unjust claims to Bassano, Belluno, and Feltre. Moving to recent events, the reply described the cruel murder of its unarmed herald at Vicenza and the unwarranted siege of Cologna Veneta, which was part of Vicenza's contado. In short, Venice's Senate asserted that the lord of Padua's "ingratitude and inconstancy have given us most just cause to enlist in our pay men-at-arms, cavalry and infantry, for the preservation of our honor."[101] Ordering its commander at Rovigo, Francesco Giustinian, to cut the dikes on the Adige at Anguillara and thus flood the southern Padovano, Venice declared war on the lord and commune of Padua on 25 June 1404, committing itself to a fight to the finish.

The war began with the usual closing of frontiers and garrisoning of border strongholds. Initial skirmishes were favorable to the Paduan cause, whose forces repulsed attacks at Oriago, Gambarare, and Gorgo on the eastern frontier. In the western theater, the troops of Jacopo dal Verme were defeated outside Verona and those of Venice's ally Francesco Gonzaga at Peschiera. In September Niccolò III d'Este sharply rejected Venice's call for negotiation and alliance, affirming that he was bound by friendship and blood to the lord of Padua, who, in any case, was not at fault in the present conflict.[102] Emboldened by these initial successes, the lord of Ferrara attacked Venice's strongholds in the Polesine, sending a ripple of alarm through the Ducal Council and Senate. In retaliation, Venice recalled Azzone d'Este from exile in Crete and replaced its ineffective commander Malatesta Malatesta with the popular Roman condottiere Paolo Savelli.

That fall Venice stationed large mercenary companies under Jacopo dal Verme, Francesco Gonzaga, and Ottobuono Terzi in the Valpolicella, with instructions to burn and ravish the Veronese countryside, bringing terror to the peasants, nominally under Carrara protection. Repulsed at Limina near the Vicentine frontier in September, Paolo Savelli moved the main Venetian army before Camponogara, occupying that town in November and moving to attack Ronchi. Driven back by troops under the command of Francesco III, Savelli invested the defenses of Piove di Sacco. When Francesco Novello ordered his troops to counterattack late in December, the Romagnol condottiere Manfredi da Barbiano refused. Perhaps already in Venice's pay, Manfredi was charged with treason and dismissed, only to join Venetian forces that winter.

The loss of Piove di Sacco marked the turning point in the war. Thereafter, the Carrara forces were on the defensive, fighting from strongholds in the Padovano and Veronese. The Venetian forces were swelled by the arrival of Azzone d'Este with troops from Candia in October and the hiring of Obizzo da Polenta and his mercenary company in December. At the end of 1404, the Senate bolstered the morale of its troops by putting a price on the head of the Carrara lord and his sons, promising a reward of 10,000 ducats, with a life annuity of 1,000 ducats, for the capture of Francesco Novello and 6,000 ducats with 500 a year for each of his sons.[103] At the beginning of 1405, the Venetian government combined diplomacy, bribery, terror, and war to bring about the fall of the Carrara.[104]

The death of the ruling lord's consort, Taddea d'Este, in Padua on 3 November 1404 weakened the already tenuous relations with the young lord of Ferrara. Further reverses early in 1405 convinced Niccolò III that the Paduan cause was hopeless, and he sent envoys to Venice late in February to negotiate a separate peace.[105] The terms set by Venice were aimed at restoring the status quo: frontiers were to be the same as before the war, and all strongholds taken in the Polesine were to be turned over to Venice, with no further aid sent to the Carrara. The harshest penalty, an indemnity of 100,000 ducats to pay for Venice's war expenses, was, in the end, canceled. By the end of March Niccolò III had been effectively removed from the alliance, leaving Francesco Novello to face Venice's might alone.

Since the start of the war the lord of Padua had sought aid from his traditional allies. Florence, however, was too concerned with removing Visconti regimes from Tuscany and the conquest of Pisa to pay more than lip service to Padua's pleas for help. Hopeful of eliciting aid from Genoa's patron the king of France, Francesco Novello sent his finest orator, Francesco Zabarella, to Paris late in 1404, pleading on behalf of the lord and commune of Padua with King Charles VI to honor the old alliances between his state and Genoa.[106] In January Francesco Novello appointed two envoys, Gherardo Boiardo and the canon lawyer Giovanni Ubaldini, abbot of S. Maria di Praglia, to form an alliance with the pretender to the Hungarian throne, King Ladislaus of Naples, and the next month he made Enrico Gallo his proctor to conclude pacts with any and all friendly powers. On 25 April 1405, the lord of Padua appointed Bonifacio Guarnerini his agent to procure a loan of 20,000 ducats from Genoa and enlist the mercenary captain Alberico da

Barbiano in his service, but in May Venice bid higher, enrolling the condottiere with eight hundred lances and three hundred foot for three months' service.[107] But Genoese pleas for Venice to make peace fell on deaf ears in the Senate. As all of Francesco Novello's diplomatic ploys failed, Venice's military campaign against Padua grew ever stronger.[108]

By the late spring of 1405 Venice's scorched-earth policy in the Veronese was having its desired effect. Local peasants were angry with the Carrara rulers, who had proved incapable of protecting the lives and property of their subjects in the countryside. By early May Venetian forces reached the walls of Verona itself, beginning a bombardment of the city early in June. Realizing the situation was hopeless, a committee of Veronese notables handed the city over to the Venetian commander Jacopo dal Verme, with Giacomo da Carrara and his Paduan garrison taking refuge in the Cittadella. On 22 June Gabriele Emo and Francesco Gonzaga took possession of Verona in the name of Venice. A few days later young Giacomo da Carrara and Paolo Lion escaped from Verona, only to be captured near Legnago and taken to prison in Venice.

Faced with the loss of Verona and its contado, Francesco Novello also had to cope with treachery from within. That spring the Senate had authorized its agents to negotiate with the ruling lord's half brother Giacomo da Carrara for the surrender of Padua, with a reward of 1,000 ducats if the city was taken and an annuity of 50 ducats for his efforts. But Giacomo's sons Antonio and Bonifacio informed Francesco Novello of their father's treason, and he was arrested and executed. Meanwhile, as plague raged and famine threatened in Padua, Venetian forces besieged the strongholds of the contado. Castelcarro fell at the end of May; Bovolenta a week later. Desperate for the safety of his family, Francesco Novello sent Stefano da Carrara and all his younger offspring to Florence, where they arrived destitute early in June. Recognizing the ancient devotion of the House of Carrara for the commune of Florence, the *signoria* voted a subsidy of 600 florins to be paid over the next six months, so that the Carrara children could meet the cost of food and housing.[109] When the fall of Verona placed Giacomo da Carrara in Venetian custody and with an army at the gates of Padua, Francesco Novello began to consider abdication.

In July Paduan agents suggested to the Senate that the Carrara lord was ready to sell Padua to Venice for 50,000 ducats, with continued enjoyment of his Paduan property and safe-conduct to Ferrara. This brought a mixed reaction in the Venetian Senate, with hard-liners, such as Niccolò Foscari, holding out for unconditional surrender. As the Venetian army approached the city walls late in August, Francesco Novello send Luca Lion to discuss with the Venetian *provveditore* Carlo Zen terms for his abdication: 50,000 ducats for Padua, liberation of Giacomo da Carrara and Paolo Lion imprisoned in Venice, safe-conduct and transport of all his munitions and moveables from Padua to Ferrara, confirmation of his sales and gifts to favorites over the past fifteen years, continued ownership of land in the Padovano, and Venice's promise to respect the commune of Padua's ancient rights and customs. After hearing explanations by Carlo Zen and Luca Lion, on 26 August the Senate voted overwhelmingly to accept Francesco Novello's offer. Carlo Zen even volunteered to take the favorable response back to Padua and negotiate a settlement.[110] But it turned out that the offer was a hoax. Carlo Zen was in the pay of the lord of Padua, as he played for time, hoping for a miracle.

That summer Francesco Novello prepared for his final defense by selling all his property to supporters and clients just as he had to raise cash in the autumn of 1388. But this time Carrara wealth was much reduced, the buyers were few, and, according to later Venetian estimates, Carrara real estate was sold for perhaps a sixth of its true value. Thus, the sales of 1405 netted much less cash that those of 1388.[111] Carrara resistance crumbled that autumn, with the surrender of Este and Montagnana followed by the fall of Camposampiero, Cittadella, Castelbaldo, and Monselice. Not even the death of the popular commander Paolo Savelli early in October could stop the momentum of Venice's campaign. Enlisting the aid of Paduan exiles who had been persecuted by Francesco Novello since his restoration, such as the da Peraga, Scrovegni, Sanguinacci, and Niccolò da Lazara, the Venetian commanders brought up bombards and munitions for the final assault. Concentrating their forces at S. Croce and Ognissanti, the Venetian captains had their engineers construct trenches to undermine the walls. Reminding the Paduans how brutally Venice had crushed rebellions at Zara and Candia within living memory, the Venetian commanders called for immediate surrender. When Padua was about to fall into Venetian hands, on 18 November Francesco Novello entered the enemy camp to negotiate the surrender of Padua and his own freedom. Meanwhile, his erstwhile supporters, including Francesco Dotti and Fredo Malizia, raised the banner of S. Marco in the city, calling for death to the Carrara. Convinced the cause was hopeless, a board of six ambassadors for the Paduan commune surrendered their city to Venice, hoping to obtain the best possible terms from the Senate. Francesco Novello and his eldest son, Francesco III, were arrested and brought to Venice to join Giacomo in captivity.

Ambition and Destruction

Epilogue: The Extinction of the House of Carrara

Venice had achieved another "bloodless" victory. Meeting on 27 November 1405, by unanimous vote the Maggior Consiglio proclaimed a general thanksgiving for the great triumph over Padua. All prisoners with less than a year to serve were set free, and the rest had one year deducted from their sentences, excepting those who had been condemned for political crimes by the Council of Ten.[112] The three Carrara lords were brought before the Council of Ten, tried, and convicted of treason against the state. Venice's argument was that since the Carrara lords were Venetian citizens, members of its nobility and of the Great Council, the declaration of war of 1404 had violated their oath of fidelity and, hence, Francesco Novello, with his sons, was to be treated as "our rebel and traitor" [rebellem et proditorem nostrum].[113] The councils of the Venetian government debated the proper punishment. Jacopo dal Verme, who had fought the Carraresi in many battles and several wars, argued for their execution, because they were ambitious and able men who could always raise another army and always try to build another state. The government agreed, and the stage was set for the ultimate sanction. Andrea Gatari has vividly reconstructed the final scene:[114]

> [Dal Verme's] advice was adopted by the Council of Ten which decreed that the Carrara lord and his sons must die. The Signoria sent for Fra Zuan Benedetto, an old servant of God, so that the Carrara lord could confess his sins, and the friar was ordered to go to the prison and announce his fate to the lord. And this he did, and when the Carrara lord heard he spoke these words: "Why do I have to die? Isn't it bad enough that you've taken my lordship and my lands and goods and thrown me unjustly into prison with my sons, and threaten my life? I am in your power and you can do with me as you wish. And still if you really want, you can stop this from happening." But Fra Zuan Benedetto simply comforted him and confessed his sins once more and had him devoutly receive the blessed body of Christ. With the lord shedding many tears, the friar left. When he had left, into the prison entered two men from the Council of Ten, two heads of the Forty, and two Ducal Councillors with many others, including Bernardo Priuli with about twenty cutthroats. And then the door of the Carrara lord's cell was opened, and in came Bernardo Priuli with his followers. And the lord put up a great defense against them. But with great force, they beat him with clubs on his feet and arms, and pushed him around, and stripped off his clothes, and hit him in the face and on the head. And they threw him to the ground, hitting and punching him as he lay there. And they wound a double cord around his throat and strangled him with such force that his soul departed his body, and in that way [the Carrara lord] ended his life.

FIG. 35. *Defaced* carro *stemma, Gate of Castelfranco. Photograph courtesy of Judith C. Kohl*

The next day the two sons were also executed and buried secretly. The *signoria* circulated a rumor that the Carraresi had died of natural causes. The old proverb attached to the demise of the family—dead men don't make wars—suggests that contemporaries knew the truth. Venice now embarked on the creation of a *terraferma* state that was to alter its own destiny. The Carrara dynasty had been removed from power. Its despised and feared *carro* was stricken from the monuments of the former Carrara domains, to be revived in moments of rebellion over the next century as the defiant emblem of an independence that Padua had lost forever.

APPENDIXES

Appendix 1

Contrade of Padua (1320) and Villages of the Padovano (1281)

PART I.
Census of Padua in 1320

Neighborhood	Families	Men	Citizens (+ minors)
QUARTER OF DUOMO			
Centenario Duomo	56	—	7 (+ 8)
S. Prosdocimo to S. Benedetto	65	—	9 (+ 2)
S. Prosdocimo to Ponte Tadi	31	—	13
Ponte Tadi to Ponte S. Giovanni	27	—	2 (+ 2)
Ponte S. Giovanni to S. Daniele	37	—	7 (+ 12)
Androna Enselmini to Porta S. Giovanni	37	—	13 (+ 14)
Concariola	19	—	2
Porta Rustigelli to Porta Tadi	76	—	16 (+ 10)
Porta Tadi to Duomo	53	—	17 (+ 10)
Piazza del Duomo	11	—	2
Borgo Nuovo	38	—	1
Ambrolo	17	—	1
Centenario S. Urbano	193	—	16 (+ 5)
Centenario S. Nicolò	90	—	33 (+ 11)
Centenario S. Nicolò (men from contado)	162	129	26 (+ 16)
Centenario S. Lucia	20	—	4 (+ 1)
Contrada Pozzo dei Pescatori	190	—	33 (+ 7)
Centenario S. Tommaso	32	—	11 (+ 9)
Near S. Urbano	19	—	3 (+ 2)
Canton della Mandeferro	32	—	7 (+ 3)
Canton della Mandeferro, Duomo	14	—	1
Contrada del Ghetto	18	—	0
Ca' Malizia, near Salone	24	—	6 (+ 10)
Near S. Cecilia	12	—	2

(Continued)

Appendix 1

(Continued)

Neighborhood	Families	Men	Citizens (+ minors)
S. Cecilia to Ca' Rodolfi	8	—	2
Toward S. Tommaso	44	—	7 (+ 6)
S. Tommaso to S. Cecilia	14	—	0
Canton della Mandeferro to S. Giovanni Evangelista	64	—	6 (+ 3)
Borgo Todosco	72	—	2
Brondolo	25	—	4 (+ 3)
Porta S. Agostino to S. Giovanni	20	—	3
Ponte S. Giovanni to Spaldo	60	—	3 (+ 1)
Totals	1,580	129	259 (+ 135)
Quarter Torricelle			
Centenario S. Martino	193	376	32
Centenario S. Egidio	167	299	19 (+ 4)
S. Luca	30	50	9 (+ 2)
Borgo dei Rogati *extra murum*	54	90	8 (+ 8)
S. Maria in Vanzo to S. Michele	29	51	1 (+ 3)
Borgo della Paglia	88	52	2 (+ 1)
Borgo della Stufa	18	332	1 (+ 1)
S. Agostino to Saracinesca	72	132	3 (+ 6)
"In Gualdagnio"	18	35	0
Centenario Rudena	103	219	26 (+ 36)
Ponte Peochioso	96	184	6 (+ 10)
Androna Pozzo Campion	67	119	7 (+ 13)
Via Vignali	40	103	1 (+ 2)
Borgo Pieve	37	69	3 (+ 1)
Ponte dell'Abbate to Santo	19	30	1
Piazza del Santo to Ponte S. Daniele	54	2	4
Borgo dei Capelli	40	101	8 (+ 10)
Borgonuovo	18	94	0
Ponte S. Daniele to Crosara del Santo	68	139	10 (+ 10)
Ponte S. Daniele to Ponte S. Lorenzo	51	90	15 (+ 13)
Borgo delle Nogare	29	46	7
Piazza del Santo	23	41	4 (+ 2)
Piazza del Santo to Via Zabarella	98	—	16 (+ 20)
Centenario S. Daniele	88	—	19 (+ 32)
Near Prato della Valle	78	—	11 (+ 18)
Androna Cigolo	16	—	0
Via Nova	21	—	0

City and District of Padua

(Continued)

Neighborhood	Families	Men	Citizens (+ minors)
Contrada S. Leonino	26	—	2
Businello	37	—	0
S. Maria de Betlemme	31	6	6 (+ 7)
Centenario S. Croce	91	—	14 (+19)
Vanzo	24	—	4 (+ 3)
Porta S. Croce to Prato della Valle	125	—	17 (+ 19)
Androna Boschetto	42	—	3 (+ 1)
Totals	2,014	3,020	240 (+ 241)
QUARTER PONTE ALTINATE			
Centenario S. Biagio	194	—	33 (+ 28)
Burgo dei Pievani	32	—	5 (+ 3)
S. Margherita to Ponte S. Lorenzo	104	—	16 (+ 16)
House of Giacomo da Carrara (Ca' Zabarella) to House of Pietro Rossi (Ca' Pisani)	44	—	13 (+ 8)
Toward S. Sofia	—	12	5 (+ 3)
"In Burgo Agnus Dei"	—	32	1
Borgo Zocco	9	54	1
Casa di Dio to S. Bernardino	—	86	7 (+ 2)
Borgo Pozzo Bonello	—	34	7 (+ 5)
Centenario S. Sofia	—	495	47 (+ 44)
Centenario S. Matteo	—	380	47 (+ 25)
Centenario S. Andrea	—	330	25 (+ 28)
Centenario Arena	—	512	4 (+ 7)
S. Bartolomeo to Ponte Porciglia	—	—	6 (+ 3)
"In Burgo Tascherio"	—	—	15 (+ 3)
"In Canale Domini Rio"	—	—	1 (+ 2)
Via S. Bernardo	—	—	3 (+ 3)
Ponte Contarini to Ponte Altinate	—	—	6 (+ 2)
Totals	383	2,058	240 (+ 181)
QUARTER OF PONTE MOLINO			
Centenario S. Fermo	—	244	42 (+ 32)
Extra Portam	—	67	9 (+ 5)
Centenario Ponte Molin	—	310	30 (+ 8)
Centenario S. Leonardo	—	174	39 (+ 48)

(Continued)

Appendix 1

(Continued)

Neighborhood	Families	Men	Citizens (+ minors)
Extra murum	—	42	4 (+ 4)
Borgo S. Benedetto	—	71	2 (+ 3)
Porta Savonarola toward Spaldo	—	78	2 (+ 3)
Porta Spaldi to S. Leonardo	—	97	2 (+ 5)
S. Antonio di Vienne to S. Maria Mater Domini	—	117	8 (+ 7)
S. Leonardo	—	122	7 (+ 4)
Borgo Zodìo	28	—	0
Borgo Novo, toward Arzere	—	98	6 (+ 3)
Centenario S. Giacomo	—	276	37 (+ 10)
Centenario Codalunga	—	248	16 (+ 20)
Totals	28	1,933	194 (+ 152)
City totals	4,005	7,140	956 (+ 709)

Source: "Descritione delli huomeni da factione della città do Padova," in G. Grion, ed., *Delle rime volgari Trattato di Antonio da Tempo, giudice padovano* (Bologna, 1869), 254–88.

PART 2.
Hearth Assessments of Villages of the Padovano in 1281, Arranged by Quarter and Podesteria and Vicariate of 1370

Total number of villages in campanea and district: 396
Total number of hearths in these villages: 13,812
Ratio of hearths per village: 35

QUARTER OF THE DUOMO. Area to the south and west of Padua, including the Euganean Hills (Pedeventa) and land along the Bacchiglione River to the Vicentine border, divided between the vicariates of Teolo to the north and Arquà to the south.
Total number of villages with hearths given: 57
Total number of hearths: 2,417
Ratio of hearths per village: 43

CAMPANEA:
Total number of villages with hearths given: 8
Number of hearths: 214
Ratio of hearths per village: 27
Brusegana 24
Cantone 20
Domus a Curioli Fratrum usque ad molendinum Rivella 30

City and District of Padua

*Homines S. Benedicti et Pontis Archini
  ad Curiolum Fratrum* 16
Mandria with Guizza and Casalta 37
Mandria toward Abano 27

Sarmeola 25
Tencarola 35
Volta Brusegana, no hearths given

VICARIATE OF TEOLO: The northern half of the Euganean Hills and the area west of Padua in the valley of the Bacchiglione River, bounded on the south by the vicariate of Arquà, on the west by the Vicentine border, on the east by Padua, and on the north by the Padua-Vicenza Road. See Gloria, *Territorio,* 2:62–63.

Total number of villages: 29
Total number of hearths: 1302
Ratio of hearths per village: 45

Arlesega 20
Arselda 20
Boccon 76
Carbonara 10
Castelnuovo 14
Cervarese 128
Cortelà 31
Costa, near Zovon 16
Creola 40
Domus Cantoni Henrici 20
Luvigliano 56
Mestrino 60
Montecchio 15
Montemerlo 26
Monterosso 13

Praglia 32
Rovolon 175
Rubano 16
Saccolongo 19
Selvano (S. Benedetto delle Selve) 6
Selvazzano 50
Teolo and Villa 210
Torreglia 95
Trambacche 20
Tramonte 45
Villa. See Teolo
Villa del Bosco 9
Vò 44
Zovon 36

VICARIATE OF ARQUÀ: The southern part of the Euganean Hills, bounded on the west by the Vicentine, the north by the vicariate of Teolo, the east by the Padua-Monselice Canal, and the south by Este and Monselice. See Gloria, *Territorio,* 3:173.

Number of villages: 20
Total number of hearths: 901
Ratio of hearths per village: 45

Abano 175
Arquà 120
Baone 45
Cinto Euganeo 35
Cornoleda and Rusta 25
Faedo 36
Fontana Fredda and Viminelle 26
Galzignano 110
Lozzo (Valbona) 35
Monteortone 18

San Pietro Montagnone, and
  Montegrotto, Corte and Villa
  Ranza 102
Montegrotto. See San Pietro
  Montagnone
Nogaredo 50
Valle S. Giorgio and Tormeno 95
Valsanzibio 29
Vimenelle. See Fontana Fredda

Appendix 1

QUARTER OF TORRICELLE. The most populous quarter of the Padovano comprised three podesteria, Montagnana, the chief town of Scodosia, Este to the east, and Monselice, the largest town of the Padovano, and the vicariate of Conselve.
  Total number of villages: 98
  Total number of hearths: 5,835
  Ratio of hearths per village: 60

CAMPANEA
  Number of villages: 6
  Number of hearths: 121
  Ratio of hearths per village: 20
  Mandria di Roncon 12   Salboro 18
  Rio 26   Spassano 34
  Roncaglia 18   Volta Barozzo 13

PODESTERIA OF MONTAGNANA in Scodosia: bounded on the north by the Guà River, on the west by the Fratta River, on the south by the Adige River, and on the east by the road from Piacenza d'Adige to Saletto. See Gloria, *Territorio,* 2:138.
  Number of villages: 12
  Number of hearths: 935
  Ratio of hearths per village: 78
  Altaura 3   Merlara 28
  Argarano, near Urbana 27   Montagnana 410
  Barbuglio 20   Saletto di Scodosia 76
  Casale di Scodosia 46   S. Salvaro *extra foveam* 14
  Megliadino San Fidenzio with   Urbana and San Salvaro *intra*
     Santa Margherita 180   *foveam* 131

PODESTERIA OF ESTE. See Gloria, *Territorio,* 3:16.
  Number of villages: 18
  Number of hearths: 1,078
  Ratio of hearths per village: 60
  Calaone 85   Lusia 8
  Calcatonega 13   Passiva. See Carmignano
  Carceri 10   Ponso and Vigo di Este 26
  Carmignano and Passiva 35   Schiavonia 18
  Domus domini Alioti que sunt   Solesino and Sant'Elena 110
     Marchionis 5   Vescovana 42
  Este 642   Vighizzolo and Gazzolo 45
  Finale 3   Vigo di Este. See Ponso
  Gazzolo. See Vighizzolo   Villa Estense 36

PODESTERIA OF MONSELICE. See Gloria, *Territorio,* 3:138.
  Town and villages: 4
  Hearths: 1,120
  Monselice 1,093   Vanzo di Storta 3
  Pozzoveggiani 14   Vetta 10

City and District of Padua

VICARIATE OF CONSELVE: The southeastern part of Torricelle Quarter comprised the vicariate of Conselve, bounded on the west by the Rovigo-Monselice Road, on the south by the Adige River, and on the north and east by the Bacchiglione River, which flowed from Padua at Volta Barozzo, turning at Bovolenta to flow into the lagoon near Chioggia. See Gloria, *Territorio*, 3:215.

Total number of villages: 58
Total number of hearths: 2,581
Ratio of hearths per village: 45

Agna 44
Albignasego 40
Anguillara 63
Arre 50
Arzercavalli 32
Bagnoli di Sopra 55
Bagnoli di Sotto 35
Bertipaglia 78
Borgoforte with Cesso and Sardello 24
Bovolenta 175
Braida 18
Brenta dell'Abbà 6
Ca' Ferrante 7
Cagnola 23
Camurà 11
Candiana 42
Carpanedo 20
Carrara 40
Cartura 106
Casalserugo 65
Cazzago 12
Cesso. See Borgoforte
Chiusure 10
Civè 24
Cona 42
Concadalbero 18
Conselve 290
Cornegliana 42
Correzzola 21
Desman 6

Domus Becharelli, near Lion 2
Domus Buschi 15
Domus domini Aylini 4
Domus domini Egidioli de Ezzelino, near Ponte San Niccolò 13
Domus domini Olderici [de Sparando] 7
Fossale 5
Fossalta 5
Frascà, near Bovolenta 7
Gorgo 27
Lion 32
Maserà 102
Pernumia 310
Pontecasale 50
Pontelongo 48
Roncaiette 52
Ronchi Ca' Trevisan, near Pontelongo 18
Ronchi dell'Abbà 10
Roncon 12
S. Pelagio. See Terradura
S. Siro 25
Sardello. See Borgoforte
Scardevara 6
Terradura and S. Pelagio 41
Terrassa 70
Tribano 224
Villa Banza 7
Villa del Bosco 22
Vò Castellano 18

Appendix 1

QUARTER OF PONTE ALTINATE largely corresponded to the Saccisica, with its podesteria in the major town of Piove di Sacco, bounded on the west and south by the Bacchiglione River, on the east by the Venetian lagoon, and on the north by the Brenta River and Canal. See Gloria, *Territorio*, 3:323.

Total number of towns and villages: 72
Total number of hearths: 2,989
Ratio of hearths per village: 42

Arzergrande 77
Boion 42
Bosco di Sacco 40
Brenta Secca 15
Calcinara 11
Cambroso 7
Camin 14
Campagna Lupia 75
Campagnola 85
Campolongo di Liettoli 45
Campolongo Maggiore 96
Camponogara 81
Campoverardo 18
Castel di Brenta 6
Celeseo 25
Codevigo 75
Conche 5
Corte 126
Curano 8
Domus qd. Petri de Andrioto 3
Domus Branchuze 2
Domus de Galmarellis 3
Domus Guilielmi Nigri 7
Fossò 41
Frassenedo di Vico Bergan 31
Frassenedo di Villatora 20
Galta 4
Guasti. See S. Agata
Isola Bernù 9
Isola dell'Abbà 32
Lavezzolo 10
Legnaro dell'Abbà 40
Legnaro del Vescovo 175
Lova 10
Lugo 6
Melara, near Codevigo 29
Nogara 27
Paluello 8
Piove di Sacco 775
Polverara Maggiore 127
Polverarola 45
Ponte S. Nicolò 22
Porto 8
Premaore 20
Prozzolo 40
Ronchi di Concelodo 5
Rosara 22
Sabbioncello 27
Sandon 18
S. Agata with Guasti 40
S. Angelo di Piove di Sacco 36
S. Bruson with Sabbion and
  Altura 43
S. Ilario 4
S. Margherita 3
S. Maria di Lugo 6
Saonara 40
Scandalò 75
Sermazza 41
Sopracornio 38
Strà 45
Terranova 21
Tognana 24
Tombelle 10
Vallonga 29
Vigonovo 29
Vigorovea 32
Villa Maura 13
Villanova di Sopracornio 9
Villa Ranza, near Premaore 8
Villa Surti 5
Villatora 6
Villa Zizogna di Sopracornio 15

City and District of Padua

QUARTER OF PONTE MOLINO: The region of the Oltrebrenta was divided into the vicariate of Camposampiero and the podesteria of Cittadella.
    Total number of villages: 168
    Total number of hearths: 2,571
    Ratio of hearths per village: 15

CAMPANEA of Ponte Molino:
    Total number of villages: 6
    Total number of hearths: 122
    Ratio of hearths per village: 20

Altichiero 21	Ponte di Brenta toward Padua 14
Noventa 19	S. Vito 20
Ponte di Brenta 44	Torre 4

VICARIATE OF CAMPOSAMPIERO was bounded on the west by the road from Padua to Camposampiero, on the north by the Musone River and Trevisan border, on the east by the Venetian lagoon and *dogado*, and on the south by the Brenta River and Canal. Area of Roman centuriated fields and farmsteads rather than large rural villages. See Gloria, *Territorio*, 2:207.
    Total number of villages: 102
    Total number of hearths: 1,260
    Ratio of hearths per village: 12

Albarea 3	Caselle 11
Arino 11	Caselle di Bagnoli 5
Arsego 42	Caselle di Sopra 8
Ballò 8	Caselle di Sotto 5
Bagnoli di Peraga 10	Cavorliega 4
Boara 6	Centa 4
Borbiago 1	Codiverno 14
Borghetto di Scandolara 4	Codivernarolo 5
Borgoricco 44	Covenzago 9
Bronzola 9	Desmano 7
Buschavana 11	Favariego 2
Cadoneghe 4	Fiesso 5
Cagnano 10	Fiesso Minor 16
Caltana 21	Fiumicello 18
Caltanella 21	Fornace 6
Camenzago 13	Fossalovara 15
Campo Ceserano 9	Fossalta 3
Campocroce di Mirano 22	Fratte di Caselle 5
Campodarsego 25	Fratte di Mirano 6
Camposampiero 39	Loreggia 27
Campremarino 11	Loreggiola 2
Canacedum 9	Massanzago 22
Carpanè 25	*Maxinczigus*, near Rustega 9

Appendix 1

Meianiga di Brenta 25
Mellaredo 12
Mirano 28
Morenzago 9
Murelle 24
Onedo 2
Oriago 10
Panigale 5
Peraga 40
Perarolo 13
Pianiga 25
Pionca 5
Ponteclese 15
Reschigliano 4
Rio Bianco 4
Rivale 12
Rivaletto 11
Ronchi di Bertaldo 9
Ronchi di S. Eufemia 4
Ronchi di Transalgardino 7
Ronco Morello 3
Rossignago 5
Rostello 3
Rustega 7
Sabbioncello (Oltrebrenta) 4
Sala 29
Salcello 5
Saletto 4
S. Andrea 5
S. Angelo di Sala 26
S. Eufemia di Borgoricco 12
S. Eufemia Abbazia 4
S. Giorgio delle Pertiche 9
S. Giovanni di Lusor 2
S. Giustina in Colle 25
S. Maria di Peraga 5
S. Michele delle Badesse 23
S. Prosdocimo, near Arino 3
Scaltanigo 9
Scortegara 4
Solagna 3
Sorriva 6
Stigliano 8
Stornapria 9
Tao, not given
Trebaseleghe 12
Veternigo 22
Vetrego 20
Vigodarzere 46
Vigonza 16
Villa del Conte 47
Villa Desman 2
Villa Nova degli Alvarroti 5
Villanova di Camposampiero 12
Zeminiana 15
Zianigo 18

PODESTERIA OF CITTADELLA comprised the Brenta Valley in the northern Padovano, bounded on the east by the road from Padua to Camposampiero and the Trevisano, on the south by the Padua-Vicenza Road, on the west by the Vicentine border on the Ceresone River, and on the north by Cittadella's contado. See Gloria, *Territorio*, 2:264.

Total number of villages: 60
Total number of hearths: 1,189
Ratio of hearths per village: 20

Abbazia [Pisano] 4
Baschiera 18
Bevadore 28
Burri 5
Busiago Dandolo 2
Busiago di Ca' Mussato 13
Busiago Ronco 6
Busiago Vecchio 13
Campastrino 2
Campo S. Martino 35
Campreto 14
Carmignano 32
Carturo di Sopra 22
Carturo di Sotto 30
Cazzago 11
Cittadella 225

City and District of Padua

Curtarolo 77
Fontaniva 42
Gazzo 22
Grantorto 17
Limena 51
Lissaro 20
Lobia 6
Marsango 10
Monastiero 2
Non 13
Oltrarsego 6
Ottavello 13
Ottavo, near Tavo 11
Parolo 18
Paviola 11
Piazzola sul Brenta 42
Pligava 3
Pontevigodarzere 14
Porciglia 17
Presina 9
Ronchi di Engelerio 6
Ronchi Nuovi del Vescovo 21
Rovettera 6

S. Colomba 12
S. Giorgio in Bosco 49
S. Giorgio in Brenta 10
S. Lucia 6
S. Margherita 8
S. Maria di Non 11
S. Martino di Lupari 12
Sorriva 21
Teggì di Sopra, Teggì di Sotto 17
Tergola 13
Tergolina 12
Tremignon 39
Vaccarino 13
Villa Bagassa 3
Villa Bozza 6
Villa Cicogna 5
Villaguatera 20
Villa Muza 7
Villa Nova di Pieve di S. Prosdocimo 9
Villapapara 3
Villaranza 8
Villarappa 8

Source: *Stat. Car.*, fols. 241r–93r.

Note: Those villages and hamlets for which no modern equivalent has been found are given in the original Latin in italics.

Appendix 2

Podestà and Vicars of Padua, 1318–1405

Term of Office	Podestà and City (Number of Terms)	Vicar and City
1 Dec. 1318–21 Jan. 1320	Marco Gradenigo, Venice (2)	
31 Jan. 1320–31 July 1320	Altiniero Azzoni, Treviso (1)	
2 Aug. 1320–30 Apr. 1321	Nigrisolo Ansoldi, Cremona (2)	
1 May 1321–30 Apr. 1322	Gerardo Dalmaela, Treviso (2)	Arriverio Toscanelli
1 May 1322–29 June 1323	Tebaldo Castelnovo, Perugia (2)	Albertino Turisendi, Parma
July 1323	Armanino Persico, Cremona (1)	
1 Aug. 1323–1 Mar. 1324	Altiniero Azzoni, Treviso (1)	Nicolino Dosino, Cremona
1 Mar. 1324–22 Aug. 1324	Rinaldo Zinci, Cesena (1)	Giovanni Sassi, Modena
1 Sept. 1324–25 Mar. 1325	Beraldino Caserio, Treviso (1)	
1 Apr. 1325–24 Sept. 1325	Napoleone Beccadelli, Bologna (1)	
29 Sept. 1325–30 Apr. 1326	Corradino Bocchi, Brescia (1)	Matteo Gotesaldi, Parma
1 May 1326–15 Nov. 1326	Bonaccorso Ruggieri, Parma (1)	Andriolo Zanoni, Parma
15 Nov. 1326–12 May 1327	Tebaldo Castelnovo, Perugia (1)	Nicolino Dosino, Cremona
12 May 1327–31 Oct. 1327	Pasini Griffi, Brescia (1)	Pietro Allegri, Florence
1 Nov. 1327–15 July 1328	Gerardo Morosini, Venice (1)	
6 Aug. 1328–3 Sept. 1328	Griffon von Villanders, Germany (1)	
3–21 Sept. 1328	Marsilio Rossi, Parma (1)	
21 Sept. 1328–31 Oct. 1329	Bernardo Ervari, Verona (2)	Ughetto Carrari, Bologna; Francesco Nichisola, Verona; Forese Falconieri, Florence
10 Nov. 1329–19 Apr. 1330	Galeotto Maggi, Brescia (1)	Albertino Albertini, Brescia

Podestà and Vicars of Padua

(Continued)

Term of Office	Podestà and City (Number of Terms)	Vicar and City
19 Apr. 1330–30 Apr. 1332	Baliardino Nogarola, Verona (4)	Giovanni della Vazzola, Treviso; Fioravante Borso, Treviso, Zenobio Cipriani, Florence; Pietro Valle, Bologna; Lanfranco Gorzoni, Pavia
1 May 1332–31 Oct. 1332	Taddeo Uberti, Florence (1)	
1 Nov. 1332–31 Oct. 1333	Pietro del Mesa, Verona (2)	Jacopo dall'Arena, Parma; Niccolò Gonessa; Arriverio Toscanelli; Giovanni Tatario, Parma; Gerardo Zavati, Parma
1 Nov. 1334–9 May 1335	Federico Uberti, Florence (1)	Uguccione da Forlì; Zenobio Cipriani, Florence
9 May 1335–8 June 1336	Baliardino Nogarola, Verona (2)	Lanzaroto Spagnoli; Niccolò Gonessa
22 June 1336–5 Jan. 1337	Federico Cavalli, Verona (1)	
5 Jan. 1337–3 Aug. 1337	Guidoriccio da Fogliano, Reggio (1)	Niccolò Lolla
1 Sept. 1337–29 Feb. 1338	Marco Corner, Venice (2)	Bettini Sassi, Mantua
1 Mar. 1338–28 Feb. 1339	Marino Falier, Venice (2)	Pietro Quartari, Parma; Giovanni della Vazzola, Treviso
1 Mar. 1339–31 Aug. 1339	Giovanni Contarini, Venice (1)	
1 Sept. 1339–28 Feb. 1340	Pietro Badoer, Venice (1)	
1 Mar. 1340–31 Aug. 1340	Giovanni Sanudo, Venice (1)	Alberto della Stufa, Bologna
1 Sept. 1340–4 Mar. 1342	Pietro Zen, Venice (3)	Matteo Castelsampietro, Bologna; Leonardo Certoni, Parma
4 Mar. 1342–31 Aug. 1343	Giovanni Gradenigo, Venice (3)	Filippo Megliorato, Reggio; Lomo Candolfini, Rimini
1 Sept. 1343–30 Sept. 1344	Pietro Zen, Venice (2)	Lomo Candolfini, Rimini; Matteo Castelsampiero, Bologna
1 Oct. 1344–30 Sept. 1345	Bernardo Giustinian, Venice (2)	Lomo Candolfini, Rimini
1 Oct. 1345–28 Feb. 1346	Guido Cardinali, Pesaro (vice-podestà)	
1 Mar. 1346–28 Feb. 1347	Giovanni Dandolo, Venice (2)	Guido Cardinali, Pesaro
1 Mar. 1347–June 1348	Andreasio Morosini, Venice (2)	Guido Cardinali, Pesaro

(Continued)

APPENDIX 2

(Continued)

Term of Office	Podestà and City (Number of Terms)	Vicar and City
June–1 Sept. 1348	Guido Cardinali, Pesaro (vice-podestà)	
1 Sept. 1348–31 Aug. 1349	Pietro Badoer, Venice (2)	Guido Cardinali, Pesaro
1 Sept. 1349–28 Feb. 1350	Giovanni Contarini, Venice (1)	
1 Mar. 1350–31 Aug. 1350	Maffeo Contarini, Venice (1)	
1 Sept. 1350–31 Aug. 1351	Marino Falier, Venice (2)	Rolando Bracchi, Modena
1 Sept. 1351–1 Mar. 1353	Giovanni Foscari, Venice (3)	Rolando Bracchi, Modena;
1 Mar.–31 Aug. 1353	Ognibene Giudici, Mantua (vice-podestà)	Ambrogio Farisci, Parma
1 Sept. 1353–6 Mar. 1355	Pietro Badoer, Venice (3)	Bartolommeo da Rimini; Ambrogio Farisei, Parma
6 Mar. 1355–31 Aug. 1355	Maffeo Contarini, Venice (1)	
1 Sept. 1355–31 Aug. 1356	Marco Corner, Venice (2)	Ambrogio Farisei, Parma
1 Sept. 1356–31 Jan. 1357	Marco Morosini, Venice (1)	
1 Feb. 1357–31 Aug. 1361	Giovanni Manfredi, Reggio (9)	Ambrogio Farisei, Parma; Giovanni Salgardi, Feltre
1 Sept. 1361–31 May 1362	Giovanni Salgardi, Feltre (vice-podestà)	
1 June 1362–30 Nov. 1363	Guelfo Gerardini, Florence (2)	Giovanni Salgardi, Feltre
1 Dec. 1363–30 Aug. 1364	Giovanni Salgardi, Feltre (vice-podestà)	Ambrogio Farisei, Parma
1 Sept. 1364–28 Feb. 1368	Simone Lupi, Parma (9)	Giovanni Salgardi, Feltre
1 Mar. 1368–28 Feb. 1369	Onofrio Rossi, Florence (2)	Giovanni Salgardi, Feltre
1 March 1369–Oct. 1369	Ansedisio Loiano, Bologna (1)	Giovanni Salgardi, Feltre
Oct. 1369–28 Feb. 1370	Giovanni Salgardi, Feltre (vice-podestà)	
1 Mar. 1370–31 Aug. 1371	Scolaio Cavalcanti, Florence (3)	
1 Sept. 1371–31 Aug. 1373	Federico Lavellongo, Brescia (4)	Antonio Zecchi, Piedmont
1 Sept.–5 Nov. 1373	Cortesia Lambertini, Bologna (vice-podestà)	
5 Nov. 1373–5 May 1375	Giacomo Rangoni, Modena (3)	Cortesia Lambertini, Bologna
5 May 1375–6 May 1382	Rizzardo Sambonifacio, Verona (14)	Benedetto Girlandi, Siena
6 May 1382–6 May 1383	Roberto Mario Camporini, Ascoli (2)	Benedetto Girlandi, Siena
6 May 1383–6 Nov. 1384	Marino Memmo, Venice (3)	Benedetto Girlandi, Siena
6 Nov. 1384–10 Jan. 1385	Simone Lupi, Parma (1)	Bonifacio Cantelli, Parma
11 Jan. 1385–14 May 1385	Valerano Lambardi, Cetona (1)	

Podestà and Vicars of Padua

(Continued)

Term of Office	Podestà and City (Number of Terms)	Vicar and City
15 May 1385–14 May 1386	Andrea di Tebaldo da Bitonio, Siena (2)	Tommaso di S. Giovanni, Bologna
14 May 1386–14 May 1387	Ugolino de' Prete, Bologna (2)	Tommaso Camanzati, Florence; Daniele Cambio, Bologna; Niccolò Morano, Modena
15 May 1387–27 Feb. 1388	Jacopo Azzoni, Treviso (2)	Benedetto Girlandi, Siena
27 Feb. 1388–18 Dec. 1388	Ugolino de' Prete, Bologna (1)	Benedetto Girlandi, Siena; Antonio Sartori, Trent
24 Dec. 1388–20 July 1389	Ubertetto Visconti, Milan (1)	Giovanni Quartari, Parma
20 July 1389–21 June 1390	Guglielmo Soardi, Bergamo (2)	Bartolommeo Volpe, Soncino
21 June 1390–10 Aug. 1390	Giovanni Porcellini, Padua (1)	
10 Aug. 1390–6 Apr. 1393	Rizzardo Sambonifacio, Verona (5)	Andrea Poltroni, Rome; Antonio Romena, Florence; Rosso Orlandi, Florence
6 Apr. 1393–30 Nov. 1393	Jacopo Gradenigo, Venice (1)	Antonio Romena, Florence
30 Nov. 1393–18 May 1395	Maffeo Memmo, Venice (3)	Niccolò da Montecatino; Paolo dall'Aquila
18 May 1395–18 May 1399	Pietro Pisani, Venice (8)	Antonio Romena, Florence; Benedetto Girlandi, Siena
18 May 1399–18 May 1400	Jacopo Gradenigo, Venice (2)	Benedetto Girlandi, Siena
18 May 1400–18 May 1401	Francesco Bembo, Venice (2)	Benedetto Girlandi, Siena
18 May 1401–30 June 1402	Guglielmo della Scala, Verona (2)	Benedetto Girlandi, Siena
30 June 1402–15 Oct. 1402	Benedetto Girlandi, Siena (vice-podestà)	
15 Oct. 1402–15 Oct. 1403	Antonio Bembo, Venice (1)	Benedetto Girlandi, Siena
15 Oct. 1403–30 Nov. 1404	Andrea Vettori, Florence (2)	Benedetto Girlandi, Siena
30 Nov. 1404–19 Nov. 1405	Nerio Vettori, Florence (2)	Benedetto Girlandi, Siena

Source: Gloria, *Monumenti* (1318–1405), 1:2–46, passim. Until regular six-month terms were instituted in 1337, the terms of service were irregular, with the podestà assuming office at different times of the year.

Appendix 3

Sales and Gifts of Carrara Property, June–November 1388

Source and Date	Price and Buyer	Property
Codice Lion, 136v–38r, 29 June	Francesco il Vecchio and Francesco Novello name Naimerio Conti proctor to sell property	
AN, 5:251–52, 5 July	£900 Donato *linarolo* qd. Guilielmo	2 houses in Ponte dei Tadi
Codice Lion, 135–36, 10 July	Francesco il Vecchio names Francesco Novello his proctor to sell property in Padua and district	
AN, 118:158, 10 July	£2,000 Galvano, curial notary	110 *campi* in Tribano
AN, 118:159, 10 July	£100 Lorenzo da Gazo, notary	house cont. S. Croce
AN, 118:159v, 11 July	Gift to Bartolomeo Cermisone of Parma	2 houses in Burgo Novo
AN, 118:160, 18 July	£2,000 Bartolomeo Cermisone of Parma	110 *campi* Spassano
AN, 118:160v, 20 July	Gift to Tebaldo *mercarius* qd. Giovanni	house cont. S. Matteo
AN, 5:261v, 21 July	£1,000 Suffredo detto Pisano di Vanni da Montecatino	house cont. S. Caterina, 8 *campi* Monselice
AN, 118:161, 22 July	£500 Ugolino qd. Domenico	house cont. Allorum
AN, 118:161, 30 July	£160 Manfredo Crescenzio	40 *campi* Galzignano
AN, 118:161v, 10 Aug.	Gift to Bartolomeo qd. Giovanni Savonarola	house cont. Savonarola
AN, 118:161v, 11 Aug.	Gift to Maria qd. Almerico da Curtarolo	32 *campi* Terranegra
AD, 9124, 16 Aug.	£200 Bartolomeo d'Este	house cont. S. Anna
Codice Lion, 138v, 28 Aug.	Francesco Novello names Paolo qd. Checcho da Lion his proctor to sell property in Padua and district	

Sales and Gifts of Carrara Property

(Continued)

Source and Date	Price and Buyer	Property
Codice Lion, 126–30, 31 Aug.	4,500 ducats Guglielmo qd. Traverso Ongarelli	382 *campi* with 13 houses in Noventa
AN, 5:265, 31 Aug.	Niccolò qd. Niccolò da Monselice	31 *campi* in Pernumia
AN, 118:163, 4 Sept.	3,000 ducats Benedetto qd. Giacomo Dondi dall'Orolgio	729 *campi* in 222 parcels in Piove di Sacco
AN, 118:163v, 4 Sept.	2,500 ducats Manno qd. Manno Donati of Florence	756 *campi* Creola and Saccolongo
AN, 118:164, 8 Sept.	Gift Albertino qd. Alberto Goffo	42 *campi Villa Domorum Ser Ceti*
AN, 45:1, 8 Sept.	Gift to Pietro qd. Engolfo, M.D. of Pernumia	14 *campi* Sarmeola, 4 *campi* Arquà
AN, 5:276–77, 12 Sept.	£200 Drudone qd. Stefano da Ravenna	house Selvazzano
AN, 118:164v, 17 Sept.	£4,500 Giovanni qd. Michele Savonarola	168 *campi* Piove di Sacco and Vallonga
AN, 525bis:3, 17 Sept.	Gift Giovanni qd. Niccolò Salimbene of Cremona for faithful service 15 years	house cont. Duomo worth under 500 ducats
AN, 525bis:5v, 21 Sept.	Gift Giovanni qd. Luca *Enzegnerati* for father's faithful service	tithes: 22 parcels Pernumia, 9 parcels Battaglia
AN, 118:165, 21 Sept.	300 ducats Stefano qd. Marino da Augusto	57 *campi* Crose supra Brenta
AN, 45:1, 21 Sept.	75 ducats Aginorio da Corte of Parma	9½ *campi* in Monselice and Montericco
AN, 118:165v, 23 Sept.	£2,000 Matteo di Andrea da Colle	101 *campi* in Motta, Este, Monselice area
AN, 45:1, 25 Sept.	£3,000 Giovanni da Sala	houses cont. S. Lucia, 122 *campi* Creola, 6 *campi* Arquà
AN, 45:1, 27 Sept.	£8,000 Giovanni qd. Michele Savonarola	26 *campi* and house Galzignano
AN, 45:1, 29 Sept.	£1,000 Partinipeo di Prando Descalzi	16 *campi* Villa Fabredi?
AN, 40:78, 30 Sept.	29 ducats Bonanova *telarolo* of Arezzo	house cont. Duomo
AN, 118:166, 30 Sept.	22 ducats Prosdocimo di Bartolomeo Brazolo	4 *campi* Galzignano
AN, 118:166v, 30 Sept.	£1,000 Giovanni di Ugozone da Montagnana	45 *campi* Piove di Sacco, 7 *campi* Saccolongo

(Continued)

Appendix 3

(Continued)

Source and Date	Price and Buyer	Property
AN, 5:277v, also 290–96, 2 Oct.	£20,000 Arcoano Buzzacarini	439 *campi* Polverara and Saonara plus grazing rights on 200 *campi* there
AN, 45:1, 6 Oct.	£4,600 Bartolomeo Casalino and brother Lazaro	25 small houses cont. Ambrioli, and 6 S. Lucia
AN, 45:1v, 6 Oct.	£200 Stefano Spadari	house S. Lucia
AN, 45:1v, 8 Oct.	£200 Beleto qd. Giovanni da Urbana	house, 3 *campi* Montericco
AN, 45:1v, 9 Oct.	£2,000 Grazioso Legnaro	60 *campi* Piove di Sacco
AN, 45:1v, 9 Oct.	6 ducats Marco a Columbini qd. Niccolò	house cont. S. Croce
AN, 45:1v, 9 Oct.	£300 Bagnesio da Firenze, *famulus* Francesco il Vecchio	house cont. S. Matteo
AN, 169:59, 10 Oct.	Gift Zilio Calvi da Montagnana, curial notary	house of father Facino Calvi in Montagnana, confiscated earlier by Francesco il Vecchio
AN, 45:1v, 11 Oct.	£90 Bernardo qd. Bartolomeo	vineyard Baone
AN, 699:186, 14 Oct.	600 ducats Guglielmo qd. Leone da Camerino and Musato qd. Manoele da Perugia, Jews	house cont. S. Andrea
AN, 45:1v, 17 Oct.	£300 Antonio qd. Pietro Polastro	house cont. Duomo, *sedimen garbum* Arquà
AN, 45:2, 17 Oct.	£100, Giovanni qd. Antonio Masinio of Arquà	one *campo* Arquà
AN, 45:2, 17 Oct.	£225 Giovanni qd. Antonio Bazaleri, for mother, Grasenda	house cont. Ponte Tadi
AN, 45:2, 17 Oct.	Gift Giovanni Francesco qd. Salvatore	house cont. Parencii and 40 *campi* Gambarare
AN, 45:1v, 20 Oct.	£50 Donato qd. Andrea da Pernumia	house Monselice
AN, 45:2, 31 Oct.	£125 Veri qd. Agostino Donato *negociator* of Florence	house cont. S. Lucia
AN, 45:2, 31 Oct.	£60 Niccolò qd. Pietro of Trento	house Monselice
AN, 525bis, 10–11v, late Oct.	Gift of tithes from estate qd. Bartolomeo Volpe to Giovanni qd. Niccolò Salimbene of Cremma	50 parcels Villa del Conte

Sales and Gifts of Carrara Property

(Continued)

Source and Date	Price and Buyer	Property
AN, 45:2, 1 Nov.	50 ducats plus £200 Raisio detto Archariso qd. Guidone of Bologna	house Piazza dei Signori
AN, 45:158, 1 Nov.	Gift to Giovanna qd. Giovanni Feltrino, widow of Pietro Alresio of Arquà	*sedimen garbum* Arquà
AN, 45:2, 2 Nov.	£1,500 Giberto Casalino	"sedimen garbum ubi solebat esse domus gastalderie domini" tithes Cervarese and Campo S. Martino
AN, 45:2, 3 Nov.	£200 Paolo qd. Bensegnario	8 *campi* Valnogaredo
AN, 45:2v, 3 Nov.	£300 Rigo qd. Filippo Leone	5 *campi* Baone
AN, 45:2v, 3 Nov.	£550 Domenico *sartor* qd. Daniele	house Piazza dei Signori
AN, 45:95rv, 6 Nov.	£300 Cristoforo qd. Dusio Maccaruffi	8 houses cont. Torricelle
AN, 45:2v, 11 Nov.	Gift Bersanino qd. Corne of Brescia	house in cont. Pontecorvo
AN, 45:2v, 15 Nov.	£6,000 Giovanni qd. Ugotone da Montagnana and Giovanni qd. Michele Savonarola	mill Villa Carrara, cont. Battaglia
AN, 45:2v, 15 Nov.	300 ducats Giovanni qd. Uberto Porcellini	lease on furrier shop near Salone
AN, 45:2v, 15 Nov.	2,000 ducats Pietro and Francesco qd. Bonafede dall'Olio	*duas postas molendinorum* cont. Ponte Molino
AN, 45:2v, 15 Nov.	1,000 ducats Giovanni qd. Michele Savorarola	546 *campi* and tithes in Arsego
AN, 45:2v, 15 Nov.	£300 Giovanni qd. Giacomo Terrazzo	7 *campi* and house, Baone
AN, 37:177v, 18 Nov.	£6,000 Biago Ovetari	all Carrara lands in S. Giorgio in Bosco
AN, 45:3, 20 Nov.	2,100 ducats Fredo di Francesco Piombioli	parcels Pontecasale, Polverara, Arquà, Polverarola, house, cont. Rudena
AN, 45:3, 20 Nov.	£1,500 Cristoforo qd. Dusio Maccaruffi	house, cont. S. Daniele, 40 *campi* Conselve, Arquà
AN, 45:3, 20 Nov.	£300 Cristoforo qd. Dusio Maccaruffi	8 *domunculas,* cont. Torricelle
AN, 45:3, 20 Nov.	£200 Giovanni qd. Engolfo	house, cont. Torricelle

(Continued)

Appendix 3

(Continued)

Source and Date	Price and Buyer	Property
	Conti, buying for Matteo Belcaro	
AN, 45:3, 20 Nov.	40 ducats Gerardo and Daniele Candelle and Giovanni qd. Giacomo da Tempo	house, cont. S. Canciano
AN, 45:3, 20 Nov.	£200 Giovanni Porcellini	33½ *campi* in Piazzola
AN, 45:3, 20 Nov.	£4,500 Conforte *expeditori domini* qd. Ser Uzeri	170 *campi* in Boane, Supracornio, Villa del Bosco, Sacco, Gorgo, Valsanzibio
AN, 45:3, 20 Nov.	£600 Michele Pignolati	11½ *campi* vines, olives, Arquà
AN, 45:241, 20 Nov.	*donatio inter vivos* to Pietro qd. Francesco Brentella	6 houses, vineyard Montagnana
AN, 45:246, 20 Nov.	£700 Zufredino qd. Ledorte	mills on Tergola, Caselle, sawmill and 20 *campi* Burri
AN, 37:175, 20 Nov.	1,500 ducats Paolo Lion	mills Montagnana on Frassine
AN, 37:176, 20 Nov.	£3,500 Paganino Sala	woods toward Oriago
AN, 37:176v, 20 Nov.	1,000 ducats Paganino Sala	woods Piazzola, which Jacopo Capodivacca held
AN, 37:177v, 20 Nov.	3,000 ducats Zilio Calvi	house where he lives, 13 *campi* Cinto, Carrara property in Saletto and Megliadino
AN, 37:176, 20 Nov.	16,000 ducats Bonifacio Lupi	Carrara possessions and tithes, Bovolenta, Brugine
AN, 37:176, 20 Nov.	Exchange with Biago Ovetari	Ovetari gets house of Marsilio da Carrara, while Francesco Novello gets house cont. S. Fermo
AN, 37:176, 20 Nov.	£1,000 Biago Ovetari	parcels Arquà
AN, 37:177v, 20 Nov.	£1,000 Novello qd. Guglielmo da Marano, M.D.	*mansus,* tithes Oriago
AN, 37:177, 20 Nov.	3,300 ducats Guglielmo Curtarolo	houses, cont. S. Leonardo, property in Curtarolo
AN, 118:167, 20 Nov.	Gift Niccolò qd. Guzolino Mussato	house, cont. S. Pietro
AN, 118:167, 20 Nov.	600 ducats Bartolomeo Zirmepono?	2 houses, Piazza dei Signori
AN, 118:167v, 20 Nov.	£2,000 Bartolomeo Tubeta of Genoa	152 *campi* Monselice, Tribano
AN, 118:167v, 20 Nov.	£8,000 Cabrietto di Rolandino of Parma	all Carrara property in Piove S. Prosdocimo, Villanova, Desmano, S. Michele di Ba-

Sales and Gifts of Carrara Property

(Continued)

Source and Date	Price and Buyer	Property
		desse, Fiumicello, S. Andrea, Murelle, S. Angelo di Sala; all property that Zufredo d'Abano used to hold in Montagnana, Monselice, Montegrotto
AN, 118:168, 20 Nov.	Gift to Jacopo di Ser Rigo	40 *campi*, Villa Tremignon
AN, 100:347v–50, 20 Nov.	£1,500 Francesco Dotti	6 houses, cont. S. Andrea
AN, 100:350v–53v, 20 Nov.	Gift to Nascimbene qd. Alberto della Ricca of Cittadella	935 *campi*, woods, arable, pasture in S. Giorgio in Brenta, Cittadella, Fontaniva
AN, 5:297v, 20 Nov.	£30,000 Michele Rabatta	all property and houses of Conte da Carrara
AN, 5:297v, 20 Nov.	£7,000 Biagio Ovetari	all property in Cittadella
AN, 5:315, 20 Nov.	£200 Biagio Ovetari	"una possessio super Aggerem"
AN, 5:315v, 20 Nov.	£60 Biagio Ovetari, buying for Agnese da Fontaniva	parcel S. Margherita
AN, 5:315v, 20 Nov.	£1,000 Marco qd. Niccolò Guarnerini	84 *campi* Carrara and S. Margherita
AN, 5:317, 20 Nov.	Gift to Nicoletto d'Alessio	house Burgo Lapido, tithes Bertipaglia
AN, 5:317v, 20 Nov.	Gift to Paganino Sala	47 *campi*, Bosco Altichiero, campanea
AN, 5:317v, 20 Nov.	£3,000 Bandino Brazzi	120 *campi*, Abano, 37 *campi* and mills, Montaone
AN, 5:318, also 351–53v, 20 Nov.	£10,000 Francesco Beningrado	"omnes possessiones gastaldie Terrasse"
AN, 5:318, 20 Nov.	£10,000 Ludovico Buzzacarini buying for father, Arcoano Buzzacarini	property in Arzercavelli plus house and stables, all once owned by Fina Buzzacarini
AN, 5:318, 20 Nov.	2,000 ducats Francesco Turchetto	all property in Camponogara and S. Elena and house in Este
AN, 5:318v, 20 Nov.	500 ducats Paganino Sala, buying for Marsilio Motta	house, cont. Fallaroti, where Motta lives
AN, 5:318v, 20 Nov.	£800 Bernardo Lazara	possession in Pontelongo and Bovolenta, which belonged to Jacopino Gaffarello
AN, 5:318v, 20 Nov.	£450 Bartolomeo qd. Francesco, curial notary	2 houses, cont. S. Lucia

(Continued)

Appendix 3

(Continued)

Source and Date	Price and Buyer	Property
AN, 5:348, 20 Nov.	Gift Bartolomeo qd. Francesco, curial notary for work in chancery	house, cont. S. Matteo, valued at £450
AN, 5:319, 20 Nov.	2,000 ducats Giovanni qd. Ugoccione da Montagnana	houses and parcels, Merlara, Castelbaldo
AN, 5:319, 20 Nov.	£1,200 Niccolò di Angelo	3 houses, cont. S. Andrea
AN, 5:319v, 20 Nov.	£3,000 Francesco da Rustega	40 *campi*, house Cinto
AN, 5:320, 20 Nov.	300 ducats Bartolomeo da Lendinara	2 houses, Monselice, 2 houses, Padua, house, Este, 300 *campi*, Conselve, 31 *campi*, Rovolon, 6 *campi*, Arquà
AN, 5:320, 20 Nov.	£127 Giovanni Frabaldi buying for Antonio da Pio, lord of Carpi	9½ *campi*, Tribano
AN, 5:320v, 20 Nov.	70 ducats Matteo da Bugeli of Monselice	2 houses, 2 *campi* in Monselice
AN, 5:321, 20 Nov.	£300 Arimondo di Solimano da Ponte buying for Bartolomeo Zacco	18 *campi*, Luvigliano
AN, 5:321, 20 Nov.	3,000 ducats Francesco da Rustega	all property and tithes in Gutico(?)
AN, 5:321v, 20 Nov.	£2,000 Priore qd. Niccolò Trapolino	inheritance of Maria Trapolino, widow of Tebaldo Cortelliero, 24 *campi* Camin
AN, 5:321v, 20 Nov.	£2,000 Priore qd. Niccolò Trapolino	property and tithes in Massanzago
AN, 5:321v, 20 Nov.	£4,000 Pietro Zabarella, buying for father, Andrea	property in Arquà, paying annual livello of £440
AN, 5:323, 20 Nov.	£11,000 Benedetto da Montagnana	house, cont. Duomo, 15 *campi*, Padua, 362 *campi*, woods, meadow, Terradura, 99 *campi*, Arzergrande, 145 *campi*, S. Michele Valdebrama, 194 *campi*, Cicogna, 267 *campi*, Franchesi, 40 *campi*, Baone, 20 *campi*, Calcarola
AN, 5:323v, 20 Nov.	£2,000 Alberto di Zordano of Merlara	house, cont. Ponte Molino
AN, 5:323v, 20 Nov.	£6,000 Pietro Curtarolo	land in Tribano
AN, 5:325, 20 Nov.	£3,000 Giovanni Conti	5 houses, near Carrara Reggia

Sales and Gifts of Carrara Property

(Continued)

Source and Date	Price and Buyer	Property
AN, 5:325, 20 Nov.	2,000 ducats Giovanni qd. Antonio Turchetto	all property in Casale di Scodosia
AN, 5:325v, 20 Nov.	£5,000 Giacomo Enselmini	ovens, houses in Mira, property inherited from Fina Buzzacarini in S. Bruson
AN, 5:326v, 20 Nov.	£1,000 Nicoletto d'Alessio	5 houses, cont. S. Urbano
AN, 5:326v, 20 Nov.	£800 Bartolomeo qd. Francesco Strazarolo	house, cont. Domorum Aletis
AN, 5:358–63, 20 Nov.	£1,600 Giovanni Bassanello	property from legacy of deceased Arzencio, *campsor*
AN, 525bis:17, 21 Nov.	Gift Biagio Ovetari for faithful service	all Carrara property now in Ovetari's possession
AN, 5:327, 22 Nov.	1,500 ducats Pietro Zabarella, for sister Caterina	house, oven, cont. S. Canciano
AN, 5:327, 22 Nov.	1,000 ducats Rizzardo Sambonifacio	house where he lives, cont. Salone
AN, 5:327v, 22 Nov.	£3,000 Simone Macerii of Parma	land, tithes Villa del Conte, *mansus*, Camin, Massanzago, 48 *campi*, Malcantone, 250 *campi*, woods, S. Michele, 14 *campi*, Montericco
AN, 5:328, 22 Nov.	200 ducats, Ser Nardo Cajano	house, where he lives, cont. S. Giovanni delle Navi *intra portam*
AN, 5:328, 22 Nov.	£3,000 Simeone dagli Statuti	82 *campi* Villa Rampazzo, Paduan campanea
AN, 5:328v, 22 Nov.	2,000 ducats Simeone dagli Statuti	Albergo Bo, and another house, cont. S. Martino
AN, 5:328v, 22 Nov.	£1,200 Giovanni Frabaldi	house, cont. S. Urbano
AN, 5:328v, 22 Nov.	Gift Stefano Berti da Merlo	house, Piazza dei Signori
AN, 5:329, 22 Nov.	£30,000 Giovanni Parisino Mezzoconti da Este	butcher shops of Padua, Carrara loan office, house, Prato della Valle, house of Michele Rabatta, tithe of Saccolongo, oil warehouse, furrier's house at S. Antonio, bath (*stuva olim Cecilie*), *domus a Salizata*, meadows of Anguillara, Vighizzolo and Vescovana

(Continued)

Appendix 3

(Continued)

Source and Date	Price and Buyer	Property
AN, 5:329v, also 384, 22 Nov.	Gift Giovanni Parasino Mezzoconti da Este	*iura proprietatis*, S. Clemente, where German soldier Squarzmarz lives
AN, 5:329v, 22 Nov.	£700 Giacomo dalla Crosara	9 *campi*, Galzignano
AN, 5:330, 22 Nov.	£7,000 Alberto qd. Bartolomeo Spazza, for himself and nephew, Manfredo	Possessions qd. Artusino Spazza in Rovolon, S. Angelo di Sala, 22 *campi* Fiumicello, Camin
AN, 5:330v, 22 Nov.	£1,600 Giovanni Bassanello	houses and lands, cont. S. Croce, Bassanello
AN, 5:331, 22 Nov.	£500 Drudone qd. Stefano da Ravenna	house where he lives, cont. S. Leonardo
AN, 5:331, 22 Nov.	400 ducats Francesco Dotti	all property and tithes Cinto, not already sold
AN, 5:331v, 22 Nov.	£3,000 Prosdocimo qd. Martino Barbario	4 *campi*, Vimenelle, 3 *campi*, Fontanafreddo, and parcels Montecchio
AN, 5:332v, 22 Nov.	£100 Paganino Sala, buying for Alvarotto Alvarotti	house, cont. S. Niccolò
AN, 5:333, 22 Nov.	£1,500 Federico qd. Filippo da Bavaria, schoolmaster	4 houses, Piazza dei Signori
AN, 5:333, 22 Nov.	300 ducats Bartolomeo Zaccaria	3 houses, Padua, lands Baone, Galzignano, Este
AN, 5:334, 22 Nov.	£500 Biagio qd. Francesco Spazza	12 *campi*, Tergola, 14 *campi*, S. Eufemia
AN, 5:334v, 22 Nov.	£300 Giovanni qd. Jacopo Teiracio	4 houses, gardens, cont. S. Michele
AN, 5:334v, 22 Nov.	£500 Facio detto Faciolo qd. Giovanni, painter	house, cont. S. Urbano
AN, 5:334v, 22 Nov.	£50 Facio detto Faciolo qd. Giovanni, painter	*iura proprietatis*, house, cont. S. Urbano
AN, 5:335, 22 Nov.	2,000 ducats, Antonio and Niccolò qd. Giovanni Cortusi, and Marco qd. Albrigeto Cortusi	legacy of Giovanni Cortusi, not already sold to Giacomo Dotti, Paganino Sala
AN, 5:335, 22 Nov.	£1,000 Carlo goldsmith	house, cont. S. Stefano *extra portam*
AN, 5:335v, 22 Nov.	£200 Pietro qd. Giovanni Nene	2 houses, cont. Parencii and S. Agata
AN, 5:335v, 22 Nov.	£300 Francesco Furlana	house, cont. Parencii
AN, 5:336, 22 Nov.	Restoration to Cristoforo Mac-	house, cont. S. Lucia

Sales and Gifts of Carrara Property

(Continued)

Source and Date	Price and Buyer	Property
	caruffi, for Giovanna qd. Acotano Rossi, and wife Pietro Maconia	
AN, 37:177v, 22 Nov.	1,000 ducats Niccolò da Vigonza	house, Padua, where he lives
AN, 43:170v, 22 Nov.	£3,000 Ugolino Preti da Bologna	shops of smiths, craftsmen, Porte Tadi, Borgo Todoschi
AN, 45:99rv, 22 Nov.	Unstated price Giovanni Bassanello buying for Bonifacio qd. Niccolo Torcolo	67 *campi,* Stanghella
AN, 45:97v, 22 Nov.	Unstated price Pietro qd. Tomasino, M.D.	16 *campi,* Montagnana
AN, 84:250, 22 Nov.	£1,000 Pietro di Domenico da Anquillara	mills in Este
AN, 169:53, 22 Nov.	£600 Fruzerino qd. Aicardino Capodivacca	*motte,* 6 *campi* Trambacche
AN, 5:336v, 23 Nov.	400 ducats Bandino Brazzi	house, cont. Ponte Molino
AN, 5:337, 23 Nov.	Gift Benedetto Galmarelli	property of Biancafiore qd. Francesco Iselberti
AN, 5:337, 23 Nov.	1,000 ducats Antonio qd. Padovano Chierigati	house, Camposampiero next to Castello
AN, 5:337v, 23 Nov.	1,000 ducats Niccolò qd. Checchino Sanguinazzi	house, tower, cont. S. Bartolomeo
AN, 5:338, 23 Nov.	£400 Benedetto qd. Bartolomeo of Padua	houses, *Ripa Salis,* Padua
AN, 5:338v, 23 Nov.	1,000 ducats Ugolino Preti of Bologna, podestà	shops where dazii exacted "omnes stationes daciorum Padue in quibus dacia exigebantur"
AN, 5:338v, 23 Nov.	£2,000 Gasparino da Montagnana	rights in territory of Montagnana "*ultra foveam*"
AN, 5:339, 23 Nov.	1,500 ducats Pietro Brentella	Stronghold S. Martino of Serramonte
AN, 5:339, 23 Nov.	£1,200 Stechino Capodivacca	all possessions in Campolongo not already sold
AN, 5:339v, 23 Nov.	200 ducats Giovanni qd. Baldasare da Montagnana	all property of Paolo Enzeleni in Montagnana not already sold
AN, 5:339v, 23 Nov.	500 ducats Tisone San Angelo	all possessions in Torreglia not already sold

(Continued)

APPENDIX 3

(Continued)

Source and Date	Price and Buyer	Property
AN, 5:340, 23 Nov.	£800 Zanino qd. Niccolò Bellarini	house, cont. S. Agata, "laborerium a Bugatis"
AN, 5:340v, 23 Nov.	£2,000 Ugone di Giovanni Ubaldini	house, Porte Tadi
AN, 5:340v, 23 Nov.	£150 Jacopino da Montagnana, knight	"unam muragliam cum sedimine ubi erant granaria," at Albergo Bo
AN, 5:341, 23 Nov.	£1,500 Andrea qd. Pietro *lanario* of Milan, buying for Maria da Torreglia, wife of Pietro Salomone	51 parcels in Cortelà
AN, 17:116, 23 Nov.	£500 Aldegarda, niece of qd. Caterina, widow Engeleno a Balneo	house, bath 2 *campi*, Montegrotto
AN, 37:177v, 23 Nov.	£500 Isengarde, wife of Bartolomeo Pellizzari	house, cont. S. Maria in Vanzo, house, 10 *campi*, Montegrotto
AN, 46:249, 23 Nov.	Gift Giovanni qd. Pace da Bertipaglia	house, parcels in Bertipaglia
AN, 308:37–8, 23 Nov.	*Donatio inter vivos* Bonaventura qd. Jacopo Curte	house, cont. S. Antonio
AN, 506:27, 23 Nov.	Gift Prosdocimo qd. Martino Barbario	6 *sedimina garba*, facing Piazza del Santo
AN, 525bis:18, 23 Nov.	Gift Niccolò Sdalfs, Carrara familiar	house, cont. Ognissanti, 10 *campi*, Galzignano
AN, 525bis:19v, 23 Nov.	£700 Carlo qd. Pagano Capodivacca	15 *campi*, Terranegra
AN, 48:110, 24 Nov.	Giacomo di Francesco il Vecchio takes possession of property given by father	Property in Teolo, Camposampiero, Agna, Piove di Sacco, Monselice, Anquillara, Camponogara
AN, 118:168, 24 Nov.	Gift Paolo Strazzarolo	house, cont. S. Andrea
AN, 118:168v, 24 Nov.	Gift Sambono qd. Oliviero	house, cont. Borgo Lapido
AN, 525bis:18v, 24 Nov.	Exchange between Tommaso di Jacopo Guarnerini and Francesco Novello	Tommaso gets land in Galzagnano; Francesco Novello, £500 and land in Faedo
AN, 525bis:19rv, 24 Nov.	Gift Tisone San Angelo	five houses and edifices near Porta Trevisana in Cittadella

Notes

Abbreviations

AD	Archivio Diplomatico, Archivio di Stato, Padua, cited by parchment number and date.
AN	Archivio Notarile, Archivio di Stato, Padua, cited by register number, folio, and date.
DBI	*Dizionario biografico degli Italiani,* 46 vols. to date. Rome, 1960–.
Gennari	G. Gennari, ed., *Codice Diplomatico Padovano,* Biblioteca Seminario, Padua, MS 582, vol. 8, eighteenth-century copies.
Gloria	A. Gloria, *Monumenti della Università di Padova (1318–1405)* (Padua, 1888), cited by volume, page, paragraph number, and date.
Ljubiċ	S. Ljubiċ, ed., *Monumenta spectantia historiam slavorum meridionalium,* vols. 2–5 (Zagreb, 1868–74), cited by volume, page, document number, and date.
Papafava	G. B. Papafava, ed., *Documenti per servire la storia dei Carraresi,* Biblioteca Civica, Padua, MS B.P. 928, 5 vols, eighteenth-century copies of Carrara documents, cited by volume, page, and date.
Predelli	R. Predelli, ed., *I libri Commemoriali della Repubblica di Venezia,* Monumenti storici della R. Deputazione veneta di storia patria, ser. 1, vols. 1–3 (Venice, 1880–83), cited by volume, page, document number, and date.
Stat. Car.	*Statuta communis Padue, 1362* (also *Statuti carraresi),* Biblioteca Civica, Padua, MS B.P. 1237.
Stat. Com.	A. Gloria, ed., *Statuti del comune di Padova dal secolo XII all'anno 1285* (Padua, 1873), cited by page and paragraph number.
Verci	G. B. Verci, *Storia della marca trevigiana e veronese,* 20 vols. (Venice, 1786–91), cited by volume of documents, document number, and date; vol. and pp. alone refers to volume of narrative.
Wenzel	G. Wenzel, ed., *Monumenta Hungariae historica: Acta extera,* 3 vols. (Budapest, 1874–76), cited by volume, page, document number, and date.

Introduction

1. For an overview of the Renaissance signori, see John E. Law, *The Lords of Renaissance Italy: The Signori, 1250–1500*, General Studies, 102 (London: Historical Association, 1981).

2. Chris Given-Wilson, *The Royal Household and the King's Affinity: Service, Politics, and Finance in England, 1360–1413* (New Haven: Yale University Press, 1986), 203.

3. See Jane Laurent, "Feudalismo e Signorie," *Archivio storico italiano* 137 (1979): 155–75, and Trevor Dean, "Lords, Vassals, and Clients in Renaissance Ferrara," *English Historical Review* 100 (1985): 106–19.

4. For full citations of the works mentioned here, see the Bibliography, Printed Primary Sources, and, for a survey of historians and authors at the Carrara court, L. Capo, "I cronisti di Venezia e della Marca Trevisana," in *Storia della cultura veneta: Il Trecento* (Vicenza: Neri Pozza, 1976), 311–27.

Chapter 1 Late Medieval Padua: The Setting

1. On the urban development of Padua, I follow the recent account of Tim Benton, "Three Cities Compared," 15–23, as well as Hyde, *Padua in the Age of Dante*, 29–34, and C. Gasparotto's detailed "Padova ecclesiastica, 1239," 17–191.

2. On the public buildings of medieval Padua, see Colin Cunningham, "The Honour and Beauty of the City," 49–53, and on the markets, Hyde, *Padua in the Age of Dante*, 42–43.

3. On policing in the centenari, see *Stat. Car.*, fol. 153r (1276), requiring the heads of each neighborhood to report violent crimes to the podestà, and for militia service, the muster roll for S. Tommaso, in the quarter of the Duomo, AD, 5383, 7 Dec. 1321.

4. See Grion, "Ruoli di cittadini," 254, and arguments of Hyde, *Padua in the Age of Dante*, 34–36, and Bortolami, "Acque, mulini e folloni," 280.

5. See Luzzatto, "Popolazione del territorio padovano," 373–84, and note 10 below.

6. On the Paduan campanea, see the fundamental study of Bortolami, "Pieve e 'Territorium Civitatis' nel Medioevo," 1–94, esp. 45–55.

7. See *Stat. Car.*, fol. 225v, ed. in Beda, *Ubertino da Carrara*, 187.

8. On the medieval Padovano, see C. Comello, "Padova, sviluppo politico e strutture urbane e territoriali," in *Città, contado e feudi nell'urbanistica medievale*, ed. E. Guidone (Rome: Multigrafica Editrice, 1974), 13–18, and, in general, the wealth of information in Gloria, *Territorio*, vol. 1. For a definition of the *mansus* in 1339, see *Stat. Car.*, fol. 146r.

9. On soil types of the Padovano, see P. Principi, *I terreni italiani* (Rome: Ramo Editoriale degli Agricoltori, 1961), 61, 68–69, 72–73, and G. Trevisan, *Proprietà e impresa nella campagna padovano all'inizio dell'Ottocento* (Verona: Regione Veneto, 1980), 8–9. On the *patriarcati* stretching from Conselve to Carrara, see *Stat. Car.*, fol. 143r.

10. This figure accords with the older estimate of Gino Luzzato, "Popolazione del territorio padovano," 373–84, who undercounted the number of hearths as 12,660 but used a multiplier of five to arrive at the same total of 62,000. See also Hyde, *Padua in Age of Dante,* 48.

11. On the commune's higher jurisdiction in the contado, see *Stat. Car.*, fols. 1v, 50v–52v, and Hyde, *Padua in the Age of Dante,* 47–48.

12. See *Stat. Car.*, fol. 328r, with discussion in Gallo, "L'epoca delle signorie," 186–87.

13. See, for example, a letter of 23 Sept. 1402 in *Copialettere,* 413, no. 772, listing five podestà and eight vicars.

14. The hydrography of the medieval Padovano is a complex matter that has yet to receive definitive treatment. Still useful are the older studies of G. Gennari, *Dell'antico corso de fiumi in Padova e nei suoi contorni* (Venice, 1778), 1–36, and Gloria, "Argini dei fiumi," 11–22. Indispensable for plotting the location of shipping canals, embankments, and dikes is the rubric "De navigiis, riveriis et restariis," in *Stat. Car.*, fols. 230r–32v. The 1281 corvées for the drainage canals have been published from *Stat. Car.*, fols. 259r–94r, in Gloria, *Della agricoltura,* 2:161–252, which forms the basis for the calculation of numbers and total length given in Bortolami, "Acque, mulini e folloni," 300.

15. The key provisions for governing the territorial state are contained in the rubric "De jurisdictione," *Stat. Car.*, fols. 50r–51v and 120v–21r for the *ingrossatores,* fols. 130v–32r for the *saltuarii* (rural police). My analysis of government of the rural communes is based on the surviving statutes: "Statuti di Pernumia," edited by Bortolami, 179–240; *Statuti di Cittadella,* edited by Ortalli et al., 47–137; and Rome, Biblioteca del Senato, MS 271, *Statuti di Montagnana,* partial edition from another MS in Gloria, *Della agricoltura,* 1:105–31. See also A. Giacomelli, "Sugli statuti del Comune di Montagnana," *BMCP* 50 (1961): 136–87.

16. AD, 5832, 30 Nov. 1321 for Camin, AD, 6453, 18 July 1330 for Polverara.

17. On medieval Paduan agriculture, I am much indebted to the work of Sante Bortolami, especially his monograph on Pernumia, *Territorio e società in un comune rurale veneto,* chaps. 3–4, and the essays of the late V. V. Samarkin, "Evolyutsiya libell-yarnogo derzhaniya v severo-vertochnoy Italii v XII–XIV vekakh" (Evolution of Livello holdings in Northeastern Italy in the 12th–14th centuries) and "Evolyutsiya khozyaystvennykh rasporyadkov paduanskoy derevni v XII–XIV vekakh" (Evolution of land use in the Paduan countryside in the 12th–14th centuries), studied with the aid of Italian translations deposited in the Dipartimento di Studi Storici of the University of Padua. I am also indebted to my colleague Nellie Ohr for aid in the interpretation and citation of Samarkin's essays.

18. See the examples of various agricultural contracts given in Roberti, *Un formulario inedito di notaio padovano,* 69–72.

19. See Samarkin, "Evolyutsiya libellyarnogo," 70–73.

20. The nature and extent of Venetian investment in the *terraferma* before the conquests of the early Quattrocento has been little studied; for the Padovano, see the essay of Ling, "Presenza fondiaria veneziana nel Padovano," 305–20; on Venice's

regulations governing acquisition of property on the mainland, the studies of Lazzarini, *Proprietà e feudi,* 9–48; and for a case study of Trecento monastic investment, Modzeleweski, "Beni fondari del monastero di San Zaccaria di Venezia," pt. 2:46–63

21. On the analogous use of the communal government in Este Ferrara, see Trevor Dean, "Commune and Despot," 183–97, and on the myth of the impartial podestà, S. Bertelli, *Il potere oligarchico nello stato-città medievale* (Florence: La Nuova Italia, 1978), 56–60.

22. See *Stat. Com.*, 41–42, no. 113, also in *Stat. Car.*, fol. 5v.

23. The duties of the podestà, his staff, and the communal judiciary, officials, and councils are spelled out in detail in Liber I of the *Stat. Car.*, fols. 1r–49v.

24. *Stat. Car.*, fol. 20v: "cum potestates Padue et plurimum sint milites layci et ignoranti iuris, teneantur omnes contempnationes et absolutiones facere de consilio sue curie."

25. On similar duties the neighboring Este signoria left to the commune of Ferrara, see Dean, "Commune and Despot," 191–93, and on Padua's communal taxes, Hyde, *Padua in the Age of Dante,* 53–56.

26. On communal property in the Trecento, see *Stat. Car.*, fols. 212v–15v. See also Savioli, *Compendio,* 68–71, which defines from Venetian records of 1421 the nature of the estimo in the Carrara period.

27. See Sambin, *L'ordinamento parrocchiale di Padova,* 77–83, for the parishes and Rigon, *Clero e città,* 245–47, on the right of collation.

28. Historians have scarcely examined this issue; the standard work is still the older essay of L. A. Botteghi, "Clero e comune in Padova nel secolo XIII," 215–72.

29. This agreement was incorporated in the Carrara lord's revision of the Paduan statutes of 1362, thus affirming its defining importance in the late Trecento; see *Stat. Car.*, fols 116v–119r; edition in Gloria, *Controversie fra il clero e il comune di Padova del secolo decimoterzo* (Padua, 1855), 13–23, with discussion in Botteghi, "Clero e comune," 262–65.

30. *Stat. Car.*, fols. 301v–8v, for the bulls, and fols. 11v–12v, for the podestà's duties to curb heresy.

31. See Sambin, "Famiglia di un vescovo italiano del '300," 237–47, for Conti's household, and for his career, idem, "Amico del Petrarca," and my entry "Conti, Ildebrandino," in the *DBI,* 437–40.

32. See Sambin, "Amico del Petrarca," 18–21.

33. For a complete list of canons, see Dondi dall'Orologio, *Serie cronologico-storica,* and for an analysis of canons under the later Carrara regime, see Collodo, "Lo sfruttamento dei benefici canonicali," in *Società in trasformazione,* 277–96.

34. On the lay tithe in medieval Italy, see the classic account of Catherine E. Boyd, *Tithes and Parishes in Medieval Italy,* esp. chaps. 9–11, and two recent surveys by Andrea Castagnetti, "La decima da reddito signorile a privilegio economico de ceti cittadini," 215–33, and "Le decime e i laici," 509–30, esp. 520–25.

35. See Montobbio, *Splendore e utopia nella Padova dei Carraresi,* 244–54, for a list of some of the tithes granted to the Carrara and their favorites, culled from the

registers of Feudorum of the Archivio della Curia Vescovile, Padua. Specific examples of the fiefs granted to Carrara family and its affinity are given from the same source throughout this book.

36. See discussion in Boyd, *Tithes and Parishes*, 187–88, 203, based on legislation in *Stat. Com.*, 216–17, nos. 659–662I, which was incorporated in 1362 in the *Stat. Car.*, fol. 126rv, under the new rubric "De decimis."

37. See Castagnetti, "Le decime e i laici," 525.

38. AD, 7442, 3 Nov. 1345, excerpt in Gloria, 2:25, no. 1147.

39. Although there is no detailed treatment of the diocesan church in Trecento Padua, two recent studies help to fill that gap. See Rigon, *Clero e città*, chap. 5, on various aspects of diocesan and parish organization, and, on the bishops of Carrara Padua, Gaffuri and Gallo, "Signoria ed episcopato a Padova nel Trecento," 2:923–56.

40. See Stacul, *Il cardinale Pileo da Prata*, 4–15.

41. See Sambin, *Ricerche di storia monastica*, 23–24, and Rigon, "Esigenze di riforma e ribellione di monaci nel Trecento," 71–87, for reforms of S. Giovanni del Venda, S. Maria del Monte delle Croci, and S. Maria di Porciglia.

42. On Giacomo II, see Gloria, 2:31, no. 1159, 7 July 1350; Francesco il Vecchio's dispensations are calendared in Gloria, *Documenti relativi alla storia padovana*, 8–11; AD, 8069, 9 July 1361, for S. Agostino.

43. On the political role of Paduan guilds, see Roberti, *Corporazioni padovane*, 55–61; Hyde, *Padua in the Age of Dante*, 44–45, 207–10; and, in great detail, Zorzi, *L'ordinamento comunale padovano nella seconda metà del secolo XIII*, 140–78.

44. See *Stat. Car.*, fols. 76v–77v.

45. See Hyde, *Padua in the Age of Dante*, 125–30, and Roberti, "Corporazione dei Giudici di Palazzo," 330–49, for an edition of statutes, from Padua, Archivio Antico Universitario, MS 123, *Statuta et matricula collegii iudicum*.

46. See the list in *Statuta et matricula collegii iudicum*, fol. 207r, and Gloria, 2:51, no. 1211. A similar list from 1372 (fol. 196v) adds Alvarotto Alvarotti, Giovanni Porcellini, and Pizzacomino Pizzacomini as members of the college.

47. On notaries in Padua, see Hyde, *Padua in the Age of Dante*, 49–50, 153–63. Figures for attendance of meetings are taken from Padua, Biblioteca Civica, MS B.P. 825, *Reformationes frataleae notariorum*, fols. 4v, 8rv, 40rv, and for the membership on the eve of the Black Death, MS B.P. 1480I, *Liber modularum omnium not. fratalee*, fols. 10r–15v, giving a total of 328 members in 1345–48.

48. My analysis is based on statutes from 1261 to 1341, "Statuti della Fraglia dei Notai," edited in Roberti, *Corporazioni padovane*, 157–83, supplemented by the compilation made in 1419 by Sicco Polenton: Padua, Biblioteca Civica, MS B.P. 339, *Statuta notariorum Patavii*.

49. See AN, 699, fols. 23v–24r, March 1371.

50. See *Stat. Car.*, fols. 26v–30r, for notaries' role in communal record keeping.

51. My account is based on the recent work of Collodo on the Paduan woolen industry in her *Società in trasformazione*, 329–85; the older study of R. Cessi, *Corporazioni dei mercanti di panni*, 42–55; and his edition of the "Statuti dell'Arte della Lana," 105–65.

52. See *Reformationes frataleae notariorum*, fols. 97r–98r, for the interventions of 1360, and *Liber modularum omnium not. fratalee*, fols. 31v–32v, for the lord's appointment of convicted and foreign notaries in 1373.

53. See *Stat. Car.*, fol. 329r (1366), and Roberti, *Corporazioni padovane*, 111–13, for the new assessments.

54. See *Stat. Com.*, 375–79, and *Stat. Car.*, fols. 228r–30r, with discussion in Kibre, *Scholarly Privileges*, 56–61.

55. On the organization of the Paduan *studium* before 1350, see Siraisi, *Arts and Sciences at Padua*, chap. 1, on which I draw heavily.

56. See the edition of Denifle, "Statuten," 309–562.

57. Quoted from ibid., 431.

58. Based largely on Andrea Gloria's edition of "Antichi statuti del collegio padovano," 355–402.

59. On the settlements of 1360 and 1399, see Gloria, 2:48, 342–45, nos. 1205 and 2049, and discussion in Kibre, *Scholarly Privileges*, 65–66, and Siraisi, *Arts and Sciences at Padua*, 23, 25.

60. On Padua's college system, see Kibre, *Scholarly Privileges*, 66–68.

61. My dicussion of the size of the professoriate and student body is based on the data in Gloria, *Monumenti* (1318–1405), 1:115–517.

62. See Cessi, "La signoria comitale dei Carraresi nel secolo XII," in his *Padova medioevale*, 1:125–37.

63. See Hyde, *Padua in the Age of Dante*, 82–85, 312–14, for the statute of 1278.

64. My account of the emergence of Giacomo il Grande owes much to Collodo, "Il ceto dominante padovano," 25–39, especially 36–39.

Chapter 2   Under Foreign Domination, 1318–1337

1. For the election, see Cortusi, *Chronica*, 26–27, and Gatari, *Cronaca carrarese*, 11, and for an edition of the statute, Colle, *Storia scientifico-letteraria*, 1:29–31, *Stat. Com.*, 431, no. 1382, establishes the *palio*. For the provisional nature of Giacomo's power, subject to ultimate revocation by the Maggior Consigilio, see Salzer, *Ueber die Anfänge der Signorie in Oberitalien*, 140–41.

2. See Hyde, *Padua in the Age of Dante*, 270–71, and Cortusi, *Chronica*, 25–27.

3. Quoted in Cortusi, *Chronica*, 29.

4. Ibid., 30.

5. Verci, 8:184–87, no. 934.

6. *Constitutiones*, 1313–24, 5:445–45, no. 556, December 1319.

7. Ibid., 5:446–47, no. 557, 5 Jan. 1320.

8. Ibid., 5:449–50, no. 561, 27 Feb. 1320.

9. Ibid., 5:456–57, no. 589, 29 May 1320.

10. Cortusi, *Chronica*, 35–37, and Reidmann, "La Marca e Venezia," 364–66.

11. Cortusi, *Chronica*, 31.

12. AD, 5735, 6 Aug. 1320; cf. Hyde, *Padua in the Age of Dante*, 115.

13. See Bortolami, "Statuto padovano del 1320," 389–90, 395–400, which describes these procedures in detail.
14. See Mueller, "Camera del frumento," 328.
15. AD, 6161, May–November 1326.
16. Predelli, 2:12, no. 77, 13 Mar. 1326.
17. Cortusi, *Chronica*, 39–40; *Constitutiones*, 1313–24, 5:498–99, no. 629, 19 July 1321.
18. *Constitutiones*, 1313–24, 5:504–6, nos. 637–39, 5–6 Sept. 1321.
19. Bortolami, "Statuto padovano del 1320," 394, 400–402.
20. Cortusi, *Chronica*, 40.
21. Gloria, 2:12–13, no. 1123, 4 May 1323.
22. AD, 5933, 2 June 1323, excerpt in Gloria, 2:14, no. 1124; ed. in Gloria, "Documenti inediti intorno a Francesco Petrarca a Albertino Mussato," 43–44.
23. AD, 5938, 7 July 1323; ed. in *Forschungen zur Reichs- und Rechtsgeschichte Italiens*, ed. J. Ficker (Innsbruck, 1874), 4:516–17, no. 506.
24. AD, 6077, 27 June 1325.
25. Mussato, *De traditione*, col. 725 and passim; Vergerio, *De principibus Carrariensibus*, 416; Conversini, *De dilectione regnantium*, 152.
26. See Riedmann, *Beziehungen der Grafen und Landesfürsten*, 358–60, and 544–55 for the documents from which the figures are derived.
27. Cortusi, *Chronica*, 41–42.
28. Gloria, *Monumenti* (1222–1318), 2:87, no. 654, 20 Jan. 1325.
29. AD, 6127, 18 Apr. 1326: "in camera vel extra cameram domini Regis vel in canipis communis Padue."
30. See Riedmann, *Beziehungen der Grafen und Landesfürsten*, 371, 372 n. 204: "significavimus domino nostro Karinthia duci sine cuius conscensu [sic] nichil facere possumus."
31. See Verci, 11:74, no. 991; also in *Constitutiones*, 1325–30, 6:54, no. 77, 23 Aug. 1325.
32. Cortusi, *Chronica*, 43–45, and *Chronicon Patavinum*, col. 1159.
33. Mussato, *De traditione*, col. 725.
34. Cortusi, *Chronica*, 51, and Mussato, *De traditione*, col. 726.
35. Dondi dall'Orologio, *Dissertazione ottava*, 59–69 and 116–18, doc. 68, 23 Mar. 1327.
36. Mussato, *De traditione*, col. 726, and Dondi dall'Orologio, *Dissertazione ottava*, 62–63.
37. AD, 6138, 28 May 1326.
38. Cortusi, *Chronica*, 45.
39. Ibid., 46, and Mussato, *De traditione*, col. 729.
40. Mussato, *De traditione*, col. 732: "Vir ingentis in genii, magna vi animi et corporis, factiosus. Cui a iuventute exosa urbis sue communitas legum statutorum coarctatio. Audax, formidolosus, sed semper varius, dominii cupidus, insolens, facundie mediocris, astutia quam sapientia inbutus."

41. Quoted in Riedmann, *Beziehungen der Grafen und Landesfürsten*, 374: "propter multa obsequia et beneficia per ipsum dominum Henricum colata comuni Padue."
42. Cortusi, *Chronica*, 51.
43. Verci, 10:45, no. 1103, 3 Sept. 1328.
44. Mussato, *De traditione*, cols. 753-55. On Cangrande's rule in Padua, now see the authoritative account of Varanini, "Della Scala, Cangrande," 402-4, and Collodo's insightful analysis in *Società in trasformazione*, 188-91.
45. *Constitutiones*, 1325-30, 6:172-73, no. 265.
46. Mussato, *De traditione*, col. 757, and Hyde, *Padua in the Age of Dante*, 278-79, which I follow closely.
47. Archivio di Stato, Florence, Missivi della Prima Cancellaria, reg. 3, fols. 74v-75r, 20 Sept. 1328; mentioned in Allen, *History of Verona*, 212.
48. See Cipolla, "Degli atti diplomatici," 229-35, and for the feasts, Gloria, 2:13-14, no. 1125, 16 Oct. 1328; Gloria, *Monumenti* (1222-1318), 2:90, no. 657, 19 Apr. 1329.
49. *Annales patavini*, 250, and Hyde, *Padua in the Age of Dante*, 279.
50. See Mussato, *De traditione*, cols. 746-47, and *Gesta magnifica domus Carrariensis*, 42.
51. See Cipolla, "Degli atti diplomatici," 235-39; a complete edition of the Paduan statutes under the Scaligeri has been published by B. Cessi, "Gli statuti padovani durante la dominazione scaligera in Padova," 66-124.
52. See the essay of Collodo, "Padova e gli Scaligeri," in *Società in trasformazione*, 169-91, with quotation on 189.
53. Mussato, *De traditione*, col. 763.
54. Cortusi, *Chronica*, 67-68; Verci, 9:44, no. 1260; and on the conditions of the second marriage, Collodo, *Società in trasformazione*, 190-91.
55. Cortusi, *Chronica*, 73-74.
56. Predelli, 2:27, no. 158, 12 Mar. 1329.
57. Vararini, "Pietro dal Verme," 75-80.
58. Archivio della Curia Vescovile, Padua, Feudorum, vol. 5, fol. 48r, 4 Aug. 1333.
59. Predelli, 2:57, no. 340, Dec. 1334.
60. I have based my account of the origins of this conflict on the important essay of Simeoni, "Origini del conflitto veneto-fiorentino-scaligero," esp. 15-25, and the contemporary account in Cortusi, *Chronica*, 75-80.
61. Archivio di Stato, Venice, Senato, Misti, vol. 17, fols. 42v and 43r, 8 and 19 Jan. 1336 (1335 *more veneto*).
62. Documents in Simeoni, "Origini del conflitto veneto-fiorentino-scaligero," 58-59, nos. 11-12.
63. G. Villani, *Cronica*, 418-19 (bk. 11, chap. 49). See also discussion and documents in Simeoni, "Origini del conflitto veneto-fiorentino-scaligero," 29-37, 61-64.
64. AD, 6878, 2 Apr. 1336.
65. AN, 1849, no. 3, 2 Apr. 1336.
66. Senato, Misti, reg. 17, fol. 57v, 30 Apr. 1336.
67. Piacentino, *Cronica*, 39-44.

68. Ibid., 53–55.
69. Ibid., 57–60, 62–65.
70. Ibid., 70–80.
71. Lazzarini, "Storia di un trattato," 245–49, text on 273–82; see also Piacentino, *Cronica*, 84–86.
72. See accounts in Vergerio, *De principibus Carrariensibus*, 402–8, and Cortusi, *Chronica*, 83–85.
73. Piacentino, *Cronica*, 87.

Chapter 3   Venice's *Status Noster*, 1337–1355

1. Cessi, *Padova medioevale*, 1:145 n. 19, quoting Biblioteca Civica, Padua, MS B.P. 825, fol. 15r, 30 Sept. 1337: "dicti gastaldiones fecerunt depingi in ecclesia palacii et portas palacii et dicto palacio signa et armaturas communium Veneciarum, Florencie, Padue et magnifici domini domini Marsilii de Carraria."
2. Cortusi, *Chronica*, 84.
3. Ibid., 84–85.
4. See Gonzati, *Basilica di S. Antonio*, 2:37–41.
5. Piacentino, *Cronica*, 90–100.
6. Cortusi, *Chronica*, 89–90.
7. Lazzarini, "Storia di un trattato," 251–53, 266–82.
8. On the siege of Monselice, see Cortusi, *Chronica*, 90; Bortolami, "Monselice 'Oppidum opulentissimum,'" 158–60.
9. Piacentino, *Cronica*, 105–11, 116.
10. Cortusi, *Chronica*, 92–93; Piacentino, *Cronica*, 114–15.
11. See Cessi, *Padova medioevale*, 1:149–51.
12. See G. Villani, *Cronica*, 438–40 (bk. 11, chap. 89), and Perrens, *Histoire de Florence*, 4:209–13. Excerpts from the original text of the treaty found in Archivio di Stato, Venice, Pacta, vol. 5, fols. 59r–64r, have been published in Cappelletti, *Storia della Repubblica di Venezia*, 4:125–56. There is a much abridged version in Verci, 11:124–28, doc. 1324.
13. Lazzarini, "Storia di un trattato," 251.
14. Dondi dall'Orologio, *Dissertazione ottava*, 127–28, doc. 77.
15. The numerous statutes promulgated at the end of Falier's podesteria in February 1339 have been published from *Stat. Car.* in Beda, *Ubertino da Carrara*, 129–90, with discussion on 75–105.
16. Archivio di Stato, Venice, Senato, Misti, reg. 18, fol. 5v, 28 Feb. 1339 (1338 *more veneto*); see also Beda, *Ubertino da Carrara*, 38–39.
17. For this background, see Cortusi, *Chronica*, 99–100, and the entries by Barile "Camposampiero, Guglielmo da" and "Camposampiero, Tiso da," in the *DBI*.
18. Senato, Misti, reg. 18, fols. 8r and 14r, 6 and 18 March 1339, and Predelli, 2:83–84, no. 483, 24 Mar. 1340.
19. See Archivio di Stato, Venice, Maggior Consiglio, Grazie, reg. 8, fol. 90r, 16 Feb. 1341. On the recommendation of the Council of Forty, the Maggior Con-

siglio voted "quod dictus nobilis Guilielmus de Campo Sancti Petri cum suis heredibus . . . ad dictam gratiam et honorem nostre citadinantis . . . assumatur."

20. See Senato, Misti, reg. 20, fol. 38r, 7 Mar. 1342, and Verci, 11:23, doc. 1401, 27 Feb. 1342.

21. Senato, Misti, reg. 20, fol. 82r, 82v, 14 and 16 Sept. 1342.

22. Cortusi, *Chronica,* 99–100; Senato, Misti, reg. 21, fol. 58r, 22 Aug. 1343.

23. See Beda, *Ubertino da Carrara,* 35–36, and Lazzarini, "Storia di un trattato," 252–53 and doc. on 279–82, from Archivio di Stato, Venice, Pacta, vol. 5, fol. 72rv.

24. Senato, Misti, reg. 18, fol. 58r, 19 Aug. 1339, for the initial appointment of the savi, and Beda, *Ubertino da Carrara,* 37–39, 109–110, doc. 1, for the recommendations.

25. Senato, Misti, reg. 18, fol. 40r, 8 June 1339.

26. Maggior Consiglio, Spiritus, fol. 97r, 8 July 1339: "non debet intelligi quod civitas Padue sit ad conditionem tyrampnorum, quia potest dici quod est nostrum statum proprium." There is an abridged and inaccurate text in Verci, 11:119, no. 1329. See also Lazzarini, "Storia di un trattato," 257–58.

27. Maggior Consiglio, Grazie, reg. 8, fols. 36v, late 1339, 45v, 15 Feb. 1340, and F. C. Lane, *Venice and History* (Baltimore: Johns Hopkins Press, 1966), 65.

28. My account of the Dente vendetta follows Lazzarini's essay "Aneddoti di storia carrarese," 475–90, which is based on exhaustive research in Venetian archival sources. Guido Ruggiero has also discussed these incidents in his *Violence in Early Renaissance Venice,* 170–71, without, however, the benefit of having read Lazzarini's essay.

29. The story is told in *Historiae romanae fragmenta,* col. 288, and repeated with relish in Brown's "The Carraresi," 1:119.

30. See Cortusi, *Chronica,* 102–3, and Cipolla, *Documenti per la storia delle relazioni diplomatiche,* 324–25.

31. Senato, Misti, reg. 18, fol. 70r, 5 Oct. 1339, fol. 92v, 2 Mar. 1340. Cf. Beda, *Ubertino da Carrara,* 46–48.

32. Senato, Misti, reg. 19, fol. 26v, 6 July 1340; Predelli, 2:87–88, no. 502, 10 July 1340.

33. Senato, Misti, reg. 19, fol. 35r, 2 Oct. 1340: "quia non cessant querelle pro parte illorum de la Scala et suorum contra dominum Ubertinum et suos, et ergo que futigunt [?] nos multum et adducunt scandalum et errorem inter partes."

34. Senato, Misti, reg. 19, fol. 51r, 31 Dec. 1340: "quod nos desiderantes honorem et quietum statum ipsius domini Ubertini ut nostrum, . . . in hoc operati id boni quod poterimus cum omni honore et conservatione domini Ubertini."

35. Text in Cipolla, *Documenti per la storia delle relazioni diplomatiche,* 341–42, no. 124.

36. Senato, Misti, reg. 19, fols. 80v, 87r, 21 May and 19 June 1341.

37. Beda, *Ubertino da Carrara,* 118–19, doc. 5, 1 Aug. 1341.

38. Senato, Misti, reg. 20, fol. 4v, 20 Aug. 1341: "sperimus de eo [Ubertino] in omnibus, sicut de nobis ipsis, quia suum bonum est nostrum, et nostrum est suum."

39. Ibid., fol. 11r, 2 Oct. 1341.

40. See Beda, *Ubertino da Carrara*, 56–58, and Senato, Misti, reg. 21, fol. 21v, 24 Mar. 1343.
41. Senato, Misti, reg. 21, fol. 31v, 27 Apr. 1343, and Cortusi, *Chronica*, 106.
42. B. Zendrini, *Memorie storiche delle lagune di Venezia*, 2 vols. (Venice, 1809), 1:15, 30–31.
43. Verci, 11:175, no. 1371, 16 Mar. 1340, and Senato, Misti, reg. 20, fol. 15rv, 22 Oct. 1341.
44. Senato, Misti, reg. 21, fol. 12r, 10 Feb. 1343, with discussion in Beda, *Ubertino da Carrara*, 59. Full text of the doge's reply to the Paduan ambassador in ibid., 119–21, doc. 5.
45. Senato, Misti, reg. 20, fol. 55r, 18 May 1342, and Predelli, 2:101–2, no. 572, 20 May 1342; cf. Beda, *Ubertino da Carrara*, 110–12.
46. Maggior Consiglio, Grazie, reg. 9, fol. 67v, 9 Dec. 1342; fol. 69r, 12 Jan. 1343.
47. Senato, Misti, reg. 22, fol. 21v, 10 May 1344.
48. Ibid., fol. 13v, 12 Apr. 1344, fol. 26v, 27 May 1344; see also Beda, *Ubertino da Carrara*, 59–62.
49. Senato, Misti, reg. 22, fol. 53v, 56v, 26 Oct. and 12 Nov. 1344.
50. Ibid., fol. 64v, 22 Dec. 1344; fols. 68r, 69r, 71r, 10 Jan., 16 Jan., and 20 Jan. 1345.
51. Senato, Misti, reg. 22, fol. 61v, 12 Feb. 1344: "prout scribit potestas noster Castelfranchi, speloncha latronum appellari potest." Cf. Beda, *Ubertino da Carrara*, 44–45.
52. Vergerio, *De principibus Carrariensibus*, 434: "nimium usum genitalis membri morbum incurrit."
53. Ibid., 435–37, and in general on Marsilietto and others of the Papafava branch, see Ceoldo, *Albero della famiglia Papafava*, 85–97.
54. Maggior Consiglio, Grazie, reg. 7, fol. 26v, 22 Mar. 1338, cited in Lazzarini, "Storia di un trattato," 260.
55. Senato, Misti, reg. 22, fol. 89v–90r, 16 Apr. 1345, discussed in Lazzarini, "Storia di un trattato," 261–62.
56. Text in Archivio di Stato, Venice, Pacta, vol. 5, fol. 74rv, 20 Apr. 1345, cited in Lazzarini, "Storia di un trattato," 262: "Item quod commune Venetiarum habebit et tenebit ipsum dominum Marsilium et comune Padue et districtum in sua protectione et defensione contra quamlibet persone de mundo."
57. V. Lazzarini, *Proprietà e feudi*, 26–27, doc. 13, publishing Maggior Consiglio, Spiritus, fol. 142v, 17 Apr. 1345.
58. Senato, Misti, reg. 23, fol. 1r, 3 May 1345.
59. Cortusi, *Chronica*, 111–13.
60. In general on Giacomo II's rule, see the entry by Ganguzza Billanovich "Carrara, Giacomo da," 673–75, along with the older studies of Frison, *Principato di Giacomo II*, and Zennari, "Giacomo II da Carrara," 101–23 on domestic affairs, and 1–27 on reforms and relations with Venice.
61. Senato, Misti, reg. 23, fol. 9v, 23 May 1345: "Respondeatur ambaxatoribus

domini Padue cum decentibus verbis quod nos habemus ad bonum id quod nobis ipse dominus notificavit, et credimus quod eius responsio sit bona pro bono et pacifico statu civitatis Padue, que desideramus omni tempore."

62. See Beda, "Un trattato di estradizione," 32–44, which publishes the text of the treaty on 39–44.

63. Senato, Misti, reg. 23, fols. 18r, 25 June; 23r, 29 June; 27v, 25 July 1345.

64. Senato, Misti, reg. 23, fol. 32r, 14 Aug. 1345; Verci, 12:68, doc. 1433, 14 Aug. 1345.

65. Zennari, "Giacomo II," 17–18, and Clement VI, *Lettres closes, patentes et curiales*, 2:184, no. 2589, 15 June 1346.

66. Cortusi, *Chronica*, 112–14, and Senato, Misti, reg. 23, fol. 42v, 8 Dec. 1345; see also Verci, 12:69, doc. 1435, abridged version of same act.

67. Maggior Consiglio, Grazie, vol. 11, fol. 43r, 26 and 30 Oct. 1345, published in Lazzarini, "Storia di un trattato," 264–65.

68. Cortusi, *Chronica*, 115, and Archivio di Stato, Venice, Senato, Secreta, reg. A, fol. 19r, ed. in Ljubić, 2:297, no. 493, 6 Dec. 1345.

69. See Cortusi, *Chronica*, 114–15, and for the appropriation of the 1,000 ducats for the gifts, Maggior Consiglio, Grazie, vol. 11, fol. 56v, 14, 16 Jan. 1346.

70. Ljubić, 2:448, no. 705, 21 Apr. 1347, ed. of Senato, Secreta, reg. A, fol. 75r: "considerato etiam pacto, quod habuimus cum communi Padue et predecessoribus suis, et habemus ad presens, videlicet de habendo pro inimicis inimicos nostros, et nos haberemus pro inimicis inimicos suos. Quare magnificentiam suam requirimus et rogamus, quod, premissis debite pensatis, debeat se abstinare a dando aliquam fidantiam vel promissionem gentibus dicti regis per literas vel aliter, et si iam dedisset, studeat illas pro bono suo et nostro revocare per illum modum, quem viderit expedire."

71. Cortusi, *Chronica*, 117.

72. *Deliberazioni del Consiglio del XL della Repubblica di Venezia*, ed. A. Lombardo, Monumenti Storici della Deputazione di Storia Patria per le Venezie, n.s., vol. 12 (Venice: Deputazione Editrice, 1958), 2:7, no. 23, May 1347.

73. Senato, Secreta, reg. A, fol. 79r, 12 June 1347; quotation in ibid., fol. 83r, 19 July 1347, ed. in Ljubić, 3:9, no. 12.

74. Cortusi, *Chronica*, 117–18.

75. Senato, Misti, reg. 24, fol. 30r, 19 Aug. 1347, and cf. Zennari, "Giacomo II," 116.

76. Clement VI, *Lettres closes, patentes et curiales*, 2:399, no. 3547, 23 Oct. 1347.

77. *Constitutiones*, 1345–48, ed. Zeumer and Salomon, 8:606–12, nos. 600–601, 4–5 June 1348.

78. See the accounts in Cortusi, *Chronica*, 122–23, and Verci, 13:69–74, and Verci, 12:107–8, no. 1463, 12 Jan. 1349.

79. AN, 256, fol. 15r, 13 July 1350.

80. Senato, Misti, reg. 26, fol. 27r, 25 May 1350.

81. Ibid., fol. 32v, 25 June 1350, and Cortusi, *Chronica*, 127.

82. See Senato, Secreta, reg. B, fol. 16r, 14 Sept. 1348, fol. 31r, 6 Nov. 1348, pub-

lished in Cesca, *Sollevazione di Capodistria,* 34, 111, docs. 8, 56, and Cortusi, *Chronica,* 123, on the value of the palace.

83. Senato, Secreta, reg. B (copia), fols. 12v–13r, 4 May 1348.

84. See Frison, *Principato di Giacomo II,* 29–32, Zardo, *Petrarca e i Carraresi,* 16–21, and Cortusi, *Chronica,* 125–35.

85. Cipolla, *Document per la storia delle relazioni diplomatiche,* 477–78, no. 197, and 483–88, no. 199.

86. Clement VI, *Lettres closes, patents et curiales,* 2:327–28, nos. 2343–50, 27 Nov. 1350, abridged version in Verci, 12:159–60, no. 1498.

87. Cortusi, *Chronica,* 127–28; Gatari, *Cronaca carrarese,* 28–31.

88. The text of the statute from Archivio Papafava, Padua, Codice 35, Parchment 2, is published with discussion in Lazzarini, "Statuto che conferisce la signoria a Francesco I da Carrara," 284–90. Francesco and Giacomino are already called imperial vicars in documents from March and December 1354; see *Constitutiones,* 1354–56, ed. Fritz, 11:68, 176–77, nos. 104, 322, but I have found no record of Charles IV's bestowal of the vicariate.

89. Lazzarini, "Storia di un trattato," 266–67, citing Senato, Secreta, reg. B, fols. 69r, 88v, 20 Sept. and 20 Dec. 1350.

90. Predelli, 2:200, no. 456, 19 June 1353.

91. Senato, Misti, reg. 26, fols. 58v, 59r, 8 May 1351.

92. See Predelli, 2:218–20, nos. 27–29, 10, 12 Jan. 1354.

93. Cortusi, *Chronica,* 133–38, and reporting the knightings, *Gesta magnifica domus Carrariensis,* 70–71.

94. Gatari, *Cronaca carrarese,* 30–32. Cortusi, *Chronica,* 140–41, Gallo, "L'epoca delle signorie," 180, 183.

95. See, most conveniently, the account in Lazzarini, *Marino Falier,* 230–231, and also documents in Verci, 13:47–48, no. 1543, 18 Nov. 1355, and Predelli, 2:234–36, 237, 238, nos. 104, 118, 120, Nov. 1355.

96. See Cortusi, *Chronica,* 140, and Joppi, "Documenti goriziani del secolo XIV (1890)," 23–25.

97. Senato, Misti, reg. 27, fol. 50v, 22 Dec. 1355, ed. in Ljubič, 3:297, no. 440, and Wenzel, 2:459–60, no. 370; "licet optaverit et optet amorem et benivolentiam domini regis Hungarie, ipsum tamen optavit et optat semper cum honore et bono dominii nostri Veneciarum, cuius statum reputat suum et reputaret in omni casu suum proprium, sicut e converso dominium Veneciarum fecit et faciet erga ipsum."

98. Gloria, 2:41, no. 1184, 13 June 1356, from a copy made in the eighteenth century by G. Brunacci. I have not, however, found this diploma in Charles IV's *Constitutiones,* 1354–56, ed. Fritz, cited in note 88 above.

Chapter 4 Seeking Other Allies, 1356–1376

1. Archivio di Stato, Venice, Collegio, Segreti, vol. 1, fol. 11r, no. 38, 3 Aug. 1356.

2. Cortusi, *Chronica,* 143–44, and Collegio, Segreti, vol. 1, fol. 12r, no. 42, 9 Aug. 1356.

3. Maggior Consiglio, Deliberazioni, Spiritus, fol. 49r [60r], 27 Nov. 1356; the preamble reads: "cum antiqui nostri cognoverint utile et salubre fore pro conservatione status nostri quod cives nostri non possent acceptare vel ire rectores in terras tyrampnorum." The earlier prohibition of 1327 is discussed and edited in Lazzarini, *Proprietà e feudi*, 14, 25.

4. Collegio, Segreti, vol. 1, fol. 25rv, no. 77, 30 Dec. 1356 (1357 *more paduano*).

5. Collegio, Segreti, vol. 1, fol. 28r, no. 86, 25 May 1357: "tractent cum quibuscumque personis sibi videbuntur, excepto domino Padue, per quem modum possemus exire de Trevisana, cum minore onore et maiori avantagio nostro et nostrum possemus."

6. Collegio, Segreti, vol. 1, fol. 30r, nos. 98–99, 10 Aug. 1357.

7. Senato, Misti, reg. 28, fol. 8, 15 July 1357, ed. in Ljubić, 3:346, no. 516, on war damage, and Predelli, 2:268, no. 261, 20 Sept. 1357, protest of Venetian ambassadors in Padua; witnesses include Pataro Buzzacarini, Bartolomeo Piacentini, and Checco Lion.

8. Cortusi, *Chronica*, 144; Gatari, *Cronaca carrarese*, 35.

9. See discussion in Romanin, *Storia documentata di Venezia*, 3:146–51. The text of the negotiations and treaty is in the Archivio di Stato, Venice, Pacta, vol. 5, fols. 154r–63r, Feb. 1358, editions in Wenzel, 2:490–522, no. 390, and Ljubić, 3:361–81.

10. A text of grant is incorporated in Cortusi, *Chronica*, 145–46; partial edition from another source in Gloria, 2:43, no. 1189, 5 May 1358.

11. Collegio, Secreti, vol. 1, fols. 40v, 41r, nos. 127, 129, 26 May, 4 June 1358; the two passages quoted read: "quod dominus and commune Padue et sui sucessori possint emere et emi facere de sale Clugie quantum erit sibi necessarii per usu civitatis et districtus Padue," and "intendimus vivere cum eo [i.e. Francisco] in omni amore et caritate sicut cum fratre."

12. Cortusi, *Chronica*, 145; the texts of the treaty ratified separately with Francesco il Vecchio and the Paduan commune are edited in Cappelletti, *Storia di Padova*, 1:283–94, from Pacta, vol. 5, fols. 164r–65v.

13. See AN, 256, fols. 137v–38r, 2 Dec. 1358, the original contract with Paolo Dotti serving as general factor for Francesco il Vecchio, and ibid., fol. 225r, 17 Jan. 1359, for final delivery of the grain.

14. See Lazzarini, "Principio della dominazione carrarese a Feltre e a Belluno," 1–4, which includes an edition of the act of cession of 1 Nov. 1360 from AN, 5, fol. 2rv.

15. Verci, 14:3–4, no. 1594, 1 Jan. 1363.

16. The case can be followed from abstracts in Predelli, 2:285, no. 46, 29 Aug. 1358; 2:286, no. 50, 2 Sept. 1358; 2:289, no. 69, 6 Oct. 1358; 2:291, no. 80, 18 Nov. 1358; 2:292, no. 85, 30 Nov. 1358; and 2:313–14, no. 206, 19 June 1360. See also Senato, Misti, reg. 28, fol. 74v, 20 Sept. 1358, fol. 94r, 14 March 1359, fol. 101v, 11 Apr. 1359.

17. Senato, Misti, reg. 28, fol. 60v, 16 June 1358: "procedatur ad alia super differencia confinium que est inter dominum Padue et communem Clugie sic diligenter examinare."

18. Ibid., fol. 98v, 30 March 1359; reg. 29, fol. 28v, 10 Oct. 1359; fol. 29v, 20 Oct. 1359, an update on instructions to the ambassador.

19. Ibid., fol. 86r, 19 Oct. 1360; fol. 114v, 27 April 1361.

20. Predelli, 2:333, no. 317, 19 May 1362, on the grain deal, and Senato, Misti, reg. 30, fols. 77v, 86v, 24 May and 18 June 1362, on the Carrara retinue to Istria.

21. Senato, Misti, reg. 30, fol. 79r, 24 May 1362.

22. See Gatari, *Cronaca carrarese,* 40, and on Montagnana, Collodo, "Castello di Montagnana," 106.

23. Senato, Misti, reg. 30, fol. 84r, 9 June 1362.

24. See the text of the *Commemoriali,* vol. 7, fol. 11r, 18 Sept. 1362, recording the Carrara lord's response to a Venetian ambassador explaining his government's position edited in Gloria, "Documenti inediti intorno a Francesco Petrarca," 36–38, doc. 1; summary in Predelli, 3:8, no. 21. See also *Additamentum primum ad Chronicon Cortusiorum,* cols. 965–66.

25. Senato, Misti, reg. 30, fol. 109v, 19 Sept. 1362; fol. 111r, 3 Oct. 1362.

26. For the Carrara lord's appointment on 8 April of Manno Donati and Bartolomeo Piacentini as his ambassadors to join the anti-Visconti league and the text of the treaty ratified at Ferrara on 16 April, see Cipolla, *Storia scaligera secondo i documenti,* 94–95, no. 23, and 103–18, no. 24; another version of that treaty is in Verci, 13:88–92, no. 1590, 16 Apr. 1362.

27. On the policies of Rudolf, see Cusin, "Rudolfo IV d'Absburgo," 68–75, 107–36; Venice's denial is found in Senato, Misti, reg. 30, fol. 121r, 10 Dec. 1362, ed. in Zahn, *Austro-Friulana,* 187–88, no. 148.

28. Collegio, Secreti, vol. 1, fol. 99v, 24 Feb. 1363, ed. in Zahn, *Austro-Friulana,* pp. 188–89, no. 149.

29. Verci, 14:4–10, no. 1595, contract of [spring] 1363.

30. Cusin, "Rudolfo IV d'Absburgo," 109–11, and Urban V, *Lettres communes,* 1:27, no. 223, 4 Mar. 1363.

31. Collegio, Secreti, vol. 1, fol. 102rv, nos. 186–88, 7 June, letter to captains on deserters, 8 June 1363, letter to count of Spilimbergo and the Este embassy; fol. 103r, no. 193, 14 June 1363, on the deployment of troops.

32. Ibid., fol. 107rv, 27 June 1363, ed. in Zahn, *Austro-Friulana,* 195–98, no. 156, quotation on 197: "in casu quo civitas Padue subtraheretur de manibus dicti domini [de Carraria], et ipse deponeretur de statu suo, ipsa civitas et castra et loca paduani districtus debeant dimitti in libertate et regi per commune."

33. Text edited in Cappelletti, *Storia di Padova,* 1:296–98, from Archivio di Stato, Venice, Pacta, vol. 5, fols. 164r–65v, 6 July 1362.

34. Verci, 14:10, no. 1596, 7 July 1363.

35. Senato, Misti, reg. 30, fol. 40r, 17 Sept., fol. 42v, 11 Oct., fol. 47v, 30 Nov. 1363, ed. in Zahn, *Austro-Friulana,* 211, 215–16, 218–19, nos. 166, 171, 175, respectively.

36. Maggior Consiglio, Grazie, reg. 15, fol. 86v, December 1363; see also Predelli, 2:23, no. 115, 9 Dec. 1363.

37. Treaty of 3 Mar. 1364 between Pope Urban V with his allies and Bernabò Visconti in Verci, 14:15–18, no. 1599.

38. Urban V, *Lettres communes,* 1:132 and 192–93, nos. 888, 1210, 10 Apr. and 3 Aug. 1364.

39. Zahn, *Austro-Friulana,* 226–32, no. 184, 13 Aug. 1364.

40. Ibid., 239–40, nos. 191–92, 11 Sept. 1364; other papal letters urged Charles IV, Holy Roman Emperor, and Rudolf himself to assist in the peace efforts: Urban V, *Lettres communes,* 1:195–96, nos. 1223–25, 11 Sept. 1364.

41. See Zahn, *Austro-Friulana,* 241–42, no. 194, on 13 Sept. 1364, on the refusal of safe-conduct to Paduan troops; Senato, Misti, reg. 31, fol. 88v, 21 Dec. 1364, on the counterfeit ducats from Padua.

42. See Zahn, *Austro-Friulana,* 275–76, 278–79, nos. 210, 212–13, 8 and 12 Jan. and 4 Feb. 1365.

43. On this diplomacy, see Cusin, "Rudolfo IV d'Absburgo," 116–21, with documents from Florence printed on 129–32. See also the account in Brucker, *Florentine Politics and Society,* 225–26.

44. On the Florentine troops, see Cusin, "Rodulfo IV d'Absburgo," 136, doc. 11, 3 Aug. 1365; on the Spilimberg oath, Zahn, *Austro-Friulana,* 294–99, no. 228, 4 Sept. 1365.

45. See *Additamentum primum ad Chronicon Cortusiorum,* col. 973, and Lazzarini, "Prestito di Francesco il Vecchio da Carrara," 229–30.

46. Archivio di Stato, Florence, Missivi della Prima Cancellaria, reg. 13, fol. 72v, 25 Oct. 1365; AN, 1158, fols. 75r–76r, 15 Aug. 1366, excerpt in Gloria 2:64, no. 1252; and AN, 1158, fols. 77r–78v, 10 Jan. 1367.

47. Missivi della Prima Cancellaria, reg. 13, fol. 69v, 6 Oct. 1365, and reg. 14, fol. 20r, 8 Aug. 1366.

48. See Meek, *Lucca, 1369–1400,* 29, 54; Molà, *Comunità dei Lucchesi a Venezia,* 84–86, and AN, 31, fol. 70r, 2 Feb. 1370, contract of the loan to Lucca.

49. Padua, Archivio Papafava, Cod. 35, perg. 3, 8 Feb. 1370.

50. See Praga, "Prestito di Francesco il Vecchio da Carrara," 471–81, with document of 31 May 1366 on 480–81; and Papafava, vol. 5, fol. 39r, 30 Oct. 1366.

51. Gloria, 2:64, no. 1251, 1 Aug. 1366, from Prague.

52. Senato, Misti, reg. 32, fol. 30r, 23 Dec. 1366, and fol. 32v, 9 Feb. 1367, ed. in Ljubić, 4:90, no. 156, and Wenzel, 2:654, no. 490.

53. Gloria, 2:68, no. 1261, 1 Aug. and 9 Aug. 1367.

54. For the emperor, see Mommsen, *Italienische Analekten zur Reichsgeschichte,* 136, no. 322, 16 May 1367, and on the meeting at Bologna, AN, 398, fol. 1r, 4 Apr. 1367, excerpt in Gloria, 2:66, no. 1257.

55. The text of the treaty of 4 Aug. 1367 is in Theiner, *Codex diplomaticus,* 2:445–50, no. 429; on Florentine policy, see Brucker, *Florentine Politics and Society,* 231–34.

56. On Charles' second descent, see the exhaustive study of Pirchan, *Italien und Kaiser IV,* with account of the visit to Padua on 1:139–44.

57. Verci, 14:34–40, no. 1371, 15 Mar. 1369; ratified at the house of Albertello Marmito of Parma at Montagnana on 3 Apr. 1369, see AN, 31, fol. 9rv.

58. For a clear description of Urban's movements and policy in these years, see Partner, *Lands of St Peter,* 353–57.

59. Senato, Misti, reg. 32, fol. 28r, 10 Dec. 1366; fol. 68v, 12 Aug. 1367.
60. Ibid., reg. 33, fol. 22v, 9 June 1369, fol. 23v, 12 June, fol. 24v, 19 June, and fol. 29r, 30 July; see Predelli, 3:81–82, nos. 500–502.
61. Predelli, 3:87, nos. 528–29.
62. AN, 31, fol. 94v, 29 Dec. 1369, excerpt in Gloria 2:80, no. 1298: "omnes et quarumcumque pecuniarum quantitates quas recipere debet quibuscumque mercatoribus et habitatoribus in civitate Venetiarum."
63. Verci, 14:54–55, no. 1641, 14 Sept. 1370; Senato, Misti, reg. 33, fol. 80v, 6 Oct. 1370; Verci, 14:56, no. 1643, 1 Nov. 1370; Pacta, vol. 5, fols. 176v–77r, 8 Dec. 1370.
64. Senato, Misti, reg. 33, fol. 95r, 28 Feb. 1371; fol. 96v, 11 Mar. 1371: "punire taliter subditos suos quod transeat aliis in exemplum de non committendo talis, que sunt contra honorem nostrum." See also Verci, 14:71, no. 1648, on border commission appointed by the Carrara lord.
65. Senato, Misti, reg. 33, fol. 143rv, 27 Oct. 1371; Predelli, 3:100–101, no. 646, 30 Oct. 1371.
66. Archvio di Stato, Padua, Pergamene diverse, busta 54, no. 1123, 30 Dec. 1371.
67. Verci, 14:74–75, nos. 1654–55, 30 Dec. 1371 and 6 Feb. 1372.
68. See Vararini, "Della Scala, Cansignorio," 413, on these negotiations; Gatari, *Cronaca carrarese,* 47–48, stresses the lord of Verona's venality.
69. Senato, Misti, reg. 34, fol. 3v, 29 Mar. 1372, which was actually instructions granting permission to the Dione brothers from Paduan domains to enter Venetian service, despite the usual prohibition against employing Paduans in Treviso.
70. My account of the war is based on Paolo Sambin's standard monograph "La guerra del 1372–73," 1–76, and the two major chronicles that he utilized, d'Alessio, *Storia della guerra,* and Gatari, *Cronaca carrarese,* 60–125. A shorter contemporary account from the Venetian viewpoint, full of invectives against Francesco il Vecchio's ingratitude and treachery, is Caresini, *Chronica,* 20–27.
71. Gregory XI, *Lettres secrètes et curiales intéressant le pays autres que la France,* no. 588, 19 Mar. 1372, no. 620, 6 Apr. 1372.
72. Predelli, 2:102, no. 658, text in Wenzel, 3:21–22, no. 19, 12 Apr. 1272: "Dominus Paduanus fecit dirui domos, placone destrui, et turrim Sancti Baldi, demolitis omnibus edificiis circa ipsam a tempore orte discordie factis, in pristinum statum restitui."
73. My account of the Carrara plots of spring 1372 is based on the authoritative essay of Lazzarini, "Storie vecchie e nuove," 325–63.
74. The popular reaction in Venice is recorded most fully in Caroldo's largely unedited chronicle, of which largely excerpts have been published in Cappelletti, *Storia di Padova,* 1:303–6. The letter to Niccolò d'Este is printed in Lazzarini, "Storie vecchie et nuove," 358–60, doc. 3.
75. Gatari, *Cronaca carrarese,* 56; safe-conduct to the count of Veglia, Senato, Misti, reg. 34, fol. 11r, 28 May 1372, ed. in Ljubić, 4:101, no. 189.
76. Verci, 14:76–77, no. 1661, 19 June 1372.
77. Letter of Gregory XI to Louis to Hungary in Wenzel, 3:22–23, no. 21, 14 May 1372.

78. Theiner, *Vetera monumenta historica Hungariam sacram illustrantia*, 2:118, no. 223, 27 June 1372: "Duces Austrie et Canissegnorius de Lascala se contra dictum Franciscum [de Carraria] cum eisdem Venetiis colligarent, cupimus amputare."

79. Gatari, *Cronaca carrarese*, 63–65, on the council. Only on 27 December did the Anziani authorize partial repayment; see Molà, *Comunità dei Lucchesi a Venezia*, 85–86.

80. Gatari, *Cronaca carrarese*, 60–65.

81. See G. Mollat, "Thomas de Frignano, O.F.M., et la diplomatie pontificale," *Archivum Franciscanum Historicum* 55 (1962): 521–23.

82. Theiner, *Vetera monumenta historica Hungariam sacram illustrantia*, 2:122–23, no. 243, 27 Sept. 1372; another ed. in Wenzel, 3:33–34, no. 31.

83. I follow the accounts in d'Alessio, *Storia della guerra*, 118–22, and Gatari, *Cronaca carrarese*, 103–11.

84. Gloria, 2:38, no. 1175, 16 Oct. 1354; much of this account of the plot of 1373 and its background follows my longer narrative in "Fedeltà e tradimento nello stato carrarese," 43–48.

85. See AN, 165, fols. 145r–47v, 30 and 31 Aug. 1363, for the tithes and *Additamentum primum ad Chronicon Cortusiorum*, cols. 976–77, for the division of the patrimony.

86. AN, 141, fol. 1rv, 16 Sept. 1368; on Marsilio's career, see the entry by Ganguzza Billanovich "Carrara, Marsilio da" in the *DBI*, 691–93.

87. AN, 33, fols. 237v–39r, 29 Oct. 1368.

88. AN, 346, fols. 6v–7v, 17 June 1369, rent of a house in Padua for £68 annually; fol. 11v, 10 Sept. 1369, a fief at Anguillara; fols. 15v–16v, 28 Oct. 1369; *locatio* for five years of all property in Agna, Cona, and Borgoforte for annual income of £800 and *onori;* fol. 21v–22r, 22 Dec. 1369, lease of a house in contrada S. Canciano for annual rents of £132; fols. 31v–32r, 13 Feb. 1370, rent of property in Conselve for £875 at Christmas and 50 *moggi* of grain delivered to Padua on the feast of S. Margherita (22 July); fols. 33v–34r, 24 Feb. 1370, rents in Pernumia.

89. AN, 346, fols. 12v–13r, 27 Sept. 1369, purchase from Margherita, widow of professor of medicine Bartolomeo Campo, of house in contrada S. Canciano and 14 *campi* in Monselice and Valsanzibio; fol. 63r, 25 Mar. 1371, sale for £2,000 of 60 *campi* in Villa Campagna.

90. AN, 346, fol. 66r, 1 Aug. 1371, fol. 68r, 7 Nov. 1371.

91. Biblioteca Civica, Padua, MS B.P. 990, *Documenti carraresi*, perg. 54, 11 Jan. 1373, at Ferrentino in the Roman Campagna, Pietro Paolo Crivelli deposited 136 ducats with Marsilio qd. Pietro Merlara of Padua.

92. AN, 346, fol. 77r, 15 Jan. 1373, fol. 78r, 19 Mar. 1373.

93. See Gatari, *Cronaca carrarese*, 120–24, and Sambin, "La guerra del 1372–73," 68–69, 73–75.

94. A list of those to be ransomed is given in Wenzel, 3:52–53, no. 48, 1 July 1373; another version in Ljubić, 4:105–6, no. 204.

95. See the discussion in Sambin, "La guerra del 1372–73," 71–4.

96. See Lazzarini, "Seconda ambasceria di Francesco Petrarca a Venezia," 173–83,

which includes an edition of the speech in Paduan dialect from Nicoletto d'Alessio's chronicle; the same passage is also available in his *Storia della guerra*, 160.

97. Archivio di Stato, Florence, Provvisioni, reg. 61, fol. 155r, 19 Oct. 1373: "ordinare de reddendo et reddi et restitui faciendo magnifico et egregio militi domino Francischo condam Jacobi de Carraria, dominatori civitatis Padue, vel de sibi mutuando et mutuari faciendo 20,000 et usque in 20,000 florenos auri." I wish to thank Reinhold Mueller for providing notice of this text in a letter of 19 Feb. 1972.

98. Verci, 14:90–95, no. 1675, 13 Mar. 1374.

99. AN, 34, fol. 3rv, 10 Apr. 1374, excerpt in Gloria 2:102, no. 1363.

100. AN, 31, 237v–38v, 19 July 1374, another copy in Gennari, 8:1126; the Carrara treasurer, Jacopino Gaffarello, then resident in the Carrara palace in Venice, received the loan "a provido viro magistro Jacobo Saraceno, regie maiestatis Hungarie domestico et servitore."

101. Gregory XI, *Lettres secrètes et curiales relatives à la France (1370–1378)*, 1107, no. 3471, 1 Aug. 1374.

102. AN, 33, fols. 415v–16v, 25 Oct. 1373, excerpt in Gloria, 2:100, no. 1355; fol. 420rv, 27 Oct. 1373, fols. 421v–22r, 27 Oct. 1373.

103. AN, 31, fols. 216r–17r, 5 Mar. 1374. Despencer's sureties were two English knights: "Symon Curson, filius viri nobilis Rizerii de Anglia, Stephanus qd. Johannis de Anglia," both resident in Bologna.

104. AN, 31, fol. 241rv, 24 Aug. 1374.

105. *Statuti di Verona del 1327*, ed. S. A. Bianchi et al., 2 vols. (Rome: Jouvence, 1992), 2:720–23, treaty of 11–12 Nov. 1374.

106. AN, 346, fol. 79r, 6 Nov. 1373.

107. See AN, 31, fol. 243r, 8 Sept. 1374, a act in Monselice, where Niccolò da Carrara appointed Francesco Raini proctor to recover 1,750 ducats from Guido III da Polenta, apparently part of the inheritance that was never paid.

108. The text of Petrarch's letter, probably written in January 1374, is available in a critical edition by Ussani, "Rerum Senilium liber XIV, epistola II," 297–301.

109. Cf. *Additamentum secundum ad Chronicon Cortusiorum*, col. 984, which dates the tourneys on 1 January, which is too early according to Verci, 14:238.

110. Lazzarini, "Storie vecchie e nuove," 353–54.

111. Senato, Misti, reg. 34, fol. 98v, 15 Apr. 1374.

112. See, for example, AN, 35, fol. 19v, 28 Jan. 1377, Marsilio da Carrara's factor, Leonardo Riniero da Venezia's grant a livello of a house in contrada Brondolo, Padua; AN, 178, fol. 167r, 30 Apr. 1377, rent of property in Castelbaldo and Merlara; Verci, 14:19–21, 1 Mar. 1379, sale for 600 ducats by Marsilio da Carrara of huge fief in Godega in the Trevisano to his factor, Leonardo Riniero, as a reward for faithful service.

113. Theiner, *Codex diplomaticus*, 2:559–60, no. 566; see also Brucker, *Florentine Politics and Society*, 284–85.

114. Missivi della Prima Cancellaria, reg. 16, fol. 19v–20r, 6 Sept. 1375, ed. in Wenzel, 3:112–13, no. 94.

115. Cipolla, *Storia scaligera secondo i documenti*, 158–62, no. 31, 20 Aug. 1375.
116. Senato, Secreta, reg. D, fols. 5r, 8r, 15 May 1376, fol. 15r, 30 May.
117. See Archivio Papafava, Padua, cod. 29, fols. 65r–67r, 9 July 1376, and AN, 34, fol. 430rv, 19 July 1376, excerpt in Gloria, 2:117, no. 1408.
118. On these negotiations, see Senato, Secreta, reg. D, fols. 8rv, 11v–12v, 15v–18v, June and July 1376, edited as an appendix to *Calendar of State Papers, Venetian, 1534–1554*, ed. R. Brown (London, 1873), 600–609.
119. Senato, Secreta, reg. D, fols. 25v–26v, 6 Aug. 1376, quoted passage reads: "est contentus dominus dux et commune Veneciarum tenere et reputare effectualiter dictum dominum Padue, et filium et statum suum, pro intimis filiis, veris et puris amicis, et pro bonis vicinis suis, favorabiliter et benigne et sine aliquo rancore."
120. Text in Verci, 15:9–11, 7 Nov. 1376.

Chapter 5 Signorial Government and Carrara Wealth

1. Text from *Stat. Car.*, fols. 80r–81v, ed. in Roberti, *Corporazioni padovane*, 123–26.
2. Still valuable on Francesco Novello's education is Levi, *Poesie di popolo e poesia di corte nel Trecento*, 219–37.
3. See the capsule biographies in Gloria, 1:129–36, nos. 284–97.
4. See, in general, Sambin, "Alessio, Nicoletto d'," in the *DBI*, which overlooks, however, the sentence and pardon in Venice, on which see Senato, Misti, reg. 25, fol. 70r, 29 Dec. 1349, reg. 26, fol. 26r, 18 May 1350, and Avogaria di Comun, Raspe, vol. 3642, fasc. 3, fol. 18r.
5. See Gloria, 2:34, no. 1165, 13 Oct. 1351, citing AD, 7741.
6. See Gloria, 2:38, no. 1175, 16 Oct. 1354, which gives the location as "in contrada S. Nicolai in curia magnificorum D. d. Jacobini et Francisci de Carrara . . . in camera stipendiariorum . . . in qua habitat Naximbene de Grumpo officialis."
7. See Archivio di Stato, Padua, Archivi Privati Diversi, Grompo, reg. 173, no. 5276, 28 Oct. 1357.
8. See AN, 394, fols. 7r–36r, 20 Oct. 1392, inventory of Arimondo da Ponte real estate and banking interests.
9. On Paduan banking practices during the Trecento, see Zen Benetti, "Prestatori ebraici e cristiani," 629–50, and Cessi's older essay "La condizione degli ebrei banchieri in Padova nel secolo XIV (1907)," in his *Padova medioevale*, 2:319–35.
10. AN, 31, fols. 265v–66r, 268r, 30 Jan. 1372, 12 Apr. 1375, deposits with Padovano. The total of £140,000 is given in my entry "Carrara, Francesco, il Vecchio," in the *DBI*, 652, from AN, 257, fols. 228v–67v, passim, 1366–68; AN, 31, fols. 24rv, 74r, 97r, 145r, 228v, 234r, 252v, 1368, 1371–72, 1374; AN, 47, fols. 17v–18v, 7 Dec. 1369, AN, 6, fol. 6v, 15 Feb. 1370; and AN, 258, fol. 186r, 2 Jan. 1371.
11. See Ciscato, *Gli ebrei in Padova*, 18–23, 230–40.
12. See AD, 7515, 23 Jan. 1346, act on legacies to the Tomb of S. Antonio and the Franciscan house of S. Maria of Monselice.

13. See AD, 8237, 12 Feb. 1365; AN, 31, fol. 41r, 30 July 1369, excerpt in Gloria 2:79, no. 1293, and Collodo, *Società in trasformazione*, 304.

14. See AN, 1158, fol. 55rv, 23 Aug. 1346 = Papafava, 4:340.

15. See AN, 211, fols. 332v–33r, 9 July 1356 = Papafava, 4:256–57, and Gennari, 8:1253.

16. AN, 256, fol. 128v, 22 Dec. 1358.

17. AN, 210, fol. 363r, 22 Aug. 1356 = Papafava, 4:257–58.

18. AN, 256, fols. 134v–135r, 16 Oct. 1358, edited in Levi, *Francesco di Vannozzo e la lirica nelle corti lombarde*, 461–62.

19. See *Stat. Car.*, fol. 315v; only murderers and traitors were excluded from this general pardon.

20. *Stat. Car.*, fol. 190rv, 1360, under podestà Giovanni Manfredi; see the discussion in Cessi, *Corporazioni dei mercanti di panni*, 47–48, 73–74.

21. Cessi, *Corporazioni dei mercanti di panni*, 84–85, for the document, and analysis on 48–50.

22. On these policies, see Rizzoli, "L'università dell'arte della lana," 175–80, and Collodo, *Società in trasformazione*, 383–98.

23. Calculations from Biblioteca Civica, Padua, MS B.P. 169, Matricola, Arte della Lana, fols. 1r–6r.

24. AN, 256, fols. 290rv, 323rv, 7 and 23 July 1361.

25. AN, 257, fol. 118v, 30 May 1365.

26. AN, 257, fol. 224r, 21 Nov. 1365, lease to the grocer Antonio; AN, 258, fol. 177v, 22 Apr. 1371, renunciation of lease by Antonio and grant of property to the weaver Leonardo.

27. AN, 39, fol. 57r, 8 Sept. 1376.

28. See AN, 31, fol. 77v, 1 July 1370, decree to permit one Lotto Strazoruolo to sell at wholesale or retail all sorts of cloths, skins, and furs in Padua and its district, and AN, 398, fol. 42rv, 7 Apr. 1362, rental for five years by Luca da Casale as factor for Francesco il Vecchio of house and smithery in contrada S. Prosdocimo to make nails and hammers.

29. AN, 256, fols. 156r–63v, 23 June–Aug. and 9 Nov. 1357.

30. On the meaning of *vadum*, with examples of this sort of fief, see Lazzarini, "Della voce 'vadum' nei documenti padovani," in his *Scritti di paleografia e diplomatica*, 308–26.

31. See the grant made for five years on 24 June 1357 of a *vadum maserandi*, measuring 20 by 30 Paduan feet, at Terrenegra to one Giovanni a Sale of Pontecorvo "extra portam," AN, 256, fol. 156r. The Carrara lord continued to grant fiefs of *vada maserandi* over the next few years, at Pontelongo on the Bacchiglione in June 1362 and at Terranuova and Terranegra outside Padua in the summer of 1363: see AN, 257, fols. 11r, 18 June 1362, 138rv and 141rv, 24 June and 4 July 1363.

32. See AN, 256, fol. 235r, 8 May 1360.

33. The imperial grant from Viterbo is recorded in Gloria, 2:68, no. 1184, 1 Aug. 1367. The first twenty grants of fishing rights to local *piscatores*, mainly residing in

Ponte Peochioso in Padua, are to be found in AN, 257, fols. 250v–59v, 1 July–16 Oct. 1367.

34. AN, 257, fol. 268rv, July 1368: "in vigore iuris et gratia a domino Serenissimo Imperatore et eius predecessoribus per prefatum dominum et antecessores de domo sua."

35. AN, 257, fol. 227v, 19 May 1369; AN 258, fol. 169v, 30 Sept. 1370, fol. 187v, 1 July 1371, fol. 189rv, 10 and 13 July 1371, fol. 195v, 17 Feb. 1372, fol. 206v, 14 May 1372, fol. 208v, 23 Aug. 1372, fol. 210r, 17 July 1372.

36. AN, 258, fol. 161v, 20 Jan. 1370, with the rent due in two payments, half at Easter and half at Christmas.

37. The following is based on an analysis of three registers of the curial notary Pietro Saraceno, AN, 256–258 for the years 1356 to 1371, and some score of entries of Alberto Figario in AN, 1158, mainly from 1370.

38. AN, 257, fols. 59r–61r, March 1362, with leases of three more parcels rented to sharecroppers in June, ibid., fols. 74r–75v; on 17 June 1362, the Carrara brothers leased for five years all tithes in the village for annual rent of £50, ibid., fol. 9v.

39. AN, 257, fols. 76r–94r, summer 1362.

40. Ibid., fol. 242rv, April 1367.

41. Ibid., fols. 273r, 275r, October 1368, 2 Feb. 1369; half the rent was payable at Shrovetide 1369 and half at the feast of S. Margherita, 20 July 1369.

42. AN, 1158, fols. 111r–48v, April 1372.

43. AN, 256, fols. 268r–70r, 31 Jan. 1361; on the tendency to develop larger blocks in the decades following the Black Death, see Samarkin, "Evolyutsiya khozyaystvennykh," 48–58.

44. AN, 257. fols. 265r–66v, 272v–272r, 4 May and 4 Dec. 1368.

45. AN, 258, fol. 164v, 8 June 1370.

46. Ibid., fols. 165r, 175r, 4 July and 25 Dec. 1370.

47. Ibid., fol. 176v, 26 Jan. 1371.

48. See Gloria, 2:86, no. 1314, 30 Jan. 1371, for the exchange; Papafava, 4:352–53, 1 Mar. 1371, for the purchase; and AN, 258, fols. 177r–78r, 9 and 11 March, for taking possession.

49. AN, 258, fols. 184r–85r, 200r, 23 June 1371 and 1 Mar. 1372.

50. See F. C. Lane's appendix in Luzzatto, *Debito pubblico della Repubblica di Venezia*, 283; Becker, *Florence in Transition*, 2:178, and Meek, *Lucca, 1363–1400*, 63.

51. See AN, 178, fol. 73r, which is an undated scrap of paper bearing the guild names and figures given in the text. Its placement in the cartulary suggests that the assessment was made about 1375.

52. On similar development at the Este court in Ferrara, see T. Dean, "Notes on the Ferrarese Court in the Later Middle Ages," *Renaissance Studies* 3 (1989): 362–67.

53. See the capsule biography in Gloria, 2:138–39, nos. 303–5.

54. AN, 33, fols. 340r–41v, 1 Oct. 1372, purchase of eleven parcels, held a livello for an annual rent of £20 (2.5 percent) and 18 *staia* of wheat and 22 of rye, beans, millet, and other crops.

55. For a biographical sketch, see Gloria, 1:152–53, nos. 331–32, and the grant of Paduan citizenship in ibid., 2:88, no. 1320, 19 May 1371, excerpt of AD, 8500.

56. See AN, 34, fols. 73r–74r, 5 Sept. 1374, fol. 80r, 30 Sept. 1373, and fol. 427v, 19 Dec. 1376, acts of procuration to collect debts in Lucca, Bassano, and Genoa, respectively, and Gloria, 2:146, no. 1499, 2 Aug. 1380, son Grisolfo appoints proctor at father's home in contrada Duomo.

57. See Gloria, 2:266, no. 1834, 12 Aug. 1392, another son, Manuele, residing in contrada S. Lucia, with Antonio given as *quondam* (deceased).

58. Gloria, 2:132, no. 1453, 12 Oct. 1378.

59. AN, 5, fol. 92r, 5 Oct. 1382, for the farm in Brusegana, with Zilio Calvi serving both as witness and notary; ibid., fol. 134rv, 20 June 1384.

60. Ibid., fols. 156r–157r, 23 Jan. 1385, livello granted in the interior chancery by Niccolò Curtarolo, factor general for Francesco Novello, who is styled "Carrarie Dux et Padue, Tarvisii, etc."

61. AN, 34, 58v–60r, 26 July 1374.

62. Pietro Saraceno's notarial registers, which provide much of the information of Carrara holdings, survive in AN, 256–258.

63. These survive as AN, 31–32; further, Campolongo appeared often as a witness in the chancery, for example, in AN, 35, fol. 72r, 18 Dec. 1377.

64. See Ghirardini's entry "Brazzi, Bandino" in the *DBI* and several notices in Gloria, 2:67, no. 1259, 28 May 1367, and 2:89, no. 1323, 29 July 1371.

65. See Gloria, 2:80, no. 1297, 9 Dec. 1369, for Marco as scribe in the Carrara chancery, and AN, 34, fols. 88v–89r, 21 Nov. 1374 and fol. 426v, 15 Dec. 1376, for the lease in Este and soceda in Corte, respectively.

66. See Calvi's first register, AN, 5, fols. 29–73, passim, which documents his work as a notary for the Paduan business community as well as in his native Montagnana.

67. AN, 256, fol. 166r, March 1364, and AN, 258, fol. 177v, marginal note without date, but the sale in question took place in 1370.

68. AD, 8461, 23 June 1370.

69. AN, 34, fol. 136r, 9 Feb. 1375, act in the Carrara chancery in Padua.

70. See the account of his career in Collodo, *Società in trasformazione*, 299–304.

71. AN, 398, fol. 209r, 10 June 1374; meeting in Vicenza with Cavalli and other high officials, Turchetto read a transcription of the account of Giacomo dall'Olio, where it is admitted that "dictos denarios dictus Jacobus plus recepit quam expendit de dictis rationibus thesaurarie et massarie prefati domini." Giacomo then acknowledged his debt and agreed to pay in full.

72. AN, 35, fols. 56r–57v, 16 Apr. 1377, *instrumentum confessionis*, drawn up by Bandino Brazzi.

73. AN, 34, fols. 31r–32v, 25 June 1374.

74. AN, 166, fols. 377v–378v, 9 Jan. 1371, purchase of land in Torre; AN, 35, fols. 203v, 204r, 2, 3, Apr. 1380, leases in Villa Estense; AN, 525, fol. 4r, 25 Feb. 1387, deposit of £538 made "sub logia cancellarie domini."

75. For Fina's life, see discussion with partial edition of her will from AN, 35, fols. 95v–98v, in my "Giusto de' Menabuoi," 13–30. On her patronage, see the essays of Plant, "Patronage in the Circle of the Carrara Family," and Warr, "Painting in Late Fourteenth-Century Padua."

76. AN, 416, fols. 120v–22r, 31 Mar. 1375 = Papafava, 5:117–119.

77. AN, 416, fols. 126v–27r, 21 Aug. 1375 = Papafava, 5:119–120.

78. See AN, 34, fol. 30v, 1374, for the loan of 300 ducats; ibid., fols. 346v–47r, 5, 7 Apr. 1376, for the land purchases; and AN, 35, fol. 205r, 5 Apr. 1380, for the role as peacemaker.

79. Gloria, 2:162–63. no. 1544: "Montursius de Montursio familiaris in ipsius aula tener nutritus."

80. Conversini's account of life at the Carrara court, *De primo eius introitu ad aulam*, addressed in 1385 to a Venetian friend, Marco di Pietro Giustinian, has been edited with translation by Kohl and Day, *Two Court Treatises*, 22–83, with the description of his "typical" day at court on 34–37.

81. Ibid., 32–33.

82. Gloria, 2:139, no. 1474, 17 Sept. 1379, purchase of the ship; AN, 35, fol. 365r, 2 Mar. 1382, witness at mint transfer; and Gloria, 2:160, no. 1536, 22 July 1382, dowry for niece.

83. See Conversini, *De primo eius introitu*, 57, 59, 67.

84. Ibid., 61–65, and AN, 43, fol. 9r, 9 Feb. 1381, which shows Gaiardo, a recent immigrant from Cittadella, enjoyed income from tithes in Vicenza; AN, 43, fols. 125v–26r, 24 Nov. 1386, purchase for £1,000 from Niccolò Curtarolo of farmland in the campanea.

85. Conversini, *De primo eius introitu*, 49, 55, 57.

86. The formulary, largely unedited, Codice 23 of the Archivio Papafava dei Carraresi, now in the Biblioteca of the Accademia Patavina, Padua, is a valuable document for Carrara diplomacy in the time of the Chioggia war.

87. Text in Rizzoli and Perini, *Monete di Padova*, 110, doc. 16.

88. See ibid., 109, doc. 15, where the authors have misdated the decree giving as the date 1378 (*more veneto*) instead of 1379; better text in *Il "Capitolar dalle Broche,"* 38–39. On the fineness of the Venetian *grosso*, see Lane and Mueller, *Money and Banking in Medieval and Renaissance Venice*, 1:511, 527. I am much indebted to Alan Stahl of the American Numismatic Society, who has reviewed my analysis of the operation of the Carrara mint and saved me from several errors. Any mistakes remaining are of my own making.

89. Texts in Rizzoli and Perini, *Monete di Padova*, 111–15, docs. 18–19, 28 Jan. 1381 and 2 Mar. 1382.

90. Ibid., 109, doc. 14, 8 Jan. 1384, and Rizzoli, "Nuovi documenti sulla zecca padovana," 66–67, doc. 5, 17 Aug. 1384.

91. Rizzoli and Perini, *Monete di Padova*, 95, 99.

92. Ibid., 132–34.

93. Matteo da Ferrara's account is published in ibid., 99–108, February 1386 to July 1388.

94. On the redaction of 1362, see Varanini, *Comuni cittadini e stato regionale*, 17–19, and the essay of Magliani, "I tre manoscritti degli statuti comunali," 155–64, who is preparing a critical edition of that code. Only two MS witnesses survive: Biblioteca Civica, Padua, MS B.P. 1237, which was probably kept in the Carrara chancery, and a later version that perhaps belonged to the Paduan Collegio dei Giudici, Biblioteca Marciana, Venice, Lat. V, 37 (=2306), which was redacted shortly after 1366, since the statutes of Simone Lupi, podestà in that year, are integrated into the text.

95. See the discussion in A. Liva, *La gerarchia delle fonti di diritto nelle città dell'Italia settentrionale* (Milan: Giuffrè, 1976), 18–19, quoting *Stat. Car.*, fol. 2v: "secundum formam statutorum et ordinamentorum communis Padue et ubi deficerent secundum formam iuris comunis et bonarum et antiquarum consuetudinum civitatis Padue," followed by, "et plus et minus aut aliter aut preter secundum beneplacita et voluntatem ipsius domini."

96. *Stat. Car.*, fol. 330r (1366).

97. On the creation of the office in Verona under the Visconti, see Varanini, *Comuni cittadini e stato regionale*, 188–90, and in Padua under Venetian rule my "Government and Society," 215–17.

98. On Cittadella and its statutes, see the essays of G. Ortalli and M. Pozza in *Statuti di Cittadella*, 10–16 and 24–31, with the corrections of Bortolami, "Cittadella e le sue mura," in *Città murate del Veneto*, 181–88.

99. On the government, see *Statuti di Cittadella*, 47–70 passim, and for income and expenses from 1353 to 1388 the ledger *Introitus comunis . . . Cittadelle*, Archivio di Stato, Padua, Territorio, no. 480. I am much indebted to Sante Bortolami for informing me of the existence of this valuable record of local government and sharing his notes and transcriptions, which greatly facilitated my consultation and analysis of the ledger.

100. See *Introitus comunis . . . Cittadelle*, fols. 1v–5r.

101. See the list published by Ronchi, "Contributo alla serie dei podestà di Cittadella," 108–9.

102. *Introitus comunis . . . Cittadelle*, fols. 11r, 37rv, for the inventory of 1371 and the addition and list of 1388.

103. Ibid., fols. 37v, 39v, Buzzacarini's letter of 18 Mar. 1379, Zecchi's of 21 Nov. 1379, obliging villages to pay prorated taxes: "in faciendo reductum sive receptum iuxta terram Cittadelle."

104. Ibid., fol. 39r, May 1386.

Chapter 6   Creating the Carrara Affinity

1. AN, 159, fol. 1rv, 21 Oct. 1351, act of Piove di Sacco's council, summoned by Dotti as podestà; Archivio Corona 6482, 16 May 1358, the Carrara lord appoints Paolo Dotti of contrada S. Andrea his factor general.

2. AN, 256, fols. 102r, 103r, 105r, 14 Sept. 6 and 9 Nov. 1356.

3. AD, 7869A, 6 Jan. 1357, confirmation of the sentence given by the podestà of

Padua, Marco Cornaro, and AN, 212, fol. 280v, 14 June 1360, grant of provisions for life to Zambon's widow.

4. AN, 256, fol. 123v, 6 Dec. 1357, for the house, fol. 134r, 20 Aug. 1358, for the deposit.

5. AD, 8118A, 12 June 1362.

6. AN, 668, fol. 28v, 23 Sept. 1363; Predelli, 3:21, no. 97, 4 Nov. 1363, and AN, 33, fol. 223r, 13 Aug. 1368.

7. AN, 203, fols. 35r–36v, 10 Feb. 1365, the first will, AN, 33, fols. 149r–50v, 7 Jan. 1368, the second will.

8. See Biblioteca Civica, Padua, MS B.P. 990, *Documenti carraresi*, perg. 50, 16 May 1366, negotiation on dowry of £1,200 between Ansedisio and Antonia qd. Giovanni da Peraga, his wife.

9. See Archivio di Stato, Padua, Archivi Privati Diversi, no. 189, Lion, vol. 1 = *Codice Lion*, fols. 61r, 62r, April 1359 and May 1360.

10. On Albertino Papafava, see discussion with documents in Ceoldo, *Albero della famiglia Papafava*, 97–105.

11. *Documenti Carraresi*, perg. 49, 29 July 1364, excerpt in Gloria, 2:59, no. 1235. In her discussion of Badoer acquisitions in the Padovano, Leslie Ling, "Presenza fondiaria veneziana nel Padovano," 311, suggests that this was a pretended sale.

12. *Documenti carraresi*, perg. 49bis, 1364, parchment ledger of 31 fols.

13. See ibid., perg. 56, 28 July 1374, for the sentence, and AN, 34, fol. 34v, 1 July 1374, for dealings with Giorgio Resta, who was acting as Marco's executor in Venice.

14. For Arcoano Buzzacarini's career, see "Buzzacarini, Arcoano," on which I draw freely.

15. Archivio della Curia Vescovile, Padua, Feudorum, reg. 7A, fols. 58v–61r, 4 Jan. 1372, and AN, 165, fols. 150v–54r, 30 Aug. 1363.

16. AN, 258, fol. 160v, 2 Mar. 1370, purchases of parcels from peasants in Noventa, fol. 207rv, 8 July 1372, inventory of holdings in Arquà.

17. See the edition and summary of Fina's will of 22 Sept. 1378 in my "Giusto de' Menabuoi," 25, where the bequest is mentioned.

18. See Medin, "Maddalena degli Scrovegni," 246–49, 253–54; Collodo, *Società in trasformazione*, 56–58, 216–18, and my "Scrovegni in Carrara Padua," which includes an English version of Enrico's testament.

19. Cortusi, *Chronica*, 131.

20. Gloria, 2:43, no. 1189, 29 May 1358, Archivio della Curia Vescovile, Padua, Feudorum, reg. 6, fols. 64r–66v, 9 Nov. 1359, and AN, 256, fols. 338r–39r, 1362.

21. AN, 202, fols. 304v–5v, 10 Jan. 1360; Lazzarini, "Principio della dominazione carrarese a Feltre e Belluno," 1–4.

22. AN, 1158, fol. 116rv, 10 Jan. 1370; Ugolino is listed as residing in contrada Arena.

23. See Gloria, 2:113, no. 1396, 20 Jan. 1376, and 2:149, no. 1506, 10 Jan. 1381.

24. AN, 56, fols. 124v–25r, 4 Feb. 1380, for the house in S. Tomà, and AN, 99, fol. 420rv, 10 June 1381, for the suit.

25. Senato, Misti, reg. 37, fol. 53v, 3 Mar. 1382; AN, 699, fols. 358v–59r, 27 Mar. 1382, and fol. 80r, 10 Oct. 1386. On the Corner connection, see da Mosto, *Dogi di Venezia,* 137.

26. On Bonifacio Lupi's career and patronage, see Pistoia, "Bonifacio Lupi di Soragna," 23–43, and Billanovich, "Amico del Petrarca," 259–78.

27. AN, 257, fols. 132rv and 134r, 6 and 28 Feb. 1363.

28. See Gloria, 2:58, no. 1230, 8 Mar. 1364, on the exchange, and Archivi Privati Diversi, 106, Dondi, reg. 1, 12 July 1364, for a description of the Dondi's new property.

29. Gloria, 2:72, no. 1273, 17 May 1368.

30. AN, 407, fol. 53r, Dec. 1370, excerpt in Sartori, "Note su Altichiero," 322–23.

31. AN, 407, fols. 55v–56v, 6 Nov. 1373, fols. 59v–60r, 15 Aug. 1376.

32. Gloria, 2:56, no. 1225, 22 July 1363.

33. See AN, 34, fol. 129r, Jan. 1375, where it is mentioned that Lupi had received from Francesco il Vecchio the privilege of Paduan citizenship.

34. On Lupi's career in service to the Carrara, see Gatari, *Cronaca carrarese,* 101–2, 114–16, 190, 206, 215, and my summary in "Fedeltà e tradimento nello stato carrarese," 51–53.

35. See Cenci, "Bonifacio Lupi di Soragna," 90–91, and Billanovich, "Amico del Petrarca," 268–74.

36. On Altichiero's commissions in Padua, see Simon, "Altichiero versus Avanzo," 252–71, which makes sense of the massive archival studies of Sartori, "Note su Altichiero," and "Capella di S. Giacomo al Santo di Padova."

37. See Plant, "Portraits and Politics in Late Trecento Padua," 406–25, and Norman, "Those Who Pay, Those Who Pray, and Those Who Paint," 2:179–93.

38. AN, 407, fols. 91v–92v, 20 Mar. 1380.

39. AN, 407, fol. 93r, 5 Apr. 1380, and sentence at fols. 93v–95v, 10 Apr. 1380, by which Lupi himself acquired part of the contested legacy at bargain prices.

40. AN, 407 fols. 100r–102r, 19, 20 Feb. 1381.

41. Ibid., fols. 102v–3v, 2 Mar. 1381, fol. 106r, 15 June 1383.

42. See, for example, Gloria, 2:63, 65, 69, 71, nos. 1247–48, 1253, 1264–66, 1269, 26 Feb., 13 Apr., and 9 Dec. 1366, 23 Oct., 13 Nov., and 1 Dec. 1367, 31 Jan. 1368, for numerous decisions at Sigillo and Aquila rendered by Simone Lupi's vicars.

43. See Liberali, *Dominazione carrarese in Treviso,* 53–54.

44. See *Stat. Car.,* fol. 1v, for the podestà's monthly salary of £1,000; Feudorum, reg. 8, fol. 57v, 28 Jan. 1376, award of 83 *campi* of decimal fiefs in Piove di Sacco; AD, 8731, 21 Apr. 1376, Francesco il Vecchio through his proctor Manfredino Conti sold Simone four farmsteads on 40 *campi* in Volta Brusegana in the Paduan campanea for £3,735; AN, 407, fols. 83v–84v, 8 Nov. 1379, Simone, with brother Antonio and sister Franceschina, appointed Giovanni di Tibero, archpriest of S. Pancrazio in Parma, their proctor to collect rents and renew leases; AN, 35, fols. 397v–98r, 22 May 1382, Simone appointed another agent to collect rents and make leases in Parma.

45. See AN, 31, fols. 76v–77r, 18 June 1370, on acquisition of house near Duomo;

AD, 9039, 7 Jan. 1385, for the will; and AN, 5, fol. 162rv, 9 Apr. 1385, for Francesco il Vecchio's dispensation to Bengarda, witnessed by Arsendino Arsendi, Paganino Sala, and Francesco Turchetto in the "Camera a Quadris."

46. AN, 31, fol. 144v, 30 Aug. 1371, for the will, and AN, 80, fol. 255r, 9 July 1372, for the agent, excerpt in Gloria 2:95, no. 1339.

47. See Gatari, *Cronaca carrarese*, 155, and AN, 407, fol. 91v, 13 May 1380; see ibid., fol. 165rv, 25 Feb. 1386, where Antonio, residing in Mantua, sold to Bonifacio Lupi his interest in land held pro indiviso in Soragna.

48. See AN, 42, fol. 281r, 3 Nov. 1378, for a small parcel on a vineyard from the prior of the local monastery of S. Maria della Mandria, and, for the large block, AN, 407, fols. 116r–17r, 10 July 1381, where the earlier purchases are mentioned.

49. AN, 407, fol. 127rv, 16 Mar. 1382; fol. 132v, 21 Nov. 1382, partial ed. in Sartori, "Note su Altichiero," 320–21.

50. AN, 407, fols. 135r–36r, 3 Mar. 1383, for Monte shares; fol. 164r, 26 Dec. 1385, Caterina's Venetian citizenship; fol. 184r, 17 Mar. 1387, Bonifacio's purchase of a house in Venice, fol. 186r, 22 May 1387, Caterina's house there.

51. Ibid., fols. 138v–40r, 8 Apr. 1383, for the nieces' legacy, and fols. 145v–46v, 19 May 1384, for Verde Franzesi's marriage.

52. Ibid., fol. 164r, partial ed. in Sartori, "Note su Altichiero," 309.

53. AN, 31, fol. 159rv, 23 Jan. 1372.

54. See Gatari, *Cronaca carrarese*, 88–89, 95–97, 101–2, and 124, and Gonzati, *Basilica di S. Antonio*, 2:70–73.

55. Gatari, *Cronaca carrarese*, 72–73, 91–93, 112–14, 119.

56. See AN, 31, fols. 160r–62r, 24, 27 Jan. 1372, leases and loans to sharecroppers in Lendinara and Carmignano.

57. See, for example, AN, 47, fols. 293r, 316r, 10 Mar. and 16 Nov. 1377.

58. AN, 72, fol. 67r, 7 Feb. 1378 = Gennari, 8:1142.

59. AN, 357, fol. 227r, 4 Oct. 1386.

60. See the record of the knighthood of 22 Feb. 1337 in G. Salvemini, *La dignità cavalleresca nel comune di Firenze* (Florence, 1896), 106–7.

61. See *Gesta magnifica domus carrariensis*, 66, 76, and, in general, my entry "Donati, Manno," in the *DBI*, 47–49, on which this account of his career draws freely.

62. See the arguments put forth by Wilkins, "Petrarch and Manno Donati," 381–93.

63. See the text published in R. W. Witt, *Coluccio Salutati and His Public Letters* (Geneva: Droz, 1976), 99: "nobilis quondam et egregius miles, dominus Mannus de Donatis, quod dolenter recolimus, in servitiis Sante Matris ecclesie contra mediolanenses dominos militando diem clausit extremum."

64. AN, 348, fols. 137v–38v, 22 Jan. 1378, on claims in Venice, and Archivi Privati Diversi, no. 190, Lion, perg. no. 4, 25 Sept. 1382.

65. AN, 36, fol. 399rv, 23 Dec. 1386, excerpt in Gloria, 2:193, no. 1633.

66. See AN, 669, fols. 122v–23r, 29 Nov. 1397, rent of farmland in Tergola.

67. For notices of his career, see Gatari, *Cronaca carrarese*, 63, 115–16, 214, 238,

264–72 passim, 293–94, and Gloria, 2:91, no. 1328, 28 Sept. 1371, for his witnessing Ovetari's will.

68. AN, 525, fols. 22v–23r, 13 Aug. 1387.

69. See Hyde, *Padua in the Age of Dante*, 257–58, 313.

70. Archivio di Stato, Venice, Procuratori di San Marco, de ultra, busta 185, sub anno, 28 July 1338.

71. AD, 7592, 1 Apr. 1348, Feudorum, reg. 5, fols. 105v–7r, 5 Mar. and 17 Dec. 1348, reg. 6, fols. 10v–13r, 23 July 1354.

72. See *Gesta magnifica domus Carrariensis*, 70–71.

73. Gloria, 2:77, 79, nos. 1287, 1293, 2 Mar. and 30 June 1369.

74. Ibid., 2:81, no. 1299, 1370, for embassy to Belluno, and Gatari, *Cronaca carrarese*, 54, 59, 61–64.

75. Gatari, *Cronaca carrarese*, 72–73, 95, 101–2.

76. Gloria, 2:56, no. 1226, 2 Oct. 1363, for the dowry, 2:65, no. 1254, 31 Dec. 1366, and 2:83, no. 1307, 28 July 1370, for Niccolò Cremaschi's last testament.

77. Feudorum, reg. 7B, fols. 120r–21v, another copy in Procuratori di San Marco, de ultra, busta 185, sub anno.

78. Procuratori di San Marco, de ultra, busta 185, 29 Apr. 1372.

79. Gatari, *Cronaca carrarese*, 130–34.

80. See Gloria, 2:125, no. 1432, 22 Nov. 1377, 2:137, no. 1467, 20 May 1379, excerpt from AN, 304, fol. 84v, for the annuity.

81. AN, 352, fol. 62r, 4 Sept. 1386.

82. On Alvise's popularity with the *popolo minuto*, see Gatari, *Cronaca carrarese*, 134, and on Francesco il Vecchio's false accusation, see Capodilista, *De viris illustribus familiae*, 60.

83. AD, 6089, 5 Sept. 1325, purchase, and AD, 6199, 2 Mar. 1327, livello to peasants.

84. Gatari, *Cronaca carrarese*, 15–16.

85. Cortusi, *Chronica*, 131, mistakenly given as 1357 in the chronicle.

86. Papafava, 4:401–2, 17 Aug. 1356.

87. Archivio di Stato, Venice, Avogaria di Comun, Raspe, reg. 3643, fols. 5v–6r, 20 Apr. 1361.

88. See Gatari, *Cronaca carrarese*, 65–68, 93–94, 101–16.

89. AN, 31, fols. 203r–5r, 27 Oct. 1373, excerpt in Gloria, 2:100, no. 1356, and request to the Carrara lord: "Item precatur magnificum et potentum dominum dominum Franciscum de Carraria Padue, etc. quod in hoc suo ultimo testamento mandare dignetur legata et debita predicta per dictos suos commissarios executioni mandari."

90. AN, 31, fols. 273r–75v, 15 July 1375, excerpt in Gloria, 2:110, no. 1385, with bequest to Francesco il Vecchio on fol. 274v: "terrenum Mirani super quo magnificus dominus construi fecit duas fortilitias, magnam et parvam, tempore guerre quam habuit cum Venetis, et omnes domos tam de muro quam de lignarie intra dictas fortilitias existentes, libere et expedite."

91. See Gloria, 2:110, no. 1387, 5 Sept. 1375, where Francesco il Vecchio appointed a proctor for the speedy settlement of Zanino da Peraga's estate.

92. AN, 31, fols. 208–12, 7 Dec. 1373, the purchases from della Torre heirs; fol. 264r, 6 Mar. 1375, for tithes, and fol. 258rv, 18 Feb. 1375, grants of fiefs to new vassals.

93. See AD, 6519, 16 Jan. 1331, for uncle Fruzerino.

94. On Aicardino's career see Hyde, *Padua in the Age of Dante*, 278–79, and Gatari, *Cronaca carrarese*, 15; on the restitution of the dowry, AD, 6872, 11 Feb. 1336; and on the tithes, Feudorum, reg. 5, fol. 110v, May 1336, copy in Archivio Papafava, Cod. 27.

95. On Fruzerino and the Scrovegni, see Collodo, *Società in trasformazione*, 218, 258–59, and on his banking interests, Gloria, 2:38, no. 1176, 21 Feb. 1355.

96. Gatari, *Cronaca carrarese*, 41, 45, 52–53.

97. Feudorum, reg. 7B, fol. 127rv, 5 June 1373, and reg. 8, fol. 97rv, 3 Jan. 1375.

98. See AN, 6, fol. 107rv, 18 Jan. 1384, for Vigonovo, and AN, 684, fols. 46v–47r, 20 Nov. 1380, for holdings in Trambacche.

99. AN, 169, fols. 53r–54v, 22 Nov. 1388, for £600 the lord of Padua sold "unam motam super quam erat castrum Transbagnis campos sex cum uno curtivo magno cum orto intus, et cum uno prato."

100. Gloria, 2:267, nos. 1838–39, 21 Sept. and 1 Oct. 1392.

101. See Grion, "Ruoli dei cittadini," 257, and AD, 5528, 30 Oct. 1321, will of Lina, wife of Negro di Guido de' Negri.

102. See *Gesta magnifica domus carrariensis*, 70–71, and for the treason, Collodo, *Società in trasformazione*, 43–44.

103. AN, 141, fols. 10v–11r, 18 May 1365, and fol. 47r, 30 Aug. 1366.

104. Gatari, *Cronaca carrarese*, 107, 115–17, and d'Alessio, *Storia della guerra*, 129.

105. AN, 141, fols. 153v–54r, 10 Apr. 1375, fol. 156r, 13 Mar. 1377, for the sale of the small house, and fol. 158v, 11 May 1377, for sale in Carpenedo, lauded by Prosdocimo, fol. 160r, 29 July.

106. AN, 141, fols. 227r–28r, 6 Feb. 1382, and AN, 364, fol. 266r, 3 Dec. 1384, Prosdocimo's restitution of Beatrice's dowry from his home at "Volta illorum de Negris."

107. AN, 56, fol. 147rv, 30 Jan. 1383, for the will, and AN, 141, fol. 235v, 14 May 1383, purchase of land in Selvazzano by Polentesia, daughter of Albertino da Peraga and wife of Negro di Gherardo Negri, which confirmed her identity.

108. See AN, 141, fols. 256, 21 Jan. 1385, 267r, 16 Apr. 1387, on Prosdocimo appointing proctors to claim tithes from the bishop of Vicenza and S. Giorgio Maggiore in the Padovano. For the Negro's loan to his brother, AN, 699, fol. 104v–5r, 10 Jan. 1387; he is listed as "quondam" by 1 Mar. 1388, see Gloria, 2:211, no. 1674.

109. AD, 8914, 28 Feb. 1381, sale of 4 *campi* in Padovano; AN, 117, fols. 139v–40r, 11 Sept. 1383, will of Francesco detto Checcho di Donati Lion; and Salomonio, *Urbis Patavinae inscriptiones*, 58, for the inscription.

110. AN, 119, fols. 106r–7v, 172r–74r, 10 May 1391, 18 Mar. 1394.

111. See Archivi Privati Diversi, no. 189, Lion, vol. 1 = *Codice Lion*, fols. 1r–7r, 75r–76r, for the purchases from the Gottola brothers and resale to Checcho Lion, 96rv, as patron of S. Giacomo. For recent interpretations of Lion's acquisitions, see Rigon, *Clero e città*, 156–58, and Collodo, *Società in trasformazione*, 387.

112. This data is assembled from *Codice Lion.*

113. See *Codice Lion,* fols. 8v, 67v, July, May 1361, for tithes renounced by Ansedisio Schinelli, and Feudorum, reg. 7A, fols. 3rv, 131r, 18 Aug. 1371 and 22 May 1372, for further tithes in Montagnana.

114. *Codice Lion,* fols. 20v, 155r–56v, 28 Aug. 1364, 2 Dec. 1366.

115. Ibid., fols. 162r–63v, 9 Dec. 1366

116. For his career, see Abbondanza, "Arsendi, Arsendino," and the older sketch in Gloria, 1:126–29, nos. 279–283, with supporting documents.

117. Mommsen, *Italienische Analekten zur Reichsgeschichte,* 141–43.

118. For the son Giovanni and father Jacopo, see the authoritative entries of T. Pesenti in the *DBI* 41 (1991): 96–104, 104–11.

119. See Lazzarini, "I libri, gli argenti, le vesti di Giovanni Dondi dall'Orologio," in *Scritti di paleografia,* 253–73.

120. See my entry "Curtarolo, Niccolò" and that on the nephew Guglielmo, both in the *DBI.*

121. See Medin, "Familiare dei Carraresi," 171–92, esp. 185–92, for the text of the will, and AN, 525bis, fol. 25r, Jan. 1389, for division of the estate.

122. On Cortelerio, see the sketch in Gloria, 1:236, no. 493, and the release from the guardianship, AN, 5, fol. 12rv, 3 May 1370. For the earliest mention of Maria as a widow, living near the Casa di Dio, see Gloria, 2:99, no. 1352, 20 July 1373.

123. On Pietro and Maria, see Gatari, *Cronaca carrarese,* 338, 379, 389, and 472, and for Maria's business deals, AN, 34, fol. 401r, 5 Oct. 1376, sale of parcel in Polverara, AN, 35, fol. 248r, 20 Dec. 1383, purchase of houses in S. Andrea, AN, 191, fol. 181r, 21 July 1389, appointment of proctor to collect debts, AN, 38, fols. 5v–6r, 3 Mar. 1395, investment with Guglielmo Curtarolo, and AN, 40, fols. 492v–93v, 29 Nov. 1406, donation of land in Valsanzibio by Stefano da Carrara. For her death on 18 July 1410, see Mazzatinti, *Obituario del convento di S. Agostino,* 30–31.

124. See AN, 256, fol. 274r, 28 May 1359, for contract as moneylender, and AN, 388, fol. 144v, 20 Apr. 1377, purchase for £160 of 5 *campi* in Monselice by his wife, Antonia di Giacomo Basilio.

125. AN, 115, fol. 96r, 28 Apr. 1366, lease of house and land in Teolo, fol. 281r, 24 May 1370, lease of three small vineyards in Faedo.

126. AN, 668, fol. 148v, 27 Oct. 1375; extensive holdings in the village of Pontelongo are confirmed in Gaffarello's will of 21 Aug. 1387, AN, 188, fol. 118r, another copy AD, 9103.

127. AN, 34, fols. 31r–32v, 25 June 1374, purchase in Carrara chancery for more than 378 ducats of Pietro Lando's *iura* to land on the Brenta; AN, 166, fols. 377v–78v, 9 Jan. 1371, disguised loan of 500 ducats with land as collateral; AN, 178, fols. 82v–83r, 23 Dec. 1375, loan to rector of S. Daniele, fols. 271v–72e, 27 Nov. 1379, payments at executor of estates.

128. On his career, see Gloria, 1:146–49, nos. 318–26, Gatari, *Cronaca carrarese,* 183–85, 194, 215, 304, and Archivio Papafava, Codice 23, fol. 12v, no. 57, letter from Guglielmo Curtarolo and Michele Rabatta praising Sala as an orator.

129. See AN, 33, 223v–25r, 9 Aug. 1368, excerpt in Gloria, 2:73, no. 1278.

130. For the Naseri family, see Collodo's reconstruction in her *Società in trasformazione*, 301–26, and on Bonacorso, 243–46.

131. See the short biography in Gloria, 1:166–67, nos. 363–67, and also Gatari, *Cronaca carrarese*, 50–52, 185, 193–95, 304.

132. AN, 257, fol. 269r, 24 Aug. 1368, and on benefits the Turchetti gained from the Carrara, Collodo, *Società in trasformazione*, 247–49.

133. See Archivio di Stato, Padua, Ospedale S. Francesco, 590, parchment ledger.

134. AN, 5, fols. 231rv, 232rv, 24 Apr. 1387.

Chapter 7 Venice's Mortal Enemy, 1377–1388

1. See the accounts in *Additamentum secundum ad Chronicon Cortusiorum*, col. 984, and Gatari, *Cronaca carrarese*, 142–43. The appointment of the Venetian ambassadors is documented in Maggior Consiglio, Novella, fol. 161r, 19 May 1377.

2. See the text in Maniaco, *Historia Belli Forojuliensis*, 1223–26, 21 June 1376, and discussion in Paschini, *Storia di Friuli*, 2:175–76.

3. *Dispacci di Pietro Cornaro*, 147–52, doc. 1, 14 Nov. 1377.

4. Gloria, 2:128, no. 1438, 3 Mar. 1378.

5. Thomas and Predelli, *Diplomatarium veneto-levantinum*, 2:178–81, no. 105, 6 Mar. 1378.

6. Gatari, *Cronaca carrarese*, 149–50, and Seneca, "Diplomatico gorziano," 160.

7. Verci, 15:12, no. 1698, 12 June 1378, date of the receipt of the letter of *diffidatio*.

8. The events of the Chioggia war are described in detail in two nearly contemporary chronicles: Gatari, *Cronaca carrarese*, 151–204, provides the Paduan viewpoint, while Chinazzo, *Cronaca de la guerra da Veniciani a Zenovesi*, is a narrative from an eyewitness of events in Venice and Chioggia. Among recent accounts in English, three narratives stand out: Goy, *Chioggia and the Villages of the Venetian Lagoon*, 34–39, mainly based on Gatari's account; Lane, *Venice*, 189–96, best on the war at sea and the exploits of Vettor Pisani; and Norwich, *History of Venice*, 246–56, by far the most colorful and dramatic.

9. Maggior Consiglio, Novella, fol. 163v, 22 Aug. 1378.

10. See Rizzoli and Perini, *Monete di Padova*, 35–36, 97–98. See also account in chap. 5 above.

11. Ibid., 109, ed. of Senato, Misti, vol. 36, fol. 72v, 18 Jan. 1379; the penalty read in part: "omnes quibus tales monete nove facte in Padue, vel cararini novi et veteres reperti fuerunt, tam falsi quam boni, debeant perdere predictos omnes." Another ed. in *Il "Capitolar dalle Broche,"* 37–38.

12. See V. Mistruzzi, "Note biografiche su Gidino da Sommacampagna," *Nuovo Archivio Veneto*, n.s., 31 (1916): 111, 146–48, doc. 6, edition of AN, 35, fol. 107r, 4 June 1379.

13. See Lane, *Venice*, 191–92, and Lazzarini, "Battaglia di Pola," 177–98, with documents of the trial on 190–94.

14. Dondi dall'Orologio, *Dissertazione ottava*, 120.

15. Gatari, *Cronaca carrarese*, 176–77, following the translation in Goy, *Chioggia and the Villages of the Venetian Lagoon*, 36–37.

16. I follow the detailed account in Lazzarini, "Presa di Chioggia," 53–74; the estimates of Venetian prisoners seized vary widely, from 3,800 according to Gatari to only 980 according to the Genoese chronicler Giorgio Stella.

17. Gatari, *Cronaca carrarese*, 179; the retort, which was, in effect, a demand for unconditional surrender, has been attributed to both Francesco il Vecchio da Carrara and the Genoese commander Pietro Doria.

18. See Lazzarini, "Presa di Chioggia," 64, and the report of the Venetian ambassadors on the incident in Wenzel, 3:212–13, 31 Aug. 1379.

19. The following account of negotiations between Venice and Charles of Durazzo and other allied leaders is based on the ambassadorial reports to the doge from August to late October 1379 edited from Venice, Biblioteca Nazionale Marciana, cl. lat. X, 299 (= 3512), in Wenzel, 3:161–314.

20. Ibid., 235–45, no. 27, 9 Sept. 1379.

21. Ibid., 280–86, no. 36, 28 Sept. 1379.

22. Ibid., 287–90, no. 38, 3 Oct. 1379.

23. The Genoese plans were reported in a secret dispatch to the doge on 8 Sept. 1379 by the Venetian envoys in the Hungarian camp; see ibid., 231, no. 25.

24. See Lazzarini, "Frammento di registro," 124–32, on the events of autumn 1379, and the account in Caresini, *Chronica*, 38–41, which provides a list of the noble commanders of each galley.

25. *Dispacci di Pietro Cornaro*, 4–7, 9–10.

26. Archivio di Stato, Florence, Missivi della Prima Cancellaria, reg. 18, fol. 22rv, 11 June 1379.

27. Ibid., fol. 60v, 1 Sept. 1379, "in quo concilio quid aliud nisi de straga civitatis."

28. Ibid., fol. 73rv, 14 Oct. 1379.

29. On the earlier loans, see Lazzarini, "Prestito di Francesco il Vecchio da Carrara," 229, and for the loan to Genoa, AN, 35, fols. 160r–62r, 24 Sept. 1379, excerpt in Gloria, 2:140–41, no. 1475.

30. AN, 32, fol. 76r, 18 Nov. 1379.

31. Ibid., fol. 77r, 8 Dec. 1379, excerpt in Gloria, 2:141, no. 1478.

32. AN, 35, fol. 185r, 11 Dec. 1379.

33. AN, 32, fol. 78rv, 20 Dec. 1379.

34. Ibid., fol. 85v, 13 Jan. 1380.

35. Ibid., fol. 90v, 23 Jan. 1380, excerpt in Gloria, 2:143, no. 1483.

36. Ibid., fol. 87v, 3 Feb. 1380.

37. *Dispacci di Pietro Cornaro*, 16–18, 26–31.

38. Ibid., 54–70.

39. Gatari, *Cronaca carrarese*, 194, following the translation in Goy, *Chioggia and the Villages of the Venetian Lagoon*, 39. The contemporary Venetian chancellor and historian Caresini, *Chronica*, 45, confirms the same dire straits of the allied forces in Chioggia.

40. Missivi della Prima Cancellaria, reg. 18, fols. 161v–62r, 26 May 1380. The pretext for seizing the woolen cloth was that it had been improperly sealed at customs.

41. See the account in Caresini, *Chronica,* 48–50, which Norwich, *History of Venice,* 254–55, follows closely.

42. Missivi della Primi Cancellaria, reg. 18, fol. 134rv, 3 Apr. 1380; reg. 19, fol. 52r, 26 Sept. 1380.

43. Collino, "Politica fiorentino-bolognese," 118 and 157, doc. 17, ed. of letter of 3 May 1381 from the Missivi della Prima Cancellaria, reg. 19, fol. 127r.

44. See Wenzel, 3:426–28, no. 206, 26 June 1381.

45. The text of the Peace of Turin is edited in Ljubič, 4:119–63, no. 241, with provisions on Padua on 135–39; there is another edition in Verci, 15:71–112, no. 1769, with provisions on Padua on 90–94.

46. Maggior Consiglio, Grazie, vol. 17, fol. 121r, 1381, no day or month.

47. AN, 35, fol. 286rv, 22 Aug. 1381, excerpt in Gloria, 2:153, no. 1518.

48. Archivio di Stato, Venice, Pacta, vol. 5, fol. 61rv.

49. See Gatari, *Cronaca carrarese,* 207–9, on the coming of peace; and Zonta, *Zabarella,* 137–39, for the text of Zabarella's speech.

50. Predelli, 3:151, no. 101, 4 Oct. 1381.

51. Senato, Misti, reg. 37, fol. 7r, 22 Sept. 1381: fort had to be razed "quia ipsa bastita facta fuit in locis in quibus per formam illorum pactorum non potest fieri aliqua fortilicia et illa pacta vera sunt approbata et confirmata per istam pacem novam."

52. Ibid., fol. 14rv, 10 Oct. 1381, for the instructions from the Senate to Luca Contarini, who had been elected ambassador on 1 October; and ibid., fol. 11r, 1 Oct. 1381.

53. Ibid., fol. 19r, 21 Oct. 1381, for the election of the savi; fol. 35r, 3 Dec. 1381, for the appropriation of 50 ducats; AN, 83, fol. 1v, also Gennari, 8:1144, 18 Mar. 1382, extension to Pentecost; Verci, 16:24–30, no. 1775, 3 June 1382, settlement at Cona; Senato, Misti, reg. 37, fol. 107r, 17 Aug. 1382: syndication in Venice "ad approbandum, ratificandum et emologandum omnia et singula facta per magnificum dominum Nicolaum Estensem Marchionem seu per commissarios suos in determinatione et assignatione confinium inter nos, ex una parte, et magnificum dominum Padue, ex altera."

54. Louis's letter of late December 1381 is edited in Ljubič, 4:183–84, no. 254, dated 30 Dec. 1381; the Senate's reply is to be found in Senato, Misti, reg. 37, fol. 41r, 30 Jan. 1382, eds. in Ljubič, 4:184–85, no. 255, and Wenzel, 3:463–64, no. 227.

55. Documents in Wenzel, 3:465–67, no. 228, March 1382, 472–74, no. 235, 1 Apr. 1382, and 480–81, no. 244, 16 May 1382, with summaries in Predelli, 3:159, nos. 133–36. Appointment of Carrara proctor in AN, 35, fols. 515r–16r, 15 Oct. 1382, excerpt in Gloria, 2:158, no. 1530, and AN, 35, fol. 518r, 16 May 1382, for notice of the receipt from Caresini for payment of 16,666⅔ ducats.

56. On the Carrara heralds and request for aid, see Verci, 16:6–8, no. 1762, 30 Aug. 1381, and on the sorry state of Treviso, see the contemporary account of Redusio, *Chronicon Tarvisinum,* cols. 776–78.

57. Verci, 16:12–15, no. 1767, 18 Jan. 1382.

58. See Lazzarini, "Prestito di Francesco il Vecchio da Carrara," 229–36, which includes an edition of the loan contract from AN, 35, fol. 364rv, 1 Apr. 1382.

59. AN, 35, fols. 318r–19r, 320v, 329v, 19, 23, 29 Jan. 1382; on the podestaship of Pietro Giustinian in Chioggia, see Goy, *Chioggia and the Villages of the Lagoon*, 41–43.

60. Senato, Misti, reg. 37, fol. 68v, 12 Apr. 1382: "que fuit inter progenitores suos et magnificam domum suam et nos et communem nostrum, sicut in temporibus preteritis." For background, see Cessi, "Venezia e la preparazione," 415–23, and Surdich, *Genova e Venezia*, 25–31.

61. AN, 35, fol. 512, 14 Apr. 1382, excerpt in Gloria, 2:156, no. 1528.

62. See Archivio Papafava, Padua, Cod. 23, fol. 2r, no. 10, June 1382.

63. On the marriage of Gigliola, see Gatari, *Cronaca Carrarese*, 39, and *Ystoria de mesier Francesco Zovene*, 177; on Caterina, Gatari, *Cronaca carrarese*, 58–60, 392, and *Ystoria de Mesier Francesco Zovene*, 182: the editors of Gatari's chronicle, Medin and Tolomei, are sometimes imprecise in their annotations on the marriages of the women of the Carrara family.

64. On the wedding, see *Guerra da Trivixo*, 264; for the dowry contract, AN, 35, fols. 408r–11v, 26 June 1382, excerpt in Gloria, 2:159, no. 1533.

65. My account of the Trevisan war is based on the three principal contemporary accounts: Gatari, *Cronaca carresese*, 210–26; the anonymous *Guerra da Trivixo*, 247–64, very full on diplomacy, written in Paduan dialect by a member of the Carrara court; and Redusio, *Chronicon Tarvisinum*, cols. 775–80. The report of the taking of Serra Carrarese is found in Gatari, *Cronaca carrarese*, 210–11, and the Este contibution to the war effort in *Guerra da Trivixo*, 247.

66. Predelli, 3:161, no. 141, 18 Aug. 1382.

67. Senato, Misti, reg. 37, fol. 240r, 17 Oct. 1382, ed. in Wenzel, 3:486–87, no. 252: "nuper cum Januensibus et Domino Padue fecimus et firmavimus bonam et perpetuam pacem, et similiter habemus cum aliis principibus, communibus et dominis mundi pacem . . . , quod ullo modo cum honore nostro possemus ad istam ligam generalem attendere."

68. AN, 35, fol. 436v, 28 Sept. 1382: "ad acquirendum in civitate Venetiarum a quacumque persona, una vel pluribus, ecclesiasticis vel secularibus, comuni, collegio, vel universitate de omnem quantitatem imprestitorum usque ad quantamcumque summam, et pro eo foro et precio, prout ipsi procuratori videbitur." On the value of the shares and sale to mainland lords that spring, see Luzzatto, *Debito pubblico della Repubblica di Venezia*, 168–69, 178.

69. Senato, Misti, reg. 37, fol. 124v, 9 Dec. 1382.

70. Ibid., reg. 38, fol. 9r, 16 Feb. 1383 (1382 *more veneto*).

71. Predelli, 3:163, no. 153, 20 Mar. 1383 on the forts, no. 154, 30 Mar. 1383, on the Venetians in Povegliano.

72. See Senato, Misti, reg. 38, fol. 14r, 27 Mar. 1383, and fol. 28r, 13 May 1383, granting permission to the Carrara lord to transport huge quantities of supplies up the Sile, paying the usual custom duties.

73. *Guerra da Trivixo,* 259–61.

74. Verci, 16:58–59, no. 1802, 14 Aug. 1383: "quod territorium totum citra Plavium meum est, . . . et per me acquisitum non sine magnis laboribus et expensis."

75. Senato, Misti, reg. 38, fol. 56r, 10 July 1383, and fol. 77r, 24 Sept. 1383, permission from the Senate to the lord of Padua to transport vast quantities of munitions, foodstuffs, and supplies for the siege of Treviso.

76. Verci, 16:61–63, no. 1806, 15 Oct. 1383.

77. Sources differ on the amount paid for Treviso; see the review of the evidence in Gloria, 1:36, and on the entry into Treviso, Gatari, *Cronaca carrarese,* 220–26, and Redusio, *Chronicon Tarvisinum,* cols. 779–80. It is very unlikely that Duke Leopold of Austria was on hand to greet the Paduan lord, as Gatari erroneously asserted on 226.

78. Senato, Misti, reg. 38, fol. 102v, 19 Feb. 1384: "notificandum nobis sub brevitate de nuptiis filie filii sui, cum filio domini ducis Leopoldi, et de pace et concordia quod fecit cum eo."

79. See Verci, 16:69–70, no. 1815, 11 Feb. 1384, granting permission for Padua to have a Venetian as podestà "pro executione pacis facte inter dominum Regem Hungarie, et adherentes, . . . ex una parte, et nos." The document should probably be dated 1383, a few months before Memmo assumed office.

80. Gloria, 2:169, no. 1560, 17 Oct. 1383.

81. Senato Misti, reg. 38, fol. 98r, 11 Feb. 1384, permission to ship from Musestre to Treviso 10,000 *staia* of grain and another 10,000 of millet, with lesser amounts of rye, spelt, sorghum, and vegetables, with the lord of Padua paying the usual Venetian customs.

82. Ibid., fol. 117r, 22 Apr. 1384.

83. See Gatari, *Cronaca carrarese,* 227–28; the favorites were Enrico Gallo, Niccolò Curtarolo, Matteo da Ferrara, and Pietro da Montagnana, who was prior of S. Maria delle Carceri.

84. See Gloria, 1:36 n, where a tax on the druggists guild of 300 ducats is documented for 14 Feb. 1384 and one of 600 ducats on 26 July 1387.

85. Senato Misti, reg. 38, fols. 131r and 137v, 27 May and 12 June 1384, and Liberali, *Dominazione carrarese a Treviso,* 54–56.

86. Senato Misti, reg. 38, fol. 155r, 8 Aug. 1384.

87. The basic studies of the first phase of Paduan involvement in Friuli until open hostilities with Venice in the summer of 1385 are Cogo, "Patriarcato d'Aquileia," 220–50, Cessi, "Venezia e la preparazione," 414–45, and, for background, Paschini, *Storia del Friuli,* 2:195–210.

88. See the letters in Verci, 16:63–54, nos. 1807–8, 5 and 19 Nov. 1383.

89. See Cogo, "Patriarcato d'Aquileia," 238 and 309–10, doc. 1.

90. Collegio, Secreti, vol. 3, fol. 24r, 4 July 1384, analyzed and quoted in part in Cessi, "Venezia and la preparazione," 427.

91. See Cogo, "Patriarcato d'Aquileia," 239–40, and text in Verci, 16:77–81, no. 1822, 31 July 1384.

92. Collegio, Secreti, vol. 3, fol. 37v, 30 Aug. 1384: "dominus Cardinalis et Patri-

archa clare dicit omnibus volentibus audire quod intendit quod dominus Padue sit patriarcha Aquilegensis," quoted in Cogo, "Patriarcato d'Aquileia," 241 n. 2.

93. AN, 36, fol. 104r, 9 Feb. 1384, fol. 115rv, 31 Mar. 1384, and fol. 237rv, 14 Sept. 1384.

94. Ibid., fol. 105r, 14 Feb. 1384.

95. See ibid., fol. 181rv, 27 June 1384, on the Seta inheritance, and fol. 249r, 30 Sept. 1384, on the banking interests in Venice with the Medici.

96. Senato, Misti, reg. 38, fol. 111r, 27 Sept. 1384.

97. AN, 36, fol. 256r, 23 Oct. 1384, other copies in Papafava, 4:113v–115v, and Gennari, 8:1016–19; on the panic caused by the sire de Coucy's occupation of Arezzo, Brucker, *Civic World*, 104–5.

98. AN, 36, fol. 280rv, 10 Dec. 1384.

99. Senato, Misti, reg. 39, fol. 46r, 3 Feb. 1385; the Carrara envoy was an official from Treviso, Giacomello Zancani.

100. See Cessi, "Venezia e la preparazione," 442.

101. See Predelli, 2:247 and 322, 30 May 1356 and 25 May 1361, on service for the Della Scala; 3:89–90, 9 Jan. and 6 Mar. 1370, proctor to Abbey of Rosazzo in Friuli; 3:106, 15 Apr. 1372, as podestà of Conegliano, and 3:120–21, 30 July and 4 Oct. 1375, in Grain Office; Senato, Secreta, reg. D, fols. 7v, 9r, and 10v–11r, 17 May, 27 May, 2 June 1376, envoy to the Della Scala.

102. Senato, Misti, reg. 36, fol. 6v, 8 May 1377, where, as recent ambassador to Genoa, he was appointed to give expert opinion to the Senate, and ibid., fol. 62r, 9 July 1378, as ducal councillor.

103. On service as Avogador di Comun, see Archivio di Stato, Venice, Avogaria di Comun, Raspe 3644 (= reg.4), fols. 58r, 72r, 73r. For the reply to Carrara ambassadors, see Senato, Misti, reg. 39, fol. 60r, 20 Mar. 1385: "Omnia negotia consilii de X debent teneri et tenentur secretissima nec possunt revellari alicui ullo modo," ed. in Cogo, "Patriarcato d'Aquileia," 249. On the execution, see Sanuto, *Vite de' Duchi*, col. 755; notices on Pietro Giustinian are also found in Venice, Biblioteca Nazionale Marciana, It. VII, 128A (8639), G. Caroldo, *Cronaca veneta*, fols. 350r, 382rv, and 455r.

104. See, in general, Cogo, "Patriarcato d'Aquileia," 250–56, with text of final treaty of 11 May on 310–16, doc. 2; Senato, Misti, reg. 39, fols. 65v–66r, 6 Apr. 1385, and Collegio, Secreti, vol. 3, fols. 77r–79v, 22 Apr. 1385. See also Cessi, "Venezia e la preparazione," 450–52.

105. Senato, Misti, reg. 39, fol. 65r, 6 Apr. 1385.

106. See Pastorello, *Nuove ricerche*, 131–33, doc. 1, 24 June 1385, from the act of procuration, from AN, 5, fol. 177rv, and Lünig, *Codex Italiae diplomaticus*, 3:339–48, for the text of the treaty. In general, see Bueno de Mesquita, *Giangaleazzo Visconti*, 332, app. 3.

107. See Bueno de Mesquita, *Giangaleazzo Visconti*, 69–71; and, on the uprising in Ferrara, Law, "Popular Unrest in Ferrara," 41–60.

108. See Cessi, "Venezia e la preparazione," 459–62, and Verci, 16:95–98, 27 May 1385, for the Carrara lord's reply to the Veronese embassy.

109. Senato, Misti, reg. 39, fols. 101v–2r, 26 June 1385: "quod dominatio nostra multum mirabitur et gravabitur de tali responsione quia non putabat ipsum dominum Padue debere taliter respondere et quod non poterimus facere cum minori pro honore nostri dominii quam providere sicut nobis videbitur pro conservatione nostrorum [civium]."

110. Senato, Misti, reg. 39, fol. 117rv, 24 and 26 July 1385, fol. 128r, 24 Aug. 1385.

111. Ibid., fol. 147r, 13 Sept. 1385: in response to Padua's request for safe-conduct for its envoys at Portogruaro, Venice denied henceforth the right of any persons of the lord of Padua to travel through Venetian territories to reach Friuli; and AN, 32, fol. 165r, 7 Oct. 1385, appointment of Giovanni Francesco qd. Salvatore as proctor to collect "prode imprestitorum ipsius magnifici domini Padue," due that September.

112. Principal narrative sources for the conflict are Gatari, *Cronaca carrarese*, 230–320, and, from the Udinese viewpoint, Maniaco, *Historia Belli Forojuliensis*, cols. 1194–1220. The standard modern monograph on the war in Friuli is Seneca, "L'intervento veneto-carrarese," esp. 27–81, from the beginning of the war to the fall of the Carrara. See also Cessi, "Venezia e la preparazione," 462–73, for the events of summer 1385, and Cogo, "Patriarcato d'Aquileia," 250–95, for a detailed narrative. Invaluable for background, utilizing manuscript sources from Udine, is Paschini, *Storia di Friuli*, vol. 2, chaps. 9 and 10. On the role of the Scaliger lords in the conflict, see Law, "Caduta degli Scaligeri," 83–98, and Soldi Rondinini's entry "Della Scala, Antonio" in the *DBI*.

113. See Seneca, "Diplomatico goriziano," 153–55, and Cessi, *Padova medioevale* 1:156, 164. By early 1388, Rabatta was back in Padua residing in contrada Duomo; see AN, 525, fols. 42v–43r, 12 Feb. 1388, where he appears as guardian to his niece, Isabella qd. Enrico Rabatta.

114. AN, 45, fols. 206rv, 208r–9v, excerpt in Gloria, 2:185–86, nos. 1611–12, 1 Mar. 1386, record of dispute over oral deposition made by the mortally wounded Cerdolini at Montagnana.

115. AN, 36, fols. 355r–56r, 7 and 8 Mar. 1386, excerpt in Gloria 2:186, no. 1612–13.

116. AN, 36, 357v–58r, 21 Mar. 1386, excerpt in Gloria 2:187, no. 1614.

117. Gatari, *Cronaca carrarese*, 245.

118. See the letter of 18 May from Guglielmo Curtarolo to the Paduan captain at S. Vito, Bartolomeo da Verona, detailing the recent triumphs, in Suttina, "Per la storia della guerra," 139–45.

119. I follow the detailed account in Gatari, *Cronaca carrarese*, 246–55, and the useful summary in Allen, *History of Verona*, 315–16.

120. *Stat. Car.*, fol. 105r, ed. in A. Gloria, *Annua festività de' padovani per la grande vittoria avuta nel 1386 sulle armi di Antonio della Scala* (Padua, 1850), 7–8.

121. See Cessi's essay "Prigionieri illustri durante la guerra fra Scaligeri e Carraresi (1386)," in his *Padova medioevale* 1:153–70, and the list of captains in Gatari, *Cronaca carrarese*, 252–53.

122. On Venice's occupation of Corfu in 1386, see Lane, *Venice*, 198; D. M. Nicol, *Byzantium and Venice* (Cambridge: Cambridge University Press, 1988), 322–24; and

the documents in Predelli, 3:178–79, no. 221, 28 May 1386 and 184–85, no. 246, 8 Jan. 1387.

123. See the act of procuration for the loan in AN, 36, fol. 71rv, 14 Nov. 1386, and appointment of Turchetto in AN, 5, fol. 208rv, 14 Jan. 1387, both edited in Pastorello, *Nuove ricerche.* 140–44, doc. 6 and 7.

124. I follow the detailed account in Temple-Leader and Marcotti, *Sir John Hawkwood,* 195–204, based mainly on Gatari, *Cronaca carrarese,* 270–77. There is a summary of the battle in Allen, *History of Verona,* 317–20.

125. See AN, 37, fol. 12rv, 13 Apr. 1387, excerpt in Gloria 2:199–200, no. 1646, and Gatari, *Cronaca carrarese,* 284–85, on Giangaleazzo hiring Ubaldini's company of 350 soldiers for 7,000 ducats a month (or 20 ducats per man) for service against the Scaligeri.

126. On the first four freed on 22 Apr. 1387, see Cessi, "Prigionieri illustri," 1:160 and 169–70, doc. 6, edited from AN, 37, fol. 15r; on the release of Antonio di Toma Obizi, see AN, 1849, no. 12, 14 Apr. 1387, excerpt in Gloria, 2:200, no. 1647.

127. I follow the account in Bueno de Mesquita, *Giangaleazzo Visconti,* 74–77; see Gatari, *Cronaca carrarese,* 278–79, for a summary of the treaty.

128. See Seneca, "L'intervento veneto-carrarese," 57–60, and the correspondence in Verci, 16:142–47, nos. 1892–1895, 7, 14 July 1387.

129. On the conquest of these towns, see Gatari, *Cronaca carrarese,* 297–300, and Cogo, "Patriarcato d'Aquileia," 277–82. The acts of procuration for Sala are AN, 37, fol. 89rv, 23 Sept. 1387, excerpt in Gloria, 2:206, no. 1663 for Sacile, and AN, 37, fol. 97rv, 26 Sept. 1387, for Caneva; the text of the pact with Caneva is in ibid., fols. 98r–99r, 27 Sept. 1387, with printed version from another source in Verci, 16:154–59, no. 1904. The appointment of Francesco Dotti to confirm the pact with Aviano is found in AN, 37, fol. 103rv, 10 Oct. 1387.

130. The text of pact with Aviano is in AN, 37, fols. 104r–105r, 13 Sept. 1387, edited in Cogo, "Patriarcato d'Aquileia," 317–18, doc. 5: "quod in terris et districtibus suis cives Aviani tractabuntur dulciter et benigne ut tractantur alii sui subditi tam paduani quam tervisini."

131. See Verci, 17:3, no. 1906, 18 Oct. 1387.

132. See Law, "Caduta degli Scaligeri," 94–96.

133. See Pastorello, *Nuove ricerche,* 146–50, doc. 9–10.

134. AN, 699, fols. 116v–17r, 24 Jan. 1388; the Great Council of Padua, meeting in the Chapel of the Salone, named Alberto Aproiano proctor to reappoint Ugolino as podestà of Padua.

135. For the events of late 1387 and early 1388 leading to the isolation and fall of the Carrara, see the detailed essays of Collino, "La guerra viscontea-veneto," esp. 138–157, and Cessi, "Venezia e la prima caduta dei Carraresi," in his *Padova medioevale,* 1:171–90.

136. See Missivi della Prima Cancellaria, reg. 21, fols. 18v–19r, 29 Mar. 1388, where the Paduan lord is warned to expect no military aid from Florence but to bend to the necessities of the times and avoid the misfortunes of war by making peace.

137. See Senato, Secreta, reg. E, fol. 13v, 19 Apr. 1388, ed. in Cogo, "Patriarcato d'Aquileia," 318–19, doc. 6.

138. See the appointment of envoys in Pastorello, *Nuove ricerche*, 150–56, nos. 11–12, and the text of the treaty of 29 May in ibid., 156–69, no. 13.

139. See Salutati's letter of 12 May 1388 in *Staatsbriefe Coluccio Salutatis*, 227–28, no. 88.

140. Pastorello, *Nuove ricerche*, 169, doc. 14, 30 May 1388, partial edition of AN, 36, fol. 153r.

141. See text in Corio, *Storia di Milano*, 1:897–98.

142. See Sambin, "Statuti padovani editi II," 69–93.

Chapter 8 Exile and Restoration, 1388–1392

1. See the account in Gatari, *Cronaca carrarese*, 316.

2. See the discussion in Sambin, "Statuti padovani inediti II," 77–79, with text quoted on 92: "domini de Cararia . . . sunt et fuisse et esse intelligantur nunc et in preteritum et futuram legibus tam comunibus quam municipalibus absoluti et omnibus privilegiis, comodis, favoribus et honoribus imperialibus decorati."

3. AN, 525, fols. 52v–54v, 29 June 1388, in the Carrara chancery.

4. See Joppi, *Ultime relazioni dei Carraresi col Friuli*, 9–11, doc. 1.

5. Pastorello, *Nuove ricerche*, 172–75, nos. 16–17, both 30 June 1388.

6. Appointment of Francesco Allegro as envoy is in AN, 5, fol. 246rv, edited in Pastorello, *Nuove Ricerche*, 175–77, no. 18, and letter in Missivi della Prima Cancellaria, reg. 21, fol. 31v, 6 July 1388, edited in Collino, "Guerra veneto-viscontea contro i Carraresi," 6.

7. See Cessi, "Venezia e la prima caduta del Carraresi," in his *Padova medioevale*, 1:185 n, citing Senato, Secreta, reg. E, fol. 33v: "pro bono statu Italie de procurando quod civitas Padue regeretur ad comune—quod dominus Padue esset contentus vivere civiliter ut comunis persona."

8. Senato, Secreta, reg. E, fol. 34r, 16 Aug. 1388: "Informati sumus quod ipse dominus Padue publicus hostis noster."

9. *Staatsbriefe Coluccio Salutatis*, 233–34, no. 94, 26 Aug. 1388.

10. The main contemporary narrative of the military campaign leading to the fall of Padua in November 1388 is Gatari, *Cronaca carrarese*, 320–33, supplemented by Caresini, *Chronica*, 70–72, for the Venetian viewpoint, and the anonymous *Cronaca volgare*, 61–64, for Florence. Older detailed analyses are Cogo, "Patriarcato di Aquileia," 289–99, and Cessi, "Venezia e la prima caduta dei Carraresi," in his *Padova medioevale*, 1:183–90.

11. See Appendix 3, "Sales and Gifts of Carrara Property, June–November 1388," where full documentation from the Archivio di Stato, Padua, is provided.

12. Verci, 17:15–17, no. 1915, 2 Nov. 1388.

13. *Cronaca volgare*, 63.

14. See Verci, 17:18–21. no. 1916, letter of 27 Nov. 1388 from Giangaleazzo Visconti to the doge of Venice.

15. See AN, 169, fols. 49r–50r, 22 Nov. 1388, for the act in the chancery, AN, 699, fols. 235v–36r, 22 Nov. 1388: texts reading "propter metuum et tyranniden ipsorum Carrariensium" and "ipse Mannus et dictus eius genitor fuerunt male fide in possessionis et absque ullo legiptimo iure teneantur eam."

16. Ibid., fols. 236v–38r, 22 Nov. 1388.

17. *Cronaca volgare*, 63.

18. Quoted in Cessi, "Tumulto di Treviso," in *Padova medioevale*, 1:191–214, at 214.

19. *Staatsbriefe Coluccio Salutatis*, 236, no. 96, 5 Dec. 1388.

20. See Gatari, *Cronaca carrarese*, 344–348, for lists of the eight Anziani, board of nine, twelve ambassadors, and new officials of the communal bureaucracy: the notary Oliviero di Giovanni Lenguazzi as chancellor, Serafino di Benvenuto of Arquà as seneschal, Luchino of Milan as *spenditore*, and Bernardo da Lazara, a great favorite of Francesco il Vecchio, as provveditore.

21. My account is based on the audit of 24 Dec. 1388, conducted in the communal palace at the court of Sigillo, as described in AN, 100, fols. 355r–57v.

22. The articles of surrender proposed to Giangaleazzo Visconti are given in Gatari, *Cronaca carrarese*, 349–56, in the original Latin, drawn up by Bonacorso Naseri.

23. In making these accommodations, the Visconti lord used in Padua the same strategy of limited direct intervention in local institutions which he had employed in Vicenza; see Varanini, "Vicenza nel Trecento," 240–43.

24. The principal account of the first six months of Francesco Novello's exile, until his entry into Florence in April 1389, is Gatari, *Cronaca carrarese*, 360–80, to be supplemented by the later poem, sometimes attributed to Zenone da Pistoia, edited by Giorgio Rosconi as *Poemetto storico carrarese*, 36–50, cap. 3–7. In a letter of November 1390, Coluccio Salutati summarized Francesco Novello's many adventures leading to his reconquest of Padua, *Epistolario*, 2:252–64. G. Andenne offers a concise account in her entry on Francesco Novello's wife: "Este, Taddea d'," in *DBI* 43 (1993), 437–39.

25. See Gatari, *Cronaca carrarese*, 379–80 and notes.

26. Ibid., 380–83.

27. Vergerio, *Epistolario*, 31–32, no. 16, August 1389.

28. Francesco Novello's second trip of his exile is described in Gatari, *Cronaca carrarese*, 388–406, and *Poemetto storico carrarese*, 50–74, cap. 8–15. The fullest narrative is in Verci, 18:66–109.

29. See Bueno de Mesquita, *Giangaleazzo Visconti*, chap. 9, and Brucker, *Civic World*, 132–35, for the diplomacy leading up to the First Visconti War.

30. See the detailed account in Frati, "Lega dei Bolognesi e dei Fiorentini," 5–24.

31. The Latin letter is edited by Medin as "Littera dominae Maddelanae . . . domino Jacobo dal Verme," in his "Maddalena degli Scrovegni," 260–62, with an English translation in M. King and A. Rabil, eds., *Her Immaculate Hand* (Binghamton, N.Y.: CEMERS, 1980), 33–35.

32. AN, 407, fols. 220r–24, March 1389, bank deposits; fol. 217r, 15 Feb. 1389,

purchase of house; fols. 223r, 232r, 30 May 1389 and 13 Mar. 1390, acts concerning the hospital, also discussed in Billanovich, "Amico del Petrarca," 274.

33. AN, 407, fol. 223r, 30 July 1389; see the discussion of Lombardo della Seta's circle with partial transcription of this act in Billanovich and Pellegrin, "Nuova lettere di Lombardo della Seta," 230–31.

34. Archivi Privati Diversi, reg. 173, Grompo, perg. 5276, 23 Oct. 1357.

35. Gloria, 2:141–42, no. 1477, 19 Nov. 1379.

36. On appearance at court, see ibid., 2:170, no. 1568, 18 Jan. 1384, and on Pietro's career, Gatari, *Cronaca carrarese*, 303.

37. Archivi Privati Diversi, reg. 175, Grompo, perg. 5316, 30 June 1380, and pergs. 5323–24, 8 Jan. 1388.

38. Archivio Papafava, cod. 37, perg. 23, 22 Nov. 1388, and Gatari, *Cronaca carrarese*, 403, 405, 412.

39. Senato, Misti, reg. 40, fol. 175v, 10 Apr. 1389: "iam multis annis adhesit domino Francisco de Carraria, quondam domino Padua, naturali et perfido hosti nostro."

40. Ibid., reg. 41, fol. 21r, 15 July 1389: "sicut omnibus notus est, dictus dominus Ugolinus in quocumque tempore et casu, tam prospero quam adverso, semper laudabiliter se gessit ad honorem et statum nostrum."

41. AN, 699, fols. 210v–11v, 8 June 1389, fols. 243r–44r, 12 Apr. 1390.

42. See AN, 525, fols. 25v, 37v, 46r, 31 Aug. and 18 Dec. 1387, 28 Apr. 1388, three acts of procuration, redacted in the Carrara chancery.

43. For his career, see Mallett, "Cermisone, Bartolomeo," and AN, 118, fols. 159v, 160r, 11 and 18 July 1388, for gift and sale; Gloria, 2:228–29, no. 1728, 21 Aug. 1389, gives extracts from the legal case against Cermisone and the Visconti letter.

44. Collodo, *Società in trasformazione*, 322.

45. AN, 191, fol. 99r, 15 Dec. 1387.

46. On canon by June 1365, see Dondi dall'Orologio, *Serie cronologico-storica*, 79; for interests in Brusegena, see AN, 678, fols. 15v–16r, 23 May 1374; in Galzignano and Rubano, AN, 42, fol. 127r, 19 Feb. 1376, and fol. 327r, 2 May 1379, respectively.

47. On his numerous promotions of 12 June 1388, probably to clear a backlog of candidates for clerical orders created by the vacancy of the Paduan see, see Sambin, "Altri chierici ordinati a Padova," 403–4; for his presence as bishop at the examination on 20 Nov. 1388, see Gloria, 2:214, no. 1685. A document from the episcopal curia of 14 July 1388 seems, however, to report the bishopric as "sede vacante," see Gloria 2:212, no. 1679.

48. AN, 39, fols. 192r–201r, 21 Apr. 1390, forty-five tithes held pro indiviso in Piove di Sacco.

49. See tithes listed in Archivio della Curia Vescovile, Padua, Feudorum, vol. 9, fol. 79rv, 17 Feb. 1389, for Paolo and Luca Lion, vol. 10, fol. 2r, 18 Sept. 1389, for Gianfrancesco and Manfredo Piombioli, vol. 9, fols. 82r–85v, 8 Apr. 1389, to Daniele and Niccolò da Rio, fols. 62v–63r, 7 July 1389, to Turchetto, fols. 15v, 30v, 4 June and 4 Nov. 1389, to Vitaliani.

50. See AN, 40, fol. 138r, 15 Nov. 1389, for the Pizzacomini brothers, and fol. 139rv, 10 Mar. 1390, for Cortusi.

51. Ibid., fol. 227r, 26 June 1389, several parcels that had belonged to S. Agostino of Bovolenta.

52. Feudorum, vol. 9, fol. 58r, 8 May 1389, for Solesino, and AN, 40, fol. 16r, 24 July 1389, on Este right of patronage.

53. Feudorum, vol. 9, fols. 20v, 42r, 7 Nov. 1389.

54. Sambin, "Altri chierici ordinati a Padova," 404–5.

55. Gloria, 2:236, no. 1749, 9 Feb. 1390, and 241, no. 1762, 30 Apr. 1390.

56. See Gatari, *Cronaca carrarese*, 104, 177–78, 293.

57. See, for example, rural contracts redacted at Africano's home in contrada Salone: soceda contract on cows in Brentasicca, AN, 290, fol. 43v, 2 Dec. 1374; leases at Strà, AN, 42, fol. 404v, 17 Mar. 1380; rent of 34 *campi* in Fiesso for £60 per annum and 6 *moggi* of grain on 20 July, pork at Christmas, ham at Carnival, two capons and eggs at Easter, and two chickens in August, AN, 42, fol. 424r, 7 June 1380; and purchase of farmstead of 23 *campi* in Villanova from Pietro Querini for £1,000, AN, 43, fol. 50r, 6 May 1382.

58. AN, 188, fol. 153v, for rent of house, and fol. 177v, for lease in Fiesso.

59. Gloria, 2:242, no. 1764, 16 May 1390.

60. Gatari, *Cronaca carrarese*, 403.

61. The basic narrative of plans and operations of the reconquest of Padua is ibid., 394–420; on the role of Stephen of Bavaria, see Rambaldi, "Stefano III," 286–326.

62. See the text in *Staatsbriefe Coluccio Salutatis*, 255–56, no. 109.

63. Ibid., 256–258, no. 110, 1 May 1390, declaration of war on Giangaleazzo Visconti, and 261–65, no. 114, 25 May 1390, to all Italians.

64. See, for example, Predelli, 3:204, no. 332, 19 Feb. 1390; in response to Venice's demands, Giangaleazzo ordered his officials to pay dues on flax traditionally owed Venice by the villages of Corte and Piove di Sacco.

65. See Cessi, "Politica veneziana di terraferma," 194–97.

66. Gatari, *Cronaca carrarese*, 418.

67. Letter of 29 June 1390 in Bueno de Mesquita, *Giangaleazzo Visconti*, 346, app. 5, doc. 4.

68. Verci, 18:33, 36, nos. 1927, 1931, 30 June and 3 July.

69. *Staatsbriefe Coluccio Salutatis*, 268–69, no. 118, 11 July 1390.

70. See the contemporary judgment in *Cronaca volgare*, 106–7, and two dispatches of August 1390 to Francesco Gonzaga, showing that Stephen was in Visconti pay: Rambaldi, "Stefano III," 319–26.

71. On the medals, see the older essay of Guiffrey, "Les médailles de Carrare, seigneurs de Padoue," 17–25, and R. Weiss, *Pisanello's Medallion of the Emperor John VIII Palaeologus*, 10–12, 30. I take my descriptions from the exhibition catalogue *Da Giotto al Mantegna*, 210. On the composition of these lives, see Cessi's introduction to his edition of the *Gesta*, xxxv–xxxvi and passim.

72. *Stat. Car.,* fol. 54v, November 1390.

73. Ibid., fols. 100v–101r, 1390.

74. Archivio di Stato, Padua, Ospedale Civile, S. Francesco, reg. 964, fols. 12r–17r, copy of judicial act of October 1390.

75. *Stat. Car.,* fol. 159v, 1391.

76. Ibid., fol. 156v, December 1390, on foreign creditors, fol. 119rv, 1391, on the church, and fol. 127v, on renting to university students, which is published in Gloria, 2:241, no. 1768, 1390.

77. AN, 525, fols. 56v–72r, with reference to Marco Guarnerini's recording the creation of a citizen in 1391 in AN, 395, fol. 21v, May 1400. The creation of two other citizens is to be found in AN, 45, fols. 133v–34v, 21 Apr. and 13 July 1391.

78. See Pastorello, *Nuove ricerche,* 50–51.

79. The lists are given in AN, 5453, *Liber Officialium,* 1390–92.

80. AN, 45, fols. 251r–261v, 3 Nov. 1390, for the large sale, and fol. 128v, 3 Nov. 1390, for list of witnesses in the Carrara curia to both transactions and the sale of the two houses.

81. AN, 119, fols. 96r–98v, 21 Apr. 1391.

82. AN, 45, fols. 136r–37r, 10 June 1391, for Goffonario, fols. 244r–46r, 14 June 1392, for Nascimbene, and fol. 247r, 17 June 1392, for Michele.

83. Ibid., fols. 226r–28v, 231rv, 12 Oct. 1390.

84. Ibid., fol. 138rv, 4 Mar. 1392, ed. in Ciscato, *Ebrei in Padova,* 229–31.

85. AN, 45, fol. 135r, for Ferrara, and fol. 134v, for Venice, excerpt in Gloria, 2:252, no. 1795.

86. Three contemporary accounts describe the events of the final year of the First Visconti War leading to the Peace of Genoa in January 1392, from the viewpoints of the major protagonists: Gatari, *Cronaca carrarese,* 433–37, for Padua; *Annales Mediolanenses,* cols. 813–820, for Milan; and *Cronica volgare,* 124–27, 130–35, for Florence. Bueno de Mesquita, *Giangaleazzo Visconti,* 124–36, provides a detailed and accurate narrative.

87. Vergerio, *Epistolario,* 46–53, at 48: "societas hec populorum et principum."

88. Ibid., 52 n.

89. *Cronica volgare,* 124.

90. I follow the detailed and vivid account of this campaign given by Pier Paolo Vergerio in a letter of 19 July to Giovanni da Bologna, *Epistolario,* 66–78, no. 34.

91. Missive della Prima Cancellaria, reg. 22, fol. 151v, 4 Aug. 1391: "conveniens quidem munus domino intrepidi cordis et audacie leonine, congruens principi guelfo et popolo paduano."

92. See the detailed account of the negotiations in Delaville Le Roulx, "Anti-grand-maistre de l'ordre de Saint Jean de Jérusalem," 525–44.

93. Critical edition of the Peace of Genoa in C. Santoro, *La politica finanziera dei Visconti,* vol. 2, *Documenti, 1385-1412* (Milan: Arti Grafiche Colombo, 1979), 162–209, no. 244, January 1392, abridged text in Verci, 18:54–62, no. 1941.

94. Missivi della Prima Cancellaria, reg. 22, fols. 182v–83r, 24 Jan. 1392; Senato,

Secreta, reg. E, fol. 72v, 3 Feb. 1392: "nos consilium prestaremus ipsi domino Francisco secundum quod nobis pro statu suo bonum et utile videtur."

95. Maggior Consilio, Deliberazione, Leona, fol. 58v, 10 Mar. 1392, ed. in Pastorello, *Nuove ricerche*, 201, proposal to pay large expenses for entertainment of Francesco Novello passed by six ducal coucillors, three heads, and thirty-four members of the Forty and three-quarters of the Great Council.

Chapter 9   Reconstituting the Carrara Regime

1. AN, 45, fols. 229r–30r, 19 Mar. 1391; Descalzi is styled official "super prestantiis stipendiariorum massarie, seu introytibus possessionum et bonorum prefati domini, super datiisque et introitibus portam civitatis Padue, massarusque fonticum bladorum eiusdem domini, demum superstes et officialis super datiis et gabellis."

2. Ibid., fols. 164r–65r, 20 Nov. 1392, payment of 1,400 ducats, fols. 172r–73r, also 20 Nov. 1392, syndication and *finis* where Ton is described: "super suo bancho presiti denariorumque et bonorum dicti banchi ac rationum et utilis tocius ipsius presiti superstes et officialis deputatus."

3. Ibid., fols. 178rv, 179r, 12 Apr. 1393.

4. AN, 180, fol. 5rv, 9 Nov. 1390, and Archivio di Stato, Padua, Archivio Giudiziari Civili, Aquila, busta 5 sub anno, 30 Oct. 1391.

5. AN, 7, fol. 309v, 21 Nov. 1397; on Bernardo Lazera's status as Carrara supporter, see Collodo, *Società in trasformazione*, 299, and on Vanzerio's career as jurist and official, Gloria, 1:365, no. 702.

6. AN, 101, fols. 321r–22v, 15 Nov. 1395: "miserium et officium bullandi et iustandi omnes et singulas mensuras, statras, balancias, marchas, campiones, et omnes aliud pondus . . . civitatis Padue."

7. AN, 669, fol. 359v = Papafava, 5:54–55, 14 Oct. 1400; AN, 1, fol. 151r, 12 Apr. 1403.

8. Collodo provides a good sketch of Francesco Novello's relations with the textile industry in her *Società in trasformazione*, 399–403, revising the earlier work of Cessi, *Corporazioni dei mercanti*, 53–55, who published documents from the period on 86–98.

9. Padua, Biblioteca Civica, MS B.P. 169, Matricola, Arte della Lana, fols. 6r–25r.

10. Text from AN, 38, fols. 214r–17r, 18 June 1395, edited in Cessi, *Corporazioni dei mercanti*, 92–97, doc. 12.

11. AN, 7, fols. 252v–54rv, 21 Apr. 1397.

12. AN, 8, fols. 225v–28r, 5 Feb. 1400, fols. 255r–56r, 14 Apr. 1400.

13. Ibid., fols. 411v–13r, 20 Aug. 1400; on Bonjacopo's career, see Cessi, *Padova medioevale*, 2:573–75; Collodo, *Società in trasformazione*, 340, 343.

14. AN, 119, fols. 194v–95r, 29 Nov. 1394.

15. AN, 525, fol. 79v, 19 Mar. 1398: "mutuum gratuitum de bono et puro amore."

16. AN, 383, fols. 56v–57, 20 Jan. 1404.

17. See AN, 119, fols. 111r–212r, work of the curial notary Salimbene Zennari.

Though doubtless incomplete, Zennari's data, which included sales and fiefs, provide some insight into the nature and extent of the lord's landed wealth after his restoration.

18. AN, 119, fol. 145rv, 7 May 1393; the buyer was the former leasee, who had earlier contracted to pay £10 rent.

19. Ibid., fols. 42rv and 46v–47v, 9 Nov. and 12 Dec. 1390.

20. Ibid., fols. 48r–49r, 16 Dec. 1390; fols. 60r–61r, 10 Jan. 1391; and fols. 116r–17v, 26 June 1391.

21. Ibid., fols. 150r–51r, 26 May 1393, exchange, fols. 210v–11r, 1 Apr. 1395, sale of *dominium perpetuum*.

22. Ibid., fol. 131v–32r, 151v–54r, 4 Sept. 1392, 29 May 1393.

23. Ibid., fols. 141v–44r, 176r–77r, 200r–201r, 26 Apr. 1393, 4 May 1394, 9 Jan. 1395, purchases in and near Castelbaldo.

24. AN, 157, fols. 134r–37r, 4 Dec. 1393; Mueller, "Veronesi e capitali veronesi," 370–71, discusses the will, providing a partial edition from another MS.

25. AN, 7, fol. 273rv, 10 July 1394, excerpt in Gloria, 2:287, no. 1894, appointment of Lion to petition for Venetian citizenship; AN, 38, fols. 415r–17r, 1398, excerpt in Gloria, 2:321, no. 1991, sale of part of Taddea's inheritance.

26. AN, 525, fols. 144v–45v, 9 Jan. 1400.

27. See Rizzoli and Perini, *Moneta di Padova*, 137–38, no. 45, for the contract, with discussion in Cessi, *Padova medievale*, 1:293. See AN, 180, fols. 105r–6r, 20 May 1394, sale of Pietro dall'Olio's land in Monselice.

28. Rizzoli and Perini, *Moneta di Padova*, 116–20, no. 22, 11 Aug. 1394, with discussion on 42.

29. Ibid., 120–21, no. 23, 20 Oct. 1396, with discussion on 42.

30. See the discussion and texts in Rizzoli, "Nuovi documenti," 62 and 69–73, nos. 8–10, 10 June and 21 Aug. 1399.

31. Rizzoli and Perini, *Moneta di Padova*, 46, 56–57, with document on 121–25, no. 24, 5 June 1398.

32. On the aftermath of the murder of Giovanni dall'Argento, see ibid., 135–37, nos. 43–44, 19 Apr., 13 Aug. 1399, with discussion on 57–58.

33. Text in Cessi, "Nuovi documenti sulla zecca carrarese," in *Padova medioevale*, 1:294–97, with brief discussion on 292.

34. See Rizzoli and Perini, *Moneta di Padova*, 135, no. 42, 2 Oct. 1403, Pietro Bovi's testimony in the mint in contrada S. Canziano.

35. See Romanin, *Storia documentata*, 3:236, and the text of the Peace of Genoa with later modifications in Verci, 17:54–62, no. 1941.

36. Archivio di Stato, Padua, Ospedale Civile, S. Francesco, reg. 964, fols. 70r–73r.

37. Ibid., fol. 70v: "dominus Franciscus volebat quod illi tenerent et possiderent dicta bona quibus dederat dicta bona, et quod non volebat quod aliqui existentes extra Padua and paduano districtu et amici domini Comitis Virtutum gauderent aliquibus bonis suis, nonobstante dicta sententia."

38. Ibid., fol. 71r: "ad hospicium in Padua quidam Nicolaus de Stransoldo fuit ad ipsum dominum Johannem et sibi dixit, 'Tu venisti gratiam recuperandi bona exilorum. Per fidem meam nisi recedas de civitate Padue, ego occidam te per fruste.' Quo audito, idem dominus Johannes maxime timore recessit de Padue et fuit in Lombardia, nec unquam fuit ausus reverti."

39. Ibid., fols. 72r–73r.

40. AN, 6, fols. 194r–95r, 22 June 1392, priest from Faenza; fols. 248v–49v, 15 June 1393, inheritance in Monselice; fol. 246r, right of the *districtualis* from Monselice to buy land in Padua.

41. AN, 7, fol. 335r, 1 Oct. 1397: "magnifico domino vigili, studio et cura incessanter exhibivit."

42. Ibid., fols. 119r–20r, 4 Jan. 1395: "intentum esse debet studium principantis, ut subiecti multiplicentur in virtutibus, . . . quando quidem Aristotele teste, 'meliorum subditorum, melior est principantis.'"

43. AN, 45, fols. 176r, 177r, 177v, 10 and 12 Feb. and 8 Apr. 1393.

44. AN, 6, fol. 245r, 3 May 1393.

45. Archivi Giudiziari Civili, Aquila, busta 10, 31 Oct. 1398, in home of the noble Giacomo Salamone in contrada S. Pietro.

46. AN, 6, fols. 221r–22v, 1 Feb. 1393.

47. Archivi Giudiziari Civili, Aquila, busta 5, sub anno 1391.

48. Ibid., busta 5, sub anno 1392, 29 March.

49. AN, 352, fol. 108r, 27 May 1396.

50. Archivi Giudiziari Civili, Aquila, busta 10, sub anno 1401.

51. AN, 8, fol. 157r, 21 Aug. 1399.

52. AN, 38, fols. 199r–200v, 28 May 1395, excerpt in Gloria, 2:296, no. 1920.

53. AN, 38, fols. 136r–139r, 10 and 12 Feb. 1395; the accusation treated "de gestis et administratis per eum de bonis, rebus and reddibus canipe dicte maioris eccelsie paduane."

54. AN, 45, fols. 184r–87r, 3 Feb. 1394.

55. AN, 525, fol. 135v, 6 Oct. 1399: "per ora singulatim alterius trium se obsculantes et manus tangentes, bonam, tranquillam et perpetuam pacem et concordiam."

56. AN, 1, fols. 77v–78v, 24 June 1403.

57. AN, 119, fol. 31v, 27 November, the mason, fols. 37v–38r, 7 December, Pietro Neve, fols. 43v–44r, 10 Dec. 1390, Giacomo da Ferrara.

58. AN, 119, fols. 30r–31r, 27 Nov. 1390, fief to Silvestro; fols. 38r–41v, 8 Dec. 1390, fiefs in Este to Margherita; fols. 67v–69r, 5 Feb. 1391, fiefs to Niccolò Lattuga for "contra quamcumque premium fidelitatis et sacramentum homagii."

59. Ibid., fol. 121r, 19 July 1391, house of the count of Lavagna, fols. 159rv, 160r–62r, 24 June 1392, and 13 July 1405, fief and gift of lands in Paduan campanea.

60. AN, 38, fols. 75r–77r, 17 Sept. 1395; on his career, see Gloria, 1:434–35, nos. 831–32, which documents his membership in the Carrara elite.

61. AN, 45, fol. 163rv, 13 Jan. 1393: "de sue plentitudine potestatis ac omni auctoritiate quam fungitur."

62. AN, 7, fols. 104r–85v, 23 Nov. 1394: "propter servitorum pluralitatem eidem magnifico domino et olim magnifico genitori suo et inclite domui carrariensis die noctuque non sine magna mentis anxietate et corporis laboribus."

63. AN, 38, fol. 237rv, October 1395.

64. Gatari, *Cronaca Carrarese*, 442.

65. See AN, 37, fol. 468v, 16 May 1394, excerpt in Gloria, 2:285, no. 1888, for Collalto brothers, AN, 38, fol. 214r, 18 June 1395, published in Cessi, *Corporazioni dei mercanti*, 92. These titles were also used in a grant to Enrico Gallo, AN, 40, fol. 125r, 10 Feb. 1400.

66. See the account of Francesco Novello's court in Conversini's autobiography, *Rationarium vite*, 166–68.

67. This treatise remains unedited; I rely on the discussion with brief extracts in Sabbadini, *Giovanni da Ravenna*, 89–90, 180.

68. See Cattini and Romani, "Corti parallele," 1:55–56.

69. See Gloria, 1:159–61, 150–52, nos. 350–355, 327–30, on Girlandi and Saliceto, respectively.

70. Gundersheimer, *Ferrara*, 55, which provides a brief discussion of the organization of the contemporary Este court at Ferrara.

71. See Pastorello's introduction to her edition of *Copialettere*, xiv–xvii and passim, for examples.

72. See ibid., xv–xvi for the statistics and 365–66, and Lazzarini, "Due sigilli di Franxcesco Novello [1900]," in *Scritti di paleografia e diplomatica*, 239–43, for the seals.

73. In his *Apologia* of 1399 discussed with extracts published in Sabbadini, *Giovanni da Ravenna*, 89, 179.

74. For Giovanni Conversini's criticism, see his *Dragmalogia*, 67–107, and for the advanced state of the Carrara chancery, J. K. Hyde, *Literacy and Its Uses: Studies on Late Medieval Italy* (Manchester: Manchester University Press, 1993), 254–56.

75. For his career, see Franceschini, "Carrara, Conte da," and on his mother's family, the Maconia, Collodo, *Società in trasformazione*, 223–25.

76. AN, 5, fol. 297v, 20 Nov. 1388, record of sale of all of Conte's property, not described, to Michele Rabatta.

77. See AN, 45, fol. 229r–30r, 19 Mar. 1391, where Conte of contrada Arena witnessed in the Carrara "Camera ab Armis" the settlement of debt of Domenichino Descalzi from 1388.

78. AN, 952, fol. 143v–44r, 22 Aug. 1395, AN, 366, fols. 304v, 319r, 7 Feb and 14 March 1400 = Papafava, 4:318–19.

79. Papafava, 4:326–27, May and August 1400.

80. AN, 794, fol. 53r, 16 Sept. 1400, for the rural *canipa* in Valsanzibio.

81. AN, 286, fol. 113v, 5 Mar. 1399, appointment was made on the authority of Francesco Zabarella.

82. AN, 142, fol. 245r, 15 Jan. 1399.

83. AN, 8, fol. 199r, 28 Dec. 1399.

84. AN, 367, fol. 81r, 6 July 1402, for lease of tithes for £600 at Christmas and

£600 at Easter, and fol. 126v, 25 Feb. 1404, for rent of tithes on mills in Pernumia "que spectant ad canonicatum domini Ardizoni de Carraria."

85. See Camerini, *Piazzola*, 125–30, for Carrara interests in the area, and xxi–xxvi, doc. 22, for an edition of the grant made on 14 Oct. 1391. On his life, see Ganguzza Billanovich, "Carrara, Giacomo da," 675–76, which omits any notice of his career from 1391 to 1404.

86. AN, 39, fols. 237v–38r, 20 May 1392.

87. AN, 180, fols. 279r–80r, 23 June 1401, for act of legitimation, and Gatari, *Cronaca carrarese*, 379, who states that in April 1389 the brothers, nearly grown, were living in hiding in Venice.

88. AN, 330, fol. 181v, 4 Sept. 1394, rent of 30 *campi* in eight parcels; AN, 685, fol. 149r, 22 May 1395.

89. AN, 38, fol. 42rv, 13 July 1395, excerpt in Gloria, 2:296–97, no. 1922.

90. See AN, 794, fol. 43rv, 10 Jan. 1399, for record of Caterina purchasing for £8,000 real estate from her cousin, Dorotea di Boninsegna Bocassi, in the home of Giacomo da Carrara, and AN, 180, fol. 180v, 16 Aug. 1399, Caterina's will.

91. See AN, 8, fol. 392r, 1400 [no month given] for terms of dowry.

92. AN, 9, fols. 3r–5r, 16 Mar. 1401, excerpt in Gloria, 2:380, no. 2145.

93. On Bonifacio's service, see *Copialettere*, 347, no. 636. On Giacomo's attempted treason in April 1405, see Gatari, *Cronaca carrarese*, 551–52. According to another version, after he was arrested, Giacomo took his own life.

94. AN, 132, fol. 219r, 11 July 1405.

95. On Rodolfo's career, see Gatari, *Cronaca carrarese*, 415, 430, 435, 450, on his residence in S. Giustina and landed interests, AN, 338, fols. 48v, 86r, 5 Sept. 1399 and 4 May 1400.

96. For the career, see Gatari, *Cronaca carrarese*, 472, 481, 548, and AN, 794, fols. 52r, 53v, 18 Nov. and 12 Oct. 1400 for the vineyards in Valsanzibio.

97. AN, 286, fols. 16r, 20r, 6 June and 26 Oct. 1396, two collations of benefices by Andrea da Carrara as abbot of S. Giustina, AN, 669, fol. 154r, 10 Mar. 1398, appointment of agent to collect rents.

98. See *Copialettere*, 243, 348, for evidence on Andrea as Francesco il Vecchio's bastard and the letter to the Este lord. Sambin, *Ricerche di storia monastica medioevale*, 70–71, 73, emphasizes Andrea's disastrous leadership, mistakingly dating the beginning of his abbacy from 1402.

99. Lacking a modern biography, one must use the older study of Dondi dall'Orologio, *Dissertazione ottava*, 137–52. See also the brief discussions of Stefano da Carrara's career in Gaffuri and Gallo, "Signoria ed episcopato a Padova nel Trecento," 952–54, and Collodo, *Società in trasformazione*, 287, 291. Gatari, *Cronaca carrarese*, 474–75, 513, 534, 553–54, traces his career in service of the Carrara regime, with the editors (p. 474) placing his birth in 1370, when his father would have been eleven years (!) old.

100. See the discussion in Gaffuri and Gallo, "Signoria ed episcopato a Padova nel Trecento," 934–38.

101. Collodo, "Lo sfruttamento dei benefici canonicali," in *Società in trasformazione,* 277–96.

102. See Posenato, "Chierici ordinati a Padova dal 1396 al 1419," 29–30, and Dondi dall'Orologio, *Dissertazione ottava,* 270–71.

103. *Documenti carraresi,* no. 173, 28 Jan. 1399; AN, 8, fol. 256v, 14 May 1400, Nascimbene to receive "investituram omnium et singulorum feudorum que ipse magnificus dominus recognoscit ab ecclesia paduana."

104. See *Copialettere,* 306–7, 325–6, for letters of exchange, and 329–30, notes, for payments to the Papal Camera and College of Cardinals.

105. See AN, 1, fol. 74v, 5 May 1403.

106. AN, 43, fol. 230r, 26 Dec. 1395.

107. AN, 45, fol. 156rv, 31 Oct. 1392, fols. 158r–61r, 1 Nov. 1392, excerpt in Gloria, 2:269, no. 1841, with later documents included: "quamcumque iurisdictionem patronatus spectantis et debitus, tam de iure quam de consuetudine, in ipsis loco et ecclesia." See also the essay, with many of notarial acts cited here edited as appendixes, L. Bertazzo, "Origini dei Servi a Padova," in Bertazzo and Montagna, *Santa Maria dei Servi a Padova,* 9–58.

108. AN, 6, fols. 247r–48v, 16 Apr. 1393.

Chapter 10   Ambition and Destruction, 1392–1405

1. The only adequate survey of Padua's political history from 1392 to 1405 is Simioni's *Storia di Padova,* 552–69, though Ganguzza Billanovich's entry "Carrara, Francesco Novello," in *DBI* 20, 956–62, provides an accurate summary. For the Florentine foreign affairs in the same period, see Brucker, *Civic World,* 144–205; for Milan until late 1402, Bueno de Mesquita, *Giangaleazzo Visconti.* I am deeply indebted to these authoritative accounts for my own narrative.

2. On Italian politics leading to the Treaty of Bologna, see Brucker, *Civic World,* 147–49; Bueno de Mesquita, *Giangaleazzo Visconti,* 143–48; and Pastorello, *Nuove ricerche,* 77–82.

3. See AN, 6, 191r, 12 June 1392, excerpt in Gloria, 2:264, no. 1828.

4. Vergerio, "Ad Franciscum Juniorem de Carraria," cols. 209–15, discussed in Montobbio, *Splendore e utopia,* 150–51.

5. Archivio di Stato, Florence, Missivi della Prima Cancellaria, reg. 23, fol. 18r, 28 Apr. 1392; fol. 48r, 25 Sept. 1392, ed. in Pastorello, *Nuove ricerche,* 209–10, no. 46; and fols. 49v–50r, 28 Sept. 1392, ed. in *Staatsbriefe Coluccio Salutatis,* 296–98, no. 135.

6. Missivi della Prima Cancellaria, reg. 23, fol. 51r, 12 Oct. 1392, ed. in Pastorello, *Nuove ricerche,* 210–11, no. 47.

7. See AN, 45, fol. 140rv, 26 May 1392, excerpt in Gloria, 2:262–63, no. 1825, for appointment of Carrara proctor to ensure peace, and Jones, *Malatesta of Rimini,* 109–10, for context.

8. *Chronicon Estense,* cols. 527–28, and Gatari, *Cronaca carrarese,* 439.

9. Maggior Consiglio, Leona, fol. 61v, 24 Nov. 1392: "Franciscus Junior de Car-

raria intimus amicus nostri dominii, . . . assumatur in civem, et nostrum nobilem Veneciarum de nostro Maiori Consilio, cum suis filiis et heredibus, de gratia speciali," ed. in M. Sanuto, *Vite dei Dogi*, ed. G. Monticolo, Rerum italicarum scriptores, new ed., vol. 22, t. 4 (Città di Castello: S. Lapi, 1900), 52 n. See Lazzarini, "Trattato," 269–70, for the significance.

10. Senato, Privilegi, reg. 1, fol. 105r, 20 Mar. 1393, for Caterina and Elisabeth, fols. 106v, 107r, 10 June and 13 July 1393, Capodivacca and Santa Sofia, fols. 111r, 112r, 7 and 31 May, 12 July 1394, Della Scala and Visconti.

11. See accounts in the *Chronicon Estense*, cols. 531–34, and Delaito, *Annales Estenses*, cols. 907–8.

12. See B. Cessi, *Venezia e Padova*, 53–56 and 124–29, docs. 2–4, 31 July and 9, 12 Aug. 1393.

13. Conversini, *Memorandarum rerum liber*, 244.

14. Senato, Misti, reg. 42, fol. 139r, 23 Oct. 1393; Missivi della Prima Cancellaria, reg. 23, fol. 161v, 5 Nov. 1393.

15. See the accounts in Gatari, *Cronaca carrarese*, 441–44, and Vergerio, "De dignissimo funebri apparatu," cols. 190–94.

16. Vergerio, "Oratio in funere Francisci senioris de Carraria," cols. 195–208, and Giovanni Lodovico Lambertazzi, "Sermo in morte magni domini Francisci senioris de Carraria," eds. in Gatari, *Cronaca carrarese*, 443–46 n, and in Zardo, *Petrarca e i Carraresi*, 295–305.

17. Salutati's four letters of fall 1393 to the "dominus paduanus" are in Missivi della Prima Cancellaria, reg. 23, fols. 165r, 170r, 175r, 175v, 14 and 29 Nov., 18 and 22 Dec. 1393, the first is edited in Pastorello, *Nuove ricerche*, 212–13, no. 50.

18. Senato, Misti, reg. 42, fol. 141v, 4 Dec. 1393: "pro servando amorem et benivolentiam dicti domini Padue," the Senate voted to send an envoy to secure Conte's release; see also Esch, *Bonifaz IX*, 119–20.

19. AN, 37, fol. 487v, 11 June 1394, excerpt in Gloria, 2:286, no. 1890, partial ed. in Billanovich and Billanovich, "Gli ultimi Estensi di Padova," 150–51.

20. Letters of April and May 1394 edited in Pastorello, *Nuove ricerche*, 214–7, nos. 52–54, 56, with discussion on 86.

21. AN, 7, fol. 8rv, 29 June 1394, excerpt in Gloria, 2:287, no. 1893, ed. from another MS in Verci, 17:77–79, no. 1951.

22. For events in Ferrara in 1395, see Delaito, *Annales Estenses*, cols. 921–28; B. Cessi, *Venezia e Padova*, 62–74; and Verci, 17:82–88, no. 1955, 3 Apr. 1395, on the terms of the loan.

23. These terms are reported in Gatari, *Cronaca carrarese*, 448.

24. On his marriage, see the older study of L. Olivi, "Del matrimonio del Marchese Nicolò III d'Este," 335–76, which published a number of documents. Quotation is from Senato, Secreta, reg. E, fol. 131r, 27 Sept. 1396: "placeret nobis valde, quia cognoscimus . . . quod ipsa foret conservativa amoris et status utriusque partis."

25. For a contemporary account on the privileges of the office and ceremonies of installation, see *Annales Mediolanenses*, cols. 821–30; a modern edition of this re-

port is given in R. Elze, "Die Erhebung Giangaleazzo Viscontis zum Herzog von Mailand," in *Società, istituzioni, spirtualità: Studi in onore di Cinzio Violante*, 2 vols. (Spoleto: Centro italiano di Studi sull'Alto Medioevo, 1994), 1:291–304.

26. On Venice's envoys, see Senato, Misti, reg. 43, fol. 74v, 27 July 1395, and on Florence, *Cronaca volgare*, 199–200, and Herde, "Politische Verhaltensweisen," 225.

27. On the loan, see Theiner, *Codex diplomaticus*, 2:88, no. 35, 8 Aug. 1394, and on the events, *Cronaca volgare*, 197–98, Brucker, *Civic World*, 153–55; Esch, *Bonifaz IX*, 139–41; and, most fully, Bolognini, "Relazioni tra la repubbliche di Firenze e Venezia," 81–95.

28. Report of decision limiting Florence's presence in the Romagna, AN, 7, fols. 291r–92r, 29 Jan. 1397, excerpt in Gloria, 2:313, no. 1968.

29. On the episode, see Bueno de Mesquita, *Giangaleazzo Visconti*, 199–200, and the letter in Seville, Biblioteca Columbina, Cod. 5.5.8, fol. 32r.

30. On Conte in papal service, see Esch, *Bonifaz IX*, 166–67, and for the permits, Senato, Misti, reg. 43, fols. 127v, 137v, 3 May and 22 July 1396.

31. *Staatsbriefe Coluccio Salutatis*, 323–24, no. 155, 31 Oct. 1396.

32. AN, 7, fol. 221rv, 27 Sept. 1396, excerpt in Gloria, 2:308, no. 1956.

33. Senato, Secreta, reg. E, fol. 143r, 13 Mar. 1397, for the surety; Senato, Misti, reg. 43, fol. 185v, 20 May 1397, on the ambassador; and Maggior Consiglio, Leona, fol. 95r, 5 July 1397, for the gift.

34. Predelli, 3:246, no. 64, 2 Aug. 1397; AN, 7, fols. 348r–49r, 28 Nov. 1397, proctorship of Naimiero Conti to Venice.

35. Contemporary accounts of the Mantuan War include Gatari, *Cronaca carrarese*, 451–64, and *Cronaca volgare*, 220–24; among secondary works, see Frati, "Guerra di Giangaleazzo Visconti," 241–63; Bueno de Mesquita, *Giangaleazzo Visconti*, chap. 15; and Jones, *Malatesta of Rimini*, 114–15.

36. Biblioteca Columbina, Cod. 5.5.8, fols. 54r, 64v, 30 Dec. 1396 and 6 Apr. 1397. On the pilgrimage, see Senato, Misti, reg. 43, fol. 144r, 8 Aug. 1396, permission to Michele Rabatta and Count Morando to take a commercial galley to the Holy Land.

37. Frati, "Guerra di Giangaleazzo Visconti," 270–72.

38. Vatican City, Archivio Segreto Vaticano, Reg. Vat. 315, fols. 251r–52r, 27 Oct. 1397, with discussion in Esch, *Bonifaz IX*, 205–6.

39. For Salutati's letter, see Biblioteca Columbina, Cod. 5.5.8, fol. 82r, 1 Mar. 1398; for text of the league, see Verci, 17:97–112, no. 1615, 21 Mar. 1398, with contributions discussed in Frati, "Guerra di Giangaleazzo Visconti," 254–55; and Truce of Pavia in Predelli, 3:258, no. 109, 11 May 1398.

40. On the treaties, see Bolognini, "Relazioni tra le Repubbliche di Firenze e di Venezia," 100–107, and for the text of Zabarella's speech, Zonta, *Francesco Zabarella*, 141–42.

41. AN, 7, fol. 354r, 15 Mar. 1398, excerpt in Gloria, 2:324, no. 2001, and fol. 384r, 2 June 1398, ed. in Joppi, "Documenti goriziani del secolo XIV" (1891), 311–13.

42. On Carrara policy in Friuli, see Paschini, *Storia del Friuli*, 2:266–70, and Cusin, *Confine orientale*, 157–59; on Carrara influence in Ferrara, Delaito, *Annales Estenses*, cols. 934–35.

43. Gloria, 2:333, no. 2024, 14 Oct. 1398, appointment of Giacomo Panico as proctor for Francesco Novello at the baptism.

44. Senato, Misti, reg. 43, fol. 197r, 7 Apr. 1397.

45. Ibid., reg. 44, fols. 84r–87r, 17 Dec. 1398, 22 and 28 Jan. 1399, appointment of and instructions to Leonardo Dandolo, fol. 92rv, 13 Mar. 1399, reply to Francesco Novello's proposed customs to raise 20,000 ducats.

46. Pacta, reg. 6, fol. 129v, 14 Mar. 1399, fols. 127r–29v, treaty of 5 Aug. 1399, ed. in Pastorello, *Nuove ricerche*, 237–49.

47. Gloria, 2:357, 365, nos. 2085, 2104, 29 Jan. and 14 May 1400.

48. Ibid. 2:348, no. 2060, 7 July 1399, first mission for hand of Sveva Caetani; 2:381, no. 2147, 3 Apr. 1401, second mission to Sveva; 2:397, no. 2183, 4 Mar. 1402, to betroth Belfiore da Varano; 2:367, no. 2109, 12 June 1400, for daughter of duke of Atri and count of Flaviano.

49. Predelli, 3:273, no. 174, 21 Mar. 1400, and Gloria, 2:363, no. 2099, 28 Apr. 1400, for Padua's ratification.

50. See *Staatsbriefe Coluccio Salutatis*, 351–52, nos. 167–168, 20 Oct. and 10 Nov. 1400.

51. Senato, Misti, reg. 45, fol. 38r, 9 Nov. 1400, fol. 67r, 5 Apr. 1401, at the visit of the Byzantine emperor.

52. Senato, Secreti, reg. 1, fol. 5rv, 17 June 1401, ed. in *Deutsche Reichstagsakten*, 4:371–72, no. 310.

53. Senato, Secreti, reg. 1, fol. 1r, 15 Apr. 1401, ed. in Pastorello, *Nuove ricerche*, 253–54; Missivi della Prima Cancellaria, reg. 25, fol. 46v, 21 July 1401, ed. in *"Consulte" e "Pratiche,"* 192.

54. For narratives of Rupert's Italian descent and the encounter at Brescia, see Gatari, *Cronaca carrarese*, 469–73, which greatly exaggerates the size of the "battle"; *Annales Mediolanenses*, cols. 834–40, which emphasizes Giangaleazzo's desperate financial straits; and *Cronaca volgare*, 265–67, which heaps blame on Rupert for the defeat.

55. Senato, Secreti, reg. 1, fol. 19v–20v, 20 Sept. 1401, ed. in *Deutsche Reichstagsakten*, 5:85–88, no. 9. See also Pastorello, *Nuove ricerche*, 103.

56. On Rupert's movements in Italy, see Gatari, *Cronaca carrarese*, 474–78, and the calendar in *Regesten der Pfalzgrafen am Rhein, 1214-1508*, vol. 2, ed. Count L. von Oberndorff (Innsbruck: Verlag der Wagner'schen Universitäts-Buchhandlung, 1939), 118–25. The speech had been edited in *Oratio Petri de Alvarotis ad Rupertum regem Romanorum* (Padua, 1555).

57. *"Consulte" e "Pratiche,"* 275–78, and Brucker, *Civic World*, 176–78. Venice's expenses incurred by Rupert's stay are reported in *Deutsche Reichstagsakten*, 4:127–28, no. 69.

58. *Annales Mediolanenses*, col. 835.

59. For a clear, concise account of Bolognese politics in this era, see Ady, *Bentivoglio of Bologna*, 6–10, and Bueno de Mesquita, *Giangaleazzo Visconti*, 272–80.

60. Senato, Secreti, reg. 1, fols. 29r–30r, 4, 8, 11 Nov. 1401.

61. *"Consulte" e "pratiche,"* 41–42, ed. of Missivi della Prima Cancellaria, reg. 25, fols. 25v, 33v, 16 Dec. 1400, 17 Jan. 1401, to Carrara lord.

62. Ibid., fol. 62r, 7 Oct. 1401, Florence's claim of payment; *Copialettere,* 1, no. 1, 8 Jan. 1402.

63. Pastorello, *Nuove ricerche,* 111–12, and *Copialettere,* 6–7, 15, 26–27, 39, nos. 10, 25, 41, 63–64, January and February 1402.

64. Senato, Secreti, reg. 1, fol. 52v, 14 Feb. 1402, promise to hired lances, ed. in Pastorello, *Nuove ricerche,* 255–56; *Copialettere,* 42–43, no. 70, 16 February, Carrara lord's fawning letter of thanks.

65. *Copialettere,* 34–35, no. 55, 11 Feb. 1402.

66. Senato, Misti, reg. 46, fol. 2r, 3 Mar. 1402, permission to Venetian proprietors to take herds to Ravenna; *Copialettere,* 55, no. 87, 2 March.

67. AN, 9, fol. 83rv, agent for debts, fols. 80r–81r, 4 Mar. 1402, proctor for sale of Ca' Corner, ed. in *Copialettere,* 54. On the 11th, the Carrara lord issued a letter patent empowering Donato to collect 2,000 ducats from Venetian bankers.

68. See Gatari, *Cronaca carrarese,* 478–79, for the texts of the declaration, and 481–90, for the war in Bologna that summer.

69. Senato, Secreti, reg. 1, fols. 55r, 57v, 18 and 22 Apr. 1402, eds. in *Copialettere,* 96–97, 123.

70. *Copialettere,* 131–32, nos. 202–3, 24 Apr. 1402, for the letter to Este, and 138–39, no. 216, 26 Apr. 1402, to lord of Bologna on Bernardon's talent.

71. See ibid., 88–90, on the capture of the envoys, 124 on the Brenta dam, 160–61 on Este relations, and also Pastorello, *Nuove ricerche,* 112–18.

72. See *Copialettere,* 230–32, nos. 384–386, 10 June 1402, letters to Rudolf of Saxony, his mother, Gigliola, and Venice.

73. Ibid., 236–37, nos. 397–99, 13 June 1402.

74. Ibid., 250–53, no. 429, 19 June 1402.

75. The battle is described in detail in several chronicles: *Corpus chronicorum Bononiensium,* 480–88; Griffoni, *Memoriale,* 91–93; and Gatari, *Cronaca Carrarese,* 484–88. Pastorello, *Nuove ricerche,* 258–60, provides a list of Paduans captured from an unedited chronicle. On the fate of the lord of Bologna, see Ady, *Bentivolgio of Bologna,* 9–10.

76. *Copialettere,* 272–78, 28–29 June 1402, letters pleading for aid.

77. Ibid., 287, no. 502, 2 July 1402: "quod civitas Bononie in duobus diebus tria dominia permutavit—quia, occisso domino Bononie, populus ancianos dominos procreavit; post que gentes ducis Mediolani, privatis ancianis, terram nomine dicti ducis currentes clamaverunt."

78. AN, 3, fol. 103r, 7 July 1402, ed. from another MS in Pastorello, *Nuove ricerche,* 261–63, no. 77: "tractandum de pace aut liga, seu treugua vel concordio, cum illustri et excelso domino, domino Ioanne Galeaz de Vicecomitibus."

79. *Copialettere,* 328, no. 603, 25 July 1402.

80. Ibid., 329–30, notes, edition of documents from Archivio Segreto Vaticano, Obligationes et solutiones, reg. 57, fol. 40v.

81. Ibid., 388–99, letters of 6–10 Sept. 1402.

82. Missivi della Prima Cancellaria, reg. 25, fol. 83v, 13 Sept. 1402: "imoque verum est, ducem Mediolani nature debitum exsolvisse, speramus amodo Italiam annis plurimis quieturam. Et providendum esse cognoscimus, ne cum vipereum semen excreverit, in eadem periculo recidamus."

83. See Gatari, *Cronaca carrarese*, 503; Gloria, 2:407, no. 2211, 14 Oct. 1402, appointment of the two envoys; and Romano, "Pace tra Milano e i Carraresi nel 1402," 841–57, with text of the treaty on 846–52.

84. *Copialettere*, 441–47, 456–64, November and December 1402, exchange of letters on propriety and legality of Giacomo's escape.

85. Maggior Consiglio, Leona, fol. 126v, 18 June 1402, and *Copialettere*, 259–60, no. 441–43, with ed. of Senato, Misti, reg. 46, fol. 30r, 26 June 1402.

86. *Copialettere*, 277, 366, nos. 479, 675, 29 June, 16 Aug. 1402.

87. See Gatari, *Cronaca carrarese*, 498–501, for a detailed description of the celebration, and Senato, Misti, reg. 46, fol. 64v, 4 Feb. 1403, for the loan of the galley.

88. For example, AN, 670, 227v, 1 Oct. 1402, advance to German captain, Frezelino Gumdolzen for 500 ducats; AN 9, fols. 129r, 131r, 8 and 9 Jan. 1403, loan for one year of 4,000 ducats to Count Jacques Bourbon of France, with banker Francesco Martini advancing money in exchange for all rights to the soldier's credits in Venice.

89. Maggior Consiglio, Leona, fols. 131v–32r, 17 June 1403, partial ed. in Lazzarini, *Proprietà e feudi*, 28, discussion on 17.

90. Missivi della Prima Cancellarie, reg. 26, fol. 10r, 6 June 1403.

91. See Rupert's letter of 23 July 1403 in *Deutsche Reichstagsakten*, 5:524–25, no. 379, urging Francesco Novello to side with Pope Boniface IX against Caterina Visconti and her sons.

92. Vergerio, *Epistolario*, 263–67, no. 102, 11 Aug. 1403.

93. See the account of the Brescia campaign in a letter of Count Morando da Porcia of October 1403 in Verci, 18:49–52, no. 2020.

94. AN, 9, fols. 148r–49r, 11 Oct. 1403, excerpt in Gloria, 2:421, no. 2246.

95. Senato, Secreti, reg. 1, fol. 109v, 25 Oct. 1403; Missivi della Prima Cancellaria, reg. 26, fol. 24r, December 1403, ed. in *Staatsbriefe Coluccio Salutatis*, 363, no. 178.

96. On Venice's struggle with Genoa in the Levant in the early Quattrocento, see Lane, *Venice*, 198–201, and, in great detail, Surdich, *Genova e Venezia*, 42–72.

97. For biographies of these last Scaligers, see the entries by Strnad, "Della Scala, Antonio," and "Della Scala, Brunoro," and Varanini, "Della Scala, Guglielmo," in the *DBI*.

98. On the conquest of Verona in 1404, see the contemporary accounts in "Cronichetta di Verona," in Verci, 18:57–61, no. 2025; Gatari, *Cronaca carrarese*, 512–27; and Marzagaia, *De gestis modernis*, 175–77; secondary works include Soldi Rondinini, "Dominazione viscontea a Verona," pt. 1:222–28; Allen, *History of Verona*, 330–34; and J. Law, "The Cittadella of Verona," in *War, Culture, and Society in Renaissance Venice: Essays in Honour of John Hale*, ed. D. S. Chambers et al. (London: Hambledon Press, 1993), 9–27, at 14–15.

99. On Venice's takeover of Vicenza in the spring of 1404, the best account is Menniti Ippolito, "'Fedeltà' vicentina e Venezia," pt. 1:31–35. See also Raulich, *Ca-*

duta dei Carraresi, 14–20; both are based on discussions reported in Senato, Secreti, reg. 1, fols. 139r–44r, April 1404.

100. Senato, Secreti, reg. 2, fols. 1r, 4r, 7r, 1, 9, and 16 May 1404, ed. of the first reply in Raulich, *Caduta dei Carraresi*, 118, doc. 6.

101. On the Florentine legation, see Rubinstein, "Italian Reactions to Terraferma Expansion," 199, 210, and for the reply, Senato, Secreti, reg. 2, fol. 13v: "ingratitudines suas . . . et inconstancia sua dederunt nobis iustissimam causam conducendi ad stipendia nostra gentes armigeras, equestres et pedestres, pro conservatione honoris nostri."

102. B. Cessi, *Venezia e Padova*, 106–11, for Este's role in the conflict, and 153–54, no. 19, for his letter of 6 Sept. 1404 rejecting Venice's demands.

103. Senato, Secreti, reg. 2, fols. 69r, 74r, 80r, 20 oct., 4 Dec., and 27 Dec. 1404, safe-conduct for Azzone d'Este, payment to Obizzo Polenta, and price placed on heads of Francesco Novello and sons.

104. Though biased and sometimes unreliable, the most valuable and detailed contemporary account of the events of 1405 is Gatari, *Cronaca carrarese*, 550–77; the Venetian viewpoint is refracted through Jacopo Zen's apologetic biography of Zen, *Vita Caroli Zeni*, 114–18. Though outdated in method, the best modern treatment remains Raulich's monograph, *Caduta dei Carraresi*, 67–103. See also Romanin, *Storia documentata di Venezia*, 4:18–26, and Simioni, *Storia di Padova*, 562–68.

105. See B. Cessi, *Venezia e Padova*, 112–16, 153–54.

106. Texts of speeches of 31 Dec. 1404 and 25 Feb. 1405 in Zonta, *Francesco Zabarella*, 144–47.

107. See AN, 9, fol. 174r, 19 Jan. 1405, excerpt in Gloria, 2:432, no. 2277, on mission to Ladislaus; Gloria, 2:433, no. 2279, 5 Feb. 1405, on Gallo's proctorship; and AN, 9, fols. 194r, 195r, 25 Apr. 1405, excerpt in Gloria, 2:436, no. 2287, loan from Genoa to enlist Alberico; Predelli, 3:310, 14 May 1405, terms of Venice's contract with Alberico.

108. On Genoese diplomacy on behalf of Padua, beginning in the summer of 1404, see Surdich, *Genova e Venezia*, 101–2, 211–12.

109. Text in Raulich, *Caduta dei Carraresi*, 118–19, 5 June 1405.

110. See Raulich, *Caduta dei Carraresi*, 82–84, 85–86, for discussion, and Senato, Secreti, reg. 2, fols. 122r, 132r, 29 June and 31 July 1405, for response to initial offer, fols. 140r, 144r–45r, 25 Aug. and 4 Sept. 1405, for Senate's vote to accept and Zen's offer to convey response.

111. The sales are recorded by Sicco Polenton, AN, 1, fols. 161v–382r, passim, and confirmed in Archivio di Stato, Venice, Pacta, vol. 7, fols. 92r–133r, May–December 1406. Venice's estimate of reduced sale prices is contained in a proclamation of 27 Dec. 1405, where buyers must declare property acquired from the Carrara or have it confiscated, Maggior Consiglio, Leona, fols. 149v–50r.

112. Maggior Consiglio, Leona, fol. 148v, 27 Nov. 1405.

113. See Lazzarini, "Trattato," 272, and on the trial of the Carrara lord, Raulich, *Caduta dei Carraresi*, 99–106.

114. Gatari, *Cronaca carrarese*, 579.

Glossary

Anziani ("elders"). Council of fourteen in communal and early signorial Padua, responsible for policymaking. In many ways analogous to the Pregadi (Senate) in contemporary Venice.

Arengo. Assembly of citizens, in Padua, Venice, and other cities, usually convened to ratify the election of a chief official, such as the Carrara lord or the doge.

Campanea (also *campione*). Suburbs of Padua within 6 kilometers of the city center, marked by boundary stones and not subject to same taxes as the *contado*.

Canipa. Office for disbursing communal moneys in Padua and in the major towns of the district, also in bishop's curia.

Caniparia. Denotes the office of Paduan communal cashier, bishop's cashier, warehouse, or of the owner of a rural village in the Padovano.

Catavero. Communal magistrate in Padua and in the rural villages who investigated conduct of public officials and misuse of communal property and money.

Centenario. Basic political subdivision of the four quarters of Padua, headed by a *capo*, who was assisted by a *menevello*.

Condotta. Contract for hire of soldiers; the captain who signs the contract agreeing to provide troops is called a *condottiere*.

Contado. The countryside around a city or town and subject to its jurisdiction, also called the district or the Padovano.

Contrada. Neighborhood, smallest political subdivision of Padua and villages of the district, often named after parish church, for example, contrada S. Martino, and usually but not necessarily coterminous with the parish boundaries.

Dacia (*dazio*). Excise tax levied on basic commodities and activities, for example, wine by the cup, bread, flour, prostitutes. Also internal custom duties, originally also a direct personal tax, later called the *estimo*.

District. The Paduan *contado*, or Padovano.

Donatio inter vivos. Gift made when the donor expects that he will die before the legatee. It becomes effective at the donor's death but is invalid if the legatee dies before the donor. The gift usually functioned as a legacy, modifying terms of the testament.

Dowry (Latin: *dos*). Endowment of the bride by her family of origin, by her guardian, or by herself. The dowry was usually administered by the husband during

Glossary

marriage, but it was returned to the wife if the husband predeceased her without surviving offspring. If the wife predeceased the husband without surviving offspring, the husband retained only a portion of the dowry, the rest of which was returned to the wife's family.

Estimo. Tax on a citizen's real and moveable property, usually a percentage of the declared value of real estate, lease, merchandise, bank deposits, credits, animals, and personal property.

Gastaldaria. Business office and warehouse in rural villages, where lord of village collected and stored rents in kind, sometimes called *caniparia*.

Gastaldo. A factor or manager of an estate; head of a guild or confraternity. The fifteen *gastaldi* were a committee of guildsmen, equivalent to the Anziani, which functioned as a policymaking body in the Paduan communal government of the early fourteenth century.

Lineage. A unilateral descent group or clan, that is, a grouping defined by its descent from a supposed common ancestor. Often called a *domus,* or house, as in *domus Carrariensis.*

Livello (Latin: *libellus*). A long-term lease of twenty-nine years, often with high entry fine or fee but low customary rents. Used by religious corporations to ensure some income without the necessity of close supervision.

Locatio. Lease of determined length, one, five, or ten years, for both urban and rural property. In latter case, the landlord rented parcels to peasant tenant(s) in return for a portion (usually one-half) of the major crops, with *onori* and money payments often also required. The *locatio* was the contract on which sharecropping (*mezzadria*) in the Padovano was based.

Maggior Consiglio. The Great Council of the Paduan commune, which continued to meet under the Carrara to appoint the *podestà* and certain communal officials, such as envoys. The same term was used for Venice's Great Council.

Maleablata. Misdeeds or misgotten profits. Testators made donations to the poor or favorite churches or monasteries to atone for this income, often gained from the practice of usury.

Mansus. Parcel of land or farmstead, usually defined as 30 Paduan *campi* of arable land or 5 of vineyards.

Massaro (Latin: *massarius*). Paduan communal comptroller, that is, the official responsible for the collection and handling of communal revenues; same term used for official overseeing accounts in the Carrara household government, a lay superintendent charged with the upkeep of fabric of churches, and the treasurer of guilds and confraternities.

Merum et mixtum imperium. Full powers of public jurisdiction, both civil and criminal, held by the Carrara lord.

Mezzadria. A form of sharecropping in which the landlord leased land to a peasant tenant and gave him half the seed for cultivation. In return, the landlord received half of the crop.

Onori (Latin: *honores*). Small dues in kind, for example, eggs, cakes, or hams, usually due from peasant to landlord on major feasts.

Glossary

Podestà. Chief executive officer of Padua, also commander of the communal army in early Trecento, elected for a term of six months with eligibility for reelection, subject to approval of the Carrara *signore* after the middle of the century. Chief magistrate of the subject communes of the Padovano, with general military and judicial powers. Sometimes vicars held analogous office in certain towns of the *contado*. *Podestaria* indicates both the office and term of a podestà and the area under his jurisdiction.

Precones. Town criers, or messengers for the communal government, charged with serving writs, making proclamations, and arresting criminals.

Pro indiviso ("**undivided**"). Holding in common property that was difficult to divide, such as palaces, marshes, or pasture rights, often by brothers or other common heirs.

Provveditore. Venetian civil commissioner, appointed to oversee and supervise mercenary troops in the field; also head of various Venetian civil offices, such as the Grain Office.

Referendario. The treasurer of the Carrara household government.

Rocca. Castle or citadel, often within a walled town, as the Rocca di Monselice.

Saltuarii. Agrarian police, usually elected by a village council and charged with the upkeep of roads, bridges, and canals and controlling damages to crops from grazing animals and hunters.

Savio, savi (Latin: ***sapiens, sapientes;*** "the wise"). In Padua and Venice *savi* were citizens and notables elected to ad hoc boards and committees to handle specific missions, tasks, and needs. In Venice, they also served as overseers of dominions, such as the *savi* of Istria or Treviso.

Sedimen. Land with residence or homestead. A *sedimen garbum* was a vacant lot or unimproved property.

Signore (Latin: ***dominus***). In general any "lord," or ruler of a city, but mainly used specifically to mean "lord of Padua."

Signoria (Latin: ***dominium***): Lordship, signory, or dominion, used here mainly to indicate fully legitimate one-man governments, such as the Carrara *signoria*. *Signoria* also can denote the doge, Ducal Council, and three heads of the Forty who formed Venice's central government. *Signoria* is also used to indicate the priorate, or highest magistracy of Florence.

Soceda. Contract for the leasing of grazing animals (mainly sheep and cattle), often by landlords to peasant tenants, in exchange for payment in money or kind and half of the offspring.

Spenditore. Official in charge of purveyance in Carrara household; also bookkeeper there.

Suprastans. One of those Paduan communal officials charged with the supervision of public works in city and district, especially construction and/or maintenance of roads, bridges, and canals.

Syndication. Investigation, or audit, of the conduct and accounts of an official, especially the *podestà*, at end of his term.

Bibliography

Archival and Manuscript Sources

Florence, Archivio di Stato
   Provvisioni, Register 61, 1373
   Signori, Carteggi, Missivi della Prima Cancellaria
   Registers 3–26, 1327–1405
Padua, Accademia Patavina, Archivio Papafava dei Carraresi
   Codice 23, Formulario della Cancellaria, 1381–85
   Codici 29, 35–37, Atti notarili
Padua, Archivio Antico Universitario
   Register 123, *Statuta et matricula collegii Iudicum*
Padua, Archivio della Curia Vescovile
   Feudorum libri, Registers 4–13, 1318–1405
Padua, Archivio di Stato
   Archivio Corona
      Pergamene 6369–9745, 1350–90
   Archivio Diplomatico (AD)
      Pergamene 5570–9205, 1318–89
   Archivi Giudiziari Civili
      Ufficio dell' Aquila, *Liber datiorum*, 1383
      Aquila, busta 5, 1361–99, busta 10, 1401–7
      Sigillo, Compromessi, Registers 1–4, 1356–1408
   Archivio Notarile (AN)
      Register Number with Name of Notary

1–4	Polenton, Sicco
5–10	Calvi, Zilio
14–19	Roverini, Marsilio
31–32	Campolongo, Giovanni da
33–38	Brazzi, Bandino
39–43	Nicolini, Bartolomeo
45–46	Beccari, Giovanni Francesco
47–51	Lenguazzi, Rizzardo
54–62, 72	Lenguazzi, Olivierio

Bibliography

77–86	Marostica, Ottone
99–101	Pessalato, Giovanni
115–19	Zennari, Salimbene
132	Treviso, Nicoli da
141	Ponte da Vigodarzere, Giovanni
142	Bon, Pietro
143, 147	Spazza, Manfredo
157–58	Boaria, Enrico
159	Campagnola, Giovanni
165	Mondo fu Domenico
165	Persuzio fu Francesco
165	Da S. Marino, Semprebene
165	Martini, Pietro
165	Micheli, Francesco
165	Da Vallonga, Giacomo
166	Da Caselle, Bartolomeo
166	Da Lendenara, Francesco
166	Zaratini, Silvestro
169	Strazzarolo, Bartolomeo di Francesco
178–81	Stuva, Giovanni
191–93	Este, Giovanni Enrico
202–08	Canonici, Giovanni
209–12, 214	Canonici, Paolo
256–58	Saraceno, Pietro
260–66	Torri, Giacomo
286, 288	Albertini, Giacomo
295	Ton, Francesco
309–13	Lamberti, Nicolò
330	Squassa, Francesco Melchiore
337–39	Fornasiero, Bellone
340	Mazari, Giovanni Nicolò
346–49	Spassono, Bartolomeo
350–56	Fantelli, Fantello
357–58, 364–67	Borghese, Pietro
388	Bonetto, Antonio
388	Bragero, Giovanni
388	Dal Burgo Todesio, Antonio
397	Ugone
398	Floriani
398	Pernumia, Giovanni da
398	Pascio fu Franceschino
398	Squassino, Giovanni
405	Fossadolce, Francesco
405	Faliveti, Bartolomeo

Bibliography

407	Marostica, Enrico
407	Montagnana, Antonio da
407	Codagnelli, Antonio
416	Preve, Giovanni
506	Da' Segni, Bartolomeo
506	Cortellieri, Gerardino
522–24	Spazza, Giacomo
525	Guarnerini, Marco
525bis	Guarnerini, Marco
668	Giacomino fu Ture
668	Ton, Francesco, da Piove di Sacco
668	Pietro fu Ugolino
668	Dalesmanini, Gregorio
669–70	Vigonza, Francesco da
678	Pilei, Pileo
678	Curiaepiscopale, Bartolomeo da
678	Villanova, Francesco
678	Da Montagnana, Francesco
679	Dalle Donne, Antonio
684	Viviani, Nicolò
685–86	PontediBrenta, Boninsegna da
699–703	Statuti, Zilberto dagli
1158	Figaro, Nicolò
1158	Figario, Alberto
1158	Bagnello, Enzeliero
1158	Franzone, Enrico
5453	*Liber officialium*

Archivi Privati Diversi
    Register 106   Dondi, reg. 1, 1333–69
    Register 173   Grompo, 1356–75
    Register 174   Grompo, 1375–80
    Register 175   Grompo, 1380–1406
    Register 189   *Codice Lion* 1360–89
    Register 190   Lion Pergamene, vol. 1, 1213–1405

Ospedale Civile, S. Francesco
    Registers 590, 964

Pergamene Diverse
    Busta 54

Territorio
    Register 480, *Liber Introitus et racionum comunis Citadelle*

Padua, Biblioteca Civica
    B.P. 124, XXII   *Liber cimeriorum dominorum de Carraria*, sec. XIV
    B.P. 158   Pier Paolo Vergerio, *De principibus Carrariensibus*
    B.P. 169   *Matricola, Arte della lana*

Bibliography

    B.P. 339   *Statuta notariorum Patavii, 1419*
    B.P. 410II   *Catalogo dei rettori e fratelli, Arte della Lana*
    B.P. 825   *Reformationes frataleae notariorum Padue*
    B.P. 928   G. B. Papafava, ed. *Documenti per servire la storia dei Carraresi*, 5 vols.
    B.P. 990   *Documenti Carraresi*, 2 vols.
    B.P. 1236   *Codex statutorum reformatorum, 1420*
    B.P. 1237   *Liber statutorum communis Padue, 1362* (Statuti Carraresi)
    B.P. 1480I   *Liber modularum omnium not. fratalee*

Padua, Biblioteca del Seminario
    MS 11   Giovanni da Nono, *De generatione aliquorum civium urbis Padue*, Sec. XIV.
    MS 582   G. Gennari, *Codice diplomatico padovano*, vol. 8

Rome, Biblioteca del Senato
    MS 271   *Statuti di Montagnana*

Seville, Biblioteca Columbina
    MS 5.5.8   Letter Book of Florentine Chancery, 1394–1406

Vatican City, Archivio Segreto Vaticano
    Reg. Vat. 315, 1397

Venice, Archivio di Stato
  Avogaria di Comun, Raspe
    Registers 3642–45
  Collegio
    Segreti, vol. 1, 1354–63, vol. 2, 1375–77, vol. 3, 1382–88, Lettere Secrete, 1363–66
  Maggior Consiglio, Deliberazioni
    Registers: Spiritus, Novella, Leona
  Maggior Consiglio, Grazie
    Registers 7–19
  Pacta
    Volumes 5–7
  Procuratori di San Marco, de ultra, busta 185, Forzatè papers
  Senato, Deliberazioni, Misti
    Registers 15–46
  Senato, Privilegi
    Register 1, 1375–1425
  Senato, Secreta consilii Rogatorum
    Register A, 29 August 1345–24 March 1348
    Register B, 27 March 1348–28 February 1351
    Register D, 14 May 1376–3 February 1377
    Register E, 3 March 1388–30 April 1397
  Senato, Secreti
    Register 1, April 1400–April 1404
    Register 2, May 1404–February 1406

Bibliography

Venice, Biblioteca Nazionale Marciana
    Ital. VII, 128A (8639), G. Caroldo, *Cronaca veneta*
    Lat. X, 381 (2803), *Gesta magnifica domus carrariensis*

Printed Primary Sources

Entries listed under Printed Primary Sources and under Secondary Sources (below) include only sources cited more than once and those used extensively in the preparation of this book. Publishers are provided only for works issued in the twentieth century. The following abbreviations are used:

AMAP	*Atti e Memorie dell'Accademia patavina di scienze, lettere ed arti*
BMCP	*Bollettino del Museo Civico di Padova*
DBI	*Dizionario biografico degli Italiani*

Additamentum primum ad Chronicon Cortusiorum. Rerum italicarum scriptores 12, cols. 959–82. Milan, 1728.

Additamentum secundum ad Chronicon Cortusiorum. Rerum italicarum scriptores 12, cols. 983–88. Milan, 1728.

Annales Forolivienses ab origine urbis usque ad annum MCCCCLXXIII. Edited by G. Mazzatini. Rerum italicarum scriptores, new ed., vol. 22, pt. 2. Città di Castello: S. Lapi, 1903–9.

Annales Mediolanenses. Rerum italicarum scriptores, vol. 16. Milan, 1730.

Annales Patavini. Edited by Antonio Bonardi. Rerum italicarum scriptores, new ed., vol. 8, pt. 1:175–265. Città di Castello: S. Lapi, 1906.

Il "Capitolar dalle Broche" della Zecca di Venezia (1358–1556). Edited by Giorgetta Bonfiglio Dosio. Padua: Antenore, 1984.

Capodilista, Gian Francesco. *De viris illustribus familiae Transelgadorum, Forzatè et Capitis Listae.* Edited by Mirella Blason Berton. Rome: Edindustria Editoriale, 1972.

Caresini, Raphayni. *Chronica, 1343–1388.* Edited by Ester Pasterello. Rerum italicarum scriptores, new ed., vol. 12, pt. 1. Bologna: Zanichelli, 1922.

Cessi, Benvenuto, ed. "Gli statuti padovani durante la dominazione saligera in Padova." *Atti dell'Accademia scientifica veneto-trentino-istriana,* n.s., 2 (1907): 66–124.

Chinazzo, Daniele. *Cronaca de la guerra da Veneciani a Zenovesi.* Edited by Vittorio Lazzarini. Monumenti Storici della Deputazione di Storia Patria per le Venezie, n.s., vol 11. Venice: A Spese della Deputazione, 1958.

Chronicon Estense. Rerum italicarum scriptores, vol. 15. Milan, 1731.

Chronicon Patavinum (1174–1399). In *Antiquitates italicae Medii Aevi,* edited by L. A. Muratori, 4:1120–68. Milan, 1741.

Cipolla, Carlo, ed. "Degli atti diplomatici riguardanti il dominio di Cangrande I in Padova." *Rendiconti della R. Accademia de Lincei, classe di scienze morali, storiche e filologiche* 10 (1901): 229–38.

———, ed. *Documenti per la storia delle relazioni diplomatiche fra Verona e Mantova nel secolo XIV*. Miscellanea di Storia Veneta della R. Deputazione Veneta di Storia Patria, ser. 2, vol. 12. Venice: A spese della Società, 1907.

———, ed. *La storia scaligera secondo i documenti degli Archivi di Modena e di Reggio Emilia*. Miscellanea di Storia Veneta della R. Deputazione Veneta di Storia Patria, ser. 2, vol. 9. Venice: A spese della Società, 1903.

Clement VI. *Lettres closes, patentes et curiales se rapportant à la France*. Edited by E. Déprez, J. Glenisson, and G. Mollat. 3 vols. Paris: E. de Boccard, 1910–61.

Constitutiones et acta publica imperatorum et regum, MCCCXIII ad MCCCXXIV. Edited by J. Schwalm. Monumenta Germaniae historica, Leges, Sectio 4, Bd. 5, Hannover: Impensis Bibliopolii Hahniani, 1909–13.

Constitutiones et acta publica imperatorum et regum, MCCCXXV ad MCCCXXX. Edited by J. Schwalm. Monumenta Germaniae historica, Leges, Sectio 4, Bd. 6, Hannover: Impensis Bibliopolii Hahniani, 1914–27.

Constitutiones et acta publica imperatorum et regum, MCCCXLV ad MCCCXLVIII. Edited by K. Zeumer and R. Salomon. Monumenta Germaniae historica, Leges, Sectio 4, Bd. 8, Hannover: Impensis Bibliopolii Hahniani, 1910–26.

Constitutiones et acta publica imperatorum et regum, 1354–56. Edited by W. Fritz. Monumenta Germaniae historica, Leges, Sectio 4, Bd. 11. Weimar: Hermann Bohlaus Nachfolger, 1978–92.

Le "Consulte" e "Pratiche" della Repubblica fiorentina nel Quattrocento, 1 (1401): Cancellierato di Coluccio Salutati. Edited by Elio Conti et al. Pisa: Giardini Editori, 1981.

Conversini, Giovanni. *De dilectione regnantium*. In *Two Court Treatises*, edited by B. G. Kohl and J. Day, 93–249. Munich: Wilhelm Fink Verlag, 1987.

———. *De primo eius introitu ad aulam*. In *Two Court Treatises*, edited by B. G. Kohl and J. Day, 21–83. Munich: Wilhelm Fink Verlag, 1987.

———. *Dragmalogia de eligibili vite genere*. Edited by H. L. Eaker with intro. and notes by B. G. Kohl. Lewisburg, Penn.: Bucknell University Press, 1980.

———. *Memorandarum rerum liber*. In V. Zaccaria, "Il *Memorandarum rerum liber* di Giovanni Conversini da Ravenna." *Atti dell'Istituto Veneto* 106, pt. 2 (1947–48): 221–50.

———. *Rationarium vite*. Edited by Vittore Nason. Florence: Leo S. Olschki, 1986.

Il copialettere marciano della cancelleria carrarese, 1402–1403. Edited by Ester Pasterello. Monumenti storici della R. Deputazione Veneta di Storia Patria, ser. 1, vol. 19. Venice: A spese della Società, 1915.

Corio, Bernardino. *Storia di Milano*. Edited by A. M. Guerra. 2 vols. Turin: UTET, 1978.

Corpus chronicorum Bononiensium. Edited by A. Sorbelli. Rerum italicarum scriptores, new ed., vol. 18, pt. 1. Città di Castello: S. Lapi, 1911.

Cortusi, Guglielmo. *Chronica de Novitatibus Padue et Lombardie*. Edited by B. Pagnin. Rerum italicarum scriptores, new ed., vol. 12, pt. 5. Bologna: Zanichelli, 1941–64.

Crescini, Vincenzo, ed. "Documenti padovani del periodo carrarese." *Atti dell'Istituto Veneto* 66 (1906–7): 611–24.

Cronaca volgare di Anonimo fiorentino dall'anno 1385 al 1409. Edited by E. Bellondi.

Bibliography

Rerum italicarum scriptores, new ed., vol. 27, pt. 2. Città di Castello: S. Lapi, 1915–18.

D'Alessio, Nicoletto. *La storia della guerra per i confini (1372–1373)*. Edited by Roberto Cessi. Rerum italicarum scriptores, new ed., vol. 17, pt. 1, tome 3:1–172. Bologna: Zanichelli, 1964.

Dandolo, Andrea. *Chronica per extensum descripta*. Edited by Ester Pastorello. Rerum italicarum scriptores, new ed., vol. 12, pt. 1. Bologna: Zanichelli, 1938.

Delaito, Jacopus de. *Annales Estenses*. Rerum italicarum scriptores, vol. 18. Milan, 1731.

Denifle, Hans, ed. "Die Statuten der Juristen-Universität Padua vom Jahr 1331." *Archiv für Literatur- und Kirchengeschichte des Mittelalters* 6 (1892): 309–562.

Deutsche Reichstagsakten unter König Ruprecht, 1400–1405. Edited by J. Weizsäcker. Deutsche Reichstagsakten, vols. 4–5. 2d. ed. Göttingen: Vanderhoeck & Ruprecht, 1956.

Dispacci di Pietro Cornaro, ambasciatore a Milano durante la guerra di Chioggia. Edited by Vittorio Lazzarini. Monumenti storici della R. Deputazione Veneta di Storia Patria, ser. 1, vol. 20. Venice: Deputazione Editrice, 1939.

Gatari, Galeazzo, with Bartolomeo and Andrea. *Cronaca carrarese*. Edited by A. Medin and G. Tolomei. Rerum italicarum scriptores, new ed., vol. 17, pt. 1. Bologna: Zanichelli, 1909–32.

Gesta magnifica domus Carrariensis. Edited by Roberto Cessi. Rerum italicarum scriptores, new ed., vol. 17, pt. 1, tome 2. Bologna: Zanichelli, 1942–48.

Giovanni da Nono. "*Visio Egidii Regis Patavie*, edited by Giovanni Fabris." *BMCP* 10–11 (1934–39): 1–20. Reprinted in G. Fabris, *Cronache e cronisti padovani*, 139–58. Padua: Rebellato Editore, 1977.

Gloria, Andrea, ed. "Antichi statuti del collegio padovano dei dottori giuristi." *Atti dell'Istituto Veneto*, ser. 6, 7 (1889): 355–402.

———, ed. "Documenti inediti intorno a Francesco Petrarca e Albertino Mussato." *Atti dell'Istituto Veneto*, ser. 5, 6 (1879–80): 17–52.

———, ed. *Documenti inediti intorno al Petrarca con alcuni cenni della casa di lui in Arquà e della reggia dei da Carrara in Padova*. Padua, 1867.

———, ed. *Documenti relativi alla storia padovana*. Padua, 1867.

———, ed. *Intorno ai diplomi dei principi da Carrara, disquisizioni paleografiche*. Per nozze Papafava-Cittadella Vigoarzere. Padua, 1859.

———, ed. *Sull'epistole della repubblica di Padova e dei principi da Carrara raffronate con quelle di altri comuni e principi italiani, disquisizioni paleografiche*. Per nozze Papafava-Cittadella. Padua, 1850.

Gregory XI. *Lettres secrètes et curiales intéressant les pays autres que la France*. Edited by G. Mollat. Paris: E. de Boccard, 1962–65.

Gregory XI. *Lettres secrètes et curiales relatives á la France (1370–1378)*. Edited by G. Mirot et al. Paris: E. de Boccard, 1935–57.

Griffoni, Matteo. *Memoriale historicum de rebus bononiensium*. Edited by L. Frati and A. Sorbelli. Rerum italicarum scriptores, new ed., vol. 18, pt. 2. Città di Castello: S. Lapi, 1902.

Bibliography

Grion, Giusto, ed. "Ruoli dei cittadini di Padova del 1275, 1320 e 1321." In *Delle rime volgari di Antonio da Tempo,* 248–88. Collezione di opere inedite o rare, 17. Bolgona, 1869. Reprint, Bologna: Forni, 1970.

La guerra da Trivixo (1383). Edited by Robert Cessi. Rerum italicarum scriptores, new ed., vol. 17, pt. 1, tome 3:227–66. Bologna: Zanichelli, 1964.

Historiae Romanae fragmenta. In *Antiquitates italicae Medii Aevi,* edited by L. A. Muratori, 3:251–546. Milan, 1740.

Jacopo Piacentino. *Cronaca della guerra Veneto-Scaligera.* Edited by Luigi Simeoni. Miscellanea di Storia Veneta della R. Deputazione di Storia Patria, vol. 5. Venice: Deputazione Editrice, 1931.

Liber regiminum Padue. Edited by Antonio Bonardi. Rerum italicarum scriptores, new ed. vol. 8, pt. 1:286–376. Città di Castello: S. Lapi, 1908.

Ljubič, Sime, ed. *Monumenta spectantia historiam slavorum meridionalium.* Vols. 2–5. Zagreb, 1868–74.

Lünig, J. C. *Codex Italiae diplomaticus.* 4 vols. Frankfurt, 1725–35.

Maniaco, J. A. *Historia Belli Forojuliensis, 1366–1388.* In *Antiquitates italicae Medii Aevi,* edited by L. A. Muratori, 3:1187–1242. Milan, 1740.

Marzagaia. *De gestis modernis.* In *Antiche cronache veronesi,* vol. 1, edited by C. Cipolla, Monumenti Storici della Deputazione Veneta di Storia Patria, ser. 3, vol. 2. Venice, 1890.

Mazzatinti, G., ed. *Obituario del convento di S. Agostino in Padova.* Miscellanea di Storia Veneta della R. Deputazione Veneta di Storia Patria, ser. 2, vol. 2, fasc. 4. Venice, 1894.

Mommsen, Theodor E., ed. *Italienische Analekten zur Reichsgeschichte des 14. Jahrhundert, 1310–1378.* Schriften der Monumenta Germaniae Historica, 11. Stuttgart, 1952.

Mussato, Albertino. *Il principato di Giacomo da Carrara, primo signore di Padova, narrazione scelta dalle storie inedite di Albertino Mussato.* Edited by Luigi Padrin. Padua, 1891.

———. *De traditione Patavii ad Canem Grandem.* Rerum italicarum scriptores, vol. 12, cols. 715–68. Milan, 1727.

Petrarca, Francesco. *Rerum Senilium liber XIIII: Ad magnificum Franciscum de Carraria Padue dominum: Epistola I. Qualis esse debeat qui rem publicam regit.* Edited by V. Ussani. Padua, 1922.

———. "Rerum Senilium liber XIIII: Ad magnificum Franciscum de Carraria Padue dominum: Epistola II, ed. V. Ussani." *Atti dell'Istituto Veneto* 83 (1923–24): 295–301.

Poemetto storico carrarese [on Francesco Novello's exile]. In Giorgio Rosconi, *Francesco Novello e la riconquesta di Padova (1390), poemetto storico carrarese edito dell'esemplare Vaticano,* 36–74. Padua: La Garangola, 1994.

Predelli, R., ed. *I libri commemoriali della Repubblica di Venezia.* Monumenti Storici della R. Deputazione Veneta di Storia Patria, ser. 1, vols. 1–3. Venice, 1880–83.

Redusio, Andrea. *Chronicon Tarvisinum.* Rerum italicarum scriptores, vol. 19, cols. 741–866. Milan, 1731.

Bibliography

Roberti, Melchiorre, ed. *Un formulario inedito di un notaio padovano del 1223*. Memorie del R. Istituto Veneto, vol. 27, no. 6. Venice, 1903.

Rolandino Patavino. *Cronaca in factis e circa facta Marchie Trivixiane*. Edited by Antonio Bonardi. Rerum italicarum scriptores, new ed., vol. 8, pt. 1. Città di Castello: S. Lapi, 1906.

Salutati, Coluccio. *Epistolario*. 4 vols. Edited by Francesco Novati. Fonti per la storia d'Italia, 15-18. Rome: Tipografia del Senato, 1891-1911.

———. *Die Staatsbriefe des Coluccio Salutatis*. Edited by Hermann Langkabel. Archiv für Schriftgeschichte, Sigel- und Wappenkunde, 3. Cologne: Böhlau Verlag, 1981.

Sanuto, Marino. *Vite de' Duchi di Venezia*. Rerum italicarum scriptores, vol. 22. Milan, 1733.

Sella, Pietro, and Giuseppe Vale, eds. *Rationes decimarum Italiae nel secoli XIII e XIV, Venetiae-Histria Dalmatia*. Studi e Testi, 96. Vatican City: Biblioteca Apostolica Vaticana, 1941.

Statuti del comune di Padova dal secolo XII al 1285. Edited by A. Gloria. Padua, 1873.

Statuti del comune di Treviso (sec. XIII-XIV). Edited by B. Betti. 2 vols. Fonti per la storia d'Italia, 111. Rome: Nella sede dell'Istituto, 1986.

"Statuti della Fraglia dei Notai." In Roberti, *Corporazioni padovane d'arti e mestieri*, 157-83.

"Statuti dell'Arte della Lana." In Cessi, *Corporazioni dei mercanti di panni e della lana in Padova*, 105-65.

Statuti di Cittadella del secolo XIV. Edited by Gherardo Ortalli et al. Corpus statuario delle Venezie, 1. Rome: Jouvence, 1984.

"Statuti di Pernumia." In Bortolami, *Territorio e società in un comune rurale veneto*, 179-240.

Theiner, Augustin, ed. *Codex diplomaticus dominii temporalis S. Sedis*. 3 vols. Rome, 1862-63.

———, ed. *Vetera monumenta historica Hungariam sacram illustrantia*. 2 vols. Rome, 1859-60.

Thomas, G. M., and R. Predelli, eds. *Diplomatarium veneto-levantinum, sive acta et diplomata res venetas, graecas atque levantis illustrantia*. 2 vols. Venice, 1870-79.

Urban V. *Lettres communes (1362-1370)*. Edited by M. H. Laurent et al. 2 vols. Rome: Ecole française de Rome, 1955-85.

Vergerio, Pier Paolo. "Ad Franciscum Juniorem de Carraria." In *Orationes*. Rerum italicarum scriptores, vol. 16, cols. 209-15. Milan, 1730.

———. "De dignissimo funebri apparatu in exequiis clarissimi omnium principis Francisci Senioris de Carraria." In *Orationes*. Rerum italicarum scriptores, vol. 16, cols. 189-94. Milan, 1730.

———. "Oratio in funere Francisci Senioris de Carraria." In *Orationes*. Rerum italicarum scriptores, vol. 16, cols. 195-208. Milan, 1730.

———. "*De principibus Carrariensibus et gestis eorum*, ed. A. Gnesotto." *AMAP* 41 (1924-25): 327-475.

———. *Epistolario*. Edited by Leonardo Smith. Fonti per la Storia d'Italia, 74. Rome: Tipografia del Senato, 1935.

Villani, Giovanni. *Cronica*. Edited by A. Mauri. Milan, 1834.
Wenzel, Gustav, ed. *Monumenta Hungariae historica: Acta extera*. 3 vols. Budapest, 1874–76.
Ystoria de mesier Francesco Zovene. Edited by Roberto Cessi. Rerum italicarum scriptores, new ed., vol. 17, pt. 1, tome 3:173–226. Bologna: Zanichelli, 1964.
Zahn, Josef von, ed. *Austro-Friulana: Sammlung von Actenstücken zur Geschichte des Conflictes Herzog Rudolfs IV von Österreich mit dem Patriarchate von Aquileja, 1358–1365*. Fontes Rerum Austriacarum. 2te Abteilung, Diplomataria et Acta, 40. Vienna, 1877.
Zen, Jacopo. *Vita Caroli Zeni*. Edited by G. Zonta. Rerum italicarum scriptores, new ed., vol. 19, pt. 6. Bologna: Zanichelli, 1941.

Secondary Sources

Abbondanza, R. "Arsendi, Arsendino." In *DBI* 4 (1962), 331–33.
Ady, C. M. *The Bentivoglio of Bologna: A Study in Despotism*. Oxford: Oxford University Press, 1937.
Allen, A. M. *A History of Verona*. London: Methuen, 1910.
Baggio Collavo, Rita. "Archivio di Stato di Padova." In *Guida generale degli Archivi di Stato italiani*, 2:221–85. Rome: Ministero per i beni culturali e ambientali, Ufficio centrale per i beni archivistici, 1986.
Barile, E. "Camposampiero, Guglielmo." In *DBI* 17 (1974), 608–9.
———. "Camposampiero, Tiso." In *DBI* 17 (1974), 617–19.
"Beccari, Niccolò." In *DBI* 7 (1965), 437–40.
Becker, Marvin B. *Florence in Transition*. 2 vols. Baltimore: Johns Hopkins Press, 1967–68.
Beda, Gioacchino. "Un trattato di estradizione fra Padova e Venezia." In *In memoria di Oddone Ravenna*, edited by Benvenuto Cessi and Vincenzo Crescini, 31–44. Padua: Gallina, 1904.
———. *Ubertino da Carrara, signore di Padova*. Città di Castello: S. Lapi, 1906.
Benton, Tim. "The Three Cities Compared." In *Siena, Florence, and Padua*, 2:7–27.
Bertazzo, L., and D. M. Montagna. *Santa Maria dei Servi a Padova, note sulla fondazione (1374–1406) e il primo secolo*. Vicenza: Neri Pozza, 1981.
Billanovich, E., and M. Billanovich. "Gli ultimi Estensi di Padova." *Italia medioevale ed umanistica* 30 (1987): 149–77.
Billanovich, Giuseppe, and Elisabeth Pellegrin. "Una nuova lettera di Lombardo della Seta e la prima fortuna delle opere del Petrarca." In *Classical, Medieval, and Renaissance Studies in Honor of Berthold Louis Ullman*, edited by Charles Henderson Jr., 215–36. Rome: Storia e letteratura, 1964.
Billanovich, M. C. "Un amico del Petrarca, Bonfacio Lupi e le sue opere di carità." *Studi petrarcheschi*, n.s., 6 (1989): 257–78. (See also Ganguzza Billanovich, M. C.)
Biscaro, Gerolamo. "Le tombe di Ubertino e di Jacobo da Carrara." *L'arte* 2 (1899): 88–97.

Bibliography

Bolognini, G. "Le relazioni fra le repubbliche di Firenze e Venezia nell'ultimo ventennio del secolo XIV." *Nuovo archivio veneto* 9 (1895): 5–109.

Bortolami, Sante. "Acque, mulini e folloni nella formazione del paesaggio urbano medievale (secoli XI–XIV): l'esempio di Padova." In *Paesaggi urbani dell'Italia padana nei secoli VIII–XIV,* 277–330. Bologna: Cappelli Editore, 1988.

———. "Monselice, 'Oppidum opulentissimum' Formazione e primi sviluppi di una comunità semiurbana del Veneto medioevale." In *Monselice: Storia, cultura e arte di un centro "minore" del Veneto,* 101–71.

———. "Per la storia della storiografia comunale: il 'Chronicon de potestatibus Padue.'" *Archivio veneto,* ser. 5, 105 (1979): 69–121.

———. "Pieve e 'Territorium civitatis' nel Medioevo, ricerche sul campione padovano." In *Pievi, parrocchie, e clero nel Veneto dal X al XV secolo,* edited by Paolo Sambin, 1–94. Miscellanea di Studi e Memorie della Deputazione di Storia Patria per le Venezie, 24. Venice: Deputazione Editrice, 1987.

———. *Signoria cittadina e comuni rurali nel medioevo padovano, San Michele delle Badesse, 1377.* Biblioteca comunale di Borgoricco, Quaterni di storia locale, 2. Borgoricco (Padova), 1980.

———. "Lo statuto padovano del 1320 'Super Bonis Rebellium.'" *AMAP, classe di scienze morali, lettere ed arti* 87 (1974–75): 385–402.

———. *Territorio e società in un comune rurale veneto (sec. X–XIII): Pernumia e i suoi statuti.* Miscellanea di Studi e Memorie della Deputazione di Storia Patria per le Venezie, 18. Venice: Deputazione Editrice, 1978.

Botteghi, L. A. "Clero e comune in Padova nel secolo XIII." *Nuovo archivio veneto* 9 (1905): 215–72.

Boyd, Catherine E. *Tithes and Parishes in Medieval Italy: The Historical Roots of a Modern Problem.* Ithaca, N.Y.: Cornell University Press, 1952.

Brown, Horatio. "The Carraresi." In *Studies in the History of Venice,* 1:107–51. New York: Dutton, 1907.

Brucker, Gene A. *The Civic World of Early Renaissance Florence.* Princeton: Princeton University Press, 1977.

———. *Florentine Politics and Society, 1343–1378.* Princeton: Princeton University Press, 1962.

Bueno de Mesquita, D. M. *Giangaleazzo Visconti, Duke of Milan (1351–1402): A Study of the Political Career of an Italian Despot.* Cambridge: Cambridge University Press, 1941.

"Buzzacarini, Arcoano." In *DBI* 15 (1973), 636–39.

"Buzzacarini, Francesco." In *DBI* 15 (1973), 640–41.

"Buzzacarini, Ludovico." In *DBI* 15 (1973), 643–46.

Camerini, Paolo. *Piazzola.* Milan: Alfieri & Lacroix, 1925.

Capitano, Ovidio, et al. *Comuni e signorie: Istituzioni, società e lotte per l'egemonia.* Storia d'Italia, 4. Turin: UTET, 1981.

Cappelletti, Giuseppe. *Storia della repubblica di Venezia.* 13 vols. Venice, 1848–55.

———. *Storia di Padova.* 2 vols. Padua, 1874–75. Reprint, Bologna: Eurografica ATESA, 1972.

Castagnetti, Andrea. "La decima da reddito signorile a privilegio economico dei ceti cittadini: Linea di ricerca." In *Pieve e parrochie in Italia nel Basso Medioevo*, 1:215–33.

———. "Le decime e i laici." In *Storia d'Italia, Annali 9*, 509–30. Turin: Einaudi, 1986.

Cattini, M., and M. A. Romani. "Le corte parallele: Per una tipologia delle corte padane." In *Le corte e lo spazio: Ferrara estense*, 1:47–82. Rome: Bulzoni, 1987.

Cenci, Cesare. "Bonifacio Lupi di Soragna e i frati minori." *Archivum Franciscum Historicum* 57 (964): 90–109.

Cenni storici sulle famiglie di Padova e sui monumenti dell' Università, premesso un breve trattato sull'arte araldica. 2 vols. Padua, 1842.

Ceoldo, Pietro. *Albero della famiglia Papafava nobile di Padova compilato con le sue prove*. Venice, 1801.

———. *Memorie della Chiesa ed abbazia di S. Stefano di Carrara*. Venice, 1802.

Cesca, Giovanni. *La sollevazione di Capodistria nel 1348*. Verona, 1882.

Cessi, Benvenuto. "Un trattato di pace tra Carraresi ed Estensi (1354)." *Nuovo archivio veneto*, n.s., 7, pt. 2 (1904): 401–17.

———. *Venezia e Padova e il Polesine di Rovigo, secolo XIV*. Città di Castello: S. Lapi, 1904.

Cessi, Roberto. *Le corporazioni dei mercanti di panni e delle lana in Padova fino a tutto il secolo XIV*. Memorie del R. Istituto Veneto, vol. 28, no. 2. Venice, 1908.

———. *Padova medioevale: Studi e documenti*. Edited by Donato Gallo with intro. by Paolo Sambin. 2 vols. Padua: Edizioni Erredici, 1985.

———. "La politica veneziana di terraferma dalla caduta dei Carraresi al lodo di Genova." *Memorie storiche forogiuliesi* 5 (1909): 127–44, 193–209.

———. "Venezia e la preparazione della guerra friuliana (1381-1385)." *Memorie storiche forogiuliesi* 10 (1914): 414–73.

———. "Venezia neutrale nella seconda lega anti-viscontea." *Nuovo archivio veneto*, n.s., 28 (1914): 233–307.

Checchi, Marcello, L. Gaudenzio, and L. Grossato. *Padova: Guida ai monumenti e alle opere d'arte*. Venice: Neri Pozza, 1961.

Ciscato, Antonio. *Gli Ebrei in Padova (1300-1800)*. Padua, 1901. Reprint, Bologna: Forni, 1985.

Cittadella, Giovanni. *Storia della dominazione carrarese in Padova*. 2 vols. Padua, 1842.

Città murate del Veneto. Edited by Sante Bortolami. Milan: Silvana Editoriale, 1988.

Cogo, Gaetano. "Di Ognibene Scola, umanista padovano." *Nuovo archivio veneto* 8 (1894): 115–71.

———. "Il patriarcato di Aquileia e le aspirazioni dei Carraresi al possesso del Friuli." *Nuovo archivio veneto* 16 (1898): 223–320.

Colle, Francesco Maria. *Storia scientifico-letteraria dello Studio di Padova*. 4 vols. Padua, 1824–25.

Collino, Giovanni. "La guerra veneto-viscontea contro i Carraresi nelle relazioni di Firenze e di Bologna col Conte di Virtù (1388)." *Archivio storico lombardo* 36 (1909): 5–58, 315–86.

Bibliography

———. "La guerra viscontea contro gli Scaligeri nelle relazione di Firenze e di Bologna col Conte di Virtù." *Archivio storico lombardo* 34 (1908): 105–59.

———. "La politica fiorentino-bolognese dall'avvento dal principato del Conte di Virtù alle sue prime guerre di conquista." *Memorie della R. Accademia delle Scienze di Torino,* ser. 2, 54 (1904): 109–84.

Collodo, Silvana. "Il castello di Montagnana." In *Città murate del Veneto,* 103–106.

———. "Il ceto dominante padovano, dal comune alla Signoria (secolo XII–XIV)." In *Istituzioni, società e potere nella Marca trevigiana e veronese,* 25–39.

———. *Una società in trasformazione: Padova tra XI e XV Secolo.* Padua: Antenore, 1990.

Cunningham, Colin. "The Honor and Beauty of the City: The Design of the Town Hall." In *Siena, Florence, and Padua,* 2:29–53.

Cusin, Fabio. *Il confine orientale d'Italia nella politica europea del XIV e XV secolo.* 2 vols. Milan, 1937–38. Reprint, Trieste: LINT, 1977.

———. "Rodolfo IV d'Absburgo, la curia avignonese e la politica italiana nel 1363–65." *Archivio storico italiano* 98 (1940): 68–75, 107–36.

Da Giotto al Mantegna. Edited by Lucio Grossato. Milan: Electa, 1974.

Da Mosto, Andrea. *I dogi di Venezia nella vita pubblica e privata.* Florence: Giunti Martello, 1977.

Dean, Trevor. "Commune and Despot: The Commune of Ferrara under Este Rule, 1300–1450." In *City and Countryside in Late Medieval and Renaissance Italy: Essays Presented to Philip Jones,* edited by Trevor Dean and Chris Wickham, 183–97. London: Hambleton Press, 1990.

———. *Land and Power in Late Medieval Ferrara: The Rule of the Este, 1350–1450.* Cambridge: Cambridge University Press, 1988.

Delaville Le Roulx, C. "Un anti Grand-maistre de l'Ordre de Saint Jean de Jérusalem, médiateur de la paix conclue entre Jean Galéaz Visconti e la République de Florence, 1391–1392." *Bibliothèque de l'Ecole des Chartes* 40 (1879): 525–44.

Dondi dall'Orologio, Francesco Scipione. *Dissertazione ottava sopra l'Istoria ecclesiastica di Padova.* Padua, 1813.

———. *Serie cronologico-storica de' canonici di Padova.* Padua, 1802.

Ercole, Francesco. "Comuni e signori nel Veneto (Scaligeri, Caminesi, Carraresi): Saggio storico-giuridico." *Nuovo archivio veneto,* n.s., 19 (1910): 255–337.

Esch, Arnold. *Bonifaz IX und der Kirchenstaat.* Tübingen: Max Niemeyer Verlag, 1969.

Fabris, Giovanni. *Cronache e cronisti padovani.* Padua: Rebellato Editore, 1977.

———. *Scritti di arte e storia padovana.* Padua: Rebellato Editore, 1977.

Fasoli, G. "Domenico di Benintendi di Firenze, ingegnere del secolo XIV." *Archivio veneto,* ser. 5, 1 (1927): 145–80.

Filippini, F. *Il cardinale Egidio Albornoz.* Bologna: Zanichelli, 1933.

Franceschini, M. "Carrara, Conte da." In *DBI* 20 (1977), 646–49.

Frati, Luigi. "La guerra di Gian Galeazo Visconti contro Mantova nel 1397." *Archivio storico lombardo* 14 (1887): 241–77.

———. "La lega dei Bolognesi e dei Fiorentini contro Gian Galeazzo Visconti (1389–1390)." *Archivio storico lombardo* 16 (1889): 5–24.

Frison, Vito. *Il principato di Giacomo II da Carrara, signore di Padova, con appendice e albero genealogico della famiglia da Carrara (1345–1350)*. Legnano: E. Narcati, 1906.

Gaffuri, Laura, and Donato Gallo, "Signoria ed episcopato a Padova nel Trecento: Spunti per una ricerca." In *Vescovi e diocesi in Italia dal XIV alla meta del XVI secolo*, edited by G. De Sandre Gasparini et al., 2:923–56. Rome: Herder, 1990.

Gallo, Donato. "L'epoca delle signorie: Scaligeri e Carraresi (1317–1405)." In *Monselice: Storia, cultura e arte di un centro "minore" del Veneto*, 173–89.

Ganguzza Billanovich, Maria Chiara. "Carrara, Francesco Novello." In *DBI* 20 (1977), 656–62.

———. "Carrara, Giacomo da." In *DBI* 20 (1977), 671–73.

———. "Carrara, Giacomo da." In *DBI* 20 (1977), 673–75.

———. "Carrara, Giacomo da." In *DBI* 20 (1977), 675–76.

———. "Carrara, Marsilietto Papafava da." In *DBI* 20 (1977), 687–88.

———. "Carrara, Marsilio da." In *DBI* 20 (1977), 688–91.

———. "Carrara, Marsilio da." In *DBI* 20 (1977), 691–93.

———. "Carrara, Marsilio da." In *DBI* 20 (1977), 693–95.

———. "Carrara, Nicolò da." In *DBI* 20 (1977), 696–98.

———. "Carrara, Ubertino da." In *DBI* 20 (1977), 700–702.

———. "Padova trecentesca: Dalla signoria carrarese al dominio veneziano." In *Da Giotto al Mantegna*, edited by L. Grossato, 19–22. Milan: Electa, 1974.

Gasparotto, Cesira. "Padova ecclesiastica, 1239, note topografico-storiche." *Fonti e ricerche di storia ecclesiatica padovana* 1 (1967): 13–195.

———. "La reggia dei Da Carrara, il Palazzo di Ubertino e le nuove stanze dell'Accademia Patavina." *AMAP* 79, pt. 1 (1966–67): 71–116.

———. "L'ultimi affreschi venuti in luce nella reggia dei Da Carrara e una documentazione inedita sulla camera di Camillo." *AMAP* 81, pt. 3 (1968–69): 243–61.

Ghirardini, L. L. "Brazzi, Bandino." In *DBI* 14 (1972), 84–85.

Gloria, Andrea. *Annua festività de' padovani per la grande vittoria avuta nel 1386 sulle armi di Antonio della Scala, documento inedito illustrato*. Padua, 1850.

———. "Gli argini dei fiumi dai tempi romani alla fine del secolo XII." *AMAP*, n.s., 6 (1889–90): 11–22.

———. "Dei podestà che furono in Padova durante la dominazione carrarese, serie cronologica provata co' documenti." *Rivista periodica dell'Accademia di Padova* 7 (1858–59).

———. *Della agricoltura nel Padovano: Leggi e cenni storici*. 2 vols. Padua, 1855.

———. *Monumenti della Università di Padova (1222–1318)*. 2 vols. Venice, 1884. Reprint, Bologna: Forni, 1972.

———. *Monumenti della Università di Padova (1318–1405)*. 2 vols. Padua, 1888. Reprint, Bologna: Forni, 1972.

———. *La pace del 1323 tra i padovani intrinseci ed estrinseci e l'annua solennita per essa ordinata: Documenti inediti illustrati*. Padua, 1851.

———. *Il territorio padovano illustrato*. 4 vols. Padua, 1862–63. Reprint, Bologna: Forni, 1974.

Bibliography

Gonzati, Bernardo. *La basilica di S. Antonio di Padova, descritta ed illustrata.* 2 vols. Padua, 1852–53.

Goy, Richard J. *Chioggia and the Villages of the Venetian Lagoon: Studies in Urban History.* Cambridge: Cambridge University Press, 1985.

Guiffrey, J. "Les médailles de Carrare, seigneurs de Padoue, exécutées vers 1390." *Revue numismatique,* ser. 3, 9 (1891): 17–25.

Gundersheimer, Werner. *Ferrara: The Style of a Renaissance Despotism.* Princeton: Princeton University Press, 1973.

Herde, Peter. "Politische Verhaltensweisen der Florentiner Oligarchie 1382–1402." In *Geschichte und Verfassungsgefüge: Frankfurter Festgabe für Walter Schlesinger,* 156–249. Wiesbaden: Steiner, 1973.

Hyde, J. K. *Literacy and Its Use: Studies in Late Medieval Italy.* Edited by D. Waley. Manchester: Manchester University Press, 1993.

———. *Padua in the Age of Dante.* Manchester: Manchester University Press, 1966.

———. *Society and Politics in Medieval Italy: The Evolution of the Civil Life, 1000–1350.* New York: St. Martin's Press, 1973.

Istituzioni, società e potere nella Marca trevigiana e veronese (secoli XIII–XIV), sulle tracce di G. B. Verci. Edited by Gherardo Ortalli and Michael Knapton. Istituto storico italiano per il Medio Evo, Studi storici, 199–200. Rome: Nella sede dell'Istituto, 1988.

Jones, P. J. "Communes and Despots: The City State in Late-Medieval Italy." *Transactions of the Royal Historical Society,* ser. 5, 15 (1965): 71–96.

———. *The Malatesta of Rimini and the Papal State: A Political History.* Cambridge: Cambridge University Press, 1974.

Joppi, Vincenzo. *I Carraresi ed il Friuli: Nuovi documenti.* Udine, 1888.

———. "Documenti goriziani del secolo XIV." *Archeografo triestino,* n.s., 16 (1890): 5–54, 345–76; 17 (1891): 5–41, 293–324.

———. *Ultime relazioni dei Carraresi col Friuli, documenti del 1388–1421.* Udine, 1879.

Kibre, Pearl. *Scholarly Privileges in the Middle Ages.* Cambridge, Mass.: Mediaeval Academy of America, 1962.

Knapton, Michael. "Dalesmanini, Manfredo." In *DBI* 31 (1985), 727–29.

———. "Venezia e Treviso nel Trecento: Proposte per una ricerca sul primo dominio veneziano a Treviso." In *Tomaso da Modena e il suo tempo,* 41–78. Treviso: Comitato Manifestazioni Tomaso da Modena, 1980.

Kohl, Benjamin G. "Carrara, Francesco, il Vecchio." In *DBI* 20 (1977), 649–56.

———. "Conti, Ildebrandino." In *DBI* 28 (1983), 438–40.

———. "Conti, Prosdocimo." In *DBI* 28 (1983), 463–65.

———. "Conversini, Giovanni." In *DBI* 28 (1983), 574–78.

———. "Curtarolo, Guglielmo." In *DBI* 31 (1985), 471–73.

———. "Curtarolo, Nicolò." In *DBI* 31 (1985), 473–74.

———. "Descalzi, Ottonello." In *DBI* 34 (1989), 344–46.

———. "Donato, Manno." In *DBI* 41 (1992), 47–49.

———. "Dotti, Francesco." In *DBI* 41 (1992), 538–40.

Bibliography

———. "Fedeltà e tradimento nello stato carrarese." In *Istituzioni, società e potere nella Marca trevigiana e veronese*, 41–63.

———. "Giusto de' Menabuoi e il mecenatismo artistico in Padova." In *Giusto de' Menabuoi nel Battistero di Padova*, edited by A. M. Spazzi, 13–30. Trieste: LINT, 1990.

———. "Government and Society in Renaissance Padua." *Journal of Medieval and Renaissance Studies* 2 (1972): 205–21.

———. "The Scrovegni in Carrara Padua." *Apollo* 142, no. 406 (December 1995): 43–47.

Lane, Frederic C. *Venice: A Maritime Republic*. Baltimore: Johns Hopkins University Press, 1973.

Lane, Frederic C., and Reinhold C. Mueller. *Money and Banking in Medieval and Renaissance Venice*. Vol. 1, *Coins and Moneys of Account*. Baltimore: Johns Hopkins University Press, 1985.

Larner, John. *Italy in the Age of Dante and Petrarch, 1216–1380*. London: Longman, 1980.

———. *The Lords of Romagna: Romagnol Society and the Origins of the Signorie*. Ithaca, N.Y.: Cornell University Press, 1965.

Law, John E. "La caduta degli Scaligeri." In *Istituzioni, società e potere nella Marca trevigiana e veronese*, 83–97.

———. "Popular Unrest in Ferrara in 1385." In *The Renaissance in Ferrara and Its European Horizons*, edited by J. Salmons, 41–60. Cardiff: University of Wales Press, 1984.

Lazzarini, Vittorio. "Aneddoti di storia carrarese." *Nuovo archivio veneto* 3 (1892): 475–90.

———. "La battaglia di Pola e il processo di Vettor Pisani." *Nuovo archivio veneto*, new ser., 25 (1913): 177–98.

———. "Beni carraresi e proprietari veneziani." In *Studi in onore di Gino Luzzatto*, 1:274–80. 2 vols. Milan: Giuffrè, 1949.

———. "Frammento di registro del tempo della guerra di Chioggia." *Archivio veneto*, ser. 5, 21 (1937): 124–52.

———. *Marino Faliero. Avanti il Dogado, La Congiura, Appendici*. Florence: Sansoni, 1963.

———. "La presa di Chioggia (16 agosto 1379)." *Archivio veneto*, ser. 5, 48–49 (1950): 53–74.

———. "Un prestito di Francesco il Vecchio da Carrara al comune di Trieste." In *Miscellanea di studi in onore di Attilio Hortis*, 229–36. Trieste: G. Caprin, 1910.

———. "Il principio della dominazione carrarese a Feltro e a Belluno." *Archivio storico di Belluno, Feltre e Cadore* 1 (1929): 1–4.

———. *Proprietà e feudi, offizi, grazoni, carcerati in antique leggi veneziane*. Storia e economia, 6. Rome: Storia e Letteratura, 1960.

———. *Scritti di paleografia e diplomatica*. 2d ed. Medioevo e umanesimo, 6. Padua: Antenore, 1969.

———. "La seconda ambasceria di Francesco Petrarca a Venezia." In *Miscellanea di*

Bibliography

studi critici pubblicati in onore di Guido Mazzoni, 1:173–83. 2 vols. Florence: Galileiana, 1907.

———. "Statuto che conferisce la signoria a Francesco I da Carrara." *Archivio veneto*, ser. 5, 16 (1934): 284–90.

———. "Storia di un trattato tra Venezia, Firenze e i Carraresi, 1337–1399." *Nuovo archivio veneto* 18 (1899): 243–82.

———. "Storie vecchie e nuove intorno a Francesco il Vecchio da Carrara." *Nuovo archivio veneto* 10 (1895): 325–63.

Levi, Ezio. *Francesco di Vannozzi e la lirica nelle corti lombarde durante la seconda metà del secolo XIV.* Florence: Tip. Calletti e Cocci, 1908.

———. *Poesia di popolo e poesia di corte nel Trecento.* Livorno: R. Giusti, 1915.

Liberali, Giuseppe. *La dominazione carrarese in Treviso.* Padua: CEDAM, 1935.

Ling, Lesley A. "La presenza fondiaria veneziana nel Padovano (secoli XIII–XIV)." In *Istituzioni, società e potere nella Marca trevigiana e veronese*, 305–21.

Luzzatto, Gino. *Il debito pubblico della Repubblica di Venezia dagli ultimi decenni del XII secolo alla fine del XV.* Milan: Istituto Editoriale Cisalpino, 1963.

———. "La popolazione del territorio padovano nel 1281." *Nuovo archivio veneto*, n.s., 3 (1902): 373–84.

Magliani, M. "I tre manoscritti degli statuti comunali di Padova (sec. XIII–XV) conservati nella Biblioteca del Museo Civico: Note storiche e codicologiche." *BMCP* 78 (1989): 155–64.

Mallett, M. E. "Cermisone, Bartolomeo." In *DBI* 23 (1979), 774–76.

———. "Dal Verme, Iacopo." In *DBI* 32 (1986), 262–67.

———. *Mercenaries and Their Masters: Warfare in Renaissance Italy.* Totowa, N.J.: Rowman and Littlefield, 1974.

Medin, Antonio. "Un familiare dei Carraresi: Nicolò da Curtarolo." *AMAP*, n.s., 31 (1915–16): 171–92.

———. "Maddalena degli Scrovegni e le discordie fra i Carraresi e gli Scrovegni." *AMAP*, n.s., 12 (1896): 243–72.

———. "I ritratti autentici di Francesco il Vecchio e di Francesco Novello da Carrara, ultimi principi di Padova." *BMCP* 2 (1908): 100–104.

Meek, Christine. *Lucca, 1369–1400.* Oxford: Oxford University Press, 1978.

Menniti Ippolito, Antonio. "La 'fedeltà' vicentina e Venezia la dedizione del 1404." In *Storia di Vicenza*, 3, pt. 1:29–43. Vicenza: Neri Pozza, 1988.

Modzelewski, Karol. "Le Vicende della 'pars dominica' nei beni fondari del monastero di San Zaccaria di Venezia (sec. X–XIV)." *Bollettino dell'Istituto di storia della società e dello stato veneziano* 4 (1962): 42–79; 5–6 (1963–64): 15–63.

Molà, Luca. *La comunità dei Lucchesi a Venezia.* Memorie dell'Istituto Veneto di scienze, lettere ed art, Classe di scienze morali, lettere ed arti, vol. 53. Venice, 1994.

Monselice: Storia, cultura e arte di un centro "minore" del Veneto. Edited by Antonio Rigon. Treviso: Canova, 1994.

Montobbio, Luigi. *Splendore e utopia nella Padova dei Carraresi.* Padua: Corbo e Fiore Editori, 1989.

Mueller, Reinhold C. "La Camera del frumento: Un 'banco pubblico' veneziano e 'gruzzoli' dei signori di terraferma." In *Istituzioni, società e potere nella Marca trevigiana e veronese*, 321–60.

———. *The Procuratori di San Marco and the Venetian Money Market*. New York: Arno Press, 1977.

———. "Veronesi e capitali veronesi a Venezia in epoca scaligera." In *Gli Scaligeri, 1277–1387*, edited by G. M. Varanini, 369–76. Verona: Mondadori, 1988.

Le mura ritrovate: Fortificazioni di Padova in età comunale e carrarese. Edited by A. Verdi. Padua: Panda Edizioni, 1989.

Norman, Diana. "The Three Cities Compared: Patrons, Politics, and Art." In *Siena, Florence, and Padua*, 1:2–27.

———. "Splendid Models and Examples from the Past: Carrara Patronage of Art." In *Siena, Florence, and Padua*, 1:155–75.

———. "Those Who Pay, Those Who Pray, and Those Who Paint: Two Funerary Chapels." In *Siena, Florence, and Padua*, 2:169–93.

Norwich, John Julius. *A History of Venice*. New York: Knopf, 1982.

Olivi, Luigi. "Del matrimonio di Marchese Niccolò III d'Este con Gigliola figlia di Francesco Novello da Carrara." *Atti e Memorie della R. Deputazione di storia patria di Modena e Parma*, ser. 3, 5 (1888): 335–76.

Olivieri, Dante. *Toponomastica veneta*. Florence: Leo S. Olschki, 1977.

Padova, basiliche e chiese. Edited by C. Bellinati and L. Puppi. 2 vols. Vicenza: Neri Pozza, 1975.

Padova, case e palazzi. Edited by L. Puppi and F. Zuliani. Vicenza: Neri Pozza, 1977.

Partner, Peter. *The Lands of St. Peter*. Berkeley: University of California Press, 1973.

Paschini, Pio. *La storia del Friuli*. 2d ed. 2 vols. Udine: Istituto delle Edizioni Accademiche, 1953.

Pastorello, Ester. *Nuove ricerche sulla storia di Padova e dei principi da Carrara al tempo di Gian Galeazzo Visconti*. Padua: Tip. Fratelli Gallina, 1908.

———. "Un'orazione inedita del card. Zabarella per la nozze di Belfiore Verano con Giacomo da Carrara." *Atti e Memorie della R Deputazione di Storia patria per le Marche*, new ser., 8 (1912): 121–28.

———. "I preliminari della pace fra Milano e i Carraresi nel 1402." *Nuovo archivio veneto*, n.s., 22 (1911): 289–305.

———. "Sfida di Francesco II da Carrara e Caterina Visconti." *Nuovo archivio veneto*, n.s., 25 (1913): 489–90.

Perrens, F. T. *Histoire de Florence, depuis ses origines jusqu'a la domination des Medicis*. 2d ed. Vol. 4. Paris: A. Fontemoing, 1902.

Pieri, P. "Alberico da Barbiano." In *DBI* 1 (1960), 639–42.

Pieve e parrocchie in Italia nel Basso Medioevo (sec. XIII–XIV): Atti del VI convegno di storia della chiesa in Italia (Firenze, 21–25 settembre 1981). 2 vols. Italia Sacra, 35–36. Rome: Herder, 1984.

Pirchan, G. *Italien und Kaiser Karl IV in der Zeit seiner zweiten Romfahrt*. 2 vols. Prague: Deutsche Gesellschaft der Wissenschaften und Künste für die Tschechoslowakische Republic, 1930.

Bibliography

Pistoia, Ugo. "Bonifacio Lupi di Soragna, signore di Primiero (1349–1373)." *Civis* 14, no. 40 (1990): 23–34.

Plant, Margaret. "Patronage in the Circle of the Carrara Family: Padua, 1337–1405." In *Patronage, Art, and Society in Renaissance Italy,* edited by F. W. Kent and P. Simons, 177–99. Oxford: Clarendon Press, 1987.

———. "Portraits and Politics in Late Trecento Padua: Altichiero's Frescoes in S. Felice Chapel, San Antonio." *Art Bulletin* 63 (1981): 406–25.

Portenari, Angelo. *Della Felicità di Padova.* Padua, 1623. Reprint, Bologna: Forni, 1973.

Posenato, Pietro. "Chierici ordinati a Padova dal 1396 al 1419." *Fonti e ricerche di storia ecclesiastica padovana* 2 (1969): 11–106.

Praga, Giuseppe. "Un prestito di Francesco il Vecchio da Carrara al Comune di Zara (1366)." *Archivio storico per la Dalmazia,* fasc. 58 (1931): 1–11.

Puppi, Lionello, and Giuseppe Toffanin. *Guida di Padova, arte e storia tra vie e piazze.* Trieste: LINT, 1983.

Rambaldi, P. L. "Frammenti carraresi: I documenti inediti del ms. comunale padovano, B.P. 1013, XVII." *AMAP* 13 (1897): 207–12.

———. "Stefano III duca di Baviera al servizio della lega contro Gian Galeazzo Visconti (luglio–agosto 1390)." *Archivio storico lombardo* 28 (1901): 286–321.

Raulich, Italo. *La caduta dei Carraresi, signori di Padova.* Padua, 1890.

Riedmann, Josef. *Die Beziehungen der Grafen und Landesfürsten von Tirol zu Italien bis zum Jahre 1335,* Sitzungsberichte, Osterreichische Akademie der Wissenschaften, Philosophisch-Historische Klasse, vol. 307. Vienna: Verlag der Osterreichische Akademie der Wissenschaften, 1977.

———. "La Marca e Venezia nella politica dei conti di Gorizia e dei conti del Tirolo (secoli XIII–XIV)." In *Istituzioni, società e potere nella Marca trevigiana e veronese,* 361–68.

Rigon, Antonio. *Clero e città, "fratalea cappellanorum," parroci, cura d'anime in Padova dal XII al XV secolo.* Fonti e ricerche di storia ecclesiastica padovana, 22. Padua: Istituto per la Storia Ecclesiastica Padovana, 1988.

———. "Esigenze di riforma e ribellione di monaci nel Trecento." *Atti e memorie del sodalizio vangadisciense,* 71–87. Badia Polesine, 1982.

———. "Le istituzioni ecclesiastiche e la vita religiosa." In *Monselice: Storia, cultura e arte di un cetro "minore" del Veneto,* 211–35.

———. *San Giacomo di Monselice nel Medio Evo (sec. XII–XV), ospedale, monastero, collegiata.* Fonti e ricerche di storia ecclesiastica padovana, 4. Padua: Istituto per la Storia Ecclesiastica Padovana, 1972.

Rizzoli, Luigi, Jr. "Artisti alla zecca dei principi da Carrara." *Rivista italiana di numismatica* 13 (1900): 225–39.

———. "Nuovi document sulla zecca padovana dell'epoca carrarese." *Nuovo archivio veneto,* n.s., 34 (1917): 55–74.

———. "Per la storia della zecca carrarese in Padova, nuovi documenti." *AMAP,* n.s., 19 (1902–3): 257–70.

———. "Ritratti di Francesco il Vecchio e Francesco Novello da Carrara in medaglie ed affreschi padovani del secolo XIV." *BMCP* 25 (1932): 104–14.

———. "Sulle più antiche monete di Padova e sulle origini della zecca." *Studi medioevali*, n.s., 1 (1928): 505–14.

———. "Teche e medaglie murali carraresi." *BMCP* 2 (1899): 56–58.

———. "L'università dell'arte della lana." *BMCP* 20 (1927): 166–229.

Rizzoli, Luigi, Jr., and Quintilio Perini. *Le monete di Padova*. Rovereto: Ugo Grande, 1903. Reprint, with intro. by Giovanni Gorini, Padua: Aldo Ausilio, 1973.

Roberti, Melchiorre. "La corporazione dei Giudici di Palazzo e la sua lotta contro il comune popolare nel Padova." *Ateneo Veneto* 26 (1903): 90–107, 330–49.

———. *Le corporazioni padovane d'arti e mestieri, studio giuridico con documenti e statuti inediti*. Memorie del R. Istituto Veneto, vol. 26, no. 8. Venice, 1902.

Romanin, Samuele. *Storia documentata di Venezia*. 3d ed. 10 vols. Venice: Libraria Filippi Editore, 1973.

Romano, G. "La pace tra Milano ed i Carraresi nel 1402." *Archivio storico lombardo*, n.s., 18 (1891): 841–57.

Ronchi, O. "Contributo alla serie dei Podestà di Cittadella." *AMAP, Memorie della classe di scienze morali, lettere ed arti*, n.s., 64 (1951–52): 107–12.

Rubinstein, Nicolai. "Italian Reactions to Terraferma Expansion in the Fifteenth Century." In *Renaissance Venice*, edited by J. R. Hale, 197–217. London: Faber & Faber, 1973.

Ruffino, O. "Capodivacca, Bartolomeo." In *DBI* 18 (1975), 643–45.

Ruggiero, Guido. *Violence in Early Renaissance Venice*. New Brunswick, N.J.: Rutgers University Press, 1980.

Rusconi, Giacomo. "Il 'traghetto' della Reggia Carrarese." *AMAP*, n.s., 45 (1928–35): 153–86.

Sabbadini, Remigio. *Giovanni da Ravenna, insigne figura d'umanista (1343–1408)*. Como, 1924. Reprint, Turin: Bottega d'Erasmo, 1961.

Salomonio, J. *Agri Patavini inscriptiones*. Edited by J. P. Tommasini. Padua, 1696.

———. *Urbis Patavinae inscriptiones*. Edited by J. P. Tommasini. Padua, 1701.

Salzer, Ernst. *Ueber die Anfänge der Signorie in Oberitalien*. Historische Studien, 14. Berlin, 1900.

Samarkin, V. V. "Evolyutsiya khozyaystvennykh rasporyadkov paduanskoy derevni v XII–XIV vekakh" (Evolution of land use in the Paduan countryside in the 12th–14th centuries). *Vestnik Moskovskogo Universiteta* 11, no. 6 (1966): 48–58.

———. "Evolyutsiya libellyarnogo derzhaniya v severo-vertochnoy Italii v XII–XIV vekakh" (Evolution of Livello holdings in Northeastern Italy in the 12th–14th centuries). *Vestnik Moskovskogo Universiteta* 9, no. 3 (1964): 68–78.

Sambin, Paolo. "Alessio, Nicoletto d'." In *DBI* 2 (1960), 247–48.

———. "Altri chierici ordinati a Padova nella seconda metà del secolo XIV." *Rivista di storia della Chiesa in Italia* 6 (1952): 386–407.

———. "Un amico del Petrarca: Ildebrandino Conti e la sua attività spirituale e culturale." In *Studi di storia padovana e veneta*, edited by P. Sambin, F. Seneca, and

Bibliography

M. Cessi Drudi, 1–57. Miscellanea di studi e memorie della Deputazione di storia patria per le Venezie, vol. 8, pt. 1. Venice, Deputazione Editrice, 1952.

———. "Chierici ordinati a Padova alle fine del Trecento." *Rivista di storia della Chiesa in Italia* 2 (1948): 381–402.

———. "La famiglia di un vescovo italiano del '300." *Rivista di storia della Chiesa in Italia* 4 (1950): 237–47.

———. "La guerra del 1372–1373 tra Venezia e Padova." *Archivio veneto,* ser. 5, 38–41 (1946–47): 1–76.

———. *L'ordinamento parrocchiale di Padova nel Medioevo.* Padua: CEDAM, 1941.

———. *Ricerche di storia monastica medioevale.* Miscellanea erudita, 11. Padua: Editrice Antenore, 1959.

———. "Statuti padovani inediti, II: Il conferimento della signoria a Francesco II da Carrara (1388)." *AMAP, Memorie della classe di scienze morale, lettere ed arti* 73 (1960–61): 69–93.

Sartore, T. "Biancardo, Ugolotto." In *DBI* 10 (1968), 39–41.

Sartori, Antonio. "La Cappella di S. Giacomo al Santo di Padova." *Il Santo* 6 (1966): 267–359.

———. "Note su Altichiero." *Il Santo* 3 (1963): 291–326.

Savioli, Pietro. *Compendio delle origini e relazioni degli estimi della città di Padova.* Padua, 1667.

Scardeone, Bernardo. *De antiquitate urbis Patavii.* Basilea, 1560. Reprint, Bologna: Forni, 1974.

Seneca, Federico. "Un diplomatico goriziano a cavaliere dei secoli XIV e XV: Michele da Rabatta." *Memorie storiche forogiuliesi* 40 (1952–53): 138–74.

———. "L'intervento veneto-carrarese nella crisi friuliana (1384–1389)." In *Studi di storia padovana e veneta,* edited by P. Sambin, F. Seneca, and M. Cessi Drudi. Miscellanae di studi e memorie della Deputazione di storia patria per le Venezie, vol. 8, pt. 2. Venice: Deputazione Editrice, 1952.

Sestan, Ernesto. *Italia medievale.* Naples: Edizioni Scientifiche Italiane, 1966.

Siena, Florence, and Padua: Art, Society, and Religion, 1280–1400. Edited by Diana Norman. 2 vols. New Haven: Yale University Press, 1995.

Simeoni, Luigi. "Le origini del conflitto veneto-fiorentino-scaligero (1336–1339)." *Memorie della R. Accademia delle scienze dell'Istituto di Bologna, classe di scienze morali,* ser. 3, 4 (1930): 4–65.

———. *Le signorie.* 2 vols. Milan: F. Vallardi, 1950.

Simioni, Attilio. *Storia di Padova.* Padua: Randi, 1969.

Simon, Robin. "Altichiero versus Avanzo." *Papers of the British School at Rome* 45 (1977): 252–71.

Siraisi, Nancy G. *Arts and Sciences at Padua: The Studium before 1350.* Studies and Texts, 25. Toronto: Pontifical Institute of Mediaeval Studies, 1973.

Soldi Rondinini, G. "Della Scala, Antonio." In *DBI* 37 (1989), 377–80.

———. "Della Scala, Bartolomeo." In *DBI* 37 (1989), 386–87.

———. "La dominazione viscontea a Verona (1387–1404)." In *Verona e il suo territorio.* Vol. 4, pt. 1:3–237. Verona: Istituto per gli Studi Storici Veronesi, 1981.

Stacul, Paolo. *Il cardinale Pileo da Prata*. Rome: Presso la Società alla Biblioteca Vallicelliana, 1957.
Strnad, A. A. "Della Scala, Antonio." In *DBI* 37 (1989), 380–81.
———. "Della Scala, Brunoro." In *DBI* 37 (1989), 389–93.
Surdich, Francesco. *Genova e Venezia fra Tre e Quattrocento*. Genoa: Fratelli Buzzi, 1970.
Suttina, L. "Per la storia della guerra fra Scaligeri e Carraresi nell'anno 1386." *Memorie storiche cividalesi* 2 (1906): 139–45.
Temple-Leader, John, and Giuseppe Marcotti. *Sir John Hawkwood*. London, 1889.
Varanini, Gian Maria. *Comuni cittadini e stato regionale: ricerche sulla Terraferma veneta nel Quattrocento*. Verona: Libreria Editrice Universitaria, 1992.
———. "Della Scala, Cangrande I." In *DBI* 37 (1989), 393–406.
———. "Della Scala, Cangrande II." In *DBI* 37 (1989), 406–11.
———. "Della Scala, Cansignorio." In *DBI* 37 (1989), 411–16.
———. "Della Scala, Guglielmo." In *DBI* 37 (1989), 435–38.
———. "Pietro dal Verme podestà scaligero di Treviso (1329–1336)." In *Istituzioni, società e potere nella Marca trevigiana e veronese*, 65–81.
———. "Vicenza nel Trecento: Istituzioni, classe dirgente, economia (1312–1404)." In *Storia di Vicenza*. Vol. 2, *L'età medievale*, ed. G. Cracco, 139–245. Vicenza: Nera Pozzi, 1988.
Vasoin, Gigi. *La signoria dei Carraresi nella Padova del '300*. Padua: La Garangola, 1988.
Ventura, Angelo. *Nobiltà e popolo nella società veneta del '400 e '500*. Bari: Laterza, 1964.
Verci, G. B. *Storia della Marca trivigiana e veronese*. 20 vols. Venice, 1786–91. Reprint, Bologna: Forni, 1979–85.
Warr, Cordelia. "Painting in Late Fourteenth-Century Padua: The Patronage of Fina Buzzacarini." *Renaissance Studies* 10 (1996): 139–55.
Weiss, Roberto. *Pisanello's Madallion of the Emperor John VIII Palaeologus*. London: British Museum, 1966.
Wilkins, E. H. "Petrarch and Manno Donato." *Speculum* 35 (1960): 381–93.
Zardo, A. *Il Petrarca e i Carraresi*. Milan, 1887.
Zen Benetti, Francesca. "Prestatori ebraici e cristiani nel Padovano fra Trecento e Quattrocento." In *Gli Ebrei e Venezia, secoli XIV–XVIII*, edited by G. Cozzi, 629–50. Milan: Edizione di Comunità, 1987.
Zennari, Jacopo. "Giacomo II da Carrara, signore di Padova, 1345–1350." *BMCP* 13 (1910): 101–23; 14 (1911): 1–55.
Zonta, G. *Francesco Zabarella, 1360–1417*. Padua: Tip. del Seminario, 1915.
Zorzi, Maria Antonietta. *L'ordinamento comunale padovano nella seconda metà del secolo XIII, studio storico con documenti inediti*. Miscellanea di Storia Veneta della R. Deputazione di Storia Patria, ser. 4, vol. 5. Venice: Deputazione Editrice, 1931.

Index

Abano, 56, 194, 292
Adige River, 3, 10, 13, 21, 56, 71, 83–84, 90, 123, 126, 216, 237–38, 240–41, 331
Adorno, Antoniotto, doge of Genoa, 274
affinity, Carrara: defined, xix, 171–73; under Francesco il Vecchio, 149, 171–74, 178, 193
Agapito, bishop of Asolo, 113
Agna, 35, 125, 171
Agrapati, Domenico, 41
Albignasego, 198
Albizzi, Maso degli, 310
Albornoz, Egidio, 112, 116–17
Aldobrandino, Roberto, 231
Aldrigetto da Montagnana, 71
Alessandria, 256; battle of, 273–74
Alidosi, Lodovico, lord of Imola, 303
Alidosio da Ferrara (tailor), 280
Allegro: Francesco, 231, 248, 255, 257, 262; Simone, 189
Alreim di Bruni, Niccolò, bishop of Trent, 93
Altichiero, 170, 179
Altichini: family, 38, 59; Francesca di Pietro, 195
Alvarotti: Aicardino, 301; Alvarotto, 34, 245, 247–48, 251, 253; Giacomo, 41, 49, 301; Pietro, 320, 325
Amadeus VI, count of Savoy, 117, 218–19, 259
Andrea di Francesco da Cittadella, 156
Andrea di Pace da Arezzo, 127
Andrew of Hungary, 91, 210
Anguillara, 13, 35, 125–26, 196, 331

Antonia "de Solutiis" (mistress of Giacomo di Francesco il Vecchio da Carrara), 299
Antonino of Langusco, Count Palatine, 261
Antonio da Cartura, 270
Antonio da Lio, 41
Antonio da Siena (mercenary), 238
Antonio di Gerardo da Modena (Carrara vassal), 247
Aproino, Alberto, 253
Aquileia, patriarch of, 93, 98, 106–8, 112–14, 205, 229–31, 234, 240, 248, 265–66, 297, 315, 325; in Chioggia war, 210, 214, 217, 222–23
Arena, 22, 125–26, 251, 266, 297, 299
Arena Chapel, 174–75, 297
Armagnac, Jean II, count of, 273
Armelina (Lupi servant), 285
Arquà, 35, 48, 147, 174–75, 198, 203, 272, 280
Arsendi: family, 152, 199; Arsendino, 118, 120, 122, 127, 131, 199; Caterina, 199; Rainiero, 199; Ubertino, 199
Arzercavalli, 145, 147, 152
Asolo, 66, 90, 103, 107, 112–13, 118, 222
Aspermont, Henvarardo, 104
Assale, Andrea, 277
Asti, 256–57
Aufenstein, Konrad von, 48–49, 51, 53, 56
Augustinian Hermits. *See* Eremitani
Austria, duke of. *See* Habsburg dukes of Austria
Avalista, Antonio, 280

447

Index

Aviano, 239–40
Avignon, 23, 24, 114, 116–17, 124, 256, 260
Avogadori di Comun, 232
Azzoguido, Taddeo, 220

Bacanzani, Baldo, 151
Bacchiglione River, 3–4, 10, 13–14, 43, 73, 110, 143–44, 195, 235, 327, 333
Badoer: Bonaventura, 170, 194; Bonsembiente, 170; Matteo, 170
Badoer: Venetian family, 171, 192; Andriolo di Stefano, 171; Balzanello, 192; Marco Zeno, 192
Baldani, Bartolomeo, 191–92
Baldo, Leonardo and Marino (Carrara proctors), 272–73
Baptistery, 154, 200, 307
Barbiano: Alberico, 218, 304, 321, 332–33; Giovanni, 243, 273, 308–9, 311, 313; Manfredi, 332
Barbo, Pantaleone, 120–21
Bartolomeo (*precone*), 147
Bartolomeo detto Guastopane (official in Cittadella), 166
Bartolomeo detto Scrivano di Jacobo (wool merchant), 272
Bartolomeo di Benedetto (Carrara proctor), 272, 277
Basilio: family, 201; Aleardo, 43–45, 47
Bassanello, 43; Scaliger camp at, 45–46
Bassanello, Giovanni, 276
Bassano, 12, 36–37, 43, 46, 56, 66, 71, 75, 84, 93, 97, 118, 121–23, 165, 195–96, 198, 209, 321, 323, 325, 328, 330–31
Battaglia Canal, 14, 20
Battifolle, Parte di Guido, 199
Bazaleri, Andrea (druggist), 268
Bazzano (papal fortress), 313
Beaufort, Elias de (bishop of Padua), 25
Becari, Antonio detto Radico, 143
Beccadello, Napoleone, 53–54
Beccari: Antonio, 295; Niccolò, 133
Beccarice, Aluisa di Tomasino, 183–84
Belengero (Carrara bodyguard), 276
Belluno, 59, 91–92, 93, 98, 115, 119–20, 131, 219, 235, 247, 251; under Carrara rule, 108, 111, 119, 161–62, 175, 235, 240–41; under Habsburg dukes, 123, 149, 203, 206; podestà of, 175, 196; under Visconti rule, 326, 328–32
Bembo: Antonio, 328; Francesco, 293, 313; Giovanni, 221
Benedetto (carder), 278
Benedetto da Padova, friar, 121
Benedict XII, pope, 75, 77
Beningrado, Francesco, 29, 271, 278, 294, 301
Bentivoglio: Bente, 324; Giovanni, 320–24
Berini, Pasquale, 150
Bernardo, Piero di, 121
Bernardon de Serres (Breton mercenary), 323–24
Bertipaglia, 35, 198, 280
Berto d'Areoldi, 283
Bertono, Bartolomeo, 283–84
Bevilacqua: family, 61; Guglielmo, 239, 256
Biancardo: Agnese, 178; Antonio, 185, 234; Ugolotto, 185–86, 238, 249, 252, 261, 265, 267, 312–13, 329
Bibi, Alberto, 169
bishops: of Asolo, 113; of Fermo, 103; of Padua, 22–25, 33, 55, 85, 264–65, 325; of Trento, 93; of Treviso, 85
Black Death, 15, 25, 132–33, 175, 191
Bocassi, Caterina (wife of Bonifacio di Giacomo da Carrara), 299–300
Boiardo, Gherardo, 315, 317, 322, 332
Boion, 186, 191
Bologna: diplomacy of, 42, 63, 122, 260, 310–12, 314, 317–18; relations with Carrara lords, 63, 83–84, 94, 113, 116–20, 129, 241–42, 248, 259, 303–4, 318–19; and Visconti wars, 265–67, 273–74, 320–25
Bolzano, 44, 328
Bonafari, Baldo, 203, 257, 276, 278, 290, 294, 299
Bonifacio IX, pope, 274, 297, 304, 311, 313, 327
Bonjacopo di Ognibene da Mantova, 279
Border War of 1372–1373, xxi, 25, 121–26, 135, 174, 178, 193, 195; outbreak of, 119–21, 147

Index

borgo (Padua): Nuovo, 8, 262–63; Paglia, 8; Rogati, 8; S. Benedetto, 8; S. Croce, 43; Todesco, 279
Borgoforte, on Adige, 124, 125–26, 171, 207, 249
Borgoforte, on Po, 116–18, 304, 306
Borgoricco, 194, 264
Boto, Giovanni, 284
Boucicault, Marshal, 328
Boulogne, Gui de (cardinal), 94, 136
Bovolenta, 14, 35, 56, 65, 110, 145, 178, 198
Brancaleone di Casteldurante, Niccolò Filippo, 186
Brandenburg, Marquis of, 93, 197
Brazolo, Prosdocimo, 164
Brazzi, Bandino, 150–51, 220, 292
Brendoli, Barto (brickmaker), 279
Brenta Canal, 10, 13–14, 51, 85, 123–24, 143–44
Brenta River, 3–4, 12, 13–14, 51, 85, 110, 123, 152, 165, 187, 202, 235, 249, 266, 321–23, 325, 327–28
Brentasecca, 174, 264
Brentelle, battle of, 191, 200, 235–36
Brentelle Canale, 13, 123, 279
Brescia, 59, 62, 71, 114, 116, 256, 322, 328; battle of, 300, 319–20
Brocardo, Giovanni (*campsor*), 115, 207, 276
Brondolo, 109, 209, 216
Brugine, 145, 147, 152, 207, 250
Brugnacchi, Becaro, 41
Brugnera, 234
Brunacci, G., xxiii–xxiv
Brusegana, 13, 150, 235, 263
Buda (Hungary), 127, 178, 207
Buonconforte, battle of, 124–26, 183, 184, 186, 196
Butchers' guild, 142–43, 154, 250
Buti of Urbana, Buto and Oberto, 55
Buzzacarini: family, 97, 113, 167, 174, 288; Anna, 154; Arcoano, 113, 122, 129, 147, 166, 174, 209, 250, 296; Bonfemina di Pataro, 193–94; Boscarino, 118, 124, 129, 174, 224, 255, 264; Buzzacarina di Dusio, 195; Dusio, 43, 67, 75, 87, 89; Francesco di Arcoano, 174, 238, 249, 263, 278, 296, 317–18, 327; Imperatrice di Pataro, 192; Ludovico di Pataro, 174, 263, 295, 296, 324, 325; Pantaleone, 45, 48; Pataro di Arcoano, 174, 238, 249, 296, 313; Pataro di Dusio, 89, 95, 97, 104, 108, 175; Venceslao, 174
Buzzacarini, Fina, 89, 97, 152, 154, 212, 219, 230, 306; Florentine citizenship of, 115; household of, 133, 136, 152–54; landed wealth of, 145, 147, 151–52; Venetian citizenship of, 113

Caetani: Antonio, patriarch of Aquileia, 315, 317; Sveva, 317
Cagnoli, Nerio, da Cortona (goldsmith), 277
Caldonazzo, Sicco (mercenary), 91, 187
Caligine: Giovanni, 45; Prosdocimo, 55
Calvi, Zilio, 151, 250, 292, 295
Camerino, 300, 317, 324, 327
Camino: family, 36–37; Guecello da, 37, 61–62; Rizzardo, 56
Campagna, Roman, 124–25
Campagnola (village), 177, 281
Campagnola: Marco da, 89; Petro da, 41, 53, 71, 87, 89; Sachetto da, 87
campanea, Paduan, 8–10, 13, 24, 25, 150, 203
Campo, Bartolomeo, 34
Campo S. Martino, 196, 300; peacemaking in, 290
Campolongo, 195; peacemaking in, 290
Campolongo, Giovanni da, 150
Camponogara, 98, 331
Camporini, Roberto Mario, 224
Camposampiero (village), 12, 66, 78, 95, 122, 125, 126, 152, 192, 266, 334
Camposampiero: family, 12, 15, 54, 61, 64, 66–67, 77–79, 284–85; Giacomo, 78, 200; Giovanni, 44, 47–48, 51, 53–54, 58; Giovanni di Guglielmo, 270; Guglielmo, 66, 78; Sara, 78–79; Tiso (VII), 37, 59, 61, 64, 77–78; Tiso Novello (VIII), 64, 77–78
Cane: Facino, 236, 313, 319, 325, 329; Niccolò, 203
Caneva, 239–40
canons, cathedral chapter of, 22, 24, 148, 181, 263–64, 296–97, 299, 301

Index

Capelli, Pasquino, 213
Capodistria, 81, 94, 109, 135, 150
Capodivacca: family, 152, 167, 194–95; Agnese, 202; Aicardino di Marco, 56, 59, 194–95; Bartolomeo, 23, 33, 195; Beatrice, 196; Francesco, 59; Francesco, 304, 306; Francesco di Francesco, 306; Fruzerino di Aicardino, 120, 124, 189, 191, 194–95, 196, 253; Fulcone, 143; Gian Enrico, 143; Jacopo, 67; Lodovico Paradisi, 159–61, 175; Niccolò di Antonio, 55, 143, 195; Pagano, 282; Paradiso, 74; Rambaldo, 306
Caracciolo, Riccardo, 274
Caresini, Raffaino, 222
Caresino, Rigo di Giovanni, 177
Carlo da Genova (moneyer), 161, 283–84
Carmelites, 22, 193
Carmignano, 183–84, 264
Caronelli, Leonardo, 108
Carpanedo (near Este), 196
Carpenedo (near Mestre), 207
Carrara (village), 35, 144, 302, 307
Carrara, Agnese di Francesco Novello, 279, 296
Carrara, Andrea di Francesco il Vecchio, 257, 296, 300–301
Carrara, Anna (abbess), 264
Carrara, Antonio di Giacomo, 299, 333
Carrara, Ardizzone di Conte, 297, 299, 301
Carrara, Bonifacio (d. 1307), 192
Carrara, Bonifacio di Giacomo (d. 1425), 296, 299–300, 333
Carrara, Bonifacio di Giacomo II, 129
Carrara, Carlo Ubertino, 124
Carrara, Caterina, countess of Veglia, 121, 133, 152, 191, 224, 259, 265, 322, 325; Venetian citizenship of, 304
Carrara, Conte, 231, 238, 240, 249–50, 268, 273, 276, 296–97, 299, 301, 308, 311–13, 325, 327
Carrara, Cunizza, 59, 60, 64, 77–78
Carrara, Donzella, 64, 129
Carrara, Fina. See Buzzacarini, Fina
Carrara, Francesco il Vecchio: abdication of, 243, 245, 247; in Border war, 120–27; captivity of, 129–30, 201, 247, 252, 304, 306; and Chioggia war, 203–18; and church, 25–26; court of, 133–39, 156–58; death and funeral of, 291, 306–7; and economy, 31, 132–33; and Florence, 114–15, 126–27, 140–41; Florentine citizenship of, 115; and Friuli, 229–31, 233–34, 239–42; and Louis of Hungary, 103–4, 106–7, 111–14, 121–27, 131, 158, 210–12, 221; marriage of, 89, 133, 152, 154; offspring of, 121, 133, 296–302; plots against, 124–25, 129; portraits of, 181–82; powers as lord of Padua, 95–97, 116, 165, 171; and university, 3, 199–200; Venetian citizenship of, 91, 113; wealth of, 139–45, 158–62, 198; and woolen industry, 31, 140–41
Carrara, Francesco Novello: early career of, 124–26, 189, 226, 235–38; education of, 133; execution of, 335; exile of, 250–51, 253, 256–60, 265; and Florence, 284, 303–4, 311–13, 318–19, 327–38, 333; marriage of, 130, 205; offspring of, 257–58, 296–97, 333; powers as lord of Padua, 247, 268–72, 287–92; and reconquest of Padua, 266–68, 273–75; regime of, 272–76, 292–96; and Scaliger lord, 306, 308–10, 313, 318, 332; and university, 33, 291; Venetian citizenship of, 304, 335; and Venice, 274, 315–18, 322–25, 329–35; wealth of, 154, 272–73, 275–76, 279–84; and woolen industry, 277–79
Carrara, Francesco III, 257, 295, 300–301, 304, 310–11, 323–25, 330–33, 335–36
Carrara, Gentile, 85
Carrara, Giacomino, 56, 86–87, 93, 124, 133; lordship of Padua, 94–97
Carrara, Giacomo (d. 1240), 35, 269
Carrara, Giacomo (il Grande), xviii, 17, 37–38, 44, 49; election of, 38, 39–42, 44; lordship of Padua, 42–43, 45, 69
Carrara, Giacomo II, 24, 54, 56, 86–87, 124, 132, 167, 191; imperial vicar, 93; lordship of Padua, 89–95, 135; Venetian citizenship of, 91; and woolen industry, 140–41
Carrara, Giacomo di Francesco il Vecchio

450

Index

(d. 1405), 236, 238, 249, 257, 266, 296, 299–300, 333
Carrara, Giacomo di Francesco Novello (d. 1406), 257, 296, 300–301, 333–34, 335–36
Carrara, Giacomo di Giacomino, 97
Carrara: Gigliola di Francesco il Vecchio, duchess of Saxony, 116, 133, 152, 187, 224, 248, 324; Gigliola di Francesco Novello, marquise of Ferrara, 257, 310, 318; Gigliola di Giacomo II, 93
Carrara, Gionata di Francesco Novello, 257
Carrara, Guglielmo, 95, 167
Carrara, Leonardo, 23
Carrara, Lieta di Francesco il Vecchio, 133, 152, 224, 265
Carrara, Lieta di Giacomo II, 96, 109, 224
Carrara, Lotolfo, 268
Carrara, Margherita, 154
Carrara, Marsilio (il Grande), 37, 44–45, 47–49, 54–56, 77–78, 99, 174, 191, 195; as Della Scala vicar, 57–59, 61; lordship of Padua, 68–71; in Scaliger War, 64–67
Carrara, Marsilio di Francesco Novello, 257
Carrara, Marsilio di Giacomo II, 95, 124–26, 129–30, 192, 198, 212, 219
Carrara, Niccolò (d. 1344), 44, 47, 54–56, 59, 86, 89
Carrara, Niccolò di Giacomo, 296, 301
Carrara, Niccolò di Giacomo II, 124–25, 129, 198
Carrara, Paolo di Giacomo, 300–301
Carrara, Pierconte, 51
Carrara, Pietro detto Perenzano, 23, 51, 64, 71
Carrara, Pietro di Francesco il Vecchio, 201, 257, 300
Carrara, Rodolfo, 256–57, 259, 266, 296, 299–300
Carrara, Servio di Francesco il Vecchio, 257, 296, 302
Carrara, Sofia di Bonifacio, 192
Carrara, Stefano di Francesco Novello, 25, 257, 296, 301–2, 320, 325, 333
Carrara, Taddea, 42, 57–59, 193

Carrara, Ubertino, 51–55, 59, 61–62, 66–67, 69, 136, 174; death of, 86–87; foreign policy of 82–86; lordship of Padua, 71–74, 77–78, 86–87; relations with Scaliger lords, 82–85; relations with Venice, 78–82, 85–86; and university, 199; Venetian citizenship of, 77, 82; and woolen industry, 31, 140–42
Carrara, Ubertino Fiorentino, 257, 296
Carrara, Ubertino il Vecchio, 51
Carrara espionage, in Venice, 81–82, 121, 130–31, 219, 223
Carrara family, early, 4, 15, 24, 35, 37, 49–53
Carrara palaces, in Padua: S. Andrea 124–25, 133; S. Lorenzo, 39, 49. *See also* Reggia
Carrara palaces, in Venice: Ca' Corner, 316, 318, 322; on Campo S. Polo, 94, 107, 118, 124, 154, 156, 223, 231, 234
Carturo, 21, 299–300
Casale (village), 169, 261
Casale: Antonio da, 177; Biancafiore da, 202; Giovanni da, 141; Luca da, 136, 143, 151; Pietro da, 272
Casalserugo, 198
Caselle di Bagoto, 247
Casone, Ugotone, 289
Castagnaro, battle of, 238–39
Castelbaldo, 10, 13, 44, 66, 75, 83, 192, 237, 273, 281, 321–22, 324, 334
Castelbarco, Antonio da, 236
Castelcarro, near Chioggia, 110, 119, 126, 207, 219, 232, 250, 333
Castelfranco, 12, 78, 86, 98, 118, 122, 211, 220, 222; podestà of, 195
Castello (Padua's citadel), 4, 162, 167–68, 253, 291
Castello: Doimo da, 231; Nicoletto da, 231
Castelnuovo: family, 38; Margherita di Antonio da, 192–93
Castelnuovo of Boccadella, 177
Casteltealdo, Francesco, 122
Castiglionchio, Lapo da, 214
Castiglione, Bernardo da, 93
Castrocaro, near Forlì, 311, 321
Castronovo, Guidone, 97

Index

Caterina, wife of Giovanni di Prato, 147
Cateruzza (Venetian prostitute), 121
Cavalcanti: Matteo, 263, 299; Scolaio, 115
Cavalli, Nicola, 152
Cavarzere, 82, 109, 123, 212, 214, 220
Celsi, Lorenzo, doge, 112–13
Ceneda, 81, 106, 161, 228, 251
centenari (of Padua), 6–7, 164, 271–72
Cerdolini, Tommaso (mercenary), 234
Cermisione, Bartolomeo, 228, 238, 239, 262–63, 284
Cesana, 118, 201
Cetto: Gualperto, 141–43, 202; Sibilia, 203–4
chancery, Carrara, 135–36, 150–51, 163, 178, 250, 294–96, 324–25; letterbook of, 295–96; notaries of, 150–51, 295; records of, 150–51, 295–96
Charles IV, Holy Roman Emperor, 91–93, 94, 97–99, 106, 108, 115; descent into Italy, first, 97–99, 174, 177, 191, 196; —, second, 115–17, 174, 199; and Friuli, 113–14; grants to Carrara lord, 93, 96, 114, 144
Charles VI, king of France, 218, 312
Charles of Durazzo, 203, 210–12, 218, 236
Chioggia, 10, 14, 54, 56, 109–10, 118, 123, 199, 223; podestà of, 209, 223, 232
Chioggia War, xix, 131, 149, 157–59, 165–66, 174, 196, 202–3, 207–18; alliances before, 205–6; outbreak of, 206–8
citizenship, Paduan, Carrara lord grants of, 133, 149, 151, 198, 271, 277, 287, 292
citizenship, Venetian, grants of, 134, 169, 177, 185, 285, 304, 306
Cittadella, 12–13, 15, 21, 41, 44–45, 66, 85, 93, 126; government of, 164–66; parley, in 1380, 166, 178, 203, 217; —, in 1381, 218; statutes of, 14–15, 164
Cittadella (Verona's citadel), 329–30, 333
Cividale, 112, 265
Clement V, pope, 37
Clement VI, pope, 90–91, 92, 94–95
Clement VII, antipope, 256, 260
Codevigo, 191–92, 194
coins, Paduan: *carrarese*, 158, 161–62, 207; *carrarino*, 158–62, 207, 282–84; *grosso aquilino*, 53; *piccolo*, 282–84; *quattrino*, 162, 284; *sestino*, 282–84; *soldino*, 282–84
Collalto: family, 192, 292; Manfredo, 192
College of Judges, 20, 133, 148, 202
College of Jurist Doctors, 33, 148
Collegio, Venice, 103, 106–7, 111–12, 230, 232
Collodo, S., xxiii–xxiv, 263, 301
Compagni: Nerio (moneyer), 160–62; Niccolò (moneyer), 159–62
Cona, 125, 171, 220, 221
Conegliano, 66, 103, 104, 107, 119, 211, 226, 228; podestà of, 232
Conio, Bengarda (wife of Simone Lupi), 183
Conselve, 10, 12–13, 14, 35, 48, 125, 249
Conselve, Francesco, 29, 33, 271, 274
Contarini: family, 108; Andrea, doge, 117, 119, 121, 125–26; —, in Chioggia War, 210–11, 213, 217, 221; Angelberto, 108; Giovanni, 281; Luca, 220; Lucia (wife of Giacomo di Francesco il Vecchio), 296, 299–300; Niccolò, 209; Pietro, 310; Pirano, 108; Zaccaria, 210–12, 213, 217, 220
Conti: family, 10; Arturo, 256; Engolfo, 145, 151; Manfredino, 145; Naimiero, 154, 202, 255, 264, 276–77, 283; Naimiero di Naimiero, 289, 294, 312; Prosdocimo, 263, 289, 294, 300, 301
Conti, Ildebrandino, bishop of Padua, 23, 85
contrada (in Padua), defined, 7–8
Contrari, Uguccione, 324
Conversini: Conversino di Giovanni, 292; Giovanni, da Ravenna, 51, 132, 156–57, 292–96, 306; Israele di Giovanni, 157
Corfu, 236–37
Corner: family, 175; Francesco, 130, 310; Marcia, 177; Marco, doge, 175, 177; Pietro, 213–14, 216–18
Correggio: family, 59; Azzo, 62–64, 84; Beatrice, 61; Giacomina, 81–82; Gilberto, 123–24; Guido, 62–64
Corte, 98, 151

Index

Corte, Francesco, 147
Cortellerio: Bartolomeo Taddeo, 201; Tebaldo, 29
Cortusi: Guglielmo, xxi, 29, 61–62, 107, 217; Lodovico di Giovanni, 194, 271
Costabile family, 152
Coucy, Enguerrand, sire of, 231
Council of Anziani (Padua), 27, 40–42, 45, 54, 59–60, 245
Council of Forty (Venice), 81–82, 91, 104, 130, 193, 219, 232
Council of Francesco Novello, 289–90, 293–94
Council of Sixty (Padua), 59–60
Council of Ten, xxii, 98, 121, 122, 232, 331
Council of War of 1372, 122, 171–73, 204
Count Palatine, 30, 116, 149, 182, 262
Court: of Aquila, 19, 141, 254, 288–89; of Cavallo, 289; of Draco, 277; of Sigillo, 19; of Vettovalgio, 19, 30, 132, 254
court system, in Padua, 19–20, 96, 132–33, 163, 271–72; appeals from, 96, 163, 288–90
Crema, 177, 217
Cremaschi, Niccolò, 191–92
Cremona, 97, 116, 217, 328
Cremona, Bernardo da, 43
Creola, 195, 251, 252
Crescenzio: Agnese, 157; Antonio, 157; Manfredo, 157–58
Crete, 85, 113–14, 212, 331–32
Cristoforo di Jacopo da Padova (Carrara vassal), 247
Crivello, Pietro Paolo, 125, 289, 316
Curan, 122, 125, 212, 219, 316
Curtarolo (village), 51, 66, 192, 196, 201, 235
Curtarolo: family, 167, 200–201; Alberto, 201; Enrico, 200; Enrico di Pietro, 279; Francesco, 201; Francesco di Matteo, 201; Guglielmo, 29, 128, 200–201, 221, 230, 239–40, 250, 251, 255, 289, 290, 315; India, 200; Maria di Almerico, 201; Niccolò di Enrico, 157–58, 200–201, 223; Niccolò di Niccolò, 201; Pantisilia, 200; Piero Piccinino di Pietro, 201; Pietro di Enrico, 200
Curtivo, Rolando, 281–82
Cyprus, 34, 122, 124–25, 206, 219

da Peraga: family, 167, 192–94, 284–85, 334; Albertina di Filippo, 193; Albertino di Marco, 192, 193; Albertino di Marino, 194; Alice, 193; Antonia di Giovanni, 171; Bartolomea di Marco, 169, 192; Bartolomeo detto Peragino di Marino, 194, 249; Filippa di Filippo, 193–94; Filippo di Marco, 56, 192–93; Francesco, 194; Geremia di Marino, 194, 253; Giacomino, 54, 67, 74, 194; Giovanni di Marino, 194; Marino di Filippo, 193, 194; Polentesia di Albertino, 194, 196; Ursula di Filippo, 193; Zanino di Filippo, 104, 122, 127, 171, 189, 193–94, 196
da Ponte: family, 247; Arimondo di Solimano, 139, 200; Solimano, 136–37, 143
dal Verme: Jacopo, 129, 251–53, 260, 262, 267, 313, 328, 330–35; Pietro, 72, 74
d'Alençon, Philippe, patriarch of Aquileia, 223, 229–30, 231, 234, 240
Dalesmanini: Azzo, 92; Traverso, 42
d'Alessio: Carlo, 150; Giovanni, 150; Guidone, 150; Niccoletto, xxi, 135, 150–51, 157, 292; Pandolfo, 150
Dall'Argento, Giovanni (moneyer), 283–84
Dalle Ave, Francesco, 268, 289
Dalle Calze, Reprandino, 289
Dall'Olio: Bartolomeo, 282–83; Francesco, 151–52, 284; Giacomo, 151–52; Pietro, 281–82
Dalmatia, 91, 98, 103, 106–7, 116, 123
Dandolo: Andrea, doge, 85, 89, 91; Francesco, 220; Jacopo, 220; Leonardo, 223, 315; Niccolò, 220; Simeone, 103
De la Roche, Andrion, 116–17
Del Bene: bankers, 179, 185; Betto, 179, 185; Franceschino, 179
Della Ricca, Nascimbene, 270–71
Della Scala: Alberto, 59, 62–64, 66–67, 68–70, 73–75, 81, 82–84; Antonio,

INDEX

Della Scala (cont.)
207, 232–37, 239–40; Antonio di Guglielmo, 329–30; Bartolomeo, 206, 209; Brunoro di Guglielmo, 329–30; Cangrande II, 106, 187, 329; Cansignorio II, 116, 120–21, 122, 129–30; Fregnano, 62, 97, 187; Giovanni, 97; Mastino II, 42, 57, 59, 62–64, 66, 69–72, 73–75, 82, 83–85, 90, 94–95, 193; Regina, wife of Bernabò Visconti, 217, 240; Tainaldo, 62; Viride, 281

Della Scala, Cangrande, 37–38, 39, 41–43, 45, 52–53, 55–56, 62, 83, 195; lord of Padua, 57–59, 69; Venetian citizenship of, 62

Della Scala, lords of Verona, 35–36, 38, 83–84, 94–95, 152; court at Verona, 58–59, 61–62, 195

Della Seta: Lombardo, 179, 181, 185, 261; Pellegrino, 261

Della Stuva, Giovanni (notary), 148

Della Torre: Febo, 266; Federico, 193; Geremia, 194; Lodovico, patriarch of Aquileia, 108, 111, 113–14; Marino, 194

Della Torre, of Milan, 37

Dente: family, 51, 53–54, 58–59, 81–82; Caterina, 78–79; Guglielmo, 53–54, 67, 82; Lemizio, 82; Paolo, 53–54; Vitaliano, 78, 81–82

Descalzi: Domenichino, 247, 276, 278, 284; Ottonello, 29, 33, 247, 268, 271

Despencer, Hugh qd. Edward, 126

despot, Renaissance, concept of, xvii–xviii

dogado, 81–82, 207–11, 225–26, 274

Dolfin: Dorde, 83; Giovanni, doge, 103

Domenico da Bergamo (canon), 263

Dominicans, 25, 193

Donati: family, 187–88; Manno, 104, 187–89, 252; Manno di Mammo, 188–89, 252; Pazzino, 186, 187–89, 257

Dondi dall'Orologio: family, 178, 199–200; Giovanni, 120, 191, 194, 199–200; Jacopo, 199–200; Jacopa di Giovanni, 139, 200; Orsola di Giovanni, 200

Dorde de Gaubert (Carrara seneschal), 317, 318

Doria: Luciano, 208–9; Pietro, 208, 210, 212–13, 216–17

Doto, Schinella da, 41, 47–48, 54

Dotti: family, 152, 168–70; Antonio, 169–70; Beatrice, 170; Diamante, 170; Francesco di Paolo, 34, 124, 169–70, 218, 229, 239–40, 255, 294, 307, 334; Francesco di Zambon, 192; Giacomo, 97; Gionata, 170; Giovanna, 170; Paolo, 97, 141, 143–44, 167, 169–70; Paolo di Francesco, 294; Zambon, 97, 169, 191, 192

Dottori, Alessandro, 29, 253, 271

dowries, 170, 171, 188, 191, 193–94, 195, 196, 198, 224, 287–88, 312

Drudone da Ravenna, 204

druggist guild, 149, 229

Dubrovnik, 107, 240

Duino, Hugh, count of, 222–23, 257

Dulcino, Michele, 301

Duomo, 3–4, 9, 21–22, 55, 74, 129, 220; archpriests of, 23, 195; of Chioggia, 216; quarter of, 6–7, 19, 252, 272. *See also* canons, cathedral chapter of

Elisabeth (daughter of Louis of Hungary), 114–15

Elisabeth, queen of Hungary, 225, 229–30, 234

Emo: Gabriele, 329, 333; Pietro, 307

Engleschi: Antonio, 45; Tebaldo, 143

Enselmini: family, 263–64; Africano, 253, 264–65; Giovanni, bishop of Padua, 164–66; Jacopo, 164, 166, 265

Eremitani (church), 22, 25, 170, 174, 193, 266

Eremitani (order), 169–70, 193

Ermanno (Carrara agent in Venice), 323

Este (town), 10, 11–13, 19, 38, 44–45, 48, 65–66, 83, 139, 185, 235, 334; Castello of, 185

Este, lords of Ferrara: dynasty, 10, 36, 42, 44, 66, 71, 95–97, 261; Alberto, 241, 264, 303–6; Azzone, 297, 308–9, 331–32; Francesco, 37, 175; Giacomina, 174–75; Niccolò I, 66, 75, 84; Niccolò II, 112–13, 117, 121, 130, 177, 191, 205, 221,

Index

223, 225, 233, 240–41, 281; Niccolò III, 281, 297, 306, 309–10, 315, 327, 329, 330–31; Obizzo I, 36; Obizzo II, 66, 75, 83–84, 90, 175; Rinaldo, 175; Taddea, wife of Francesco Novello, 130, 205, 251, 256–58, 281, 304, 306, 308, 318, 332
Euganean Hills, 10, 19, 124–25, 139, 171, 175, 201–2, 272
exiles, from Padua: confiscation of property, 45–46, 58–59; Papafava family, 90, 170–71; in 1320s, 45–49, 51, 54–56, 175; in 1390s, 269–70, 284–85, 334
extradition, to Venice, 86, 89–90, 109–11, 129, 142, 219; treaty, 89–90, 241; treaty with Verona, 129
Ezzelino da Romano, 35, 191, 269

Fabriano, Ruzierio, 55
Faedo, 124, 197, 202, 280
Faenza, 174, 175, 237, 273
Falier: Marino, as podestà, 71, 74, 77, 81, 95–96, 162–63, 270; —, as doge, 98; Niccolò, 118
Fantelli: Fantello, 295; Padovano, 277, 282
feast days, in Padua: Sant'Alò, 236; S. Giustina, 58; St. James the More, 39, 42; St. Louis of Toulouse, 74; St. Peter Martyr, 48–49, 53, 58; S. Prosdocimo, 58; S. Stefano, 302
Felice Unione (anti-Carrara league in Friuli), 231, 234–35, 239
Feltre, 57, 59, 91–92, 93, 98, 114, 119–20, 131, 206, 219, 235, 239, 247, 251; under Carrara rule, 108, 111, 115, 161–62, 175, 235, 240–41; under Habsburg dukes, 123, 149, 203, 206; under Visconti rule, 326, 328–29, 330–32
Ferdinand, patriarch of Jerusalem, 237, 239
Ferrara, 36–37, 42, 66, 84, 90, 96–97, 122, 130, 205, 233, 272, 332–33; council of regency in, 306, 309–10; Este court at, 205, 294, 315
Fiesco: family, 37; Isabella, 92
Fiesso, 156, 264
Filippo da Pisa (mercenary), 322

Fioremonte da Verina (wool worker), 141
Florence: and Carrara lords, 66–67, 71–72, 113–15, 122, 140–41, 207, 214, 241–42, 248, 257, 265, 303–4, 318–19, 333; diplomacy of, 42, 58, 63, 75, 84, 120, 177, 259–60, 310–12, 314, 318, 332; in Scaliger War (1336–1339), 66–67, 75–76; in Visconti wars, 265–66, 273–75, 320–25
Fondaco dei Panni (Carrara lord's), 141–43, 158, 171, 277
Fondaco delle Biave, in Padua, 4, 140, 151, 154, 158, 216, 230, 251, 276
Fontaniva, 21, 93
forced loans (*prestiti*), Padua, 136, 147–49
fortifications, of Padovano, 110, 119–20, 126, 165–66, 175, 186, 194–95, 206, 219–20, 226, 232, 241, 250
Forzatè: family, 55, 167, 189–92; Aledusio, 192; Alvise, 97, 129, 143, 189, 191–92; Enrico, 191; Filippino, 129, 191–92; Forzatè, 189; Giordano (Zordano), 55, 87, 89, 191–92; Giovanni, 189, 191, 192; Lieta di Marco, 191; Marco, 42, 55, 191–92; Palma di Alvise, 191; Ziliola di Giovanni, 192
Foscari, Niccolò, 333
Fracassini, Lorenzo (Florentine envoy), 231
Franceschino da Alessandria (mercenary), 238
Francesco da Monselice (Lozzo accomplice), 90
Francesco di Francesco, archpriest of Ferrara, 156
Francesco di S. Zilio (notary), 276
Franciscans, 22–23, 193, 202
Frankapan, Elisabeth, 304, 322
Frankapan, Stefan, count of Veglia and lord of Segni, 121, 191, 224, 257, 259
Franzesi: Aloisio, 182; Rainiero, 185; Stefano, 185; Verde, 185
Franzesi, Caterina, da Staggia (wife of Bonifacio Lupi), 178, 181–82, 185–86, 285–86; Venetian citizenship of, 185
Frassalasta, Francesco, 67
Frederick, count of Cilli, 322

INDEX

Frederick II, Holy Roman Emperor, 35, 89
Frederick the Handsome, duke of Austria, 42–45, 47–48, 69
Friuli, 93–94, 98, 111–14, 127, 130, 161, 222–23, 229–31, 233–34, 237, 239–40, 248–49, 265–67, 297, 315
Friuli War (1385–1387), xix, 161, 189, 231–42

Gabatori, Paolino, of Milan (priest), 264
Gaffarello, Jacopino, 120, 136, 139, 151–52, 201–2
Gaiardo (Carrara butcher), 157, 288
Gallicano, Niccolò da (mercenary), 209–11
Gallo: Enrico, 29, 247, 255, 257, 278, 285, 292, 294, 315, 322–25; Oliviero, 264
Gallucci, Baldo (mercenary), 209–10
Galluzzi, Francesco (mercenary), 238
Galmarelli, Carletto, 156
Gambacorta, Pietro, 159–60
Gambarare, 122, 232, 331
Ganimberti, Raimondo, bishop of Padua, 24, 130, 195, 256, 263
Garzerie, 4; *Nuove*, 278–79
Gatari: Andrea, xxi, 235, 309–10, 335; Bartolomeo, xxi; Galeazzo, xxi, 122, 187, 207, 209, 217, 247, 253, 326
Genoa, 97, 116, 122, 178, 200, 205–6, 240–41, 274, 311–12, 328–29, 331–32
Genoese War, Third, 96–98
Genoese War, Fourth. *See* Chioggia War
Gentile, Loenzo (Genoese official), 216
Gerardo di Antonio (wool merchant), 271
German garrison, in Padua, 51–53, 55–56. *See also* mercenaries: German
German vicars, in Padua, 44–49, 53–57. *See also* Aufenstein, Konrad von; Villanders: Engelmar von; Walsee, Ulrich von
Gesta magnifica domus Carrariensis, xxi, 268
Ghibelline factions: in Bologna, 320–22; in Padua, 42, 55–56
Ghibellinism, xix, 35–37, 218
Giacomo di Ser Niccolò detto Terrazzo, 141

Giovanni (abbot of S. Benedetto), 230, 261
Giovanni Andrea (Duomo custos), 289–90
Giovanni "a Pallata" (*campsor*), 289
Giovanni Benedetto, Fra, 335
Giovanni Cavosia da Sarmeola (Carrara assassin), 82
Giovanni Cestario da Piove di Sacco (Carrara assassin), 82
Giovanni da Bologna (scholar), 273
Giovanni da Carpi (mercenary), 214
Giovanni da Cremona (mercenary), 270
Giovanni da Milano (mercenary), 238–39
Giovanni da Montagnana (Carrara advisor), 283, 289
Giovanni da Nono (Visconti envoy), 285
Giovanni da Portogruaro (Carrara agent), 175
Giovanni di Pietro (rector of S. Andrea), 198
Giovanni di Saltimberto da Cremona, 270
Girlandi, Benedetto, 161, 175, 278, 283, 289–90, 293, 302
Giustinian: Bernardo, 89; Francesco, 331; Giustinian, 63; Lorenzo di Bernardo, 196; Pantaleone, 221; Pietro di Marco, 96, 130, 223, 231–32; Taddeo, 120–21, 123, 151, 209, 213
Gloria, Nicola, 289
Goffonario, Bartolomeo, 272
Gonzaga: Alda, 304, 309, 312; Francesco, 177, 189, 225, 233, 239–41, 303–4, 312–14, 321–23, 324–26, 331; Lodovico (Luigi I), 55, 61–72, 74, 75, 83–84, 94; Luigi I, 116; Margherita, wife of Giacomino da Carrara, 97
Gorgo, 35, 144, 272, 331
Gorizia, 94, 112, 318
Gorizia: counts of, 93–94, 114, 315; Enrico II, 43–45, 47, 93; Enrico III, 315; Giovanni Mainardi, 315; Meynard, 114
Gottola, Albertino (Carrara agent), 89, 198
Gottola, Albertino (moneylender), 284
Governolo, battle of, 313

456

Index

Gozzadini, Nanni, 320
Gradenigo: family, 37; Andrea, 217; Giacomo 63; Giovanni (Venetian diplomat), 106–7, 210–12, 220, 232; Giovanni, doge, 81, 98, 103, 132; Jacopo, 293; Marco, 43
Grado, 82, 208; patriarch of, 122–23, 230–31
Grain Office (Venice), 47, 109, 120, 169, 177, 212, 230
Grain Warehouse (Padua). See Fondaco delle Biave
Great Council. See Maggior Consiglio
Gregory XI, pope, 25, 120, 122, 124, 126, 130, 188
Grimoard, Anglic, 117
Grompo: family, xxiii, 15, 136, 261; Gombertino, 261; Nascimbene, 136, 187, 261; Poetro, 136, 261–62, 266, 285; Rolando, 261; Ubertino, 136, 261–62, 270–71, 284
Grosso, Giacomo (Lozzo accomplice), 90
Guarnerini: Bonifacio, 316, 317, 328, 332; Marco, 150–51, 271
Guelf factions: in Bologna, 320–22; in Padua, 35–38, 42, 77
Guelfism, xix, 23, 63, 73, 111–14, 130, 205, 218, 259–60, 265. See also Ghibellinism
Guidone, abbot of S. Maria in Vanzo, 48, 51
guilds, in Padua, 27–31, 41, 74, 132–33; assessments on, 31, 148–49, 229. See also various guilds

Habsburg dukes of Austria, 93, 111–14, 122–23, 149, 195, 203, 206; as lords of Belluno and Feltre, 123, 149, 203, 206; Albert, 113–14, 115, 122–23, 235, 239, 249–50; Leopold, 113–14, 122–23, 130–31, 179, 189, 200, 202; —, as lord of Treviso, 218–20, 222–26, 228; —, as lord of Trieste, 223; Rudolf IV, 106, 111–14, 165, 196
Halfinstaign, Louis of, 229
Hawkwood, Sir John, 117, 122, 127, 131, 189, 206, 267, 300; in pay of Carrara lord, 237–38, 273

Heinrich, duke of Carinthia, 44, 47–48, 51, 53, 56–57, 69, 193, 195
Henry IV, king of England, 322
Henry VII, Holy Roman Emperor, 37, 45, 93, 177
Hermann (German mercenary), 214, 216
Hermann, count of Cilli, 224, 248
household, Carrara, 133–36, 149–51; balance sheets of, 136–37, 138, 147–48; notaries of, 150–51; offices of, under Francesco il Vecchio, 133–36, 156–58; —, under Francesco Novello, 276–77, 289–90, 292–94; provisioning of, 136, 144–45, 154, 155–57; vicars in, 133–35, 149–50. See also chancery, Carrara; Reggia

imperial vicariate, in Padua, 93, 94, 96, 247
indemnities: from Border War of 1372–1373, 126–27, 212, 219; from Chioggia War, 219–20; payment of, 221–22; from Peace of Genoa, 274, 303, 311, 314, 317–19
Isola, Giovanni da, 238
Isola della Scala (fortress at Bassanello), 42–43, 46

Jacobo da Ferrara (priest), 263
Jacobo di Zero (moneyer), 282–83
Jacomelli, Milano, called Malabarba, 162, 255, 270, 276
Jacopo Piacentino, 67
Janos Chur, 207
Jews, in Padua, as moneylenders, 28, 140, 254, 272, 288–89
Joanna, queen of Naples, 115, 206, 210
John XXII, pope, 55
jousts, as celebrations, 129, 187, 205, 304, 311
judges, delegation by Carrara lord, 175–76, 289–90. See also court system, in Padua: appeals from

knighthoods, bestowed, 59, 97, 117, 124, 187, 195, 196, 200, 238, 266

Ladislaus, king of Naples, 332

Index

Lambardi, Valerano, 152, 189
Lambertazzi, Giovanni Lodovico, 34, 253, 271, 308
Lambertini, Cortesia, 171
Lana, Alberto di Francesco, 141
Landau: Conrad von, 206, 308; Lucius von, 236–37
Lando, Pietro, 152
Lanzarotti, Lanzarotto, 164
Lariolo, Petrucci, 185
Lattuga, Galvano, 276
Latuga, Niccolò, 291
Lavellongo, Federico, 149, 163, 186
Lazera, Bernardo, 277
League of Bologna, 260, 303–4, 306, 308, 310, 312, 314, 317
Lemici family. *See* Dente: family
Lendinara (village), 46, 66, 83, 186–87, 321–22
Lendinara, Rizzardo detto Tartaro da, 45, 53–54, 58–59, 67, 72
Lenguazzo: family, 284–85; Daniele, 270, 285; Lion, 253; Riccardo, 285
Leone da Brescia (mercenary), 216
Leti, Bono (Florentine banker), 283–84
Levico (Valsugana), 93, 187
Lewis of Bavaria, Holy Roman Emperor, 42, 71, 73, 91, 92
Lido, 209–10, 213
Limena, 13, 123, 249
Linaroli, Donato, 322
linen industry, 30, 143–44
linseed oil industry, 144, 277
Lion: family, xxiii, 135, 197–99, 255, 264, 267; Aleta di Checcho, 198; Francesco detto Checcho di Pietro, 142, 171, 194, 197–99, 207, 325; Jacopa di Checcho, 198; Luca di Checcho, 197, 255, 276–77, 278, 322–23, 325, 328, 333–34; Paolo di Checcho, 197, 200, 250, 255, 278–79, 294, 312, 325, 333–34
Lion: Antonio di Checcho di Donati, 197; Checcho di Donati, 197; Giacomo di Checcho di Donati, 197
Lion, Niccolò, of Venice, 255
Lischi, Guglielmo, 234
Livernza River, 229, 231
loans, of Carrara lords to other states:
Aquileia, patriarch of, 214; Belluno, 140; Della Scala lord, 207; Dubrovnik, 214; Feltre, 114; Florence, 114, 126–27, 140; Genoa, 214; Louis of Hungary, 140, 214, 221; Lucca, 114, 122, 140; papacy, 127; Pirano, 77; Trieste, 140, 223; Venice, 96; Zara, 114, 140
Lombardo, Valeriano, 233
Loredan, Marco, 68
Lorenzo da Camponogara (Carrara assassin), 82
Louis, duke of Anjou, 218, 231
Louis, king of Hungary, xix, 90, 91–94, 98–99, 116–17, 134–35; ally of Carrara lord, 104, 106–7, 111–14, 116, 121–24, 126–27, 131, 158, 175, 224; in Chioggia War, 205–7, 210–12, 214, 221; portrait of, 180–81; war with Venice (1354–1356), 103–4, 205
Lova, battle of, 123–25, 183, 186, 191–92, 196
Lozzo (castle), 90, 145, 281
Lozzo: family, branch of Maltraversi, 10, 37–38, 90–91; Antonioda, 67; Enrico da, 87, 90; Francesco da, 90; Guido di Niccolò, 174; Niccolò da, 37–38, 89, 90–91
Lucca, 58, 61, 64, 75, 84, 115, 122, 260
Lupi: family, 167, 171, 177, 179, 181–85; Antonio, 122, 182–83, 185; Bartolomea, 178; Conradino, 214; Giovanni, 181; Guido, 182; Raimondino, 177, 179, 181, 185; Simone, 122, 133, 163, 175, 182–83, 224, 226, 228–29, 271; Ugolino di Manfredino, 214; Ugolotto di Bonifacio, 177
Lupi, Bonifacio di Ugolotto, 116, 122, 131, 177–82, 185–86, 189, 217, 250–51, 253, 285; Florentine service of, 177–78; and Louis of Hungary, 178–80, 198–99; Paduan citizenship of, 178; Venetian citizenship of, 177, 185; in Visconti Padua, 250–51, 253, 261, 266; wealth of, 177–79, 182, 185–86

Maccaruffi: family, 47, 51, 58–59; Bartolomeo detto Maccaruffo, 38, 42, 45;

Index

Marino, 54; Piera, née Sambonifacio, 54; Prosdocimo, 276
Maconia, Giustina (mistress of Francesco il Vecchio), 296
Maggior Consiglio, Paduan, 40–41, 46, 48–49, 77, 169, 198, 220–21; meetings of, 44, 67, 89, 131, 207, 245
Maggior Consiglio, Venetian, 64, 80–81, 86, 87, 91, 104, 111–13, 126, 207, 221, 304, 312, 327, 335
Magneto, Giacomo, da Imola (Carrara agent), 129
Malamacco, 209, 213
Malaspina, Spinetta, 61, 239, 251
Malatesta: family, 95; Carlo, 259, 297, 304, 312–13; Galeotto, 104, 273; Jacopa, 192–93; Pandolfo, 324, 329; Polentesia, 193
Malempensa, Giovanni di Canzelari (moneyer), 158
Malizia: Aicardini, 54; Fredo, 253, 334
Mandria, 185, 194, 285
Manfredi: Aimerico di Giovanni, 317; Astorre, 273, 303, 309; Francesco, 175; Giovanni, 104, 175; Manfredo, 41; Nobilia, 174
mansus, defined, 10, 15
Manthelor: Federico, 104; Gherardo, 209, 230
Mantua, 66, 97, 116–17, 178, 185, 305, 313–14
Mantuan War, 299, 310, 312–15, 318
Manuel II, Byzantine emperor, 318
Manzone, Giacomo (wool merchant), 278
Maresa, Donato, 223
marriage alliances, of Carrara family: with Buzzacarini, 89, 167; with counts of Cilli, 224, 248; with Della Scala, 42, 57, 58–59, 193; with Este, 130, 205, 310; with Stefan Frankapan, 121, 133, 191, 224; with Gonzaga, 304, 309, 312–13; with count of Gorizia, 93; with count of Ortenburg, 96, 133, 152, 223; with duke of Saxony, 116, 133, 152, 187, 224; with Varano, lords of Camerino, 300, 317
marriage alliances, of Carrara family (proposed): with duke of Atri, 317; with Caetani family, 317; with Habsburg duke, 228; with Visconti of Milan, 309–10
Marseilles, 116, 256, 263
Maruffo, Marco (mercenary), 217
Masini, Tommaso, 185
Matteo Andrea, duke of Atri, 317
Matteo da Ferrara (Carrara accountant), 162, 255, 276
Matteo "de Buleis," 276
Medici, Vieri de', 231
Mel, 119, 200–201
Melzi, Filippo, 263–64
Memmo, Marino, 104, 161, 182, 228, 293
Menabuoi, Giusto de', 154
Meneghini, Antonio (Carrara agent), 223, 225, 230–32
mercenaries, 65, 68, 72–73, 78, 117, 129, 131, 186–87, 233–34, 265–67; Carrara office of, 135–36, 157–58; in Chioggia War, 208–10, 214, 216–18; English, 127, 131, 216, 218, 237–38, 313; German, 68, 72–73, 106, 111–12, 206, 236–37, 308, 319–20; in Mantuan War, 312–14; pay rates of, 65, 127, 215, 265, 322. *See also individual mercenary captains*
merchants, foreign, in Padua: from Florence, 48, 141–42, 185, 207, 217; from Lucca, 135; from Milan, 141; from Parma, 178, 181–82, 186; from Tuscany, 28, 178, 181–82, 185
merchants court, 132–33, 278
Merlara, 191, 203, 291
Mestre, 43, 71, 112, 119, 207, 209, 211, 225, 315, 316, 322
Mezzoconti, Giovanni Parsino, 250, 255, 289, 315, 321; Mezzoconte, 271
Milan, 97, 111–13, 114, 213, 216–17, 256, 263, 273, 326–28
mint, in Padua: under duke of Carinthia, 53; under Francesco il Vecchio, 158–62, 185, 207; under Francesco Novello, 281–84
Mirano, 13, 122, 126, 193, 194, 202
Mocenigo, Tommaso, doge, 310
Modigliano, Giacomo, count of, 189
Modon, battle of, 329
Molin: Alvise, 121; Giovanni, 41

Index

Monaco, 256, 259
moneylenders (*campsores*), 27–28, 61, 115, 137, 139–40, 152, 182, 195, 201–2; guild of, 61, 159
Monfiore, Ugo, count of, 313
Monfumo, Manfredo, 108
Monselice, 10, 12–14, 19, 38, 42, 44–45, 51, 66, 95, 119, 175, 251, 287, 321–22, 334; Carrara property in, 97, 125, 175, 281; siege of, 69–74, 83, 87
Montagnana, 10, 12–13, 35, 38, 42, 44–45, 66, 88, 175, 198, 234–35, 261, 334; Carrara property in, 125; fortification of, 110; peace of May 1343 at, 85; podestà of, 321; statutes of, 14–15, 164
Monte, Venetian, 177, 185, 225, 230–31, 262; Carrara investment in, 203, 212, 219, 224, 231, 234–35
Montecchio, 72–73
Montefeltro, Antonio, count of Urbino, 310
Montegrotto, 20, 35, 199, 201
Montericco, 175, 280
Monterosso, 194, 291
Montferrato, Teodoro II, marquis of, 310
Montorso, Montorso, 156, 255, 276
Monza, 259, 304, 306
Morando, Porcia, count of, 234, 278, 313
Moro, Jacopo, 120
Morosini: Fantin, 96; Gherardo, 56; Leonardo, 121; Marco, 63; Marino, 104; Michele, doge, 220, 224; Niccolò, 83, 210–12; Paolo, 175, 177; Roberto, 223
Motta, 106, 226, 229, 232
Munich, 259–60
Musestre, 225, 226
Musone River, 3, 13, 21, 64, 119, 123, 315
Mussato, Albertino, 38, 47–48, 51, 53–54, 59; Giovanni (Carrara official), 282–83; Gualpertino, 53–55

Naples, 91–93, 114, 210, 218, 231
Nascimbene da Rodi, 279
Nascimbene di Zambono, 272, 282–84, 301
Naseri: family, 115, 167, 202–3; Antoni, bishop of Belluno and Feltre, 202, 263; Bonacorso, 202–3, 220, 224, 261, 263;
Giovanni, 115, 118, 136, 141, 143–44, 145, 169, 177, 202, 263, 270
Negri: family, 167, 195–97; Bonfrancesco, 67, 74, 89; Daniele, 196; Gherardo, 97, 196–97, 253; Giovanni, 124; Giovanni di Bonfrancesco, 194, 196; Guido di Bonfrancesco, 194, 196; Jacopa di Negro, 196; Negro, 124, 126, 129, 185, 189, 194–97; Negro di Guido, 195–96; Prosdocimo, 196
Nervesa, 106, 123, 226
Neumarkt-Em, Gottschalk von, 56
Niccoli, Niccolò, 259
Niccolò da Fano, 291
Niccolò da Portogruaro, 301
Niccolò di Spado, 178
Nicholas of Luxembourg, patriarch of Aquileia, 98, 108
Noale, 79, 112, 119, 209, 211, 222, 223, 226, 240, 315; podestà of, 261
Noellet, Guillaume, 130
Nonantola (papal fortress), 313
notaries, xxiv, 20, 29–30, 149–51; guild of, 29–30, 53, 68, 74
Noventa, 67, 145, 147, 152, 174
Novi, Tommaso (castellan of Castrocaro), 311

Obizi, Antonio, of Lucca, 239
Obizzi: Gherardo (mercenary), 207; Giovanni (mercenary), 313
Ognissanti, 27, 249, 277, 288
Oltrebrenta, 10, 12, 14–15, 21, 23, 65, 78–79, 164–66, 186, 192, 194, 249, 277
Ongarelli, Guglielmo, 250, 282–83
onori (gifts in kind), 16, 145, 154, 279
Ordelaffi, Giovanni, 235, 237–38, 317
Oriago, 13, 85, 91, 110, 118–19, 126, 207, 219, 232, 315, 331
Orsini, Giovanni, bishop of Padua, 24
Ortenburg, counts of: Frederick IV, 224, 265; Otto IV, 96, 109, 224
Osio, Manfredino (Milanese banker), 283–84
Ostiglia, 62, 75
Ottolino da Monselice (Carrara councillor), 283, 289

Index

Ovetari: Albertobono, 189; Biagio, 157, 200, 250, 276; Giovanni, 166

Padovano: administration of, xxi, 12–13, 14–15; agriculture of, 10, 12, 14–16; boundaries of, 3, 13, 21; geography of, 10, 12–14, population of, 12–13, app. 1; Venetian investment in, 16, 62, 72, 75, 87, 106, 109–10, 266, 315–17
Padua: civic buildings of, 4, 6, 20, 27; in early Middle Ages, 3–4; geography of, 3–7; markets of, 4, 6, 20; population of, 7–8, app. 1
Paduan commune, xxviii–xxi, 4, 6–7, 70–72, 75, 80, 87, 98, 131, 205–6, 211–22, 245–46, 254–55, 334; government of, 17–21, 151, 162–63; podestà of, 17–19, 131, 163, 181–83, 186, app. 2; taxes of, 19–21, 29, 72, 79–80, 276, 290–91, 316; treasury of, 40–41, 46–47, 51, 141. *See also* court system in Padua; statutes, Paduan
Paganelli, Guidone di Collacio, 135
Palazzi, in Padua: Anziani, 4, 6, 54; Bo, 4, 278; Podestà, 5, 6, 18, 187
Palma, Gabreotto, of Parma, 186
Paolo da Bologna (mercenary), 228
Paolo da Dugnano (priest), 264
Paolo qd. Ture (Carrara agent), 230, 234
Papafava dei Carraresi: family, xxiv, 35, 55–56, 89, 167, 170–72; Albertino, 74, 86, 89, 171, 255; Beatrice di Fava, 194–95; Caterina, 171; Cubitosa di Jacopino, 191; Jacopino, 6, 54, 59, 67, 89; Leita, 90; Obizzo, 59
Papafava dei Carraresi, Marsilietto, 54, 56, 59, 67, 69; assassination of, 90, 167; lordship of Padua, 86–87, 89, 170; Venetian citizenship of, 87
Papino (Paduan subject), 157
Papino, Bartolomeo di Giovanni, 280
Parliament of Friuli, 205–6
Parma, 61, 63, 75, 84, 116, 177–78, 181–83, 262
Partinopea, Giovanni da, 44
Parzili, Bertolozzo, 175
Pasini: Anna, 147; Bartolomeo, 280
Patriarcati, 10, 198, 291

Pavanello, Antonio, 161, 231, 255, 282
Pavia, 185, 200, 233, 240, 248, 250, 267
Peace of Genoa, 274, 284–85, 294, 303, 309
Peace of Turin, 140, 149, 211, 225, 230, 316; terms of, 218–23, 228
Pegolotti, Filippo, 145
Pelicani, Biagio, 235–36
Pepolo, Taddeo, 83–84, 92–94
Pernumia, 12, 19, 48, 125, 264
Perugia, 260, 317, 326
Peruzzi, Benedetto, 214
Peschiera sul Garda, 71, 331
Petazzi, Adelmo de', 222
Peter II, king of Cyprus, 206
Petrarca, Francesco, 117, 126, 129, 181, 187, 200
Pezzogoti, Antonia, 288
Piacentini: Bartolomeo, 29, 104, 116, 133–35, 142, 149, 199; Leonizio, 133
Piave River, 63, 65, 106, 108, 123, 207, 222, 226
Piazza, in Padua: Biave, 54, 210, 249; Erbe, 4; Frutta, 4, 277; Legne, 4; Noli, 4; Signori, 157
Piazzola (village), 299–300
Piazzola, Rolando da, 41, 43, 44, 48
Pignolati, Michele, 272
Pinarollo, Fermerina (poulterer), 154, 156
Piombioli family, 185, 264
Piove di Sacco, 4, 10, 12–13, 62, 65, 86, 110, 118, 145, 147, 174, 178, 186, 192, 250, 272, 332; podestà of, 118, 169
Piovego Canal, 4, 13
Pisa, 84, 122, 177–78, 259–60, 311, 317, 318, 319, 332
Pisano, Pietro, 293
Pisano, Vettor, 207–9, 210, 213, 218
Pizzacomini: Matteo, 264; Padovano, 264
Plant, M., 181
Po River, 62–63, 64, 75, 116–17, 216–17, 306, 309, 313
podestà, of Padua: duties of, 14, 17–18, 40–41, 58, 104, 163–64; geographic origins of, 18–19, app. 2; staff of, 18–20; in towns of Padovano, 14–15, 41, 44, 164–66
Pola, battle of, 208–9

Index

Polenta: family, 95; Costainza, 124; Guidone III, 125; Obizzo, 322, 323; Ostasio, 75, 125, 235–36, 238, 303; Pietro, 303

Polenton, Sicco, 295–96

Polesine, 66, 306, 308, 309, 322, 331

Poliavolo, Fiora and Pariano (peasants), 129

Polverara, 15, 198, 201, 250

Ponte Altinate, quarter of, 6–7, 10, 19, 253, 272

Ponte Corvo, 4, 8, 31, 67, 140–41, 144, 204, 279

Ponte dei Tadi, 4, 41, 183, 280

Pontelongo, 65–66, 202

Ponte Molino, 4, 8, 22, 31, 266; quarter of, 6–7, 12, 19, 253, 272

Ponte Peochioso, 144

Ponte S. Niccolò, 14, 143, 144, 169, 204, 327

Porcellini: Giovanni, 200, 253, 269, 271, 272, 278, 290, 300; Margherita, 185

Porciglia, gate of, 266

Portomaggiore, near Ferrara, 309

Portonuovo, 119, 126

Pozzoveggiano, Padovano da (Jewish banker), 140

Praglia, 90, 129

Prague, 92, 99, 116, 117, 177

Prampero, Francesco, 23

Prata: Pileo da, bishop of Padua, 24, 34, 117, 124, 198; Toberto da, 124

Prato della Valle, 8, 31, 171, 273

precones (communal police), 19–20; guild of, 149

Preti, Ugolino, 241, 249, 253–54

Pretoni: Bartolomeo, 182; Bernardo, 182; Franceschino, 182; Maffeo, 182; Pietro, 182

Priuli: Bernardo, 335; Jacopo, 120

Prosdocimo da Chioggia, 118

Prosperi, Corrado (mercenary), 313

provisionati, 228, 238–39, 319, 323, 328

public debt: at end of Border War, 147–48; of Florence, 148; of Lucca, 148; of Padua, 135; of Venice, 148, 177

Quero, 130–31, 219, 222

Rabatta: Enrico di Antonio, 150, 248; Michele, 200, 207, 230, 234, 248, 250, 274, 307, 315, 325; Pietro, 299

Raini, Antonia di Gerardo, 280

Ramiro, king of Oviedo, 179–81

Randek, Marquardo of, patriarch of Aquileia, 144, 205–6, 223, 229

Rangoni, Jacopo, 163

Ravenna, 124–25, 196, 323

Ravignani, Benintendi dei, 87, 103, 106–7

Reggia (Carrara complex), 41, 61, 81, 88–89, 97, 127, 152, 154, 220, 266–67, 292–93; Camera Lucrezia, 220; Camera Nerone, 133; Camino Ercole, 289–90, 292; construction of, 133, 149, 161; Palazzo di Levante, 133, 136, 152; Sala dei Viri Illustri, 152, 266, 292; Stuveta, 162, 276. *See also* chancery, Carrara; household, Carrara

Reggio, 62, 66

Renaldino, Giovanni (Carrara offical), 283

Renaldino di Martino (*campsor*), 284

Resta, Marco, 143, 171

Rhodes, 124, 274

Rio: family, 264; Bartolomeo, 279, 282, 290; Daniele da, 278; Niccolò, 288

Rizollo, Colonbano (wool guild rector), 278

Robert, king of Naples, 37

Roberti, Ugone, bishop of Padua, 301

Rocca: degli Alberi, 110; di Garda, 29; di Monselice, 73–74, 97, 129, 330

Roccabruna (Valsugana), 93

Rome, 92, 94, 116–17, 322–23, 325

Ronchi (village), 331

Ronchi family, 38, 59

Roncon (village), 297

Rosara, 191–92

Rosazzo (abbey), 230, 232

Rossi (of Parma): family, 61, 64, 79, 177; Beltrando di Rolando, 79; Giacomo, 104; Lusia di Pietro, 175, 182; Marsilio, 57, 63–67, 70–71, 179; Pietro, 61, 63–65, 69–71, 179, 187; Rolando, 61, 63–65, 70–72, 78–79; Scanuzzi, 185

Rosta (village), 147, 177

Rothegnanz, Lunardo (Carrara tutor), 133

Rottenburg, Siegfried von, 53

Index

Rovigo, 268, 331
Rovolon, 38, 171
Rubano, 263
Rudena, 4, 8, 202, 290
Rudolf III, duke of Saxony, 324
Rupert of Bavaria, king of the Romans, 318–20, 322–25, 329
Rusconi, Luchino, 253
Rustega, 64

S. Agata (convent), 55, 147
S. Agnese (convent), 25
S. Agostino, 22, 25, 49, 53, 58, 87
S. Anna (convent), 45–47, 49
St. Anthony of Padua, 22, 94
St. Anthony of Vienne, 256
S. Antonio (basilica), 8, 22, 70–71, 74, 125, 179–81, 255
S. Benedetto (convent), 152, 261
S. Boldo (fortress), 119–20, 219
S. Bruson, 108, 123
S. Clemente, 41, 236
S. Croce, gate of, 8, 43, 49, 56, 67, 110, 154, 279, 334
S. Daniele, 202; hospital of, 150
S. Francesco, 25
S. Giacomo (chapel), 179–81
S. Giorgio (oratory), 179, 181–84
S. Giorgio di Bosco (village), 196, 279
S. Giorgio Maggiore (Venetian abbey), 74, 196
S. Giovanni Battista (Florentine hospital), 179, 261, 285
S. Giovanni Battista del Venda, 25, 183
S. Giovanni delle Navi, 4, 14, 49
S. Giovanni Evangelista (Venetian monastery), 119
S. Giustina (abbey), 4, 8, 10, 22, 24, 53, 55, 109, 197, 296, 300–301
S. Ilario, 92, 121–22, 183, 211; border disputes at, 86, 110–12, 220–21, 228
S. Lorenzo (church), 4, 39, 49
S. Marco (basilica), 75, 209–10
S. Maria dei Servi, 154, 302
S. Maria di Monteoliveto, 183
S. Maria di Non, 203–4
S. Maria in Vanzo, 4, 8, 48, 51, 55
S. Martino di Lupari, 86
S. Massimo (hospital), 288
S. Michele (oratory), 154
S. Niccolò di Lido, 210, 213
S. Pelagio (village), 146, 280
S. Pietro (convent), 22, 25
S. Siro (village), 35, 171
S. Stefano, in Carrara, 26, 55, 75, 296, 301
S. Stefano, in Este, 24
S. Teche, in Este, 24
S. Zaccaria (Venetian monastery), 16
Sabbioncello, 174, 247
Saccolongo, 195, 251–52
Sacile, 231, 239–40, 262
Sala (village), 202
Sala: family, 202; Corrado, 202; Giovanni, 250; Paganino, 118, 175, 179, 202–3, 217, 239–40, 245, 250–51, 263, 270
sale, of Carrara property: in 1388, 195, 197, 249–50, 257, 272, 275–76, app. 3; in 1405, 334
Saletto, 195
Salgardi, Giovanni, 115, 149, 163
Salgeri, Francesco, 140
Saliceto, Bartolomeo, 289, 293
Salone (city hall), 4, 19–20, 39, 41, 43, 55, 68–69, 154, 204, 245, 268
salt monopoly, Venetian, 63–64, 80, 107, 109, 210–11, 241
Salutati, Coluccio, letters of, 188, 214, 241, 265, 267–68, 274, 307, 308, 311, 314, 318–19, 325–26, 328, 330
Sambonifacio: family, 58, 186; Bonifacio, 186; Lina di Vinci, 195; Manfredo, 186–87; Rizzardo, 131, 186–87, 269–70, 293; Vinciguerra, 38, 54, 174
San Angelo, Antonio, 271, 272, 289
Sanguinacci: family, 284, 334; Francesco, 55; Giovanni, 143; Ilario, 164
Santa Croce, Giacomo, 29, 33, 34, 92–94, 98, 104, 133–34, 149; as Conte Palatine, 115–16; Venetian citizenship of, 134
Santa Sofia, Marsilio, 181, 306
Santi: Androili de', 179; Giovanni de', 179
Saonara, 174, 250
Saraceno: Giovanni, 127; Pietro, 136, 150–51
Saracinesca, gate, 110, 154, 251, 279

Index

Savelli, Pietro, 331–32, 334
Savonarola, Giovanni, 250, 278, 280, 283–84, 289
Savorgnan, Federico, 191, 231, 279
Scadelato, Biagio, 147
Scaliger state, in 1330s, 57–60, 62–63
Scaliger War (1336–1339), 63–67, 69–75, 78, 187
Scaliger War (1385–1387), 185, 189, 232–36, 238–40, 297
Scaltanigo, Giacomo (mercenary), 321
Schici, Francesco, 110
Schinelli: family, 10, 38, 171; Ansedisio, 198; Caterina, 171
Scodosia, 10, 14, 15, 19, 195, 203, 264
Scola, Ognibene, 279, 295, 317, 318–19, 325–26
Scolari: family, 189; Bernardo, 135, 189, 233, 235, 238; Caterina, 189; Filippo di Bernardo, 189; Giovanna, 189; Mabilla, 189; Rainiero, 186, 189; Taddeo di Bernardo, 189
Scrovegni: family, 14, 58–59, 167, 172, 174–77; Adelaita, 86; Alice, 191; Bartolomea, 61, 177, 186; Capellina, 174; Caterina, 174, 177; Enrico di Rinaldo, 58, 174; Enrico di Ugolino, 125, 175, Francesco, 81–82; Giacomo di Ugolino, 175, 177; Giovanna, 175, 177; Maddalena, 175, 177; Orsina, 175; Pietro di Ugolino, 187; Renaldo II, 58; Ugolino, 97, 119, 175, 177, 178, 182
Serafino di Benvenuto, 276, 302
Serega, Cortesia, 235–36
Sermazza, 175, 297
Serravalle (Trevisano), 106–7, 112, 119, 228, 248
Seta: Bartolomeo, 231; Nicola, 277
Sforza, Muzio Attendolo, 321–22
sharecropping, 15–16, 145, 147, 150, 195, 280
Siena, 257, 260, 311, 317, 326
signori di notte, 111, 121, 193
Sile River, 222, 225–26, 228–29, 233
Simeone, Pietro, 189
Simone da Noventa, 147
Sobieslaw, John, patriarch of Aquileia, 240, 248, 265–66

Solagna, 21, 93, 126, 165, 191
Solesino, 35, 203, 264
Soranzo, Gabriele, 281
Spilimbergo: counts of, 112, 114; Bertold, 222; Niccolò, 230; Venceslao, 231; Walterpertoldo, 114
Spinelli, Francesco, 141
Spini, Cristofano, 310
Spisser, Hermann (mercenary), 266
Squarcialupi, Francesco, 297
statutes, Paduan, reforms of, 17, 77, 96–97, 149, 162–64
Statuti: Giovanni dagli, 175; Simeone dagli, 143, 216, 250, 299–300; Zilberto dagli, 30
Stefano de Franchino, 75
Steinberg, Golford (mercenary), 65
Steno, Michele, doge, 315, 324
Stephen, duke of Bavaria, 259–60, 265, 267–68
Stephen, voivode of Transylvania, 123–24, 126, 207
Strà, 4, 10, 13, 85, 175, 264
Strassoldo, Niccolò, 285
Strazzarolo, Berto, 288
Suriano, Giacomo, 330

Tagliamento River, 265
Tempesta: Guecello, 61–62, 71, 78; Meliaduse, 78–79
Tenedos, 206, 219, 223
Teolo, 202, 290
Teolo, Paolo da, 41, 45
Terence, quoted, 126
Tergola River, 13, 14, 119
Terradura family, 58, 59
Terranegra, 141, 144, 278–79, 281
Terzi, Ottobuono, 331
Tesino River, 91, 195
tithes, lay: defined, 23–24; fiefs of, granted, 23–24, 62, 64, 85, 93, 124, 171, 175, 182, 191, 195–96, 198, 261–62, 264
Tolomei, Andrea (mercenary), 253
Tommaso da Frignano, patriarch of Grado, 122–23
Tommaso da Mantova, 321
Ton, Francesco (Carrara notary), 276

464

Index

Torre, 44–45, 55, 152, 202, 232
Torcoli: Antonio, 247; Gabriele, 281
Torlone, Giacomo, 141
Torricelle, 3, 31, 43, 140; quarter of, 6–7, 19, 253, 266, 272
Tortona, Tommaso da, 233
Trambacche (village), 195
Trambacche, Gherardo da, 130
Trambachino, Giacomo, 285
Trapolino, Enrico, 290
treasury, Carrara household, 136–37, 139, 147–48, 151–52, 157–58, 201–3; embezzlement from, 151–52
treaties, between Padua and Venice: of 14 July 1337, 66–67, 68, 71, 79, 87, 115; of 5 May 1338, 71–72, 87; of 24 Jan. 1339, 75, 84; of 17 Apr. 1339, 79–80, 87; of 20 Apr. 1345, 87; of 21 June 1345, 89–90; of 7 June 1358, 107, 109; of 6 July 1363, 112–13; of 21 Sept. 1373, 126–30, 140, 219; of Aug. 1399, 316–17. *See also* Peace of Turin
Trent, 13, 91, 93
Treville, 54, 66, 78–79
Trevisan War (1382–1384), xix, 189, 222–28
Trevisano, 64–65, 78–79, 80, 103, 120–21, 130–31, 221–22, 240–42; in Chioggia War, 207, 209–10; Venetian proprietors in, 220, 225–26, 229, 234, 267
Treviso, 33–37, 51, 81, 106, 108, 233, 240–42; in Border War, 119–23; Carrara lordship of, 161, 182, 200, 228–29; in Chioggia War, 209–12, 218–19; under German vicars, 42–44; Habsburg rule over, 218–20, 222–26, 228, 233, 249; podestà of, 222, 229; Scaliger rule over, 59, 61–66; Venetian rule over, 74–75, 78–79, 81, 103, 106–7, 112, 252–53, 267
Tribano, 48, 192, 196
Trieste, 140, 211, 218, 222–24
Trincher, Nicholas (mercenary), 266
Truce of Pavia, 314–15
Turchetto: family, 167, 203–4, 255, 264; Antonio, 203; Francesco, 130, 151, 189, 203–4, 207, 233, 255; Giacomo, 151, 203–4, 217, 220–21, 240, 255; Giovanni, 255, 276; Marsilio, 122

tyrant: defined, xvii–xviii; use of term, 80–81, 82, 104, 327–28
Tyrol, 93–94, 111

Ubaldini, Giovanni, abbot of Praglia, 332
Ubaldini, Giovanni Azzo degli, 233–37, 238, 248, 251, 267
Udine, 117, 229, 231, 233–34
Ugolino da Prato (Carrara agent), 297, 299
University of Padua, 31–34, 135, 202, 292, 320; college system of, 34; legal faculty of, 32–33, 167, 172, 199; medical faculty of, 33, 172, 199–200, 202
Urban V, pope, 111, 113–14, 116–17, 122, 135, 199
Urban VI, pope, 230–31, 237, 240, 263
Urbana, 136, 195, 261

Valbona, 129, 145–46
Valcherich, Enrico, 104
Valle, Daniele da, 234
Vallonga, 191–92
Valmareno, 112
Valpolicello, 331
Valsanzibio, 125, 280, 297
Valsugana, 93, 123, 131, 187
Valvasone (castle), 265–66
Valvasone: Bernardo, 321; Giacomo, 266; Rizzardo, 266
Vannozzo, Francesco, 141
Vanzerio, Bartolomeo, 220, 277
Varano: Belfiore da, 317, 327; Gentile da, 308; Rodolfo da, 324, 327
Vasco, Rainiero, 122–23
Veglia, 191, 265
Venetian podestà, of Padua, 56, 71, 74, 77, 81, 96, 104, 182, 278, 293, 370
Venetian proprietors, in Padovano, taxes on, 62–63, 67, 72, 79–80, 87, 211–12, 219–20, 225, 228, 233–34, 242, 315–16
Venice: border disputes with Padua, 90–92, 110–12, 118–20, 220–21, 306; and Francesco il Vecchio da Carrara, 96–99, 103–4, 107, 115, 120–21, 129–31, 209–12, 216–17, 220–26, 228–29, 231–34, 237–42, 248, 252; and Francesco Novello da Carrara, 126, 259, 266, 303–

Index

Venice (cont.)
  4, 308–10, 312–18, 323–25, 327–36; and Giacomo II, 89–94; and Marsilio il Grande, 62–69; as model for Carrara regime, 68–69, 99; and Ubertino, 71–72, 78–82; wars with Padua, 37–38, 122–26, 207–18, 241–42, 248, 251, 329–36. See also treaties, between Padua and Venice
Venier, Antonio, doge, 304, 309
Venturi, Jacopo, 231
Vergerio, Pier Paolo, xxi, 51, 86, 259, 273, 298, 328; speeches of, 303–4, 307–8
Verona, 35–37, 62, 75, 81, 84, 187, 232–33, 328–30; Carrara rule over, 329–30; Scaliger court at, 56, 61–62, 232; Venetian rule over, 333–34; Visconti rule over, 239–41, 267, 329
Veronese, 62–67, 72–73, 237, 331–33
Vettore, Andrea, 328
Vicenza, 35, 56–57, 71, 83–84, 152, 236, 326; Paduan rule over, 36–37; Scaliger rule over, 61–62, 75, 83; Venetian rule over, 330–31; Visconti rule over, 202, 240–41, 326
Vicentino, 97, 144–45, 174
Vigenzone Canal, 14, 143–44
Vighizzolo, 48, 90
Vigonza: family, 15; Bonzanello da, 126, 216; Corrado da, 54–55; Francesco da, 57; Giovanni da, 47, 49
Villa, peacemaking in, 290
Villa Estense, 136, 152, 261
Villanders: Engelmar von, 53–57, 83, 91; Griffo von, 57
Villanova, 119, 264
Visconti: family, 66, 71, 84, 92, 94–95, 114; Agnese, 312; Azzo, 66, 71, 75; Bernabò, 111, 113–14, 116–17, 123, 130, 135, 187–88, 225, 233, 258; —, in Chioggia War, 206–7, 213, 216–18; Bertetto, 253; Caterina, 240, 326–28, 330; Filippo Maria, 326, 328; Gabriele, 310; Galeazzo II, 187–88; Giovanni Maria, 326, 328; Luchino, 66, 83–84, 92; Verde, 114

Visconti, Giangaleazzo, 186, 189, 200, 203, 223; and Carrara lord, 309–11, 312–14, 317–24; and conquest of Padua, 240–42, 248–51, 253–55; his court at Pavia, 200, 259–60; death and funeral of, 325–26; as duke of Milan, 300, 311; as lord of Padua, 255, 260–65, 288
Visconti War, First (1390–1392), 265–68, 273–74, 288, 297
Visconti War, Second (1400–1402), 300–301, 318–28
Vitaliani: family, 264; Bicco, 124; Vitaliano, 124
Volta Barozzo, 204, 281
Volta dei Negri, 196

Walsee, Ulrich von, 43–47, 53
War of the Eight Saints, 130, 214, 218
War with Venice (1403–1405), 327–34
Wenceslaus, duke of Saxony, 116, 187, 224
Wenceslaus, king of the Romans, 239–40, 310, 322, 348
wool guild, 27, 30–31, 141–42, 277; membership of, 142, 271, 277–78
wool retailers guild, 277–78, 291
woolen industry, 27, 30–31, 61, 140–42, 196, 270–71, 277–79

Zabarella: family, 152; Andrea di Daniele, 272; Francesco, 34, 220, 283, 289, 301; —, orations of, 220, 314, 333–34; Giovanni di Andrea, 281, 284; Pietro, 295
Zacchi: Bartolomeo, 194; Corrado, 143; Giacomo, 194, 247, 284
Zambeccari, Carlo, 320
Zano, Lorenzo, 121
Zara, 90–91, 106–7, 114–15, 140, 247
Zecchi: Antonio, 127, 131, 149–50, 166, 182, 220–21, 224; Grisoldo, 150; Manuele, 149
Zen, Carlo, 208, 216–17, 329, 333–34
Zennari, Salimbene, 140
Zerdo, Filippo, 288–89
Zorzi, Giovanni, 96

Library of Congress Cataloging-in-Publication Data

Kohl, Benjamin G.
Padua under the Carrara, 1318–1405 / Benjamin G. Kohl.
p. cm.
Includes bibliographical references and index.
ISBN 0-8018-5703-1 (alk. paper)
1. Padua (Italy)—History. 2. Carrara family. 3. Padua (Italy)—Kings and rulers—History. 4. Padua (Italy)—Foreign relations. 5. Cities and towns—Renaissance—Italy—Padua. I. Title.
DG975.P15K64 1998
945'.32—dc21 97-30172
CIP

WITHDRAWN